College Writing Skills with Readings

ELEVENTH EDITION

Zoé L. Albright

Metropolitan Community College—Longview

John Langan

Atlantic Cape Community College

COLLEGE WRITING SKILLS WITH READINGS

Published by McGraw Hill LLC, 1325 Avenue of the Americas, New York, NY 10019. Copyright ©2023 by McGraw Hill LLC. All rights reserved. Printed in the United States of America. No part of this publication may be reproduced or distributed in any form or by any means, or stored in a database or retrieval system, without the prior written consent of McGraw Hill LLC, including, but not limited to, in any network or other electronic storage or transmission, or broadcast for distance learning.

Some ancillaries, including electronic and print components, may not be available to customers outside the United States.

This book is printed on acid-free paper.

1 2 3 4 5 6 7 8 9 LCR 27 26 25 24 23 22

ISBN 978-1-265-22659-6
MHID 1-265-22659-8

Cover Image: *Nana_studio/Shutterstock*

mheducation.com/highered

ABOUT THE AUTHORS

Zoé L. Albright has been involved in diverse aspects of education for twenty-five years. For the last twenty-one years, she has been a faculty member at Metropolitan Community College–Longview, teaching developmental writing, composition, and literature. She has created and implemented traditional and online curricula for high school and college English and composition courses and for a variety of literature courses. She continues to research new educational theory and practices. In addition to this extensive teaching experience, Zoé served as co-author of the previous edition of *College Writing Skills with Readings* and has most recently served as co-author of *English Skills with Readings*, tenth edition, and *Exploring Writing*, fourth edition. She has also been a contributing author to other John Langan texts, including earlier editions of the *Exploring Writing* books and *College Writing Skills with Readings*. She received her M.A. from Goldsmiths, University of London; B.S. and B.A. from the University of Idaho; and A.A. from Cottey College. She holds a Ph.D. in Curriculum and Instruction from the University of Kansas, where her focus was on developmental writers and their identities. Zoé currently resides near Kansas City, Missouri, with her family.

Zoé L. Albright
Courtesy of
Zoé L. Albright

John Langan has taught reading and writing at Atlantic Cape Community College near Atlantic City, New Jersey, for more than twenty-five years. The author of a popular series of college textbooks on both writing and reading, John enjoys the challenge of developing materials that teach skills in an especially clear and lively way. Before teaching, he earned advanced degrees in writing at Rutgers University and in reading at Rowan University. He also spent a year writing fiction that, he says, "is now at the back of a drawer waiting to be discovered and acclaimed posthumously." While in school, he supported himself by working as a truck driver, a machinist, a battery assembler, a hospital attendant, and an apple packer. John now lives with his wife, Judith Nadell, near Philadelphia. In addition to his wife and Philly sports teams, his passions include reading and turning on nonreaders to the pleasure and power of books. Through Townsend Press, his educational publishing company, he has developed the nonprofit "Townsend Library"—a collection of more than one hundred new and classic stories that appeal to readers of any age.

John Langan
Courtesy of
John Langan

BRIEF CONTENTS

CONTENTS

READINGS LISTED BY RHETORICAL MODE

Note: Some selections are cross-listed because they illustrate more than one rhetorical method of development.

DESCRIPTION

NARRATION

EXEMPLIFICATION

PROCESS

CAUSE AND/OR EFFECT

COMPARISON AND/OR CONTRAST

The skills of writing and thinking critically about one's world are not only important to a successful college career, they are also important to success in life. Especially now, as misinformation and disinformation run rampant, the ability to critically evaluate what we are reading and writing about is more essential than ever. It is because of these shifting needs that I have worked hard to increase the critical thinking lessons throughout this text while still emphasizing the strong pedagogy surrounding good writing. Students are introduced to topics that will challenge their perceptions and beliefs, including a new research essay titled "Environmental Health" that examines food waste. Many of the new readings are from marginalized voices. For some students, these readings will serve as an introduction to unfamiliar points of view, and for other students, these readings may echo their own lived experiences. These new essays and readings should encourage lively discussions in the classroom.

As an educator who has been in the classroom for almost three decades, I have seen my students' and colleagues' needs change. Strong grammar foundations have been shaken by social media use and texting. Search engines and databases have affected the art of research and the incorporation of research into writing. The constant bombardment of new information has had a negative impact on the ability to think through a topic slowly. This new edition of *College Writing Skills with Readings* was developed with the goal of addressing these changes. Its lessons are designed to help students gain the strong foundational skills that they need to navigate what it means to be not only a college student in the twenty-first century but also an active and responsible citizen of the world.

Preface

College Writing Skills with Readings is designed to help students gain the strong foundational skills that they need to succeed in college and in their lives beyond college. It does this by focusing on the four bases of unity, support, coherence, and sentence skills; emphasizing writing for personal, academic, and workplace settings; focusing on information literacy and research writing; and demonstrating for students how the stages of the writing process work together.

Mastering the Four Bases: Unity, Support, Coherence, Sentence Skills

College Writing Skills with Readings, eleventh edition, emphasizes writing skills and process. By referring to a set of four skills for effective writing, *College Writing Skills with Readings,* eleventh edition, encourages new writers to see writing as a skill that can be learned and a process that must be explored. The four skills, or bases, for effective writing are as follows:

- **Unity:** Discover a clearly stated point, or topic sentence, and make sure that all other information in the paragraph or essay supports that point.

- **Support:** Support the points with specific evidence, and plenty of it.

- **Coherence:** Organize and connect supporting evidence so that paragraphs and essays transition smoothly from one bit of supporting information to the next.

- **Sentence skills:** Revise and edit so that sentences are error-free for clearer and more effective communication.

The four bases are essential to effective writing, whether it be a narrative paragraph, a cover letter for a job application, or an essay assignment.

Twenty-seven professional readings support the development of the four bases by modeling effective writing, as well as inspiring lively class discussion and providing a continuing source of high-interest material for a wide range of writing assignments. Reflecting the diversity of backgrounds, experiences, and identities of the college writing classroom and students' broader communities, 50 percent of the readings are written by authors of historically marginalized groups. For some students, these readings will serve as an introduction to unfamiliar points of view, and for other students, their own lived experiences may be echoed by these readings.

UNITY

Discover a clearly stated point, or topic sentence, and make sure that all other information in the paragraph or essay supports that point.

SUPPORT

Support the points with specific evidence, and plenty of it.

COHERENCE

Organize and connect supporting evidence so that paragraphs and essays transition smoothly from one bit of supporting evidence to the next.

SENTENCE SKILLS

Revise and edit so that sentences are error-free for clearer and more effective communication.

Personal, Academic, and Workplace Writing

College Writing Skills with Readings, eleventh edition, is flexible and emphasizes personal learning, academic learning, and workplace preparation. Students are exposed to examples of writing that reflect these three key realms of their lives to help them understand the critical way in which writing will have an impact on the many facets of their lives.

To help students learn the different characteristics of each type of writing, icons identifying specific writing pieces, examples, and assignments are integrated throughout the chapters.

Writings that employ first-person point of view, narrative, and/or an informal tone are marked "Personal." Writings that employ a third-person point of view, a formal tone, and focus on academic topics are identified as "Academic." Writings that employ a third-person point of view, a formal tone, and focus on employment-related topics are marked "Work."

In addition to these abundant examples, there are writing assignments and activities emphasizing each of these categories throughout the chapters and readings anthology, so students can gain practice writing for a variety of audiences and situations. This variety provides flexibility in the kinds of assignments you may wish to give.

Emphasis on Information Literacy and Research Writing

College Writing Skills with Readings, eleventh edition, continues to focus strongly on information literacy, research, and source-based essay writing. Students are introduced to using and locating online sources effectively and efficiently and employing critical thinking skills to determine the reliability and validity of sources found. Resources available at most college libraries—including the expertise of resource librarians and how to make best use of that expertise—are discussed in detail. In addition to learning how to choose sources, students are exposed to a new, more detailed look at the skills of paraphrasing and summarizing. As well, students are given an in-depth experience devoted to source-based essay writing and research, including how to create a plan to meet deadlines set by instructors; how to take good notes; how to incorporate sources to avoid plagiarism; and how to use proper MLA format. Along with a full-length sample research paper, students are also given the opportunity to read several source-based literary analyses throughout the textbook.

The Writing Process in Action

College Writing Skills with Readings, eleventh edition, provides strong writing pedagogy. To help students see the whole picture and walk actively through the steps of the entire writing process, Chapter 7 provides an extended example of one student's complete writing process, demonstrating the student's prewriting, organizing, drafting, revision, editing, and resulting (but still evolving) final draft. This chapter culminates Part 1, in which the six preceding chapters offer in-depth instruction about different facets and steps of the writing process from prewriting through revision. Chapter 1 explains why writing is important in all aspects of life. Chapter 2 offers an overview of the writing process. Chapters 3, 4, and 5 break down the steps of the writing process, providing explanations and extensive activities to help students practice, and Chapter 6 helps students understand and apply the Four Bases for revising.

CHAPTER-BY-CHAPTER CHANGES

The eleventh edition of *College Writing Skills with Readings* includes the following chapter-by-chapter changes:

Part 1: Essay Writing

- Revised and updated section on using technology to write and study efficiently
- Revised and updated coverage of MLA guidelines, including such key areas as inclusive language and formatting in research writing
- Reorganized and augmented coverage of purpose and audience
- Enhanced discussion of peer and personal review
- More clearly identified steps and stages in Chapter 7's full length student essay, which demonstrates the writing process from prewriting through peer review, self-evaluation, and revising

Part 2: Patterns of Essay Development

- All student essays and Writing Assignments thoroughly examined and revised as needed for sensitivity to culture, gender, and differences in ability
- Several Model Essays repositioned to better fit within a particular pattern, each incorporating new pedagogy
- Continued emphasis on essays with more than three supporting paragraphs
- More clearly called-out and identified examples of Literary Analysis
- All Four Bases Checklists thoroughly examined and revised as necessary, to insure focus on the specific needs of the targeted mode

Part 3: Researching, Writing, and Documenting

- Full and updated coverage of students' use of the Internet, technology, and the library in the digital age
- Revised, newly focused, and enhanced treatment of paraphrasing
- Expanded coverage of note-taking that fully illustrates and explains two different methods
- New discussion of misinformation and disinformation

- New full length student research paper that illustrates key research skills including the essential steps in writing a good research paper
- Revised and updated examples of correct source citation per recent MLA guidelines
- Updated and increased coverage of identifying and avoiding plagiarism
- More clearly called-out and identified examples of Rhetorical Analysis and Literary Analysis
- Text explanations and discussions formatted to make them more accessible to students

Part 4: Handbook of Sentence Skills

- All grammar activities, exercises, and Review Tests thoroughly updated for currency
- Pronoun instruction and examples reworked and updated to reflect gender-neutral usage
- Grammar activities, exercises, and Review Tests continue to incorporate personal, academic, and workplace-related themes
- Many tests and activities focused on single issue so that each reads as a unified passage

Part 5: Readings for Writers

- Readings updated to include selections by diverse voices
- New readings with accompanying questions and assignments include:
  - "Colleges Must Confront Structural Racism" by Kevin V. Collymore
  - "What Academics Misunderstand about 'Public Writing'" by Irina Dumitrescu
  - "Purposefully Mispronouncing Kamala Harris's Name is Racist, Plain and Simple" by Duaa Israr
  - "Memes and the Art of Nonsense" by Serena G. Pellegrino
  - "A Memoir Reflects on What Happens to the 'Fairest' of Them All" by Hope Wabuke

Connect Writing for *College Writing Skills with Readings*

Connect is a highly reliable, easy-to-use homework and learning management solution that embeds learning science and award-winning adaptive tools to improve student results. Connect Writing offers comprehensive, reliable writing and research content that is designed to actively engage students and help prepare them to be successful writers. This is done through Connect components such as Adaptive Learning Assignment, Power of Process, the College Writing Skills with Readings eBook, and Writing Assignment Plus.

Adaptive Learning Assignment

Adaptive Learning Assignment provides each student a personalized path to learning concepts instructors assign in their course. The assignments continually adapt to the individual, identifying knowledge gaps and focusing on areas where remediation is needed. All adaptive content—including questions and integrated concept resources—is specifically targeted to, and directly aligned with, the individual learning objectives being assessed in the course.

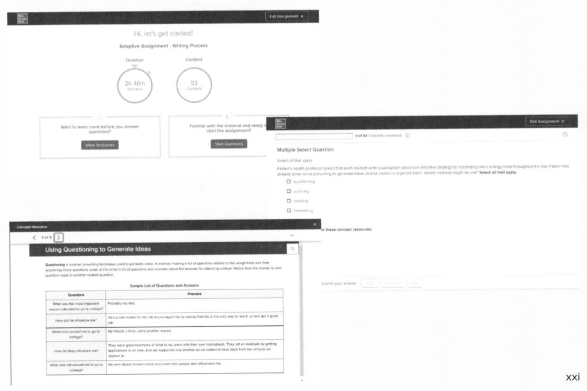

Power of Process

One overarching goal is at the heart of Power of Process: for students to become self-regulating, strategic readers and writers. Power of Process facilitates engaged reading and writing processes using research-based best practices suggested by major professional reading and writing organizations. Instructors can choose from a bank of carefully chosen readings within Power of Process, readings from *College Writing Skills with Readings,* or upload their own readings. As with the professional readings in the text, 50 percent of the forty-six additional readings in Power of Process are written by Black, Indigenous, and People of Color (BIPOC) authors.

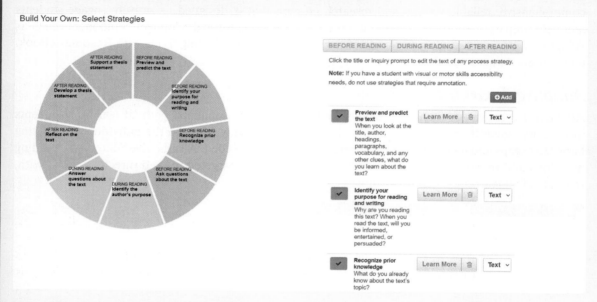

College Writing Skills with Readings eBook

The entire *College Writing Skills with Readings* text can be accessed through Connect or as a stand-alone ebook. At McGraw Hill Higher Education, our mission is to accelerate learning through intuitive, engaging, efficient, and effective experiences, grounded in research. Assignments in Connect are WCAG compliant, and updates to the ebook of the eleventh edition of *College Writing Skills* go beyond WCAG compliance to create an improved reading experience for all learners. These enhancements include improved functionality for viewing annotated readings and editing marks. We are committed to creating universally accessible products that unlock the full potential of each learner, including individuals with disabilities.

Writing Assignment Plus

McGraw Hill's new Writing Assignment Plus tool delivers a learning experience that improves students' written communication skills and conceptual understanding with every assignment. Assign, monitor, and provide feedback on writing more efficiently and grade assignments within

McGraw Hill Connect®. Writing Assignment Plus gives you time-saving tools with just-in-time basic writing and originality checker.

Text-Specific Resources for Instructors

The Annotated Instructor's Edition consists of the student text, including answers to all activities and tests, as well as a complete Instructor's Guide.

Available within Connect are a number of instructional materials, including the instructor's manual, chapter quizzes, a variety of handouts, and PowerPoint® slides that may be tailored to course needs.

Learning Management System Integration Services

Connect Writing integrates with your local Learning Management System (Blackboard, Canvas, and others).

McGraw Hill provides a one-stop teaching and learning experience to users of any learning management system. This complimentary integration allows faculty and students to enjoy single sign-on (SSO) access to all McGraw Hill Higher Education materials and synchronized gradebooks with our award-winning McGraw Hill Connect platform. For more information on learning management system integration, please visit our website at www.mhcampus.com or contact your local McGraw Hill representative to find out more about installations on your campus.

ACKNOWLEDGMENTS

Manuscript Reviewers

The quality of *College Writing Skills with Readings,* eleventh edition, is a testament to the suggestions and insights from instructors around the country. Many thanks to all of those who helped improve this project.

Emory Abbott, *Georgia State University*

Valerie Ambrose, *Shasta College*

Rhonda Fabrizi, *Cuyahoga Community College*

Joseph Fly, *South Plains College*

Karen Griscom, *Community College of Rhode Island*

Beth Gulley, *Johnson County Community College*

Kendra Haggard, *Northeastern State University*

Olga Han Hardy, *Gwinnett College*

Keith Haynes, *Yavapai College*

Mindy Hodge, *Beckfield College*

Karen Holley, *Georgia State University-Perimeter College*

Tonia Humphrey, *Kennedy-King College*

Robbyn Lamb, *Colby Community College*

L. Marie Lumpkin, *Wayne County Community College*

Anna Maheshwari, *Schoolcraft College*

Cassandra Powell, *Richard J. Daley College*

Barbara Rubinstein, *Community College of Rhode Island*

Becky Samberg, *Housatonic Community College*

Cherise Shane, *Community College of Philadelphia*

Lesley Shelton, *South Plain College*

Laurie Sherman, *Community College of Rhode Island*

Barbara Smith, *Hillsborough Community College*

Tammy Teague, *Tulsa Community College*

Eileen Thompson, *Edison State Community College*

Priscilla Underwood, *Quinsigamond Community College*

Beverly Vick, *Tulsa Community College*

Maria Villar, *Miami Dade College*

Gledy Wariebi, *Prince George's Community*

Sabrina Walters, *Miami Dade College*

Bradley Waltman, *College of Southern Nevada*

Jaime West, *University of Northern Iowa*

Personal Acknowledgments

We are incredibly grateful for the talent and support of our developmental team without which this edition would not have happened. Thank you to Brianna Kirschbaum, Kristin Piljay, and their team for their hard work in obtaining text and photo permissions. Thank you to Mary Powers, who handled the production process skillfully. To Byron Kanoti, thank you for all your research and planning to market this new edition. Beth Blech, thank you for the great design. To Oakley Clark and to George Theofanopoulos, thank you for your work managing the development and build of the digital experience and supplements. To Erin Cosyn and Cara Labell—thank you for keeping us on schedule, troubleshooting, and filling our Wednesday mornings with some great chats. Finally, to Merryl Maleska Wilbur, a colleague and friend, thank you for pushing and developing our abilities as writers and thinkers; we have grown beyond our imagination and remain immensely grateful.

Zoé L. Albright

John Langan

Essay Writing

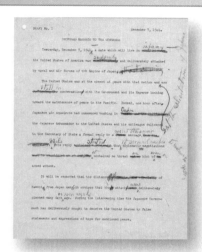

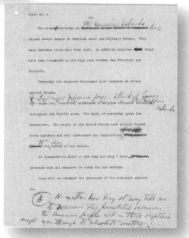

PREVIEW

Even accomplished political leaders like Franklin D. Roosevelt have to write several drafts of speeches before creating the final product. Study this excerpted draft of FDR's address to Congress asking for a declaration of war after Pearl Harbor was attacked by the Japanese during World War II. Choose one aspect of this revision and explain why and how it makes the speech more effective.

Courtesy of the Franklin D. Roosevelt Presidential Library and Museum, Hyde Park, New York

An Introduction to Writing

This chapter will explain and illustrate

- the importance of supporting a point in writing
- the structure of the traditional essay
- the benefits of writing the traditional essay

This chapter also

- presents writing as both a skill and a process of discovery
- suggests keeping a journal

What is your ideal job? Write two or more paragraphs about what your ideal job would be and what your daily activities on the job would entail. Be sure to include your reasons for wanting such a job.

Erickson Stock/Alamy Stock Photo

Observations from co-author John Langan: The experience I had writing my first college essay helped shape this book. I received a C− for the essay. Scrawled beside the grade was the comment "Not badly written, but ill-conceived." I remember going to the instructor after class, asking about his comment as well as the word *Log* that he had added in the margin at various spots. "What are all these logs you put in my paper?" I asked, trying to make a joke of it. He looked at me a little wonderingly. "Logic, Mr. Langan," he answered, "logic." He went on to explain that I had not thought out my paper clearly. There were actually two ideas rather than one in my thesis, one supporting paragraph had nothing to do with either idea, another paragraph lacked a topic sentence, and so on. I've never forgotten his last words: "If you don't think clearly," he said, "you won't write clearly."

I was speechless, and I felt confused and angry. I didn't like being told that I didn't know how to think. I went back to my room and read over my paper several times. Eventually, I decided that my instructor was right. "No more logs," I said to myself. "I'm going to get these logs out of my papers."

My instructor's advice was invaluable. I learned that clear, disciplined thinking is the key to effective writing. *College Writing Skills with Readings* develops this idea by breaking down the writing process into a series of four logical, easily followed steps. These steps, combined with practical advice about prewriting and revision, will help you write strong papers.

Here are the four steps in a nutshell:

1. Discover a clearly stated point, or thesis.
2. Provide logical, detailed support for your thesis.
3. Organize and connect your supporting material.
4. Revise and edit so that your sentences are effective and error-free.

Part 1 of this book explains each of these steps in detail and provides many practice materials to help you master them.

Point and Support

An Important Difference between Writing and Talking

In everyday conversation, you make all kinds of points or assertions. You say, for example, "My boss is a hard person to work for," "It's not safe to walk in our neighborhood after dark," or "Poor study habits keep getting me into trouble." The points that you make concern personal matters as well as, at times, outside issues: "That trade will be a disaster for the team," "Many advertisements are degrading to women," "Students are better off working for a year before attending college."

The people you are talking with do not always challenge you to give reasons for your statements. They may know why you feel as you do, or they may already agree with you, or they simply may not want to put you on the spot; and so they do not always ask why. But the people who read what you write may not know you, agree with you, or feel in any way obliged to you. If you want to communicate effectively with readers, you must provide solid evidence for any point you make. An important difference, then, between writing and talking is this: *In writing, any idea that you advance must be supported with specific reasons or details.*

Think of your readers as reasonable people. They will not simply accept your views, but they are willing to accept what you say as long as you support it. Therefore, remember to support with specific evidence any point that you make.

Point and Support in a Paragraph

In conversation, you might say to a friend who has suggested a movie, "No, thanks. Going to the movies is just too much of a hassle. Parking, people, everything." From shared past experiences, your friend may know what you are talking about so that you will not have to explain your statement. But in writing, your point would have to be backed up, or supported, with specific reasons and details.

Below is a paragraph, written by a student named Finley Woods, on why moviegoing is a nuisance. A *paragraph* is a short paper of around 150 to 200 words. It usually consists of an opening point, called a *topic sentence,* followed by a series of sentences that support that point.

The Hazards of Moviegoing

Personal

Although I love movies, I've found that there are drawbacks to moviegoing. One problem is just the inconvenience of it all. To get to the theater, I have to drive for at least fifteen minutes, or more if traffic is bad. It can take forever to find a parking spot, and then I have to walk across a huge parking lot to the theater. There I encounter long lines, sold-out shows, and ever-increasing prices. And I hate sitting with my feet sticking to the floor because of other people's spilled snacks. Another problem is my lack of self-control at the theater. I often stuff myself with unhealthy calorie-laden snacks. My choices might include a bucket of popcorn, a box of Milk Duds, a giant soda, or all three. The worst problem is some of the other moviegoers. Kids run up and down the aisle. Teenagers laugh and shout at the screen. People of all ages drop soda cups and popcorn tubs, cough and burp, and talk to one another. All in all, I would rather stay home and stream a movie in the comfort of my own living room.

Notice what the supporting evidence does here. It provides you, the reader, with a basis for understanding *why* the writer makes the point that is made. Through this specific evidence, the writer has explained and successfully communicated the idea that moviegoing can be a nuisance.

The evidence that supports the point in a paper often consists of a series of reasons followed by examples and details that support the reasons. That is true of the paragraph above: three reasons are provided, with examples and details that back up those reasons. Supporting evidence in a paper can also consist of anecdotes, personal experiences, facts, studies, statistics, and the opinions of experts.

The paragraph on moviegoing, like almost any piece of effective writing, has two essential parts: (1) a point is advanced, and (2) that point is then supported. Taking a minute to outline "The Hazards of Moviegoing" will help you understand these basic parts. Write in the following space the point that has been advanced in the paragraph. Then add the words needed to complete the paragraph's outline.

ACTIVITY 1

_____   **Point**

1. _____   **Support**

    a. Fifteen-minute drive to theater

    b. _____

    c. Long lines, sold-out shows, and increasing prices

    d. _____

2. Lack of self-control

    a. Often stuff myself with unhealthy snacks

    b. Might have popcorn, candy, soda, or all three

3. _____

    a. _____

    b. _____

    c. People of all ages make noise.

Point and Support in an Essay

An excellent way to learn how to write clearly and logically is to practice composing the traditional college *essay*—a paper of about five hundred words that typically consists of an introductory paragraph, three or more supporting paragraphs, and a concluding paragraph. The central idea, or point, developed in any essay is called a *thesis statement* (rather than, as in a paragraph, a *topic sentence*). The thesis appears in the introductory paragraph, and the specific support for the thesis appears in the paragraphs that follow. The supporting paragraphs allow for a fuller treatment of the evidence that backs up the central point than would be possible in a single-paragraph paper. Unlike paragraphs that are usually developed using one mode of writing, like description, essays are usually developed using several modes of writing to support the single point.

Structure of the Traditional Essay

A Model Essay

The following model will help you understand the form of an essay. Finley Woods, the writer of the paragraph on moviegoing, later decided to develop her subject more fully. Here is the essay that resulted.

Personal

Introductory paragraph

First supporting paragraph

Second supporting paragraph

The Hazards of Moviegoing

I am a movie fanatic. My friends count on me to know movie trivia (who was the pigtailed little girl in *E.T.: The Extra-Terrestrial*? Drew Barrymore) and to remember every big Oscar awarded since I was in grade school (Best Picture, 2020? *Parasite*). My friends, though, have stopped asking me if I want to go out to the movies. While I love movies as much as ever, the inconvenience of going out, the temptations of the concession stand, and the behavior of some patrons are reasons for me to wait and stream the film.

To begin with, I just don't enjoy the general hassle of the evening. Since small local movie theaters are a thing of the past, I have to drive for fifteen minutes to get to the nearest multiplex. The parking lot is shared with several restaurants and a supermarket, so it's always jammed. I have to drive around at a snail's pace until I spot another driver backing out. Then it's time to stand in an endless line, waiting to have our tickets scanned, so we can enter. Once we do get in, we often find our reserved seats are occupied. We then have to find an employee to help us access our seats. I have to shell out a ridiculous amount of money—up to $11—for a ticket. That entitles me to sit while my shoes seal themselves to a sticky floor coated with spilled soda, bubble gum, and crushed Raisinets.

Second, the theater offers tempting snacks that I really don't need. Like most of us, I have to battle an expanding waistline. At home I do pretty well by simply not buying stuff that is bad for me. I can make do with snacks like celery and carrot sticks because there is no ice cream in the freezer. Going to the theater, however, is like spending my evening in a 7-Eleven that's been equipped with a movie screen and

---

continued

comfortable seats. As I try to persuade myself to just have a sparkling water, the smell of fresh popcorn dripping with butter soon overcomes me. Chocolate bars the size of small automobiles seem to jump into my hands. I risk pulling out my fillings as I chew enormous mouthfuls of Milk Duds. By the time I leave the theater, I feel bloated and full.

Many of the other patrons are even more of a problem than the concession stand. Little kids race up and down the aisles, usually in giggling packs. Teenagers try to impress their friends by talking back to the screen, whistling, and making what they consider to be hilarious noises. Adults act as if they were at home in their own living room. They comment loudly on the ages of the stars and reveal plot twists that are supposed to be a secret until the film's end. Additionally, people of all ages create disgusting messes and rude distractions. They leave tacky remnants of candy on the hand rests, stick gum on their seats, and drop popcorn tubs or cups of crushed ice and soda on the floor. They also cough and burp, squirm endlessly in their seats, file out for repeated trips to the restrooms or concession stands, and elbow me out of the armrest on either side of my seat.

Third supporting paragraph

After arriving home from the movies one night, I decided that I was not going to be a moviegoer anymore. I was tired of the problems involved in getting to the theater, resisting unhealthy snacks, and dealing with the patrons. The next day, I subscribed to Disney+, Netflix, and Hulu. I may now see movies a bit later than other people, but I'll be more relaxed watching box office hits in the comfort of my own living room.

Concluding paragraph

Parts of an Essay

"The Hazards of Moviegoing" is a good example of the standard short essay you will write in college English. It is a composition of over five hundred words that consists of a one-paragraph introduction, a three-paragraph body, and a one-paragraph conclusion. The roles of these paragraphs are described and illustrated below.

Introductory Paragraph

The introductory paragraph of an essay should start with several sentences that attract the reader's interest. It should then advance the central idea, or *thesis*, that will be developed in the essay. The thesis often includes a *plan of development*—a "preview" of the major points that will support the thesis. These supporting points should be listed in the order in which they will appear in the essay. Such a thesis might assert, "Winter is my favorite season because I like the weather, the holidays, and the sports," leading to an essay that has a paragraph about weather, followed by a paragraph about winter holidays, and so on. In some cases, however, the plan of development is omitted. For example, a thesis that claims, "Education can be a key to socioeconomic security" doesn't state how the essay will be developed but still advances a central idea.

ACTIVITY 2

1. In "The Hazards of Moviegoing," which sentence or sentences are used to attract the reader's interest?
   a. First sentence
   b. First two sentences
   c. First three sentences

2. In which sentence is the thesis of the essay presented?
   a. Third sentence
   b. Fourth sentence

3. Does the thesis include a plan of development?
   a. Yes
   b. No

4. Write the words in the thesis that announce the three major supporting points in the essay:
   a. _____
   b. _____
   c. _____

Body: Supporting Paragraphs

Many essays have three supporting points, developed at length over three separate paragraphs. However, more developed essays require four or more body paragraphs to support the thesis. This is very common in essays with thesis statements that omit a plan of development. Each of the supporting paragraphs should begin with a *topic sentence* that states the point to be detailed in that paragraph. Just as a thesis provides a focus for the entire essay, the topic sentence provides a focus for a supporting paragraph.

ACTIVITY 3

1. What is the topic sentence for the first supporting paragraph of the model essay?

   _____

   _____

2. The first topic sentence is then supported by the following details (fill in the missing details):
   a. Have to drive fifteen minutes
   b. _____

    c. Endless ticket line

    d. _____

    e. _____

    f. Sticky floor

3. What is the topic sentence for the second supporting paragraph of the essay?

    _____

    _____

4. The second topic sentence is then supported by the following details:

    a. At home, only snacks are celery and carrot sticks.

    b. Theater is like a 7-Eleven with seats.

       (1) Fresh popcorn

       (2) _____

       (3) _____

5. What is the topic sentence for the third supporting paragraph of the essay?

    _____

    _____

    _____

6. The third topic sentence is then supported by the following details:

    a. _____

    b. _____

    c. Adults talk loudly and reveal plot twists.

    d. People of all ages create disgusting messes and rude distractions.

Concluding Paragraph

The concluding paragraph often summarizes the essay by briefly restating the thesis and, at times, the main supporting points. In addition, the writer often presents a concluding thought about the subject of the paper.

1. Which two sentences in the concluding paragraph restate the thesis and supporting points of the essay?

    a. First and second

    b. Second and third

    c. Third and fourth

ACTIVITY 4

2. Which sentence in the concluding paragraph contains the final thought of the essay?
   a. Second
   b. Third
   c. Fourth

Diagram of an Essay

The following diagram shows you at a glance the different parts of a standard college essay, also known as a *one-three-one essay*. This diagram will serve as a helpful guide when you are writing or evaluating essays.

TITLE OF THE ESSAY

Introduction

Opening remarks to catch reader's interest
Thesis statement
Plan of development (optional)

Body

Topic sentence 1 (supporting point 1)
Specific evidence

Topic sentence 2 (supporting point 2)
Specific evidence

Topic sentence 3 (supporting point 3)
Specific evidence

Conclusion

Summary (optional)
General closing remarks
(Or both)

You now have an overview of the traditional form of the essay. In Chapter 2, you will learn *how* to go about writing an effective essay. First, though, it will be helpful to consider the following: the benefits of writing traditional essays, the advantage of seeing writing as both a skill and a process of discovery, the value of keeping a journal, and the ways a computer can enhance the writing process.

Benefits of Writing the Traditional Essay

Learning to write a traditional essay offers at least three benefits. First of all, mastering the traditional essay will help make you a better writer. For other courses, you'll often compose papers that will be variations on the essay form—for example, examination essays, reports, and research papers. Becoming comfortable with the basic structure of the traditional essay, with its emphasis on a clear point and well-organized, logical support, will help with almost every kind of writing that you have to do.

Second, the discipline of writing an essay will strengthen your skills as a reader and listener. As a reader, you'll become more critically aware of other writers' ideas and the evidence they provide (or fail to provide) to support those ideas. Essay writing will also help you become a better speaker. You'll be more prepared to develop the three basic parts of an effective speech—an appealing introduction, a solidly developed body, and a well-rounded conclusion—because of your experience writing three-part essays.

Most important, essay writing will make you a stronger thinker. Writing a solidly reasoned traditional essay requires mental discipline and close attention to a set of logical rules. Creating an essay in which there is an overall thesis statement and in which each of three supporting paragraphs begins with a topic sentence is more challenging than writing a free-form or expressive paper. Such an essay obliges you to carefully sort out, think through, and organize your ideas. You'll learn to discover and express just what your ideas are and to develop those ideas in a logical, reasoned way. Traditional essay writing, in short, will train your mind to think clearly, and that ability will prove to be of value in every phase of your life.

Writing as a Skill

A realistic attitude about writing must build on the idea that *writing is a skill,* not a "natural gift." It is a skill like driving, typing, or cooking; like any skill, it can be learned. If you have the determination to learn, this book will give you the extensive practice needed to develop your writing skills.

People often fear they are the only ones for whom writing is unbearably difficult. They believe that everyone else finds writing easy or at least tolerable. Such people typically say, "I'm not any good at writing," or "English was not one of my good subjects." They imply that they simply do not have a talent for writing, while others do. Often, the result of this attitude is that people try to avoid writing, and when they do write, they don't try their best. Their attitude then becomes a self-fulfilling prophecy: their writing fails chiefly because they have brainwashed themselves into thinking that they don't have the "natural talent" needed to write.

Many people find it difficult to do the intense, active thinking that clear writing demands. It is frightening to sit down before a blank sheet of paper or computer screen and know that an hour later, nothing on it may be worth keeping. It is frustrating to discover how much of a challenge it is to transfer thoughts and feelings from one's head onto the page. It is upsetting to find that an apparently simple subject often turns out to be complicated. But writing is not an automatic process: we will not get something for nothing—and we should not expect to. For almost everyone, competent writing comes from plain hard work—from determination, sweat, and struggle. The good news is that the skill of writing can be mastered, and if you are ready to work, you will learn what you need to know.

Writing as a Process of Discovery

In addition to believing that writing is a natural gift, many people falsely believe that writing should flow in a simple, straight line from the writer's head onto the written page. But writing is seldom an easy, one-step journey in which a finished paper comes out in a first draft. The truth is that *writing is a process of discovery* involving a series of steps, and those steps are very often a zigzag journey. Look at the following illustrations of the writing process:

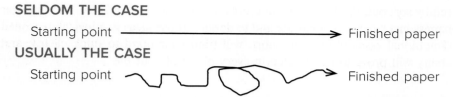

Very often, writers do not discover just what they want to write about until they explore their thoughts in writing. For example, Finley Woods (the author of the paragraph and essay on moviegoing) had been assigned to write about an annoyance in everyday life. She did not know what annoyance she would choose; instead, she just began writing about annoyances in general, in order to discover a topic. One of those annoyances was traffic, which seemed promising, so she began putting down ideas and details that came to her about traffic. One detail was the traffic she had to deal with in going to the movies. That made her think of the traffic in the parking lot at the theater complex. At that point, she realized that moviegoing itself was an annoyance. She switched the focus and began writing down ideas and details about moviegoing.

As Finley wrote, she realized how much other moviegoers annoyed her, and she began thinking that other movie patrons might be her main idea in a paper. But when she was writing about patrons who loudly drop popcorn tubs onto the floor, she realized how much all the snacks at the concession stand tempted her. She changed direction again, thinking now that maybe she could talk about patrons and tempting snacks. She kept writing, just putting down more and more details about her movie experiences, still not having figured out exactly how she would fit both patrons and snacks into the paper. Even though her paper had not quite jelled, she was not worried, because she knew that if she kept writing, it would eventually come together.

The point is that writing is often a process of continuing discovery; as you write, you may suddenly switch direction or double back. You may be working on a topic sentence and realize suddenly that it could be your concluding thought. Or you may be developing a supporting idea and then decide that it should be the main point of your paper. Chapter 2 will treat the writing process more directly. What is important to remember here is that writers frequently do not know their exact destination as they begin to write. Very often they discover the direction and shape of a paper during the process of writing.

Writing as a Way to Communicate with Others

When you talk, chances are you do not treat everyone the same. For example, you are unlikely to speak to your boss in the same way that you chat with a young child. Instead, you adjust what you say to suit the people who are listening to you—your *audience*. Similarly, you probably change your speech each day to suit whatever *purpose* you have in mind when you are speaking. For instance, if you wanted to tell someone how to get to your new apartment, you would speak differently than if you were describing your favorite movie.

To communicate effectively, people must constantly adjust their speech to suit their purpose and audience. This same idea is true for writing. When you write for others, it is crucial to know both your purpose for writing and the audience who will be reading your work. The ability to adjust your writing to suit your purpose and audience will serve you well not only in the classroom but also in the workplace and beyond.

Chapter 7 will provide a more detailed explanation of purpose and audience and how to use this knowledge to better develop your writing.

Keeping a Journal

Because writing is a skill, it makes sense that the more you practice writing, the better you will write. One excellent way to get practice in writing, even before you begin composing essays, is to keep a daily or almost daily journal. Writing in a journal will help you develop the habit of thinking on paper and will show you how ideas can be discovered in the process of writing. A journal can make writing a familiar part of your life and can serve as a continuing source of ideas for papers.

At some point during the day—perhaps during a study period after your last class of the day, or right before dinner, or right before going to bed—spend fifteen minutes or so writing in your journal. Keep in mind that you do not have to plan what to write about, or be in the mood to write, or worry about making mistakes as you write; just write down whatever words come out. You should write at least one page in each session.

You may want to use a notebook that you can easily carry with you so that you can write any time ideas present themselves. Or you may decide to write on loose-leaf paper that can be transferred later to a journal folder on your desk. Many students choose to keep their journals on their home computer or laptop. No matter how you proceed, be sure to date all entries.

Your instructor may ask you to make journal entries a specific number of times a week, for a specific number of weeks. They may have you turn in your journal every so

Getty Images

often for review and feedback. If you are keeping the journal on your own, try to make entries three to five times a week every week of the semester.

Using Technology to Work Efficiently

- If you are using computers at your school to work on your essays, allow enough time. You may have to wait for a computer or printer to be available. In addition, you may need several sessions at a computer and printer to complete your paper.

- There are numerous programs you can use to type and save your work. Google Docs, Pages, Open Office, and Microsoft Office are all programs that offer helpful features for typing and saving students' papers.

- Every program allows you to save your writing by clicking one or more icons. Save your work frequently as you write your draft. A saved file is stored safely on the computer or network. A file that is not saved will be lost if the computer crashes or if there is a loss of power.

- Always keep copies of your work in at least two places. Some local options include your computer's hard drive or a USB flash drive, while some remote options include cloud options like Google Drive or your school's network storage.

- If you have a hard time proofreading on screen, print out your paper, so you can proofread by hand. This also gives you an additional hard copy backup in case something happens to your electronic backups.

- Work in single spacing so that you can see as much of your writing on the screen at one time as possible. Just before you print out your work, change to double spacing.

- Before making major changes in a paper, create a copy of your file. For example, if your file is titled "Worst Job," create a file called "Worst Job 2." Then make all your changes in that new file. If the changes don't work out, you can always go back to the original file.

Using Technology to Communicate Effectively

Much communication that takes place between instructors and students occurs electronically, through either e-mail or a discussion forum on a learning management system like Blackboard, Canvas, or Schoology.

While students are used to texting friends and corresponding through social media, they should remember that correspondence with a professor should be treated differently. E-mails and other correspondence with an instructor should be seen as a more formal type of writing.

A Proper Formal E-mail

Students should keep the following points in mind when corresponding via e-mail with an instructor. (An example of a properly formatted e-mail follows this list.)

- E-mail should be treated like a formal writing assignment.
- You should include a subject line, a formal greeting, an explanation of who you are and what class you are enrolled in, a detailed message, and a formal closing.
- You should revise for clarity and edit for mistakes prior to sending your message.
- You should not expect immediate responses from instructors. You may have to wait up to forty-eight hours before hearing back from an instructor.

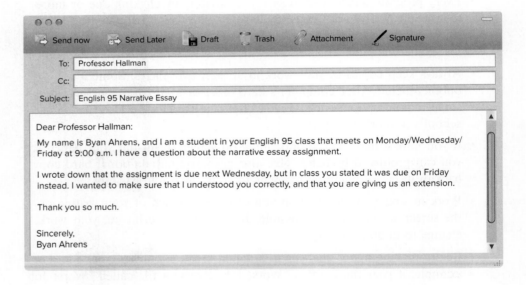

| Send now | Send Later | Draft | Trash | Attachment | Signature |

To: Professor Hallman

Cc:

Subject: English 95 Narrative Essay

Dear Professor Hallman:

My name is Byan Ahrens, and I am a student in your English 95 class that meets on Monday/Wednesday/Friday at 9:00 a.m. I have a question about the narrative essay assignment.

I wrote down that the assignment is due next Wednesday, but in class you stated it was due on Friday instead. I wanted to make sure that I understood you correctly, and that you are giving us an extension.

Thank you so much.

Sincerely,
Byan Ahrens

A Proper Discussion Forum Post

Students should keep the following points in mind when posting on a discussion forum. (An example of a properly formatted forum post follows this list.)

- Discussion forums should be treated like formal writing assignments.
- You should include a title line that explains what the post will be about.
- You don't need to explain who you are and what class you are in, as forums are set up in individual classes and are automatically attached to students' accounts.

- Revise for clarity and edit for mistakes prior to sending your message.
- You should not expect immediate responses from instructors. You may have to wait up to forty-eight hours before hearing back from an instructor.

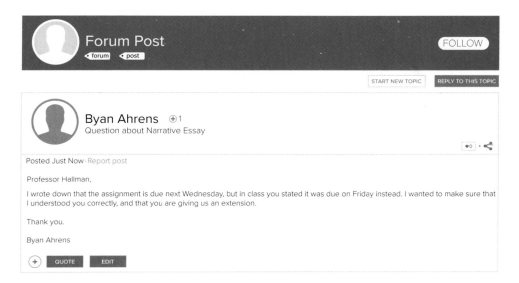

Either write a formal e-mail to your instructor or post the following information to your class discussion forum.

ACTIVITY 5

Your formal e-mail should include:

- full name
- class you are enrolled in
- class schedule
- work schedule
- concerns about the class

Your discussion forum post should include:

- class schedule
- work schedule
- concerns about the class

Using a Computer at Each Stage of the Writing Process

Following are some ways to make computer use a part of your writing. Note that this section may be more meaningful *after* you have worked through Chapter 2 of this book.

Prewriting

If you're a fast typist, many kinds of prewriting will work well on a computer. With freewriting in particular, you can get ideas onto the screen almost as quickly as they occur to you. (See Chapter 2 for an explanation of prewriting and free-writing.) A passing thought that could be productive is not likely to get lost. You may even find it helpful, when freewriting, to dim the monitor screen so that you can't see what you're typing. If you temporarily can't see the screen, you won't have to worry about grammar or spelling or typing errors (all of which do not matter in prewriting); instead, you can concentrate on getting down as many ideas and details as possible about your subject.

After any initial freewriting, questioning, and list-making on a computer, it's often very helpful to print out a hard copy of what you've done. With a clean printout in front of you, you'll be able to see everything at once and revise and expand your work with handwritten comments in the margins of the paper. Don't underestimate the power of working on a printed copy. By allowing yourself the freedom to mark up the printed copy, you will free up more ideas.

If you have prepared a list of items, you may be able to turn that list into a scratch outline right on the screen. Create a copy of your list below the original, and then using the copy, delete the ideas you feel should not be in your paper, and add any new ideas that occur to you. Then use the cut and paste functions to shuffle the supporting ideas around until you find the best order for your paper. If you find that you accidentally deleted an idea that would now work, you can use the copy and paste feature to take that idea from your original list and place it in your scratch outline.

Using the computer also makes it easy for you to experiment with the wording of the point of your paper. You can try a number of versions in a short time. After you have decided on the version that works best, you can easily delete the other versions—or simply move them to a temporary "leftover" section at the end of the paper.

At any point in the prewriting, outlining, or drafting process, you might experience writer's block or need some inspiration. One way to get ideas flowing is to do some Google searches based on keywords in your topic. For instance, you could do a search for "worst jobs" and find some funny lists or sad stories on the topic, and one of these stories could remind you of a bad job experience. It's easy to get caught up in Web searching for hours, so restrict your search to ten or twenty minutes. Set an alarm so that you won't go over your time limit.

If you are trying to find a new topic or can't think of one, try reviewing recent e-mails, text messages, posts on Twitter or Facebook, or even your school library website. What have you been talking about with friends, family, or classmates? What topics have been hotly discussed on your campus? Write about something that interests you.

Writing Your First Draft

Like many writers, you may want to write out your first draft by hand and then type it into the computer for the next steps in writing. Even as you type your handwritten draft, you may find yourself making some changes and improvements. And once you have a draft on the screen, or printed out, you will find it much easier to revise than a handwritten one.

If you feel comfortable composing directly on a computer and you typed your prewriting, you can benefit from its special features. For example, if you have written an anecdote in your freewriting that you plan to use in your paper, simply copy the story from your freewriting file and insert it where it fits in your paper. You can refine it then or later. Or if you discover while typing that a sentence is out of place, cut it out from where it is and paste it wherever you wish. And if while writing you realize that an earlier sentence can be expanded, just move your cursor back to that point and type in the additional material.

Revising

It is during revision that the advantages of using a computer really shine. All substituting, adding, deleting, and rearranging can be done easily within an existing file. All changes instantly take their proper places within the paper, not scribbled above the line or squeezed into the margin. You can concentrate on each change you want to make, because you never have to type from scratch or work on a messy draft. You can carefully go through your paper to check that all your supporting evidence is relevant and to add new support as needed here and there. Anything you decide to eliminate can be deleted in a keystroke. Anything you add can be inserted precisely where you choose. If you change your mind, all you have to do is delete or cut and paste. Then you can sweep through the paper, focusing on other changes, such as improving word choice, increasing sentence variety, and eliminating wordiness.

Editing and Proofreading

Editing and proofreading also benefit richly from computers. Most programs have spell-checker and grammar-checker features. If your own program doesn't have these options, your college computers will likely provide them, or you can use an online program like Grammarly or SpellCheckPlus.

The spell-checker function tells you when a word is not in the program's dictionary. Keep in mind, however, that the spell-checker cannot tell you how to spell a name correctly or when you have mistakenly used, for example, *their* instead of *there*. To a spell-checker, *Thank ewe four the complement* is as correct as *Thank you for the compliment*. The grammar-checker is a good feature, but use it with caution. It will look for mistakes like fragments and run-ons, but it isn't always correct. Any errors it doesn't uncover are still your responsibility.

Once you have checked your essay, you should print it out for a final read-through. Reading aloud, slowly, will help you catch any typos or awkward sentences the programs didn't identify.

A printed paper, with its clean appearance and handsome formatting, often looks so good that you may feel it is in better shape than it really is. Do not be fooled. Take sufficient time to review your grammar, punctuation, and spelling carefully.

Even after you hand in your paper, save the computer file. Your teacher may ask you to do some revising, and then the file will save you from having to completely retype the paper.

TIP

In future assignments, you may be asked to incorporate images or links into a paper. Think of these as garnishes on a dinner plate or lemon slices in glasses of water—they are there to add a bit of color and flavor, not to overwhelm the main dish. Incorporate visuals or links into a paper only with your instructor's approval and guidance.

Know and follow rules, both legal and ethical, about when and how to use others' images as well as how to credit them. You probably know the saying, "A picture speaks a thousand words." Remember this when selecting an image; you should aim to find one that illustrates or supports your paper's main idea.

Links should be used when they provide useful information that enhances the content of your paper. As with images, avoid links that might distract readers from the central point of your paper.

MLA Format

Essays in English classes must be submitted in MLA format. While many students might think this applies only to the use of citations within resource-based essays, MLA format also dictates the formal characteristics of the paper including paper size, margins, spacing, and font. All essays should be formatted like this:

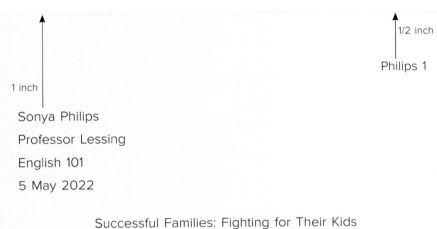

1/2 inch

Philips 1

Model First Page of MLA-Style Paper

1 inch

Sonya Philips

Professor Lessing

English 101

5 May 2022

Successful Families: Fighting for Their Kids

It's a terrible time to be a teenager, or even a teenager's parent. That message is everywhere. Television, magazines, and newspapers are all full of frightening stories about teenagers and families. They say that America's families are falling apart, that kids don't care about anything, and that parents have trouble doing anything. . . .

Double-space lines. Leave a one-inch margin on all sides.

Here is a checklist you should use when preparing a paper:

- Is the paper full-size, 8½ by 11 inches?
- Is there a heading that includes your name, your professor's name, your class, and date?
- Is there a header with your last name and the page number?
- Are your margins one inch all around the paper?

- Is the title of your paper about two inches from the top of the page, centered, and separate from the body of the essay? Have you been careful *not* to put quotation marks around the title and *not* to underline or boldface it? Have you capitalized all the words in the title except short connecting words like *of, for, the, and, it,* and *to*?

- Have you skipped a line between the title and the first line of your paper?

- Have you indented the first line of each paragraph five spaces (half an inch or tab) from the left-hand margin?

- Is your essay double-spaced?

- Have you turned off the hyphenation feature in your word processing program so words are not divided at the end of a line?

- Does your essay use an easy-to-read typeface (e. g., Times New Roman or Calibri) in a 12-point font throughout, including the title? (Have you checked your professor's requirements?)

Also ask yourself these important questions about the title and the first sentence of your paper:

- Is your title a phrase, not a complete sentence? Is your title made up of several words that tell what the paper is about? (The title should hint at the topic, not focus on what assignment it fulfills.)

- Does the first sentence of your paper stand independent of the title? (The reader should *not* have to use the words in the title to make sense of the opening sentence.)

Part 3 will explain MLA format in much more detail, including integration and documentation of sources, proper citation, and proper format of papers that integrate outside sources. Additionally, Chapter 20 includes a properly formatted, complete research essay.

Review Activities

ACTIVITY 6   Answering the following questions will help you evaluate your attitude about writing.

1. How much practice were you given writing compositions in high school?

    _____ Much _____ Some _____ Little

2. How much feedback (positive or negative comments) from teachers were you given on your compositions?

    _____ Much _____ Some _____ Little

3. How did your teachers seem to regard your writing?

    _____ Good _____ Fair _____ Poor

4. Do you feel that some people simply have a gift for writing and others do not?

    _____ Yes _____ Sometimes _____ No

5. When do you start writing a paper?

    _____ Several days before it is due

    _____ About a day before it is due

    _____ At the last possible minute

EXPLANATION: Many people who answer *Little* to questions 1 and 2 often answer *Poor, Yes,* and *At the last possible minute* to questions 3, 4, and 5. On the other hand, people who answer *Much* or *Some* to questions 1 and 2 also tend to have more favorable responses to the other questions. The point is that people with little practice in the skill of writing often have understandably negative feelings about their writing ability. They need not have such feelings, however, because writing is a skill that they can learn with practice.

---

6. What kinds of writing do you do on a computer? What additional types of writing might you want to undertake on the computer?

    _____

    _____

    _____

7. Have you ever kept a diary or journal like the one explained in this chapter? If so, what kinds of ideas, images, or other information have you put into your journal? If you have never kept a journal, why not? Does this fact have anything to do with how you think of writing?

    _____

    _____

    _____

8. In your own words, explain what it means to say that writing is often a zigzag journey rather than a straight-line journey.

    _____

    _____

    _____

    _____

ACTIVITY 7   Following is an excerpt from Finley's journal. As you read, look for a general point and supporting material that could be the basis for an interesting paper.

September 12

I received the results of my first history test today. I really thought I had studied a lot, but my grade was terrible. In high school, I never needed to study much, and I still received As and Bs. My teachers always provided a study guide of some sort, and working through it usually guaranteed a good grade. My history professor didn't give us anything to study from. When I asked about a study guide, I was told that our text, notes, and PowerPoints were the study guide. How was I supposed to figure out what was and wasn't important? At first I was really angry at my professor that she hadn't helped me more. It was hard to sit through the class listening to her go over the exam and reprimanding the class for not doing well. I felt like telling her that maybe it was her fault if so many people did poorly. When class was over, I ended up storming out, promising myself that I was going to complain to the dean. I headed to the dean's office to formally complain, but was told by the assistant that if I hadn't spoken to my professor first, the dean wasn't going to listen to my complaint. As upset as I was, I headed back to my professor's office and waited for her. When she arrived, she seemed really pleased to see me. I was totally surprised! She told me she was happy that I was coming in to talk about my test and would be more than pleased to show me where I had gone wrong. After forty-five minutes, I completely understood what I had missed and what I needed to do for future tests. Our meeting ended with my professor making me promise to visit her again—before the next

continued

exam—to make sure I understood the material. I learned a lot more from this test than just history! I now realize that professors expect us to take responsibility for our learning, which means going to see them for help and not waiting for them to spoon-feed us.

1. If Finley was looking for ideas for an essay, she could probably find several in this single entry. For example, she might write a story about the differences between high school teachers and college professors. See if you can find an idea in the entry that might be the basis for an interesting essay, and write your point in the space below.

    _____

2. Take fifteen minutes now to write a journal entry on this day in your life. On a separate sheet of paper, just start writing about anything that you have seen, said, heard, thought, or felt today, and let your thoughts take you where they may.

Using This Text

Here is a suggested sequence for using this book if you are working on your own.

1. After completing this introduction, read Chapters 2 through 7 in Part 1 and work through as many of the activities as you need to master the ideas in these chapters. By the end of Part 1, you will have covered all the basic theory needed to write effective papers.

2. Work through some of the chapters in Part 2, which describe a number of ways to organize and develop essays. You may want to integrate "Exemplification," "Process," and "Argument." Each chapter opens with a brief introduction to a specific pattern, followed by two student essays and one model essay written in a way that emphasizes that pattern. Included are a series of questions so that you can evaluate the essays in terms of the basic principles of writing explained in Part 1. Finally, a number of writing topics are presented, along with hints about prewriting and revising to help you plan and write an effective paper.

3. Turn to Part 3 as needed for help with skills essential to academic writing in college: information literacy, summarizing and paraphrasing, writing source-based essays, and writing research papers. You will see

that these kinds of writing are variations of the essay form you have already learned in Part 1 and have further explored in Part 2.

4. In addition, refer to Part 4 as needed for review and practice in the skills needed to write effective, error-free sentences.

5. Finally, read some of the selections in Part 5 and respond to the activities that follow the selections.

For your convenience, the book includes the following:

• At the back of the book, there is a checklist of the four basic steps in effective writing.

• At the end of Part 4, there is a list of commonly used correction symbols.

Get into the habit of regularly referring to these guides; they'll help you produce clearly thought-out, well-written essays.

College Writing Skills with Readings will help you learn, practice, and apply the thinking and writing skills you need to communicate effectively. But the starting point must be your own determination to do the work needed to become a strong writer. The ability to express yourself clearly and logically can open doors of opportunity for you, both in school and in your career. If you decide—and only you can decide—that you want such language power, this book will help you reach that goal.

The Writing Process

This chapter will explain and illustrate

- the sequence of steps in writing an effective essay
- prewriting
- drafting
- revising
- editing

Think about an electronic device you use every day; it could be your cell phone, radio, computer, music player, tablet, etc. See if you can write for ten minutes about why you couldn't live without it. Don't worry about spelling and punctuation; just get your thoughts down on paper.
Purestock/SuperStock

Chapter 1 introduced you to the essay form and to some basics of writing. This chapter explains and illustrates the sequence of steps in writing an effective essay. In particular, the chapter focuses on prewriting and revising—strategies that can help with every essay you write.

For many people, writing is a process that involves the following steps:

1. Discovering a thesis—often through prewriting.

2. Developing solid support for the thesis—often through more prewriting.

3.   Organizing the thesis and supporting material and writing it out in a first draft.

4.   Revising and then editing carefully to ensure an effective, error-free essay.

Learning this sequence will help give you confidence when the time comes to write. You'll know that you can use prewriting as a way to think on paper and to gradually discover just what ideas you want to develop. You'll understand that there are four clear-cut goals—unity, support, organization, and error-free sentences—to aim for in your writing. You'll realize that you can use revision to rework an essay until it is a strong and effective piece of writing. And you'll be able to edit your writing so that your sentences are clear and error free.

Prewriting

If you are like many people, you may have trouble getting started with writing. A mental block may develop when you sit down before a blank sheet of paper or an empty computer screen. You may not be able to think of an interesting topic or thesis. Or you may have trouble coming up with relevant details to support a possible thesis. And even after starting an essay, you may hit snags—moments when you wonder, What else can I say? or Where do I go next?

The following pages describe five prewriting techniques that will help you think about and develop a topic and get words written down: (1) freewriting, (2) questioning, (3) making a list, (4) clustering, and (5) preparing a scratch outline. These techniques help you think about and create material, and they are a central part of the writing process.

Technique 1: Freewriting

Freewriting means jotting down in rough sentences or phrases everything that comes to mind about a possible topic. See if you can write nonstop for ten minutes or more. Do not worry about spelling or punctuating correctly, about erasing mistakes, about organizing material, or about finding exact words. Instead, explore an idea by putting down whatever pops into your head. If you get stuck for words, repeat yourself until more words come. There is no need to feel inhibited, since mistakes *do not count* and you do not have to hand in your freewriting.

Freewriting will limber up your writing muscles and make you familiar with the act of writing. It is a way to break through mental blocks about writing. Since you do not have to worry about mistakes, you can focus on discovering what you want to say about a subject. Your initial ideas and impressions will often become clearer after you have gotten them written down, and they may lead to other impressions and ideas. Through continued practice in freewriting, you will develop the habit of thinking as you write. And you will learn a helpful technique for getting started on almost any writing you have to do.

Freewriting: A Student Model

Finley Woods's essay "The Hazards of Moviegoing" in Chapter 1 was developed in response to an assignment to write about some annoyance in everyday life. Finley began by doing some general freewriting and thinking about things that annoy her. Here is her freewriting:

There are lots of things I get annoyed by. One of them that comes to mind is politishans, in fact I am so annoyed by them that I don't want to say anything about them the last thing I want is to write about them. Another thing that bothers me are people who keep complaining about everything. If you're having trouble, do something about it just don't keep complaining and just talking. I am really annoyed by traffic. There are too many cars in our block and its not surprising. Everyone has a car, the parents have cars and the parents are just too induljent and the kids have cars, and theyre all coming and going all the time and often driving too fast. Speeding up and down the street. We need a speed limit sign but here I am back with politiks again. I am really bothered when I have to drive to the movies all the congestion along the way plus there are just so many cars there at the mall. No space even though the parking lot is huge it just fills up with cars. Movies are a bother anyway because the people can be annoying who are sitting there in the theater with you, talking and dropping popcorn cups and acting like they're at home when they're not.

At this point, Finley read over her notes and, as she later commented, "I realized that I had several potential topics. I said to myself, 'What point can I make that I can cover in an essay? What do I have the most information about?' I decided that maybe I could narrow my topic down to the annoyances involved in going to the movies. I figured I would have more details for that topic." Finley then did more focused freewriting to accumulate details for an essay on problems with moviegoing:

> I really find it annoying to go see movies anymore. Even though I love films. Traffic to Cinema Six is awful. I hate looking for a parking place, the lot isn't big enough for the theaters and other stores. You just keep driving to find a parking space and hoping someone will pull out and no one else will pull in ahead of you. Then you don't want there to be a long line and end up finding out someone is sitting in your seat. Then I'm in the theater with the smell of popcorn all around. Sitting there smelling it trying to ignore it and just wanting to pour a whole bucket of popcorn with melted butter down my throat. I can't stop thinking about the choclate bars either. I love the stuff but I don't need it. The people who are there sometimes drive me nuts. Talking and laughing, kids running around, packs of teens hollaring, who can listen to the movie? And I might run into my old boyfriend—the last thing I need. Also sitting thru all the previews and commercals. If I arrive late enough to miss that junk I have to try and find my seat in the dark.

Notice that there are errors in spelling, grammar, and punctuation in Finley's freewriting. Finley is not worried about such matters, nor should she be. At this stage, she just wants to do some thinking and get some material down on the page. She knows that this is a good first step, a good way of getting started, and that she will then be able to go on and shape the material.

You should take the same approach when freewriting: explore your topic without worrying at all about being correct. Figuring out what you want to say and getting raw material down on the page should have all of your attention at this early stage of the writing process.

ACTIVITY 1   To get a sense of the freewriting process, take a sheet of paper and freewrite about some of the everyday annoyances in your life. See how much material you can accumulate in ten minutes. And remember not to worry about mistakes; you're just thinking on paper.

Technique 2: Questioning

In *questioning,* you generate ideas and details by asking questions about your subject. Such questions include *why, when, where, who, what,* and *how.* Ask as many questions as you can think of.

Questioning: A Student Model

Here are some questions that Finley Woods might have asked while developing her essay.

QUESTIONS	ANSWERS
<u>Why</u> don't I like to go to a movie?	Just too many problems involved.
<u>When</u> is going to the movies a problem?	Could be any time—when a movie is popular, the theater is too crowded; when traffic is bad, the trip is a drag.
<u>Where</u> are problems with moviegoing?	On the highway, in the parking lot, at the concession stand, in the theater itself.
<u>Who</u> creates the problems?	I do by wanting to eat too much. The patrons do by creating disturbances. The theater owners do by not having enough parking space and showing too many commercials.
<u>How</u> can I deal with the problem?	I can stay home and stream movies.

Asking questions can be an effective way of getting yourself to think about a topic from a number of different angles. The questions can really help you generate details about a topic.

To get a sense of the questioning process, use a sheet of paper to ask yourself a series of questions about a good or bad experience that you have had recently. See how many details you can accumulate in ten minutes. And remember again not to be concerned about mistakes, because you are just thinking on paper.

ACTIVITY 2

Technique 3: Making a List

In *making a list*, also known as *brainstorming*, you collect ideas and details that relate to your subject. Pile these items up, one after another, without trying to sort out major details from minor ones or trying to put the details in any special order. Your goal is just to make a list of everything about your subject that occurs to you.

Making a List: A Student Model

After Finley did her freewriting about moviegoing, she made up the following list of details.

Traffic is bad between my house and theater

Noisy patrons

Don't want to run into Jeremy

Hard to be on a diet

Kids running in aisles

I'm crowded into seats between strangers who push me off armrests

Not enough parking

Parking lot needs to be expanded

Too many previews

Can't pause or fast-forward as you can when you stream

Long lines

High ticket prices

Too many temptatons at snack stand

Commercials for food on the screen

Can prepare healthy snacks for myself at home

Tubs of popcorn with butter

Huge choclate bars

Candy has always been my downfall

People who've seen movie before talk along with actors and give away plot twists

People coughing and sneezing

Icky stuff on floor

Teenagers yelling and showing off

One detail led to another as Finley expanded her list. Slowly but surely, more details emerged, some of which she could use in developing her paper. By the time she was done with her list, she was ready to plan an outline of her paragraph and then to write her first draft.

To get a sense of list-making, list on a sheet of paper a series of realistic goals, major or minor, that you would like to accomplish between today and one year from today. Your goals can be personal, academic, or career-related.

ACTIVITY 3

Technique 4: Clustering

Clustering, also known as *diagramming* or *mapping*, is another strategy that can be used to generate material for an essay. This method is helpful for people who like to do their thinking in a visual way. In clustering, you use lines, boxes, arrows, and circles to show relationships among the ideas and details that occur to you.

Begin by stating your subject in a few words in the center of a blank sheet of paper. Then, as ideas and details come to you, put them in boxes or circles around the subject and draw lines to connect them to each other and to the subject. Put minor ideas or details in smaller boxes or circles, and use connecting lines to show how they relate as well.

Clustering: A Student Model

Keep in mind that there is no right or wrong way of clustering or diagramming. It is a way to think on paper about how various ideas and details relate to one another. Below is an example of what Finley might have done to develop her ideas.

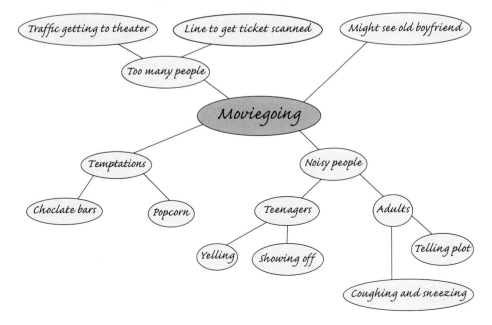

> In addition to helping generate material, clustering can give you an early sense of how ideas and details relate to one another. For example, the cluster for Finley's essay suggests that different kinds of noisy people could be the focus of one paragraph and that different kinds of temptations could be the focus of another paragraph.

ACTIVITY 4   Use clustering (diagramming) to organize the list of year-ahead goals that you created for the previous activity (Activity 3).

Technique 5: Preparing a Scratch Outline

A *scratch outline*, or informal outline, is an excellent sequel to the first four prewriting techniques. A scratch outline often follows freewriting, questioning, list-making, or diagramming; or it may gradually emerge in the midst of these strategies. In fact, trying to make a scratch outline is a good way to see if you need to do more prewriting. If you cannot come up with a solid outline, then you know you need to do more prewriting to clarify your main point or its several kinds of support.

In a scratch outline, you think carefully about the point you are making, the supporting items for that point, and the order in which you will arrange those items. The scratch outline is a plan or blueprint to help you achieve a unified, supported, well-organized essay.

Scratch Outline: A Student Model

As Finley was working on her list of details, she suddenly realized what the plan of her essay could be. She could organize many of her details into one of three supporting groups: (1) annoyances in going out, (2) too many tempting snacks, and (3) other people. She then went back to the list, crossed out items that she now saw did not fit, and numbered the items according to the group where they fit. Here is what Finley did with her list:

> 1   *Traffic is bad between my house and the theater*
>
> 3   *Noisy patrons*
>
>   *Don't want to run into Jeremy*

continued

2	Hard to be on a diet
3	Kids running in aisles
3	I'm crowded into seats between strangers who push me off armrests
1	Not enough parking
1	Parking lot needs to be expanded
1	Too many previews
	~~Can't pause or fast forward as you can when you stream~~
1	Long lines
1	High ticket prices
2	Too many temptations at snack stand
	~~Commercials for food on the screen~~
2	Can prepare healthy snacks for myself at home
2	Tubs of popcorn with butter
	~~Candy has always been my downfall~~
2	Huge choclate bars
3	People who've seen movie before talk along with actors and give away plot twists
3	People coughing and sneezing
1	Icky stuff on floor
3	Teenagers yelling and showing off

Under the list, Finley was now able to prepare her scratch outline:

Moviegoing a problem
- inconvenience of going out
- tempting snacks
- other moviegoers

After all her prewriting, Finley was pleased. She knew that she had a promising essay—one with a clear point and solid support. She saw that she could organize the material into a strong essay consisting of an introduction, several supporting paragraphs, and a conclusion. She was now ready to write the first draft of her essay, using her outline as a guide.

TIP ▶ Chances are that if you do enough prewriting and thinking on paper, you will eventually discover the point and support of your essay.

ACTIVITY 5 Create a scratch outline that could serve as a guide if you were to write an essay about your year-ahead goals.

Writing a First Draft

When you write a first draft, be prepared to put in additional thoughts and details that did not emerge during prewriting. And don't worry if you hit a snag. Just leave a blank space or add a comment such as "Do later" and press on to finish the essay. Also, don't worry yet about grammar, punctuation, or spelling. You don't want to take time correcting words or sentences that you may decide to remove later. Instead, make it your goal to state your thesis clearly and develop the content of your essay with plenty of specific details.

Writing a First Draft: A Student Model

Here is Finley's first draft:

Even though I love movies, my friends have stopped asking me to go. There are just too many problems involved in going to the movies.
There are no small theaters anymore, I have to drive fifteen minutes to a big multaplex. Because of a supermarket and restarants, the parking lot is filled. I have to keep driving around to find a space. Then I have to stand in a long line. Waiting to get my tickets scanned. Finally, I have to pay too much money for a ticket. Putting out that much money, I should not have to deal with a floor that ~~is sticky~~ seems coated with rubber cement. By the end of a movie, my shoes are often sealed to a mix of spilled soda, bubble gum, and other stuff.

continued

The theater offers temptations in the form of snacks I really don't need. Like most of us I have to worry about weight gain. At home I do pretty well by simply watching what I keep in the house and not buying stuff that is bad for me. I can make do with healthy snacks because there is nothing in the house. Going to the theater is like spending my evening in a ~~market~~ 7-Eleven that's been equiped with a movie screen and there are seats which are comfortable. I try to persuade myself to just have a sparkling water. The smell of popcorn soon overcomes me. My friends are as tempted as I am. Choclate bars seem to jump into your hands, I am eating enormous mouthfuls of milk duds. By the time I leave the theater I feel sick.

Some of the other moviegoers are the worst problem. There are teenagers who try to impress their friends in one way or another. Little kids race up and down the aisles, gigling and laughing. Adults act as if they're watching the movie at home. They talk loudly about the ages of the stars and give away the plot. Other people are droping popcorn tubs or cups of ~~soda~~ crushed ice and soda on the floor. Also coughing a lot and doing other stuff—bms!

I decided one night that I was not going to be a moviegoer anymore. I joined Netflix, and I'll watch movies comfortable in my own living room.

> After Finley finished the first draft, she was able to put it aside until the next day. You will benefit as well if you can allow some time between finishing a draft and starting to revise.

TIP

Team up with someone in your class and see if you can fill in the missing words in the following explanation of Finley's first draft.

ACTIVITY 6

Jacob Lund/ Shutterstock

1. Finley has a very brief introduction—no more than an opening sentence and a second sentence that states the _____. She knows she can develop the introduction more fully in a later draft.

2. Of Finley's three supporting paragraphs, only the _____ paragraph lacks a topic sentence. She realizes that this is something to work on in the next draft. _____

3. There are some misspellings—for example, _____. Finley doesn't worry about spelling at this point. She just wants to get down as much of the substance of her paper as possible.

4. There are various punctuation errors, such as the run-on sentences in the _____ paragraphs. Again, Finley is focusing on content; she knows she can attend to punctuation and grammar later.

5. At several points in the essay, Finley revises on the spot to make images more _____: she changes "is sticky" to "seems coated with rubber cement," "market" to "7-Eleven," and "cups of soda" to "cups of crushed ice and soda."

6. Near the end of her essay, Finley can't think of added details to insert, so she simply puts the letters "_____" at that point to remind herself to "be more specific" in the next draft. She then goes on to finish her first draft.

7. Her _____ is as brief as her introduction. Finley knows she can round off her essay more fully during revision.

Revising

Revising is as much a stage in the writing process as prewriting, outlining, and doing the first draft. *Revising* means rewriting an essay, building on what has already been done, to make it stronger. One writer has said about revision, "It's like cleaning house—getting rid of all the junk and putting things in the right order." But it is not just "straightening up"; instead, you must be ready to roll up your sleeves and do whatever is needed to create an effective essay. Too many students think that the first draft *is* the essay. They start to become writers when they realize that revising a rough draft three or four times is often at the heart of the writing process.

Here are some quick hints that can help make revision easier. First, set your first draft aside for a while. A few hours will do, but a day or two would be better. You can then come back to the draft with a fresh, more objective point of view. Second, work from typed or printed text. You'll be able to see the essay more impartially in this way than if you were just looking at your own familiar handwriting. Next, read your draft aloud. Hearing how your writing sounds will help you pick up problems with meaning as well as with style. Finally, as you do all these things, add your thoughts and changes above the lines or in the margins of your essay. Your written comments can serve as a guide when you work on the next draft.

There are two stages to the revising process:

- revising content
- revising sentences

Revising Content

To revise the content of your essay, ask these questions:

1. Is my essay **unified**?
   - Do I have a thesis that is clearly stated or implied in the introductory paragraph of my essay?
   - Do all my supporting paragraphs truly support and back up my thesis?
2. Is my essay **supported**?
   - Are there three separate supporting points for the thesis?
   - Do I have specific evidence for each of the three supporting points?
   - Is there plenty of specific evidence for each supporting point?
3. Is my essay **organized**?
   - Do I have an interesting introduction, a solid conclusion, and an accurate title?
   - Do I have a clear method of organizing my essay?
   - Do I use transitions and other connecting words?

Chapters 3 and 4 will give you practice in achieving **unity, support,** and **organization** in your writing.

Revising Sentences

To revise sentences in your essay, ask yourself the following questions:

1. Do I use parallelism to balance my words and ideas?
2. Do I have a consistent point of view?
3. Do I use specific words?
4. Do I use active verbs?
5. Do I use words effectively by avoiding slang, clichés, pretentious language, and wordiness?
6. Do I vary my sentences?

Chapter 5 will give you practice in revising sentences.

Editing

After you have revised your essay for content and style, you are ready to *edit*—check for and correct—errors in grammar, punctuation, capitalization, sentence structure, word usage, and spelling. Students often find it hard to edit their writing carefully. They have put so much, or so little, work into their writing that it's almost painful for them to look at the essay one more time. You may simply have to *will* yourself to perform this important closing step in the writing process. Remember that eliminating sentence-skill mistakes will improve an average essay and help ensure a strong grade on a good essay. Further, as you get into the habit of checking your writing, you will also get into the habit of using the sentence skills consistently. They are an integral part of clear and effective writing.

Once you have completed your editing, you should always double-check everything by proofreading what you have written. During proofreading you look out for small errors like typos and spacing issues. Proofreading focuses on correcting careless mistakes rather than on the essay's contents.

Chapter 5 and Part 4 of this book will serve as a guide while you are editing your essay for mistakes in **sentence skills.**

An Illustration of the Revising and Editing Processes

Revising with a Second Draft: A Student Model

Since Finley Woods was working on a computer, she was able to print out a double-spaced version of her essay about movies, leaving her plenty of room for revisions. Here is one of her revised paragraphs:

> *Second,*   *tempting*
> ∧ The theater offers ~~temptations in the form of~~ snacks I really don't
>   *battle an expanding waistline.*
> need. Like most of us I have to ~~worry about weight gain.~~ At home I do
>
> pretty well by simply ~~watching what I keep in the house and~~ not buying
>   *like celery and carrot sticks*
> stuff that is bad for me. I can make do with ~~healthy~~ snacks ∧ because there
>   *no ice cream*   *however*
> is ~~nothing~~ in the freezer. Going to the theater ∧ is like spending my evening
>   *comfortable*
> in a 7-Eleven that's been equiped with a movie screen and ~~there are~~
>   *As*
> seats ~~which are comfortable.~~ ∧ I try to persuade myself to just have a
>   *t*   *dripping with butter*
> sparkling water, ∧ The smell of fresh popcorn ∧ soon overcomes me. ~~My~~
>   *risk pulling out my fillings as I chew*   *my*
> ~~friends are as tempted as I am.~~ Choclate bars seem to jump into ~~your~~
>
> hands. I ~~am eating~~ enormous mouthfuls of milk duds. By the time I leave
>   *bloated and full.*
> the theater I feel ~~sick.~~ ∧

Finley made her changes in longhand as she worked on the second draft. As you will see when you complete the activity below, her revision serves to make the paragraph more unified, better supported, and better organized.

Fill in the missing words.

1. To achieve better organization, Finley adds at the beginning of the paragraph the transitional phrase "_____," making it very clear that her second supporting idea is tempting snacks.

2. Finley also adds the transition "_____" to show clearly the difference between being at home and being in the theater.

3. In the interest of (*unity, support, organization*) _____, Finley crosses out the sentence "_____." She realizes this sentence is not a relevant detail but really another topic.

4. To add more (*unity, support, organization*) _____, Finley changes "healthy snacks" to "_____"; she changes "nothing in the freezer" to "_____"; she adds "_____" after "popcorn"; and she changes "am eating" to "_____."

5. In the interest of eliminating wordiness, she removes the words "_____" from the third sentence.

6. In the interest of parallelism, Finley changes "and there are seats which are comfortable" to "_____."

7. For greater sentence variety, Finley combines two short sentences, beginning the first sentence with the subordinating word "_____."

8. To create a consistent point of view, Finley changes "jump into your hands" to "_____."

9. Finally, Finley replaces the vague "sick" with the more precise "_____."

Editing: A Student Model

After typing in the changes to her document and saving it as a second draft, Finley printed out another clean draft of the essay. The paragraph on tempting snacks required almost no more revision, so Finley turned her attention mostly to editing changes, illustrated below with her work on the second supporting paragraph:

> Second, the theater offers tempting snacks I really don't need. Like most of us, I have to battle an expanding waistline. At home I do pretty well by simply not buying stuff that is bad for me. I can make do with snacks like celery and carrot sticks because there is no ice cream in the freezer. Going to the theater, however, is like spending my evening in a 7-Eleven that's been ~~equiped~~ *equipped* with a movie screen and comfortable seats. As I try to persuade myself to just have a sparkling water, the smell of fresh popcorn dripping with butter soon overcomes me. ~~Choclate~~ *Chocolate* bars *the size of small automobiles* seem to jump into my hands. I risk pulling out my fillings as I chew enormous mouthfuls of ~~milk duds~~ *M D*. By the time I leave the theater, I feel bloated and full.

Once again, Finley makes her changes in longhand right on the printout of her essay. To note these changes, complete the activity below.

ACTIVITY 8   Fill in the missing words.

1. As part of her editing, Finley checked and corrected the _____ of two words, *equipped* and *chocolate*.

2. She added _____ to set off two introductory phrases ("Like most of us" in the second sentence and "By the time I leave the theater" in the final sentence) and also to set off the interrupting word *however* in the fifth sentence.

3. She realized that "milk duds" is a brand name and added _____ to make it "Milk Duds."

4. And since revision can occur at any stage of the writing process, including editing, she made one of her details more vivid by adding the descriptive words "_____."

Review Activities

You now have a good overview of the writing process, from prewriting to first draft to revising to editing. The remaining chapters in Part 1 will deepen your sense of the four goals of effective writing: unity, support, organization or coherence, and sentence skills.

To reinforce the information about the writing process that you have learned in this chapter, you can now work through the following activities:

- taking a writing inventory
- prewriting
- outlining
- revising

Taking a Writing Inventory

Answer the questions below to evaluate your approach to the writing process. This activity is not a test, so try to be as honest as possible. Becoming aware of your writing habits will help you realize changes that may be helpful.

ACTIVITY 9

1. When you start work on an essay, do you typically do any prewriting?

    _____ Yes   _____ Sometimes   _____ No

2. If so, which prewriting techniques do you use?

    _____ Freewriting   _____ Diagramming

    _____ Questioning   _____ Scratch outline

    _____ List-making   _____ Other (please describe)

    _____

3. Which prewriting technique or techniques work best for you, or which do you think will work best for you?

4. Many students say they find it helpful to handwrite a first draft and then type that draft on a computer. They then print out the draft and revise it by hand. Describe the way you proceed in drafting and revising an essay.

5. After you write the first draft of an essay, do you have time to set it aside for a while so that you can come back to it with a fresh eye?

    _____ Yes   _____ No

6. How many drafts do you typically write when working on an essay? _____

7. When you revise, are you aware that you should be working toward an essay that is unified, solidly supported, and clearly organized? Has this chapter given you a better sense that unity, support, and organization are goals to aim for?

8. Do you revise an essay for the effectiveness of its sentences as well as for its content?

   _____ Yes   _____ No

9. Do you typically do any editing of the almost-final draft of an essay, or do you tend to "hope for the best" and hand it in without careful checking?

   _____ Edit   _____ Hope for the best

10. What (if any) information has this chapter given you about *prewriting* that you will try to apply in your writing?

11. What (if any) information has this chapter given you about *revising* that you will try to apply in your writing?

12. What (if any) information has this chapter given you about *editing* that you will try to apply in your writing?

Prewriting

ACTIVITY 10

On the following pages are examples of how the five prewriting techniques could be used to develop the topic "Problems of Combining Work and College." Identify each technique by writing F (for freewriting), Q (for questioning), L (for list-making), C (for clustering), or SO (for the scratch outline) in the answer space.

_____   Never enough time

Miss campus parties

Had to study (only two free hours a night)

Give up activities with friends

No time to rewrite papers

Can't stay at school to play video games or talk to friends

Friends don't call me to go out anymore

Sunday no longer relaxed day—have to study
Missing sleep I should be getting
Grades aren't as good as they could be
Can't watch favorite TV shows or stream YouTube
Really need the extra money
Tired when I sit down to study at nine o'clock

<u>What</u> are some of the problems of combining work and school?

Schoolwork suffers because I don't have time to study or rewrite papers. I've had to give up things I enjoy, like sleep and touch football. I can't get into the social life at college, because I have to work right after class.

<u>How</u> have these problems changed my life?

My grades aren't as good as they were when I didn't work. Some of my friends have stopped calling me. My relationship with a girl I liked fell apart because I couldn't spend much time with her. I miss TV and YouTube.

<u>What</u> do I do in a typical day?

I get up at 7 to make an 8 A.M. class. I have classes till 1:30, and then I drive to the supermarket where I work. I work till 7 P.M., and then I drive home and eat dinner. After I take a shower and relax for a half hour, it's about 9. This gives me only a couple of hours to study—read textbooks, do math exercises, write essays. My eyes start to close well before I go to bed at 11.

<u>Why</u> do I keep up this schedule?

I can't afford to go to school without working, and I need a degree to get the accounting job I want. If I invest my time now, I'll have a better future.

major difficulties juggling job and college
- little time for studying
  - textbooks not read
  - papers no revision
  - no study time for tests

- no time for socializing
  - during school
  - after school
- no time for personal pleasures
  - TV shows and YouTube videos
  - Monday Night Football
  - sleeping in

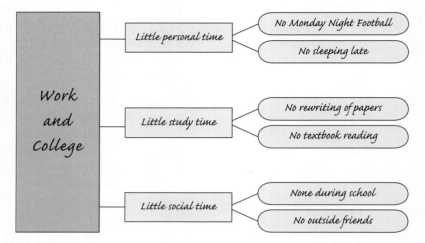

It's hard working and going to school at the same time. I never realized how much I'd have to give up. I won't be quitting my job
because I need the money. And the people are friendly at the place
where I work. I've had to give up a lot more than I thought. We
used to play touch football games every Sunday. They were fun and
we'd go out for drinks afterwards. Sundays now are for catch-up
work with my courses. I have to catch up because I don't get home
every day until 7, I have to eat dinner first before studying. Sometimes I'm so hungry I just eat cookies or chips. Anyway, by the time
I take a shower it's 9 P.M. or later and I'm already feeling tired. I've
been up since 7 A.M. Sometimes I write an English paper in twenty
minutes and don't even read it over. I feel that I'm missing out on a
lot in college. The other day some people I like were sitting in the
cafeteria listening to music and talking. I would have given anything
to stay and not have to go to work. I almost called in sick. I used to
get invited to parties, I don't much anymore. My friends know I'm
not going to be able to make it, so they don't bother. I can't sleep
late on weekends or watch TV and YouTube videos during the week.

Outlining

As already mentioned, outlining is central to writing a good essay. An outline lets you see, and work on, the bare bones of an essay, without the distraction of a clutter of words and sentences. It develops your ability to think clearly and logically. Outlining provides a quick check on whether your essay will be *unified*. It also suggests right at the start whether your essay will be adequately *supported*. And it shows you how to plan an essay that is *well organized*.

There are two types of outlines that will help you create strong essays. The first is a scratch, or informal, outline. As we have seen earlier in this chapter, it can be a very helpful tool in the prewriting stage. The second, a formal outline, is useful during the drafting and revision stages. You should have a working thesis before you begin a formal outline. Unlike a scratch outline, a formal outline employs specific formatting and uses complete sentences.

Another way to use a formal outline is as a check. Once you have written your draft, you can go through and outline your essay. This will help you decide whether you have information that is out of place and will help you find a better location for that information.

The following two exercises will help you develop the two different outlining skills so important to planning and writing a solid essay.

One key to effective outlining is the ability to distinguish between major ideas and details that fit under those ideas. In each of the four lists below, major and supporting items are mixed together. Working in pairs, put the items into logical order by filling in the scratch or formal outline that follows each list.

ACTIVITY 11

Jacob Lund/
Shutterstock

1. Working thesis idea: high school had three major problems

    Involved with drugs
    Leaky ceilings
    Students
    Unwilling to help after class
    Formed cliques
    Teachers
    Buildings
    Ill-equipped gym
    Much too strict

    • _____

    • _____

    • _____

    • _____

    • _____

    • _____

    • _____

    • _____

    • _____

2. Working thesis idea: worst job was as dishwasher

Ten-hour shifts
Heat in kitchen
Working conditions
Minimum wage
Hours changed every week
No bonus for overtime
Hours
Pay
Noisy work area

• _____

• _____

• _____

• _____

• _____

• _____

• _____

• _____

• _____

3. Thesis: Running is an ideal way to get needed exercise.

It's a great way to keep fit.
No special equipment is needed;
    there are no gym fees.
People can run while listening to
    music on headphones.
People can run with friends.
It burns calories and is great for
    weight loss.
It's great for the heart and lungs
    and builds leg muscles.
It is inexpensive.
No special clothing is needed,
    except sneakers.
It's not boring.

A. _____

1. _____

   _____

2. _____

   _____

B. _____

1. _____

   _____

2. _____

   _____

C. _____

1. _____

   _____

2. _____

4. Thesis: The Internet is an invaluable tool for college students.

They can e-mail instructors and classmates.

A. _____
_____

Conducting research online can be stress-free.

1. _____
_____

Students can take online courses.

Many learning centers have online resources, so students can easily get extra help.

2. _____
_____
_____

There is a lot of information online to help with term papers.

3. _____
_____

There are many test preparation sites and practice exercises available.

_____

B. _____
_____

Schedules can be more flexible if all studying is online.

1. _____
_____

It is easy to find additional information on important topics.

2. _____
_____

Students can save money and time traveling to class.

Students can keep up in any course even if they are absent.

C. _____
_____

1. _____
_____

2. _____
_____

Read the following essay and create a formal outline in the spaces provided. One item is done for you as an example.

ACTIVITY 12

Losing Touch

Instead of commuting to an office, Julian stays home on workdays. From the comfort of his home office, he logs into his computer, communicates with his co-workers via e-mail, and submits his reports through a company server. In the evenings, he streams music or movies, or surfs the Internet. On many days, Julian doesn't talk to any other human beings, and he doesn't see any people except those on television or his electronic devices. Julian is imaginary, but his lifestyle is very common. More and more, the inventions of modern technology seem to be cutting us off from contact with our fellow human beings.

Thesis: _____

_____

> The world of business is one area in which technology is isolating us. Many people now work alone at home. With access to a large central computer, employees such as secretaries, insurance agents, and accountants do their jobs at display terminals in their own homes. They no longer have to actually see the people they're dealing with, except for the occasional Zoom meeting. In addition, employees are often paid in an impersonal way. Workers' salaries are automatically credited to their bank accounts, eliminating the need for paychecks. Fewer people stand in line with their coworkers to receive their pay or cash their checks. Finally, personal banking is becoming a detached process. Customers interact with machines rather than people to deposit or withdraw money from their accounts. Even some bank loans are approved or rejected, not in an interview with a loan officer, but by a computer program or app.

First topic sentence: _____

_____

Support: 1. Many people now work alone at home.

2. _____

_____

3. _____

_____

a. _____

_____

b. _____

_____

Another area that technology is changing is entertainment. Music, for instance, was once a group experience. People listened to music in concert halls or at small social gatherings. For many people now, however, music is a solitary experience. Walking along the street or sitting in their living rooms, they wear headphones to build a wall of music around them. Movie entertainment is changing, too. Movies used to be social events. Now, some people are not going out to see a movie. Some are choosing to wait for a film to appear on Netflix or Hulu. Instead of being involved with the laughter, applause, or hisses of the audience, viewers watch movies in the isolation of their own living rooms.

Second topic sentence: _____

_____

Support: 1. _____

_____

2. _____

_____

Education is a third important area in which technology is separating us from others. From elementary schools to colleges, students spend more and more time sitting by themselves in front of computers. The computers give them feedback, while teachers spend more time tending the computers and less time interacting with their classes. A similar problem occurs in homes. As more families buy tablets and computers, increasing numbers of students practice their math and reading skills with apps and programs instead of with their friends, brothers and sisters, and parents. Last, alienation is occurring as a result of YouTube and through Zoom. People are streaming videos and meeting virtually about subjects such as cooking, real estate investment, speaking, and learning a second language. They then practice their skills at home rather than by taking classes in which a rich human interaction can occur.

Third topic sentence: _____

_____

Support: 1. _____

_____

2. _____

_____

3. _____

_____

Technology, then, seems to be driving human beings apart. Soon, we may no longer need to communicate with other human beings to do our work, entertain ourselves, or pursue an education. Machines will be the coworkers and companions of the future.

Revising

ACTIVITY 13

Following is the second supporting paragraph from an essay called "Problems of Combining School and Work." The paragraph is shown in four different stages of development: (1) first draft, (2) revised second draft, (3) edited next-to-final draft, (4) final draft. The four stages appear in scrambled order. Write the number 1 in the answer blank for the first draft, and number the remaining stages in sequence. To help you get started, a few comments about the changes made in draft 2 are included here. Add to these, but also record the changes made in drafts 3 and 4.

Changes in draft 2: *Adds information about sports he/she used to play.* _____

Removes sentence beginning "Psychologists say . . ." _____

_____

Changes in draft 3: _____

_____

_____

_____

Changes in draft 4: _____

_____

_____ I have also given up some personal pleasures in my life. On sundays for example I used to play softball or football, now I use the entire day to study. Good old-fashioned sleep is another lost pleasure for me now. I never get as much as I like because their just isn't time. Finally I miss having the chance to just sit in front of the TV or stream my favorite YouTube videos, on weeknights. In order to watch the whole lineup of movies and sports that I used to watch regularly. These sound like small pleasures, but you realize how important they are when you have to give them up.

_____ I've had to give up pleasures in my life. I use to spend sundays playing games, now I have to study. Im the sort of person who needs a lot of sleep, but I dont have the time for that either. Sleeping nine or ten hours a night woul'dnt be unusual for me. Psycologists say that each individual need a different amount of sleep, some people need as little as five hours, some need as much as nine or ten. So I'm not unusual in that. But Ive given up that pleasure too. And I can't watch the TV shows or YouTube videos I use to enjoy. This is another personal pleasure Ive lost because of doing work and school. These may seem like small things, but you realize how good they are when you give them up.

_____ Besides missing the social side of college life, I've also had to give up some of my special personal pleasures. I used to spend Sunday after-noons, for example, playing lob-pitch softball or touch football depend-ing on the season. Now I use Sunday as a catch-up day for my studies. Another pleasure I've lost is sleeping late on days off and weekends. I once loved mornings when I could check the clock, bury my head in the pillow, and drift off for another hour. These days I'm forced to crawl out of bed the minute the alarm lets out its piercing ring. Finally, I no longer have the chance to just sit watching the movies and sports programs that I enjoy. A leisurely night of *Monday Night Football* or a Dwayne Johnson movie is a pleasure of the past for me now.

_____ Besides missing the social side of college life, I've also had to give up some of my special personal pleasures. I used to spend sunday after-noons, for example playing lob-pitch softball or touch football depend-ing on the season. Now I use the day as a catch-up day for my studies. Another pleasure I've lost is sleeping late on days off and weekends. I once loved mornings when I could check the clock, then burying my head in the pillow, and you drift off to sleep for another hour. These days I'm forced to get out of bed the minute the alarm lets out it's ring. Finally I no longer have the chance to just sit watching the movies and also programs with sports that I enjoy. A leisurely night of Monday Night Football or a Dwayne Johnson movie is a pleasure of the past for me now.

After you have done that, explain why you think that drafts 2, 3, and 4 are each better than the one that preceded them. In other words, explain what improvements that writer has made to each. As you do this, consider the following questions:

1. Is this version of the paragraph better unified, supported, and organized than the previous one? (Review the Revising Content questions presented earlier in this chapter.)

2. Has the student revised sentences? (Review the Revising Sentences questions presented earlier in this chapter.)

3. Has the student edited for mistakes in grammar, punctuation, and spelling? Which ones?

The First and Second Steps in Essay Writing

Describe a favorite childhood place that made you feel secure, safe, private, or in a world of your own. Begin with a thesis statement, something like this: "_____ was a place that made me feel _____ when I was a child." Remember to keep the point of your thesis statement in mind as you describe this place. Include only details that will support the idea that your place was one of security, safety, privacy, or the like.
Pixel-Shot/Shutterstock

This chapter will show you how to

- start an essay with a point, or thesis
- support that point, or thesis, with specific evidence

Chapter 2 emphasized how prewriting and revising can help you become an effective writer. This chapter focuses on the first two steps in writing an effective essay:

1. Begin with a point, or thesis.

2. Support the thesis with specific evidence.

The chapters that follow will focus on the third and fourth steps in writing:

3. Organize and connect the specific evidence (Chapter 4).

4. Write clear, error-free sentences (Chapter 5).

Step 1: Begin with a Point, or Thesis

Your first step in writing is to discover what point you want to make and to write that point out as a single sentence. There are two reasons for doing this. You want to know right from the start if you have a clear and workable thesis. Also, you will be able to use the thesis as a guide while writing your essay. At any stage you can ask yourself, Does this support my thesis? With the thesis as a guide, the danger of drifting away from the point of the essay is greatly reduced.

Understanding Thesis Statements

In Chapter 1, you learned that effective essays center around a thesis, or main point, that a writer wishes to express. This central idea is usually presented as a *thesis statement* in an essay's introductory paragraph.

A good thesis statement does two things. First, it tells readers an essay's *topic*. Second, it presents the writer's *attitude, opinion, idea,* or *point* about that topic. This is often referred to as the *author's claim.* For example, look at the following thesis statement:

Owning a pet has several important benefits.

In this thesis statement, the topic is *owning a pet;* the writer's main point is that owning a pet *has several important benefits.*

ACTIVITY 1   For each thesis statement below, single-underline the topic and double-underline the main point that the writer wishes to express about the topic.

EXAMPLES

Our company president should be fired for three main reasons.
The Internet has led to new kinds of frustration in everyday life.

1. Having to care for a child requires hard work, commitment, and patience.

2. Celebrities are often poor role models because of the ways they dress, talk, and behave.

3. My first night as a security guard turned out to be one of the most frightening experiences of my life.

4. SUVs are inferior to cars because they are harder to control, more expensive, and dangerous to the environment.

5. The twentieth century produced three inventions that dramatically changed the lives of all Americans.

6. Stress in the fast-food workplace has led to serious physical, psychological, and emotional problems for employees.

7. Advertisers target young people when marketing e-cigarettes, cell phones, and trendy clothing.

8. Christian Bale's varied film roles demonstrate his versatility as an actor.

9. American carmakers need to produce vehicles that are electric, safe, and less expensive.

10. Being successful at any job requires punctuality, dependability, and ambition.

Writing a Good Thesis I

Now that you know how thesis statements work, you can begin writing your own. To start, you need a topic that is neither too broad nor too narrow. Suppose, for example, that an instructor asks you to write a paper on marriage. Such a subject is too broad to cover in a five-hundred-word essay. You would have to write a book to support adequately any point you might make about the general subject of marriage. What you would need to do, then, is limit your subject. Narrow it down until you have a thesis that you can deal with specifically in about five hundred words. In the box that follows are (1) several general subjects, (2) a limited version of each general subject, and (3) a thesis statement about each limited subject.

General Subject	Limited Subject	Thesis
Marriage	Honeymoon	A honeymoon is perhaps the worst way to begin a marriage.
Family	Older sister	My older sister helped me overcome my shyness.
Television	Educational programming	Television stations offer many great educational programs for young children.
Children	Children helping with chores	My spouse and I have several creative ways to encourage our children to complete household duties.
Sports	Players' salaries	Players' high salaries are bad for the game, for the fans, and for the values our children are developing.

Sometimes a subject must go through several stages of limiting before it is narrow enough to write about. Below are four lists reflecting several stages that writers went through in moving from a general subject to a narrow thesis statement. Number the stages in each list from 1 to 5, with 1 marking the broadest stage and 5 marking the thesis.

LIST 1

_____ Major league baseball players

_____ Athletes

_____ Major league pitchers' salaries too high

_____ Professional athletes

_____ Major league pitchers

LIST 2

_____ John Philip Sousa

_____ American composers

_____ Music 101 taught me to appreciate Sousa's band music.

_____ Music

_____ Band music

LIST 3

_____ Retail companies

_____ Supermarkets

_____ Dealing with customers

_____ Working in a supermarket

_____ I've learned how to handle unpleasant supermarket customers.

LIST 4

_____ Camping

_____ First camping trip

_____ Summer vacation

_____ My first camping trip was a disastrous experience.

_____ Vacations

Later in this chapter, you will get more practice in narrowing general subjects to thesis statements.

How to Limit and Focus Your Thesis

You have just learned that it is important to _limit_ a topic. One way to do this is by clustering, which is also a good way to gather information. (If necessary, turn back to Chapter 2 to review how to cluster.) Let's say your instructor assigns a paper on physical exercise. Obviously, this is far too broad a topic for a short paper. Therefore, you can try to cluster ideas around this topic as a way to limit it to an aspect of the topic that you know most about or that you are most interested in. Here's an example of how one student began to use this method to limit her topic:

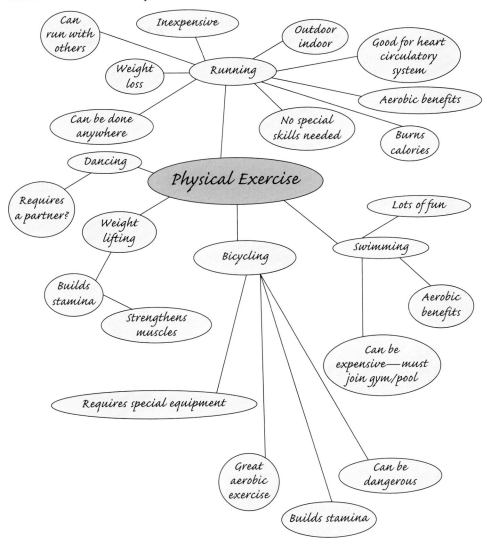

Immediately after completing this exercise, the student realized that the type of physical exercise she knew most about was running. So, she decided to limit her essay to that topic. However, she also knew that she would have to *focus* on a main point about running and that her clustering suggested several different main points. Here are just three:

- Running <u>is an easy way to get needed exercise: it is inexpensive, can be done almost anywhere, and requires few special skills.</u>

- Running <u>benefits the lungs, circulatory system, and the leg muscles.</u>
- Running <u>burns calories and helps maintain a healthy weight.</u>

To determine which of these three main points she could most easily write about, the student used another prewriting technique, making a list. (If necessary, turn back to Chapter 2 to review list making.) In fact, she listed everything she knew about each of her three potential thesis statements:

Easy way to get exercise	Benefits circulatory system, lungs, muscles	Helps maintain a healthy weight
Can be done outside or inside	Strengthens heart muscle	Lost 20 pounds in one year running three times a week
No special training needed	Strengthens lungs, improves breathing	
Inexpensive	Slows pulse rate	
No special location needed	Increases blood supply	
No uniform or special clothing required		
Can be done with others		
Can be done while listening to music on headset		

It is obvious from what we see here that the interests of the student favor writing about why running is an easy way to get exercise.

As you can see, limiting or narrowing a topic is extremely important. However, you will also have to *focus* on a main point. Writers should always be committed to the ideas they are discussing. So, if possible, always write about the main point that you know most about, that you are most interested in, or that you are most passionate about.

Below is a list of thesis statements that make or focus on different main points about the same topic. Each can be the foundation of a very different essay.

Topic	Main Point
Some professional athletes	act as negative role models for young people.
Some professional athletes	have to train year round.

Topic	Main Point
Some professional athletes	have caused themselves harm by taking steroids.
Some professional athletes	contribute time and money to worthy causes.
Some professional athletes	forget they are members of a team that needs to work together.
Going to college	demands careful time management.
Going to college	enables people to appreciate different cultures and lifestyles.
Going to college	provides students with analytical skills that can lead to rewarding careers.
Going to college	requires study habits different from those used in high school.
Conserving energy at home	saves residents a great deal of money.
Conserving energy at home	reduces air pollution caused by the burning of fossil fuels.
Conserving energy at home	doesn't require a change in lifestyle.
Conserving energy at home	reduces our dependence on foreign sources of energy.
The Internet	should be regulated to protect children.
The Internet	is an inexpensive way to transmit information.
The Internet	is a valuable academic tool.
The Internet	enables millions of people to speak out on important social and political issues.

As you can see, you can write several different thesis statements about the same topic. In each case, of course, your purpose will help determine your main point and may even help shape the organization of your paper. Below is a list of several different thesis statements written on "heating costs." Each serves a different purpose.

Purpose	Thesis
To analyze	A home energy audit revealed that we can reduce home heating costs by $500 a year.
To explain a cause	Our home heating costs were high because of poor insulation, drafty windows, and an inefficient furnace.

Purpose	Thesis
To contrast	Homes using passive solar energy have lower heating bills than others.
To explain an effect	Higher heating costs have made architects design more energy-efficient homes.
To explain a process	Lowering home heating costs is easy if one follows three basic steps.
To offer a solution	People who own older homes should have an energy audit to find ways to reduce heating costs.
To classify	Heating costs can be reduced by using fossil-fuel alternatives: solar, wind, and geothermal.
To explain advantages	Reducing heating costs not only saves money, but it also increases the value of a home and helps the environment.
To explain disadvantages	Installing solar panels will reduce heating costs, but they are unsightly and expensive.

Writing a Good Thesis II

When writing thesis statements, people often make mistakes that undermine their chances of producing an effective essay. One mistake is to simply announce the subject rather than state a true thesis. A second mistake is to write a thesis that is too broad, and a third is to write a thesis that is too narrow. A fourth error is to write a thesis containing more than one idea. Here are tips for avoiding such mistakes and writing good thesis statements.

1 Write Statements, Not Announcements

The subject of this paper will be my parents.

I want to talk about the crime wave in our country.

The millennial generation is the concern of this essay.

In this first group, the sentences are not thesis statements but announcements of a topic. For instance, "The subject of this paper will be my parents" does not make a point about the parents but merely tells, in a rather weak and unimaginative way, the writer's general subject. Remember, a thesis statement must make a point about a limited subject. Effective thesis statements based on the above sentences could be as follows:

My parents each struggled with personal demons.

The recent crime wave in our city has several apparent causes.

The millennial generation has changed American society in key ways.

2 Avoid Statements That Are Too Broad

Disease has shaped human history.

Insects are fascinating creatures.

Men and women are very different.

In the preceding examples, each statement is too broad to be supported adequately in a student essay. For instance, "Disease has shaped human history" would require far more than a five-hundred-word essay. In fact, there are many lengthy books written on the exact same topic. Remember, your thesis statement should be focused enough that it can be effectively supported in a five-paragraph essay. Revised thesis statements based on the topics in the above sentences could be as follows:

In 2020, Covid-19 changed people's views about regularly wearing face masks when in public.

Strength, organization, and communication make the ant one of nature's most successful insects.

Men and women are often treated very differently in the workplace.

3 Avoid Statements That Are Too Narrow

Here are three statements that are too narrow:

The speed limit near my home is sixty-five miles per hour.

A hurricane hit southern Florida last summer.

A person must be at least thirty-five years old to be elected president of the United States.

In this third group, there is no room in any of the three statements for support to be given. For instance, "The speed limit near my home is sixty-five miles per hour" is too narrow to be expanded into a paper. It is a simple fact that does not require any support. Such a statement is sometimes called a *dead-end statement:* there is no place to go with it. Remember, a thesis statement must be broad enough to require support in an essay. Successful thesis statements based on the preceding sentences are as follows:

The speed limit near my home should be lowered to fifty-five miles per hour for several reasons.

Federal officials made a number of mistakes in their response to the recent Florida hurricane.

The requirement that a U.S. president must be at least thirty-five years old is unfair and unreasonable.

4 Make Sure Statements Develop Only One Idea

Here are three statements that contain more than one idea:

> One of the most serious problems affecting young people today is bullying, and it is time more kids learned the value of helping others.

> Studying with others has several benefits, but it also has drawbacks and can be difficult to schedule.

> Teachers have played an important role in my life, but they were not as important as my parents.

In this fourth group, each statement contains more than one idea. For instance, "One of the most serious problems affecting young people today is bullying, *and* it is time more kids learned the value of helping others" clearly has two separate ideas ("One of the most serious problems affecting young people today is bullying" *and* "it is time more kids learned the value of helping others"). The reader is asked to focus on two separate points, each of which more logically belongs in an essay of its own. Remember, the point of an essay is to communicate a *single* main idea to readers. To be as clear as possible, then, try to limit your thesis statement to the single key idea you want your readers to know. Revised thesis statements based on each of the examples above are as follows:

> One of the most serious problems affecting young people today is bullying.

> Studying with others has several benefits.

> Teachers have played an important role in my life.

ACTIVITY 3

Write *TN* in the space next to the two statements that are too narrow to be developed in an essay. Write *TB* beside the two statements that are too broad to be covered in an essay. Then, in the spaces provided, revise one of the too-narrow statements and one of the too-broad statements to make them each an effective thesis.

_____ 1. The way our society treats elderly people is unbelievable.

_____

_____ 2. Enrollment at Freestone State College increased by 10 percent.

_____

_____

_____ 3. California has much to offer the tourist.

_____

_____

_____   4. I failed my biology course.

_____

_____

Step 2: Support the Thesis with Specific Evidence

The first essential step in writing a successful essay is to formulate a clearly stated thesis. The second basic step is to support the thesis with specific reasons or details.

To ensure that your essay will have adequate support, you may find an informal outline very helpful. Write down a brief version of your thesis idea, and then work out and jot down the three points that will support the thesis.

Here is the scratch outline that was prepared by the author of the earlier essay on moviegoing:

Moviegoing a problem

- _inconvenience of going out_

- _tempting snacks_

- _other moviegoers_

A scratch outline like this one looks simple, but developing it often requires a great deal of careful thinking. The time spent on developing a logical outline is invaluable, though. Once you have planned the steps that logically support your thesis, you will be in an excellent position to go on to write an effective essay.

Activities in this section will give you practice in the crucial skill of planning an essay clearly.

Following are ten informal outlines. Working with a partner, complete any five of them by adding a third logical supporting point (_c_) that will parallel the two already provided (_a_ and _b_).

1. Difficulties of first day on job

    a. Meeting new people

    b. Finding your way around a new place

    c. _____

ACTIVITY 4

Jacob Lund/
Shutterstock

2. Stepmother's admirable qualities

   a. Patience

   b. Thoughtfulness

   c. _____

3. Advantages of summer job on landscaping crew

   a. Learned how to follow directions

   b. Great people to work for

   c. _____

4. Living at home while in college

   a. Stay in touch with family

   b. Avoid distractions of dorm or apartment life

   c. _____

5. Bussing tables worst job ever

   a. Difficult boss

   b. Poor pay

   c. _____

6. College stressors

   a. Worry about grades

   b. Worry about being accepted

   c. _____

7. My excellent high school algebra teacher

   a. Extra help after class

   b. Great practice handouts for tests

   c. _____

8. College library best place to study

   a. Quiet and well-lit

   b. Nothing to tempt me away from my books

   c. _____

 9. Used cars better than new

   a. Less likely to be stolen than new cars

   b. Don't lose their value as quickly as most new cars

   c. _____

10. Companies' annoying practices to increase sales

   a. Junk mail

   b. Spam e-mail

   c. _____

The Importance of *Specific* Details

Just as a thesis must be developed with at least three supporting points, each supporting point must be developed with specific details. Specific details are valuable in two key ways. First, details excite the reader's interest. They make writing a pleasure to read, for we all enjoy learning particulars about people, places, and things. Second, details serve to explain a writer's points. They give the evidence needed for us to see and understand general ideas.

All too often, the body paragraphs in essays contain only vague generalities, rather than the specific supporting details that are needed to engage and convince a reader. Here is what one of the paragraphs in "The Hazards of Moviegoing" would have looked like if the writer had not detailed her supporting evidence vividly:

> Some of the other patrons are even more of a problem than the theater itself. Many people in the theater often show themselves to be inconsiderate. They make noises and create disturbances at their seats. Included are people in every age group, from the young to the old. Some act as if they were at home in their own living room watching TV. And people are often messy, so that you're constantly aware of all the food they're eating. People are also always moving around near you, creating a disturbance and interrupting your enjoyment of the movie.

The following box contrasts the vague support in the preceding paragraph with the specific support in the essay.

Vague Support	Specific Support
1. Many people in the theater show themselves to be inconsiderate. They make noises and create disturbances at their seats. Included are people in every age group, from the young to the old. Some act as if they were at home in their own living room watching TV.	1. Little kids race up and down the aisles, usually in giggling packs. Teenagers try to impress their friends by talking back to the screen, whistling, and making what they consider to be hilarious noises. Adults act as if they were at home in their own living room and comment loudly on the ages of the stars or why movies aren't as good anymore.
2. And people are often messy, so that you're constantly aware of all the food they're eating.	2. And people of all ages leave tacky remnants of candy on the hand rests, stick gum on their seats, and drop popcorn tubs or cups of crushed ice and soda on the floor.
3. People are also always moving around near you, creating a disturbance and interrupting your enjoyment of the movie.	3. They also cough and burp, squirm endlessly in their seats, file out for repeated trips to the restrooms or concession stand, and elbow you out of the armrest on either side of your seat.

The effective paragraph from the essay provides details that make vividly clear the statement that patrons are a problem in the theater. The writer specifies the exact age groups (little kids, teenagers, and adults) and the offenses of each (giggling, talking and whistling, and loud comments). She specifies the various food excesses (tacky remnants of candy, gum on seats, dropped popcorn and soda containers). Finally, she provides concrete details that enable us to see and hear other disturbances (coughs and burps, squirming, constant trips to restrooms, jostling for elbow room). The ineffective paragraph asks us to guess about these details; the effective paragraph describes the details in a specific and lively way.

In the strong paragraph, then, sharp details capture our interest and enable us to share the writer's experience. They provide pictures that make us feel we are there. The particulars also enable us to understand clearly the writer's point that patrons are a problem. Aim to make your own writing equally convincing by providing detailed support.

Write *S* in front of the two selections below that provide specific evidence to support the opening point. Write *X* in front of the two selections in which the opening point is followed by vague, general, wordy sentences.

_____   1. The tree house my father and I built was a masterpiece.

It had three floors, each of which was about seventy-five square feet. There were two windows made of real glass on each floor, allowing sunlight to flood in and making the place pleasant and cheerful. The walls were made of sweet-smelling cedar planks Dad and I salvaged from a landfill. On the bottom floor was a small cast-iron stove, which gave off enough heat to keep us toasty on the coldest winter day. The second floor had an old rocking chair on which I read my favorite comics every summer afternoon. On the top floor, Dad had set up a telescope from which we observed the glories of the night sky.

_____   2. Our first camping trip in Keystone State Forest was disappointing.

Many of the animals we had hoped to see on our walk just weren't there. Some smaller animals were, but we had seen them before in our backyards. The forest was rather quiet. It was not what we had expected. The weather didn't cooperate either. It was dreadful for most of our stay. Then there were the bugs! We had planned for the trip well, spending a lot of money on provisions and special equipment, but much of it was a waste because we left much earlier than we had intended. We came home frustrated and soured on the whole idea of camping.

_____   3. Some things are worse when they're "improved."

A good cheesecake, for one thing, is perfect. It doesn't need pineapple, cherries, blueberries, or whipped cream smeared all over it. Plain old American blue jeans, the ones with five pockets and copper rivets, are perfect too. Manufacturers only made them worse when they added flared legs, took away the pockets, tightened the fit, and plastered white logos and designers' names all over them.

_____   4. Pets can be more trouble than children.

My dog, unlike my children, has never been completely housebroken. When he's excited or nervous, he still has an occasional problem. My dog, unlike my children, has never learned how to take care of himself when we're away, despite the fact that we've given him plenty of time to do so. We don't have to worry about our grown children anymore. However, we still have to hire a dog-sitter.

The Importance of *Adequate* Details

One of the most common and most serious problems in students' writing is inadequate development. You must provide *enough* specific details to fully support the point in a body paragraph of an essay. You could not, for example, include a paragraph about a friend's unreliability and provide only a one- or two-sentence example. You would have to extend the example or add several other examples showing your friend as an unreliable person. Without such additional support, your paragraph would be underdeveloped.

Students may try to disguise unsupported paragraphs through repetition and generalities. Do not fall into this "wordiness trap." Be prepared to do the plain hard work needed to ensure that each paragraph has solid support.

ACTIVITY 6 Both of the following body paragraphs were written on the same topic, and each has a clear opening point. Which paragraph is adequately developed? Which one has only several particulars and uses mostly vague, general, wordy sentences to conceal that it is starved for specific details?

Eternal Youth?—No, Thanks

I wouldn't want to be a teenager again, first of all, because I wouldn't want to worry about talking to girls. I still remember how scary it was to call up a girl and ask her out. My heart would race, my pulse would pound, and perspiration would trickle down my face, adding to my acne by the second. I never knew whether my voice would come out sounding calm and confident or nervous and shaky. Then there were the questions: Would she be at home? If she was, would she want to talk to me? And if she did, what would I say? The one time I did get up the nerve to take a girl in my homeroom to a movie, I was so tongue-tied that I stared silently at the box of popcorn in my lap until the feature finally started. Needless to say, I wasn't very interesting company.

Terrors of My Teenage Years

I wouldn't want to be a teenager again, first of all, because I wouldn't want to worry about talking to girls. Calling up a girl to ask her out was something that I completely dreaded. I didn't know what words to express or how to express them. I would have all the symptoms of nervousness when I got on the phone. I worried a great deal about how I would sound, and I had a lot of doubts about the girl's reaction. Once, I managed to call up a girl to go out, but the evening turned out to be a disaster. I was too unsure of myself to act in a confident way. I couldn't think of anything to say and just kept quiet. Now that I look back on it, I really made a fool of myself. Agonizing over my attempts at relationships made adolescence a very uncomfortable time.

The first paragraph offers a series of well-detailed examples of the author's nerve-racking experiences, as a teenager, with girls. The second paragraph, on the other hand, is underdeveloped. For instance, the second paragraph makes only the general observation "I would have all the symptoms of nervousness when I got on the phone," but the first paragraph states, "My heart would race, my pulse would pound, and perspiration would trickle down my face."

The second paragraph makes the general statement "I worried a great deal about how I would sound," but in the first paragraph the author wonders if their voice will "come out sounding calm and confident or nervous and shaky." And the second paragraph has no specific description of the evening that turned into a disaster. In summary, the second paragraph lacks the full, detailed support needed to develop its opening point convincingly.

ACTIVITY 7

Write a paragraph supporting one of the following points:

1. My room is a mess.

2. My college offers a variety of student activities.

3. Our city has incredible parks.

4. Trader Joe's (or Whole Foods; or My local grocery store) has the best groceries in town.

Afterward, consider reading your paragraph to a small group of classmates. The best paragraphs are sure to be those with plenty of specific details.

Practice in Advancing and Supporting a Thesis

Identifying the Parts of an Essay

Each cluster below contains one topic, one thesis statement, and two supporting sentences. In the space provided, label each item as follows:

> T—topic
> TH—thesis statement
> S—supporting sentence

GROUP 1

_____ a. Films based on historical events are sometimes shown in class.

_____ b. Making history more interesting

_____ c. Some history teachers use innovative methods to increase student interest.

_____ d. Instructors ask students to write short plays dramatizing historical events.

GROUP 2

_____ a. Vegetarian diets

_____ b. Staying away from meat can reduce intake of fat and cholesterol.

_____ c. Eating vegetables helps the environment because raising veggies uses less energy than raising animals.

_____ d. Vegetarianism benefits both the individual and the environment.

GROUP 3

_____ a. Medicine

_____ b. Antibiotics have enabled doctors to control many diseases that were once fatal.

_____ c. Organ transplants have prolonged the lives of tens of thousands of people.

_____ d. Advances in modern medicine have had great success in helping people.

GROUP 4

_____ a. Reading

_____ b. Parents can take steps to encourage their children to enjoy reading.

_____ c. The adults' own behavior can influence children to become readers.

_____ d. Parents can make sure the physical environment of the home encourages reading.

GROUP 5

_____ a. Insects perform many helpful functions for human beings.

_____ b. Insects are essential to the growth of many important crops.

_____ c. Insects

_____ d. Insects protect the environment by removing wastes and controlling disease-causing germs.

This activity will sharpen your sense of the parts of an essay. The essay that follows, "Coping with the Challenges of Elderhood," has no indentations starting new paragraphs. Read this essay carefully, and then <u><u>double-underline</u></u> the thesis and <u>single-underline</u> the topic sentence for each of the three supporting paragraphs and the first sentence of the conclusion. Write the numbers of those sentences in the spaces provided at the end.

ACTIVITY 9

Coping with the Challenges of Elderhood

[1]I recently read about an area of the former Soviet Union where many people live to be well over a hundred years old. [2]Being 115 or even 125 isn't considered unusual there, and these old people continue to do productive work right up until they die. [3]The United States, however, isn't such a healthy place for older people. [4]Since I retired from my job, I've had to cope with the physical, mental, and emotional stresses of being "old." [5]For one thing, I've had to adjust to physical changes. [6]Now that I'm over seventy-five, the trusty body that carried me around for years has turned traitor. [7]Aside from the deepening wrinkles on my face and neck, and the wiry gray hairs that have replaced my brown hair, I face more frightening changes. [8]I don't have the energy I used to. [9]My eyes get tired. [10]Once in a while, I miss

continued

something that's said to me. [11]My once faithful feet seem to have lost their comfortable soles, and I sometimes feel I'm walking on marbles. [12]In order to fight against this slow decay, I exercise whenever I can. [13]I walk, I stretch, and I climb stairs. [14]I battle constantly to keep as fit as possible. [15]I'm also trying to cope with mental changes. [16]My mind was once as quick and sure as a champion gymnast. [17]I never found it difficult to memorize answers in school or to remember the names of people I met. [18]Now, I occasionally have to search my mind for the name of a close neighbor or favorite television show. [19]Because my mind needs exercise, too, I challenge it as much as I can. [20]Taking a college course like this English class, for example, forces me to concentrate. [21]The mental gymnast may be a little slow and out of shape, but he can still do a backflip or turn a somersault when he has to. [22]Finally, I must deal with the emotional impact of being old. [23]Our society typecasts old people. [24]We're supposed to be unattractive, senile, useless leftovers. [25]We're supposed to be the crazy drivers and the cranky customers. [26]At first, I was angry and frustrated that I was considered old at all. [27]And I knew that people were wrong to stereotype me. [28]Then I got depressed. [29]I even started to think that maybe I was a castoff, one of those old animals that slow down the rest of the herd. [30]But I have now decided to rebel against these negative feelings. [31]I try to have friends of all ages and to keep up with what's going on in the world. [32]I try to remember that I'm still the same person who sat at a first-grade desk, who fell in love, who comforted a child, who got a raise at work. [33]I'm not "just" an old person. [34]Coping with the changes of old age has become my latest full-time job. [35]Even though it's a job I never applied for, and one for which I had no experience, I'm trying to do the best I can.

Thesis statement in "Coping with the Challenges of Elderhood": _____

Topic sentence of first supporting paragraph: _____

Topic sentence of second supporting paragraph: _____

Topic sentence of third supporting paragraph: _____

First sentence of the conclusion: _____

Evaluating Thesis Statements

As was explained earlier, some writers announce a subject instead of stating a true thesis idea. Others write a dead-end thesis statement that is too narrow to need support or development. Contrasting with such a dead-end statement is the statement that is wide open—too broad to be adequately supported in the limited space of a five-hundred-word essay. Other thesis statements are vague or contain more than one idea. They suggest that the writer has not thought out the main point sufficiently.

Write *A* beside the sentence in each pair that is an announcement rather than a thesis statement. Write *OK* beside the statement in each pair that is a clear, limited point that could be developed in an essay.

ACTIVITY 10

1. _____ a. I want to discuss what it means to be a good citizen.

   _____ b. Being a good citizen means becoming informed about important social, environmental, and political issues.

2. _____ a. I made several mistakes in the process of trying to win the respect and affection of my teenage stepson.

   _____ b. My thesis in this paper is relationships between stepparents and stepchildren.

3. _____ a. Successfully purchasing a good used car requires four simple steps.

   _____ b. This paper explains how to purchase a good used car.

4. _____ a. This paper will be about sharing housework.

   _____ b. Deciding who will perform certain unpleasant household chores can be the crisis that makes or breaks a marriage.

5. _____ a. I want to show how cardiology has changed in the last twenty years.

   _____ b. The advances in cardiology in the last twenty years have been miraculous.

Write *TN* beside the statement in each pair that is too narrow to be developed in an essay. Write *OK* beside the statement in each pair that is a clear, limited point.

ACTIVITY 11

1. _____ a. It snowed last winter.

   _____ b. The snow last winter caused many hardships.

2. _____ a. The library is located in the center of town.

   _____ b. The library is conveniently located in the center of town.

3. _____ a. The addition of a fifty-seat computer lab at our college has made it possible to expand the computer-science, mathematics, and English curricula.

   _____ b. Our college just added a fifty-seat computer lab.

4. _____ a. Leslie Marmon Silko's novel *Gardens in the Dunes* is about a Native American girl.

_____ b. Leslie Marmon Silko's novel *Gardens in the Dunes* explores the struggles a Native American girl experiences as she navigates her identity.

5. _____ a. Americans are living longer than before because of better diets, a cleaner environment, and advanced medical care.

_____ b. The average American can now expect to live longer than before.

ACTIVITY 12

Write *TB* beside the statement in each pair that is too broad to be developed in an essay. Write *OK* beside the statement in each pair that is a clear, limited point.

1. _____ a. After-school art and athletic clubs provide healthy outlets for young people.

_____ b. After-school art and athletic clubs at Garfield Junior High School have helped reduce the number of thefts, gang wars, and acts of vandalism once common in our community.

2. _____ a. The educational system in the United States needs to be improved.

_____ b. The educational system in my hometown could be improved by eliminating the current school board, hiring more teachers, and holding parents accountable.

3. _____ a. The attacks of 9/11 dramatized the heroism we have come to expect from our police and firefighters.

_____ b. Americans responded well during the attacks of 9/11.

4. _____ a. College classes can be very challenging.

_____ b. Completing a college course requires organization, persistence, and patience.

5. _____ a. Colorado is an interesting state.

_____ b. Adventure enthusiasts can experience exhilarating outdoor activities in Colorado.

ACTIVITY 13

For each pair, write *2* beside the statement that contains more than one idea. Write *OK* beside the statement that is a clear, limited point.

1. _____ a. Working with old people changed my stereotypical ideas about the elderly.

_____ b. My life has moved in new directions since the rewarding job I had working with older people last summer.

2. _____ a. The police officers in our town do their jobs very well and the police chief is really nice.

   _____ b. Our town's police department is efficient, nice, and professional.

3. _____ a. Forest fires are one way nature creates new habitats.

   _____ b. Forest fires destroy lives and property, but they do provide some benefits to the environment.

4. _____ a. My roommate and I are compatible in most ways, but we still have conflicts at times.

   _____ b. My roommate has his own unique systems for studying, writing term papers, and cleaning our room.

5. _____ a. Although the Modern Language Department offers first-rate instruction in several European languages, many professors and students see the need to offer Arabic, Chinese, and Hindi as well.

   _____ b. Many professors and students believe there is a need for courses in Arabic, Chinese, and Hindi.

Completing Thesis Statements

Complete the following thesis statements by adding a third supporting point that will parallel the two already provided. You might want to first check the section on parallelism in Chapter 5 to make sure you understand parallel form.

ACTIVITY 14

1. A successful camping trip requires familiarity with the terrain, a good tent and sleeping bag, and _____ .

2. Our new college library building is massive, overwhelming, and _____ .

3. Successful TV shows have good actors, great writers, and _____ _____ .

4. School cafeteria food should include non-fried foods, fruits, and _____ _____ .

5. A good teacher should be compassionate, patient, and _____ .

6. Drinking tea promotes good health, a relaxed state of mind, and _____ _____ .

7. The loss of a job can result in depression, weight gain, and _____.

8. Before beginning an exercise program, a person should get a thorough physical examination, decide on his or her exercise goals, and _____

   _____.

9. The sights, sounds, and _____ of the amusement park made the visit very interesting.

10. Cats are good pets because they are easy to care for, quiet, and _____.

Writing a Thesis Statement

ACTIVITY 15

Write a thesis for each group of supporting statements. This activity will give you practice in writing an effective essay thesis—one that is neither too broad nor too narrow. It will also help you understand the logical relationship between a thesis and its supporting details.

1. Thesis: _____

   a. Most animals in animal shelters have been abandoned; therefore, they look at potential families with very sad, longing eyes.

   b. Seeing animals in cages can make a visitor feel sympathy for all the animals.

   c. Puppies and kittens are usually very cute and can easily work their way into a person's heart.

2. Thesis: _____

   a. The actors were very stiff and unbelievable.

   b. The costumes were very poorly designed.

   c. The plot was predictable and boring.

3. Thesis: _____

   a. First, I tried simply avoiding the snacks aisle of the supermarket.

   b. Then I started limiting myself to only five units of any given snack.

   c. Finally, in desperation, I began keeping the bags of snacks in a padlocked cupboard.

4. Thesis: _____

    a. Thomas Jefferson wrote the Declaration of Independence and helped lead the American Revolution.

    b. As third president of the United States, he negotiated the Louisiana Purchase, which doubled the size of the country.

    c. He provided many books to the Library of Congress in its early years.

5. Thesis: _____

    a. Many students who intend to go to law school major in English.

    b. Studying writing and literature is excellent preparation for a career in teaching.

    c. After earning undergraduate degrees in English, some students pursue a master's degree in business administration.

Limiting a Topic and Writing a Thesis Statement

The following two activities will give you practice in distinguishing general from limited subjects and in writing a thesis.

Look carefully at the ten general subjects and ten limited subjects below. Then write a thesis statement for any five of the limited subjects.

ACTIVITY 16

 HINT To create a thesis statement for a limited subject, ask yourself, What point do I want to make about_____ (*my limited subject*)?

GENERAL SUBJECT	LIMITED SUBJECT
1. Apartment	1. Sharing an apartment with a roommate
2. Self-improvement	2. Behavior toward others
3. Family	3. My mother
4. Eating	4. Fast-food restaurants
5. Automobiles	5. Bad driving habits
6. Health	6. Regular exercise

GENERAL SUBJECT	LIMITED SUBJECT
7. Owning a house	7. Do-it-yourself home repairs
8. Baseball	8. Free-agent system
9. Religion	9. Religious celebrations
10. Pollution	10. Noise pollution

Thesis statements for five of the limited subjects:

_____

_____

_____

_____

_____

_____

_____

_____

_____

_____

_____

_____

_____

_____

_____

_____

ACTIVITY 17   Here is a list of ten general subjects. Limit five of the subjects. Then write a thesis statement about each of the five limited subjects.

GENERAL SUBJECT	LIMITED SUBJECT
1. Parenting	_____
2. Cell phones	_____
3. Homework	_____
4. Happiness	_____
5. Weather	_____

6. Career   _____

7. Foreign languages   _____

8. Leadership   _____

9. Math   _____

10. Change   _____

Thesis statements for six of the limited subjects:

_____

_____

_____

_____

_____

_____

_____

_____

_____

_____

_____

_____

_____

_____

_____

Providing Specific Evidence

Provide three details that logically support each of the following points. Your details can be drawn from your own experience, or they can be invented. In each case, the details should show *specifically* what the point expresses only generally. State your details briefly in several words rather than in complete sentences.

ACTIVITY 18

Jacob Lund/
Shutterstock

EXAMPLE

We quickly spruced up the apartment before our guest arrived.

1. *Hid toys and newspapers in spare closet* _____

2. *Vacuumed pet hairs off sofa* _____

3. *Sprayed air freshener around living room* _____

1. The hike up to the mountain lookout was exciting.

   _____

   _____

   _____

2. My hometown is worth visiting.

   _____

   _____

   _____

   _____

3. There are several reasons why I put off studying.

   _____

   _____

   _____

4. Working at the hospital has taught me many valuable skills.

   _____

   _____

   _____

5. I have several ways to earn extra cash.

   _____

   _____

   _____

6. My car needs repairs.

_____

_____

_____

7. Friday evening, I didn't sit still for a minute.

_____

_____

_____

8. My best friends are very different, but I love each of them.

_____

_____

_____

_____

Identifying Adequate Supporting Evidence

The following body paragraphs were taken from student essays. Two of the paragraphs provide sufficient details to support their topic sentences convincingly. Write *AD* for *adequate development* beside those paragraphs. Three paragraphs use vague, wordy, general, or irrelevant sentences instead of real supporting details. Write *U* for *underdeveloped* beside those paragraphs.

ACTIVITY 19

_____ 1.   Another consideration in adopting a dog is the cost. Initial fees for shots and a license might add up to $100. Annual visits to the vet for heartworm pills, rabies and distemper shots, and general checkups could cost $200 or more. Then there is the cost of food. A twenty-five-pound bag of dry food (the cheapest kind) costs around $15. A large dog can eat that much in a couple of weeks.

_____ 2.   People can be cruel to pets simply by being thoughtless. They don't think about a pet's needs, or they simply ignore those needs. It never occurs to them that their pet can be experiencing a great deal of discomfort as a result of their failure to be sensitive. The cruelty is a result of the basic lack of attention and concern—qualities that should be there, but aren't.

_____ 3.   My first flight overseas was a miserable experience. To begin with, even though we boarded our flight on time, we sat on the runway for over two hours. During those two hours, we had no food, no entertainment systems, and no air conditioning. Not only was it hot and stuffy on the plane, but the lack of food and water caused a lot of passengers to get really vulgar and angry. Once we finally took off, I thought things might get better, but a group of schoolkids made the flight even more miserable. For the entire eight-hour trip, they were loud, obnoxious, and rude. They ran up and down the aisles, threw things to each other over the heads of other passengers, and ignored the flight attendants' constant reprimands. The final straw came when we were landing. Just as the wheels were about to hit the runway, the pilot pulled up sharply and we took back off. Everyone on the plane was screaming and crying. After circling for a while, we finally landed and were then told we nearly hit another airplane. If I could have swum home for my return flight, I would have.

_____ 4.   A friend's rudeness is much more damaging than a stranger's. When a friend says sharply, "I don't have time to talk to you just now," it can hurt deeply. When a friend shows up late for lunch or a shopping trip, with no good reason, it can make a person feel as if he or she is being taken for granted. Worst, though, is when a friend pretends to be listening but his or her wandering eyes show a lack of attention. This often feels like betrayal. Friends, after all, are supposed to make up for the thoughtless cruelties of strangers.

_____ 5.   Giving my first shampoo and set to a real person, after weeks of practicing on wigs, was a nerve-racking experience. The customer was a woman who acted very sure about what she came for. She tried to describe what she wanted, and I tried without much success to understand what she had in mind. Every time I did something, she seemed to be indicating in one way or another that it was not what she wanted. I got more and more nervous as I worked on her hair, and the nervousness showed. The worst part of the ordeal happened at the very end, when I added the final touches. Nothing, to this woman, had turned out right.

Adding Details to Complete an Essay

ACTIVITY 20 The following essay needs specific details to back up the ideas in the supporting paragraphs. Using the spaces provided, add a sentence or two of clear, convincing details for each supporting idea. This activity will give you practice at supplying specific details and an initial feel for writing an essay.

Life Off-Line

Introduction

When my family's Internet provider had some mechanical problems that interrupted our service for a week, my parents, my sister, and I thought we would never make it. Getting through long evenings without streaming movies, e-mails, Twitter updates, and Internet searches seemed impossible. We soon realized, though, that living off-line for a while was a stroke of good fortune. It became easy for each of us to enjoy some activities alone, to complete some postponed chores, and to spend rewarding time with each other and friends.

First supporting paragraph

First of all, now that we were disconnected, we found plenty of hours for personal interests. We all read more that week than we had read during the six months before. _____

_____

_____

We each also enjoyed some hobbies we had ignored for ages. _____

_____

_____

_____

In addition, my sister and I both stopped procrastinating with our

homework. _____

_____

_____

_____

_____

Jacob Lund/
Shutterstock

Second supporting paragraph

Second, we did chores that had been hanging over our heads for too long. There were many jobs around the house that had needed attention

for some time. _____

_____

_____

continued

We had a chance to do some long-postponed shopping. _____

_____

_____

Also, each of us did some paperwork that was long overdue. _____

_____

_____

_____

Third supporting paragraph

     Finally, and probably most important, we spent time with each other. Instead of just being in the same room together while we stared at different screens, we actually talked for many pleasant hours. _____

_____

_____

Moreover, for the first time in years my family played some card games and board games together. _____

_____

_____

_____

Because we couldn't keep up with everyone electronically, we had some family friends over one evening and spent an enjoyable time with them. _____

_____

_____

_____

continued

Conclusion

Once our Internet provider got the problems fixed, we were not prepared to go back to our previous ways. We had gained a sense of how our online activities had not only taken over our lives, but had also interrupted our family's life. We still spend time streaming movies, gaming, e-mailing, and tweeting, but we make sure to spend at least two evenings a week focusing on each other. As a result, we have found that we can enjoy our virtual lives and still have time left over for our real lives!

What are some ways besides using electronic media that you and your family or friends spend quality time together? Write about one of these activities and why you enjoy it.

Rawpixel.com/Shutterstock

The Third Step in Essay Writing

This chapter will show you how to

- organize and connect specific evidence in the body paragraphs of an essay

- begin and end an essay with effective introductory and concluding paragraphs

In the previous chapter, you helped complete one student's essay about life without electronic media. Without Internet access, the student had time to enjoy a host of other activities they otherwise would not have had time to do. Write an essay about what, in your life, keeps you from completing tasks or doing what you enjoy. Also include what you would do with your time if this obstacle was removed.

wavebreakmedia/Shutterstock

You know from Chapter 3 that the first two steps in writing an effective essay are advancing a thesis and supporting it with specific evidence. This chapter deals with the third step: organizing and connecting the supporting information in a paper. You'll also learn how to start an essay with a suitable introductory paragraph and how to finish it with a well-rounded concluding paragraph.

Step 3: Organize and Connect the Specific Evidence

As you are generating the specific details needed to support a thesis, you should be thinking about ways to organize and connect those details. All the details in your essay must *cohere,* or stick together, so that your reader will be able to move smoothly from one bit of supporting information to the next. This section shows you how to organize and connect supporting details by using (1) common methods of organization, (2) transitions, and (3) other connecting words.

Common Methods of Organization

Two common methods used to organize the supporting material in an essay are time order and emphatic order. (You will learn more specific methods of development in Part 2 of this book.)

   Time order, or *chronological order,* simply means that details are listed as they occur in time. *First* this is done; *next* this; *then* this; *after* that, this; and so on. Here is an outline of an essay in this book that uses time order:

In order to effectively market the preschool, promoting the center needs to remain at the top of our priority list and should include proper advertising, publicity, and referrals.   **Thesis**

1. *The first step is proper advertising that must start with a well-designed multi-layered website that includes general information, enrollment forms, and profiles of teachers and staff.*

2. *A second step to increasing enrollment is through concerted publicity.*

3. *The final and best way to increase enrollment is to utilize our currently enrolled families.*

Fill in the missing words: The topic sentences in the essay use the words or phrases _____, and _____ to help show time order.

   Here is one supporting paragraph from the essay:

   A second step to increasing enrollment is through concerted publicity. Publicity could include a monthly column in the local newspaper that highlights what is currently going on at the preschool.

continued

Because our curriculum is a blend of Montessori and Carden methods, we have a unique offering; calling attention to the special achievements, programs, and students in our school would offer the positive publicity needed to interest potential families. Each column's publication should be followed by an open house, so potential families can actually visit our school. These open houses should also occur during key enrollment periods to encourage greater attendance. Finally, hosting one or two major events such as a school picnic or music program will continue to raise awareness of our school within the community.

Fill in the missing words: The paragraph uses the following words to help show time order: _____, and _____.

Emphatic order is sometimes described as "saving the best till last." It is a way to put *emphasis* on the most interesting or important detail by placing it in the last part of a paragraph or in the final supporting paragraph of an essay.

TIP ▶

> In cases where all the details seem equal in importance, the writer should impose a personal order that seems logical or appropriate.

The last position in a paper is the most emphatic position because the reader is most likely to remember the last thing read. *Finally, last of all,* and *most important* are typical words or phrases showing emphasis. Here is an outline of an essay in this book that uses emphatic order:

Thesis

> When I compare the two restaurants, the advantages of eating at McDonald's are clear.
>
> 1. For one thing, going to the Chalet is more difficult than going to McDonald's.
>
> 2. Eating at the Chalet is, to me, less enjoyable than eating at McDonald's.
>
> 3. The most important difference between the Chalet and McDonald's, though, is price.

Fill in the missing words: The topic sentences in the essay use the words or phrases _____, _____, _____ to help show emphatic order.

Here is the third supporting paragraph from the essay:

> The most important difference between the Chalet and McDonald's, though, is price. Dinner for two at the Chalet, even without appetizers or desserts, would easily cost $100. And the $100 doesn't include the cost of parking the car and tipping the waiter, which can come to an additional $20. Once, I forgot to bring enough money. At McDonald's, a filling meal for two will cost around $15. With the extra $105, my wife and I can eat at McDonald's seven more times, or go to the movies five times, or buy tickets to a local theater production.

Fill in the missing phrase: The words _____ are used to mark the most emphatic detail in the paragraph.

Some essays use a combination of time order and emphatic order. For example, the essay on moviegoing in Chapter 1 includes time order: the writer first describes getting to the theater, then the theater itself, and finally the behavior of audience members during the movie. At the same time, the writer uses emphatic order, ending with the most important reason for her dislike of moviegoing: "Some of the other patrons are even more of a problem than the theater itself."

ACTIVITY 1

Part A Read the essays listed below (chapter numbers are in parentheses) and identify their method of organizing details—time order, emphatic order, or a combination of both.

1. "Taking on a Disability" (Chapter 9)

    _____

2. "A Vote for McDonald's" (Chapter 13)

    _____

3. "Paying Attention to a Death" (Chapter 10)

    _____

Part B Now see if you can complete the explanations that follow.

The essay titled "Taking on a Disability" uses (*add the missing word*) _____ order. The author begins with the challenge of learning to sit properly in the wheelchair, then moves on to learning to move in the wheelchair, and ends with several problems that occurred next, during the church service. "A Vote for McDonald's" uses (*add the missing word*) _____ order. The writer presents three advantages of eating at McDonald's and ends with the most important one: reasonable prices. "Paying Attention to a Death" uses a combination of (*add the missing words*) _____ and _____ order. It begins with a chronological overview of both the essay and the film, but then it moves into important themes and ideas presented in both pieces. It ends with the significance and impact of each of the deaths.

Transitions

Transitional Words

Transitions signal the direction of a writer's thoughts. They are like the road signs that guide travelers. In the box that follows are some common transitions, grouped according to the kind of signal they give to readers. Note that certain words provide more than one kind of signal.

Common Transitions

Addition Signals: one, first, second, the third reason, also, next, and, in addition, moreover, further, furthermore, finally, last, similarly, likewise, as well, too, besides.

Time Signals: first, then, next, after, as before, while, meanwhile, soon, now, during, finally, after a while, as soon as, at that time, by then, since, suddenly, then, thereafter, by then, in a few hours, by that time, previously, at last, later, all this time, shortly, formerly.

Space Signals: next to, across, on the opposite side, to the left, to the right, above, below, near, nearby, beside, on top of, under, over, underneath, far from.

Change-of-Direction Signals: but, however, yet, in contrast, although, otherwise, still, on the contrary, on the other hand, nevertheless, instead, nonetheless, otherwise, even though, unfortunately, alternatively.

Illustration Signals: for example, for instance, specifically, as an illustration, once, such as, accordingly.

Conclusion Signals: therefore, consequently, thus, then, as a result, in summary, to conclude, last, finally, in review.

Other Transitions: Conjunctive Adverbs and Transitional Phrases

A conjunctive adverb is a word that, when used after a semicolon, connects two independent (main) clauses. A transitional phrase is a group of words that, when used after a semicolon, connects two independent (main) clauses.

Conjunctive adverb: Napoleon successfully invaded Russia in 1812; **however,** he did not occupy it for long.

Common conjunctive adverbs: also, anyway, besides, certainly, consequently, finally, further, furthermore, however, indeed, instead, likewise, moreover, nevertheless, otherwise, similarly, still, therefore.

Transitional phrase: Jean Piaget made major contributions to child psychology; **in fact,** he proved that children and adults reason differently.

Common transitional phrases: for instance, in addition, in contrast, in spite of, in retrospect, once again, on the other hand.

Like transitional words, conjunctive adverbs and transitional phrases signal the direction of the writer's thoughts and guide the reader.

1. Underline the four *addition* signals in the following selection:

ACTIVITY 2

> Applying for financial aid is a very detailed process. First, students should fill out the Free Application for Federal Student Aid (FAFSA). This may require gathering a lot of specific information, but once it has been completed, the Student Aid Report (SAR) should arrive quickly. Second, students should review their SAR to find out how much they will be expected to pay for college and how much aid they qualify for. Next, they should compare financial aid packages offered by each of their chosen colleges. Finally, students should decide which financial aid package they are going to accept, contact the college, and prepare to fill out more paperwork to receive their financial aid.

2. Underline the three *time* signals in the following selection:

> To set up a realistic exercise regime, people need to follow a simple plan consisting of arranging time, making preparations, and starting off at a sensible pace. The first step is arranging time. Most

continued

people who don't regularly exercise have excuses for not exercising: a heavy schedule at work or school; being rushed in the morning and exhausted at night; or too many other responsibilities. One simple solution is to get up half an hour earlier in the morning. The next step is making preparations. Having necessary items like workout clothes, videos, and exercise equipment laid out and ready makes it much easier to get started. Finally, people who are just beginning an exercise regime should start off at a sensible pace. Many workout videos have different levels of exercise programs, and new exercisers should always start with level one to avoid injuries. Through careful planning and common sense, anyone can start exercising.

3. Underline the three *space* signals in the following selection:

The vegetable bin in my refrigerator contained an assortment of weird-looking items. Next to a shriveled, fuzz-coated lemon were two oranges covered with blue fur. To the right of the oranges was a bunch of carrots that had begun to sprout points, spikes, knobs, and tendrils. The carrots drooped into U shapes as I picked them up with the tips of my fingers. Near the carrots was a net bag of onions; each onion had sent curling shoots through the net until the whole thing resembled a mass of green spaghetti. The most horrible item, though, was a head of lettuce that had turned into a pool of brown goo. It had seeped out of its bag and coated the bin with a sticky, evil-smelling liquid.

4. Underline the two *change-of-direction* signals in the following selection:

Taking small children on vacation sounds like a wonderful experience for the entire family. Although this may be true for most, vacations can also be scary or emotionally overwhelming times for children. When children are taken away from their usual routine and brought to an unfamiliar place, they can become very frightened. That strange bed in the motel room or the unusual noises in Grandma's spare bedroom may cause nightmares. On vacations, too, children usually clamor to do as many things in one day as they can and to stay up past their usual bedtime. Since it is vacation time, parents may decide to give in to the children's demands. A parental

continued

attitude like this, however, can lead to problems. After a sixteen-hour day of touring the amusement park, eating in a restaurant, and seeing a movie, children can experience sensory and emotional overload. They become cranky, unhappy, or even rebellious and angry.

5. Underline the two *illustration* signals in the following selection:

    Supermarkets also use psychology to encourage people to buy. For example, in most supermarkets, the milk and the bread are either at opposite ends of the store or located far away from the first aisle. Even if a shopper stopped at the market only for staples like these, he or she must first pass hundreds of items. The odds are that instead of leaving with just a quart of milk, additional purchases will be made. Special displays, such as a pyramid of canned green beans in an aisle or a large end display of cartons of paper towels, also increase sales. Because the shopper assumes that these items are a good buy, he or she may pick them up. However, the items may not even be on sale. Store managers know that the customer is automatically attracted to a display like this, and they will use it to move an overstocked product.

6. Underline the two *conclusion* signals in the following selection:

    Finally, my grandmother was extremely thrifty. She was one of those people who hoard pieces of used aluminum foil after carefully scrubbing off the cake icing or beef gravy. She had a drawer full of old eyeglasses that dated back at least thirty years. The lens prescriptions were no longer accurate, but Gran couldn't bear to throw away "a good pair of glasses." She kept them "just in case," but we could never figure out what situation would involve a desperate need for a dozen pairs of old eyeglasses. We never realized the true extent of Gran's thriftiness, though, until after she died. Her house was to be sold; therefore, we cleaned out its dusty attic. In one corner was a cardboard box filled with two- and three-inch pieces of string. The box was labeled, in Gran's spidery hand, "String too short to be saved."

Transitional Sentences

Transitional sentences, or *linking sentences,* are used between paragraphs to help tie together the supporting paragraphs in an essay. They enable the reader to move smoothly from the idea in one paragraph to the idea in the next paragraph.

Here is the linking sentence used in the essay on moviegoing:

Many of the other patrons are even more of a problem than the concession stand.

The words *concession stand* remind us of the point of the first supporting paragraph, while *Many of the other patrons* presents the point to be developed in the second supporting paragraph.

ACTIVITY 3

Following is a partially completed diagram draft of an essay. The second and third topic sentences serve as transitional, or linking, sentences. Each reminds us of the point in the preceding paragraph and announces the point to be developed in the current paragraph. In the spaces provided, add the words needed to complete the second and third topic sentences.

Thesis

The most memorable sites I visited in Washington, D.C., were the Capitol Building, the Lincoln Memorial, and the Vietnam Memorial.

Our first stop was Capitol Hill, the very symbol of our democratic system. . . .

First supporting paragraph

After leaving the _____, we walked along the Mall to the _____ _____. . . .

Second supporting paragraph

A short distance to the right of the _____ is the _____ _____. . . .

Other Connecting Words

In addition to transitions, there are three other kinds of connecting words that help tie together the specific evidence in a paper: *repeated words, pronouns,* and *synonyms.*

Repeated Words

Many of us have been taught—correctly—not to repeat ourselves in writing. However, repeating *key* words helps tie together the flow of thought in a paper. Below, repeated words remind readers of the selection's central idea.

> One good reason for studying <u>psychology</u> is to help parents deal with their children. Perhaps a young daughter refuses to go to bed when she should and bursts into tears at the least mention of "lights out." A little knowledge of <u>psychology</u> comes in handy. If she is given a choice of staying up until 7:30 with the family or going upstairs and playing until 8:00, she gets to make the decision. In this way, she does not feel so powerless and will not resist. <u>Psychology</u> is also useful in rewarding a child for a job well done. Instead of telling a ten-year-old son what a good boy he is when he makes his own bed, good <u>psychology</u> says to focus on how neat it is and the fact that he did it by himself. The <u>psychology</u> books say that being a good boy is much harder to live up to than doing one job well.

Pronouns

Pronouns (*he, she, it, you, they, this, that,* and others) are another way to connect ideas. Also, using pronouns in place of other words can help you avoid needless repetition. (Note, however, that pronouns should be used with care to avoid the problems described in Chapter 27.) Here is a selection that makes good use of pronouns:

> Lake Bled, Slovenia, is a destination worth visiting. <u>It</u> is a small village in the Julian Alps, and the mountains surrounding the town are so magnificent that <u>they</u> inspire complete awe. In the middle of the lake is the only island in the country, and to get to <u>it</u>, visitors have to take special flat-bottom boats. While <u>they</u> are beautiful, <u>they</u> tip easily, so the boatmen are very careful about how <u>they</u> assign seats. Most visitors go to the island to visit the church, but first <u>they</u> have to ascend the Baroque stairway. <u>It</u> was built in 1655 and has ninety-nine steps leading to the church. Many visitors have to stop numerous times before <u>they</u> are able to get to the top. Luckily, the coffee shop offers <u>them</u> a place to rest before <u>they</u> finish <u>their</u> journey to the church. Once people are done visiting the island, <u>they</u> can return to the shores of the lake and visit the small town of Bled or the romantic Bled Castle.

Synonyms

Synonyms are words alike in meaning. Using synonyms can also help move the reader easily from one thought to the next. In addition, the use of synonyms increases variety and interest by avoiding needless repetition.

Note the synonyms for *method* in the following selection:

> Several methods of fund-raising work well with small organizations. One <u>technique</u> is to hold an auction, with everyone either contributing an item from home or obtaining a donation from a sympathetic local merchant. Because all the merchandise and the services of the auctioneer have been donated, the entire proceeds can be placed in the organization's treasury. A second fund-raising <u>procedure</u> is a car wash. Club members and their children get together on a Saturday and wash all the cars in the neighborhood for a few dollars apiece. A third, time-tested <u>way</u> to raise money is to hold a bake sale, with each family contributing homemade cookies, brownies, layer cakes, or cupcakes. Sold by the piece or by the box, these baked goods will satisfyingly fill both the stomach and the pocketbook.

ACTIVITY 4

Read the selection below and then answer the questions about it that follow.

> [1]When I think about my childhood in the 1930s, life today seems like the greatest of luxuries. [2]In our house, we had only a wood-burning cookstove in the kitchen to keep us warm. [3]In the morning, my father would get up in the icy cold, go downstairs, and light a fire in the black iron range. [4]When he called us, I would put off leaving my warm bed until the last possible minute and then quickly grab my school clothes. [5]The water pitcher and washing basin in my room would be layered with ice, and my breath would come out as white puffs as I ran downstairs. [6]My sisters and I would all dress—as quickly as possible—in the chilly but bearable air of the kitchen. [7]Our schoolroom, once we had arrived, didn't provide much relief from the cold. [8]Students wore woolen mitts that left their fingers free but covered their palms and wrists. [9]Even with these, we occasionally suffered chilblains. [10]The throbbing swellings on our hands made writing a painful process. [11]When we returned home in the afternoon, we spent all our indoor hours in the warm kitchen. [12]We hated to leave it at bedtime to make the return trip to those cold bedrooms and frigid sheets. [13]My mother made up hot-water bottles and gave us hot bricks to tuck under the covers, but nothing could eliminate the agony of that penetrating cold when we first slid under the bedclothes.

1. How many times is the key word *cold* used? _____

2. Write here the pronoun that is used for *father* (sentence 4): _____

3. Write here the words in sentence 3 that are used as a synonym for *cookstove:* _____; write in the words in sentence 10 that are used as a synonym for *chilblains:* _____; write in the word in sentence 12 that is used as a synonym for *cold:* _____.

Introductions, Conclusions, and Titles

So far, this chapter has discussed ways to organize and connect the supporting paragraphs of an essay. A well-organized essay, however, also needs a strong introductory paragraph, an effective concluding paragraph, and a good title.

Introductory Paragraph

Functions of the Introduction

A well-written introductory paragraph performs four important roles:

1. It attracts readers' interest, encouraging them to continue reading the essay.

2. It supplies any background information that readers may need to understand the essay.

3. It presents a thesis statement. This clear, direct statement of the main idea of the paper usually appears near the end of the introductory paragraph.

4. It indicates a plan of development. In this preview, the major supporting points for the thesis are listed in the order in which they will be presented. In some cases, the thesis and plan of development appear in the same sentence. However, writers sometimes choose not to describe the plan of development.

Common Methods of Introduction

Here are some common methods of introduction. Use any one method, or a combination of methods, to introduce your subject to the reader in an interesting way.

- **Begin with a broad, general statement of your topic and narrow it down to your thesis statement.** Broad, general statements ease the reader into your thesis statement by first introducing the topic. In the following example, the writer talks generally about categories of students and then narrows down to comments on a specific type.

> Schools divide people into categories. From the early grades, students are labeled "college track" or "vocational-technical" or "model citizen" or "trouble-maker." Students pigeonhole their fellow students, too. We've all known the "brain," the "jock," the "clown," and the "teacher's pet." In most cases, these narrow labels are misleading and inaccurate. But there is one label for a certain type of college student that says it all: "zombie."

- **Start with an idea or a situation that is the opposite of the one you will develop.** This approach works because your readers will be surprised, and then intrigued, by the contrast between the opening idea and the thesis that follows it.

> Most Americans are not alcoholics. Most do not cruise city streets looking to score cocaine or heroin. Relatively few try to con their doctors into prescribing unneeded mood-altering medications. And yet, many Americans are traveling through life with their minds slightly out of kilter. In its attempt to cope with modern life, the human mind seems to have evolved some defense strategies. Confronted with inventions like television, the shopping center, and the Internet, the mind will slip—all by itself—into an altered state.

- **Explain the importance of your topic to the reader.** If you can convince your readers that the subject in some way applies to them, or is something they should know more about, they will want to keep reading.

> Happy Child Preschool is a valuable and cherished part of our campus, but enrollment has declined dramatically over the past two years. Thus, a task force was commissioned to analyze the causes. The comparative analysis conducted by the task force uncovered numerous ways that other campus childcare centers have achieved success through advertising. The task force agrees that promotion is the number one issue that has been overlooked in the past and the area where major and immediate improvements are essential to the long-term success of the center. In order to effectively market the preschool, promoting the center needs to remain at the top of the priority chart and should include proper advertising, publicity, and referrals.

- **Use an incident or a brief story.** Stories are naturally interesting. They appeal to a reader's curiosity. In your introduction, an anecdote will grab the reader's attention right away. The story should be brief and should be related to your main idea. The incident in the story can be something that happened to you, something you have heard about, or something you have read about in a newspaper or magazine.

> Early Sunday morning, the young mother dressed her little girl warmly and gave her a candy bar, a picture book, and a well-worn stuffed rabbit. Together, they drove downtown to a Methodist church. There the mother told the little girl to wait on the stone steps until children began arriving for Sunday school. Then the young mother drove off, abandoning her five-year-old because she couldn't cope with being a parent anymore. This incident is one of thousands of cases of child neglect and abuse that occur annually. Stories like this one highlight the need for better social programs to help struggling parents.

- **Use a quotation.** A quotation can be something you have read in a book or an article. It can also be something that you have heard: a popular saying or proverb ("Never give advice to a friend"), a current or recent advertising slogan ("Can you hear me now?"), or a favorite expression used by friends or family ("My father always says . . ."). Using a quotation in your introductory paragraph lets you add someone else's voice to your own.

> "Life is not fair, but with education you have a fair chance at life," stated Tyrone J. Flowers, founder of Higher M-Pact, at the spring Excellence in Teaching awards ceremony. As I listened to him, I realized that my desire to keep teaching was stronger than ever because I believe that education is the key to changing a life. Many of my students come to my classroom underprepared and living in terrible situations, but it is my job to open their eyes to the possibilities. Before I heard Mr. Flowers speak, I had been considering getting out of education, but his words inspired in me a new desire to become a better teacher.

The box that follows summarizes the five kinds of introductions. Read the introductions that come after it and, in the space provided, write the letter of the kind of introduction used in each case.

ACTIVITY 5

A. General to narrow	D. Incident or story
B. Starting with an opposite	E. Quotation
C. Stating importance of topic	

_____ 1. The commercial begins with a shot of a beautiful, modern kitchen. The focus sweeps to the clean counters, top-of-the-line appliances, and then focuses on a shiny, industrial-strength red blender. The next shot shows an attractive, athletically trim couple surrounded by gorgeous fruits, vegetables, and leafy greens, making delicious-looking smoothies. As they add the fruits and greens to the blender, they smile and laugh as if this is the most wonderful thing to be doing in the morning. The announcer claims that using this blender is the one change that will make being healthy easy. Viewers should not be taken in. My blender turned out to be expensive, difficult to operate, and incredibly loud.

_____ 2. My father stubbornly says, "You <u>can</u> often tell a book by its cover," and when it comes to certain paperbacks, he's right. Whenever a person is browsing in the drugstore or supermarket and he or she sees a paperback featuring an attractive young woman in a low-cut dress fleeing from a handsome dark figure in a shadowy castle, it is obvious what the book will be about. Every romance novel has the same elements: an innocent heroine, an exotic setting, and a mysterious hero.

_____ 3. We humans can be incredibly lazy. Instead of cooking a simple, nourishing meal, we pop a frozen dinner into the oven. Instead of studying a daily newspaper, we are contented with the capsule summaries on the network news. Worst of all, instead of walking even a few blocks to the local convenience store, we jump into our cars. This dependence on the automobile, even for short trips, has robbed us of a valuable experience—walking. If we drove less and walked more, we would save money, become healthier, and discover fascinating things about our surroundings.

Concluding Paragraph

A concluding paragraph is your chance to remind the reader of your thesis idea and bring the paper to a natural and graceful end.

Common Methods of Conclusion

You may use any one of the methods below, or a combination of methods, to round off your paper.

- **End with a summary and final thought.** When army instructors train new recruits, each of their lessons follows a three-step formula:

  1. Tell them what you're going to tell them.
  2. Tell them.
  3. Tell them what you've told them.

  An essay that ends with a summary is not very different. After you have stated your thesis ("Tell them what you're going to tell them") and supported it ("Tell them"), you restate the thesis and supporting points ("Tell them what you've told them"). However, don't use the exact wording you used before. Here is a summary conclusion:

> Online shopping at home, then, has several advantages. Such shopping is convenient, saves money, and saves time. It is not surprising that growing numbers of people are doing the majority of their shopping on the Internet for everything from turnip seeds to televisions.

Academic

Note that the summary is accompanied by a final comment that rounds off the paper and brings the discussion to a close. This combination of a summary and a final thought is the most common method of concluding an essay.

- **Include a thought-provoking quotation.** A well-chosen quotation can be effective in re-emphasizing your point. Here is an example:

> Rude behavior has become commonplace and needs to stop. People no longer treat each other with the respect and courtesy they should. People talk on their cell phones at inappropriate times and places. Cutting off other drivers in order to save mere seconds happens more and more often. As the Dalai Lama said, "Love and kindness are the very basis of society. If we lose these feelings, society will face tremendous difficulties; the survival of humanity will be endangered."

Academic

- **End with a prediction or recommendation.** Predictions and recommendations encourage the reader to continue thinking about the essay. A prediction states what may happen in the future:

It is believed that as many as two million people are currently undiagnosed with celiac disease or gluten sensitivity. There is currently no medication to cure the disease. If doctors disregard patients who complain of symptoms of the disease, serious physical damage can occur. But if doctors listen to their patients and administer the appropriate tests, proper diagnosis can be made in a timely manner.

A recommendation suggests what should be done about a situation or problem:

Stereotypes such as the ditzy blonde, harried executive, and annoying in-law are insulting enough to begin with. In magazine ads or television commercials, they become even more insulting. Now these unfortunate characters are not just being laughed at; they are being turned into hucksters to sell products to an unsuspecting public. Consumers should boycott companies whose advertising continues to use such stereotypes.

ACTIVITY 6

In the space provided, note how each concluding paragraph ends: with a summary and final thought (write *S* in the space), with a prediction or recommendation (write *P/R*), or with a quotation (write *Q*).

_____ 1. Disappointments are unwelcome, but regular, visitors in everyone's life. We can feel depressed about them, or we can try to escape from them. The best thing, though, is to accept a disappointment and then try to use it somehow: step over the unwelcome visitor and then get on with life.

_____ 2. Saving the environment is up to each of us. Levels of harmful emissions would drop dramatically if we chose to carpool or take public transportation more often. Conserving fuel and electricity at home by sealing up leaky windows and using energy-saving light bulbs would help, too. As David Orr once wrote, "When we heal the Earth, we heal ourselves."

_____ 3. Some people dream of starring roles, their names in lights, and their pictures on the cover of *People* magazine. I'm not one of them, though. A famous person gives up private life, feels pressured all the time, and is never completely safe. So let someone else have that cover story. I'd rather lead an ordinary, but calm, life than a stress-filled one.

Titles

A title is usually a very brief summary of what your paper is about. It is often no more than several words. You may find it easier to write the title *after* you have completed your paper.

Following are the introductory paragraphs for two of the essays in this text, along with the titles of the essays.

> I'm not just a consumer—I'm a victim. If I order a product, it is sure to arrive in the wrong color, size, or quantity. If I hire people to do repairs, they never arrive on the day scheduled. If I owe a bill, the computer is bound to overcharge me. Therefore, in self-defense, I have developed the following consumer's guide to complaining effectively.

Introductory paragraph

Title: How to Complain

> Schools divide people into categories. From the early grades, students are labeled "college track" or "vocational-technical" or "model citizen" or "trouble-maker." Students pigeonhole their fellow students, too. We've all known the "brain," the "jock," the "clown," and the "teacher's pet." In most cases, these narrow labels are misleading and inaccurate. But there is one label for a certain type of college student that says it all: "zombie."

Introductory paragraph

Title: Student Zombies

Note that you should not underline the title. Nor should you put quotation marks around it. On the other hand, you should capitalize all but small connecting words in the title. Also, you should skip a space between the title and the first line of the text. (See the "MLA Format" section in Chapter 1.)

Write an appropriate title for each of the introductory paragraphs that follow.

ACTIVITY 7

1. Returning to my hometown of Mercyville after five years, I discovered several newcomers on the same street as the pharmacy, hardware store, and restaurants I had patronized. A store selling African art had opened next to my favorite pizzeria. A few doors down was a Thai take-out restaurant, and across the street a Hindu grocer had set up shop. In the storefront where Charlie's Hamburgers was once located, I found a fancy Hungarian bistro featuring an elegant New Year's Eve dinner for $90 per person.

   Title: _____

2. When my parents bought a new home in a small town outside Chicago, they decided to fence in our yard so that our two Labrador retrievers

For further practice in writing titles, write an appropriate title for the image pictured here.
StockPhotosArt/Shutterstock

wouldn't wander off. The contractor they hired informed them that they would have to apply for a permit, which would cost $150. After the shock wore off, my father went to town hall with the check, but the clerk informed him that he would have to submit an online request for the permit as well as a plot plan of our property. After struggling with the online process for two hours, he called the office, but it was closed, and he realized he would have to wait until Monday to get help. After submitting everything, he learned that the town planning committee would not meet to consider our application for two months. When they did meet, they refused to grant our permit because the proposed fence crossed a "designated wetlands" area, and they refused to refund our $150.

Title: _____

3. Having the ideal job doesn't depend only on the amount of money it pays, the working conditions, or the opportunities for advancement. It also has to do with one's fellow employees and, of course, the boss. While most people realize that bosses need to exercise careful supervision over the workplace and the employees, they prefer bosses who socialize with workers, make few demands, and look the other way when they don't perform well. Unfortunately, such supervisors too often turn out to be inefficient, disorganized, and unpredictable. A better alternative is someone who enforces rules predictably and demands that workers meet reasonable expectations.

Title: _____

Practice in Organizing and Connecting Specific Evidence

You now know the third step in effective writing: organizing the specific evidence used to support the thesis of a paper. This closing section will expand and strengthen your understanding of the third step in writing. You will work through the following series of activities:

- organizing through time or emphatic order
- providing transitions
- identifying transitions and other connecting words
- completing transitional sentences
- identifying introductions and conclusions

Organizing through Time or Emphatic Order

Use time order to organize the scrambled lists of supporting ideas below. Write *1* beside the supporting idea that should come first in time, *2* beside the idea that logically follows, and *3* beside the idea that comes last in time.

ACTIVITY 8

1. Thesis: When I was a child, Disney movies frightened me more than any other kind.

    _____   As a five-year-old, I was terrified by the movie *Pinocchio,* about a puppet transformed into a boy.

    _____   Although I saw *Bambi* when I was old enough to begin poking fun at "baby movies," the scene during which Bambi's mother is killed has stayed with me to this day.

    _____   About a year after seeing *Pinocchio,* I gripped my seat in fear as the witches and goblins of *Fantasia* flew across the screen.

2. Thesis: Observing three important rules will help students write better research papers.

    _____   Students should follow the format for including researched material required by their instructor.

    _____   They should start the project early, immediately after it is assigned.

    _____   They should record facts and ideas from their research in a document or on note cards.

3. Thesis: Applying for unemployment benefits was a confusing, frustrating experience.

    _____   It was difficult to find both the office and a place to park.

    _____   When I finally reached the head of the line after four hours of waiting, the clerk had problems processing my claim.

    _____   There was no one to direct or help me when I entered the large office, which was packed with people.

ACTIVITY 9 Use emphatic order (order of importance) to arrange the following scrambled lists of supporting ideas. For each thesis, write 1 in the blank beside the point that is perhaps less important or interesting than the other two, 2 beside the point that appears more important or interesting, and 3 beside the point that should be most emphasized.

1. Thesis: My part-time job has been an invaluable part of my life this year.

    _____   Better yet, it has taught me how to get along with many kinds of people.

    _____   Since it's in the morning, it usually keeps me from staying up too late.

    _____   Without it, I would have had to drop out of school.

2. Thesis: Our soccer team was awarded three special honors for winning the state championship.

    _____   Three of our team members won college athletic scholarships

    _____   Our victory was written up in major newspapers.

    _____   Each team member received a gold medal.

3. Thesis: Aree is my most loyal friend.

    _____   She has taken time to do special favors for me.

    _____   She's always there in real emergencies or emotional crises.

    _____   She once lent me her favorite necklace to wear on a date.

Providing Transitions

In the spaces provided, add appropriate transitions to tie together the sentences and ideas in the following essay. Draw from the words and phrases given in the boxes above the paragraphs. Use each word or phrase only once.

Personal

Annoying People

President Richard Nixon used to keep an enemies list of all the people he didn't especially like. I'm ashamed to confess it, but I, too, have an enemies list—a mental one. On this list are all the people I would gladly live without, the ones who cause my blood pressure to rise to the boiling point. The top three places on the list go to people with irritating habits, people who talk in movie theaters, and people who talk on cell phones while driving.

For example	First of all	Another	However

_____, there are the people with irritating habits.

_____, there are the ones who listen to music on their phones in class. Even though they think they are being secretive, their music is often loud enough that I can hear it, and it distracts me when I am trying to concentrate on the professor's lesson. _____ type of irritating character makes useless designs. These people bend paper clips into abstract sculptures or string the clips into necklaces as they talk.

_____, neither of these groups is as bad as the people who bring food to class. These individuals often arrive with complete meals. They proceed to pull every item out of the loud paper bag, slurp their drinks, and crumple up the garbage all while the rest of the class attempts to hear the professor.

On the contrary	Then	As a result	After	Second

A _____ category of people I would gladly do away with is the ones who talk in movie theaters. These people are not content to sit back, relax, and enjoy the film they have paid to see. _____,

continued

they feel compelled to comment loudly on everything from the hero's

hairstyle to the appropriateness of the background music. _____,

no one hears a word of any dialogue except theirs. _____ these
people have been in the theater for a while, their interest in the movie

may fade. _____ they will start discussing other things, and the
people around them will be treated to an instant replay of the latest
family scandal or soap-opera episode. These stories may be
entertaining, but they don't belong in a movie theater.

| In addition | However | Last of all |

_____, there are the people who talk on the phone while
they're driving. One of the things that bothers me about them is the way
they seem to be showing off. They're saying, "Look at me! I'm so

important I have to make phone calls in my car." _____, such
behavior is just plain dangerous. Instead of concentrating on adjusting
carefully to ever-changing traffic conditions, they're weaving all over the
road or getting much too close to the car in front of them as they gossip
with a friend, make an appointment with a doctor, or order a pizza.

So long as murder remains illegal, the late arrivers and loud
chompers, movie talkers, and cell-phone users of the world are safe

from me. _____, if I am ever granted the power to magically make
these annoyances go away, these people may want to think twice about
annoying me. I may just have to wave my magic wand.

Identifying Transitions and Other Connecting Words

ACTIVITY 11

The following sentences use connecting words to help tie ideas together. The connecting words you are to identify are set off in italics. In the space, write T for *transition,* RW for *repeated word,* S for *synonym,* or P for *pronoun.*

_____ 1. The Statue of Liberty stands watch in New York Harbor. In *her* right hand she holds the torch of freedom.

_____ 2. Plants like poinsettias and mistletoe are pretty. *They* are also poisonous.

_____ 3. A strip of strong cloth can be used as an emergency fan-belt replacement. *In addition,* a roll of duct tape can be used to patch a leaky hose temporarily.

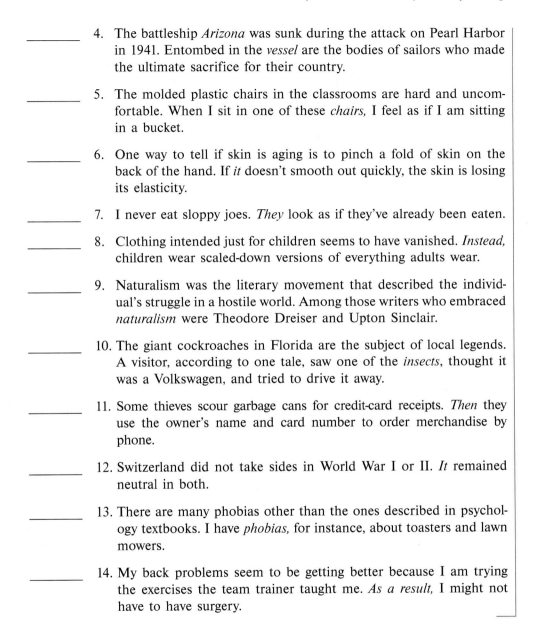

_____ 4. The battleship *Arizona* was sunk during the attack on Pearl Harbor in 1941. Entombed in the *vessel* are the bodies of sailors who made the ultimate sacrifice for their country.

_____ 5. The molded plastic chairs in the classrooms are hard and uncomfortable. When I sit in one of these *chairs,* I feel as if I am sitting in a bucket.

_____ 6. One way to tell if skin is aging is to pinch a fold of skin on the back of the hand. If *it* doesn't smooth out quickly, the skin is losing its elasticity.

_____ 7. I never eat sloppy joes. *They* look as if they've already been eaten.

_____ 8. Clothing intended just for children seems to have vanished. *Instead,* children wear scaled-down versions of everything adults wear.

_____ 9. Naturalism was the literary movement that described the individual's struggle in a hostile world. Among those writers who embraced *naturalism* were Theodore Dreiser and Upton Sinclair.

_____ 10. The giant cockroaches in Florida are the subject of local legends. A visitor, according to one tale, saw one of the *insects,* thought it was a Volkswagen, and tried to drive it away.

_____ 11. Some thieves scour garbage cans for credit-card receipts. *Then* they use the owner's name and card number to order merchandise by phone.

_____ 12. Switzerland did not take sides in World War I or II. *It* remained neutral in both.

_____ 13. There are many phobias other than the ones described in psychology textbooks. I have *phobias,* for instance, about toasters and lawn mowers.

_____ 14. My back problems seem to be getting better because I am trying the exercises the team trainer taught me. *As a result,* I might not have to have surgery.

Completing Transitional Sentences

ACTIVITY 12

Following are partially completed diagram drafts of two essays. In each example, the second and third topic sentences serve as transitional, or linking, sentences. Each reminds us of the point in the preceding paragraph and announces the point to be developed in the current paragraph. In the spaces provided, add the words needed to complete the second and third topic sentences.

Thesis 1

To prepare for a long automobile trip, a driver should check tire pressure and condition, replace worn belts and hoses, and make sure the engine oil and other fluids are at proper levels.

First supporting paragraph

To ensure safety on the trip, the tire pressure and condition of the tires should be checked first.

Second supporting paragraph

After making sure that _____ _____, the driver should _____ .

. . .

Third supporting paragraph

Once the driver is certain that _____ _____. . . .

Thesis 2

Cheaper cost, greater comfort, and superior electronic technology make watching football at home more enjoyable than attending a game at the stadium.

First supporting paragraph

For one thing, watching the game on TV eliminates the cost of attending the game. . . .

Second supporting paragraph

In addition to saving me money, watching the game at home is more _____ than sitting in a stadium. . . .

Third supporting paragraph

Even more important than _____ and _____, though, is the _____ that makes a televised game better than the "real thing." . . .

Identifying Introductions and Conclusions

The following box lists five common kinds of introductions and three common kinds of conclusions. Read the three pairs of introductory and concluding paragraphs that follow. Then, in the spaces provided for each pair, write the letters of the kind of introduction and conclusion used in each paragraph.

ACTIVITY 13

Introductions	Conclusions
A. General to narrow	F. Summary and final thought
B. Starting with an opposite	G. Quotation
C. Stating importance of topic	H. Prediction or recommendation
D. Incident or story	
E. Quotation	

Pair 1

_____   Shortly before spring break, our local elementary school sponsored a fund-raising event at which classroom pets and their babies—hamsters, guinea pigs, and chicks—were available for adoption. Afterward, as I was driving home, I saw a hand drop a baby hamster out of the car ahead of me. I barely avoided running over the tiny creature and quickly stopped to scoop it up. One of the parents had taken the pet, regretted the decision, and decided to get rid of it. Such people have never stopped to consider the real obligations involved in owning a pet.

_____   A pet cannot be thrown onto a trash heap when it is no longer wanted or tossed into a closet if it begins to bore its owner. A pet, like us, is a living thing that needs attention and care. Would-be owners, therefore, should think seriously about their responsibilities before they acquire a pet.

Pair 2

_____   All animals communicate. Some forms of communication, like that of the bee, are through movement, while others include sound and movement. Humans naturally communicate through a variety of methods, including body language and sounds, but they also communicate through methods that don't require physical proximity. Texts, phone calls, and e-mails are such forms of communication, often entailing serious drawbacks.

_____   Neither texts, phone calls, nor e-mails guarantee perfect communication. With all our sophisticated skills, we human beings often communicate less effectively than howling wolves or chattering monkeys. We always seem to find some way to foul up the message.

Pair 3

_____   "Few things are harder to put up with," said Mark Twain, "than the annoyance of a good example." Twain obviously knew the problems faced by siblings cursed with older brothers or sisters who are models of perfection. All our lives, my older sister Shelley and I have been compared. Unfortunately, in competition with my sister's virtues, my looks, talents, and accomplishments always ended up on the losing side.

_____   Although I always lost in the sibling contests of looks, talents, and accomplishments, Shelley and I have somehow managed not to turn into deadly enemies. Feeling like the dud of the family, in fact, helped me to develop a drive to succeed and a sense of humor. In our sibling rivalry, we both managed to win.

The Fourth Step in Essay Writing

What differences do you notice about the students in the photograph above? Most likely, you can identify with at least a couple of them. Thinking about your own experiences in the classroom, write an essay about one or more teachers or instructors who have conducted classes that made you glad to learn or, alternatively, left you daydreaming in class. Once you have written your first draft, read it aloud to make sure all your sentences flow smoothly and clearly.

Olena Yakobchuk/Shutterstock

Up to now, this book has emphasized the first three goals in effective writing: unity, support, and coherence. This chapter focuses on the fourth goal of writing effectively: sentence skills. You'll learn how to revise an essay so that your sentences flow smoothly and clearly. Then you'll review how to edit a paper for mistakes in grammar, punctuation, and spelling.

Revising Sentences

These strategies will help you to revise your sentences effectively:

- Use parallelism.
- Use a consistent point of view.
- Use specific words.
- Use active verbs.
- Use concise words.
- Vary your sentences.

Use Parallelism

Words in a pair or a series should have parallel structure. By balancing the items in a pair or a series so that they have the same kind of structure, you will make the sentence clearer and easier to read. Notice how the parallel sentences that follow read more smoothly than the nonparallel ones.

NONPARALLEL (NOT BALANCED)	PARALLEL (BALANCED)
My job includes checking the inventory, initialing the orders, and *to call* the suppliers.	My job includes checking the inventory, initialing the orders, and calling the suppliers. (A balanced series of *-ing* words: *checking, initialing, calling*)
The game-show contestant was told to be cheerful, charming, and *with enthusiasm*.	The game-show contestant was told to be cheerful, charming, and enthusiastic. (A balanced series of descriptive words: *cheerful, charming, enthusiastic*)
Grandmother likes to read mystery novels, to do needlepoint, and *surfing* the Internet.	Grandmother likes to read mystery novels, to do needlepoint, and to surf the Internet. (A balanced series of *to* verbs: *to read, to do, to surf*)
We painted the trim in the living room; *the wallpaper was put up by a professional*.	We painted the trim in the living room; a professional put up the wallpaper. (Balanced verbs and word order: *We painted . . . ; a professional put up . . .*)

As you look at this gymnast, consider the importance of the parallelism in the two bars. If the bars were not parallel, what would be affected in the gymnast's actions?
Master1305/Shutterstock

Balanced sentences are not a skill you need worry about when writing first drafts. But when you rewrite, you should try to put matching words and ideas into matching structures. Such parallelism will improve your writing style.

Cross out and revise the unbalanced part of each of the following sentences.

ACTIVITY 1

EXAMPLE   Chocolate makes me gain weight, lose my appetite, and ~~breaking~~ *break* out in hives.

1. Florida is famous for its wonderful weather, theme parks that are family oriented, and great fishing.

2. Many people share the same three intense fears: being in high places, working with numbers, and speeches.

3. The garden boasted a line of fruit trees that were mature, several rows of vegetables, and a large stand of rose bushes.

4. The History Channel offers many programs that are timely, well researched, and that people find interesting.

5. To become a dancer, Rhina is taking lessons, working in amateur shows, and auditioned for professional companies.

6. Juan's last job offered security; a better chance for advancement is offered by his new job.

7. Smartphones allow us to communicate, store important information, and they are used to play video games.

8. Because the woman was dignified and with courage, she won everyone's respect.

9. The candidate for governor promised that she would cut taxes, reform public education, and do something to rebuild roads and bridges.

10. If we're not careful, we'll leave the next generation polluted air, contaminated water, and forests that are dying.

Use a Consistent Point of View

Consistency with Verbs

Do not shift verb tenses unnecessarily. If you begin writing a paper in the present tense, do not shift suddenly to the past. If you begin in the past, do not shift without reason to the present. Notice the inconsistent verb tenses in the following example:

Incorrect: The gardener breaks up the hard earth with a shovel, added peat moss and other compost, then blends the soil evenly.

Correct: The gardener breaks up the hard earth with a shovel, adds peat moss and other compost, then blends the soil evenly.

Correct: The gardener broke up the hard earth with a shovel, added peat moss and other compost, then blended the soil evenly.

ACTIVITY 2   Make the verbs in each sentence consistent with the *first* verb used. Cross out the incorrect verb and write the correct form in the space at the left.

EXAMPLE

_____ran_____   Aunt Alejandra tried to kiss her little nephew, but he ~~runs~~ out of the room.

_____   1. An aggressive news photographer knocked a reporter to the ground as the movie stars arrive for the Academy Awards.

_____ 2. The winning racer in the Boston shopping cart race fell over in exhaustion and asks for some ice to soothe his blistered hands.

_____ 3. Amanda Gorman performed her poem, "The Hill We Climb," at the Inauguration Day ceremony in January 2021, but chooses to recite a different poem, "Chorus of the Captains," for the 2021 Superbowl.

_____ 4. Shirin Ebadi is a political activist who attended the University of Tehran and is awarded the Nobel Peace Prize in 2003 for her work for human rights.

_____ 5. John Steinbeck wrote his masterpiece *The Grapes of Wrath* in 1939, but he does not win the Nobel Prize until 1962.

_____ 6. Galileo (1564–1642) did not invent the telescope, but he improves upon it in order to observe the heavens better.

_____ 7. Dustin ripped open the bag of cheese puffs with his teeth, grabs handfuls of the salty orange squiggles, and stuffed them into his mouth.

_____ 8. From his perch high up on the rocky cliff, the eagle spots a white-tailed rabbit and swooped down toward his victim.

_____ 9. An American physicist was the first to measure the speed of light accurately when he calculates it at just over 186,000 miles per second.

_____ 10. When the great earthquake struck San Francisco in 1906, the entire city burns to the ground in less than twenty-four hours.

Consistency with Pronouns

When writing a paper, you should not shift your point of view unnecessarily. Be consistent in your use of first-, second-, or third-person pronouns.

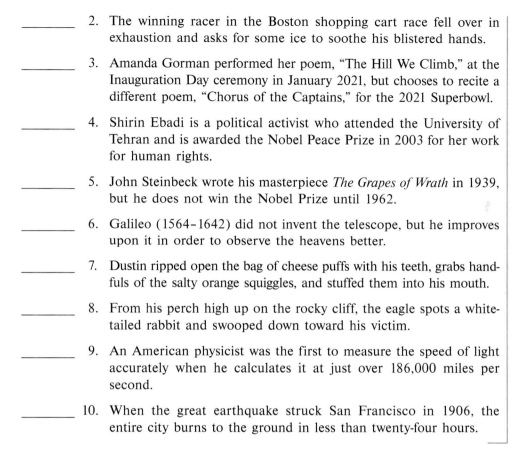

Point of View

	Singular	Plural
First-person pronouns	I (my, mine, me)	we (our, us)
Second-person pronouns	you (your)	you (your)
Third-person pronouns	they (their, them)	they (their, them)
	he (his, him)	
	she (her)	
	it (its)	

> Any person, place, or thing, as well as any indefinite pronoun such as *one,*
> *anyone, someone,* and so on (see Chapter 27), is a third-person word.

For instance, if you start writing in the first person, *I,* do not jump suddenly to the second person, *you.* Or if you are writing in the third person, *they,* do not shift unexpectedly to *you.* Look at the following examples.

INCONSISTENT	CONSISTENT
One of the fringe benefits of my job is that *you* can use a company credit card for gasoline. (The most common mistake people make is to let *you* slip into their writing after they start with another pronoun.)	One of the fringe benefits of my job is that *I* can use a company credit card for gasoline.
Though *we* like most of *our* neighbors, there are a few *you* can't get along with. (The writer begins with the first-person pronouns *we* and *our* but then shifts to the second-person *you.*)	Though *we* like most of *our* neighbors, there are a few *we* can't get along with.

ACTIVITY 3   Cross out inconsistent pronouns in the following sentences, and revise with the correct form of the pronoun above each crossed-out word.

EXAMPLE   When I examined the used car, ~~you~~ could see that one of the front fenders had been replaced.

1. Many people are ignorant of side effects that diets can have on your health.

2. I am always nervous when my dentist examines my teeth because you never know what she will find.

3. It is expensive for us to take public transportation to work every day, but what choice do you have if you can't afford a car?

4. During the border crisis, each country refused to change their aggressive stance.

5. If we go to Chicago, you should visit the Art Institute.

6. We don't have enough money to travel to Egypt, but you can learn about the pyramids on the Discovery Channel.

7. Maria loves algebra problems because solving them gives you a sense of accomplishment.

8. It's hard for us to pay for health insurance, but you don't dare go without it.

9. People often take a first-aid course so that we can learn how to help choking and heart attack victims.

10. There are several ways you can impress your new boss. For example, one should dress well, arrive at work on time, and complete tasks efficiently.

Use Specific Words

To be an effective writer, you must use specific words rather than general words. Specific words create pictures in the reader's mind. They help capture interest and make your meaning clear. Compare the following sentences:

GENERAL	SPECIFIC
The plane landed at the airport.	The United Airlines 747 landed at Reagan National Airport.
Animals came through the place.	Hungry lions padded silently through the savanna.
The man signed the paper.	The biology teacher hastily scribbled his name on the course withdrawal slip.

The specific sentences create clear pictures in our minds. The details *show* us exactly what has happened.

Here are four ways to make your sentences specific.

1. Use exact names.

   Leymah fixed the muffler on his car.

   Leymah fixed the muffler on his *2011 Chevrolet Impala*.

2. Use lively verbs.

The flag *moved* in the breeze.

The flag *fluttered* in the breeze.

3. Use descriptive words (modifiers) before nouns.

A worker strained to lift the crate.

A *brawny, perspiring* worker strained to lift the *heavy wooden* crate.

4. Use words that relate to the senses—sight, hearing, taste, smell, touch.

The tourists enjoyed a picnic lunch of cheese, bread, and olives.

The tourists enjoyed a picnic lunch of *sharp* cheese, *crusty* bread, and *spicy* olives. (*taste*)

The campers built a fire of pine and cedar.

The campers built a fire of *aromatic* pine and cedar. (*smell*)

A noise told the crowd that there were two minutes left to play.

A *piercing whistle* told the *cheering* crowd that there were two minutes left to play. (*hearing*)

When he returned, all he found in the refrigerator was bread and milk.

When he returned, all he found in the refrigerator was *stale* bread and *sour* milk. (*taste*)

Neil stroked the kitten's fur until he felt its tiny claws on his hand.

Neil stroked the kitten's *velvety* fur until he felt its tiny, *needle-sharp* claws on his hand. (*touch*)

Fran placed a sachet in her bureau drawer.

Fran placed a *lilac-scented* sachet in her bureau drawer. (*smell*)

ACTIVITY 4   Revise the following sentences, replacing vague, indefinite words with sharp, specific ones.

EXAMPLE   *Several of our appliances* broke down at the same time.

Our washer, refrigerator, and television broke . . .

1. The new home came with *energy-saving appliances*.

_____

_____

_____

2. I swept aside the *things* on my desk to spread out the road map.

_____

_____

_____

3. Large *trees* shaded the valley.

_____

_____

_____

4. *Several sections* of the newspaper were missing.

_____

_____

_____

5. The doctor examined *various parts of my body* before diagnosing my illness as bronchitis.

_____

_____

_____

Again, you will practice changing vague, indefinite writing into lively, image-filled writing that helps capture the reader's interest and makes your meaning clear. With the help of the methods described in the preceding section, add specific details to the five sentences that follow. Note the two examples.

ACTIVITY 5

EXAMPLE   The person got off the bus.

The teenage boy bounded down the steps of the shiny yellow school bus.

_____

She worked hard all summer.

All summer, Eva sorted peaches and blueberries in the hot, noisy canning factory.

_____

1. The car would not start.

_____

_____

_____

2. The desk was cluttered.

_____

_____

_____

3. The woman was overjoyed at finding her lost son.

_____

_____

_____

4. My room needs cleaning.

_____

_____

5. A vehicle blocked traffic.

_____

_____

_____

Rewrite the sign pictured here using lively, image-filled writing that will grab people's attention.
alexis84/123RF

Use Active Verbs

When the subject of a sentence performs the action of the verb, the verb is in the *active voice*. When the subject of a sentence receives the action of a verb, the verb is in the *passive voice*.

Passive voice uses a form of the verb *to be* (*am, is, are, was, were*) and the past participle of the main verb (usually the same as its past-tense form). Look at the following active and passive forms.

PASSIVE	ACTIVE
The computer *was turned on* by Hakim.	Hakim *turned on* the computer.
The car's air conditioner *was fixed* by the mechanic.	The mechanic *fixed* the car's air conditioner.
The stream *was diverted* by the engineers.	The engineers *diverted* the stream.
A Country Doctor, a novel by Sarah Orne Jewett, *was written* in 1884.	Sarah Orne Jewett *wrote* the novel *A Country Doctor* in 1884.
In World War II, France, Holland, Norway, Hungary, Poland, Russia, and other countries *were invaded* by Germany.	In World War II, Germany *invaded* France, Holland, Norway, Hungary, Poland, Russia and other countries.

In general, active verbs are more effective than passive verbs. Active verbs give your writing a simpler and more vigorous style.

Revise the following sentences, changing verbs from the passive to the active voice and making any other word changes necessary.

ACTIVITY 6

EXAMPLE   Fruits and vegetables are painted often by artists.

Artists often paint fruits and vegetables.

1. Many unhealthy foods are included in the typical American diet.

2. The North Atlantic Treaty Organization (NATO) was established by the United States, Great Britain, and nine other countries in 1949.

3. The soldier's wounds were attacked by gangrene-producing bacteria.

4. A second Nobel Prize was won by Marie Curie in 1911.

_____

5. Final grades will be determined by the instructor on the basis of class performance.

_____

Use Concise Words

Wordiness—using more words than necessary to express a meaning—is often a sign of lazy or careless writing. Your readers may resent the extra time and energy they must spend when you have not done the work needed to make your writing direct and concise.

Here are two examples of wordy sentences:

Wordy All of the employees who are new to this institution are required to attend a meeting that is scheduled for the first Friday and Saturday of August, which is August 8 and August 9.

In Ben's opinion, streaming services have changed and altered our movie and video watching habits.

Omitting needless words improves these sentences:

Clear New employees are required to attend a meeting on August 8 and 9.

Ben thinks streaming services have changed our viewing habits.

Following is a list of some wordy expressions that could be reduced to single words.

Wordy Form	Shorter Form
at this time	now
in the present	now
in the event that	if
due to the fact that	because
for the reason that	because
in every instance	always
in this day and age	today
during the time that	while
a large number of	many

continued

Wordy Form	Shorter Form
big in size	big
red in color	red
five in number	five
12 midnight/12 noon	midnight/noon
return back	return
good benefit	benefit
cooperate together	cooperate
completely unanimous	unanimous
commute back and forth	commute
postponed until later	postponed

Revise the following sentences, omitting needless words.

ACTIVITY 7

1. The bird was purple, red, orange, and yellow in color, and its body was extremely large in size.

   _____

   _____

2. Controlling the quality and level of screen time that children are exposed to is a continuing challenge to parents that they must meet on a daily basis.

   _____

   _____

3. A large number of people are now seeking out various electronic devices as presents to give to others on their birthdays.

   _____

   _____

4. In 1962, Linus Pauling, who was an American, was awarded the Nobel Prize, which was given to him for his attempts to limit the making of nuclear arms and to curtail the spread of nuclear testing.

   _____

   _____

5. I found out recently that Benito Mussolini (1883–1945), the dictator of the fascist nation of Italy for a period lasting nearly twenty-one years, was named after the Mexican political leader who went by the name of Benito Juarez (1806–1872).

_____

_____

6. In today's uncertain economic climate, it is clear that people, namely, average middle-class working people, have great difficulty saving much money or putting anything aside for emergencies.

_____

_____

7. We thought the television program that was on last night was enjoyable, whereas our parents reacted with dislike to the content of the show.

_____

_____

8. Because of the bad weather, the school district felt it would be safer to cancel classes and let everyone stay home than to risk people having accidents on the way to school.

_____

_____

9. Out of all the regrets in my life so far, one of my greatest ones to the present time is that I did not take additional art classes when I was still in high school and had a chance to do so.

_____

_____

10. It seems obvious to me, and it should be to everyone else, too, that people can be harmed as much by emotional abuse as by physical abuse, even if no one lays a hand on them.

_____

_____

Vary Your Sentences

One part of effective writing is to vary the kinds of sentences you write. If every sentence follows the same pattern, writing may become monotonous to read. This section explains four ways you can create variety and interest in your writing style. It also describes coordination and subordination—two important techniques for achieving different kinds of emphasis in writing.

The following are four methods you can use to revise simple sentences, making them more complex and sophisticated:

- Add a second complete thought (coordination).
- Add a dependent thought (subordination).
- Begin with a special opening word or phrase.
- Place adjectives or verbs in a series.

Revise by Adding a Second Complete Thought

When you add a second complete thought to a simple sentence, the result is a *compound* (or double) sentence. The two complete statements in a compound sentence are usually connected by a comma and a joining or coordinating word (*and, but, for, or, nor, so, yet*).

A compound sentence is used to give equal weight to two closely related ideas. The technique of showing that ideas have equal importance is called *coordination*. Following are some compound sentences. In each case, the sentence contains two ideas that the writer considers equal in importance.

> Anderius worked on the engine for three hours, but the car still wouldn't start.
>
> Bananas were on sale this week, so I bought a bunch for the children's lunches.
>
> We laced up our ice skates, and then we moved cautiously onto the rink.

Combine the following pairs of simple sentences into compound sentences. Use a comma and a logical joining word (*and, but, for, so*) to connect each pair of statements.

ACTIVITY 8

 If you are not sure what *and, but, for,* and *so* mean, check Chapter 23.

EXAMPLE   The weather was cold and windy.
           Remy brought a thick blanket to the football game.

The weather was cold and windy, so Remy brought a thick blanket to the football game.

1. My son can't eat peanut butter snacks or sandwiches.

    He is allergic to peanuts.

    _____

    _____

2. I tried to sleep.

    The thought of tomorrow's math exam kept me awake.

    _____

    _____

3. The poet Ezra Pound left America in 1908.

    He was dissatisfied with the artistic climate of his native country.

    _____

    _____

4. My philosophy professor believes that every student can learn.

    He spends much of his extra time tutoring his students.

    _____

    _____

5. I didn't have enough money to buy my parents an anniversary present.

    I offered to mow their lawn for the whole summer.

    _____

    _____

Revise by Adding a Dependent Thought

When you add a dependent thought to a simple sentence, the result is a *complex* sentence.* A dependent thought begins with one of the subordinating words listed in the box on the next page.

---

*The two parts of a complex sentence are sometimes called an *independent clause* and a *dependent clause*. A *clause* is simply a word group that contains a subject and a verb. An independent clause expresses a complete thought and can stand alone. A dependent clause does not express a complete thought in itself and depends on the independent clause to complete its meaning. Dependent clauses always begin with a dependent or subordinating word.

Subordinating Words

after	if, even if	when, whenever
although, though	in order that	where, wherever
as	since	whether
because	that, so that	which, whichever
before	unless	while
even though	until	who
how	what, whatever	whose

A complex sentence is used to emphasize one idea over another. Look at the following complex sentence:

Although the exam room was very quiet, I still couldn't concentrate.

The idea that the writer wishes to emphasize here—*I still couldn't concentrate*—is expressed as a complete thought. The less important idea—*Although the exam room was very quiet*—is subordinated to the complete thought. The technique of giving one idea less emphasis than another is called *subordination*.

Following are other examples of complex sentences. In each case, the part starting with the dependent word is the less emphasized part of the sentence.

Even though I was tired, I stayed up to watch the horror movie.

Before I take a bath, I check for spiders in the tub.

When Ivy feels nervous, she pulls on her earlobe.

Use logical subordinating words to combine the following pairs of simple sentences into sentences that contain a dependent thought. Place a comma after a dependent statement when it starts the sentence.

ACTIVITY 9

EXAMPLE   Rita bit into the hard taffy.
          She broke a filling.

When Rita bit into the hard taffy, she broke a filling.

_____

1. Many Americans blamed President Herbert Hoover for the Great Depression, which began in 1929.

   They elected Franklin Roosevelt president in 1932.

_____

_____

2. The bear turned over the rotten log.

   Fat white grubs crawled in every direction.

   _____

   _____

3. Europe had suffered a great deal of damage during World War II.

   The United States helped rebuild its infrastructure and economy.

   _____

   _____

4. Some people are allergic to wool.

   They buy sweaters made only from synthetic fibers.

   _____

   _____

5. A woman I know can type almost one hundred words a minute.

   She is having trouble landing a job.

   _____

   _____

Revise by Beginning with a Special Opening Word or Phrase

Among the special openers that can be used to start sentences are *-ed* words, *-ing* words, *-ly* words, *to* word groups, and prepositional phrases. Additional information can be found in Chapters 21, 22, and 26. Here are examples of all five kinds of openers:

-ed **WORD**

   Concerned about his son's fever, Paulo called a doctor.

-ing **WORD**

   Humming softly, the woman browsed through the rack of dresses.

-ly **WORD**

   Hurriedly, Sue approached the instructor's desk.

to **WORD GROUP**

To protect their hair, Alex uses the lowest setting on their blow dryer.

PREPOSITIONAL PHRASE

During the exam, drops of water fell from the ceiling.

Combine each of the following pairs of simple sentences into one sentence by using the opener shown at the left and omitting repeated words. Use a comma to set off the opener from the rest of the sentence.

ACTIVITY 10

EXAMPLE   *-ing* **word**   The pelican scooped small fish into its baggy bill. It dipped into the waves.

Dipping into the waves, the pelican scooped small fish into its baggy bill.

_____

1. Sienna signed the book contract.

   She was exuberant.

   _____

   _____

2. Eva and Olaf wanted to find the shortest route over the mountain.

   They bought a map of the local hiking trails.

   _____

   _____

3. The accused murderer grinned at the witnesses.

   He did this during the trial.

   _____

   _____

4. The vet's office was noisy and confusing.

   It was crowded with nervous pets.

   _____

   _____

5. Barry tried to find something worth watching.

   He flipped from channel to channel.

   _____

-ly **word**

to **word group**

Prepositional phrase

-ed word

-ing **word**

Revise by Placing Adjectives or Verbs in a Series

Various parts of a sentence may be placed in a series. Among these parts are adjectives (descriptive words) and verbs. (Additional information can be found in Chapter 29.) Here are examples of both in a series:

ADJECTIVES

I gently applied a *sticky new* Band-Aid to the *deep, ragged* cut on my finger.

VERBS

The truck *bounced* off a guardrail, *sideswiped* a tree, and *plunged* down the embankment.

ACTIVITY 11   Combine the simple sentences into one sentence by using adjectives or verbs in a series and by omitting repeated words. Use a comma when necessary between adjectives or verbs in a series.

EXAMPLE   Jesse spun the basketball on one finger.
            He rolled it along his arms.
            He dribbled it between his legs.

Jesse spun the basketball on one finger, rolled it along his arms, and dribbled it between his legs.

1. The bobcat sat high on a rock.
   It stared down at the unsuspecting rodent.
   It leaped upon its prey.

   _____

   _____

2. Some Native Americans lived in the desert.
   They built permanent homes.
   These homes were usually made of adobe.
   Adobe resembles stucco.

   _____

   _____

3. By 6 A.M., I had read the textbook chapter.
   I had taken notes on it.
   I had studied the notes.
   I had drunk eight cups of coffee.

   _____

   _____

4. The exterminator approached the wasps' nests hanging under the eaves.
   The nests were large.
   The nests were papery.
   The eaves were old.
   The eaves were wooden.

   _____

   _____

5. Reeds bordered the pond.
   The reeds were slim.
   The reeds were brown.
   The pond was green.
   The pond was stagnant.

   _____

   _____

Editing Sentences

After revising sentences in a paper so that they flow smoothly and clearly, you need to edit the paper for mistakes in grammar, punctuation, mechanics, usage, and spelling. Even if a paper is otherwise well written, it will make an unfavorable impression on readers if it contains such mistakes. To edit a paper, check it against the agreed-upon rules, or conventions, of written English—simply called *sentence skills* in this book. Here are the most common of these conventions:

✔   Write complete sentences rather than fragments.
✔   Do not write run-on sentences.
✔   Use verb forms correctly.
✔   Make sure that subject, verbs, and pronouns agree.

continued

✔ Eliminate faulty modifiers.

✔ Use pronoun forms correctly.

✔ Use capital letters when needed.

✔ Use the following marks of punctuation correctly: apostrophe, quotation marks, comma, semicolon, colon, hyphen, dash, parentheses.

✔ Use correct manuscript form.

✔ Eliminate slang, clichés, and pretentious words.

✔ Check for possible spelling errors.

✔ Eliminate careless errors.

These sentence skills are treated in detail in individual chapters in Part 4 of this book, and they can be referred to easily as needed, by chapter title. In addition, a checklist of sentence skills is provided at the back of the book, and a corrections symbols list is included at the end of Part 4.

Hints about Editing

These hints can help you edit the next-to-final draft of a paper for sentence-skill mistakes:

1. Have your paper fully typed and in proper MLA format before you spend time editing.

2. Run grammar- and spell-check applications: these are essential tools for editing your essays, but they are not foolproof. In addition, have a good dictionary and a grammar handbook (you can use the one in Part 4 of this text) to help you decide whether or not to accept the suggested changes from the grammar and spelling checks.

3. Print your draft. It is better to work on a printed draft rather than to make corrections electronically; use a pen with colored ink so any corrections will stand out.

4. Use a sheet of paper to cover your essay so that only one sentence at a time will be exposed. Look for errors in grammar, spelling, and typing. It may help to read each sentence out loud. If a sentence does not read clearly and smoothly, chances are something is wrong. Pay special attention to the kinds of errors you tend to make. For example, if you tend to write run-ons or fragments, be especially on the lookout for those errors.

5. Once you have worked through the printed draft, make your changes on your final draft.

> A series of editing tests appears in Chapter 39. You will probably find it most helpful to take these tests after reviewing the sentence skills in Part 4.

Proofreading

Proofreading means closely checking the final, edited draft of your paper for typos and other careless errors. A helpful strategy is to read your paper backward, from the last sentence to the first. This helps keep you from getting caught up in the flow of the paper and missing small mistakes. Here are six helpful proofing symbols:

Proofing Symbol	Meaning	Example
∧	insert missing letter or word	ach*e*ve
ℓ (curved line)	omit	draw two ~~two~~ conclusions
∽ (reverse)	reverse order of words or letters	lived happily /after\ever/
#	add space	all#right
‿	close up space	base‿ball
ⒸⒶⓅ ≡ (lc) /	Add a capital (or a ⒸⒶⓅ lowercase) letter	(lc) My ≡english ⟋lass

After you mark corrections on the page, enter them into your computer file, then reprint the page.

ACTIVITY 12

In the spaces below this paragraph, write the numbers of the ten word groups that contain fragments or run-ons. Then, in the spaces between the lines, edit by making the necessary corrections. One is done for you as an example.

Personal

A unique object in my family's living room is a vase. (lc) ⟋hich I made in second grade.   I can still remember the pride I felt.   When I presented it to my mother.   Now, I'm amazed that my parents didn't hide it away at the back of a shelf it is a remarkably ugly object.   The

Jacob Lund/
Shutterstock

vase is made out of brown clay that I had tried to mold into a perfect cylinder, unfortunately my class was only forty-five minutes long.   The best I could do was to shape it into a lopsided oval.   Its most distinc- tive feature, though, is the grooves carved into its rim.   I had theo- rized that each groove could hold a flower stem, I made at least fifty of them.   I somehow failed to consider that the only person who liked flowers in my family was my grandmother.   Who visited only twice a year.   Further, although our living room is decorated in sedate tans and blues, my vase is bright purple.   My favorite color at the time.

For variety, it has stripes around its rim they are colored neon green.

My parents have proudly displayed my little masterpiece on their cof- fee table for the past ten years.   If I ever wonder if my parents love me.   I look at that ugly vase, the answer is plain to see.

1. _____   3. _____   5. _____   7. _____   9. _____

2. _____   4. _____   6. _____   8. _____   10. _____

Practice in Revising Sentences

You now know the fourth step in effective writing: revising and editing sentences. You also know that practice in *editing* sentences is best undertaken after you have worked through the sentence skills in Part 4. The focus in this section, then, will be on *revising* sentences—using a variety of methods to ensure that your sentences flow smoothly and are clear and interesting. You will work through Review Tests on the following:

- using parallelism
- using a consistent point of view
- using specific words
- using active verbs
- using concise words
- varying your sentences

Using Parallelism

Cross out the unbalanced part of each sentence. In the space provided, revise the unbalanced part so that it matches the other item or items in the sentence.

EXAMPLE   In many ways, starting college at forty is harder than ~~to start~~ at eighteen.

starting

1. Langston Hughes (1902–1967) wrote plays, poetry, and he was an essayist.

2. Alex Haley's career included writing several short stories and essays, authoring *Roots*, the novel that made him famous, and he also edited *The Autobiography of Malcolm X*.

3. Kierra likes reading mystery novels, to listen to bluegrass, and playing golf.

4. Kanyn impressed the audience because of his clear, reasonable presentation with friendliness as well.

5. Ryan is very talented: they are a gourmet cook, a published poet, and they take great photographs.

6. Studying a little every day is more effective than to cram.

7. The keys to improving grades are to take effective notes in class, to plan study time, and preparing carefully for exams.

8. Paying college tuition and not studying is as sensible as to buy tickets to a movie and not watching it.

9. The college provides three ways to earn extra money while attending school: serve as a lab assistant, tutoring fellow students in the learning lab, and working in one of the many federally sponsored work-study programs.

_____

10. While waiting for the exam to start, small groups of nervous students glanced over their notes, drank coffee, and were whispering to each other.

_____

REVIEW TEST 2

Cross out the unbalanced part of each sentence. In the space above, revise the unbalanced part so that it matches the other item or items in the sentence.

Although there are many different majors, students who desire to be in the top 1 percent of income earners should plan on majoring in economics, biochemistry, zoology, or biology, or to follow a pre-med program.

Students who go into pre-med will then need to decide what specific sector to specialize in. General practitioners are usually paid less than oncologists, doctors who do surgery, and dermatologists. Economics majors can choose a wide variety of careers like economic consulting, law, or becoming a professor. Biochemistry majors can enter careers such as pharmacist, research scientist, or they can even become doctors of medicine. It is a degree that offers many pathways to different graduate degrees. Studying zoology doesn't mean just to work in a zoo. States like Oregon, Washington, and Maryland hire zoologists to study the management of wildlife or how the wildlife is encroaching on urban areas. Biology degrees offer the best chance of earning wages at the high end of the spectrum. Many biology majors get medical degrees, but they might choose other high-paying careers like pharmaceutical sales representative, biological scientist, or microbiologist. These majors require years of study and hard-working, but they may lead to careers with big salaries.

Using a Consistent Point of View

Change verbs as needed in the following selection so that they are consistently in the past tense. Cross out each incorrect verb and write the correct form above it, as shown in the example. You will need to make ten additional corrections.

Personal

My uncle's shopping trip last Thursday was discouraging to him.
First of all, he had to drive around for fifteen minutes until he ~~finds~~ *found* a
parking space. There was a half-price special on paper products in
the supermarket, and every spot is taken. Then, when he finally got
inside, many of the items on his list were not where he expected.
For example, the pickles he wanted are not on the same shelf as all
the other pickles. Instead, they were in a refrigerated case next to
the bacon. And the granola was not on the cereal shelves but in the
health-food section. Shopping thus proceeds slowly. About halfway
through his list, he knew there would not be time to cook dinner
and decides to pick up a barbecued chicken. The chicken, he
learned, was available at the end of the store he had already
passed. So he parks his shopping cart in an aisle, get the chicken,
and came back. After adding half a dozen more items to his cart, he
suddenly realizes it contained someone else's food. So he retraced
his steps, found his own cart, transfers the groceries, and continued
to shop. Later, when he began loading items onto the checkout
counter, he notices that the barbecued chicken was missing. He
must have left it in the other cart, certainly gone by now. Feeling
totally defeated, he returned to the deli counter and says to the
clerk, "Give me another chicken. I lost the first one." My uncle told
me that when he saw the look on the clerk's face, he felt as if he'd
flunked Food Shopping.

REVIEW TEST 4

Cross out inconsistent pronouns in the following sentences, and revise with the correct form of the pronoun above each crossed-out word.

EXAMPLE   MLA format is a way for students to format ~~your~~ *their* documents in English classes.

Students who are required to lay out his or her documents in MLA format often don't know what to do. This can be frustrating for both professors and you. However, by following a few simple rules, you can be successful. The first thing a student needs to do is open your word processing application. The next thing you should do is go to the page formatting tool. MLA standards require that the page margins are one inch around, lines are double-spaced, and the type size is a legible twelve-point font. After checking that this is correct, we should then create a header that numbers all pages in the upper-right-hand corner. Once the page layout is correct, the student should type your heading, which includes your name, instructor's name, course, and date. The final thing the student will need to do is type your essay title and essay. Following these steps won't guarantee that the essay gets an A but will mean that they will be formatted correctly.

Using Specific Words

REVIEW TEST 5

Revise the following sentences, changing vague, indefinite words to sharp, specific ones.

1. *We were exhausted* after shoveling snow all day.

_____

_____

_____

2. The *food choices* in the cafeteria were unappetizing.

_____

_____

_____

3. *Bugs* invaded our kitchen and pantry this summer.

_____

_____

_____

4. All last week, *the weather was terrible.*

_____

_____

_____

5. My mathematics teacher *is excellent.*

_____

_____

_____

REVIEW TEST 6

With the help of the methods described in the "Use Specific Details" section of this chapter, add specific details to the sentences that follow.

1. The salesperson was obnoxious.

_____

_____

_____

2. The kitchen was cheery.

_____

_____

_____

3. My city is a cultural paradise.

_____

_____

_____

4. The lounge area was busy.

_____

_____

_____

5. A passenger on the bus was acting strangely.

_____

_____

_____

Using Active Verbs

REVIEW TEST 7

Revise the following sentences, changing verbs from the passive to the active voice and making any other necessary word changes.

EXAMPLE   Soccer is played by children all over the world.

Children all over the world play soccer.
_____

1. The pizza restaurant was closed by the health inspector.

_____

2. Huge stacks of donated books were sorted by the workers in the library.

_____

3. A poem about Chicago entitled "City of Big Shoulders" was written by Carl Sandburg.

_____

4. In 1928, the antibiotic penicillin was discovered by Sir Alexander Fleming.

_____

5. Nearly a million tons of tobacco are grown by American farmers each year.

_____

6. An additional charge was placed on our phone bill by the telephone company.

_____

7. The building of a new community library was made possible by a grant from a large corporation.

_____

_____

8. Stress is relieved by physical activity, meditation, and relaxation.

_____

9. Taxes will be raised by the federal government to pay for highway improvements.

_____

10. Studies show that people's health is negatively affected by sitting for extremely long periods.

_____

_____

Using Concise Words

REVIEW TEST 8

Revise the following sentences, omitting needless words.

1. At this point in time, we are not exactly sure what the causes of Alzheimer's disease are, but we are aware of the fact that it rarely attacks younger people who are below the age of sixty.

_____

_____

2. The two identical twins wore exactly the same shoes, shirt, pants, and socks.

_____

_____

3. The salesperson advised us not to buy the laptop at this time because it was going to have a drop in price in the very near future.

   _____

   _____

4. Scientists who study botany classify or think of the tomato as a type of fruit, but most other people today think of it as a vegetable.

   _____

   _____

5. Many people are of the opinion that children should be required by law to attend school until they reach the age of sixteen years old.

   _____

   _____

6. Majoring in liberal arts during the first year in college can help a student explore various types of academic majors, and doing so will help a student decide what discipline they might want to study.

   _____

   _____

7. Many of my neighbors who believe that service is good volunteer their time at our local food bank that is located in town.

   _____

   _____

8. The primary focus of today's class will be the critiquing of one student's essay by another student.

   _____

   _____

9. It is the belief of the professor that all students enrolled in her class need to be aware of the due date for the essay focusing on the film.

   _____

   _____

10. At around the time that the clock strikes seven in the evening, we will be meeting together to view a movie.

    _____

    _____

Varying Your Sentences

Combine each of the following groups of simple sentences into one longer sentence. Omit repeated words. Various combinations are often possible, so try to find the combination in each group that flows most smoothly and clearly.

1. Jane Austen is an author.
   She is English.
   She is well known and beloved.

   _____

   _____

2. Austen wrote *Emma*.
   Emma is a novel.
   The novel is about Emma Woodhouse.

   _____

   _____

3. Emma is a matchmaker.
   Emma means well.
   Emma's matches are usually wrong.

   _____

   _____

4. Jane Austen wrote *Sense and Sensibility*.
   Sense and Sensibility is about Miss Elinor Dashwood.
   Sense and Sensibility is about Miss Marianne Dashwood.

   _____

   _____

5. The book focuses on Elinor's quest for love.
   The book focuses on Marianne's quest for love.
   The book is about the two sisters' quest for marriage.

   _____

   _____

6. Austen wrote *Mansfield Park*.
   Mansfield Park is about Fanny Price.
   Fanny Price is involved with the Bertram family.

   _____

   _____

7. Fanny Price is poor.
   She is young.
   Fanny Price is sent to live with relatives.
   Her relatives are wealthy.

   _____

   _____

8. Austen wrote *Pride and Prejudice*.
   Pride and Prejudice is Jane Austen's most famous novel.
   Pride and Prejudice is about the Bennet family.

   _____

   _____

9. Elizabeth Bennet is the main character.
   She is kind and smart.
   She is a loving person.
   She falls in love with Mr. Fitzwilliam Darcy.
   Mr. Darcy is arrogant and proud.

   _____

   _____

10. Critics used to consider Austen's books frivolous.
    Critics used to dismiss Austen's books.
    Critics now see her books as progressive and distinctive.

    _____

    _____

REVIEW TEST 10

Combine the sentences in the following paragraph into four sentences. Omit repeated words. Try to find combinations in each case that flow as smoothly and clearly as possible.

Lena and Miles wanted a vacation. They wanted a vacation that was nice. They wanted one that was quiet. They wanted one that was relaxing. They rented a small lakeside cabin. Their first day there was very peaceful. The situation quickly changed. A large family moved into a nearby cabin. They played music at top volume. They raced around in a speedboat with a loud whining engine. Lena and Miles were no longer very relaxed. They packed up their things. They drove off. They returned to their quiet apartment.

_____
_____
_____
_____
_____
_____
_____
_____
_____
_____

Four Bases for Revising Essays

This chapter will show you how to evaluate an essay for

- unity
- support
- coherence
- sentence skills

What emotions come to mind as you look at this photograph of an Oregon community destroyed by a forest fire in 2020? Write an essay about a tragic event you have experienced in your own life. What was the experience like, and how did it change you—for better or worse? After writing the first draft of your essay, check that you have covered the four bases of writing: unity, support, coherence, and sentence skills.
Ahturner/Shutterstock

In the preceding chapters, you learned four essential steps in writing an effective paper. The box on the next page shows how the steps lead to four standards, or bases, you can use in revising an essay.

Four Steps $\longrightarrow$	Four Bases
1 If you advance a single point and stick to that point,	your paper will have *unity*.
2 If you support the point with specific evidence,	your paper will have *support*.
3 If you organize and connect the specific evidence,	your paper will have *coherence*.
4 If you write clear, error-free sentences,	your paper will demonstrate effective *sentence skills*.

This chapter discusses these four bases—unity, support, coherence, and sentence skills—and shows how the four bases can be used to evaluate and revise a paper.

Base 1: Unity

Understanding Unity

The following student essays are on the topic "Problems or Pleasures of My Teenage Years." Which one makes its point more clearly and effectively, and why?

Essay 1

Personal

Teenage Antics

1   Looking back at some of the things I did as a teenager makes me break out in a sweat. The purpose of each adventure was fun, but occasionally things got out of hand. In my search for good times, I was involved in three notable incidents, ranging from fairly harmless to fairly serious.

2   The first caper proved that good, clean fun does not have to be dull. As a high school student, I was credited with making the world's largest dessert. With several friends, I spent an entire year collecting boxes of Jell-O. Entering our school's indoor pool one night, we turned the water temperature up as high as it would go and poured in box after box of the strawberry powder. The next morning, school officials arrived to find the pool filled with thirteen thousand gallons of the quivering, rubbery stuff. No one was hurt by the prank, but we did suffer through three days of a massive cleanup and had to pay for the repairs to the pump.

continued

Not all my antics were harmless, and one involved risking my life. As   3
soon as I got my driver's license, I wanted to join the Fliers' Club.
Membership in this club was limited to those who could make their cars
fly a distance of at least ten feet. The qualifying site was an old quarry
field where friends and I had built a ramp made of dirt. I drove my
battered Mercury Cougar up this ramp as fast as it would go. The
Cougar flew ten feet, but one of the tires exploded when I landed. The
car rolled on its side, and I luckily escaped with only a bruised arm.

Risking my own life was bad enough, but there was another   4
episode in which other people could have been hurt, too. On this
occasion, I accidentally set a valley on fire. Two of my friends and I were
sitting on a hill sharing a few beers. It was a warm summer night, and
there was absolutely nothing to do. The idea came like a thunderclap.
We collected a supply of large plastic trash bags, emergency highway
flares, and a half tank of helium left over from a science-fair experiment.
Then we began to construct a fleet of UFOs. Filling the bags with
helium, we tied them closed with wire and suspended several burning
flares below each bag. Our UFOs leaped into the air like an army of
invading Martians. Rising and darting in the blackness, they convinced
even us. Our fun turned into horror, though, as we watched the balloons
begin to drop onto the wooded valley below. Soon, a brushfire started
and, quickly sobered, we called the fire department. The punishment we
received for this prank put an end to my risky antics.

Every so often, I think back on the things that I did as a teenager. I   5
feel lucky that I didn't harm myself or others, though I do feel regret that
my actions had a negative impact on others. Today I'm older, wiser, and
more aware of the repercussions my actions can cause.

Essay 2

Personal

Problems of My Adolescence

In the unreal world of television situation comedies, teenagers are   1
carefree, smart, funny, wisecracking, secure kids. In fact, most of them
are more "together" than the adults on the shows. This, however, isn't
how I recall my teenage years at all. As a teen, I suffered. Every day, I
battled the terrible physical, family, and social troubles of adolescence.

For one thing, I had to deal with a demoralizing physical problem—   2
acne. Some days, I would wake up in the morning with a red bump the
size of a taillight on my nose. Since I worried constantly about my
appearance anyway, acne outbreaks could turn me into a crying,
screaming maniac. Plastering on a layer of (at the time) orange-colored
Clearasil, which didn't fool anybody, I would slink into school, hoping

continued

that the boy I had a crush on would be absent that day. Within the last few years, however, treatments for acne have improved. Now, skin doctors prescribe special drugs that clear up pimples almost immediately. An acne attack could shatter whatever small amount of self-esteem I had managed to build up.

In addition to fighting acne, I felt compelled to fight my family. As a teenager, I needed to be independent. At that time, the most important thing in life was to be close to my friends and to try out new, more adult experiences. Unfortunately, my family seemed to get in the way. My little brother, for instance, turned into my enemy. We are close now, though. In fact, Eddie recently painted my new apartment for me. Eddie used to barge into my room, make calls on my cell phone, and read my e-mail. I would threaten to tie him up and leave him in a garbage dumpster. He would scream, my mother would yell, and all hell would break loose. My parents, too, were enemies. They wouldn't let me stay out late, wear the clothes I wanted to wear, or hang around with the friends I liked. So I tried to get revenge on them by being miserable, sulky, and sarcastic at home.

Worst of all, I had to face the social traumas of being a teenager. Things that were supposed to be fun, like dates and dances, were actually horrible. On the few occasions when I had a real date, I agonized over everything—my hair, my weight, my pimples. After a date, I would come home, raid the kitchen, and drown my insecurities in a sea of junk food. Dances were also stressful events. My friends and I would sneak a couple of beers just to get up the nerve to walk into the school gym. Now I realize that teenage drinking is dangerous. I read recently that the number-one killer of teenagers is drunk driving. At dances, I never relaxed. It was too important to look exactly right, to act really cool, and to pretend I was having fun.

I'm glad I'm not a teenager anymore. I wouldn't ever want to feel so unattractive, so confused, and so insecure again. I'll gladly accept the crow's-feet and stomach bulge of adulthood in exchange for a little peace of mind.

ACTIVITY 1

Fill in the blanks.

Essay _____ makes its point more clearly and effectively because _____

_____

_____

_____

EXPLANATION: Essay 1 is more effective because it is unified. All the details in this essay are on target; they support and develop each of its three topic sentences ("The first caper proved that good, clean fun does not have to be dull"; "Not all my antics were harmless, and one involved risking my life"; and "Risking my own life was bad enough, but there was another episode where other people could have been hurt, too").

On the other hand, essay 2 contains some details irrelevant to its topic sentences. In the first supporting paragraph (paragraph 2), for example, the sentences "Within the last few years, however, treatments for acne have improved. Now, skin doctors prescribe special drugs that clear up pimples almost immediately" do not support the writer's topic statement that she had to deal with the physical problem of acne. Such details should be left out in the interest of unity.

The difference between these first two essays leads us to the first base, or standard, of effective writing: *unity*. To achieve unity is to have all the details in your paper related to your thesis and to your supporting topic sentences. Each time you think of something to put into your paper, ask yourself whether it relates to your thesis and your supporting points. If it does not, leave it out. For example, if you were writing a paper about the problems of being unemployed and then spent a couple of sentences talking about the pleasures of having a lot of free time, you would be missing the first and most essential base of good writing.

Revising for Unity

ACTIVITY 2

Go back to essay 2 and cross out the two sentences in the first supporting paragraph (paragraph 2), the one sentence in the second supporting paragraph (paragraph 3), and the two sentences in the third supporting paragraph (paragraph 4) that are off target and do not support their topic sentences.

Base 2: Support

Understanding Support

The following essays were written on the topic "Handling Disappointment." Both are unified, but one communicates more clearly and effectively. Which one, and why?

Dealing with Disappointment

One way to look at life is as a series of disappointments. Life can certainly appear that way because disappointment crops up in the life of everyone more often, it seems, than satisfaction. How disappointments are handled can have a great bearing on how life is viewed. People can react negatively by sulking or by blaming others, or they can try to understand the reasons behind the disappointment.

Sulking is one way to deal with disappointment. This attitude—Why does everything always happen to me?—is common because it is easy to adopt, but it is not very productive. Everyone has had the experience of meeting people who specialize in feeling sorry for themselves. A sulky manner will often discourage others from wanting to lend support, and it prevents the sulker from making positive moves toward self-help. It becomes easier just to sit back and sulk. Unfortunately, feeling sorry for oneself does nothing to lessen the pain of disappointment. It may, in fact, increase the pain. It certainly does not make future disappointments easier to bear.

Blaming others is another negative and unproductive way to cope with disappointment. This all-too-common response of pointing the finger at someone else doesn't help one's situation. This posture will lead only to anger, resentment, and, therefore, further unhappiness. Disappointment in another's performance does not necessarily indicate that the performer is at fault. Perhaps expectations were too high, or there could have been a misunderstanding as to what the performer actually intended to accomplish.

A positive way to handle disappointment is to try to understand the reasons behind the disappointment. An analysis of the causes of disappointment can have an excellent chance of producing desirable results. Often understanding alone can help alleviate the pain of disappointment and can help prevent future disappointments. Also, it is wise to try to remember that what would be ideal is not necessarily what is reasonable to expect in any given situation. The ability to look disappointment squarely in the face and then go on from there is the first step on the road back.

Continuous handling of disappointment in a negative manner can lead to a negative view of life itself. Chances for personal happiness in such a state of being are understandably slim. Learning not to expect perfection in an imperfect world and keeping in mind those times when expectations were actually surpassed are positive steps toward allowing the joys of life to prevail.

Essay 2

Reactions to Disappointment

Ben Franklin said that the only sure things in life are death and   1
taxes. He left something out, however: disappointment. No one gets
through life without experiencing many disappointments. Strangely,
though, most people seem unprepared for disappointment and react to
it in negative ways. They feel depressed or try to escape their troubles
instead of using disappointment as an opportunity for growth.

One negative reaction to disappointment is depression. For   2
example, Helena, a woman trying to win a promotion, works hard for
over a year in her department. Helena is so sure she will get the
promotion, in fact, that she has already picked out the car she will buy
when her salary increase comes through. However, the boss names one
of Helena's coworkers to the spot. The fact that all the other department
employees tell Helena that she is the one who really deserved the
promotion doesn't help her deal with the crushing disappointment.
Deeply depressed, Helena decides that all her goals are doomed to
defeat. She loses her enthusiasm for her job and can barely force
herself to show up every day. Helena tells herself that she is a failure
and that doing a good job just isn't worth the work.

Another negative reaction to disappointment, and one that often   3
follows depression, is the desire to escape. Jamal fails to get into the
college his brother is attending, the college that was the focus of all his
dreams, and decides to escape his disappointment. Why worry about
college at all? Instead, he covers up his real feelings by giving up on
his schoolwork and getting completely involved with friends, parties,
and "good times." Or Carla doesn't make the varsity basketball
team — something she wanted very badly — and so refuses to play
sports at all. She decides to hang around with a new set of friends who
get high every day; then she won't have to confront her disappointment
and learn to live with it.

The positive way to react to disappointment is to use it as a chance   4
for growth. This isn't easy, but it's the only useful way to deal with an
inevitable part of life. Helena, the woman who wasn't promoted, could
have handled her disappointment by looking at other options. If her
boss doesn't recognize her talent and hard work, perhaps she could
transfer to another department. Or she could ask the boss how to
improve her performance so that she would be a shoo-in for the next
promotion. Jamal, the boy who didn't get into the college of his choice,
should look into other schools. Going to another college may encourage
him to be his own person, step out of his brother's shadow, and realize
that being turned down by one college isn't a final judgment on his
abilities or potential. Rather than escape into drugs, Carla could improve

continued

her basketball skills for a year or pick up another sport—like swimming or tennis—that would probably turn out to be more useful to her as an adult.

    Disappointments are unwelcome but regular visitors to everyone's   5 life. We can feel depressed about them, or we can try to escape from them. The best thing, though, is to accept a disappointment and then try to use it somehow: step over the unwelcome visitor on the doorstep and get on with life.

Fill in the blanks.

Essay _____ makes its point more clearly and effectively because _____

_____

_____

_____

ACTIVITY 3

EXPLANATION: Here, essay 2 is more effective, for it offers specific examples of the ways people deal with disappointment. We see for ourselves the kinds of reactions people have to disappointment.

    Essay 1, on the other hand, gives us no specific evidence. The writer tells us repeatedly that sulking, blaming others, and trying to understand the reasons behind a disappointment are the reactions people have to a letdown. However, the writer never *shows* us any of these responses in action. Exactly what kinds of disappointments is the writer talking about? And how, for instance, does someone analyze the causes of disappointment? Would a person write a list of causes on a piece of paper, or review the causes with a concerned friend, or speak to a professional therapist? In an essay like this, we would want to see *examples* of how sulking and blaming others are negative ways of dealing with disappointment.

    Consideration of these two essays leads us to the second base of effective writing: *support*. After realizing the importance of specific supporting details, one student writer revised a paper they had done on being lost in the woods as the worst experience of their childhood. In the revised paper, instead of talking about "the terror of being separated from my parents," they referred to such specifics as "tears streamed down my cheeks as I pictured the faces I would never see again" and "I clutched the locket my parents had given me as if it were a lucky charm that could help me find my way back to the campsite." All your papers should include such vivid details.

Revising for Support

ACTIVITY 4

On a separate sheet of paper, revise one of the three supporting paragraphs in "Dealing with Disappointment" by providing specific supporting examples.

Base 3: Coherence

Understanding Coherence

The following two essays were written on the topic "Positive or Negative Effects of Television." Both are unified, and both are supported. However, one communicates more clearly and effectively. Which one, and why?

Essay 1

Harmful Effects of Watching Television

In a recent cartoon, one character said to another, "When you think   1
of the awesome power of television to educate, aren't you glad it doesn't?" It's true that television has the power to educate and to entertain, but unfortunately, these benefits are outweighed by the harm it does to dedicated viewers. Television is harmful because it creates passivity, discourages communication, and presents a false picture of reality.

Television makes viewers passive. Children who have an electronic   2
babysitter spend most of their waking hours in a semiconscious state. Older viewers watch tennis matches and baseball games with none of the excitement of being in the stands. Even if children are watching *Sesame Street* or *Daniel Tiger's Neighborhood*, they are being educated passively. The child actors are going on nature walks, building crafts projects, playing with animals, and participating in games, but the little viewers are simply watching. Older viewers watch guests discuss hot topics on *The View*, but the hosts don't converse with the home viewers about their opinions.

Worst of all, TV presents a false picture of reality that leaves viewers   3
frustrated because they don't have the beauty or wealth of the characters on television. Viewers absorb the idea that everyone else in the United States owns a lavish apartment, a suburban house, a sleek car, and an expensive wardrobe. Every detective, police officer, oil

continued

baron, and lawyer, male or female, is extremely good-looking and fit. The material possessions on TV shows and commercials contribute to the false image of reality. News anchors and reporters, with their perfect hair and makeup, must fit television's standard of beauty. From their modest homes or cramped apartments, many viewers tune in daily to the upper-middle-class world that TV glorifies.

Television discourages communication. Families watching television 4
do very little talking except for brief exchanges during commercials. If Uncle Scott or the next-door neighbors drop in for a visit, the most comfortable activity for everyone may be not conversation but watching ESPN. The family may not even be watching the same set; instead, in some households, all the family members head for their own rooms to watch their own sets. At dinner, plates are plopped on the coffee table in front of the set, and the meal is wolfed down during *NBC Nightly News*. During commercials, the only communication a family has all night may consist of questions like "Do we have any popcorn?" and "Where's the remote?"

Television, like cigarettes or saccharin, is harmful to our health. We 5
are becoming isolated, passive, and frustrated. And, most frightening, the average viewer now spends more time watching television than ever before.

The Benefits of Television

We hear a lot about the negative effects of television on the viewer. 1
Obviously, television can be harmful if it is watched constantly to the exclusion of other activities. It would be just as harmful to surf the Internet all the time or to eat constantly. However, when television is watched in moderation, it is extremely valuable, as it provides relaxation, entertainment, and education.

First of all, watching TV has the value of sheer relaxation. Watching 2
television can be soothing and restful after an eight-hour day of pressure, challenges, or concentration. After working hard all day, people look forward to a new episode of a favorite show or yet another showing of *Parasite* or *Captain Marvel*. This period of relaxation leaves viewers refreshed and ready to take on the world again. Watching TV also seems to reduce stress in some people. This benefit of television is just beginning to be recognized.

In addition to being relaxing, television is entertaining. Along with 3
the standard comedies, dramas, and game shows that provide

Essay 2

Academic

continued

enjoyment to viewers, television offers a variety of movies and sports events. Moreover, viewers can pay a monthly fee for services like Disney+, YouTube TV, or Sling. Viewers can watch first-run movies, rock and classical music concerts, and specialized sports events, like international soccer and pay-per-view boxing matches. Viewers can also buy or rent movies and TV shows through streaming services. Still another popular area of TV entertainment is video games. PlayStation, Xbox, and Nintendo consoles allow the owner to have a video-game arcade in the living room.

Most important, television is educational. Preschoolers learn colors,   4
numbers, and letters from public television programs, like *Sesame Street,* that use animation and puppets to make learning fun. Science shows for older children go on location to analyze everything from volcanoes to rocket launches. Adults, too, can learn from shows like *NOVA*, DIY home improvement programs, and cooking shows. Also, television widens our knowledge by covering important events and current news. Viewers can see and hear presidents' speeches, state funerals, natural disasters, and election results as they are happening.

Perhaps because television is such a powerful force, we like to   5
criticize it and search for its flaws. However, the benefits of television should not be ignored. We can use television to relax, to have fun, and to make ourselves smarter. This electronic wonder, then, is a servant, not a master.

ACTIVITY 5

Fill in the blanks.

Essay _____ makes its point more clearly and effectively because _____

_____

_____

_____

EXPLANATION: In this case, essay 2 is more effective because the material is organized clearly and logically. Using emphatic order, the writer develops three positive uses of television, ending with the most important use: television as an educational tool. The writer includes transitional words that act as signposts, making movement from one idea to the next easy to follow. The major transitions include *First of all, In addition,* and *Most important;*

continued

transitions within paragraphs include such words as *Moreover, Still another, too,* and *Also.* And this writer also uses a linking sentence ("In addition to being relaxing, television is entertaining") to tie the first and second supporting paragraphs together clearly.

Although essay 1 is unified and supported, the writer does not have any clear and consistent way of organizing the material. The most important idea (signaled by the phrase *Worst of all*) is discussed in the second supporting paragraph instead of being saved for last. None of the supporting paragraphs organizes its details in a logical fashion. The first supporting paragraph, for example, discusses older viewers, then goes to younger viewers, then jumps back to older people again. The third supporting paragraph, like the first, leaps from an opening idea (families talking only during commercials) to several intervening ideas and then back to the original idea (talking during commercials). In addition, essay 1 uses practically no transitional devices to guide the reader.

These two essays lead us to the third base of effective writing: *coherence.* All the supporting ideas and sentences in a paper must be organized so that they cohere, or "stick together." As has been discussed in Chapter 4, key techniques for tying together the material in a paper include a clear method of organization (such as time order or emphatic order), transitions, and other connecting words.

Revising for Coherence

On a separate sheet of paper, revise one of the three supporting paragraphs in "Harmful Effects of Watching Television" by providing a clear method of organizing the material and transitional words.

ACTIVITY 6

Base 4: Sentence Skills

Understanding Sentence Skills

Following are the opening paragraphs from two essays. Both are unified, supported, and organized, but one version communicates more clearly and effectively. Which one, and why?

"revenge"

[1]Revenge is one of those things that many people enjoys. [2]People don't like to talk about it, though. [3]Just the same, there is nothing more tempting, more satisfying, or with the reward of a bit of revenge. [4]The purpose is not to harm the victims. [5]But to let them know that they have been doing something that is upsetting. [6]Careful plotting can provide relief from bothersom coworkers, gossiping friends, or nagging family members.

[7]Coworkers who make comments about the fact that a person is always fifteen minutes late for work can be taken care of very simply. [8]The first thing that a person seeking revenge should do is to get up extra early one day. [9]Before the sun comes up, they should drive to each coworker's house, park near the coworker's car, reach under the hood of the car, and disconnected the wire on the pos. battery terminal. [10]The car will be unharmed, but it will not start. [11]All of the victims will be late for work on the same day. [12]If the person seeking revenge is really lucky, the boss might notice that no one else is on time and will reward the person who did show up. [13]Later if guilt becomes an issue anonymous calls to the coworkers to tell them how to get their car running again may help ease those feelings. . . .

1

2

A Bit of Revenge

Revenge is one of those things that many people enjoy. People don't like to talk about it, though. Just the same, there is nothing more tempting, more satisfying, or more rewarding than a bit of revenge. The purpose is not to harm the victims but to let them know that they have been doing something that is upsetting. Careful plotting can provide relief from bothersome coworkers, gossiping friends, or nagging family members.

Coworkers who make comments about the fact that a person is always fifteen minutes late for work can be taken care of very simply. The first thing that a person seeking revenge should do is to get up extra early one day. Before the sun comes up, they should drive to each coworker's house, park near the coworker's car, reach under the hood of the car, and disconnect the wire on the positive battery terminal. The car will be unharmed, but it will not start. All of the victims will be late for work on the same day. If the person seeking revenge is really lucky, the boss might notice that no one else is on time and will reward the person who did show up. Later, if guilt becomes an issue, anonymous calls to the coworkers to tell them how to get their cars running again may help ease those feelings. . . .

1

2

Fill in the blanks.

Essay _____ makes its point more clearly and effectively because _____

_____

_____

ACTIVITY 7

EXPLANATION: Essay 2 is more effective because it uses *sentence skills,* the fourth base of competent writing. Here are the sentence-skills mistakes in essay 1:

*   The title should not be set off in quotation marks.

*   The first letter of the title should be capitalized.

*   The plural subject *people* in sentence 1 should have a plural verb: *enjoys* should be *enjoy.*

*   There is a lack of parallelism in sentence 3: *with the reward* of should be *more rewarding.*

*   Word group 5 is a fragment; it can be corrected by attaching it to the previous sentence.

*   The word *bothersom* in sentence 6 is misspelled; it should be *bothersome.*

*   The word *disconnected* in sentence 9 should be *disconnect* to be consistent in tense with *reach,* the other verb in the sentence.

*   The abbreviation *pos.* in sentence 9 should be spelled out in full: *positive.*

*   Commas must be added in sentence 13 to set off the interrupting words.

*   The word *car* in sentence 13 needs to be changed to agree with *their* and *coworkers.*

Revising for Sentence Skills

Here are the final three paragraphs from the two essays. Edit the sentences in the first essay to make the corrections needed. Note that comparing essays 1 and 2 will help you locate the mistakes. This activity will also help you identify some of the sentence skills you may want to review in Part 4.

ACTIVITY 8

. . . [1]Gossiping friends at school are also perfect targets for a simple   3
act of revenge. [2]A way to trap friends are to leave phony messages on
their lockers. [3]The person seeking revenge should leave a message
setting up a meeting with a particular individual later that day at the coffee
shop (or other location) where the individual works. [4]When the victim
shows up, hopefully the individual working will seem confused about
meeting up. [5]The victim will be frustrated about the waste of time. [6]The
plan works equally well for male or female friends.

[7]Parents and siblings can also be victims of harmless revenge,   4
especially when they have been really annoying. [8]It may be just the way
to make them quite down for a while. [9]The dinner table, where most of
the nagging probably happens, is a likely place. [10]Just before the meal
begins, you should throw a handful of raisins into the food. [11]After about 5
minutes, once everyone has began to eat, the person should then
begin to make odd noises and yell, "Bugs!" [12]Dumping the food in the
disposal, the car, will head quickly for mcdonald's. [13]After they leave, the
meal will be quiet and peaceful.

[14]Well-planned revenge does not have to hurt anyone. [15]The object is   5
simply to let other people know that they are being a bother. [16]Anyone
who plans revenge should remember, though, to stay on guard after
completing the revenge. [17]The reason for this is simple, [18]coworkers,
friends, and family can also plan revenge.

. . . Gossiping friends at school are also perfect targets for a   3
simple act of revenge. A way to trap friends is to leave phony
messages on their lockers. The person seeking revenge should leave
a message setting up a meeting with a particular individual later that
day at the coffee shop (or other location) where the individual works.
When the victim shows up, hopefully the individual working will seem
confused about meeting up. The victim will be frustrated about the
waste of time. The plan works equally well for male or female friends.

continued

Parents and siblings can also be victims of harmless revenge,   4
especially when they have been really annoying. It may be just the
way to make them quiet down for a while. The dinner table, where
most of the nagging probably happens, is a likely place. Just before
the meal begins, the person should throw a handful of raisins into the
food. After about five minutes, once everyone has begun to eat, the
person should then begin to make odd noises and yell, "Bugs!" The
others will all dump their food in the disposal, jump into the car, and
head quickly for McDonald's. After they leave, the meal will be quiet
and peaceful.

Well-planned revenge does not have to hurt anyone. The object is   5
simply to let other people know that they are being a bother. Anyone
who plans revenge should remember, though, to stay on guard after
completing the revenge. The reason for this is simple. Coworkers,
friends, and family can also plan revenge.

Practice in Using the Four Bases

You are now familiar with four standards, or bases, of effective writing: *unity,*
support, coherence, and *sentence skills.* In this section you will expand and strengthen
your understanding of the four bases as you evaluate and revise essays for each
of them.

Revising Essays for Unity

Both of the following essays contain irrelevant sentences that do not relate to the
thesis of the essay or support the topic sentence of the paragraph in which they
appear. Cross out the irrelevant sentences and write the numbers of those sentences in the spaces provided.

ACTIVITY 9

Playing on the Browns

¹For the past three summers, I have played first base on a softball   1
team known as the Browns. ²We play a long schedule, including
playoffs, and everybody takes the games pretty seriously. ³In that
respect, we're no different from any other of the thousand or so teams
in our city. ⁴But in one respect, we <u>are</u> different. ⁵In an all-male league,
we have a woman on the team—me. ⁶Thus I've had a chance to
observe something about human nature by seeing how the men have

Essay 1

Personal

continued

treated me. [7]Some have been disbelieving; some have been patronizing; and, fortunately, some have simply accepted me.

[8]One new team in the league was particularly flabbergasted to see me start the game at first base. [9]Nobody on the Comets had commented one way or the other when he saw me warming up, but playing in the actual game was another story. [10]The Comets' first-base coach leaned over to me with a disbelieving grin and said, "You mean, you're starting, and those three guys are on the bench?" [11]I nodded and he shrugged, still amazed. [12]He probably thought I was the manager's wife. [13]When I came up to bat, the Comet pitcher smiled and called to his outfielders to move way in on me. [14]Now, I don't have a lot of power, but I'm not exactly feeble. [15]I used to work out on the exercise machines at a local health club until it closed, and now I lift weights at home a couple of times a week. [16]I wiped the smirks off their faces with a line drive double over the left fielder's head.

2

The number of the irrelevant sentence: _____

[17]The next game, we played another new team, the Argyles, and their attitude was patronizing. [18]The Argyles had seen me take batting practice, so they didn't do anything so rash as to draw their outfield way in. [19]They had respect for my ability as a player. [20]However, they tried to annoy me with phony concern. [21]For example, a redheaded Argyle got on base in the first inning and said to me, "You'd better be careful, hon. [22]When you have your foot on the bag, somebody might step on it. [23]You can get hurt in this game." [24]I was mad, but I have worked out several mental techniques to control my anger because it interferes with my playing ability. [25]Well, this delicate little girl survived the season without injury, which is more than I can say for some of the he-men on the Argyles.

3

The number of the irrelevant sentence: _____

[26]Happily, most of the teams in the league have accepted me, just as the Browns did. [27]The men on the Browns coached and criticized me (and occasionally cursed me) just like anyone else. [28]Because I'm a religious person, I don't approve of cursing, but I don't say anything about it to my teammates. [29]They are not amazed when I get a hit or

4

stretch for a wide throw. [30]My average this year was higher than the averages of several of my teammates, yet none of them acted resentful or threatened. [31]On several occasions I was taken out late in a game for a pinch runner, but other slow players on the team were also lifted at times for pinch runners. [32]Every woman should have a team like the Browns!

The number of the irrelevant sentence: _____

[33]Because I really had problems only with the new teams, I've concluded that it's when people are faced with an unfamiliar situation that they react defensively. [34]Once a rival team has gotten used to seeing me on the field, I'm no big deal. [35]Still, I suspect that the Browns secretly feel we're a little special. [36]After all, we are the only team with a woman on it.

5

The Power of the Vote

Essay 2

[1]Since 1971, in both presidential election years and in non-presidential election years, voter turn-out has been consistently lower than 70 percent. [2]Those who don't vote claim that their vote wouldn't make any difference and they are powerless to change anything. [3]However, in January 2012, websites like Wikipedia and Google demonstrated just how powerful the voices of the American people really are.

1

[4]In October 2011, two bills, the Stop Online Piracy Act (SOPA) and the Protect Intellectual Property Act (PIPA), were introduced. [5]Bills are regularly introduced in both the House and the Senate. [6]The purpose of these bills was to make it easier for the U.S. Department of Justice to block sites that sell or distribute pirated copyrighted material like music and movies as well as sites that sell counterfeit items like purses and watches. [7]Neither of the bills would have necessarily shut down the sites, but it would have allowed the U.S. Department of Justice to require Internet service providers to block access to the sites and stop providers, search engines, and advertisers from doing business with such sites. [8]Those in favor of the bills claimed the bills would protect jobs and revenue, but those against the bills saw them as an infringement of freedom of information.

2

The number of the irrelevant sentence: _____

[9]Those in favor of the bill, like many of the major Hollywood studios   3
and several news corporations, claimed the bills would protect jobs and
revenue. [10]In December 2011, Chris Dodd, Chair of the Motion Picture
Association of America (MPAA), wrote, "Indeed, the theft of intellectual
property (which costs our nation 373,000 jobs and $58 billion in
economic output each year) is itself the true threat to free speech,
because it threatens to silence the artists whose creations—and
livelihoods—are being stolen." [11]Dodd's support of the bill demonstrates
his concern for those he represents—the film industry. [12]Art industries
have also been victims of piracy. [13]The White House also maintains that
online piracy is problematic and does threaten American jobs and the
economy. [14]However, on January 14, 2012, in response to a petition
against the SOPA bill that had over 50,000 signatures, the White House
released a statement that said, "Online piracy by foreign websites is a
serious problem that requires a serious legislative response, [but] we will
not support legislation that reduces freedom of expression, increases
cybersecurity risk, or undermines the dynamic, innovative global Internet."

The number of the irrelevant sentence: _____

[15]On January 18, 2012, a coordinated service blackout was led by the   4
English Wikipedia and Reddit. [16]Reddit is a social news website founded
in 2005. [17]Other sites like Google offered a link to sign a petition, but
didn't stop service. [18]Still other sites like Twitter, MoveOn.org, and Mozilla
vocalized their protest, but didn't participate in the blackout.
[19]NetCoalition, a group that provides a platform for and represents
companies like Google, eBay, Expedia, and Amazon.com, released
national radio and print ads against SOPA and PIPA. [20]In a statement,
Google's news team said, "Like many businesses, entrepreneurs and
Web users, we oppose these bills because there are smart, targeted
ways to shut down foreign rogue websites without asking American
companies to censor the Internet. [21]So tomorrow we will be joining many
other tech companies to highlight this issue on our U.S. home page."

The number of the irrelevant sentence: _____

[22]More than four and a half million people signed Google's anti-   5
SOPA/PIPA petition. [23]As a result of the outpouring of opinion, both bills
lost congressional support and the votes were postponed pending

continued

further discussion and resolution. [24]There were a lot of people who expressed angry reactions about the bills going back to the discussion table. [25]The blackout of January 18 is a strong example of the power of the people; it is something that should inspire more people to participate in the civic responsibility of voting.

The number of the irrelevant sentence: _____

Revising Essays for Support

Both of the essays below lack supporting details at certain key points. In each essay, identify the spots where details are needed.

ACTIVITY 10

Essay 1

The Formula for Happiness

[1]The study of happiness and what creates it has become a multi-million-dollar business. [2]Some people say that happiness comes from wealth, but most researchers say that happiness comes from within. [3]In pursuit of happiness, many people create goals, but often find once they have achieved them, the expected contentment is not present. [4]Martha Beck, a life coach with a Ph.D. from Harvard, writes that "Over and over, researchers studying happiness have found that the situational elements people crave—money, social status, possessions—don't reliably lead to an experience of well-being. [5]Learning to find joy in the present moment . . . increases life satisfaction, improves health, and allows us to live longer more fulfilling lives." [6]Finding joy in the present moment might be difficult at first, but if one focuses on what truly matters, this joy can lead to a better life.

[7]The first step in learning to find joy is to learn to be in the present. [8]Instead of seeing a rainy day as a negative thing, they see a rainy day and think about splashing and jumping in puddles. [9]They see caterpillars as fascinating, not gross, objects to observe and follow. [10]They see life as a series of exciting gifts that need to be experienced. [11]Instead of always focusing on what is coming next, learning to find joy means pausing. [12]Whether it is taking a moment to deeply breathe in the aroma of that first cup of coffee or marveling at the way toothpaste foams, finding satisfaction in the little moments of the day will lead to a more positive outlook.

The spot where supporting details are needed occurs after sentence _____.

> ¹³The second step in finding joy is to focus on experiences instead of things. ¹⁴Buying a television might be exciting at first, but sitting in a room watching television alone isn't going to contribute to a sense of happiness. ¹⁵According to Thomas A. Glass, professor at Johns Hopkins Bloomberg School of Public Health, studies show that people who live longer lives have strong social connections and that people who have weak or no social connections will die earlier, despite seemingly good health.   3

The first spot where supporting details are needed occurs after sentence _____.
The second spot occurs after sentence _____.

> ¹⁶Finally, it is important to live generously. ¹⁷Many people report that when they spend more time volunteering or learning something new, they find happiness. ¹⁸This intrinsic desire to better themselves or the world around them leads people to a sense of worth and happiness.   4

The spot where supporting details are needed occurs after sentence _____.

> ¹⁹Pursuing happiness can always remain a goal, or it can become a reality. ²⁰All a person needs to do is focus on the present, focus on experiences, and live generously. ²¹Together these actions can lead to a longer, happier life.   5

Essay 2

> ### International Student Orientation Program
>
> ¹With the increase of international students on campus, it is important that the academic community be aware of the major issues these students face. ²Many international students struggle with language barriers, cultural barriers, and social barriers. ³In order to effectively educate our students, the counseling department, in conjunction with the College Orientation department and the Honors Student Ambassador Program, will be implementing an orientation program that all international students will be required to attend.   1
>
> ⁴To address the language barriers, all international students will be tested on their English language skills. ⁵If they have already taken the TOEFL, that score will be used in place of the added testing. ⁶Students who are more proficient will be partnered with students in the Student Ambassador program. ⁷These pairings will allow students to work with a peer to ask questions, have subjects clarified, and seek the necessary   2

continued

resources that will offer help. [8]This peer mentoring will be a way to increase student engagement, thus enhancing student success. [9]Students who are less fluent in English will be linked up with all the helpful elements that our ESL program can offer. [10]Not only will the orientation program offer students an opportunity to improve their English language skills, but it will offer them connections with other students and professors who are aware of the added struggles faced by international students.

The spot where supporting details are needed occurs after sentence _____.

[11]To address the cultural barriers, the orientation classes will focus specifically on American culture in comparison to the cultures represented by the students in the class. [12]Many students come from countries that view education and professors differently. [13]Specific focus will be placed on American classroom culture and the expected behavior of student-professor interaction. [14]Students will also be instructed about the many differing aspects of American social culture. [15]Students will be encouraged to share their cultures and customs to create a deeper understanding and bond within the class. [16]This type of learning will create a strong learning community that will aid in students' acclimation.   3

The spot where supporting details are needed occurs after sentence _____.

[17]The final problems many international students face are social barriers. [18]Most students attending college are forging new social connections. [19]However, it is generally much harder for international students as they are also trying to learn new customs, languages, and etiquette. [20]Within the safety of the orientation class, students will be able to form a cohort of other international students who are also facing social barriers. [21]For many reasons, the Student Ambassadors will be vital to this part of the orientation class.   4

The spot where supporting details are needed occurs after sentence _____.

[22]Our international students face many added challenges, and they give much to our college community. [23]Studies show that students who attend orientation programs often are far more successful in school. [24]Offering an orientation that is specifically geared toward the obstacles our international students face will help them to have a more positive experience, which in turn should greatly improve our retention of our international students.   5

Revising Essays for Coherence

Both of the essays that follow could be revised to improve their coherence. Answer the questions about coherence that come after each essay.

Essay 1

Academic

Noise Pollution

[1]Natural sounds—waves, wind, birdsong—are so soothing that companies sell recordings of them to anxious people seeking a relaxing atmosphere at home or in the car. [2]One reason why "environmental sounds" are big business is that ordinary citizens, especially city dwellers, are bombarded by noise pollution. [3]On the way to work, on the job, and on the way home, the typical urban resident must cope with a continuing barrage of unpleasant sounds.

[4]The noise level in an office can be unbearable. [5]From nine to five o'clock, phones and fax machines ring, computer keyboards chatter, intercoms buzz, and copy machines thump back and forth. [6]Every time the receptionists can't find people, they resort to a nerve-shattering public address system. [7]And because the managers worry about the employees' morale, they graciously provide the endless droning of canned music. [8]This effectively eliminates any possibility of a moment of blessed silence.

[9]Traveling home from work provides no relief from the noisiness of the office. [10]The ordinary sounds of blaring taxi horns and rumbling buses are occasionally punctuated by the ear-piercing screech of car brakes. [11]Taking a shortcut through the park will bring the weary worker face to face with chanting religious cults, freelance musicians, screaming children, and barking dogs. [12]None of these sounds can compare with the loud music that park visitors play. [13]Each of their devices blasts out something different, from heavy-metal rock to baseball, at decibel levels so strong that they make eardrums throb in pain. [14]If there are birds singing or wind in the trees, the harried commuter will never hear them.

[15]Even a trip to work at 6:00 or 7:00 A.M. isn't quiet. [16]No matter which route a worker takes, there is bound to be a noisy construction site somewhere along the way. [17]Hard hats will shout from third-story windows to warn their coworkers below before heaving debris out and sending it crashing to earth. [18]Huge front-end loaders will crunch into these piles of rubble and back up, their warning signals letting out loud, jarring beeps. [19]Air hammers begin an earsplitting chorus of rat-a-tat-tat sounds guaranteed to shatter sanity as well as concrete. [20]Before reaching the office, the worker is already completely frazzled.

[21]Noise pollution is as dangerous as any other kind of pollution. [22]The endless pressure of noise probably triggers countless nervous breakdowns, vicious arguments, and bouts of depression. [23]And imagine the world problems we could solve, if only the noise stopped long enough to let us think.

1. In "Noise Pollution," what is the number of the sentence to which the transition word *Also* could be added in paragraph 2? _____

2. In the last sentence of paragraph 2, to what does the pronoun *This* refer?

    _____

3. What is the number of the sentence to which the transition word *But* could be added in paragraph 3? _____

4. What is the number of the sentence to which the transition word *Then* could be added in paragraph 4? _____

5. What is the number of the sentence to which the transition word *Meanwhile* could be added in paragraph 4? _____

6. What word is used as a synonym for *debris* in paragraph 4? _____

7. How many times is the key word *sounds* used in the essay? _____

8. The time order of the three supporting paragraphs is confused. What is the number of the supporting paragraph that should come first? _____ Second? _____ Third? _____

Weight Loss

Essay 2

Personal

[1]The big fraternity party turned out to be the low point of my first year at college. [2]I was in heaven until I discovered that my date with handsome Greg, the fraternity vice president, was a hoax: he had used me to win the "ugliest date" contest. [3]I ran sobbing back to the dorm, wanting to resign from the human race. [4]Then I realized that it was time to stop kidding myself about my weight. [5]Within the next two years, I lost forty-two pounds and turned my life around. [6]Losing weight gave me self-confidence socially, emotionally, and professionally.

1

[7]I am more outgoing socially. [8]Just being able to abandon dark colors, baggy sweaters, and tent dresses in favor of bright colors, T-shirts, and designer jeans made me feel better in social situations. [9]I am able to do more things. [10]I once turned down an invitation for a great camping trip with my best friend's family, making up excuses about sun poisoning and allergies. [11]Really, I was too embarrassed to tell them that I couldn't fit into the bathroom in their Winnebago! [12]I made up for it last summer when I was one of the organizers of a college backpacking trip through the Rockies.

2

[13]Most important, losing weight helped me seek new professional goals. [14]When I was obese, I organized my whole life around my weight, as

3

continued

if it were a defect I could do nothing about. ¹⁵With my good grades, I could have chosen almost any major the college offered, but I had limited my goal to teaching kindergarten because I felt that little children wouldn't judge how I looked. ¹⁶Once I was no longer overweight, I realized that I love working with all sorts of people. ¹⁷I became a campus guide and even had small parts in college theater productions. ¹⁸As a result, last year I changed my major to public relations. ¹⁹The area fascinates me, and I now have good job prospects there.

²⁰I have also become more emotionally honest. ²¹Rose, at the college counseling center, helped me see that my "fat and jolly" personality had been false. ²²I was afraid others would reject me if I didn't always go along with their suggestions. ²³I eventually put Rose's advice to the test. ²⁴My roommates were planning an evening at a Greek restaurant. ²⁵I loved the restaurant's atmosphere, but there wasn't much I liked on the menu. ²⁶Finally, in a shaky voice I said, "Actually, I'm not crazy about lamb. ²⁷How about Chinese food?" ²⁸They scolded me for not mentioning it before, and we had dinner at a Chinese restaurant. ²⁹We all agreed it was one of our best evenings out.

4

³⁰Fortunately, the low point of my first year turned out to be the turning point, leading to what promises to be an exciting senior year. ³¹Greg's cruel joke became a strange sort of favor, and I've gone from wanting to resign from the human race to welcoming each day as a source of fresh adventure and self-discovery.

5

1. In "Weight Loss," what is the number of the sentence to which the transition words *For one thing* could be added in paragraph 2? _____

2. What is the number of the sentence to which the transition word *Also* could be added in paragraph 2? _____

3. What is the number of the sentence to which the transition word *But* could be added in paragraph 2? _____

4. In sentence 11, to what does the pronoun *them* refer? _____

5. What is the number of the sentence to which the transition word *However* could be added in paragraph 3? _____

6. What word is used as a synonym for *obese* in paragraph 3? _____

7. How many times is the keyword *weight* used in the essay? _____

8. What is the number of the supporting paragraph that should be placed in the emphatic final position? _____

Revising Essays for All Four Bases: Unity, Support, Coherence, and Sentence Skills

In this activity, you will evaluate and revise two essays in terms of all four bases: unity, support, coherence, and sentence skills. Comments follow each supporting paragraph. Circle the letter of the statement that applies in each case.

ACTIVITY 12

Essay 1

Chiggers

1   I had lived my whole life not knowing what chiggers are. I thought they were probably a type of insect someone might encounter on an Amazon River cruise. I never had any real reason to care, until one day last summer. Within twenty-four hours, I had vividly experienced what chigger bites are, learned how to treat them, and learned how to prevent them.

2   First of all, I learned that chiggers are the larvae of tiny mites found in the woods and that their bites are always multiple and cause intense itching. A beautiful summer day seemed perfect for a walk in the woods. I am definitely not a city person, for I couldn't stand to be surrounded by people, noise, and concrete. As I walked through the ferns and pines, I noticed what appeared to be a dusting of reddish seeds or pollen on my slacks. Looking more closely, I realized that each speck was a tiny insect. I casually brushed off a few and gave them no further thought. I woke up the next morning feeling like a victim staked to an anthill by an enemy wise in the ways of torture. Most of my body was speckled with measlelike bumps that at the slightest touch burned and itched like a mosquito bite raised to the twentieth power. When antiseptics and calamine lotion failed to help, I raced to my doctor for emergency aid.

a.   Paragraph 2 contains an irrelevant sentence.

b.   Paragraph 2 lacks supporting details at one key spot.

c.   Time order in paragraph 2 is confused.

d.   Paragraph 2 contains two run-ons.

3   Healing the bites of chiggers, as the doctor diagnosed them to be, is not done overnight. It seems that there is really no wonder drug or commercial product to help. The victim must rely on a primitive home remedy and mostly wait out the course of the painful bites. First, the doctor explained, the skin must be bathed carefully with warm soapy water. An antihistamine spray applied several hours later will not cure the bites but will soothe the intense itching and help prevent infection.

continued

A few days after the treatment, the bites finally healed. Although I was in pain, and desperate for relief, I followed the doctor's instructions.

a. Paragraph 3 contains an irrelevant sentence.

b. Paragraph 3 lacks supporting details at one key spot.

c. Time order in paragraph 3 is confused.

d. Paragraph 3 contains one fragment.

Most important of all, I learned what to do to prevent getting chigger   4
bites in the future. Mainly, of course, stay out of the woods in the summertime. But if the temptation is too great on an especially beautiful day, I'll be sure to wear the right type of clothing, like a long-sleeved shirt, long pants, knee socks, and closed shoes. In addition, I'll cover myself with clouds of superstrength insect repellent. I will then shower thoroughly as soon as I get home, I also will probably burn all my clothes if I notice even one suspicious red speck.

a. Paragraph 4 contains an irrelevant sentence.

b. Paragraph 4 lacks supporting details at one key spot.

c. Paragraph 4 lacks transitional words.

d. Paragraph 4 contains a run-on and a fragment.

I will never forget my lessons on the cause, cure, and prevention of   5
chigger bites. I'd gladly accept the challenge of rattlesnakes and scorpions in the wilds of the West but will never again confront a siege of chiggers in the pinewoods.

Essay 2

Navigating the Hunt for a Job

As economies fluctuate and job markets change, it is important for   1
people to know how to navigate the process of job hunting. Getting a new job starts long before the résumé or cover letter, although they are both very important. Good hunters learn about the companies they are applying to, put together strong application packets, and extensively prepare for the interviews.

Securing a good job begins even before the application process.   2
Seekers should learn about the company they are applying to because knowing information about the company shows interest and conscientiousness. Applicants who know what the company's history is, what the company does, and what is expected of employees will

continued

demonstrate desired attitudes that many companies want. Also, through research, a job seeker might learn that a potential employer spends 10 percent of the gross income each year on a specific program for underserved children. One company in Chicago spent 20 percent of its gross income on a program for children living in poverty. People who really want a job with that company will then learn about the charitable programs that are important to that company, understand that program, and accept that a job with this company will mean possibly working with that program.

a. Paragraph 2 contains an irrelevant sentence.

b. Paragraph 2 lacks supporting details at one key spot.

c. Paragraph 2 lacks transitional words.

d. Paragraph 2 contains one fragment and one run-on.

Once job seekers have researched potential employers, the next   3
step is to prepare strong application packets. This means that an applicant must understand the skills and education requirements listed in the job descriptions and properly fill out the applications. If a job requires a degree in engineering, but the applicant doesn't have a degree. This may not be the right job. After the applicant has found a job that is a right fit, it is important to properly fill out the application. An applicant should double check that every question is answered, all the information is correct, and no spelling or grammar mistakes are made. Leaving off a signature or forgetting to fill in areas will not impress the potential employer. Cover letters should also be included in the packet they are the first introduction to the applicant and should address the specifics of the job, laying out why the candidate is the best choice. Cover letters should be error free and well-articulated. Weak application packets that include cover letters and applications that are filled with spelling mistakes, grammar errors, and irrelevant material will hold the applicant back. Strong application packets will increase the chance of applicants' moving on to the final step in job hunting.

a. Paragraph 3 contains an irrelevant sentence.

b. Paragraph 3 lacks supporting details at one key spot.

c. Paragraph 3 lacks transitional words.

d. Paragraph 3 contains one fragment and one run-on.

The final step in navigating the process is preparing for the   4
interviews, which includes proper grooming and practiced interviewing skills. Clothes should be appropriate for the interview, shoes should be polished, and bodies should be groomed. It isn't necessary to go out

continued

and buy a $5,000 suit, but it is important not to wear flip-flops and shorts. By visiting the work place ahead of time, if possible, the interviewee can assess how employees are dressed and then wear a similar—or slightly nicer—outfit. Specific interviewing skills should be practiced so that when questioned, the interviewee can eloquently and intelligently respond. Proper preparation will increase the candidate's chance of being offered a job because a prepared interviewee often means that they will be a prepared employee.

a. Paragraph 4 contains an irrelevant sentence.

b. Paragraph 4 lacks supporting details at one key spot.

c. Paragraph 4 lacks transitional words.

d. Paragraph 4 contains one fragment and one run-on.

By properly navigating the process of job hunting, people who are   5 seeking a new job will stand out to potential employers. There are thousands of people looking for jobs every day, but by taking hints from the successfully employed, job seekers will have the opportunity to move from seeker to employee.

TEXT CREDIT

p. 169: Source: Beck, Martha, "Conjuring Magic: How to Set Powerful Goals" December 30, 2014. marthabeck.com/2014/12/how-to-set-powerful-goals/

Developing an Essay

Who do you believe is the intended audience of this advertisement? Write a description of that intended audience.
Dennis MacDonald/Alamy Stock Photo

This chapter will

- explain the importance of understanding the nature and length of an assignment

- explain the importance of knowing your subject, your purpose, and your audience

- explain the three different points of view used in writing

- show you how to conduct a peer review and a personal review

- provide you with a sample student essay that illustrates the writing process in action

Important Considerations in Essay Development

When you begin work on particular types of essays, keep in mind several general considerations about writing; they are discussed in the following pages.

Understanding the Nature and Length of an Assignment

In all likelihood, your college writing assignments will have a good deal of variety. Sometimes you will be able to write on a topic of your own choosing or on a point you discover within a given topic; at other times you may be given a very specific assignment. In any case, do not start writing a paper until you know exactly what is expected.

First of all, be clear about *what kind of paper* **the instructor has in mind.** Do not hesitate to ask an instructor about an assignment. If you are not sure about the nature of an assignment, other students may be confused as well. Most instructors are more than willing to provide an explanation. They would rather spend a few minutes of class time explaining an assignment than have students turn in essays that miss the mark and therefore end up with failing grades. Here are some questions to ask:

- Should it be primarily a research paper summarizing other people's ideas?
- Should it consist entirely of your own ideas?
- Should it consist of a comparison of your ideas with those of a given author?
- Should it be something else?

Second, find out right at the start *how long* **a paper is expected to be.** Many instructors will indicate the approximate length of the papers they assign. Knowing the expected length of a paper will help you decide exactly how detailed your treatment of a subject should be.

Knowing Your Subject

Whenever possible, try to write on a subject that interests you. You will then find it easier to put more time into your work. Even more important, try to write on a subject that you already know something about. If you do not have direct experience with the subject, you should at least have indirect experience— knowledge gained through thinking, reading, or talking about the subject as well as from prewriting.

If you are asked to write on a topic about which you have no experience or knowledge, do whatever research is required to gain the background information you may need. Part 3 will show you how to use sources as support in your essays. Without direct or indirect experience, or the information you gain through research, you may not be able to provide the specific evidence needed to develop an essay.

Knowing Your Purpose and Audience

As was briefly introduced in Chapter 1, it is crucial to know both your purpose for writing and the audience who will be reading your work.

Purpose

The three most common purposes of writing are *to inform, to persuade,* and *to entertain.* Each is described briefly below.

- **To inform**—to give information about a subject. Authors writing to inform want to provide facts that will explain or teach something to readers. For example, an informative paragraph about sandwiches might begin, "Eating food between two slices of bread—a sandwich—is a practice that has its origins in eighteenth-century England."

- **To persuade**—to convince the reader to agree with the author's point of view on a subject. Authors writing to persuade may give facts, but their main goal is to argue or prove a point to readers. A persuasive paragraph about sandwiches might begin, "There are good reasons why every sandwich should be made with whole grain bread."

- **To entertain**—to amuse and delight; to appeal to the reader's senses and imagination. Authors write to entertain in various ways, through fiction and nonfiction. An entertaining paragraph about sandwiches might begin, "What I wanted was a midnight snack, but what I got was better—the biggest, most magical sandwich in the entire world."

Considering Purpose within Different Contexts

Of course, the *purpose* of completing any college writing assignment is to fulfill a course requirement and get a grade. But all writing—whether done for a class, a job, or any other reason—is aimed at accomplishing something far more specific. Following are several important points to keep in mind:

- In most cases, you will be given an assignment that explains or at least hints at that purpose. You will be able to spot clues about purpose by looking for key words in the assignment such as *define, contrast, argue, illustrate,* or *explain causes and/or effects.* For example, an assignment for a history paper might ask you to *explain the causes* of World War I. An essay question on a biology midterm might call for the *definition* of photosynthesis. A political science assignment might ask you to *contrast* the parliamentary system of government used in several European nations with the federal system used in the United States. If you are enrolled in a technical writing course, you may be asked to *describe* a machine or *analyze* a natural or mechanical *process.* Each of these tasks asks you to accomplish a specific aim.

- Having a clear idea of your purpose is just as important for the writing you do outside of college (what many call "real-world writing"). For example, say your employer asks you to write a report that recommends the purchase of a laptop from a choice of three. You might have to contrast each on the basis of cost, ease of use, features, and reliability. Then you might have to argue that even though laptop A is more expensive than laptops B and C, it is preferable because it will work best with your company's software. Note that unlike a college writing assignment, the job you have been given by your employer does not specify the approaches (*contrasting and arguing*) you will have to take to complete the project. You will have to figure that out for yourself by considering the writing's purpose before you begin.

- As you start gathering information for your paragraph or essay, keep your purpose in mind. You might want to read your assignment several times, looking for key words such as those mentioned above, and then summarize your purpose in a short sentence of your own on a piece of scrap paper. Keep this sentence in front of you throughout the prewriting stage.

- As noted previously, much of the writing in this book will involve some form of argumentation or persuasion. You will advance a point or thesis and then support it in a variety of ways. To some extent, also, you will write papers to inform—to provide readers with information about a particular subject. And since, in practice, writing often combines purposes, you might also find yourself providing vivid or humorous details in order to entertain your readers.

Audience

The audience for a piece of writing is its reader or readers, and like purpose, audience should be considered early in the writing process. In college, your primary audience will be your instructor. Your instructor, though, is really representative of the larger audience you should see yourself as writing for—an audience of educated adults who expect you to present your ideas in a clear, direct, organized way.

- **Current audiences**—Some instructors will also require you to share your work with other students, either in small groups or with the class as a whole. In some cases, your writing will be judged on how well it informs or persuades your classmates. Therefore, you must keep them in mind as you write. Other academic situations in which you will want to keep your audience in mind include writing a letter to a college newspaper to express an opinion, applying for transfer to another college, or applying for a scholarship.

- **Future potential audiences**—After you graduate, you will have ample opportunity to write to a wide range of audiences. This is when you will have to pay even more attention to evaluating your audience. For example, careers in science and technology require employees to write to other experts, who may know a great deal about the subject. On the other hand, scientists and technologists are often required to write to laypersons, whose knowledge of a subject might vary from adequate to extremely rudimentary. The same is true of those who pursue careers in business, law enforcement, the legal and medical professions, the military, education, or government work.

- **One audience example**—Let's say you get a job as City Administrator and you have to suggest some cost-saving measures for the next year's budget. You may be asked to write a letter explaining to the City Council which measures need to be taken and why. Not all of the City Council members may fully understand the measures, so you will likely need to include background information, essential definitions of technical language, and reasons why these specific measures will benefit the city. You may also need to write letters to city employees about potential impacts on their jobs. In those letters, your explanation will be more straightforward and focused primarily on the needs of a particular department. Because the city is a public entity, you may need to write a presentation or explanation to help the public understand why the changes are being implemented and how these changes will benefit the public, as well as how they might result in certain adverse effects. This letter may require more of an effort to convince the readers that any inconveniences they may experience are outweighed by the cost-saving benefits.

Questions to Consider

Here are a few questions you should ask yourself when evaluating any audience. The answers to these questions will help determine your approach to any writing project.

1. *How much does the audience already know about the subject?* On the one hand, if you incorrectly assume that your readers know very little, you might bore them with too much basic information. On the other hand, if you incorrectly assume that they know more than they do, you might confuse them by using unfamiliar technical terminology or neglecting to provide enough informative detail.

   If, for example, you are writing an essay focused on the features of a computer motherboard for a digital electronics class, you wouldn't have to explain what a motherboard is. However, if you were writing that same essay for your Composition 1 class, you would need to assume that many of your classmates may not know what a motherboard is and would need an explanation before they could understand your essay.

2. *Why might the reader need or want to read this material?* In college, your English professor will use your papers to evaluate your writing skills and determine how you can strengthen them. Your professor will probably also use them to establish your course grade. If, however, you are writing to a group of residents whose public services are going to be closed at 3:00 P.M. each day, you will have to meet different expectations. They will want to know why the offices are closing earlier and what benefits they will reap

from the shortened hours. As taxpayers, they may also want to know how much the city will be saving and where these savings are going to be directed.

3. *Is your purpose simply to inform the audience? Perhaps it is to convince readers of something as well? Or perhaps you want to entertain your audience?* If your purpose is to convince or persuade, you may want to use some of the techniques for writing arguments in Chapter 16. For example, if you are writing a letter to the editor of your local newspaper in support of the new school budget, you may have to persuade voters to approve the budget even though it is sure to raise their property taxes. However, if you are writing an essay to get your audience laughing, you may need to share funny and embarrassing anecdotes and experiences to entertain them.

4. *What type of language should be used?* Are you writing to peers—other college students, or are you communicating with professors, business and community leaders, or government officials? With peers, you might want to use language that is relaxed, friendly, and informal, and that will win their confidence. If you're writing to a professor, or to a government official, or an employer, you will have to be more formal.

Determining Your Point of View

When you write, you can take any of three approaches, or points of view: first person, second person, or third person.

First-Person Approach

In the first-person approach—a strongly individualized point of view—you draw on your own experience and speak to your audience in your own voice, using pronouns like *I, me, mine, we, our,* and *us.*

The first-person approach is most common in narrative essays based on personal experience. It also suits other essays where most of the evidence presented consists of personal observation.

Here is a first-person supporting paragraph from an essay on camping:

First of all, I like comfort when I'm camping. My motor home, with its completely equipped kitchen, shower stall, toilet, double bed, and flatscreen television, resembles a mobile motel room. I can sleep on a real mattress, clean sheets, and fluffy pillows. Next to my bed are devices that make me feel at home: my cell phone, a Bluetooth speaker, and a remote control. Unlike the poor campers huddled in tents, I don't have to worry about cold, rain, heat, or annoying insects. After a hot shower, I can slide into my best pajamas, sit comfortably on my down-filled quilt, and read the latest best seller while a thunderstorm booms outside.

Second-Person Approach

In the second-person approach, the writer speaks directly to the reader, using the pronoun *you*. The second-person approach is considered appropriate for giving direct instructions and explanations to the reader. This book is written as a manual to help you become a better writer, which is why *you* is used throughout the book.

You should plan to use the second-person approach only when writing a process essay, although even for this type of essay, the third-person approach is effective. Otherwise, as a general rule, never use the word *you* in writing.

> If using *you* has been a common mistake in your writing, you should review the rule about pronoun point of view in the "Consistency with Pronouns" section in Chapter 5.

Third-Person Approach

The third-person approach is by far the most common point of view in academic writing. In the third person, the writer includes no direct references to the reader (*you*) or the self (*I, me*). Third person gets its name from the stance it suggests—that of an outsider or "third person" observing and reporting on matters of public rather than private importance. In this approach, you draw on information achieved through observation, thinking, or reading.

Here is a similar paragraph on camping, recast in the third person. Note the third-person pronouns *their, them,* and *they,* which all refer to *campers* in the first sentence.

> First of all, modern campers bring complete bedrooms with them. Winnebagos, Airstream motor homes, and Fleetwood recreational vehicles lumber into America's campgrounds every summer like mobile motel rooms. All the comforts of home are provided inside. Campers sleep on real mattresses with clean sheets and fluffy pillows. Next to their beds are the same gadgets that litter their night tables at home—cell phones, Bluetooth speakers, and remote controls. It's not necessary for them to worry about annoyances like cold, heat, rain, or buzzing insects, either. They can sit comfortably in bed and read the latest best sellers while a thunderstorm booms outside.

Using Peer Review

In addition to having your instructor as an audience for your writing, you will benefit from having other students in your class as an audience. Your instructor will most likely require that you work with another student or group of students to peer review each other's papers. This may occur during any stage of the writing

Jacob Lund/ Shutterstock

process. For some review sessions, you may be discussing your prewriting with a partner and using the questioning technique to create more ideas; for others, you may be looking just at each other's introductory paragraphs. For a formal peer review of rough drafts, you will most likely be required to bring a typed copy of your essay and work with a group of students. To properly prepare for a formal peer review, you should have gone through all the steps of writing and you should bring a clean, typed rough draft to your review. If possible, you should provide extra copies for your peer reviewer or review group to use as you work through your essay.

Many students worry that they are not strong enough writers to give constructive feedback or that they may hurt the other students' feelings. Being open to the process, both as reviewer and author, will make this a more positive experience. Your instructor is not expecting you to provide a professional-level review, but you *are* expected to read through the essays and give the best feedback you can. Both participants should look at this activity as a way to make their essays better, not as a negative criticism of their writing. The more open each person is to giving and receiving constructive feedback, the more growth both will see in their writing.

How to Get the Most Out of a Review

Being prepared is the number one way to benefit from a review. If your class is having a formal peer review of rough drafts, the more complete your draft, the more helpful the review session will be. If you show up with only an idea—or nothing—your classmates will not be able to give you the help a second (or third) set of eyes provides. Your instructor will most likely provide instructions and/or a handout for your review, but you should also practice the following strategies to get the most out of any type of peer review.

Ideally, you should read the paper aloud while your peer or group listens and follows along (if you have brought extra drafts). If reading aloud isn't practical, read it in a whisper as your peer or group looks on. As you read, both you and your partner(s) should look and listen for spots where the paper does not read smoothly and clearly. Check or circle the trouble spots where your reading snags.

If you have provided a copy of your essay for your group to work with, you should then work together through the items listed in the next section. If you have only the one copy you are reading from, give this copy to your reviewer so they can work through it, making notes on your essay. Your reviewer can also make notes on a separate sheet of paper if that is more practical.

Once a group has finished with all the essays and before leaving the classroom, students should take time to read over the feedback, make any necessary notes, and ask questions about any comments that are confusing or require clarity. Once you are home, you won't be able to ask your group members, and you may not remember the context of the suggestion.

Commenting on Others' Essays

As many people are sensitive to criticism, it is very important to be constructive with your comments. Try to avoid vague comments like "it's good"; instead offer helpful suggestions like "your topic sentence is very broad and should be narrowed down." Here are some of the general areas you should comment on while peer reviewing:

- Is there a thesis statement (or topic sentence for a paragraph) that makes a point? If not, try to suggest ways the author could improve it.

- Do the topic sentences directly relate to the thesis statement? If not, try to suggest ways the author could revise the topic sentences for better unity.

- Are there spots in the paper where you see problems with unity, support, or organization? (You'll find it helpful to refer to the Four Bases checklist at the back of this book.) If so, offer comments. For example, you might say, "More details are needed in the first supporting paragraph," or "Some of the details in the last supporting paragraph don't really back up your point."

- Make a note of at least two things the author did really well, such as good use of transitions or inclusion of an especially realistic or vivid specific detail.

- Write down at least two things the author could do to improve the paper, such as adding detail or support in specific areas or using more vibrant and active language.

- Look at the spots where your reading of the paper snagged. Try to determine the cause—is there a lack of parallel structure, is there information missing, is it a simple grammar problem? Try to figure out what the problems are and suggest ways to fix them.

- Although sentence skills are important, try not to simply edit a student's paper as you are reviewing a rough draft. Extra attention to grammar and punctuation should be given during the editing stage and not the revising stage.

Doing a Personal Review

While having someone else give constructive feedback is an important step in the writing process, being able to critique your own writing is also very important, especially as you decide what suggestions from your peer review group to incorporate as you revise your paper. This requires the ability to look at your writing and any suggestions offered in a nondefensive manner. It also requires you to step back from your writing and look at it in a less personal way. As you critique your own writing, you should treat it as you would a peer review of someone else's essay. As you critique and revise your paper, you should also:

1. Ask the same questions your reviewers asked of you to make sure you have addressed their concerns.

2. Evaluate your essay in terms of unity, support, and coherence, and find ways to strengthen these qualities.

3. Read your essay aloud to catch any small errors or readability issues.

Once you have completed your revision, you should then focus on evaluating it for *sentence skills* errors and make any final changes necessary. One last critical reading—done aloud—should help you check for any more mistakes or areas of weakness that still need additional revision.

The Writing Process in Action

In Chapters 1 through 6, you learned about the importance of supporting a point in writing, the structure of a traditional essay, and the writing process. You also practiced prewriting, creating thesis statements, developing good support, organizing your ideas, and creating effective introductions and conclusions. Finally, you learned the benefits of effective revision. The following pages illustrate the entire writing process—the complete development of an essay from prewriting through planning, drafting, peer review, revision, and final draft.

A Sample Essay

Mico created the following essay on the topic of "self-compassion" for her developmental writing class.

I **The first thing Mico did was prewrite.** She used listing for her prewriting:

- dreams, goals, self-esteem
- what made you who you are today
- loving yourself
- self-esteem
- making yourself happy
- loving others/making them happy
- accepting others for who they are
- self-compassion vs. adversity

- "stand up for what you believe in even if you are standing alone"—coach said that
- self-image
- impossible vs. realistic standards
- encouragement, kindness
- volunteering/church
- true to yourself
- health
- personal growth
- mentoring
- self-love
- being able to say no
- meditation
- honesty
- knowing limits
- not giving up
- self-confidence
- goals—set and follow through
- ok to make mistakes

Once Mico was done with her first listing exercise, she then looked to see what types of categories her ideas fell into. She came up with:

- ✔ Definition
- ✔ Treating Yourself Well
- ✔ Being True to Yourself
- ✔ Challenges

She then organized her list into her categories. While organizing, she was able to add a few more ideas. She also

Prewriting

realized that she had some ideas like "loving yourself" and "self-love" that were actually the same idea.

✓ Definition

✓ Treating Yourself Well

✓ Being True to Yourself

✓ Challenges

- dreams, goals, self-esteem
- what made you who you are today
- loving yourself
- self-esteem
- making yourself happy
- loving others/making them happy
- accepting others for who they are
- self-compassion vs. adversity
- "stand up for what you believe in even if you are standing alone"— coach said that
- self-image
- impossible vs. realistic standards
- encouragement, kindness
- volunteering/church
- true to yourself
- health
- personal growth
- mentoring
- self-love
- being able to say no
- meditation
- honesty

- knowing limits
- not giving up
- self-confidence
- goals—set and follow through
- ok to make mistakes

✔ Definition
- self-image
- self-esteem
- self-love
- honesty

✔ Treating Yourself Well
- meditation
- health/fitness
- making yourself happy
- loving others
- making others happy
- volunteering
- living essentials
- accomplishments
- being positive
- loving yourself
- personal growth, sponsorship/mentoring

✔ Being True to Yourself
- able to say no
- confidence
- church/religion
- trusting yourself
- impossible vs. realistic standards

- • staying true to yourself
- • knowing limits
- • never giving up
- • self-confidence
- • goals—setting and follow through
- • ok to make mistakes

✓ Challenges

- • adversity
- • accepting others for who they are
- • forgiveness
- • standing up for what you believe in even if you are alone

2

Formulating a thesis

II **Once Mico had her ideas grouped into categories, she worked on a thesis statement.** She started by asking herself the following questions. As she answered the questions, she began to formulate ideas for her thesis statement.

- • What is self-compassion? Self-compassion is finding ways to be true to yourself and to love yourself.
- • What does it mean to use self-compassion? Self-compassion is showing compassion to your own self, which sounds obvious, but isn't easy.
- • How can one achieve self-compassion? One can achieve self-compassion by setting goals and noticing conflicts will happen.
- • How easy is self-compassion? Some people find it difficult to have self-compassion, because they are always trying to please others.

- Why is self-compassion important? Self-compassion is important because it forms your self-identity.

- How does self-compassion relate to our daily activities? Being nice to ourselves impacts how we do things.

- Self-compassion is often described as being true to yourself. I've met many people who often offer that up as advice to me, but just how easy is it, and what exactly does it mean to be true to yourself, and to have self-compassion? It means doing what is right in my heart, but that seems difficult.

Mico then looked back over her prewriting and guiding questions to come up with several possible thesis statements:

- Self-compassion is often described as being true to yourself; however, that is not a simple thing to do.

- Self-compassion is important because it forms a person's self-identity while practicing moral values.

- Self-compassion is important because it varies from person to person and shows each person's individuality/identity.

- The best way to show self-compassion and implement it in my daily life is to be true to myself, love myself, and honesty.

- Self-compassion relates to our daily lives by being able to say no, trusting ourselves, and not giving up.

- Self-compassion is finding ways to be true to and love oneself. However it is difficult for people to have self-compassion because they are always trying to please others.

**Formulating
a thesis**

She then went through her possible thesis statements and eliminated those that were too broad, too narrow, or tried to cover too many things:

- Self-compassion is often described as being true to your-self; however, that is not a simple thing to do. (I like this one, but I don't think it is the best)
- Self-compassion is important because it forms a per-son's self-identity ~~while practicing moral values~~. (I like this one, but the moral values part doesn't seem to fit)
- ~~Self-compassion is important because it varies from per-son to person and shows each person's individuality/identity.~~ (too broad)
- ~~The best way to show self-compassion and implement it in my daily life is to be true to myself, love myself, and honesty.~~ (this seems too narrow)
- Self-compassion relates to our daily lives by being able to say no, trusting ourselves, and not giving up. (this one is ok, but not great)
- ~~Self-compassion is finding ways to be true to and love oneself. However it is difficult for people to have self-com-passion because they are always trying to please others.~~ (this one covers too many ideas)

3

III Mico selected one statement from her list and developed paragraphs based on her categories. She then created an introduction and conclusion. The statement she chose was "Self-compassion is important because it forms a person's self-identity."

**Writing the
first draft**

Introduction

Anna Quindlen has been quoted as saying "The thing
that is really hard, and really amazing, is giving up on
being perfect and beginning the work of becoming
yourself." This quote really demonstrates the idea that
self-compassion is difficult. Self-compassion is important
because it forms a person's identity.

Definition

To understand self-compassion one must be prepared to
face their own challenges. This can be a difficult task for
people who have had a hard time adjusting to change.
Self-compassion means to stay true to yourself and to
your personal values. When someone begins to reach
self-compassion, they are one step closer to personal
growth. Self-compassion is important because it forms a
person's self-identity.

Challenges

Self-compassion is important because it helps form self-
identity, however you will face challenges while learning to
embrace self-compassion. We have to start forgiving
ourselves before we can truly forgive others in order to
reach a level of self-compassion. Forgiveness is not an easy
thing to give or receive. Practicing forgiveness daily on small
things (maybe give an example?) will eventually help you to
forgive the bigger things that happen to you.

Being True to Yourself

In order to be true to yourself you need to know your
self-identity. First everyone has their own values that

stem from their beliefs and religion, but it's up to each individual to form their self-identity out of those values. Second you should be skeptical of letting others talk you out of what you believe in. As well as respecting others boundaries and limitations. "We lose our sense of self individuality if we don't respect our own opinions and the opinions of others." Third, it's ok to make mistakes, good things can come from mistakes don't let it shake your confidence.

Improving/Treating Yourself Well

Improving yourself is an important aspect of practicing self-compassion. In order to truly practice self-compassion, you must be able to recognize your strengths and weaknesses, and set yourself on a path for personal growth. Maintaining a positive attitude is paramount to improving yourself. By setting the positive goals and taking time to celebrate your achievement, you are practicing self-compassion, and creating a better you.

Conclusion

There is a lot to self-compassion. There are challenges, but if I overcome these challenges, I will be a much happier person because I will be true to myself, not society.

To understand how to become self-compassionate, a person has to be prepared to face the challenges of demonstrating self-kindness, focusing on self-improvement, and sticking to personal values.

IV With her rough draft complete, Mico engaged in peer review. She received numerous comments to help her improve her essay.

Revising:
Peer review

Mico's Paper   don't forget
                                                MLA format

I like your quote, but your introduction needs more details

Anna Quindlen has been quoted as saying "The thing that is really hard, and really amazing, is giving up on being perfect and beginning the work of becoming yourself." This quote really demonstrates the idea that self-compassion is difficult. Self-compassion is important because it forms a person's identity.

these sentences don't seem connected

can you use synonyms?

I would reorganize this paragraph

② To understand self-compassion one must be prepared to face their own challenges. This can be a difficult task for people who have had a hard time adjusting to change. Self-compassion means to stay true to yourself and to your personal values. ③ When someone begins to reach self-compassion, they are one step closer to personal growth. Self-compassion is important because it forms a person's self-identity.

what types, examples?

what do you mean?

don't repeat your thesis

revise out you

You say challenges but talk only about forgiveness—what other challenges are there?

Self-compassion is important because it helps form self-identity, however you will face challenges while learning to embrace self-compassion. We have to start forgiving ourselves before we can truly forgive others in order to reach a level of self-compassion. Forgiveness is not an easy thing to give or receive. Practicing forgiveness daily on small things (maybe give an example?) will eventually help you to forgive the bigger things that happen to you.

practice?

you say why but not how

vague word

yes

In order to be true to yourself you need to know your self-identity. First everyone has their own values that stem from their beliefs and religion, but it's up to each individual to form their self-identity out of those values. Second you should be skeptical of letting others talk you out of what you believe in, As well as respecting others boundaries and limitations. "We lose our sense of self individuality if we don't respect our own opinions and the opinions of others." Third, it's ok to make mistakes, good things can come from mistakes don't let it shake your confidence.

I wouldn't use religion

people? family?   friends?

these paragraphs need more details

who said this?

your paragraph needs a conclusion

Improving yourself is an important aspect of practicing self-compassion. In order to truly practice self-compassion, you must be able to recognize your strengths and weaknesses, and set follow

an individual   their

watch your fragments and run-ons

yourself on a path for personal growth. Maintaining a positive attitude is paramount to

. For example,

improving yourself, by setting the positive goals, and taking time to celebrate your achievement,

you are practicing self-compassion, and creating a better you.

There is a lot to self-compassion. There are challenges, but if I overcome these

challenges, I will be a much happier person because I will be true to myself, not society

your conclusion should restate the thesis and should be longer and more detailed

V   After the peer review, Mico looked over her rough draft.

She made additional comments based on her reviewers' feedback.

Anna Quindlen has been quoted as saying "The thing that is really hard, and really amazing, is giving up on being perfect and beginning the work of becoming yourself." This quote really demonstrates the idea that self-compassion is difficult. ~~Self-compassion is important because it forms a person's identity.~~ *need new thesis.*   *maybe focus on how to achieve self-compassion?*

(1) *Reorganize per peer review*   To understand self-compassion one must be prepared to face their own challenges. This can be a difficult task for people who have had a hard time adjusting to change. Self-compassion means to stay true to yourself and to your personal values. When someone begins to reach self-compassion, they are one step closer to personal growth. Self-compassion is important because it forms a person's self-identity.   *combine these?*

Self-compassion is important because it helps form self-identity, however you will face challenges while learning to embrace self-compassion. We have to start forgiving ourselves before we can truly forgive others in order to reach a level of self-compassion. Forgiveness is not an easy thing to give or receive. Practicing forgiveness daily on small things (maybe give an example?) will eventually help you to forgive the bigger things that happen to you.

(3)   In order to be~~true~~ to yourself you ~~need to know your self identity.~~ *self compassionate you need to be*   First everyone has their own values that stem from their beliefs and religion, but it's up to each individual to form their self-identity out of those values. Second you should be skeptical of letting others talk you *what about parties at college as an example?* out of what you believe in. As well as respecting others boundaries and limitations. "We lose *mom said this* our sense of self individuality if we don't respect our own opinions and the opinions of others." Third, it's ok to make mistakes, good things can come from mistakes don't let it shake your confidence.

(2)   Improving yourself is an important aspect of practicing self-compassion. In order to truly practice self-compassion, you must be able to recognize your strengths and weaknesses, and set

 give example about college

**Revising:
Personal
review**

yourself on a path for personal growth. Maintaining a positive attitude is paramount to

improving yourself, by setting the positive goals, and taking time to celebrate your achievement,

you are practicing self-compassion, and creating a better you.

    There is a lot to self-compassion. There are challenges, but if I overcome these

challenges, I will be a much happier person because I will be true to myself, not society. *make this more personal*

VI Mico then incorporated the feedback and revised and edited her essay. She submitted the following essay to her professor:

Royce 1

Mico Royce

Professor Smith

English 101 9:30

19 September 2022

Steps to Self-Compassion

Anna Quindlen has been quoted as saying "The thing that is really hard, and really amazing, is giving up on being perfect and beginning the work of becoming yourself." Many people struggle to become who they truly are because they often inflict society's standards onto themselves. To understand how to become self-compassionate, a person has to be prepared to face the challenges of demonstrating self-kindness, focusing on self-improvement, and sticking to personal values.

Self-compassion means showing compassion – love, forgiveness, kindness – to one's self. However, all people face difficulties as they practice self-compassion because society often challenges people, which can cause frustration whenever a person fails to meet society's expectations. Part of practicing self-compassion means practicing forgiveness. For instance, women are often hard on themselves when they don't fit society's ideal of beauty and often go to drastic measures to try and meet that ideal. Learning to love themselves for whom they are and ignoring outside standards will lead them to self-compassion, but it isn't easy. Becoming more forgiving of self is often very hard because people tend to expect more from themselves than they do other people. As people learn to love and forgive themselves, they often experience the personal growth that leads them toward more self-compassion.

Improving oneself is another important aspect of practicing self-compassion. To do this, a person must be able to recognize their strengths and weaknesses and maintain a positive,

Royce 2

forgiving attitude. By setting goals and taking time to reflect on how triumphs and failures, both large and small, have led toward self-improvement, a person learns to practice self-compassion. For instance, many students don't practice self-compassion during the semester. Instead of recognizing their bodies' and minds' needs, they feel they should be able to do more and often push themselves beyond their limits. By recognizing the need for sleep, healthy food, or exercise, and allowing the time to meet those needs, students will reap more benefits. Not only will they be learning to be compassionate, but also they will be improving themselves along the way.

In order to be self-compassionate people need to be true to themselves. Everyone has their own standards that stem from personal beliefs, but it is up to each individual to form a self-identity out of those values. People need to be skeptical of letting others talk them out of what they believe, but it is also important to learn to respect others' opinions, boundaries, and limitations. This can be especially difficult in college when students are confronted with new people and new sets of values. Not giving in and loving oneself enough to stick to personal values while not demeaning others' values is a way to practice self-compassion. My mother once told me, "We lose our sense of self-individuality if we don't respect our own opinions and the opinions of others."

Beginning college has been very challenging for me as I learn to navigate new people, new classes, and new values. Learning to love myself, forgive myself, improve myself, and sticking to what is in my heart will help me begin a practice of self-compassion. While there are challenges, I know that if I overcome them, I will experience great personal growth.

Mico submitted her essay on self-compassion because it was due, but she knew there were still areas that could have been improved. Either on your own or in a group, go through Mico's essay and look for weak spots. Like Mico's peer reviewers, you should focus on helping Mico improve her essay by examining the important areas first. First, look at her thesis statement and decide whether it needs to be made stronger. If so, revise the thesis and then look at the topic sentences to see if they still support your revised thesis. If not, make the changes necessary to be sure your topic sentences are advancing the claim in the thesis.

The next step is to read through the individual body paragraphs to make sure they are unified, coherent, and support the topic sentence. Any information that doesn't support the topic sentence should be eliminated and replaced with ideas that advance the main idea of the paragraph. After looking over the body of the essay, go back and read through the introduction, making any necessary changes to improve it. For example, Mico chose to start her essay with a quotation, but you might decide that a different type of introduction would make a stronger beginning.

Once you have revised the body paragraphs and introduction, read through the essay and determine whether Mico's conclusion holds up. If not, decide how you can improve it. Finally, go back through her essay and edit it as needed to make sure her sentence skills and MLA format are correct.

ACTIVITY 1

Patterns of Essay Development

PART 2

Fuse/Getty Images

COMING UP   LIVE CNN

RECORD 4,000+ COVID DEATHS IN 24 HOURS   SITUATION ROOM

Shiiko Alexander/Alamy Stock Photo

News

Fuel Prices Continue To Fall

Panther Media GmbH/ Alamy Stock Photo

What do all of the images shown here have in common? They can all be classified as news sources. Think about the many different formats available for getting the news today. Then select three formats and write an essay in which you discuss the unique qualities of each.

Introduction to Part 2

Traditionally, essay writing has been divided into the following patterns of development. However, it's important to remember that essays often emphasize one pattern while employing additional patterns to help support the thesis.

- Description
- Narration
- Exposition

Exemplification	Comparison and/or contrast
Process	Definition
Cause and/or effect	Division-classification

- Argument

Description emphasizes verbal pictures of people, places, or things. *Narration* is used when a writer tells the story of something that happened.

In *exposition*, the writer provides information about and explains a particular subject. Patterns of development often used within exposition include giving examples (*exemplification*); detailing a *process* of doing or making something; analyzing *causes* and *effects; comparing* or *contrasting; defining* a term or concept; and *dividing* something into parts or *classifying* it into categories.

Finally, in *argument*, a writer attempts to support a controversial point or to defend a position on which there is a difference of opinion.

The pages ahead present individual chapters that describe how to write essays that emphasize each pattern. You will have a chance, then, to learn nine different patterns or methods for organizing material in your papers. As you practice writing essays, keep these two points in mind:

- **While each essay that you write will involve one predominant pattern, very often one or more additional patterns may be involved.** For example, consider the two student essays in Chapter 10, "Exemplification." The first essay there, "Paying Attention to a Death," is developed through a series of anecdotes, scenes, and *examples*. But there is also an element of *comparison/contrast* because the writer is discussing two different works that treat the same theme. In the second essay, "Altered States," *exemplification* is again the predominant pattern, but in a lesser way the author is also explaining the *causes* of altered states of mind.

- **No matter which pattern or patterns you use, each essay will probably involve some form of argumentation.** You will advance a point and then go on to support that point. In "Paying Attention to a Death," for instance, the author uses *exemplification* to support their point that both the movie and the essay take a similar position about capital punishment. In "Celiac Disease Needs to Be Diagnosed to Be Controlled," a writer supports the point that celiac disease needs to be diagnosed and controlled by providing a number of *descriptive details*. In "A Night of Violence," another writer claims that a certain experience in his life was frightening and then uses a *narrative* to persuade us of the truth of this statement. Yet another author states that a fast-food restaurant can be preferable to a fancy one and then supplies *comparative information* about both to support his statement ("A Vote for McDonald's"). Much of your writing, in short, will have the purpose of persuading your reader that the idea you have advanced is valid.

The Progression in Each Chapter

In Chapters 8 through 16, after each pattern is explained, student essays and a model essay illustrating that emphasized pattern are presented, followed by questions about the essays. The questions relate to unity, support, and coherence—principles of effective writing explained earlier in this book and outlined on the inside back cover. You are then asked to write your own essay. In most cases, the first assignment has a personal focus, is fairly structured, and provides a good deal of guidance for the writing process. The other assignments typically have academic and work focuses and frequently require you to write with a specific purpose and for a specific audience. In some instances, the academic assignments require outside reading of literary works; a student model is provided for each of these assignments. Finally, some of the work assignments ask you to research local and campus issues, and in a few instances, to write about your own workplace.

Description

This chapter will explain and illustrate how to

- develop an essay with emphasis on description
- write an essay with emphasis on description
- revise an essay with emphasis on description

In addition, you will read and consider

- two student essays that emphasize description
- one professional model essay that emphasizes description

Think about your college graduation day and write an essay about what you imagine it will be like. How will you feel? What sights and sounds will surround you? Will your family and friends be there to congratulate you? Describe the day and bring it to life in your essay.

Getty Images

When you describe someone or something, you give your readers a picture in words. To make the word picture as vivid and real as possible, you must observe and record specific details that appeal to your readers' senses (sight, hearing, taste, smell, and touch). More than any other type of essay, a paper that emphasizes description needs sharp, colorful details.

Here is a sentence in which there is almost no appeal to the senses: "In the window was a fan." In contrast, here is a description rich in sense impressions: "The blades of the rusty window fan clattered and whirled as they blew out a stream of warm, soggy air." Sense impressions in this second example include sight (*rusty window fan, whirled*), hearing (*clattered*), and touch (*warm, soggy air*). The vividness and sharpness provided by the sensory details give us a clear picture of the fan and enable us to share the writer's experience.

In this chapter, you will be asked to describe a person, place, or thing sharply, by using words rich in sensory details. To prepare for this assignment, read the student essays and the model essay that follow and work through the questions that accompany each piece of writing.

Student Essays to Consider

Family Portrait

My great-grandmother, who is ninety-five years old, recently sent me a photograph of herself that I had never seen before. While cleaning out the attic of her Florida home, she came across a studio portrait she had taken about a year before she married my great-grandfather. This picture of my great-grandmother as a twenty-year-old girl and the story behind it have fascinated me from the moment I began to consider it.

Personal

The young woman in the picture has a face that resembles my own in many ways. Her face is a bit more oval than mine, but the softly waving brown hair around it is identical. The small, straight nose is the same model I was born with. My great-grandmother's mouth is closed, yet there is just the slightest hint of a smile on her full lips. I know that if she had smiled, she would have shown the same wide grin and down-curving "smile lines" that appear in my own snapshots. The most haunting feature in the photo, however, is my great-grandmother's eyes. They are an exact duplicate of my own large, dark brown ones. Her brows are plucked into thin lines, which are like two pencil strokes added to highlight those fine, luminous eyes.

I've also carefully studied the clothing and jewelry in the photograph. Although the photo was taken seventy-five years ago, my great-grandmother is wearing a blouse and skirt that could easily be worn today. The blouse is made of heavy eggshell-colored satin and reflects the light in its folds and hollows. It has a turned-down cowl collar and smocking on the shoulders and below the collar. The smocking (tiny rows of gathered material) looks hand-done. The skirt, which covers my great-grandmother's calves, is straight and made of light wool or flannel. My great-grandmother

1

2

3

continued

is wearing silver drop earrings. They are about two inches long and roughly shield-shaped. On her left wrist is a matching bracelet. My great-grandmother can't find this bracelet now, despite our having spent hours searching through the attic for it. On the third finger of her left hand is a ring with a large, square-cut stone.

The story behind the picture is as interesting to me as the young woman it captures. Great-Grandmother, who was earning twenty-five dollars a week as a file clerk, decided to give her boyfriend (my great-grandfather) a picture of herself. She spent almost two weeks' salary on the skirt and blouse, which she bought at a fancy department store downtown. She borrowed the earrings and bracelet from her older sister, Ana. The ring she wore was a present from another young man she was dating at the time. Great-Grandmother spent another chunk of her salary to pay the portrait photographer for the hand-tinted print in old-fashioned tones of brown and tan. Just before giving the picture to my great-grandfather, she scrawled at the lower left, "Sincerely, Rosa."   4

When I study this picture, I react in many ways. I think about the trouble that my great-grandmother went to in order to impress the young man who was to be my great-grandfather. I laugh when I look at the ring, which was probably worn to make him jealous. I smile at the serious, formal inscription my great-grandmother used at this stage of the budding relationship. Sometimes, I am filled with a mixture of pleasure and sadness when I look at this frozen long-ago moment. It is a moment of beauty, of love, and—in a way—of my own past.   5

Fictional Female Friends

People who read fiction often do so because the worlds inside the book covers are filled with the excitement and characters that everyday life lacks. Delving into the lives of characters of differing cultures and beliefs helps readers learn empathy, tolerance, and perseverance—traits that can transfer into their daily lives. Characters in nonfiction books are usually not as interesting as those in fiction books. Three of the best female friends a reader will find in the world of books are Hermione Granger (*Harry Potter*); Elizabeth Bennet (*Pride and Prejudice*); and Katniss Everdeen (*The Hunger Games*).   1

Hermione Granger is the girl everyone loves to hate but secretly wants to know. With her thick brown hair, which is often out of control, to her larger-than-usual front teeth, Hermione is often teased about her appearance. However, it is her intelligence and calmness that make her invaluable to those around her. Her ability to cast spells, and to remember   2

continued

the correct spells even in tense situations, saves her friends Ron and Harry numerous times. Her loyalty is another quality that inspires those around her to want to be her friend. Even under the most dreadful of circumstances, Hermione never wavers in her loyalty to her friends or those she respects. Her know-it-all attitude might be annoying at times, but her other qualities make her one of the best friends a person could ask for.

While she has what are described as expressive eyes, they are this way because they tend to reflect what is going on in Elizabeth's mind. Her intelligence and wit are often unmatched by any other woman. In fact, she often challenges men's comments and observations despite society's views that women should be secondary to men. What is most endearing, however, about Elizabeth is her love of family—despite the numerous times they make fools of themselves or of her. Her ability to love and forgive is a quality that every friend should have. Unlike Hermione, Elizabeth Bennet is described as a great beauty, but her looks are not her most important qualities.   3

Katniss Everdeen is not only a fierce warrior but also a fierce friend. She believes in doing what is right for humanity even if that means going against society's laws. Before she becomes a tribute, she spends her time focusing on surviving by hunting and trading to feed her family. While her focus is on family, she doesn't overlook the hardships others face and, in spite of danger, does what she can to help. Her desire to protect her family is what forces her to partake in the Hunger Games, a sacrifice not many would be willing to make. Once in the games, Katniss doesn't lose herself to the hatred and evil that is prevalent. Instead, she finds many ways to demonstrate her humanity—from creating a memorial for Rue, the young girl from District 11, to risking death as she challenges the Capitol to save Peeta's life. Everyone should have a friend who is as passionate as Katniss.   4

Reading books can have great impact. Opening a book and experiencing the world between the covers can transform a person's point of view and thinking. The characters inside these fictional worlds offer so much more than just their stories. Good characters can demonstrate what good friends should look like. Even though they may be fictional, they can help readers learn about the types of qualities their real-life friends should have.   5

ABOUT UNITY

1. In which supporting paragraph of "Fictional Female Friends" does the topic sentence appear at the paragraph's end, rather than the beginning?
   a. paragraph 2
   b. paragraph 3
   c. paragraph 4

2. Which sentence in paragraph 1 of "Fictional Female Friends" should be eliminated and why should it be eliminated? (*Write your answer here.*)

_____

_____

3. Which sentence in paragraph 3 of "Family Portrait" should be eliminated and why? (*Write your answer here.*)

_____

_____

ABOUT SUPPORT

4. In paragraph 3 of "Family Portrait," the writer goes beyond the mere mention of clothing and jewelry. Focus on one item and summarize the details she includes to make the object clearer to the reader. (*Write your answer here.*)

_____

_____

_____

5. Label as sight, touch, hearing, or smell all the sensory details in the following sentences taken from the two essays. The first one is done for you as an example.

   a. "Her face is a bit more oval than mine, but the softly waving brown hair around it is identical."

   b. "The blouse is made of heavy eggshell-colored satin and reflects the light in its folds and hollows."

   c. Her brows are plucked into thin lines, which are like two pencil strokes added to highlight those fine, luminous eyes.

   d. With her thick brown hair, which is often wildly out of control, to her larger-than-usual front teeth, Hermione is often teased about her appearance.

6. The author could have used additional details to provide a clearer picture of what the characters looked like. Suggest two or three you would add. (*Write your answer here.*)

_____

ABOUT COHERENCE

7. Which method of organization does paragraph 2 of "Family Portrait" use?
   a. time order
   b. emphatic order

8. What sentence in paragraph 3 of "Family Portrait" serves as a transition? (*Write the first words.*)

   _____

9. Find at least three transitions and connecting words in paragraph 2 of "Fictional Female Friends." Remember that repeated words, pronouns, and synonyms can act as connectors.

   _____

ABOUT THE INTRODUCTION AND/OR CONCLUSION

10. What method discussed in Chapter 4 is used in the introduction to "Fictional Female Friends"?

    _____

    _____

Developing an Essay with Emphasis on Description

Considering Purpose and Audience

The main purpose of an essay with an emphasis on description is to make readers see—or hear, taste, smell, or feel—what you are writing about. Vivid details are the key to good descriptions, enabling your audience to picture and, in a way, experience what you describe.

Unlike a descriptive paragraph that focuses *only* on describing the topic, an essay that emphasizes description may also contain cause and effect, comparison or contrast, or narration.

As you start to think about your own essay, choose a topic that will allow you to write descriptions that appeal strongly to at least one of your senses. Also, when selecting your topic, consider how much your audience already knows about it. If your topic is a familiar one, you can assume your audience already understands the general idea. However, if you are presenting something new or unfamiliar to your readers—perhaps a description of one of your relatives or a place where you've lived—you must provide background information.

Once you have selected your topic, focus on the goal or purpose of your essay. It is important to use the specific modes and writing techniques where and when needed. The purpose of your essay will determine what events should be told, what events should be eliminated, and what strategies should be employed when writing. What message do you hope to convey to your audience? For instance, if you chose as your topic a playground you used to visit as a child, decide what dominant impression you want to communicate. Is your goal to make readers see the park as a pleasant play area, or do you want them to see it as a dangerous place? If you choose the second option, focus on conveying that sense of danger to your audience. Then jot down any details that support that idea. You might describe broken beer bottles on the asphalt, graffiti sprayed on the metal jungle gym, or a decaying and derelict building on a nearby street corner. In this case, the details support your overall purpose, creating a threatening picture that your audience can see and understand.

Visualizing the Subject

Physical description relies solely on sense impressions. All five senses can be used when describing, and you should try to use as many as possible. One advantage that description has over other methods of development is that it allows the writer to visualize their subject before describing it in words.

If you like to draw or paint, make an image of your subject before you start writing. If possible, use different colors to reveal the complexity of your subject, apply perspective to give your picture depth and contrast, or add small details like a tiny mole, a button on a shirt, or a stain on a tie.

When you are done, use the picture as inspiration as you gather information during prewriting.

Including People and Events in the Description of a Place

Discussing the type of people who are in a place can sometimes give clues to its character and help describe it. The same can be said for what happens there. For example, a bar where middle-aged couples sip drinks and converse is one thing; a bar where young people dance to loud music is quite another.

You might even describe animals and their actions to enliven your description of a place. Say you're writing about a zoo. It might be worth discussing the antics of chimpanzees or the majestic pacing of a tiger as it struts within its habitat.

Finally, consider including dialogue. You will learn more about creating dialogue in Chapter 9, "Narration." For now just remember that dialogue can sometimes reveal a great deal about a person or a place. For example, our first clue that the owner of the café in "Lou's Place" (an essay appearing later in this chapter) is rather feisty is his response to a woman who wants to know if he's open: "I'm here, aren't I?" Later, when another customer asks for breakfast, Lou says, "I'm reading the paper. . . . Eggs are in the refrigerator."

Development through Prewriting

When Viviana, the author of "Family Portrait," sat down to think about a topic for her essay, she looked around her apartment for inspiration. First she thought about describing her own bedroom. But she had moved into the apartment only recently and hadn't done much in the way of decorating, so the room struck her as too bare and sterile. Then she looked out her window, thinking of describing the view. That seemed much more promising: she noticed the sights and sounds of children playing on the sidewalks and a group of older men playing cards, as well as smells—neighbors' cooking and exhaust from passing traffic. She was jotting down some details for such an essay when she glanced up at the framed portrait of her great-grandmother on her desk. "I stopped and stared at it, as I often do, wondering again about this twenty-year-old girl who became my great-grandmother," she said. "While I sat there studying it, I realized that the best topic of all was right under my nose."

As she looked at the photograph, Viviana began to freewrite. This is what she wrote:

> Great-Grandma is twenty in the picture. She's wearing a beautiful skirt and blouse and jewelry she borrowed from Ana. Looks a lot like me—nose, eyes, mouth. She's shorter than I am but you really can't tell in picture. Looks a lot like old photos I've seen of Grandma too—all the Diaz women resemble each other. Earrings and bracelet are of silver and they match. Ring might be amber or topaz? We've laughed about the "other man" who gave it to her. Her brown hair is down loose on her shoulders. She's smiling a little. That doesn't really look like her—her usual smile is bigger and opens her mouth. Looking at the photo makes me a little sad even though I really like it. Makes me realize how much older she's getting and I wonder how long she'll be with us. It's funny to see a picture of your great-grandmother at a younger age than you are now—stirs up all kinds of weird feelings. Picture was taken at a studio in Houston to give to Great-Grandpa. Signed "Sincerely, Rosa." So serious! Hard to imagine them being so formal with each other.

Viviana looked over her notes and thought about how she might organize her essay. First she thought only of describing how the photograph *looked*. With that in mind, she thought her main points might be (1) what her great-grandmother's face looked like and (2) what her great-grandmother was wearing. But she was stuck for a third main point.

Studying her notes again, Viviana noticed two other possible main points. One was her own emotional reaction to the photo—how it made her feel. The other was the story of the photo—how and why it was taken. Not sure which of those two she would use as her third main point, she began to write. Her first draft follows.

First Draft

Family Portrait

I have a photograph of my great-grandmother that was taken seventy-five years ago, when she was only twenty. She sent it to me only recently, and I find it very interesting.

In the photo, I see a girl who looks a good deal like I do now at twenty-two. Like most of the women in her family, including me, the girl in the picture has the Diaz family nose, waving brown hair, and large brown eyes. Her mouth is closed and she is smiling slightly. That isn't my great-grandmother's usual big grin that shows her teeth and her "smile lines."

In the photo, Great-Grandmother is wearing a very pretty skirt and blouse. They look like something that would be fashionable today. The blouse is made of heavy satin. The satin falls in lines and hollows that reflect the light. It has a turned-down cowl collar and smocking on the shoulders and under the collar. Her skirt is below her knees and looks like it is made of light wool. She is wearing jewelry. Her silver earrings and bracelet match. She had borrowed them from her sister. Ana eventually gave them both to her, but the bracelet has disappeared. On her left hand is a ring with a big yellow stone.

When I look at this photo, I feel conflicting emotions. It gives me pleasure to see my great-grandmother as a pretty young woman. It makes me sad, too, to think how quickly time passes and realize how old she is getting. It amuses me to read the inscription to my great-grandfather, her boyfriend at the time. She wrote, "Sincerely, Rosa." It's hard for me to imagine them ever being so formal with each other.

My great-grandmother had the photograph taken at a studio near where she worked in Houston. She spent nearly two weeks' salary on the outfit she wore for it. She must have really wanted to impress my great-grandfather to go to all that trouble and expense.

Development through Revising

Viviana showed this first draft to her classmate Elena, who read it and returned it with these notes jotted in the margin:

Jacob Lund/
Shutterstock

Reader's Comments

Was this the first time you'd seen it? Where's it been? And "very interesting" doesn't really say anything. Be more specific about why it interests you.

The "Diaz family nose" isn't helpful for someone who doesn't know the Diaz family—describe it!

Nice beginning, but I still can't quite picture her. Can you add more specific detail? Does anything about her face really stand out?

Color?

This is nice—I can picture the material.

What is smocking?

How—what are they like?

Family Portrait

I have a photograph of my great-grandmother that was taken seventy-five years ago, when she was only twenty. She sent it to me only recently, and I find it very interesting.

In the photo, I see a girl who looks a good deal like I do now at twenty-two. Like most of the women in her family, including me, the girl in the picture has the Diaz family nose, waving brown hair, and large brown eyes. Her mouth is closed and she is smiling slightly. That isn't my great-grandmother's usual big grin that shows her teeth and her "smile lines."

In the photo, Great-Grandmother is wearing a very pretty skirt and blouse. They took like something that would be fashionable today. The blouse is made of heavy satin. The satin falls in lines and hollows that reflect the light. It has a turned-down cowl collar and smocking on the shoulders and under the collar. Her skirt is below her knees and looks like it is made of light wool. She is wearing jewelry. Her silver earrings and bracelet match. She had borrowed them from her sister. Ana eventually gave them both to her, but the bracelet has disappeared. On her left hand is a ring with a big yellow stone.

continued

It'd make more sense for the main points of the essay to be about your great-grandma and the photo. How about making this—your reaction—the conclusion of the essay?

This is interesting stuff—she really did go to a lot of trouble to have the photo taken. I think the story of the photograph deserves to be a main point.

When I look at this photo, I feel conflicting emotions. It gives me pleasure to see my great-grandmother as a pretty young woman. It makes me sad, too, to think how quickly time passes and realize how old she is now. It amuses me to read the inscription to my great-grandfather, her boyfriend at the time. She wrote, "Sincerely, Rosa." It's hard for me to imagine them ever being so formal with each other.

My great-grandmother had the photograph taken at a studio near where she worked in Houston. She spent nearly two weeks' salary on the outfit she wore for it. She must have really wanted to impress my great-grandfather to go to all that trouble

Making use of Elena's comments and her own reactions upon rereading her essay, Viviana wrote the final draft that appears at the beginning of this chapter.

A Model Essay to Consider

Read the following essay. Then answer the questions and read the comments that follow.

Lou's Place

by Beth Johnson

Imagine a restaurant where your every whim is catered to, your every want satisfied, your every request granted without hesitation. The people on the staff live to please you. They hover anxiously as you sample your selection, waiting for your judgment. Your pleasure is their delight, your dissatisfaction their dismay. 1

Lou's isn't that kind of place. 2

At Lou's Kosy Korner Koffee Shop, the mock abuse flows like a cup of spilled 3 Folgers. Customers are yelled at, lectured, blamed, mocked, teased, and ignored. They pay for the privilege of pouring their own coffee and scrambling their own eggs. As in a fond but dysfunctional family, Lou displays his affection through criticism and insults, and his customers respond in kind. If Lou's had a slogan, it might be, "If I'm polite to you, ask yourself what's wrong."

Lou's is one of three breakfast joints located in the business district of a small 4 mid-Atlantic town. The county courthouse is nearby, supplying a steady stream of lawyers, jurors, and office workers looking for a bite to eat. A local trucking firm also provides Lou with customers as its drivers come and go in town. Lou's is on the corner. Beside it is a jewelry shop ("In Business Since 1946—Watch Repairs Our Speciality") and an upscale home accessories store that features bonsai trees and hand-painted birdhouses in its window. There's a bus stop in front of Lou's. Lou himself has been known to storm out onto the sidewalk to shoo away people who've dismounted from the bus and lingered too long on the corner.

The sign on Lou's front door says "Open 7 A.M.–3 P.M." But by 6:40 on a 5 brisk spring morning, the restaurant's lights are on, the door is unlocked, and Lou is settled in the booth nearest the door, with the *Philadelphia Inquirer* spread over the table. Lou is sunk deep into the booth's brown vinyl seat, its rips neatly mended with silver duct tape. He is studying the box scores from the night before as a would-be customer pauses on the sidewalk, unsure whether to believe the sign or her own eyes. She opens the door enough to stick her head in.

"Are you open?" she asks. 6

Without lifting his eyes from the paper, Lou answers. "I'm here, aren't I?" 7

Unsure how to interpret this remark, the woman enters and sits at a booth. 8 Lou keeps studying the paper. He begins to hum under his breath. The woman starts tracing a pattern on the glass-topped table with her fingernail. She pulls out her checkbook and pretends to balance it. After a few long minutes, Lou apparently reaches a stopping point in his reading. He rises, his eyes still on the folded newspaper he carries with him. His humming breaks into low-volume song as he trudges behind the counter. "Maaaaaaaake someone happy. . . . Make-make-maaaaaake someone happy," he croons as he lifts the steaming pot that has infused the room with the rich aroma of freshly brewed coffee. He carries it to the woman's table, fills her cup, and drops two single-serving containers of half-and-half nearby. He then peers over the tops of his reading glasses at his customer. "You want anything else, dear?" he asks, his bushy gray eyebrows rising with the question.

She shakes her head. "I'm meeting someone. I'll order when he gets here." 9

Lou nods absently, his eyes back on his paper. As he shuffles back to his 10 seat, he mutters over his shoulder, "Hope he shows up before three. I close then."

Lou reads his paper; the woman drinks her coffee and gazes around the room. 11 It's a small restaurant: just an eight-seat counter and seven padded booths. A grill, coffeepots, and a huge stainless-steel refrigerator line the wall behind the counter. Under the glass top of the tables is the breakfast menu: it offers eggs, pancakes, home fries, bacon, and sausage. A wall rack holds Kellogg's Jumbo Packs of single-serving cereals: smiling toucans and cheerful tigers offer Froot Loops and Frosted Flakes.

Two poster-size photographs hang side by side at the far wall. One is of Lou and 12 his wife on their wedding day. They appear to be in their midtwenties. He is slim, dark-haired, beaming; his arm circles the shoulders of his fair-haired bride. The other photo shows the same couple in an identical pose—only in this one, Lou looks much as he is today. His short white hair is parted at the side; a cropped white beard emphasizes his prominent red mouth. His formerly slim figure now expands to take up much of the photograph. But the smile is the same as he embraces his silver-haired wife.

The bell at the door tinkles; two sleepy-eyed men in flannel shirts, work boots, 13 and oil-company caps walk in. Lou glances up and grunts at them; they nod. One picks up an *Inquirer* from the display stand and leaves two quarters on the cash register. They drop onto seats at the counter, simultaneously swivel to look at the woman in the booth behind them, and then turn back. For a few minutes, they flip through the sports section. Lou doesn't move. One man rises from his seat and wanders behind the counter to find cups and the coffeepot. He fills the cups, returns to his seat, and immerses himself in the paper. There is no noise but the occasional slurping of men sipping hot coffee.

Minutes pass. Finally one of the men speaks. "Lou," he says. "Can I maybe 14 get some breakfast?"

"I'm reading the paper," says Lou. "Eggs are in the refrigerator." 15

The man sighs and lumbers behind the counter again. "In some restaurants, 16 they actually cook for ya," he says, selecting eggs from the carton.

Lou doesn't raise his eyes. "In some restaurants, they wouldn't let a guy with 17 a face like yours in."

The room falls silent again, except for the splatter of grease on the grill and 18 the scrape of the spatula as the customer scrambles his eggs. He heaps them onto his plate, prepares some toast, and returns to his seat. The bell at the door begins tinkling as the breakfast rush begins—men, mostly, about half in work clothes and the rest in suits. They pour in on a wave of talk and laughter. Lou reluctantly rises and goes to work behind the counter, volleying comments with the regulars:

"Three eggs, Lou," says one. 19

"Three eggs. One heart attack wasn't enough for you? You want some bacon 20 grease on top of that?"

A large red-haired man in blue jeans and a faded denim shirt walks in with 21 a newspaper, which he reads as he waits for his cup of takeout coffee. "Anything good in the paper, Dan?" Lou asks.

"Not a thing," drawls Dan. "Not a *damn* thing. The only good thing is that 22 the machine down the street got my fifty cents instead of you."

Lou flips pancakes as the restaurant fills to capacity. The hum of voices fills 23 the room as the aromas of coffee, bacon, eggs, and toasting bread mingle in the air. A group of suits* from the nearby courthouse slide into the final empty booth. After a moment one rises, goes behind the counter, and rummages in a drawer.

---

*suits: business executives or professionals (people wearing business suits).

"Whatcha need, Ben?" Lou asks, pouring more batter.   24

"Rag," Ben answers. He finds one, returns to the booth, and wipes crumbs off 25
the tabletop. A minute later he is back to drop a slice of ham on the hot grill. He
and Lou stand side by side attending to their cooking, as comfortable in their silence
as an old married couple. When the ham is sizzling and its rich fragrance reaches
the far corners of the room, Ben slides it onto a plate and returns to his booth.

Filled plate in hand, Lou approaches a woman sitting at the counter. Her 26
golden hair contrasts with her sunken cheeks and her wrinkled lips sucking an
unfiltered Camel. "You wanna I put this food in your ashtray, or are you gonna
move it?" Lou growls. The woman moves the ashtray aside.

"Sorry, Lou," she says.   27

"I'm not really yelling at you, dear," he answers.   28

"I know," says the woman. "I'm glad *you're* here this morning." She lowers 29
her voice. "That girl you've got working here sometimes, Lou—she doesn't *like*
me." Lou rolls his eyes, apparently at the poor taste of the waitress, and moves
down to the cash register. As he rings up a bill, a teenage girl enters and walks
by silently. Lou glares after her. "Start the day with a 'Good morning,' please,"
he instructs.

"Good morning, Lou," she replies obediently.   30

"*Very* nice," he mutters, still punching the cash-register buttons. "Thank you 31
so much for your concern. I get up at the crack of dawn to make your breakfast,
but don't bother saying 'good morning' to *me*."

The day's earliest arrival, the woman in the booth, has been joined by a 32
companion. They order eggs and hash browns. As Lou slides the filled plates
before them, he reverts briefly to the conventional manners he saves for first-tim-
ers. "Enjoy your meal," he says.

"Thank you," says the woman. "May I have some hot sauce?"   33

Lou's reserve of politeness is instantly exhausted. "Hot sauce. Jeez. She wants 34
hot sauce!" he announces to the room at large. "Anything else? Some caviar on
the side, maybe?" He disappears behind the counter, reemerging with an enormous red bottle. "Here you are. It's a new bottle. Don't use it all, please. I'd like
to save a little for other customers. Hey, on second thought, use it all if you want.
Then I'll know you'll like my chili." Laughing loudly at his own joke, he refills
the woman's coffee cup without being asked. Golden-brown coffee splashes into
her saucer. Lou ignores it.

Lou's waitress, Stacy, has arrived, and begins taking orders and delivering 35
meals. Lou alternates between working the grill and clearing tables. Mid-stride,
he halts before the golden-haired woman at the counter, who has pushed her plate
aside and is lighting another cigarette. "What? What is this?" he demands.

"Looouuu . . ." she begins soothingly, a stream of smoke jetting from her 36
mouth with the word.

"Don't 'Lou' me," he retorts. "You don't eat your toast, you don't eat your 37
potatoes, you barely touch your eggs. Whatcha gonna live on? Camels?"

"Awww, Lou," she says, but she pulls her plate back and eats a few more bites. 38

As the rush of customers slows to a trickle, Lou returns to the register, making 39 change and conversation, talking Phillies and the weather. One of the flannel-shirted men rises from his counter seat and heads for the door, dropping his money on the counter. "'Bye, Stacy," he says to the waitress. "Have a nice day."

"'Bye, Mel," she replies. "You too."   40

"What about me?" Lou calls after Mel.   41

Mel doesn't pause. "Who cares what kind of a day *you* have?"   42

Mel disappears into the morning sunshine; the Camel lady pulls a crossword 43 puzzle out of her purse and taps an unlit cigarette rapidly against the counter. Stacy wipes the tables and empties a wastebasket of its load of dark, wet coffee grounds. Lou butters a piece of toast and returns to his favorite booth. He spreads out his newspaper again, then glances up to catch the eye of the hot-sauce woman. "Where's your friend?" he asks.

"He left," she replies.   44

"He left you, eh?" Lou asks.   45

"No, he didn't *leave* me. He just had to go to work . . ."   46

"Dump him," Lou responds automatically. "And now, if you don't mind *very* 47 much, I would like to finish my newspaper."

QUESTIONS 2

ABOUT UNITY

1. What is the thesis of Johnson's essay? If it is stated directly, locate the relevant sentence or sentences. If it is implied, state the thesis in your own words.

2. Which statement would best serve as a topic sentence for paragraph 13?
   a. Many of Lou's customers are, like him, interested in the Philadelphia sports teams.
   b. Lou doesn't mind if customers serve themselves coffee.
   c. Lou apparently disliked the two men in oil-company caps who came into the restaurant.
   d. Regular customers at Lou's are used to taking care of themselves while Lou reads his paper.

ABOUT SUPPORT

3. In paragraph 3, Johnson claims that Lou and his customers are fond of one another. How does she support that claim in the case of the golden-haired woman who is first mentioned in paragraph 26?

4. We are told that customers enjoy the unusual atmosphere of Lou's coffee shop. What detail in paragraph 25 supports this idea?

_____

_____

5. Find a paragraph that appeals to three senses and identify those senses.

_____

ABOUT COHERENCE

6. Which sentence in paragraph 31 contains a change-of-direction signal?

_____

_____

7. Which sentence in paragraph 23 begins with a time signal? (*Write the opening words of that sentence.*)

_____

8. The sentence that makes up paragraph 38 includes which of the following types of transition?
   a. time
   b. addition
   c. change of direction
   d. conclusion

ABOUT THE INTRODUCTION AND/OR CONCLUSION

9. Johnson begins with a situation that is the opposite of the one that will be developed. Rewrite paragraph 1 using another method for introducing essays explained in Chapter 4: a broad statement that gets narrowed or a brief story.

_____

_____

10. "Lou's Place" ends with a comment by Lou that characterizes the mood of his shop. Rewrite this conclusion by using another method for concluding essays as explained in Chapter 4, summarizing the description of the shop or predicting something about the future of the shop or its owner.

_____

_____

Writing an Essay with Emphasis on Description

Write an essay that describes your strengths and weaknesses as a student. You will want to use specific details that support your purpose. You may also want to look ahead to Chapter 13, "Comparison and/or Contrast" and Chapter 16, "Argument."

PREWRITING

a. Like all essays, this essay must have a thesis. It should state your dominant impression of yourself as a college student. Write a short sentence that summarizes what kind of student you think you are. Don't worry if your thesis doesn't feel just right—you can always revise later. For now, just express your opinion. Here are a couple of examples:

I am a model college student.

Although I am in college, I haven't yet acquired good study habits.

b. Once you have written your sentence, make a list of as many details as you can to support that general impression. For example, this could be a list made by a student who thought she was a great college student:

always study assigned homework

schedule study time every day

participate in class

attend class every day

meet with professors regularly

seek tutoring when necessary

participate in several clubs

c. After creating a list, organize your paper to effectively support your purpose. If you choose emphatic order, start with your least important example and end with your most important example. This will create a more persuasive tone.

d. Use as many specific details as possible to create a full picture for your reader. For example, instead of saying, "I study at the same time every day," you might say, "Each night, I study from 7:00 P.M. until 11:00 P.M. because it is the most quiet time in my house."

e. Proceed to write the first draft of your essay.

REVISING

After you have completed the first draft of the paper, set it aside for a while—if possible, until the next day. When you review the draft, try to do so as critically as you would if it were not your own work. Ask yourself the questions in the FOUR BASES Checklist at the end of this chapter.

As you revise your essay through one or more additional drafts, continue to refer to that checklist until you can answer "yes" to each question.

WRITING ASSIGNMENT 2

Write an essay that describes and summarizes the key ideas in a chosen book or essay. The work you choose may be assigned by your instructor, or it may require your instructor's approval. You may want to check Chapter 20, "Writing a Research Essay," for proper citation of the material you reference from your work.

PREWRITING

a. Find a quote that expresses the main principle of the author's thesis.

b. Answer the following questions:
   a. What does the author want you to understand?
   b. What is the author's main purpose?
   c. What ideas does the author use to support their purpose?

c. Decide how you will organize your essay. Your decision will depend on what seems appropriate for the chosen work. You may want to describe the main ideas in the same order as they are originally presented, or you may choose to describe the ideas in emphatic order, saving the most important idea for last.

d. Make a scratch outline for your essay, based on the organization you have chosen.

e. Using your scratch outline as a guide, make a list of supporting details.

f. Use your scratch outline and list of details to write your first draft.

REVISING

Refer to the FOUR BASES Checklist provided at the end of this chapter.

Writing for a Specific Purpose and Audience

WRITING ASSIGNMENT 3

Imagine that you are working for a travel agency and have been asked to write a letter to prospective clients advertising a wonderful vacation destination you have

Wildroze/Getty Images

already visited yourself. It might be a large city, a sea-side town, an archeological site, a theme park that caters to families, a resort for honeymooners, a dude ranch, a lake, or a mountain hideaway. Then again, you might want to advertise a cruise or even a vacation that involves public service, like the kinds sponsored by Habitat for Humanity. Your purpose is, of course, to get your clients to sign up for the vacation you are advertising. Focus on a particular type of audience: college students, young professionals, families, singles, or senior citizens, for example. You may want to check Chapter 10, "Exemplification," and Chapter 16, "Argument," to create a persuasive tone that will sell your destination.

PREWRITING

a. First, gather details about the physical appearance, sounds, smells, and even tastes of the setting your clients will visit. Talk about how it feels to swim in a crystal-clear lagoon or describe the taste of a crab sandwich you bought at a straw-covered beach shack. Describe the natural setting, as well the kind of weather your clients can expect.

   Discuss what the living and dining accommodations are like as well. By the way, if you are advertising a public-service vacation, you might have to tell them about the tents they'll be sleeping in or the outdoor toilets they'll use. In any case, use as many senses as possible.

b. Keeping the type of audience you have chosen in mind, tell your readers about the kinds of people they are likely to meet, both the tourists and permanent residents. Ask yourself questions such as:

   Are the tourists mostly single, young married couples, families?

   Are most of the people young, middle-aged, older? Or is there a mix of ages?

   Are these people friendly, helpful, interesting?

   Where do they come from?

   What do they talk about?

   Are they fun-loving and active or more private and sedate?

   What about the people who work or live at the place? Are they friendly, helpful, etc.?

c. Finally, provide details about the activities your clients might pursue during the vacation. Does the place offer hang gliding, scuba diving, tours of famous landmarks? Again, if this is a public-service vacation, will your readers be digging wells, framing houses, or constructing schoolhouses?

d. After reading the notes you have gathered, write a rough outline that might look like this:

A. The place

    1. Location

    2. Accommodations

    3. Food

B. The people

    1. Other tourists

    2. Staff

    3. Locals

C. Activities

    1. Water sports

    2. Guided tours

    3. Tennis/golf

e. Now, plan your introductory and concluding sections. In your introduction, state a thesis that is intended to persuade your readers. In addition, prepare them for the points you are going to cover and the order in which you will cover them. For example, you might write:

> The setting and accommodations, the people, and the activities make a week at Crystal Bay Resort the ideal family beach vacation.

Your conclusion might summarize or remind your readers of the best reasons to book the vacation. Naturally, you will have to mention the cost of accommodations and travel as well.

DRAFTING

Write your rough draft by following your outline closely, but don't be a slave to it. If new ideas or details pop into your mind, put them down. You can fix any inconsistencies or repetitions when it comes time to revise. Just be as detailed as you can at this point.

REVISING

Read your first draft to a classmate who is willing to listen carefully and work hard at providing valuable feedback. Refer to the FOUR BASES Checklist at the end of the chapter for questions to consider while revising.

Description Checklist: THE FOUR BASES

ABOUT *UNITY*

✔ Does my essay have a clearly stated thesis, including a dominant impression?

✔ Does each paragraph, and each sentence within that paragraph, help to develop the description of my topic?

✔ Are there portions of the essay that do not support my thesis and therefore should be eliminated or rewritten?

ABOUT *SUPPORT*

✔ Have I provided rich, specific details that appeal to a variety of senses (sight, hearing, smell, taste, touch)?

✔ Have I chosen dynamic and vibrant words to enhance my description?

ABOUT *COHERENCE*

✔ Do transitional words and phrases, and linking sentences between paragraphs, help make the description clear?

✔ Does my conclusion clearly tie up the essay and explain why this topic was significant enough to describe?

ABOUT *SENTENCE SKILLS*

✔ Have I used a consistent point of view throughout my essay?

✔ Have I used specific rather than general words?

✔ Have I avoided wordiness and used concise wording?

✔ Are my sentences varied?

✔ Have I edited for spelling and other sentence skills errors, as listed in the checklist at the back of the book?

READING

p. 218: Johnson, Beth. "Lou's Place." Used by permission of Townsend Press.

Narration

Imagine that you are the owner of your own very successful company, which you have built from the ground up. You have been asked to share your experience with a group of young entrepreneurs who have hopes of owning their own businesses someday. Write a narrative of your success story, including the type of business you own, how you came up with the idea, and how you managed to make it a success.
REUTERS/Alamy Stock Photo

This chapter will explain and illustrate how to

- develop an essay with emphasis on narration

- write an essay with emphasis on narration

- revise an essay with emphasis on narration

In addition, you will read and consider

- two student essays that emphasize narration

- one professional model essay that emphasizes narration

Children beg to hear a beloved story read again and again. Over dinner, tired adults tell each other about their day. A restless class is hushed when a teacher says, "Let me tell you something strange that happened to me once." Whatever our age, we never outgrow our hunger for stories. Just as our ancestors entertained and instructed each other with tales of great hunts and battles, of angry gods and foolish humans, we still love to share our lives and learn about others through storytelling.

Narration is storytelling, whether we are relating a single story or several related ones. Through narration, we make a statement clear by relating in detail something that has happened to us. In the story we tell, we present the details in the order in which they happened. A person might say, for example, "I was really embarrassed the day I took my driver's test," and then go on to develop that statement with an account of the experience. If the story is sharply detailed, we will be able to see and understand just why the speaker felt that way.

In this chapter, you'll be asked to tell a story that illustrates a specific point. To prepare for this assignment, first read the student essays and the model essay that follow and work through the questions that accompany each piece of writing. All three essays emphasize narration to develop their points.

Student Essays to Consider

Taking on a Disability

My church recently staged a "Sensitivity Sunday" to make our congregation more aware of the problems faced by people with physical disabilities. We were asked to "take on a disability" for several hours one Sunday morning. Some members, like me, chose to use wheelchairs. Others wore sound-blocking earplugs, maneuvered around on crutches, or wore blindfolds.

Just sitting in the wheelchair was instructive. I had never considered before what it would be like to use one. As soon as I sat down, my weight made the chair begin to roll. Its wheels were not locked, and I fumbled clumsily to correct that. Something else I didn't expect was figuring out where and how to place my feet. I fumbled some more to turn the metal footrest into place. I felt psychologically challenged as well, as I took my first uneasy look at what was to be my only means of transportation for several hours. I realized that for many people, using a wheelchair is not a temporary experiment. That was a sobering thought as I sank back into my seat.

Once I sat down, I had to learn how to cope with the wheelchair. I shifted around, trying to find a comfortable position. I thought it might be restful, even kind of nice, to be pushed around for a while. I glanced around to see who would be pushing me and then realized I would have to navigate the wheelchair by myself. My palms reddened and my

continued

wrist and forearm muscles started to ache as I tugged at the heavy metal wheels. I realized, as I veered this way and that, that steering and turning were not going to be easy tasks. Trying to make a right-angle turn from one aisle to another, I steered straight into a pew. I felt as though everyone was staring at me and commenting on my clumsiness.

When the service started, other problems cropped up to frustrate me further. Every time the congregation stood up, my view was blocked. I could not see the minister, the choir, or the altar. Also, as the church's aisles were narrow, I seemed to be in the way no matter where I was. For instance, the ushers had to squeeze by me to pass the collection plate. This made me feel like a nuisance. Thanks to a new building program, however, our church will soon have the wide aisles and well-spaced pews that will make life easier for people with disabilities. After the service ended, when people stopped to talk to me, I had to strain my neck and look up at them. This made me feel like a little child being talked down to and added to my sense of powerlessness.

4

My wheelchair experiment was soon over. It's true that it made an impression on me. I no longer resent large tax expenditures for ramp-equipped buses, and I wouldn't dream of parking my car in a space marked "ADA Accessible." But I also realize how little I know about the daily life of a person with disabilities. A few hours of using a wheelchair gave me only a hint of the challenges, both physical and emotional, that people with disabilities must overcome.

5

A Night of Violence

According to my history instructor, Adolf Hitler once said that he wanted to sign up "brutal youths" to help him achieve his goals. If Hitler were still alive, he wouldn't have any trouble recruiting the brutal youths he wanted; he could get them right here in the United States. I know, because I was one of them. As a teenager, I ran with a gang. And it took a frightening incident for me to see how violent I had become.

1

The incident was planned one Thursday night when I was out with my friends. I was still going to school once in a while, but most of my friends weren't. We spent our days on the streets, talking, showing off, sometimes shoplifting a little or shaking people down for a few dollars. My friends and I were close, maybe because life hadn't been very good to any of us. On this night, we were drinking wine and vodka on the corner. For some reason, we all felt tense and restless. One of us came up with the idea of robbing one of the old people who lived in the high-rise close by. We would just knock the person over, grab the money, and party with it.

2

continued

The robbery did not go as planned. After about an hour, and after   3
more wine and vodka, we spotted an old man. He came out of the
glass door of the building and started up the street. Pine Street had a
lot of antique stores as well as apartment buildings. Stuffing our bottles
in our jacket pockets, we closed in behind him. Suddenly, the old man
whipped out a homemade wooden club from under his jacket and
began swinging. The club thudded loudly against Victor's shoulder,
making him yelp with pain. When we heard that, we went crazy. We
smashed our bottles over the old man's head. Not content with that,
Victor kicked him savagely, knocking him to the ground. As we ran, I
kept seeing him sprawled on the ground, blood from our beating
trickling into his eyes. Victor, the biggest of us, had said, "We want your
money, old man. Hand it over."

Later, at home, I had a strong reaction to the incident. My head   4
would not stop pounding, and I threw up. I wasn't afraid of getting
caught; in fact, we never did get caught. I just knew I had gone over
some kind of line. I didn't know if I could step back, now that I had
gone so far. But I knew I had to. I had seen plenty of people in my
neighborhood turn into the kind of people who hated their lives, people
who didn't care about anything, people who wound up penned in jail or
ruled by drugs. I didn't want to become one of them.

That night, I realize now, I decided not to become one of Hitler's   5
"brutal youths." I'm proud of myself for that, even though life didn't get
any easier and no one came along to pin a medal on me. I just
decided, quietly, to step off the path I was on. I hope my parents and I
will get along better now, too. Maybe the old man's pain, in some
terrible way, had a purpose.

QUESTIONS 1

ABOUT UNITY

1. Which essay lacks an opening thesis statement? *Write a thesis statement that might work for that essay.*

_____

_____

2. Which sentence in paragraph 4 of "Taking on a Disability" should be omitted in the interest of paragraph unity? (*Write the opening words.*)

_____

_____

3. What sentence in paragraph 3 of "A Night of Violence" should be omitted in the interest of paragraph unity? (*Write the opening words.*)

_____

4. Reread the conclusions to both essays. Which one contains a sentence introducing a new topic and should be eliminated? (*Write the opening words of that sentence.*)

_____

_____

ABOUT SUPPORT

5. a. Find a sentence in "Taking on a Disability" that contains words appealing to both sight and touch. (*Write the opening words.*)

_____

   b. Find a sentence in "A Night of Violence" that contains words appealing to hearing. (*Write the opening words.*)

_____

6. In a narrative, the main method of organization is time order. Which sentence in paragraph 3 of "A Night of Violence" is placed out of order? (*Write the opening words.*)

_____

7. Reread paragraph 4 of "Taking on a Disability." Then record three details that support that paragraph's topic sentence.

_____

_____

_____

ABOUT COHERENCE

8. The first stage of the writer's experience in "Taking on a Disability" might be called *sitting down in the wheelchair*. What are the other two stages of the experience?

_____

_____

9. List four transitions in paragraph 3 of "A Night of Violence." What type of transitions are they?

_____   _____   _____   _____

_____

10. What method of writing introductions explained in Chapter 4 is used in the first paragraph of "A Night of Violence"?

Developing an Essay with Emphasis on Narration

Considering Purpose and Audience

The main purpose of an essay that emphasizes narration is to make a point by incorporating one central story or several brief stories as support. Colorful details and interesting events that build up to a point of some kind make narrative essays enjoyable for readers and writers alike.

At one time or another, you have probably listened to someone tell a rambling story that didn't seem to go anywhere. You might have impatiently wondered, "Where is this story going?" or "Is there a point here?" Keep such questions in mind as you think about your own essay. To satisfy your audience, your story must have some overall purpose and point.

Also keep in mind that your essay should deal with an event or a topic that will appeal to your audience. A group of young children, for example, would probably be bored by an essay about your first job interview. They might, however, be very interested if you wrote about a time you were chased by a pack of wild dogs or when you stood up to a bully in your school. In general, essays that emphasize narration involve human conflict—internal or external—and are entertaining to readers of all ages.

Using Dialogue

In Chapter 8, you learned that including people in an essay about a place is important to communicating something about its character or atmosphere. Of course, people are essential to narration as are what they do and what they say. You can convey much about a person through the dialogue they have with others or even through the interior conversations they have while thinking silently. But dialogue can also be used to move the plot or action of the story along, to tell what happened before the story began, and to reveal other important facts that will make the story clearer, more suspenseful, or more meaningful.

For example, in "A Night of Violence" Victor's brutal tendencies become clear when he says, "We want your money, old man. Hand it over." You will also encounter dialogue in Nicholas Gage's essay "The Teacher Who Changed My Life," which appears later in this chapter. Here the narrator uses dialogue to acquaint readers with the nature of the main character, Miss Hurd, whose opening line is "What are all you goof-offs doing here?"

Some Rules for Using Dialogue

Use dialogue especially in the narrative essays you write, but remember to observe a few simple rules:

1. Place quotation marks around the words, and start a new paragraph when a new character begins speaking. For this reason, it is easy to tell that there are two different speakers in the following exchange between Lou, the owner of the restaurant in "Lou's Place" (see Chapter 8), and one of his customers.

     "You wanna I put this food in your ashtray, or are you gonna move it?" Lou growls. The woman moves the ashtray aside.

     "Sorry, Lou," she says.

     "I'm not really yelling at you, dear," he answers.

     "I know," says the woman. "I'm glad *you're* here this morning." She lowers her voice. "That girl you've got working here sometimes, Lou—she doesn't *like* me."

2. Record people's words exactly as they speak them, complete with slang and errors in grammar and punctuation. Notice that, in the dialogue quoted above, Lou says "wanna" rather than "want" and "gonna" rather than "going to." This is not the kind of writing expected in a college essay, but it is completely appropriate when you are recording dialogue. Remember that you are trying to capture the words—the very sounds—that characters uttered just as they said them.

3. Make sure your reader knows who is speaking at any given time. In the "Lou's Place" passage quoted above, Johnson uses tag lines like "she said" or "says the woman" to explain to the reader that the woman is the speaker. Later, when we read "he answers," we know it's Lou who is talking. One way to make sure that readers can identify the speaker is to use tag lines like "she said," "Lou replied," or "the man yelled."

4. Set off tag lines from quotations with commas, as in paragraph 22 of "Lou's Place": *"Not a thing," drawls Dan.* However, if a tag line is used in the middle of a quotation that is composed of two distinct sentences, place a comma before and a period after it, as in paragraph 33 of "Lou's Place": *"Thank you," says the woman. "May I have some hot sauce?"*

In the previous example and text explanation, commas and periods appear within quotation marks, but colons appear outside of them. (Semicolons follow the same rule as colons and appear outside quotation marks.) Finally, if the quotation is a question, end it with a question mark without the comma, as in paragraph 35 of "Lou's Place": *"What? What is this?" he demands.*

Development through Prewriting

Freewriting is a particularly helpful prewriting technique as you're planning your essay. As you think about the story you want to relate, many ideas will crowd into your mind. Simply writing them down in free-form style will jog loose details you may have forgotten and also help you determine what the central point of your story really is.

TIP

For more about freewriting, see the "Prewriting" section in Chapter 2.

Lisa, the writer of "Taking on a Disability," spent a half hour freewriting before she wrote the first draft of her essay. Here is what she came up with:

Our church was planning a building renovation to make the church more accessible to people with disabilities. Some people thought it was a waste of money and that those with disabilities could get along all right in the church the way it was. Not many people with disabilities come to our church anyway. Pastor Henry gave a sermon about disabilities. He suggested that we spend one Sunday experiencing what it is like to have a disability. We got to choose the type. Some people chose to experience what it is like to have blindness or to need crutches or other support to walk. I chose to use a wheelchair. I thought it might be fun to have someone push me around. It was a lot scarier and more disturbing than I expected. We borrowed wheelchairs and crutches from the local nursing home. I didn't like sitting down in the wheelchair. I didn't know how to work it right. It rolled when I didn't want it to. I felt clumsy trying to make it move. I even ran into a pew. I felt silly pretending and also sort of disrespectful because for most people sitting in a wheelchair isn't a choice. It also bothered me to think what it'd be like if I couldn't get up again. It turned out that nobody was going to push me around. I thought Paula would, but instead she put on a blindfold to experience what it is like for a person with blindness. She knocked over a cup of coffee before the morning was over. She told me later she felt really panicky when that happened. Sitting down so low in the wheelchair was weird. I couldn't see much of anything. People ignored me or talked to me like I was a little kid. I was glad when the morning was over. Making the wheels turn hurt my hands and arms.

As Lisa read over her freewriting passage, she decided that the central point of her story was her new realization of how challenging it would be to be truly disabled. To support that central point, she realized, she would need to concentrate on details that demonstrated the frustrations she felt. She created a scratch outline for the first draft of her essay:

Church experiment led to my spending the morning in a wheelchair

- *Sitting in the wheelchair*
  - *challenging because it rolled*
  - *challenging because footrest was out of place*
  - *felt psychologically challenged*
- *Moving the wheelchair*
  - *thought someone would push me*
  - *was hard to make the chair move and it hurt my hands*
  - *was difficult to steer*
- *Ways the wheelchair affected me*
  - *couldn't see*
  - *felt in the way*
  - *felt funny talking to people as they bent down over me*

Development through Revising

Lisa based her first draft on her scratch outline. Here is the draft:

Taking on a Disability

First Draft

The pastor at our church suggested that we each "take on a disability" for a few hours on Sunday morning. Some members, like me, chose to use wheelchairs. Others wore earplugs, used crutches, or wore blindfolds.

It surprised me that I felt nervous about sitting down in my wheelchair. I'm not sure why I felt scared about it. I guess I realized that most people who use wheelchairs don't do it by choice—they have to.

continued

When I sat down, I thought my friend Paula would push me around. We had talked about her doing that earlier. But she decided instead to experience what it is like to have blindness by using a blindfold. I saw her with a blindfold on, trying to fix herself a cup of coffee and knocking it off the table as she stirred it. So I had to figure out how to make the chair move by myself. It wasn't so easy. Pushing the wheels made my hands and arms sore. I also kept bumping into things. It was unexpectedly challenging. I even had trouble locking the wheels and finding the footrest.

I couldn't see well as I sat down low in my chair. When the rest of the congregation stood up, I could forget about seeing entirely. People would nod or chuckle at something that had happened up at the front of the church and I could only guess what was going on. Instead of sitting in the pew with everyone else, I was in the aisle, which was really too narrow for the chair. The new building program our church is planning will make that problem better by widening the aisles and making the pews farther apart. It's going to be expensive, but it's a worthwhile thing. Another thing I disliked was how I felt when people talked to me. They had to lean down as though I was a kid, and I had to stare up at them as though I was too. One person I talked to who seemed to understand what I was experiencing was Don Henderson, who mentioned that his brother-in-law uses a wheelchair.

Lisa read over her first draft. Then she showed it to her roommate. After hearing her roommate's comments, Lisa read the essay again. This time she made a list of comments about how she thought it could be improved:

- The introduction should explain why the pastor wanted us to take on disabilities.

- The second paragraph is sort of weak. Instead of saying, I'm not sure why I felt scared, I should try to put into specific words what was scary about the experience.

- The stuff about Paula doesn't really add to my main point. The story is about me, not Paula.

- Maybe I shouldn't talk so much about the new building program. It's related to people with disabilities, but it doesn't really support the idea that my morning in a wheelchair was enlightening.

- Eliminate the part about Don Henderson. It doesn't contribute to my feeling frustrated.

- The essay ends too abruptly. I need to wrap it up with some sort of conclusion.

With that list of comments in hand, Lisa returned to her essay. She then wrote the version that appears at the beginning of this chapter.

A Model Essay to Consider

Read the following essay. Then answer the questions and read the comments that follow.

The Teacher Who Changed My Life
by Nicholas Gage

The person who set the course of my life in the new land I entered as a young 1 war refugee—who, in fact, nearly dragged me onto the path that would bring all the blessings I've received in America—was a salty-tongued, no-nonsense schoolteacher named Marjorie Hurd. When I entered her classroom in 1953, I had been to six schools in five years, starting in the Greek village where I was born in 1939.

When I stepped off a ship in New York Harbor on a gray March day in 1949, 2 I was an undersized 9-year-old in short pants who had lost his mother and was coming to live with the father he didn't know. My mother, Eleni Gatzoyiannis, had been imprisoned, tortured and shot by Communist guerrillas for sending me and three of my four sisters to freedom. She died so that her children could go to their father in the United States.

The portly, bald, well-dressed man who met me and my sisters seemed a 3 foreign, authoritarian figure. I secretly resented him for not getting the whole family out of Greece early enough to save my mother. Ultimately, I would grow to love him and appreciate how he dealt with becoming a single parent at the age of 56, but at first our relationship was prickly, full of hostility.

As Father drove us to our new home—a tenement in Worcester, Mass.—and 4 pointed out the huge brick building that would be our first school in America, I clutched my Greek notebooks from the refugee camp, hoping that my few years of schooling would impress my teachers in this cold, crowded country. They didn't. When my father led me and my 11-year-old sister to Greendale Elementary School, the grim-faced Yankee principal put the two of us in a class for the mentally retarded. There was no facility in those days for non-English-speaking children.

By the time I met Marjorie Hurd four years later, I had learned English, been 5 placed in a normal, graded class and had even been chosen for the college preparatory track in the Worcester public school system. I was 13 years old when our father moved us yet again, and I entered Chandler Junior High shortly after the beginning of seventh grade. I found myself surrounded by richer, smarter and better-dressed classmates, who looked askance at my strange clothes and heavy accent. Shortly after I arrived, we were told to select a hobby to pursue during "club hour" on Fridays. The idea of hobbies and clubs made no sense to my immigrant ears, but I decided to follow the prettiest girl in my class—the blue-eyed daughter of the local Lutheran minister. She led me through the door marked "Newspaper Club" and into the presence of Miss Hurd, the newspaper adviser and English teacher who would become my mentor and my muse.

A formidable, solidly built woman with salt-and-pepper hair, a steely eye and 6 a flat Boston accent, Miss Hurd had no patience with layabouts. "What are all you goof-offs doing here?" she bellowed at the would-be journalists. "This is the Newspaper Club! We're going to put out a newspaper. So if there's anybody in this room who doesn't like work, I suggest you go across to the Glee Club now, because you're going to work your tails off here!"

I was soon under Miss Hurd's spell. She did indeed teach us to put out a 7 newspaper, skills I honed during my next 25 years as a journalist. Soon I asked the principal to transfer me to her English class as well. There, she drilled us on grammar until I finally began to understand the logic and structure of the English language. She assigned stories for us to read and discuss; not tales of heroes, like the Greek myths I knew, but stories of underdogs—poor people, even immigrants, who seemed ordinary until a crisis drove them to do something extraordinary. She also introduced us to the literary wealth of Greece—giving me a new perspective on my war-ravaged, impoverished homeland. I began to be proud of my origins.

One day, after discussing how writers should write about what they know, she 8 assigned us to compose an essay from our own experience. Fixing me with a stern look, she added, "Nick, I want you to write about what happened to your family in Greece." I had been trying to put those painful memories behind me and left the assignment until the last moment. Then, on a warm spring afternoon, I sat in my room with a yellow pad and pencil and stared out the window at the buds on the trees. I wrote that the coming of spring always reminded me of the last time I said goodbye to my mother on a green and gold day in 1948.

I kept writing, one line after another, telling how the Communist guerrillas 9 occupied our village, took our home and food, how my mother started planning our escape when she learned that the children were to be sent to re-education camps behind the Iron Curtain and how, at the last moment, she couldn't escape with us because the guerrillas sent her with a group of women to thresh wheat in a distant village. She promised she would try to get away on her own, she told me to be brave and hung a silver cross around my neck, and then she kissed me. I watched the line of women being led down into the ravine and up the other side, until they disappeared around the bend—my mother a tiny brown figure at the end who stopped for an instant to raise her hand in one last farewell.

I wrote about our nighttime escape down the mountain, across the minefields 10 and into the lines of the Nationalist soldiers, who sent us to a refugee camp. It was there that we learned of our mother's execution. I felt very lucky to have come to America, I concluded, but every year, the coming of spring made me feel sad because it reminded me of the last time I saw my mother.

I handed in the essay, hoping never to see it again, but Miss Hurd had it 11 published in the school paper. This mortified me at first, until I saw that my classmates reacted with sympathy and tact to my family's story. Without telling me, Miss Hurd also submitted the essay to a contest sponsored by the Freedoms Foundation at Valley Forge, Pa., and it won a medal. The Worcester paper wrote about the award and quoted my essay at length. My father, by then a "five-and-dime-store chef," as the paper described him, was ecstatic with pride, and the Worcester Greek community celebrated the honor to one of its own.

For the first time I began to understand the power of the written word. A 12 secret ambition took root in me. One day, I vowed, I would go back to Greece, find out the details of my mother's death and write about her life, so her grand-children would know of her courage. Perhaps I would even track down the men who killed her and write of their crimes. Fulfilling that ambition would take me 30 years.

Meanwhile, I followed the literary path that Miss Hurd had so forcefully set 13 me on. After junior high, I became the editor of my school paper at Classical High School and got a part-time job at the Worcester Telegram and Gazette. Although my father could only give me $50 and encouragement toward a college education, I managed to finance four years at Boston University with scholarships and part-time jobs in journalism. During my last year of college, an article I wrote about a friend who had died in the Philippines—the first person to lose his life working for the Peace Corps—led to my winning the Hearst Award for College Journalism. And the plaque was given to me in the White House by President John F. Kennedy.

For a refugee who had never seen a motorized vehicle or indoor plumbing 14 until he was 9, this was an unimaginable honor. When the Worcester paper ran a picture of me standing next to President Kennedy, my father rushed out to buy a new suit in order to be properly dressed to receive the congratulations of the Worcester Greeks. He clipped out the photograph, had it laminated in plastic and carried it in his breast pocket for the rest of his life to show everyone he met. I found the much-worn photo in his pocket on the day he died 20 years later.

In our isolated Greek village, my mother had bribed a cousin to teach her to 15 read, for girls were not supposed to attend school beyond a certain age. She had always dreamed of her children receiving an education. She couldn't be there when I graduated from Boston University, but the person who came with my father and shared our joy was my former teacher, Marjorie Hurd. We celebrated not only my bachelor's degree but also the scholarships that paid my way to

Columbia's Graduate School of Journalism. There, I met the woman who would eventually become my wife. At our wedding and at the baptisms of our three children, Marjorie Hurd was always there, dancing alongside the Greeks.

By then, she was Mrs. Rabidou, for she had married a widower when she was 16 in her early 40s. That didn't distract her from her vocation of introducing young minds to English literature, however. She taught for a total of 41 years and continually would make a "project" of some balky student in whom she spied a spark of potential. Often these were students from the most troubled homes, yet she would alternately bully and charm each one with her own special brand of tough love until the spark caught fire. She retired in 1981 at the age of 62 but still avidly follows the lives and careers of former students while overseeing her adult stepchildren and driving her husband on camping trips to New Hampshire.

Miss Hurd was one of the first to call me on Dec. 10, 1987, when President 17 Reagan, in his television address after the summit meeting with Gorbachev, told the nation that Eleni Gatzoyiannis's dying cry, "My children!" had helped inspire him to seek an arms agreement "for all the children of the world."

"I can't imagine a better monument for your mother," Miss Hurd said with 18 an uncharacteristic catch in her voice.

Although a bad hip makes it impossible for her to join in the Greek dancing, 19 Marjorie Hurd Rabidou is still an honored and enthusiastic guest at all our family celebrations, including my 50th birthday picnic last summer, where the shish kebab was cooked on spits, clarinets and bouzoukis wailed, and costumed dancers led the guests in a serpentine line around our Colonial farmhouse, only 20 minutes from my first home in Worcester.

My sisters and I felt an aching void because my father was not there to lead 20 the line, balancing a glass of wine on his head while he danced, the way he did at every celebration during his 92 years. But Miss Hurd was there, surveying the scene with quiet satisfaction. Although my parents are gone, her presence was a consolation, because I owe her so much.

This is truly the land of opportunity, and I would have enjoyed its bounty 21 even if I hadn't walked into Miss Hurd's classroom in 1953. But she was the one who directed my grief and pain into writing, and if it weren't for her, I wouldn't have become an investigative reporter and foreign correspondent, recorded the story of my mother's life and death in *Eleni* and now my father's story in *A Place for Us*, which is also a testament to the country that took us in. She was the catalyst that sent me into journalism and indirectly caused all the good things that came after. But Miss Hurd would probably deny this emphatically.

A few years ago, I answered the telephone and heard my former teacher's 22 voice telling me, in that won't-take-no-for-an-answer tone of hers, that she had decided I was to write and deliver the eulogy at her funeral. I agreed (she didn't leave me any choice), but that's one assignment I never want to do. I hope, Miss Hurd, that you'll accept this remembrance instead.

ABOUT UNITY

1. What is the thesis of Gage's essay? If it is stated directly, locate the relevant sentence or sentences. If it is implied, state the thesis in your own words.

   _____

2. Write a sentence that might serve as a topic sentence for paragraph 9.

   _____

3. What is the topic sentence of paragraph 12?

   _____

ABOUT SUPPORT

4. List several of the details Gage uses to describe Miss Hurd.

   _____
   _____

5. We can infer that the author saw Miss Hurd as a demanding but caring teacher. Find evidence to support his claim.

   _____
   _____
   _____

6. What does Gage mean by "my mentor and my muse" in paragraph 5?

   _____
   _____

7. Paragraph 9
   a. supports why Ms. Hurd is important to Nicholas Gage.
   b. explains why Nicholas and his family left his mother behind.
   c. answers the question about why Nicholas and family were refugees.
   d. defends why Nicholas didn't want to write about his experiences.

ABOUT COHERENCE

8. Because this story tells the chronology of Miss Hurd's impact, Gage uses transitions to signal the passing of time. List five that are used in the essay.

   _____   _____   _____   _____   _____

9. The author uses transitions to show change of direction in paragraph 11. List them.

   _____   _____

ABOUT THE INTRODUCTION AND/OR CONCLUSION

10. What is the relationship between the essay's first paragraph and its two concluding paragraphs?

_____

_____

_____

Writing an Essay with Emphasis on Narration

Think of an experience in your life that supports one of the statements below:

If you never have a dream, you'll never have a dream come true.
—popular saying

Before I got married I had six theories about bringing up children; now I have six children and no theories.—John Wilmot, Earl of Rochester

There are some things you learn best in calm, and some in storm.
—Willa Cather

Success is 99 percent perspiration and 1 percent inspiration.
—Thomas Edison

Be the change that you wish to see in the world.—Mahatma Gandhi

There's a sucker born every minute.—P. T. Barnum

We lie loudest when we lie to ourselves.—Eric Hoffer

You will face many defeats in life, but never let yourself be defeated.
—Maya Angelou

Hoping and praying are easier but do not produce as good results as hard work.—Andy Rooney

A little learning is a dangerous thing.—Alexander Pope

Nothing is as good as it seems beforehand.—George Eliot

Life shrinks or expands in proportion to one's courage.—Anaïs Nin

When I got to the end of my long journey in life / I realized I was the architect of my own destiny.—Amado Nervo

A fool and his money are soon parted.—popular saying

From what we get, we can make a living; what we give, however, makes a life.—Arthur Ashe

The greatest glory in living lies not in never falling, but in rising every time we fall.—Nelson Mandela

Fear not those who argue but those who dodge.—Marie von Ebner-Eschenback

Trust in Allah, but tie your camel.—old Muslim proverb

Use one of the above statements or another noteworthy saying—perhaps one that has been a guidepost for your life—to write a thesis statement for an essay with emphasis on narration about that experience. As you develop and write the essay, refer to the suggestions in the following prewriting strategies and rewriting strategies. You may also want to review Chapter 8, "Description," to help create a strong narrative with strong support.

PREWRITING

The key to the success of your essay will be your choice of an incident from your life that illustrates the truth of the statement you have chosen. Here are some guidelines to consider as you choose such an incident:

- The incident should include a *conflict,* or a source of tension. That conflict does not need to be dramatic, such as a fistfight between two characters. Equally effective is a quieter conflict, such as a conflict between a person's conscience and desires, or a decision that must be made, or a difficult situation that has no clear resolution.

- The incident should be limited in time. It would be difficult to do justice in such a brief essay to an experience that continued over several weeks or months.

- The incident should evoke a definite emotional response in you so that it might draw a similar response from your reader.

- The incident must *fully support* the statement you have chosen, not merely be linked by some of the same ideas. Do not, for example, take the statement "We lie loudest when we lie to ourselves" and then write about an incident in which someone just told a lie. The essay should demonstrate the cost of being untruthful to oneself.

Here is how one student tested whether her plan for her narrative essay was a good one:

- What statement have I chosen as my thesis?
  The chains of habit are too weak to be felt until they are too strong to be broken.—Samuel Johnson

- Does the incident I have chosen include some kind of tension?

  Yes. I am going to write about the day I tried to purchase an expensive new shirt but was told that I had maxed out my credit card. When I tried a second card and then a third, I was told that they too had reached their balance limits. What an embarrassment. That day I realized something about myself—I get the urge to buy things whenever I am lonely, depressed, or just bored. I also learned that in order to battle that urge, I would have to change my values, my outlook on life. I would have to learn that happiness does not result simply from having nice things.

- Is the incident limited in time?

  Yes. I am going to write about events that happened in one day.

- Does the incident evoke an emotional response in me?

  Yes. I was embarrassed and ashamed of myself.

- Does the incident support the statement I have chosen?

  Yes. I was a "shopaholic," but I did not realize that I was caught in the "chains" of this habit until I was embarrassed into making major changes in my outlook on life.

REVISING

After you have put your essay away for a day, read it to a friend or classmate who will give you honest feedback. You and your reader should consider the questions in the checklist that appears at the end of this chapter. Continue revising your work until you and your reader can answer "yes" to each question.

Jacob Lund/
Shutterstock

WRITING ASSIGNMENT 2

Write an essay in which you research a historical figure and come to a conclusion about that figure. The person you choose may be assigned by your instructor, or may be of your own choosing and require your instructor's approval. Options could include Malcolm X, Eva Peron, Vice-President Charles Curtis, or Queen Victoria. You may want to check Chapter 16, "Argument," and Chapter 20, "Writing a Research Essay."

PREWRITING

a. After choosing your topic, you will want to research as much information as possible. Not only should you develop a biographical understanding of your subject, but you will also want to learn about some of the more controversial ideas or actions that this figure was known for.

b. After researching, you should come to some sort of conclusion about this person. Was she maligned? Was he really as good as people thought? Did they do underhanded things to get their way? Was this person really altruistic? Your conclusion should become the basis for your thesis statement.

c. You will then want to create an outline that organizes the story of your subject's life in a manner that supports your thesis.

d. Using your outline as a guide, prepare a rough draft of your paper.

REVISING

Once you have a first draft of your essay completed, use the FOUR BASES Checklist at the end of this chapter to help you with your revision process.

Writing for a Specific Purpose and Audience

WRITING ASSIGNMENT 3

In this essay, you will write with a specific purpose and for a specific audience.
The use of narration goes beyond the classroom: people share stories online, in print, on TV, and on the radio. For stories to get noticed, however, they need to have a purpose. For instance, when the Black Lives Matter (#BlackLivesMatter) movement began, it was accompanied by many stories that illustrated why the movement was personal to different people. For this assignment, you are to write an essay that creates a campaign, complete with a hashtag or logo, to improve something in your community. First, you will want to find out what issues are affecting your community, like teen suicide, homeless veterans, or decaying parks. After you have decided on your topic, you will need to explain what the problem is and why it is important, what your campaign will be like, and what you hope to accomplish with your campaign. You may want to review Chapter 10, "Exemplification," and Chapter 12, "Cause and/or Effect."

Narration Checklist: THE FOUR BASES

ABOUT *UNITY*

✔ Have I included a thesis statement that clearly identifies a single experience or story that I am going to recount?

✔ Does each paragraph, and each sentence within that paragraph, help either to keep the action moving or to reveal important things about the characters?

✔ Are there portions of the essay that do not support my thesis and therefore should be eliminated or rewritten?

ABOUT *SUPPORT*

✔ Have I included enough vivid exact details, including dialogue, that will help my readers experience the event as it actually happened?

✔ Does my conclusion clearly tie up the story and explain why it is significant?

✔ Have I introduced any major characters within the essay?

ABOUT *COHERENCE*

✔ Do transitional words and phrases, and linking sentences between paragraphs, help make the sequence of events clear?

✔ Should I break up the essay by using bits of interesting dialogue instead of narration?

ABOUT *SENTENCE SKILLS*

✔ Have I used a consistent point of view throughout my essay?

✔ Have I used specific rather than general words?

✔ Have I avoided wordiness and used concise wording?

✔ Are my sentences varied?

✔ Have I edited for spelling and other sentence skills errors, as listed in the checklist at the back of the book?

READING

p. 239: Gage, Nicholas. "The Teacher Who Changed My Life." Reprinted by permission of the author.

Exemplification

This chapter will explain and illustrate how to

- develop an essay with emphasis on exemplification

- write an essay with emphasis on exemplification

- revise an essay with emphasis on exemplification

In addition, you will read and consider

- two student essays that emphasize exemplification

- one professional model essay that emphasizes exemplification

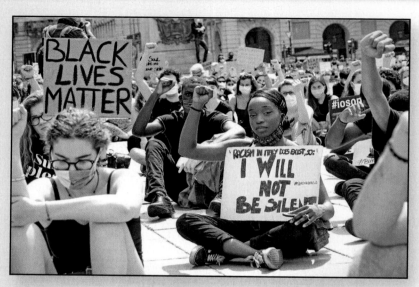

In what ways did the murder of George Floyd bring people in the United States together? In what ways have we become a more divided nation? Use examples found in the media, in this photograph, or in your own daily observations to support your point.

Michele D'Ottavio/Alamy Stock Photo

In our daily conversations, we often provide examples—details, particulars, and specific instances—to explain statements that we make. Here are several statements and supporting examples:

Statement	Examples
The first day of school was frustrating.	My sociology course was canceled. Then, I couldn't find the biology lab. And the lines at the bookstore were so long that I went home without buying my textbooks.

That washing machine is unreliable.	The water temperature can't be predicted; it stops in midcycle; and it sometimes shreds my clothing.
My brother is a thrifty person.	He washes and reuses aluminum foil. He wraps gifts in newspaper. And he's worn the same Sunday suit for twenty years.

In each case, exemplification helps us see for ourselves the truth of the statement that has been made. In essays, too, explanatory examples help your audience fully understand your point. Lively, specific examples also add interest to your paper.

In this chapter, you will be asked to emphasize exemplification to support your thesis. Read the student literary analysis essay, the second student essay, and the model essay that follow and work through the questions that accompany the essays. All three essays emphasize exemplification to develop their points.

Student Essays to Consider

Paying Attention to a Death

In "A Hanging," George Orwell narrates the execution of a Burmese 1
man in such a way that no reader can avoid realizing the enormity of
taking a human life. *The Green Mile*, a movie based on a Stephen King
novel, makes the same statement. The essay focuses on the last few
moments in the life of a man we hardly get to know. The film covers the
events of an entire year and allows us to see into the hearts of both
prisoners and guards. Nevertheless, the messages are identical: no one,
not even a legally constituted government, has the right to violate the
sanctity of human life.

The moments leading to the hanging in Orwell's essay are filled with 2
tension. Six tall guards, two of them armed with rifles, lead the prisoner,

continued

"a puny wisp of a man," who is both chained to their belts and handcuffed. Suddenly, the procession to the gallows is interrupted by a friendly dog that licks the prisoner's face and wags its "whole body wild with glee at finding so many human beings together." The scene is heavy with irony. In *The Green Mile*, a death-row prisoner called Del adopts a pet mouse that he names "Mr. Jingles." Del is a small, soft-spoken, endearing little man, who is able to train the mouse as if it were a very smart dog. He bonds with the tiny creature so poignantly that the silliness and brutality of his impending execution become clear. Here is a man who, literally, couldn't hurt a mouse—why not just keep him imprisoned for life?

In "A Hanging," Orwell mentions that the prisoner moves to avoid a puddle on his way to the gallows. Why does he do this if not from some innate human need to keep his dignity intact, even to the last? Seconds before he is killed, he begins "crying out to his god." The repeated "Ram! Ram! Ram!" is his own death knell. The guards grow gray, finally realizing that the hooded, faceless little man on the platform is, after all, a human being. In The *Green Mile*, Del is finally electrocuted, but the manner in which he dies provides us a painful reminder of the sacredness that capital punishment violates. Capital punishment is legal in thirty-two states and banned in the other eighteen states. Guard Percy Wetmore, a sadistic coward, is given the job of preparing Del for the chair. This involves placing a wet sponge on his head so that electricity will flow more efficiently through his body and result in less pain. Demonically, Wetmore decides to leave the sponge dry. When the switch is thrown, Del writhes in agony, his suffering beyond belief. Then, the chair bursts into flame in a scene from which viewers will want to turn away.

Interestingly, the author of "A Hanging" never tells about the crime for which the prisoner was executed. He leaves this information out intentionally. For Orwell, capital punishment is wrong, no matter the crime. A similar statement is made in *The Green Mile*. John Coffee, an

continued

African American, sits on death row, having been wrongly convicted of killing two white girls. Coffee is a giant—seven feet tall and muscular—but he is as gentle as Del and his mouse. Moreover, he has magical healing powers that he uses to cure Paul Edgecomb, the death-row superintendent, of a severe urinary infection, to bring Mr. Jingles back to life, and even to save the warden's wife from a deadly cancer. Near the end of the movie, we discover that the girls' real killer is another death-row inmate, and we hope for John Coffee's release. But it is not to be; the real killer dies without confessing. Yes, Edgecomb gives Coffee the option to escape, but the gentle giant declines, explaining that the world is just too evil and that he is just "dog tired."

Only a few moments after the execution of the Burmese prisoner, 5 Orwell's prison officials attempt to forget that they have just killed a man. They make silly jokes, smoke cigarettes, and take a drink, even though it is still early morning. *The Green Mile* ends with Paul Edgecomb, now 108 years old, recalling Coffee's execution and explaining that living to see all of his friends and relatives die is his punishment for letting Coffee go to the chair. "We each owe a death," he says. "There are no exceptions. But, Oh God, sometimes the Green Mile seems so long." Standing only a few yards away from the body, Orwell's warders pretend to ignore the horror they have committed. They are trying to hide the moon with a sheet, as my grandmother would say. At least Paul Edgecomb accepts the enormous significance of Coffee's wrongful death. And for that reason, we too can feel his pain and regret as if they were our own.

Works Cited

The Green Mile. Directed by Frank Darabont, performances by Tom Hanks, David Morse, Michael Clarke Duncan and Bonnie Hunt, Castle Rock Entertainment, 1999.
Orwell, George. "A Hanging." *George Orwell's Library*, 2021, orwell.ru/library/articles/hanging/english/e_hanging. Accessed 8 July 2021.

Altered States

Most Americans are not alcoholics. Most do not cruise city streets looking to score cocaine or heroin. Relatively few try to con their doctors into prescribing unneeded mood-altering medications. And yet, many Americans are traveling through life with their minds slightly out of kilter. In its attempt to cope with modern life, the human mind seems to have evolved some defense strategies. Confronted with inventions like television, the shopping center, and the Internet, the mind will slip—all by itself—into an altered state.   1

Never in the history of humanity have people been expected to sit passively for hours, staring at moving pictures emanating from an electronic box. Since too much exposure to flickering images of police officers, detectives, and talk-show hosts can be dangerous to human sanity, the mind automatically goes into a state of TV hypnosis. The eyes see the sitcom or the dog-food commercial, but the mind goes into a holding pattern. None of the televised images or sounds actually enter the brain. This is why, when questioned, people cannot remember commercials they have seen five seconds before or why the TV cops are chasing a certain suspect. In this hypnotic, trancelike state, the mind resembles an armored armadillo. It rolls up in self-defense, letting the stream of televised information pass by harmlessly.   2

If the TV watcher arises from the couch and goes to a shopping mall, they will again cope by slipping into an altered state. In the mall, the mind is bombarded with the sights, smells, and sounds of dozens of stores, restaurants, and movie theaters competing for its attention. There are hundreds of questions to be answered. Should I start with the upper or lower mall level? Which stores should I look in? Should I bother with the sweater sale at J. Crew? Should I eat fried chicken or try the healthier sounding Pita Wrap? Where is my car parked? To combat this mental overload, the mind goes into a state resembling the whiteout experienced by mountain climbers trapped in a blinding snowstorm. Suddenly, everything looks the same. The shopper is unsure where to go next and cannot remember what they came for in the first place. The mind enters this state deliberately so that the shopper has no choice but to leave. Some kids can be in a shopping mall for hours, but they are exceptions to the rule.   3

However, no part of everyday life so quickly triggers the mind's protective shutdown mode as that favorite pastime of the new millennium: Internet surfing. A computer user sits down with the intention of briefly checking e-mail or looking up a fact for a research paper. But once tapped into the immense storehouse of information, entertainment, and seemingly intimate personal connections that the Internet offers, the user loses all sense of time and priorities. Prospects flood the mind: Should I explore the rise of Nazi Germany? Play a trivia game? Hear the life story of a lonely stranger in Duluth? With a mind dazed with information overload, the user numbly hits one key after another, leaping from topic to topic, from   4

continued

distraction to distraction. Hours fly by as the user sits hunched over the keyboard, unable to account for the time that has passed.

These poor victims are merely trying to cope with the mind-numbing   5
inventions of modern life and are not responsible for their glazed eyes and robotic motions. People need to be aware of them and treat them with kindness and understanding. Going out of the way to bring these coma sufferers back to real life is the job of all those who have managed to avoid the side effects of television, shopping, and the Internet; otherwise, humanity will suffer.

ABOUT UNITY

1. Which sentence in paragraph 3 of "Altered States" should be omitted in the interest of paragraph unity? *(Write the opening words.)*

2. Which supporting paragraph in one of the essays lacks a topic sentence?

3. Find a sentence in one of the paragraphs of "Paying Attention to a Death" that does not belong in the essay. Write the opening words below, and explain why it doesn't belong.

ABOUT SUPPORT

4. Which idea in paragraph 2 of "Paying Attention to a Death" is not supported with details? Write the opening words below and explain how would you fix this problem.

5. In paragraph 4 of "Paying Attention to a Death," the author offers several examples to demonstrate that John Coffee is not a killer. What are they?

6. What three pieces of evidence does the writer of "Altered States" offer to support the statement that the Internet is an "immense storehouse of information, entertainment, and seemingly intimate personal connections"?

ABOUT COHERENCE

7. Find five transitions and connecting words in paragraph 3 of "Paying Attention to a Death." Remember that repeated words, pronouns, and synonyms
   can act as connectors. (*Write the five signals here.*)

   _____   _____   _____   _____   _____

8. What sentence in "Altered States" indicates that the author has used emphatic
   order, saving his most important point for last? (*Write the opening words.*)

   _____

ABOUT THE INTRODUCTION AND/OR CONCLUSION

9. Which of the two essays provides a clue to its development? Write the title
   of the essay and a brief outline of that plan below.

   _____

   _____

   _____

   _____

10. a. What method discussed in Chapter 4 is used in the conclusion of "Altered
       States"?

       _____

    b. What method discussed in Chapter 4 is used in the introduction of "Paying
       Attention to a Death"?

       _____

Developing an Essay with Emphasis on Exemplification

Considering Purpose and Audience

Use Various Types of Examples

All examples act as concrete representations of the abstract idea you are trying to communicate, but there are several kinds you can choose from depending on your purpose
and audience. Varying the types of examples will help make your writing interesting.
Readers would certainly become bored if you simply listed the different kinds of sports
or other extracurricular activities your college offers in an attempt to prove that there are
many good ways to spend your time. So, you might also include a couple of anecdotes
(brief stories) about the interesting club trips you have been on in the past year or the
fascinating people you met while planning a language-club fundraiser last semester.

Mention People, Places, Actions, and Things

Some effective examples refer to people, places, actions, and things that readers recognize or can relate to. If you wanted to prove that your town is making a strong effort to improve the environment, you might mention actions like the building of the new sewer treatment plant, the reduction in bus fares to encourage the use of public transportation, or the funding of an empty-lot cleanup project. If you were trying to prove that modern computers owe their existence to women, you might want to focus on the contributions of Grace Hopper.

Mention Facts and Events

You could use facts if you wanted to explain that ancient Athens was not a democracy in the modern sense because poor people could not participate in government, women had no voice in the affairs of the city, and Athenians owned slaves. You might discuss World War I, World War II, the Korean War, the Vietnam War, and the Persian Gulf War to prove that, in the twentieth century, Americans fought in many global conflicts.

Include Anecdotes

Anecdotes are brief, informative stories that can serve as examples. Although they are brief, they go beyond the mere mention of something and actually tell a genuine story that serves to make an abstract idea more understandable. There are several such stories in "Dad," an essay that appears later in this chapter.

Use Only Relevant Examples

Examples should always relate directly to the idea that they are being used to support. Let's say you are trying to prove that taking public transportation can sometimes be inconvenient. Telling your readers that you often read on the bus while traveling to work won't help you. In fact, being able to read while commuting is an advantage. Neither will it help to say that bus fares have risen lately. Remember that you are trying to explain the term "inconvenient," not "expensive." A better example would be the fact that three days this week the bus was so crowded you had to stand up for the entire half-hour trip.

Development through Prewriting

When Cedric, the student author of "Altered States," was considering a topic for his exemplification essay, he looked around his dorm for inspiration. He first considered writing about examples of some different types of people: athletes, musicians, math majors. Then he thought about examples of housekeeping in dorm rooms: the Slob Kingdom, the Neat Freak Room, and the Packrat's Place.

"But that evening I was noticing how my roommate acted as he was cruising the Internet," Cedric said. "He sat down to write his brother a brief e-mail, and three hours later he was still there, cruising from website to website. His eyes were glassy and he seemed out of touch with reality. It reminded me of how spaced out I get when I go to a busy shopping mall. I began to think about how our minds have to adjust to challenges that our grandparents didn't grow up with. I added 'watching television' as the third category, and I had a pretty good idea what my essay would be about."

Cedric had his three categories, but he needed to do some more work to generate supporting details for each. He used the technique of clustering, or diagramming, to help inspire his thinking. Here is what his diagram looked like:

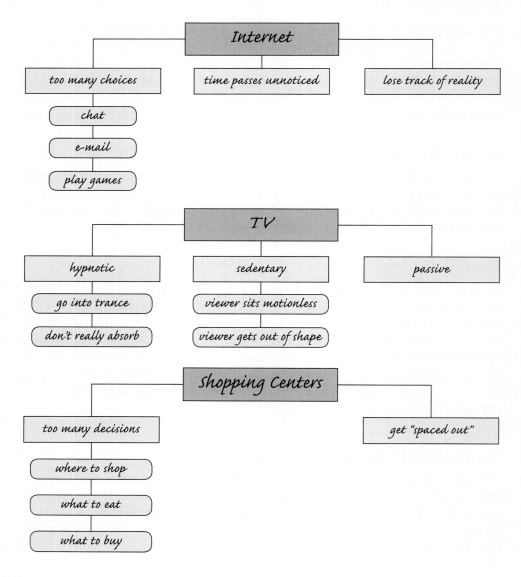

Looking at his diagram, Cedric saw that he would have no trouble supporting the thesis that people's minds go into an "altered state" when they watch TV, go to shopping centers, or use the Internet. As he quickly jotted down details in cluster form, he had easily come up with enough ideas for his essay. He started writing and produced this first draft.

First Draft

Altered States

Modern life makes demands on the human mind that no other period of history has made. As society becomes more and more complex, the mind has developed some defense mechanisms. Confronted with inventions like the Internet, television, and the shopping center, the mind will slip—all by itself—into an altered state.

Surfing the Internet can quickly make the mind slip into a strange state. A computer user sits down to check his e-mail or look up something. But once tapped into the Internet, the user loses all sense of time. He can chat with strangers, research any topic, play a game, or shop for any product. Some people begin to think of the online world and online friends as more real than the people in their own homes. While my roommate is absorbed in the Internet, he can even have brief conversations with people who come into our room, yet not be able to remember the conversations later. He sits there in a daze from information overload. He seems numb as he hits key after key, going from website to website.

Then there's TV. Growing up, our grandparents could not have imagined the idea of sitting passively for hours, staring at moving pictures emanating from a box. It's not a normal state of affairs, so the mind goes into something like a hypnotic trance. You see the sitcom or the dog-food commercial, but your mind goes into a holding pattern. You don't really absorb the pictures or sounds. Five minutes after I watch a show I can't remember commercials I've seen or why the TV cops are chasing a certain suspect.

If the TV watcher arises from the couch and journeys into the real world, he often goes to the shopping center. Here, the mind is bombarded with the sights, smells, and sounds of dozens of stores, restaurants, and movie theaters competing for its attention. Dazed shoppers begin to feel like mountain climbers trapped in a blinding snowstorm. Suddenly, everything looks the same. My father is the worst of all when it comes to shopping in an altered state. He comes back from the mall looking like he'd been through a war. After about fifteen minutes of shopping, he can't concentrate enough to know what he's looking for.

Internet surfers, TV viewers, and shoppers all have one thing in common. They're just trying to cope with the mind-numbing inventions of modern life. I hope that someday we'll turn away from such inventions and return to a simpler and more healthy way of life.

Development through Revising

Cedric showed his first-draft essay to a classmate for their critique. They returned his essay with these comments:

Jacob Lund/
Shutterstock

Reader's Comments

This seems to me like a separate topic—people's relationships with people they meet on the Internet. Sometimes you write about "a user," other times about "you," and then about "my roommate." It's confusing. Is the paragraph about your roommate on the Internet or what peole in general are like? Also, if you are talking about people in general, you should consider using "their" to be more gender neutral.

These last two sentences are good. I'd like to read more about this "altered state" you think people go into.

The idea of the "hypnotic trance" is interesting, but you need more details to back it up.

The point of view is a problem again. You skip from "you" to "I."

Altered States

Modern life makes demands on the human mind that no other period of history has made. As society becomes more and more complex, the mind has developed some defense mechanisms. Confronted with inventions like the Internet, television, and the shopping center, the mind will slip—all by itself—into an altered state.

Surfing the Internet can quickly make the mind slip into a strange state. A computer user sits down to check his e-mail or look up something. But once tapped into the Internet, the user loses all sense of time. He can chat with strangers, research any topic, play a game, or shop for any product. Some people begin to think of the online world and online friends as more real than the people in their own homes. While my roommate is absorbed in the Internet, he can even have brief conversations with people who come into our room, yet not be able to remember the conversations later. He sits there in a daze from information overload. He seems numb as he hits key after key, going from website to website.

Then there's TV. Growing up, our grandparents could not have imagined the idea of sitting passively for hours, staring at moving pictures emanating from a box. It's not a normal state of affairs, so the mind goes into something like a hypnotic trance. You see the sitcom or the dog-food commercial, but your mind goes into a holding pattern. You don't really absorb the pictures or sounds. Five minutes after I watch a show I can't remember commercials I've seen or why the TV cops are chasing a certain suspect.

If the TV watcher arises from the couch and journeys into the real world, he often goes to the shopping center. Here, the mind is bombarded with the sights, smells, and sounds of dozens of

continued

stores, restaurants, and movie theaters competing for its attention. Dazed shoppers begin to feel like mountain climbers trapped in a blinding snowstorm. Suddenly, everything looks the same. My father is the worst of all when it comes to shopping in an altered state. He comes back from the mall looking like he'd been through a war. After about fifteen minutes of shopping, he can't concentrate enough to know what he's looking for.

Good image!

I don't think this works. The essay isn't about your father. It should be about modern shoppers, not just one man.

Internet surfers, TV viewers, and shoppers all have one thing in common. They're just trying to cope with the mind-numbing inventions of modern life. I hope that someday we'll turn away from such inventions and return to a simpler and more healthy way of life.

This final sentence seems to introduce a new topic—that we shouldn't get caught up in TV and the Internet, etc.

Cedric read his classmate's comments and reviewed the essay himself. He agreed with their criticisms about point of view and the need for stronger supporting details. He also decided that the Internet was his strongest supporting point and should be saved for the last paragraph. He then wrote the final version of his essay, the version that appears at the beginning of this chapter.

A Model Essay to Consider

Read the following essay. Then answer the questions and read the comments that follow.

Dad

by Andrew H. Malcolm

The first memory I have of him—of anything, really—is his strength. It was in the 1 late afternoon in a house under construction near ours. The unfinished wood floors had large, terrifying holes whose yawning darkness I knew led to nowhere good. His powerful hands, then age thirty-three, wrapped all the way around my tiny arms, then age four, and easily swung me up to his shoulders to command all I surveyed.

The relationship between a son and his father changes over time. It may grow 2 and flourish in mutual maturity. It may sour in resented dependence or independence. With many children living in single-parent homes today, it may not even exist.

But to a little boy right after World War II, a father seemed a god with strange 3 strengths and uncanny powers enabling him to do and know things that no mortal could do or know. Amazing things, like putting a bicycle chain back on, just like that. Or building a hamster cage. Or guiding a jigsaw so it formed the letter F; I learned the alphabet that way in those pretelevision days, one letter or number every other evening plus a review of the collection. (The vowels we painted red because they were special somehow.)

He seemed to know what I thought before I did. "You look like you could 4 use a cheeseburger and a chocolate shake," he would say on hot Sunday afternoons. When, at the age of five, I broke a neighbor's garage window with a wild curveball and waited in fear for ten days to make the announcement, he seemed to know about it already and to have been waiting for something.

There were, of course, rules to learn. First came the handshake. None of those 5 fishy little finger grips, but a good firm squeeze accompanied by an equally strong gaze into the other's eyes. "The first thing anyone knows about you is your handshake," he would say. And we'd practice it each night on his return from work, the serious toddler in the battered Cleveland Indians cap running up to the giant father to shake hands again and again until it was firm enough.

When my cat killed a bird, he defused the anger of a nine-year-old with a little 6 chat about something called "instinked." The next year, when my dog got run over and the weight of sorrow was just too immense to stand, he was there, too, with his big arms and his own tears and some thoughts on the natural order of life and death, although what was natural about a speeding car that didn't stop always escaped me.

As time passed, there were other rules to learn. "Always do your best." "Do 7 it now." "NEVER LIE!" And, most important, "You can do whatever you have to do." By my teens, he wasn't telling me what to do anymore, which was scary and heady at the same time. He provided perspective, not telling me what was around the great corner of life but letting me know there was a lot more than just today and the next, which I hadn't thought of.

When the most important girl in the world—I forget her name now—turned down 8 a movie date, he just happened to walk by the kitchen phone. "This may be hard to believe right now," he said, "but someday you won't even remember her name."

One day, I realize now, there was a change. I wasn't trying to please him so 9 much as I was trying to impress him. I never asked him to come to my football games. He had a high-pressure career, and it meant driving through most of Friday night. But for all the big games, when I looked over at the sideline, there was that familiar fedora. And, by God, did the opposing team captain ever get a firm handshake and a gaze he would remember.

Then, a school fact contradicted something he said. Impossible that he could 10 be wrong, but there it was in the book. These accumulated over time, along with personal experiences, to buttress[1] my own developing sense of values. And I could tell we had each taken our own, perfectly normal paths.

I began to see, too, his blind spots, his prejudices, and his weaknesses. I never 11 threw these up at him. He hadn't to me, and, anyway, he seemed to need protection. I stopped asking his advice; the experiences he drew from no longer seemed relevant to the decisions I had to make. On the phone, he would go on about politics at times, why he would vote the way he did or why some incumbent was a jerk. And I would roll my eyes to the ceiling and smile a little, though I hid it in my voice.

He volunteered advice for a while. But then, in more recent years, politics 12 and issues gave way to talk of empty errands and, always, to ailments—his friends', my mother's, and his own, which were serious and included heart disease. He had a bedside oxygen tank, and he would ostentatiously[2] retire there during my visits, asking my help in easing his body onto the mattress. "You have very strong arms," he once noted.

From his bed, he showed me the many sores and scars on his misshapen body 13 and all the bottles of medicine. He talked of the pain and craved much sympathy. He got some. But the scene was not attractive. He told me, as the doctor had, that his condition would only deteriorate. "Sometimes," he confided, "I would just like to lie down and go to sleep and not wake up."

After much thought and practice ("You can do whatever you have to do"), 14 one night last winter, I sat down by his bed and remembered for an instant those terrifying dark holes in another house thirty-five years before. I told my father how much I loved him. I described all the things people were doing for him. But, I said, he kept eating poorly, hiding in his room, and violating other doctors' orders. No amount of love could make someone else care about life, I said: it was a two-way street. He wasn't doing his best. The decision was his.

He said he knew how hard my words had been to say and how proud he was 15 of me. "I had the best teacher," I said. "You can do whatever you have to do." He smiled a little, and we shook hands, firmly, for the last time.

Several days later, at about 4 A.M., my mother heard Dad shuffling about 16 their dark room. "I have some things I have to do," he said. He paid a bundle of bills. He composed for my mother a long list of legal and financial what-to-do's "in case of emergency." And he wrote me a note.

Then he walked back to his bed and laid himself down. He went to sleep, 17 naturally. And he did not wake up.

---

[1]*buttress:* strengthen and support.
[2]*ostentatiously:* dramatically.

ABOUT UNITY

1. What is the thesis of Malcolm's essay, "Dad"? (*Write the first words.*)

   _____

2. Which statement would best serve as a topic sentence for paragraph 6?
   a. My dad loved my dog as much as I did.
   b. Pets were a subject that drew my dad and me together.
   c. My dad helped me make sense of life's tragedies.
   d. I was angry at my cat for killing a bird.

3. Write a sentence that might serve as the topic sentence of paragraph 10.

   _____

ABOUT SUPPORT

4. List the details Malcolm uses in paragraph 3 to support the idea that his father "seemed a god with strange strengths and uncanny powers."

   _____

   _____

   _____

5. With which sentence does Malcolm support his statement in paragraph 14 that his father "wasn't doing his best"? (*Write the opening words.*)

   _____

6. What point or idea does the anecdote in paragraph 8 support?

   _____

ABOUT COHERENCE

7. What event makes Malcolm begin to see his father in more realistic, less idealized terms?

   _____

8. In paragraph 6, find each of the following:
   a. two time-transition signals

   _____   _____

   b. one addition-transition signal

   _____

   c. one change-of-direction transition signal

   _____

9. Which method of organization does Malcolm use in his essay?

   a. time order

   b. emphatic order

ABOUT THE INTRODUCTION AND/OR CONCLUSION

10. The conclusion of "Dad" is made up of

    a. a summary of the narrative and a final thought.

    b. a quotation about fatherhood.

    c. the last event of the story about Malcolm and his father.

    d. a prediction of what kind of father Malcolm hopes to be himself.

Writing an Essay with Emphasis on Exemplification

WRITING ASSIGNMENT 1

In this assignment, write an essay that exemplifies how you best learn and should study.

PREWRITING

a. Using whatever prewriting method works best for you, write down past experiences, both good and bad, of studying for tests. Note what made the experiences positive and negative.

b. Visit http://www.vark-learn.com and click on "Questionnaire." Complete the questionnaire to discover what type of learner you are. Once you have determined your type, click on "Helpsheets" to read about studying suggestions geared toward that type.

c. In order to properly present the information you have gathered, read Chapter 19, "Writing a Source-Based Essay," and Chapter 20, "Writing a Research Essay," paying attention to how to write your information and how to avoid plagiarism.

d. Using all the information you have gathered, write a topic sentence that introduces your learner type and what it means. Sample topic sentences have been provided to get you started:

   • After reading the VARK website, I understand that I am a Read/Write learner and to be successful, I need to employ specific study skills.

   • I always struggled in school because I was terrible at studying, but since I now know that I am a kinesthetic learner, I have a better idea of how I should study.

James Woodson/Getty Images

Jacob Lund/
Shutterstock

e. Write the first draft of your essay and support your thesis sentence by incorporating a definition of your study type, facts from the helpsheets, and examples or anecdotes from past studying experiences.

REVISING

After you have completed the first draft of the paper, set it aside for a while if you can. When you review it, try to do so as critically as you would if it were not your own work. Better yet, read it aloud to a friend or classmate whose judgment you trust. As you read, use the questions in the FOUR BASES Checklist at the end of this chapter as a guide to help you revise.

As you revise your essay through one or more additional drafts, continue to refer to that checklist until you can answer "yes" to each question.

WRITING ASSIGNMENT 2

Academic

Write an essay that emphasizes exemplification based upon an outside reading. It might be a selection recommended by your instructor, or it might be a piece by one of the following authors, all of whom have written books of essays that should be available in your college library.

Malcolm Gladwell	Anna Quindlen
Ellen Goodman	Marilynne Robinson
bell hooks	Richard Rodriguez
Aldous Huxley	Amy Tan
Molly Ivins	Deborah Tannen
Maxine Hong Kingston	Henry David Thoreau
Gabriel Garcia Marquez	Calvin Trillin
Vladimir Nabokov	Alice Walker
George Orwell	Marie Winn
Cynthia Ozick	Virginia Woolf
Ann Patchett	Jenny Zhang

Base your essay on an idea in the selection you have chosen, and provide a series of examples to back up your idea. Of course, you may want to draw information from the reading selection by quoting from it or making other types of references. However, you might also use examples from other sources, perhaps something else you have read, a movie you have seen, or a personal experience. You may want to review Chapter 19, "Writing a Source-Based Essay," and Chapter 20, "Writing a Research Essay," to help you properly report and document the author's original information.

The student literary analysis essay, "Paying Attention to a Death," in the beginning of the chapter offers a model essay for this assignment.

Writing for a Specific Purpose and Audience

WRITING ASSIGNMENT 3

In this essay that emphasizes exemplification, you will write with a specific purpose and for a specific audience. Your essay should present a strong explanation to your boss about exactly what you do on a daily basis and why you should be given a raise. Strive to incorporate as many specific examples of the tasks you perform every day and describe why you are good at them. For instance, perhaps you work at an animal shelter and clean kennels every day, and you have streamlined the process to be quicker and less stressful on the animals. Possibly you work as a UPS package handler and have figured out a better route plan for your territory. You may want to review Chapter 8, "Description," to help you provide specific details explaining what your daily duties are. You may also want to check Chapter 16, "Argument," to help you create a persuasive tone to your essay.

Exemplification Checklist: THE FOUR BASES

ABOUT *UNITY*

✔ Have I included a thesis statement that illustrates the topic I am going to discuss?

✔ Are there portions of the essay that do not support my thesis and therefore should be eliminated or rewritten?

ABOUT *SUPPORT*

✔ Have I included enough vivid details that will help my readers understand the point I am trying to make?

✔ Does my conclusion clearly tie up the essay and explain why my topic is significant?

ABOUT *COHERENCE*

✔ Does each paragraph support a topic sentence that connects to the thesis?

✔ Do transitional words and phrases, and linking sentences between paragraphs, help readers follow my train of thought?

ABOUT *SENTENCE SKILLS*

✔ Have I used a consistent point of view throughout my essay?

✔ Have I used specific rather than general words?

✔ Have I avoided wordiness and used concise wording?

✔ Are my sentences varied?

✔ Have I edited for spelling and other sentence skills errors, as listed in the checklist at the back of the book?

READING

p. 261: Malcolm, Andrew. "Dad." *New York Times,* January 8, 1984. Reprinted by permission of the author.

Process

Write an essay that informs a reader about how to perform a particular hobby or activity you enjoy. Depending on the hobby or activity you are writing about, you may prefer to use a humorous approach.
Dragon Images/Shutterstock

This chapter will explain and illustrate how to

- **develop an essay with emphasis on process**
- **write an essay with emphasis on process**
- **revise an essay with emphasis on process**

In addition, you will read and consider

- **two student essays that emphasize process**
- **one professional model essay that emphasizes process**

Every day we perform many activities that are *processes,* that is, series of steps carried out in a definite order. Many of these processes are familiar and automatic: for example, loading film into a camera, diapering a baby, or making an omelet. We are thus seldom aware of the sequence of steps making up each activity. In other cases—for example, when someone asks us for directions to a particular place, or when we try to read and follow directions to build an IKEA set of Billy bookcases—we may be painfully conscious of the whole series of steps involved in the process.

In this chapter, you will be asked to write an essay with emphasis on process—one that explains clearly how to do or make something.

To prepare for this assignment, you should first read the student papers and the model essay and then answer the questions that follow them.

Student Essays to Consider

Marketing Plan: Happy Child Preschool

Happy Child Preschool is a valuable and cherished part of our campus,   1
but enrollment has declined dramatically over the past two years. Thus,
a task force was commissioned to analyze the causes. The comparative
analysis conducted by the task force uncovered numerous ways that other
campus childcare centers have achieved success through marketing.
The task force agrees that promotion is the number one issue that has
been overlooked in the past and the area where major and immediate
improvements are essential to the long-term success of the center. In order
to effectively market the preschool, promoting the center needs to remain
at the top of the priority chart and should include proper advertising,
publicity, and referrals.

The first step is proper advertising that must start with a well-designed   2
multi-layered website that includes general information, enrollment forms,
and profiles of teachers and staff. The general information page should
contain the hours of operation, location, and contact information. The top
of the page should include a banner with scrolling photos of children and
staff at the center. Underneath the banner, several links, including the
enrollment forms and profiles, should be prominently placed. Having a
direct link to online enrollment and other business forms will encourage
potential families to enroll because families can fill out the application
forms when it is convenient for them, not when the center is open. Making
the application process easier than the current process should increase
interest. The page with teacher profiles is a great place to bring attention
to our quality educators. Including pictures, background information,
and education will help promote our facility because all the teachers at
our center are highly qualified. All of this information will demonstrate
our strengths and help potential families appreciate the top quality of
education our center provides.

Publicity could include a monthly column in the local newspaper   3
that highlights what is currently going on at the preschool. Because our

continued

curriculum is a blend of Montessori and Carden methods, we have a unique offering; calling attention to the special achievements, programs, and students in our school would offer the positive publicity needed to interest potential families. Each column's publication should be followed by an open house, so potential families can actually visit our school. These open houses should also occur during key enrollment periods to encourage greater attendance. In addition, hosting one or two major events will continue to raise awareness of our school within the community.

The final and best way to increase enrollment is to utilize our   4
currently enrolled families. Word-of-mouth is one of the best ways to increase enrollment. Families who are pleased with their children's schools are often more than happy to tell others. Offering referral rewards to families will help encourage families to tell others about the school. The task force looked at several referral programs and determined that a program that offers families monetary rewards that are applied to monthly fees would be a cost-effective program. Partnering with local colleges' education programs would also be a cost-effective program.

By putting these approaches into place, we project that our enrollment   5
should increase to capacity within the next two years. These key components have been overlooked in the past, so we are hopeful that the committee will accept this new direction. It will play a significant role in the future of the success of the school.

How to Complain

I'm not just a consumer—I'm a victim. If I order a product, it is sure to   1
arrive in the wrong color, size, or quantity. If I hire people to do repairs, they never arrive on the day scheduled. If I owe a bill, the computer program is bound to overcharge me. Therefore, in self-defense, I have developed the following consumer's guide to complaining effectively.

The first step is getting organized. I save all sales slips and original   2
boxes. Also, I keep a special file for warranty cards and appliance guarantees. This file does not prevent a product from falling apart the day after the guarantee runs out. One of the problems in our country is the shoddy workmanship that goes into many products. However, these facts give me the ammunition I need to make a complaint. I know the date of the purchase, the correct price (or service charge), where the item was purchased, and an exact description of the product, including model and

continued

serial numbers. When I compose my letter of complaint, I find it is not necessary to exaggerate. I just stick to the facts.

The next step is to send the complaint to the person who will get results quickly. My experience has shown that the president of the company is the best person to contact. I call the company to find out the president's name and make sure I note the proper spelling. Then I write directly to that person, and I usually get prompt action. For example, the head of AMF arranged to replace my son's ten-speed "lemon" when it fell apart piece by piece in less than a year. Another time, the president of a Philadelphia department store finally had a twenty-dollar overcharge on my bill corrected after I had spent three months arguing uselessly with a computer program.   3

If I get no response to a written complaint within ten days, I follow through with a personal telephone call. When I had a new bathtub installed a few years ago, the plumber left a gritty black substance on the bottom of the tub. No amount of scrubbing could remove it. I tried every cleanser on the supermarket shelf, but I still had a dirty tub. The plumber shrugged off my complaints and said to try Comet. The manufacturer never answered my letter or e-mail. Finally, I made a personal phone call to the president of the firm. Within days a well-dressed executive showed up at my door. In a business suit, white shirt, striped tie, and rubber gloves, he cleaned the tub. Before he left, he scolded me in an angry voice, "You didn't have to call the president." The point is, I did have to call the president. No one else cared enough to solve the problem.   4

Therefore, my advice to consumers is to keep accurate records, and if a complaint needs to be made, they should go right to the top. It has always worked for me.   5

QUESTIONS 1

ABOUT UNITY

1. The (fill in the correct answer: first, second, third) _____ supporting paragraph of "Marketing Plan" lacks a topic sentence. Write a topic sentence that expresses its main point:

   _____

   _____

2. Which sentence in paragraph 4 of "Marketing Plan" should be omitted in the interest of paragraph unity? (Write the opening words.)

   _____

   _____

3. Which sentence in paragraph 2 of "How to Complain" should be omitted in the interest of paragraph unity? (*Write the opening words.*)

_____

ABOUT SUPPORT

4. Which sentence in paragraph 3 of "Marketing Plan" needs more supporting details? (*Write the opening words.*)

_____

5. Which supporting paragraph in "How to Complain" uses one extended example? Write the number of that paragraph and tell (in just a few words) what the example was about.

_____

_____

6. Which supporting paragraph in "How to Complain" depends on two short examples? Write the number of that paragraph and tell (in just a few words) what each example was about.

_____

_____

ABOUT COHERENCE

7. Paragraph 3 of "Marketing Plan" uses several transitions. Which two types of transitions are they? _____

List them here: _____

8. In "How to Complain" what transitions are used to maintain coherence between paragraphs 1 and 2? _____

Between paragraphs 2 and 3? _____

ABOUT THE INTRODUCTION AND/OR CONCLUSION

9. Which method for writing introductions discussed in Chapter 4 is used in "Marketing Plan"?

_____

10. Which method for writing conclusions discussed in Chapter 4 is used in "Marketing Plan"?

_____

Developing an Essay with Emphasis on Process

Considering Purpose and Audience

Glance at a newsstand and you'll see magazine cover stories with titles such as "How to Impress Your Boss," "How to Add Romance to Your Life," or "How to Dress Like a Movie Star." These articles promise to give readers directions or information they can follow; they are popular versions of essays that emphasize process.

In general, essays that emphasize process explain the steps involved in a particular action, process, or event. Some of these essays focus on giving readers actual instructions, others provide information, and still others focus on persuading readers. The type of essay you write depends on the specific topic and purpose you choose.

Begin by asking yourself what you want your readers to know. If, for example, you want your audience to know how to make the ultimate chocolate chip cookie, your essay would include directions telling them what to do and how to do it. On the other hand, if you want your readers to know how a cookie is digested, you would detail the events in the body as it turns food into energy.

No matter what your main purpose, keep your audience in mind as you work. As with any essay, select a topic that will interest readers. A group of college students, for example, might be interested in reading an essay that explains how and why to get financial aid but be bored by an essay on how and why to plan for retirement.

Finally, evaluate how much your readers already know about your topic. An audience unfamiliar with your topic might require you to explain technical terms. If you are explaining how to protect your computer from viruses, for example, you might have to define "firewall." If you are explaining how to check a car's tire pressure, you might have to describe a pressure gauge.

Deciding on Structure, Content, and Style

- As with other types of papers, include a thesis. Your thesis might explain your purpose—why it is important to learn how to change the oil in your car or why learning to prepare a room for painting is worth knowing. On the other hand, it might explain something definitive about the process. For example, you might begin a paper on the digestive process by stating that "the human body is a truly marvelous machine." Then, of course, you would have to show just how marvelous it is as you explain how it digests food.

- Use language that is easy to follow and not unnecessarily complex. If you are explaining how to do something, your readers may be executing your instructions as they read them for the first time. So be as clear as you can to avoid unintentionally misleading the reader.

- In most cases, list each step in chronological or time order. (See the final section of Chapter 3 for words that signal time.)

- Explain each step in a separate paragraph. If two steps are done or occur simultaneously, connect separate paragraphs with phrases such as "At the same time."

- When giving information about a process, use the right verb tense. If you are explaining something that happened only once, use the past tense: "After Mount Vesuvius erupted, it covered the city of Pompeii with pumice and ash." However, if you are discussing something that recurs, use the present tense: "During the next phase of digestion, food passes down the esophagus to the stomach."

- If you are presenting information, as in the examples about Pompeii and digestion above, you should always write in the formal third person. If you are writing directions (something this book does), you may write in the second person, directly addressing your audience as "you," or in the third person. It's important to remember that the second person should be used very sparingly.

> For more information about third- and second-person points of view, see Chapter 7.

TIP

Development through Prewriting

An essay that emphasizes process requires the writer to think through the steps involved in an activity. As Meghan, the author of "How to Complain," thought about possible topics for her essay, she asked herself, "What are some things I do methodically, step by step?" A number of possibilities occurred to her, including getting herself and her children ready for school in the morning and shopping for groceries (from preparing a shopping list to organizing her coupons), and the one she finally settled on: effective complaining. "People tell me I'm 'so organized' when it comes to getting satisfaction on things I buy," Meghan said. "I realized that I do usually get results when I complain because I go about complaining in an organized way. To write my essay, I just needed to put those steps into words."

Meghan began by making a list of the steps she follows when she makes a complaint. This is what she wrote:

> Save sales slips and original boxes
>
> Engrave items with ID number in case of burglary
>
> Write or e-mail letter of complaint
>
> Save or make photocopy of letter
>
> Create file of warranties and guarantees
>
> Send complaint letter directly to president
>
> Call company for president's name
>
> Follow through with telephone call if no response
>
> Make thank-you call after action is taken

Next, she numbered those steps in the order in which she performs them. She struck out some items she realized weren't really necessary to the process of complaining:

> 1 Save sales slips and original boxes
>
> ~~Engrave items with ID number in case of burglary~~
>
> 4 Write or e-mail letter of complaint
>
> ~~Save or make photocopy of letter~~
>
> 2 Create file of warranties and guarantees
>
> 5 Send complaint letter directly to president
>
> 3 Call company for president's name
>
> 6 Follow through with telephone call if no response
>
> ~~Make thank-you call after action is taken~~

Next, she decided to group her items into three steps: (1) getting organized, (2) sending the complaint to the president, and (3) following up with further action.

With that preparation done, Meghan wrote her first draft.

First Draft

How to Complain

Because I find that a consumer has to watch out for herself and be ready to speak up if a product or service isn't satisfactory, I have developed the following consumer's guide to complaining effectively.

The first step is getting organized. I save all sales slips, original boxes, warranty cards, and appliance guarantees. This file does not prevent a product from falling apart the day after the guarantee runs out. One of the problems in our country is the shoddy workmanship that goes into many products. That way I know the date of the purchase, the correct price, where the item was purchased, and an exact description of the product.

The next step is to send the complaint to the person who will get results quickly. I call the company to find out the president's name and then I write directly to that person. For example, the head of AMF arranged to replace my son's bike. Another time, the president of a Philadelphia department store finally had a twenty-dollar overcharge on my bill corrected.

If I get no response to a written complaint within ten days, I follow through with a personal telephone call. When I had a new bathtub installed a few years ago, the plumber left a gritty black substance on the bottom of the tub. I tried everything to get it off. Finally, I made a personal phone call to the president of the firm. Within days a well-dressed executive showed up at my door. In a business suit, white shirt, striped tie, and rubber gloves, he cleaned the tub. Before he left, he said, "You didn't have to call the president."

Therefore, my advice to consumers is to keep accurate records, and when you have to complain, go right to the top. It has always worked for me.

Development through Revising

After she had written the first draft, Meghan set it aside for several days. When she reread it, she was able to look at it more critically. These are her comments:

I think this first draft is OK as the "bare bones" of an essay, but it needs to be fleshed out everywhere. For instance, in paragraph 2, I need to explain why it's important to know the date of purchase etc. And in paragraph 3, I need to explain more about what happened with the bike and the department store overcharge. In paragraph 4, especially, I need to explain

continued

> _how_ I tried to solve the problem with the bathtub before I called the president. I want to make it clear that I don't immediately go to the top as soon as I have a problem—I give the people at a lower level a chance to fix it first. All in all, my first draft looks as if I just rushed to get the basic ideas down on paper. Now I need to take the time to back up my main points with better support.

With that self-critique in mind, Meghan wrote the version of "How to Complain" that appears at the beginning of this chapter.

A Model Essay to Consider

Read the following essay. Then answer the questions and read the comments that follow.

How to Do Well on a Job Interview

by Glenda Davis

Ask a random selection of people for a listing of their least favorite activities, and right up there with "getting my teeth drilled" is likely to be "going to a job interview." The job interview is often regarded as a confusing, humiliating, and nerve-racking experience. First of all, you have to wait for your appointment in an outer room, often trapped there with other people applying for the same job. You sit nervously, trying not to think about the fact that only one of you may be hired. Then you are called into the interviewer's office. Faced with a complete stranger, you have to try to act both cool and friendly as you are asked all sorts of questions. Some questions are personal: "What is your greatest weakness?" Others are confusing: "Why should we hire you?" The interview probably takes about twenty minutes but seems like two hours. Finally, you go home and wait for days and even weeks. If you get the job, great. But if you don't, you're rarely given any reason why.

The job-interview "game" may not be much fun, but it is a game you _can_ win if you play it right. The name of the game is standing out of the crowd—in a positive way. If you go to the interview in a clown suit, you'll stand out of the crowd, all right, but not in a way that is likely to get you hired.

Here are guidelines to help you play the interview game to win:

Present yourself as a winner. Instantly, the way you dress, speak, and move gives the interviewer more information about you than you would think possible.

You doubt that this is true? Consider this: a professional job recruiter, meeting a series of job applicants, was asked to signal the moment he decided *not* to hire each applicant. The thumbs-down decision was often made *in less than forty-five seconds—even before the applicant thought the interview had begun.*

How can you keep from becoming a victim of an instant "no" decision?   5

- *Dress appropriately.* This means business clothing: usually a suit and tie or a conservative dress or skirt suit. Don't wear casual student clothing. On the other hand, don't overdress: you're going to a job interview, not a party. If you're not sure what's considered appropriate business attire, do some spying before the interview. Walk past your prospective place of employment at lunch or quitting time and check out how the employees are dressed. Your goal is to look as though you would fit in with that group of people.

- *Pay attention to your grooming.* Untidy hair, body odor, dandruff, unshined shoes, a hanging hem, stains on your tie, excessive makeup or cologne, a sloppy job of shaving—if the interviewer notices any of these, your prospect of being hired takes a probably fatal hit.

- *Look alert, poised, and friendly.* When that interviewer looks into the waiting room and calls your name, he or she is getting a first impression of your behavior. If you're slouched in your chair, dozing or lost in the pages of a magazine; if you look up with an annoyed "Huh?"; if you get up slowly and wander over with your hands in your pockets, the interviewer will not be favorably impressed. What *will* earn you points is rising promptly and walking briskly toward the interviewer. Smiling and looking directly at that person, extend your hand to shake theirs, saying, "I'm Regina Brown. Thank you for seeing me today."

- *Expect to make a little small talk.* This is not a waste of time; it is the interviewer's way of checking your ability to be politely sociable, and it is your opportunity to cement the good impression you've already made. The key is to follow the interviewer's lead. If the interviewer wants to chat about the weather for a few minutes, do so. But don't drag it out; as soon as you get a signal that it's time to talk about the job, be ready to get down to business.

Be ready for the interviewer's questions. The same questions come up again and 6
again in many job interviews. *You should plan ahead for all these questions!* Think carefully about each question, outline your answer, and memorize each outline. Then practice reciting the answers to yourself. Only in this way are you going to be prepared. Here are common questions, what they really mean, and how to answer them:

- *"Tell me about yourself."* This question is raised to see how organized you are. The *wrong* way to answer it is to launch into a wandering, disjointed response or—worse yet—to demand defensively, "What do you want to know?" or "What do you mean?" When this question comes up, you should be prepared to give a brief summary of your life and work experience—where you grew up, where your family lives now, where you went to school, what jobs you've had, and how you happen to be here now looking for the challenge of a new job.

- *"What are your strengths and weaknesses?"* In talking about your strong points, mention traits that will serve you well in this particular job. If you are well organized, a creative problem-solver, a good team member, or a quick learner, be ready to describe specific ways those strengths have served you in the past. Don't make the mistake of saying, "I don't have any real weaknesses." You'll come across as more believable if you admit a flaw—but make it one that an employer might actually like. For instance, admit that you are a workaholic or a perfectionist.

- *"Why should we hire you?"* Remember that it is up to *you* to convince the interviewer that you're the person for this job. If you just sit there and hope that the interviewer will magically discern your good qualities, you are likely to be disappointed. Don't be afraid to sell yourself. Tell the recruiter that from your research you have learned that the interviewer's company is one you would like to work for, and that you believe the company's needs and your skills are a great match.

- *"Why did you leave your last job?"* This may seem like a great opportunity to cry on the interviewer's shoulder about what a jerk your last boss was or how unappreciated you were. It is not. The experts agree: never bad-mouth *anyone* when you are asked this question. Say that you left in order to seek greater responsibilities or challenges. Be positive, not negative. No matter how justified you may feel about hating your last job or boss, if you give voice to those feelings in an interview, you're going to make the interviewer suspect that you're a whiner and hard to work with.

- *"Do you have any questions?"* This is the time to stress one last time how interested you are in this particular job. Ask a question or two about specific aspects of the job, pointing out again how well your talents and the company's needs are matched. Even if you're dying to know how much the job pays and how much vacation you get, don't ask. There will be time enough to cover those questions after you've been offered the job. Today, your task is to demonstrate what a good employee you would be.

Send a thank-you note. Once you've gotten past the interview, there is one   7
more chance for you to make a fine impression. As soon as you can—certainly no more than one or two days after the interview—write a note of thanks. In it, briefly remind the interviewer of when you came in and what job you applied for. As well as thanking the interviewer for seeing you, reaffirm your interest in the job and mention again why you think you are the best candidate for it. Make the note courteous, businesslike, and brief—just a paragraph or two. If the interviewer

is wavering between several equally qualified candidates, such a note could tip the scales in your favor.

No amount of preparation is going to make interviewing for a job your favorite 8 activity. But if you go in well-prepared and with a positive attitude, your potential employer can't help thinking highly of you. And the day will come when you are the one who wins the job.

ABOUT UNITY

1. Either of two sentences in "How to Do Well on a Job Interview" might serve as the thesis. Write the opening words of either of these sentences:

   _____

   _____

   _____

2. Which statement would make the best topic sentence for paragraph 4?
   a. Beauty is only skin-deep.
   b. Interviewers care only about how applicants dress.
   c. Professional job recruiters meet many applicants for a single job.
   d. You should present yourself as a winner because first impressions count a lot.

3. Write an appropriate topic sentence for the list item that talks about strengths and weaknesses in paragraph 6.

   _____

   _____

ABOUT SUPPORT

4. What does the author mean by "dress appropriately" in paragraph 5?

   _____

5. According to Davis, what is the best reason for sending a thank-you note?

   _____

   _____

ABOUT COHERENCE

6. In paragraph 1, what three transitional words or phrases are used to begin sentences as the author describes the process of interviewing?

   _____   _____   _____

7. The main method of organization of paragraph 1 is
   a. time order.
   b. emphatic order.

8. Find three change-of-direction signals in the listed items following paragraph 5. (*Write them here.*)

   _____   _____   _____

   ABOUT THE INTRODUCTION AND/OR CONCLUSION

9. Which statement best describes the introductory paragraph of "How to Do Well on a Job Interview"?
   a. It begins with a broad, general statement about job interviews and narrows it down to the thesis statement.
   b. It describes a typical job interview and its aftermath.
   c. It explains the importance of doing well on a job interview.
   d. It ends with a quotation about the importance of preparing for an interview.

10. What method for writing conclusions explained in Chapter 4 does Davis use?

Writing an Essay with Emphasis on Process

WRITING ASSIGNMENT 1

michaeljung/123RF

Everyone is an expert at something. Using your personal experiences and insights, write an essay with an emphasis on process. If you are a parent, you might write about how you taught your children to read. If you work as a sales representative, you might write about how monthly sales quotas are met. If you are a recovering addict, you might write about how the twelve-step recovery process works. If you know how to cook well, you could write about what it takes to make one of your favorite dishes. As a college student, you might write about how the registration process works at your school. Each of these topics will require you to incorporate several modes of writing, such as those discussed in Chapter 8, "Description," and Chapter 9, "Narration."

PREWRITING

a. Choose a prewriting technique that works for you, and for ten minutes use that technique to generate ideas on the topic you have tentatively chosen. Don't worry about spelling, grammar, organization, or anything other than getting your thoughts down on the page. If ideas are still flowing at the end of ten minutes, keep on writing. Once you have finished getting your thoughts down, you should have a base of raw material that you can draw on in the next phase of your work. Judging from what you have produced, do you think you have enough material to support your essay? If so, keep following the steps below. If not, choose another topic and spend about ten minutes generating ideas to see if this other topic might be a better choice.

b. Develop a single clear sentence that will serve as your thesis. Your thesis should demonstrate why it is important that your readers know about this process.

c. Make a list of the steps you are describing.

d. Number your items in time order. Strike out items that do not fit in the list; add others as they occur to you.

e. After making the list, decide how the items can be grouped into a minimum of three steps. With a topic like "How to Raise Kind Children," you might divide the process into (1) infancy and toddlerhood; (2) elementary years; and (3) teen years.

f. Use your list as a guide to write the first rough draft of your paper. Do not expect to finish your paper in one draft. You should be ready to write a series of drafts as you work toward the goals of unity, support, and coherence.

REVISING

After you have completed the first draft of the paper, set it aside for a while if you can. Then read the paper out loud to a friend or classmate whose judgment you respect. Keep in mind the points and questions in the FOUR BASES Checklist at the end of this chapter. Ask your friend to respond to them as well.

As you revise your essay through one or more additional drafts, continue to refer to the checklist until you can answer "yes" to each question.

Jacob Lund/
Shutterstock

WRITING ASSIGNMENT 2

Write an essay in which you explain how something has happened or happens rather than how to do something. Focus on a limited subject. The topic you choose may be assigned by your instructor, or it may require your instructor's approval. For example, instead of trying to discuss the workings of the U.S. government, explain the process by which a bill presented in Congress eventually becomes law. Instead of explaining how World War II happened, focus on the events that led to America's involvement. You may want to check Chapter 12, "Cause and/or Effect," Chapter 19, "Writing a Source-Based Essay," and Chapter 20, "Writing a Research Essay," for additional ways to support your thesis.

Here are other topics you might choose to explain:

- the process for conducting clinical trials of a new prescription drug
- how a virus can become a pandemic
- how a student theater production happens
- how a company like Apple became so profitable

PREWRITING

a. Select a topic you know a lot about. However, if necessary, gather more detail by reading about your topic in the library or on the Internet. Before researching, use freewriting, listing, or some other information-gathering technique to write down all the information and ideas in your head. This will help you remember what information should be cited and what information is your personal knowledge.

b. If you do need to do research, remember to check Chapter 19, "Writing a Source-Based Essay," and Chapter 20, "Writing a Research Essay," to properly cite your information and avoid plagiarism.

c. Look over your notes and make a list of steps involved in the process.

d. Organize your list to be chronological and orderly.

e. You have just prepared the beginnings of a scratch outline. Finish the outline by filling in information under each main point. Then use this outline as a guide as you write the first drafts of your paper.

REVISING

As you read through your first draft and subsequent drafts, ask yourself the questions in the FOUR BASES Checklist at the end of this chapter.

As you revise your essay through one or more additional drafts, continue to refer to this checklist until you can answer "yes" to each question.

Writing for a Specific Purpose and Audience

Many jobs require people to provide reports that make recommendations. In this essay, you will write a report that analyzes and explains a process at your job and proposes a better, more effective process. For example, you could analyze the hiring process and suggest ways to make it more efficient, or you could analyze the process a restaurant customer's order goes through and propose ways to get the food to the customer more quickly. You may want to check Chapter 16, "Argument," to help you create a persuasive tone to your essay.

Process Checklist: THE FOUR BASES

ABOUT *UNITY*

✔ Have I included a thesis statement that clearly identifies the process I am going to discuss?

✔ Does my essay describe the steps in a clear, logical way?

✔ Are there portions of the essay that do not support my thesis and therefore should be eliminated or rewritten?

ABOUT *SUPPORT*

✔ Does my essay describe the necessary steps so that a reader could perform the task described?

✔ Is essential information that could help the reader understand the process missing?

ABOUT *COHERENCE*

✔ Have I organized my essay in a consistent manner that is appropriate to my subject?

✔ Do I have a concluding paragraph that provides a summary of the process, a final thought about the process, or both?

ABOUT *SENTENCE SKILLS*

✔ Have I used a consistent point of view throughout my essay?

✔ Have I used specific rather than general words?

✔ Have I avoided wordiness and used concise wording?

✔ Are my sentences varied?

✔ Have I edited for spelling and other sentence skills errors, as listed in the checklist at the back of the book?

READING

p. 278: Davis, Glenda, "How to Do Well on a Job Interview." Used by permission of Townsend Press.

Cause and/or Effect

Write an essay in which you discuss the causes or effects of our society's fascination with reality TV. An essay on the causes would discuss why Americans are so intrigued with reality television shows. An essay on the effects would show how this fascination with reality TV has affected American society.
FOX/Getty Images

This chapter will explain and illustrate how to

- **develop an essay with emphasis on cause and/or effect**
- **write an essay with emphasis on cause and/or effect**
- **revise an essay with emphasis on cause and/or effect**

In addition, you will read and consider

- **two student essays that emphasize cause and/or effect**
- **one professional model essay that emphasizes cause and/or effect**

Why did Emma decide to move out of her parents' house? What made you quit a well-paying job? Why are horror movies so popular? Why has Benjamin missed so many classes? Why did our team fail to make the league play-offs?

Every day we ask questions like these and look for answers. We realize that many actions do not occur without causes, and we realize also that a given action can have a series of effects—good or bad. By examining the causes or effects of an action, we seek to understand and explain things that happen in our lives.

You will be asked in this chapter to do some detective work by examining the cause of something or the effects of something. First read the student essays and the model essay that follow and work through the questions that accompany the essays. All three essays support their thesis statements by explaining a series of causes or a series of effects.

Student Essays to Consider

The Joys of an Old Car

Some of my friends can't believe that my car still runs. Others laugh when they see it parked outside the house and ask if it's an antique. But they aren't being fair to my twenty-year-old Toyota Camry. In fact, my "antique" has opened my eyes to the rewards of owning an old car.   1

One obvious reward of owning my old Toyota is economy. Twenty years ago, when my husband and I were newly married and nearly broke, we bought the car—a shiny red year-old leftover—for a mere $5,000. Today it would cost four times as much. We save money on insurance, since it's no longer worthwhile for us to have collision coverage. Old age has even been kind to the Toyota's engine, which has required only three major repairs in the last several years. And it still delivers twenty-eight miles per gallon in the city and forty-one on the highway—not bad for such a mature machine!   2

I've heard that when a Toyota passes the twenty-thousand-mile mark with no problems, it will probably go on forever. I wouldn't disagree. Our Toyota breezed past that mark many years ago. Since then, I've been able to count on it to sputter to life and make its way down the driveway on the coldest, snowiest mornings. When my boss got stuck with his brand-new BMW in the worst snowstorm of the year, I sauntered into work on time. The single time my Toyota didn't start, unfortunately, was the day I had a final exam. The Toyota may have the body of an old car, but beneath its elderly hood hums the engine of a teenager.   3

Last of all, having the same car for many years offers the advantage of familiarity. When I open the door and slide into the driver's seat, the soft vinyl surrounds me like a well-worn glove. I know to the millimeter exactly how much room I have when I turn a corner or back into a curbside parking space. When my gas gauge points to "empty," I know that 1.3 gallons are still in reserve, and I can plan accordingly. The front wheels invariably   4

continued

begin to shake when I go more than sixty-five miles an hour, reminding me that I am exceeding the speed limit. With the Toyota, the only surprises I face come from other drivers.

I prize my twenty-year-old Toyota's economy and dependability, and most of all, its familiarity. It is faded, predictable, and comfortable, like a well-worn pair of jeans. And, like a well-worn pair of jeans, it will be difficult to throw away.

5

The Only Thing We Have to Fear

During the Great Depression, President Roosevelt claimed, "The only thing we have to fear is fear itself." He wanted to inspire citizens as a way to spur the economy. In his Nobel Prize acceptance speech delivered in December 1950, William Faulkner, the great American novelist, said, "The basest of all things is to be afraid." Uttered many decades ago, both these ideas still have relevance. Some young people make important life decisions based on deep-seated anxieties. They fear that they won't be accepted by others, that they won't find a mate, or that they just aren't living life to the fullest. As a result, they pervert their identities, becoming adults they don't want to become and living lives they never intended.

1

A logical question is why so many people spend money—often money they don't have—on costly toys they don't need. Deep in the pits of their stomachs is the gnawing fear that, without such toys, their friends will abandon them and they will have to sit home weekends watching sitcom reruns. They are frightened they won't fit in, so frightened, in fact, that they have become blind to the true meaning of friendship. They have forgotten that, to those of character, possessions and image are far less important than integrity, honesty, and compassion. Such people are worth knowing, and they are everywhere. To find them, all people need to do is to show a little character themselves.

2

Some individuals fear they will never be able to attract and keep a lifelong partner. Therefore, they make gargantuan efforts to re-create themselves in the Hollywood image. For example, they follow ludicrous diets, exercise for hours each day, and drink expensive commercial concoctions to curb their appetites and lose weight. Some even become anorexic. Others, looking ahead to their more mature years, plan to get collagen injections, hair plugs, and even breast implants. If people simply trusted in the goodness of someone who might love them for who they are and not for the smoothness of their skins or the fullness of their hair, their lives could be so much easier.

3

continued

However, the fear that causes the greatest damage to the human   4
spirit is the one that makes people question the value and fullness of their
own lives. Too many—young and old alike, if the truth be told—are afraid
that they might miss out on "the good life," which, the media tells us, is
part of a life fulfilled. Influenced by the glitz of Hollywood and Madison
Avenue, people equate happiness with owning the best of everything.
So, they take a second and even a third job to afford the sexiest car, the
biggest house, or the largest flat screen. This is the worst perversion of
all, for it robs human beings of their humanity. They don't own the car, the
house, the television; they are owned by the possessions. It cannot be
called anything but servitude. The irony is, of course, that, in seeking the
good life, people have lost the good life. Instead of having the luxury to
relax at home, talk to family, enjoy dinner, go for long walks, or watch the
sun set, too many people are rushing off to an evening of more work to
pay off the bills.

Cowering to silly fears, getting and taking, or changing to fit in with the   5
ridiculous images created by a plastic society is harmful, and it is blurring
American's moral vision. People need to realize once more that the true
source of happiness, the measure of a life fulfilled, is the ability to see
eternal beauty in the night sky, to become inspired by gently falling snow,
and to make those ever important human connections.

QUESTIONS 1

ABOUT UNITY

1. Which supporting paragraph in "The Joys of an Old Car" lacks a topic sentence?

   a. 2

   b. 3

   c. 4

2. Which sentence in paragraph 3 of "The Joys of an Old Car" should be omitted in the interest of paragraph unity? (*Write the opening words.*)

   _____

3. Rewrite the thesis statement of "The Joys of an Old Car" to include a plan of development.

   _____

   _____

ABOUT SUPPORT

4. In paragraph 3 of "The Only Thing We Have to Fear," how does the author support the idea that some people are afraid they won't be able to attract and keep lifelong partners?

   _____

   _____

   _____

5. After which sentence in paragraph 2 of "The Only Thing We Have to Fear" is more detail needed? (*Write the first words here.*)

   _____

6. In "The Joys of an Old Car," what examples support the topic sentence in paragraph 2?

   _____

   _____

   _____

   _____

ABOUT COHERENCE

7. Which sentence in "The Only Thing We Have to Fear" serves as a linking sentence between paragraphs? (*Write the first words.*)

   _____

8. Paragraph 3 of "The Only Thing We Have to Fear" contains two transitional words or phrases. List those words or phrases.

   _____   _____

9. What are the two transition words or phrases in "The Joys of an Old Car" that signal two major points of support for the thesis?

   _____   _____

ABOUT THE INTRODUCTION AND/OR CONCLUSION

10. Which method for concluding essays explained in Chapter 4 does "The Joys of an Old Car" use?

    a. summary and final thought

    b. thought-provoking question

    c. recommendation

Developing an Essay with Emphasis on Cause and/or Effect

Considering Purpose and Audience

The primary purpose of an essay that emphasizes cause and/or effect is to support your main point by using examples that explain (1) the causes of a particular event or situation; (2) the effects of an event or a situation; or more rarely (3) a combination of both.

The type of essay you write depends on your topic and main point. If you want to tell readers the impact a person had on your life, your essay would focus on *effects*. If you want to explain why you moved out of your family home, it would focus on *causes*.

Essays that emphasize cause and/or effect are like essays that emphasize process. However, while process explains how something happens, cause and/or effect discusses *the reasons for or results of* an event or situation. Exams in science, history, economics, and other courses include questions that demand the explanation of causes, effects, or both. For example, you might be asked to explain the economic causes of the Russian Revolution or the atmospheric effects of cutting down trees in the rain forest.

At first, this can seem simple. However, analyzing causes and effects is often complicated. For example, in the essay, "The Only Thing We Have to Fear," the writer claims that many young people desire to possess the same type of clothing or electronic gadgets that their friends have. This stems from an *ultimate* or primary cause: the fear of being alone. A more *proximate* cause (one that is closer to the effect) is the desire to be popular, part of a group. In short, the writer has not simply discussed a cause but has explained a causal chain: (1) fear of being alone (ultimate cause); (2) desire to be popular (proximate cause); (3) need to have what others have (effect). Of course, the author could have extended the chain to explain the cause behind the fear of being alone: low self-esteem, difficult family life, or peer pressure, for example.

Analyzing effects can also be tricky because one cause may lead to multiple effects. In addition, one cause may yield a long-term effect as well as an immediate effect. Take the case of a young construction worker who decided to go back to college to study architecture five years after having graduated from high school. The immediate effects of the worker's decision include (1) having to budget money more carefully to compensate for no longer being employed full-time; (2) having less time to socialize with friends; and (3) getting a lot less physical exercise. However, there are several long-term effects as well: (1) securing a high-paying position after graduation; (2) making new friends at college and at the new job; and

(3) developing new tastes in music and film as a result of taking college humanities courses.

Depending on your topic and purpose, you can decide whether to focus on causes or effects. If you want to balance your paper, you can discuss both. Consider each of the following scenarios and decide whether it requires discussing causes, effects, or both.

1. A young couple decides to buy a two-family house and rent out the top floor to tenants.

2. A new television reality show becomes an instant sensation, and the "actors" achieve instant fame.

3. Residents of an assisted living facility meet with administrators to address the increase in residents' fees.

Students writing on the first item might focus on effects; those writing on the second might discuss causes. The third item might be approached by writing about both.

Whichever approach you choose, remember that you can't discuss effects without at least mentioning causes, and vice versa. While discussing the problems that the young couple had with their tenants (effects of their decision to rent out the top floor), you might also explain their reason for becoming landlords in the first place: to earn rent money that would help them meet their mortgage payments.

As with all essays, pick a topic that appeals to your readers. An essay on the negative effects of steroids on professional athletes may interest sports fans; it might not appeal to people who dislike sports. In addition, make your main point clear so that your audience can follow the cause-and-effect relationship. You might even announce specific causes or effects by signaling them to readers: "One effect steroid use has on athletes is to . . ."

Development through Prewriting

The best essays are often those written about a topic that the author genuinely cares about. When Scarlett, the author of "The Joys of an Old Car," was assigned an essay with emphasis on cause and/or effect, she welcomed the assignment. She explains, "My husband and I believe in enjoying what we have and living simply, rather than 'keeping up with the Joneses.' Our beat-up old car is an example of that way of life. People often say to me, 'Surely you could buy a nicer car!' I enjoy explaining to them why we keep our old 'clunker.' So when I heard 'essay that emphasizes cause and/or effect,' I immediately thought of the car as a topic. Writing this essay was just an extension of a conversation I've had many times."

Although Scarlett had often praised the virtues of her old car to friends, she wasn't sure how to divide what she had to say into three main points. To get started, she made a list of all the good things about her car. Here is what she wrote:

Starts reliably

Has needed few major repairs

Reminder of Bill's and my first days of marriage

Gets good gas mileage

Don't need to worry about scratches and scrapes

I know exactly how much room I need to turn and park

Saves money on insurance

I'm very comfortable in it

No car payments

Cold weather doesn't seem to bother it

Don't worry about its being stolen

Can haul anything in it—dog, plants—and not worry about dirt

Know all its little tics and shimmies and don't worry about them

When Scarlett reviewed her list, she saw that the items fell into three major categories. They were (1) the car's economy; (2) its familiarity; and (3) its dependability. She went back and noted which category each of the items best fit. Then she crossed out those items that didn't seem to belong in any of the categories.

3   Starts reliably

1   Has needed few major repairs

~~Reminder of Bill's and my first days of marriage~~

1   Gets good gas mileage

~~Don't need to worry about scratches and scrapes~~

continued

2	*I know exactly how much room I need to turn and park*
1	*Saves money on insurance*
2	*I'm very comfortable in it*
1	*No car payments*
3	*Cold weather doesn't seem to bother it*
	~~Don't worry about its being stolen~~
	~~Can haul anything in it—dog, plants—and not worry about dirt~~
2	*Know all its little tics and shimmies and don't worry about them*

Now Scarlett had three main points and several items to support each point. She produced this as a first draft:

First Draft

The Joys of an Old Car

When people see my beat-up old car, they sometimes laugh at it. But I tell them that owning a twenty-year-old Toyota has its good points.

One obvious reward is economy. My husband and I bought the car when we were newly married. We paid $5,000 for it. That seemed like a lot of money then, but today we'd spend four times that much for a similar car. We also save money on insurance. In the twenty years we've had it, the Toyota has needed only a few major repairs. It even gets good gas mileage.

I like the familiar feel of the car. I'm so used to it that driving anything else feels very strange. When I visited my sister recently, I drove her new Prius to the grocery store. Everything was so unfamiliar! I couldn't even figure out how to turn on the radio. I was relieved to get back to my own car.

Finally, my car is very dependable. No matter how cold and snowy it is, I know the Toyota will start quickly and get me where I need to go. Unfortunately, one day it didn't start, and naturally that day I had a final exam. But otherwise it just keeps on going and going.

My Toyota reminds me of a favorite piece of clothing that you wear forever and can't bear to throw away.

Jacob Lund/
Shutterstock

Development through Revising

Scarlett traded first drafts with a classmate, KeShawn, and each critiqued the other's work before it was revised. Here is Scarlett's first draft again, with KeShawn's comments in the margins.

Reader's Comments

How? Is the insurance less expensive just because the car is old?

Here would be a good place for a specific detail—how good is the mileage?

This topic sentence doesn't tie in with the others—shouldn't it say "Second," or "Another reason I like the car. . . ."?

This is too much about your sister's car and not enough about yours.

This is a good comparison. But draw it out more—how is the car like comfortable old clothes?

The Joys of an Old Car

When people see my beat-up old car, they sometimes laugh at it. But I tell them that owning a twenty-year-old Toyota has its good points.

One obvious reward is economy. My husband and I bought the car when we were newly married. We paid $5,000 for it. That seemed like a lot of money then, but today we'd spend four times that much for a similar car. We also save money on insurance. In the twenty years we've had it, the Toyota has needed only a few major repairs. It even gets good gas mileage.

I like the familiar feel of the car. I'm so used to it that driving anything else feels very strange. When I visited my sister recently, I drove her new Prius to the grocery store. Everything was so unfamiliar! I couldn't even figure out how to turn on the radio. I was relieved to get back to my own car.

Finally, my car is very dependable. No matter how cold and snowy it is, I know the Toyota will start quickly and get me where I need to go. Unfortunately, one day it didn't start, and naturally that day I had a final exam. But otherwise it just keeps on going and going.

My Toyota reminds me of a favorite piece of clothing that you wear forever and can't bear to throw away.

Making use of KeShawn's comments, Scarlett wrote the final version of "The Joys of an Old Car" that appears at the beginning of this chapter.

A Model Essay to Consider

Read the following essay. Then answer the questions and read the comments that follow.

Shame

by Dick Gregory

I never learned hate at home, or shame. I had to go to school for that. I was about 1
seven years old when I got my first big lesson. I was in love with a little girl named
Helene Tucker, a light-complexioned little girl with pigtails and nice manners. She
was always clean and she was smart in school. I think I went to school then mostly
to look at her. I brushed my hair and even got me a little old handkerchief. It was a
lady's handkerchief, but I didn't want Helene to see me wipe my nose on my hand.
The pipes were frozen again, there was no water in the house, but I washed my socks
and shirt every night. I'd get a pot, and go over to Mister Ben's grocery store, and
stick my pot down into his soda machine. Scoop out some chopped ice. By evening
the ice melted to water for washing. I got sick a lot that winter because the fire
would go out at night before the clothes were dry. In the morning I'd put them on,
wet or dry, because they were the only clothes I had.

Everybody's got a Helene Tucker, a symbol of everything you want. I loved her 2
for her goodness, her cleanness, her popularity. She'd walk down my street and my
brothers and sisters would yell, "Here comes Helene," and I'd rub my tennis sneakers on the back of my pants and wish my hair wasn't so nappy and the white folks'
shirt fit me better. I'd run out on the street. If I knew my place and didn't come too
close, she'd wink at me and say hello. That was a good feeling. Sometimes I'd follow
her all the way home, and shovel the snow off her walk and try to make friends with
her Momma and her aunts. I'd drop money on her stoop late at night on my way
back from shining shoes in the taverns. And she had a Daddy, and he had a good
job. He was a paper hanger.

I guess I would have gotten over Helene by summertime, but something happened 3
in that classroom that made her face hang in front of me for the next twenty-two
years. When I played the drums in high school it was for Helene and when I broke
track records in college it was for Helene and when I started standing behind micro-
phones and heard applause I wished Helene could hear it, too. It wasn't until I was
twenty-nine years old and married and making money that I finally got her out of my
system. Helene was sitting in that classroom when I learned to be ashamed of myself.

It was on a Thursday. I was sitting in the back of the room, in a seat with a chalk 4
circle drawn around it. The idiot's seat, the troublemaker's seat.

The teacher thought I was stupid. Couldn't spell, couldn't read, couldn't do arith- 5
metic. Just stupid. Teachers were never interested in finding out that you couldn't

concentrate because you were so hungry, because you hadn't had any breakfast. All you could think about was noontime, would it ever come? Maybe you could sneak into the cloakroom and steal a bite of some kid's lunch out of a coat pocket. A bite of something. Paste. You can't really make a meal of paste, or put it on bread for a sandwich, but sometimes I'd scoop a few spoonfuls out of the big paste jar in the back of the room. Pregnant people get strange tastes. I was pregnant with poverty. Pregnant with dirt and pregnant with smells that made people turn away, pregnant with cold and pregnant with shoes that were never bought for me, pregnant with five other people in my bed and no Daddy in the next room, and pregnant with hunger. Paste doesn't taste too bad when you're hungry.

The teacher thought I was a troublemaker. All she saw from the front of the room was a little black boy who squirmed in his idiot's seat and made noises and poked the kids around him. I guess she couldn't see a kid who made noises because he wanted someone to know he was there. 6

It was on a Thursday, the day before the Negro payday. The eagle always flew on Friday. The teacher was asking each student how much his father would give to the Community Chest. On Friday night, each kid would get the money from his father, and on Monday he would bring it to the school. I decided I was going to buy a Daddy right then. I had money in my pocket from shining shoes and selling papers, and whatever Helene Tucker pledged for her Daddy I was going to top it. And I'd hand the money right in. I wasn't going to wait until Monday to buy me a Daddy. 7

I was shaking, scared to death. The teacher opened her book and started calling out names alphabetically. 8

"Helene Tucker?" 9

"My Daddy said he'd give two dollars and fifty cents." 10

"That's very nice, Helene. Very, very nice indeed." 11

That made me feel pretty good. It wouldn't take too much to top that. I had almost three dollars in dimes and quarters in my pocket. I stuck my hand in my pocket and held on to the money, waiting for her to call my name. But the teacher closed her book after she called everybody else in the class. 12

I stood up and raised my hand. 13

"What is it now?" 14

"You forgot me?" 15

She turned toward the blackboard. "I don't have time to be playing with you, Richard." 16

"My Daddy said he'd . . ." 17

"Sit down, Richard, you're disturbing the class." 18

"My Daddy said he'd give . . . fifteen dollars." 19

She turned around and looked mad. "We are collecting this money for you and your kind, Richard Gregory. If your Daddy can give fifteen dollars you have no business being on relief." 20

"I got it right now, I got it right now, my Daddy gave it to me to turn in today, my Daddy said . . ." 21

"And furthermore," she said, looking right at me, her nostrils getting big and 22
her lips getting thin and her eyes opening wide, "we know you don't have a Daddy."

Helene Tucker turned around, her eyes full of tears. She felt sorry for me. Then 23
I couldn't see her too well because I was crying, too.

"Sit down, Richard."   24

And I always thought the teacher kind of liked me. She always picked me to 25
wash the blackboard on Friday, after school. That was a big thrill; it made me feel
important. If I didn't wash it, come Monday the school might not function right.

"Where are you going, Richard!"   26

I walked out of school that day, and for a long time I didn't go back very often. 27
There was shame there.

Now there was shame everywhere. It seemed like the whole world had been 28
inside that classroom, everyone had heard what the teacher had said, everyone had
turned around and felt sorry for me. There was shame in going to the Worthy Boys
Annual Christmas Dinner for you and your kind, because everybody knew what a
worthy boy was. Why couldn't they just call it the Boys Annual Dinner—why'd they
have to give it a name? There was shame in wearing the brown and orange and white
plaid mackinaw[1] the welfare gave to three thousand boys. Why'd it have to be the
same for everybody so when you walked down the street the people could see you
were on relief? It was a nice warm mackinaw and it had a hood, and my Momma
beat me and called me a little rat when she found out I stuffed it in the bottom of a
pail full of garbage way over on Cottage Street. There was shame in running over to
Mister Ben's at the end of the day and asking for his rotten peaches, there was shame
in asking Mrs. Simmons for a spoonful of sugar, there was shame in running out to
meet the relief truck. I hated that truck, full of food for you and your kind. I ran into
the house and hid when it came. And then I started to sneak through alleys, to take
the long way home so the people going into White's Eat Shop wouldn't see me. Yeah,
the whole world heard the teacher that day—we all know you don't have a Daddy.

It lasted for a while, this kind of numbness. I spent a lot of time feeling sorry for 29
myself. And then one day I met this wino in a restaurant. I'd been out hustling all
day, shining shoes, selling newspapers, and I had googobs of money in my pocket.
Bought me a bowl of chili for fifteen cents, and a cheeseburger for fifteen cents, and
a Pepsi for five cents, and a piece of chocolate cake for ten cents. That was a good
meal. I was eating when this old wino came in. I love winos because they never hurt
anyone but themselves.

The old wino sat down at the counter and ordered twenty-six cents worth of food. 30
He ate it like he really enjoyed it. When the owner, Mister Williams, asked him to pay
the check, the old wino didn't lie or go through his pocket like he suddenly found a hole.

He just said: "Don't have no money."   31

The owner yelled: "Why in hell did you come in here and eat my food if you 32
don't have no money? That food cost me money."

---

[1]*mackinaw:* a short, heavy woolen coat, usually plaid and double-breasted.

Mister Williams jumped over the counter and knocked the wino off his stool 33 and beat him over the head with a pop bottle. Then he stepped back and watched the wino bleed. Then he kicked him. And he kicked him again.

I looked at the wino with blood all over his face and I went over. "Leave him 34 alone, Mister Williams. I'll pay the twenty-six cents."

The wino got up, slowly, pulling himself up to the stool, then up to the counter, 35 holding on for a minute until his legs stopped shaking so bad. He looked at me with pure hate. "Keep your twenty-six cents. You don't have to pay, not now. I just finished paying for it."

He started to walk out, and as he passed me, he reached down and touched my 36 shoulder. "Thanks, sonny, but it's too late now. Why didn't you pay it before?"

I was pretty sick about that. I waited too long to help another man.   37

QUESTIONS 2

ABOUT UNITY

1. Which of the following statements best represents the main idea of the selection?
   a. Richard felt that being poor was humiliating.
   b. Helene Tucker was a symbol of everything Richard wanted.
   c. Richard had to work hard as a child.
   d. The "wino" refused Richard's money.

2. What is the topic sentence for paragraph 2? (*Write the opening words.*)

   _____

ABOUT SUPPORT

3. In paragraphs 1 and 2, Gregory mentions several steps he took to impress Helene Tucker. What were they?

   _____

   _____

   _____

4. This essay is about Gregory's experience growing up. What is the main effect he discusses? What are some of the causes?

   The main effect _____

   The main cause _____

   _____

   A second cause _____

   _____

5. In paragraphs 5 and 6, Gregory explains his teacher thought he was stupid and a troublemaker because he couldn't read, spell, or do arithmetic, would squirm in his seat, and sometimes ate paste. What were the real causes of his inability to do well on assignments and sit still?

_____

_____

_____

ABOUT COHERENCE

6. Which method of organization does Gregory use in his essay?
   a. Time order
   b. Emphatic order

7. Gregory repeats a phrase at the beginning of two paragraphs as a way of emphasizing the importance of the incident. Which paragraphs start with the phrase, and what it is?

_____

8. How many times does Gregory use the word *shame* in paragraph 28? What effect does it have?

_____

_____

ABOUT THE INTRODUCTION AND/OR CONCLUSION

9. Which method best describes the introduction to "Shame"?
   a. quotation
   b. idea that is the opposite of the one to be developed
   c. anecdote
   d. broad, general statement narrowing to thesis

10. At the end of the essay, Gregory shifts his focus from the classroom to the scene involving the "wino" at the restaurant. What is the connection between this closing scene and the rest of the essay?

_____

_____

_____

_____

Writing an Essay with Emphasis on Cause and/or Effect

Are you as good a writer as you want to be? Write an essay analyzing the reasons you have become a good writer or explaining why you are not as good as you'd like to be. Begin by considering some factors that may have influenced your writing ability.

Your family background: Did you see people writing at home? What were the attitudes toward writing in your home?

Your school experience: Did you have good writing teachers? Did you have a history of failure or success with writing? Was writing fun, or was it a chore? Did your school emphasize writing?

Social influences: What were your friends' attitudes toward writing? What feelings about writing did you pick up from your friends? From social media? From shows or movies?

PhotoAlto/Sigrid Olsson/Getty Images

You might want to organize your essay by describing the three greatest influences on your skill (or your lack of skill) as a writer. Show how each of these has contributed to the present state of your writing. You will want to check Chapter 16, "Argument," to help create a persuasive and effective essay.

PREWRITING

a. Choose a prewriting technique that works for you, and for ten minutes use that technique to generate ideas. Don't worry about spelling, grammar, organization, or anything other than getting your thoughts down on the page. If ideas are still flowing at the end of ten minutes, keep on writing. Once you have finished getting your thoughts down, you should have a base of raw material that you can draw on in the next phase of your work. Judging from what you have produced, do you think you have enough material to support your essay? If so, keep following the steps below. If not, plan to spend at least another ten minutes generating additional ideas.

b. Develop a single clear sentence that will serve as your thesis. Your thesis should demonstrate how you feel about your writing and why.

c. Decide whether you will support each of your main points with short examples or one extended example.

d. Write a first draft of an introduction that attracts the reader's interest, states your thesis, and presents a plan of development.

REVISING

After you have completed the first draft of the paper, set it aside for a while (if possible). Then read it aloud to a friend or classmate. As you listen to your words, you should keep in mind the questions in the FOUR BASES Checklist at the end of this chapter. As you revise your essay through one or more additional drafts, continue to refer to that checklist until you can answer "yes" to each question.

Jacob Lund/
Shutterstock

WRITING ASSIGNMENT 2

Write an essay in which you advance an idea about a poem, story, play, film, literary essay, or novel. The work you choose may be assigned by your instructor or may require your instructor's approval. To develop your idea, use a series of two or more reasons and specific evidence for each reason. You may want to check Chapter 8, "Description," Chapter 18, "Summarizing and Paraphrasing," and Chapter 20, "Writing a Research Essay," to properly present and cite your information. The following student essay is a literary analysis of a short story by Willa Cather. In this essay, the student looks at the causes of a character's suicide and provides support with specific examples from the story.

Paul's Suicide

Paul, the main character in Willa Cather's short story, "Paul's Case," is a   1
young man on a collision course with death. As Cather reveals Paul's story,
we learn about elements of Paul's personality that inevitably come together
and cause his suicide. Paul takes his own life as a result of his inability to
conform to his society, his passive nature, and his emotional isolation.

First of all, Paul cannot conform to the standards of his own society.   2
At school, Paul advertises his desire to be part of another, more
glamorous world by wearing fancy clothes that set him apart from the
other students. At home on Cordelia Street, Paul despises everything
about his middle-class neighborhood. He hates the houses "permeated
by kitchen odors," the "ugliness and commonness of his own home," and
the respectable neighbors sitting on their front stoops every Sunday,
"their stomachs comfortably protruding." Paul's father hopes that Paul will
settle down and become like the young man next door, a nearsighted
clerk who works for a corporate steel magnate. Paul, however, is repelled
by the young man and all he represents. It seems inevitable, then, that
Paul will not be able to cope with the office job his father obtains for him
at the firm of Denny & Carson; and this inability to conform will, in turn,
lead to Paul's theft of $1,000.

Paul's suicide is also due, in part, to his passive nature. Throughout   3
his life, Paul has been an observer and an onlooker. Paul's only escape
from the prison of his daily life comes from his job as an usher at
Pittsburgh's Carnegie Hall; he lives for the moments when he can watch
the actors, singers, and musicians. However, Paul has no desire to *be* an
actor or musician. As Cather says, "What he wanted was to see, to be in
the atmosphere, float on the wave of it, to be carried out . . . away from
everything." Although Paul steals the money and flees to New York, these
uncharacteristic actions underscore the desperation he feels. Once at

continued

the Waldorf in New York, Paul is again content to observe the glamorous world he has craved for so long: "He had no especial desire to meet or to know any of these people; all he demanded was the right to look on and conjecture, to watch the pageant." During his brief stay in the city, Paul enjoys simply sitting in his luxurious rooms, glimpsing the show of city life through a magical curtain of snow. At the end, when the forces of ordinary life begin to close in again, Paul kills himself. But it is typical that he does not use the gun he has bought. Rather, more in keeping with his passive nature, Paul lets himself fall under the wheels of a train.

Finally, Paul ends his life because he is emotionally isolated. Throughout   4
the story, not one person makes any real contact with Paul. His teachers do not understand him and merely resent the attitude of false bravado that he uses as a defense. Paul's mother is dead; he cannot even remember her. Paul is completely alienated from his father, who obviously cares for him but who cannot feel close to this withdrawn, unhappy son. To Paul, his father is only the man waiting at the top of the stairs, "his hairy legs sticking out of his nightshirt," who will greet him with "inquiries and reproaches." When Paul meets a college boy in New York, they share a night on the town. But the "champagne friendship" ends with a "singularly cool" parting. Paul is not the kind of person who can let himself go or confide in one of his peers. For the most part, Paul's isolation is self-imposed. He has drifted so far into his fantasy life that people in the "real" world are treated like invaders. As he allows no one to enter his dream, there is no one Paul can turn to for understanding.

The combination of these personality factors—inability to conform,   5
passivity, and emotional isolation—makes Paul's tragic suicide inevitable. Before he jumps in front of the train, Paul scoops a hole in the snow and buries the carnation that he has been wearing in his buttonhole. Like a hothouse flower in the winter, Paul has a fragile nature that cannot survive in its hostile environment.

Writing for a Specific Purpose and Audience

WRITING ASSIGNMENT 3

OPTION 1

Assume that there has been a series of large cuts in your school district's budget. What might be the causes of the cuts? Where are the cuts mostly taking place? Spend some time thinking about possible causes. Then, as a principal or superintendent, write a letter to the families in your school district explaining the causes of the cuts and the decisions behind what areas were affected. Your purpose is to provide information to the families so they understand the resulting cuts.

OPTION 2

Alternatively, think about how severe school district budget cuts would have an impact on your family. Write a letter to the principal or superintendent explaining how you see the consequences of the budget cuts affecting your family and the community at large. Your purpose is to provide administrators with useful information that may be used to persuade the school board to rethink where the budget has been cut.

David Schaffer/Caiaimage/Getty Images

Cause and/or Effect Checklist: THE FOUR BASES

ABOUT *UNITY*

✓ Do I have a thesis that is narrow and focused, and contains a claim about the causes and/or effects of my topic?

✓ Are there portions of the essay that do not support my thesis and therefore should be eliminated or rewritten?

ABOUT *SUPPORT*

✓ Have I backed up each main point with one extended example or several shorter examples?

✓ Do my examples clearly support the cause, the effect, or both?

✓ Are there any repetitive areas that need to be revised?

ABOUT *COHERENCE*

✓ Have I organized my essay in a manner that clearly expresses whether this is a cause, an effect, or both?

✓ Do I have a concluding paragraph that effectively supports and completes my essay?

ABOUT *SENTENCE SKILLS*

✓ Have I used a consistent point of view throughout my essay?

✓ Have I used specific rather than general words?

✓ Have I avoided wordiness and used concise wording?

✓ Are my sentences varied?

✓ Have I edited for spelling and other sentence skills errors, as listed in the checklist at the back of the book?

READING

p. 297: "Shame." From Dick Gregory, *Nigger: An Autobiography*. Copyright ©1964 by Dick Gregory Enterprises.

13

Comparison and/or Contrast

This chapter will explain and illustrate how to

- develop an essay with emphasis on comparison and/or contrast

- write an essay with emphasis on comparison and/or contrast

- revise an essay with emphasis on comparison and/or contrast

In addition, you will read and consider

- two student essays that emphasize comparison and/or contrast

- one professional model essay that emphasizes comparison and/or contrast

Thomas Imo/Alamy Stock Photo

Looking at the two photographs above, write an essay in which you compare or contrast in-person classes with online learning.

insta_photos/Shutterstock

Comparison and contrast are two thought processes we go through constantly in everyday life. When we *compare* two things, we show how they are similar; when we *contrast* two things, we show how they are different. We may compare or contrast two brand-name products (for example, Pepsi and Coca-Cola), two television shows, two cars, two teachers, two jobs, two friends, or two possible solutions to a problem we are facing. The purpose of comparing or contrasting is to understand each of the two things more clearly and, at times, to make judgments about them.

You will be asked in this chapter to write an essay that emphasizes comparison and/or contrast. To prepare for this assignment, first read about the two methods of development you can use in writing your essay. Then read the first student essay; the student literary analysis essay; and the model essay that follow and work through the questions that accompany the essays.

Methods of Development

An essay that emphasizes comparison and/or contrast calls for one of two types of development. Details can be presented *one side at a time* or *point by point*. Each format is illustrated below.

One Side at a Time

Look at the following supporting paragraph from "A Vote for McDonald's," one of the model essays that will follow.

For one thing, going to the Chalet is more difficult than going to McDonald's. The Chalet has a jacket-and-tie rule, which means I have to dig a sport coat and tie out of the back of my closet, make sure they're semiclean, and try to steam out the wrinkles somehow. The Chalet also requires reservations. Since it is downtown, I have to leave an hour early to give myself time to find a parking space within six blocks of the restaurant. The Chalet cancels reservations if a party is more than ten minutes late. Going to McDonald's, on the other hand, is easy. I can feel comfortable wearing my jeans or warm-up suit. I don't have to do any advance planning. I can leave my house whenever I'm ready and pull into a doorside parking space within fifteen minutes.

The first half of this paragraph fully explains one side of the contrast (the difficulty of going to the Chalet). The second half of the paragraph deals entirely with the other side (the ease of going to McDonald's). When you use this method, be sure to follow the same order of points of contrast (or comparison) for each side. An outline of the paragraph shows how the points for each side are developed in a consistent sequence.

Outline

One Side at a Time

Thesis: Going to the Chalet is more difficult than going to McDonald's.

1. Chalet

   a. Dress code

   b. Advance reservations

   c. Leave an hour early

   d. Find parking space

2. McDonald's

   a. Casual dress

   b. No reservations

   c. Leave only fifteen minutes ahead of time

   d. Plenty of free parking

Point by Point

Now look at the supporting paragraph below, which is taken from a student literary analysis essay you will read, "The Lone Ranger and Tonto Fistfight with Smoke Signals":

The book and film both illustrate how desperately Victor desires his father's love. *Smoke Signals* shows this desire only through Victor's eyes, whereas *The Lone Ranger and Tonto Fistfight in Heaven* uses the collective stories and emotions of the residents on the reservation to show that Victor's desires are shared by many. In "Because My Father Always Said He Was the Only Indian Who Saw Jimi Hendrix Play 'The Star Spangled Banner' at Woodstock," the reader sees Victor's

continued

pain and longing as he sits at his drunken father's feet while listening to Hendrix. In "A Train Is an Order of Occurrence Designed to Lead to Some Result," the reader's emotions are once again tugged as Samuel, isolated and distanced from his children, lies down in front of an oncoming train. These incidents demonstrate that the father-son connection is not just Victor's problem, but a reservation problem. Like most of the book's characters, Victor doesn't have a moment of enlightenment, a true happy ending. Instead, he continues to fumble through a series of good and bad moments, much as might happen in real life. In contrast, the film focuses only on Victor's path to enlightenment from broken-hearted angry boy needing his father to a healed mature adult. With the help of the humorous Thomas, Victor travels to Phoenix to claim his father's belongings. After Victor is given his father's ashes, he realizes the anger he has clung to so tightly for fifteen years has been self-defeating. He lets the anger go and experiences a rebirth. The Victor that returns to the reservation is a new person and a man.

The paragraph contrasts a short story collection and a film point by point. The following outline illustrates the point-by-point method.

Point by Point   **Outline**

Thesis: Through Victor's story, the reader and the viewer are introduced to complex situations and emotions experienced by American Indians, but the book conveys a more comprehensive picture than the film.

1. *Victor's desire for his father's love*

    a. *Book*

    b. *Film*

2. *Victor's journey from child to adult*

    a. *Book*

    b. *Film*

When you begin writing an essay that emphasizes comparison and/or contrast, you should decide right away which format you will use: one side at a time or point by point. Use that format as you create the outline for your paper. Remember that an outline is an essential step in planning and writing a clearly organized paper.

Student Essays to Consider

A Vote for McDonald's

For my birthday this month, my wife has offered to treat me to dinner   1
at the restaurant of my choice. I think she expects me to ask for a meal at
the Chalet, the classiest, most expensive restaurant in town. However, I'm
going to eat my birthday dinner at McDonald's. When I compare the two
restaurants, the advantages of eating at McDonald's are clear.

For one thing, going to the Chalet is more difficult than going to   2
McDonald's. The Chalet has a jacket-and-tie rule, which means I have to
dig a sport coat and tie out of the back of my closet, make sure they're
semiclean, and try to steam out the wrinkles somehow. The Chalet also
requires reservations. Since it is downtown, I have to leave an hour
early to give myself time to find a parking space within six blocks of the
restaurant. The Chalet cancels reservations if a party is more than ten
minutes late. Going to McDonald's, on the other hand, is easy. I can feel
comfortable wearing my jeans or warm-up suit. I don't have to do any
advance planning. I can leave my house whenever I'm ready and pull into
a doorside parking space within fifteen minutes.

The Chalet is a dimly lit, formal place. While I'm struggling to see what's   3
on my plate, I worry that I'll knock one of the fragile glasses off the table.
The waiters at the Chalet can be uncomfortably formal, too. As I awkwardly
pronounce the French words on the menu, I get the feeling that I don't
quite live up to their standards. Even the other diners can make me feel
uncomfortable. And though the food at the Chalet is gourmet, I prefer
simpler meals. I don't like unfamiliar food swimming in a pasty white sauce.
Eating at the Chalet is, to me, less enjoyable than eating at McDonald's.
McDonald's is a pleasant place where I feel at ease. It is well lit, and the
bright-colored decor is informal. The employees serve with a smile, and
the food is easy to pronounce and identify. I know what I'm going to get
when I order a certain type of sandwich.

The most important difference between the Chalet and McDonald's,   4
though, is price. Dinner for two at the Chalet, even without appetizers or
desserts, would easily cost $100. And the $100 doesn't include the cost
of parking the car and tipping the waiter, which can come to an additional
$20. Once, I forgot to bring enough money. At McDonald's, a filling meal
for two will cost around $15. With the extra $105, my wife and I can eat
at McDonald's seven more times, or go to the movies five times, or buy
tickets to a local theater production.

So, for my birthday dinner, or any other time, I prefer to eat at   5
McDonald's. It is convenient, friendly, and cheap. And with the money my
wife saves by taking me to McDonald's, she can buy me what I really want
for my birthday—a new Sears power saw.

The Lone Ranger and Tonto Fistfight with Smoke Signals

Sherman Alexie's short story collection, *The Lone Ranger and Tonto*   1
Fistfight in Heaven, and the film, *Smoke Signals*, also written by Alexie,
expose what life is like on an Indian reservation in the twentieth century.
Both the book and the film feature Victor Joseph, a young American
Indian who is merely surviving, but continually grasping for something
better. Through Victor's life, the reader and the viewer are introduced to
complex situations and emotions experienced by American Indians, but
the book conveys a more comprehensive picture than the film.

Each work demonstrates the anger and hatred Victor feels because of   2
his situation. In *The Lone Ranger and Tonto Fistfight in Heaven*, the reader
is carried through a series of short stories that detail the incidents that
cause his anger and hatred. The book opens with "Every Little Hurricane,"
a story that describes Victor's parents' alcoholism, a problem rampant on
the reservation. Subsequent stories like "Because My Father Always Said
He Was the Only Indian Who Saw Jimi Hendrix Play 'The Star Spangled
Banner' at Woodstock" and "This Is What It Means to Say Phoenix,
Arizona" take the reader deeper into Victor's dysfunctional family and his
emotional distress. The reader experiences the abuse and alcoholism from
a profoundly first-person perspective. However, in *Smoke Signals*, based
on one of the book's short stories, "This Is What It Means to Say Phoenix,
Arizona," the viewer sees the alcoholism and abuse, but the scenes are
often preceded or followed by humor, lightening the mood. Unlike the
stories, which expose these problems as cultural and situational, the film
leads the viewer to believe these are only Victor's problems.

The book and film both illustrate how desperately Victor desires   3
his father's love. *Smoke Signals* shows this desire only through Victor's
eyes, whereas *The Lone Ranger and Tonto Fistfight in Heaven* uses the
collective stories and emotions of the residents on the reservation to

continued

show that Victor's desires are shared by many. In "Because My Father Always Said He Was the Only Indian Who Saw Jimi Hendrix Play 'The Star Spangled Banner' at Woodstock," the reader sees Victor's pain and longing as he sits at his drunken father's feet while listening to Hendrix. In "A Train Is an Order of Occurrence Designed to Lead to Some Result," the reader's emotions are once again tugged as Samuel, isolated and distanced from his children, lies down in front of the oncoming train. These incidents demonstrate that the father-son connection is not just Victor's problem, but also a reservation problem. Like most of the book's characters, Victor doesn't have a moment of enlightenment, a true happy ending. Instead, he continues to fumble through a series of good and bad moments, much as might happen in real life. In contrast, the film focuses only on Victor's path to enlightenment from broken-hearted angry boy needing his father to a healed mature adult. With the help of the humorous Thomas, Victor travels to Phoenix to claim his father's belongings. After Victor is given his father's ashes, he realizes the anger he has clung to so tightly for fifteen years has been self-defeating. He lets the anger go and experiences a rebirth. The Victor that returns to the reservation is a new person and a man.

Both works demonstrate the roller coaster of emotions that Victor experiences, but once again, the book gives a broader picture than the film. The book illustrates the fear, desperation, hope, and happiness that pervade not only Victor's life, but also the lives of those on the reservation. Many of the stories, no matter how dismal, end with the slightest bit of hope—the ever-present hope for something better. My favorite story was "Indian Education" because it actually reminded me of my education in rural Idaho. In the story, "The Only Traffic Signal on the Reservation Doesn't Flash Red Anymore," Adrian and Victor discuss how drinking has ruined so many lives, yet they demonstrate hope that someone from the

4

continued

younger generation will go on to play basketball beyond the reservation. In "The Approximate Size of My Favorite Tumor," Jimmy constantly tells jokes about his tumor, driving away his devastated wife. When she returns, it is with the knowledge that hope and humor can be found in anything—even an impending death. The film, however, omits these and other stories and focuses only on the roller coaster of Victor's growth as an adult. After Victor gains enlightenment, the film grows very positive. Life on the reservation no longer seems dismal. Victor and Thomas return home. They bond over the memory of Victor's father. Victor respects his father by spreading his ashes over the Spokane Falls, and as he does this, the viewer watches salmon jumping up the falls as they swim upstream, a reminder of new life. Victor's old life is ending and a new one is beginning.

The Lone Ranger and Tonto Fistfight in Heaven and *Smoke Signals*   5 are equally well-written pieces filled with multiple emotions. The film, however, focuses mostly on Victor and doesn't achieve the level of depth and profundity of the book. The multitude of characters created by Alexie and the clever organization of the book force the reader to experience Victor's life through many stories. Victor's story emerges as a representation of so many, and ultimately it is clear that the collective story of the reservation is what truly matters.

ABOUT UNITY

1. Which supporting paragraph in "A Vote for McDonald's" has its topic sentence within the paragraph, rather than at the beginning? (*Write the paragraph number and the opening words of the topic sentence.*)

_____

2. Which sentence in paragraph 4 of "A Vote for McDonald's" should be omitted in the interest of paragraph unity? (*Write the opening words.*)

_____

3. Which sentence in paragraph 4 in "The Lone Ranger and Tonto Fistfight with Smoke Signals" should be omitted in the interest of paragraph unity? (*Write the opening words.*)

_____

ABOUT SUPPORT

4. In paragraph 3 of "A Vote for McDonald's," what three points does the writer make to support his statement that, for him, dining at McDonald's is a more pleasant experience than dining at the Chalet?

_____

_____

_____

5. In paragraph 3 of "A Vote for McDonald's," what sentence should be followed up by supporting details? (*Write the opening words of that sentence.*)

_____

6. Which sentence in paragraph 2 of "The Lone Ranger and Tonto Fistfight with Smoke Signals" needs to be followed by more supporting details? (*Write the opening words.*)

_____

_____

ABOUT COHERENCE

7. In paragraph 2 of "A Vote for McDonald's," what "change of direction" signal does the author use to indicate that he has finished discussing the Chalet and is now going to discuss McDonald's? _____

8. Write the words in paragraph 4 of "A Vote for McDonald's" that indicate the writer has used emphatic order in organizing his supporting points.

_____

ABOUT THE INTRODUCTION AND/OR CONCLUSION

9. Which sentence best describes the opening paragraph of "The Lone Ranger and Tonto Fistfight with Smoke Signals"?

   a. It begins with a broad statement that narrows down to the thesis.
   b. It explains the importance of the topic to the reader.
   c. It uses an incident or a brief story.
   d. It begins with a quotation.

10. The conclusion of "The Lone Ranger and Tonto Fistfight with Smoke Signals" falls into which category?

   a. some observations and a prediction

   b. summary and final thought

   c. thoughtful quotation

Developing a Comparison and/or Contrast Essay

Considering Purpose and Audience

The purpose of an essay that emphasizes comparison and/or contrast is to make a point by including examples that show how distinct items or people are either similar or different. Whether you choose to use comparison or contrast depends on the specific point you want to convey to readers. Suppose, for instance, the main point of your essay is that home-cooked hamburgers are superior to fast-food burgers. To convince your audience of your claim, you might contrast the two items, pointing out those differences—price, taste, and nutrition—that make the homemade dish better. If, however, your main point is that tap water is just as good as store-bought bottled water, you could compare the two, pointing out the similarities that support your main point. Tap water and bottled water, for example, might be equally clean, fresh, and mineral-rich. In both examples above, comparing or contrasting is used to convince readers of a larger main point.

As you think about your own composition, ask yourself what type of essay would benefit from this type of support. Then determine whether you want to focus on the differences between the items or their similarities. You may even decide that you want to do both. If, say, you choose to persuade your readers that they should purchase a specific type of computer, you may include paragraphs on the similarities and differences between Mac and PC computers. But remember, no matter what topic you select, be sure that your comparison or contrast is connected to a main point that readers can see and understand.

Be sure to keep your audience in mind when planning your essay. If you were writing about Macs and PCs for computer majors, for example, you could assume your readers were familiar with the two systems. On the other hand, if your audience were made up of liberal arts majors, you could not make such an assumption, and it would be up to you to provide background information. Thinking about your audience will help you determine the tone of your essay as well. Once again, if you are writing for an audience of programmers, it is appropriate to write in an objective, technical tone. But if you are writing for a more general audience, you should assume a friendly, informal tone.

Development through Prewriting

When Jesse, one of the student writers featured earlier, had to choose a topic for his essay, the Chalet and McDonald's quickly came to mind: "My wife and I had been talking that morning about where I wanted to go for my birthday," he said. "I'd been thinking how I would explain to her that I'd really prefer McDonald's. So the comparisons and contrasts between the two restaurants were fresh in my mind."

To generate ideas for his paper, Jesse turned to the technique of freewriting. Without concerning himself with organization, finding the perfect word, or even spelling, he simply wrote whatever came into his mind as he asked himself, Why would I rather eat at McDonald's than at the Chalet? Here is what Jesse came up with:

> The Chalet is a beautiful restaurant and it's sweet of Lilly to want to take me there. But I honestly like McDonald's better. To me, food is food, and a meal at the Chalet is not seven times better than a meal at McDonald's but that's what it costs. I like a plain cheeseburger better than something I can't pronounce or identify. The waiters at the Chalet are snooty and make me feel awkward—how can you enjoy eating when you're tensed up like that? Have to wear jacket and tie to the Chalet and I've gained weight; not sure jacket will even fit. Sweats or jeans are great at McDonald's. Desserts at Chalet are great, better than McCookies or whatever they're called. Parking is a hassle at the Chalet and easy at McD's. No tipping at McD's, either. I don't know why they keep it so dark at the Chalet— guess it's supposed to be relaxing, but seems creepy to me. McD's is bright and cheerful.

As Jesse looked over his freewriting, he saw that most of what he had written fell into three categories that he could use as the three supporting points of his essay. Using these three points, he prepared this first scratch outline for the essay:

> Would rather eat my special dinner at McDonald's than at the Chalet
>
> - can wear anything I want to McD's
>
> - waiters, lighting, menu at Chalet make me feel awkward
>
> - Chalet _much_ more expensive than McD's

Next, Jesse went back and inserted some supporting details that fit in with his three main points.

Would rather eat my special dinner at McDonald's than at the Chalet

- Going to the Chalet is a hassle
  ◦ have to wear jacket, tie to Chalet
  ◦ have to make reservations
  ◦ long drive; trouble parking
- Waiters, lighting, menu at Chalet make me feel awkward
  ◦ waiters are snooty
  ◦ lighting is dim
  ◦ French names on menu don't mean anything to me
- Chalet <u>much</u> more expensive than McD's
  ◦ meal costs seven times as much
  ◦ parking, tips on top of that
  ◦ rather spend that money on other things

Working from this scratch outline, Jesse wrote the following first draft of his essay.

First Draft

A Vote for McDonald's

Lilly has offered to take me anywhere I want for my birthday dinner. She thinks I'll choose the Chalet, but instead I want to eat at McDonald's.

The Chalet has a jacket-and-tie rule, and I hate wearing a jacket and tie, and the jacket's probably too tight for me anyway. I have to dig them out of the closet and get them cleaned. I can wear any old thing to McDonald's. We'd also have to leave the house early, since the Chalet requires reservations. Since it is downtown, I have to leave an hour early so I'm sure to have time to park. The Chalet cancels reservations if a party is more than ten minutes late. Going

continued

to McDonald's, on the other hand, is easy. I don't have to do any advance planning. I can leave my house whenever I'm ready.

McDonald's is a pleasant place where I feel at ease. It is bright and well lit. The employees serve with a smile, and the food is easy to pronounce and identify. I know what I'm going to get when I order a certain type of sandwich. I like simple meals more than gourmet ones. The Chalet is dimly lit. While I'm struggling to see what's on my plate, I worry that I'll knock one of the glasses off the table. The waiters at the Chalet can be uncomfortably formal, too. I get the feeling that I don't quite live up to their standards. Even the other diners can make me feel uncomfortable.

There's a big price difference between the Chalet and McDonald's. Dinner for two at the Chalet can easily cost $100, even without any "extras" like appetizers and dessert. And the $100 doesn't include the cost of parking the car and tipping the waiter. Once, I forgot to bring enough money. At McDonald's, a meal for two will cost around $15.

So, for my birthday dinner, or any other time, I prefer to eat at McDonald's. It is convenient, friendly, and cheap.

Development through Revising

Jesse put the first draft of his essay aside and took it to his writing class the next day. His instructor asked Jesse and the other students to work in small groups reading their drafts aloud and making suggestions for revision to one another. Here are the notes Jesse made on his group's comments:

- *I need to explain that Lilly is my wife.*

- *I'm not consistent in developing my paragraphs. I forgot to do a "one side at a time" or "point by point" comparison. I think I'll try "one side at a time." I'll describe in each paragraph what the Chalet is like, then what McDonald's is like.*

- *I could use more support for some of my points, like when I say that the waiters at the Chalet make me uncomfortable. I should give some examples of what I mean by that.*

- *I want to say something about what I'd rather do with the money we save by going to McDonald's. For me that's important—we can "eat" that money at the Chalet, or do other things with it that we both enjoy.*

After making these observations about his first draft, Jesse proceeded to write the version of his essay that appears at the beginning of this chapter.

A Model Essay to Consider

Read the following essay. Then answer the questions and read the comments that follow.

Chief Seattle's Speech of 1854

by Chief Seattle

Yonder sky that has wept tears of compassion on our fathers for centuries untold, and which, to us, looks eternal, may change. Today it is fair, tomorrow it may be overcast with clouds. My words are like the stars that never set. What Seattle says, the great chief, Washington . . . can rely upon, with as much certainty as our pale-face brothers can rely upon the return of the seasons. 1

The son [a reference to Territorial Governor Stevens] of the White Chief says his father sends us greetings of friendship and good will. This is kind, for we know he has little need of our friendship in return, because his people are many. They are like the grass that covers the vast prairies, while my people are few, and resemble the scattering trees of a storm-swept plain. 2

The great, and I presume also good, white chief sends us word that he wants to buy our lands but is willing to allow us to reserve enough to live on comfortably. This indeed appears generous, for the red man no longer has rights that he need respect, and the offer may be wise, also, for we are no longer in need of a great country. 3

There Was a Time

There was a time when our people covered the whole land, as the waves of a wind-ruffled sea cover its shell-paved floor. But that time has long since passed away with the greatness of tribes now almost forgotten. I will not mourn over our untimely decay, nor reproach my pale-face brothers for hastening it, for we, too, may have been somewhat to blame. 4

When our young men grow angry at some real or imaginary wrong, and disfigure their faces with black paint, their hearts, also, are disfigured and turn black, and then their cruelty is relentless and knows no bounds, and our old men are not able to restrain them. 5

But let us hope that hostilities between the red-man and his pale-face brothers may never return. We would have everything to lose and nothing to gain. 6

True it is, that revenge, with our young braves, is considered gain, even at the 7
cost of their own lives, but old men who stay at home in times of war, and old
women, who have sons to lose, know better.

Our great father Washington, for I presume he is now our father, as well as 8
yours, since George [a reference to King George III, i.e., Great Britain] has moved
his boundaries to the north; our great and good father, I say, sends us word by his
son, who, no doubt, is a great chief among his people, that if we do as he desires,
he will protect us. His brave armies will be to us a bristling wall of strength, and his
great ships of war will fill our harbors so that our ancient enemies far to the north-
ward, the Simsiams [Tsimshian] and Hydas [Haidas], will no longer frighten our
women and old men. Then he will be our father and we will be his children.

But Can This Ever Be?

Your God loves your people and hates mine; he folds his strong arms lovingly 9
around the white man and leads him as a father leads his infant son, but he has
forsaken his red children; he makes your people wax strong every day, and soon
they will fill the land; while my people are ebbing away like a fast-receding tide,
that will never flow again. The white man's God cannot love his red children or
he would protect them. They seem to be orphans who can look nowhere for help.
How then can we become brothers? How can your father become our father and
bring us prosperity and awaken in us dreams of returning greatness?

Your God seems to us to be partial. He came to the white man. We never saw 10
Him; never even heard His voice; He gave the white man laws but He had no word
for His red children whose teeming millions filled this vast continent as the stars
fill the firmament. No, we are two distinct races and must remain ever so. There is
little in common between us. The ashes of our ancestors are sacred and their final
resting place is hallowed ground, while you wander away from the tombs of your
fathers seemingly without regret.

Your religion was written on tables of stone by the iron finger of an angry God, 11
lest you might forget it. The red man could never remember nor comprehend it.

Our religion is the traditions of our ancestors, the dreams of our old men, given 12
them by the great Spirit, and the visions of our sachems, and is written in the hearts
of our people.

Your dead cease to love you and the homes of their nativity as soon as they pass the 13
portals of the tomb. They wander far off beyond the stars, are soon forgotten, and never
return. Our dead never forget the beautiful world that gave them being. They still love its
winding rivers, its great mountains and its sequestered vales, and they ever yearn in ten-
derest affection over the lonely hearted living and often return to visit and comfort them.

Day and night cannot dwell together. The red man has ever fled the approach of 14
the white man, as the changing mists on the mountain side flee before the blazing
morning sun.

However, your proposition seems a just one, and I think my folks will accept 15
it and will retire to the reservation you offer them, and we will dwell apart and in
peace, for the words of the great white chief seem to be the voice of nature speaking
to my people out of the thick darkness that is fast gathering around them like a
dense fog floating inward from a midnight sea.

It matters but little where we pass the remainder of our days.   16

They Are Not Many

The Indian's night promises to be dark. No bright star hovers above the horizon. 17
Sad-voiced winds moan in the distance. Some grim Nemesis of our race is on the
red man's trail, and wherever he goes he will still hear the sure approaching footsteps of the fell destroyer and prepare to meet his doom, as does the wounded
doe that hears the approaching footsteps of the hunter. A few more moons, a few
more winters, and not one of all the mighty hosts that once filled this broad land
or that now roam in fragmentary bands through these vast solitudes will remain
to weep over the tombs of a people once as powerful and as hopeful as your own.

But why should we repine? Why should I murmur at the fate of my people? 18
Tribes are made up of individuals and are no better than they. Men come and go
like the waves of a sea. A tear, a tamanawus, a dirge, and they are gone from our
longing eyes forever. Even the white man, whose God walked and talked with him,
as friend to friend, is not exempt from the common destiny. We may be brothers
after all. We shall see.

We will ponder your proposition, and when we have decided we will tell you. 19
But should we accept it, I here and now make this the first condition: That we will
not be denied the privilege, without molestation, of visiting at will the graves of our
ancestors and friends. Every part of this country is sacred to my people. Every hill-
side, every valley, every plain and grove has been hallowed by some fond memory or
some sad experience of my tribe.

Even the Rocks

Even the rocks that seem to lie dumb as they swelter in the sun along the silent 20
seashore in solemn grandeur thrill with memories of past events connected with the
fate of my people, and the very dust under your feet responds more lovingly to our
footsteps than to yours, because it is the ashes of our ancestors, and our bare feet are
conscious of the sympathetic touch, for the soil is rich with the life of our kindred.

The sable braves, and fond mothers, and glad-hearted maidens, and the little 21
children who lived and rejoiced here, and whose very names are now forgotten, still
love these solitudes, and their deep fastnesses at eventide grow shadowy with the
presence of dusky spirits. And when the last red man shall have perished from the
earth and his memory among white men shall have become a myth, these shores
shall swarm with the invisible dead of my tribe, and when your children's children

shall think themselves alone in the field, the store, the shop, upon the highway or in the silence of the woods they will not be alone. In all the earth there is no place dedicated to solitude. At night, when the streets of your cities and villages shall be silent, and you think them deserted, they will throng with the returning hosts that once filled and still love this beautiful land. The white man will never be alone. Let him be just and deal kindly with my people, for the dead are not altogether powerless.

QUESTIONS 2

ABOUT UNITY

1. Which of the following statements best represents the main idea of the selection?

   a. Chief Seattle accepts that his people will have to move to a reservation but only if they can maintain rights to visit their ancestors.

   b. Chief Seattle believes that the proposition offered by the U.S. government is ultimately fair and just.

   c. Chief Seattle believes that the white man's God is more powerful than the gods of the red man.

   d. Chief Seattle envisions a time when white men and red men will harmoniously live side by side.

2. What is the topic sentence for paragraph 19? (Write the opening words.)

   _____

ABOUT SUPPORT

3. Throughout the essay, Chief Seattle employs the use of simile and metaphor. Find an example in the first section of the essay that shows comparison between the white man and the Suquamish people.

   _____

   _____

   _____

4. In paragraphs 9 through 16, Chief Seattle compares his god and religion to that of the white man. Find several examples that he uses.

   _____

   _____

   _____

5. In paragraph 17, Chief Seattle contrasts his people's fate with that of the white man to show that the white man is not immune to the same fate as that of his people. Find the sentence in which he makes this contrast and write it below.

_____

_____

_____

ABOUT COHERENCE

6. Which method of organization does Chief Seattle use in his speech?
   a. Time order
   b. Emphatic order

7. Chief Seattle breaks up his speech into sections with headings that indicate the main point of each section. How many does he have? List them here.

_____

_____

8. Chief Seattle repeats a name in paragraphs 2, 3, and 15. What is that phrase, and what is the point?

_____

_____

_____

ABOUT THE INTRODUCTION AND/OR CONCLUSION

9. Which method best describes the introduction to "Chief Seattle's Speech of 1854"?
   a. quotation
   b. idea that it is the opposite of the one to be developed
   c. anecdote
   d. broad, general statement narrowing to thesis

10. What method best describes the conclusion to "Chief Seattle's Speech of 1854"?
    a. summary and final thought
    b. thought-provoking quotation
    c. prediction or recommendation

Writing an Essay with Emphasis on Comparison and/or Contrast

Write an essay about a change (positive or negative) in a person you know, and explain the causes and process of that change. You should provide a specific description of the person both before and after the change. You will want to review Chapter 8, "Description," Chapter 11, "Process," and Chapter 12, "Cause and/or Effect," to help you provide good support for your essay.

PREWRITING

a. Gather information about the person you've selected by using a prewriting method of your choice. Write down as much information as possible within a ten-minute period. Don't worry about spelling, grammar, organization, or anything other than getting your thoughts down on the page. If ideas are still flowing at the end of ten minutes, keep on writing. Once you have finished getting your thoughts down, you should have a base of raw material that you can draw on in the next phase of your work. Judging from what you have produced, do you think you have enough material to support your essay? If so, keep following the steps below. If not, choose another person and spend about ten minutes generating ideas to see if they might be a better subject for your essay.

b. Develop a single clear sentence that will serve as your thesis. Your thesis should demonstrate why it is important that your readers know about this person and the change they went through.

c. Decide which method of development you will use to design your essay: one side at a time or point by point. Be consistent in your use of one method or the other in each of your paragraphs.

d. Write the first draft of your essay.

Jacob Lund/
Shutterstock

REVISING

Reread your essay and then show it to a friend or classmate who will give you honest feedback. You should both review it, keeping in mind the questions in the FOUR BASES Checklist at the end of this chapter. As you revise your essay through one or more additional drafts, continue to refer to that checklist until you and your reader can answer "yes" to each question.

Write an essay in which you contrast two attitudes on a controversial subject. You may want to contrast your views with those of someone else, or contrast the way you felt about the subject in the past with the way you feel now. You might consider writing about one of these subjects:

- Adopting a vegan diet
- Assisted suicide
- Climate change
- Factory farming
- Free college
- Genetically modified foods
- Immigration policies in the United States
- Legalization of marijuana
- Mandatory vaccinations
- Obligatory military service
- The public's right to know about elected officials' private lives
- Regulating social media
- Same-sex couples fostering and/or adopting children
- Standardized tests and college admissions

PREWRITING

a. To gather information for the point of view that contrasts with your own, you will need to do some research. In addition to the Internet, you'll find useful material if you go to the library and search through article indexes for recent newsmagazines. (If you need help, ask your instructor or the research librarian.) Or interview friends and acquaintances whose attitude on the subject is different from yours.

Rick_Thompson/Getty Images

b. To generate ideas for your essay, try the following two-part exercise.

- Part 1: Pretend that a visitor from Mars who has never heard of the topic of your paper has asked you to explain it, as well as why you take the attitude you do toward it. Using the technique of freewriting—not worrying about sentence structure, organization, spelling, repetition, etc.—write an answer for the Martian. Throw in every reason you can think of for your attitude.

- Part 2: Now the Martian asks you to do the same, taking the opposing point of view. Remember that it's up to you to make this interplanetary

Inti St Clair/Blend Images LLC

visitor understand both sides of the issue, so really try to put yourself in the other person's shoes as you represent the contrasting attitude.

c.   As you look over the writing on both sides of the issue you've done for the Martian, note the strongest points on both sides. From them, select your three main supporting points. Are there other thoughts in your writing that can be used as supporting details for those points?

d.   Write your three supporting paragraphs. Decide whether it is more effective to contrast your attitude and the opposing attitude point by point within each paragraph, or to devote the first half of each paragraph to one side's attitude and then contrast it with the other's.

e.   In your concluding paragraph, summarize the contrast between your attitude and the other point of view. Consider closing with a final comment that makes it clear why you stand where you do.

REVISING

Refer to the guidelines for rewriting provided in the FOUR BASES Checklist at the end of this chapter.

WRITING ASSIGNMENT 3

Write an essay that contrasts two characters or two points of view in one or more poems, stories, plays, or novels. The work you choose may be assigned by your instructor, or it may require your instructor's approval. For this assignment, your essay may have two supporting paragraphs, with each paragraph representing one side of the contrast. You will want to check Chapter 18, "Summarizing and Paraphrasing," Chapter 19, "Writing a Source-Based Essay," and Chapter 20, "Writing a Research Essay," to ensure that you properly present and cite the information from your chosen works. The following student essay is a literary analysis of a poem by Robert Frost.

Warren and Mary

In "Death of the Hired Man," Robert Frost uses a brief incident—the   1

return of Silas, an aging farmhand—to dramatize the differences between

a husband and wife. As Warren and Mary talk about Silas and reveal his

continued

story, the reader learns their story, too. By the end of the poem, Warren
and Mary emerge as contrasting personalities; one is wary and reserved,
while the other is open and giving.

   Warren is a kindly man, but his basic decency is tempered by   2
practicality and emotional reserve. Warren is upset with Mary for
sheltering Silas, who is barely useful and sometimes unreliable: "What use
he is there's no depending on." Warren feels that he has already done
his duty toward Silas by hiring him the previous summer and is under
no obligation to care for him now. "Home," says Warren, "is the place
where, when you have to go there/They have to take you in." Warren's
home is not Silas's home, so Warren does not have a legal or moral duty
to keep the shiftless old man. Warren's temperament, in turn, influences
his attitude toward Silas's arrival. Warren hints to Mary—through a
condescending smile—that Silas is somehow playing on her emotions or
faking his illness. Warren considers Silas's supposed purpose in coming
to the farm—to ditch the meadow—nothing but a flimsy excuse for a free
meal. The best that Warren can find to say about Silas is that he does
have one practical skill: the ability to build a good load of hay.

   Mary, in contrast, is distinguished by her giving nature and her   3
concentration on the workings of human emotion. In caring for Silas, Mary
sees not his lack of ability or his laziness but the fact that he is "worn out"
and needs help. To Mary, home represents not obligation ("They have to
take you in") but unconditional love: "I should have called it/Something
you somehow haven't to deserve." Mary is observant, not only of outer
appearances but also of the inner person; this is why she thinks not
that Silas is trying to trick them but that he is a desperate man trying to
salvage a little self-respect. She realizes, too, that he will never ditch the
meadow, and she knows that Silas's insecurity prompted his arguments
with the college boy who helped with the haying. Mary is also perceptive

continued

enough to see that Silas could never humble himself before his estranged brother. Mary's attitude is more sympathetic than Warren's; whereas Warren wonders why Silas and his brother don't get along, Mary thinks about how Silas "hurt my heart the way he lay/And rolled his old head on that sharp-edged chairback."

In describing Silas, Warren and Mary describe themselves. We see   4 a basically good man whose spirit has been toughened by a hard life. Warren, we learn, would have liked to pay Silas a fixed wage but simply couldn't afford to. Life has taught Warren to be practical and to rein in his emotions. In contrast, we see a nurturing woman, alert to human feelings, who could never refuse to care for a lonely, dying man. Warren and Mary are both decent people. This is the reason why, as Mary instinctively feels, Silas chooses their home for his final refuge.

Writing for a Specific Purpose and Audience

WRITING ASSIGNMENT 4

Work

In this comparison and/or contrast essay, you will write with a specific purpose and for a specific audience.

Write a letter to your boss in which you compare your abilities with those of the ideal candidate for a position to which you'd like to be promoted. Use the point-by-point method, discussing each desired qualification and then describing how well you measure up to it. Consider the requirements of a job you are familiar with, ideally a job you would really like to apply for. You may want to review Chapter 8, "Description," and Chapter 16, "Argument," to help you create a detailed persuasive essay.

Comparison and/or Contrast Checklist: THE FOUR BASES

ABOUT *UNITY*

✓ Have I included a thesis statement that clearly identifies whether I am comparing, contrasting, or using both processes to discuss my subject?

✓ Are there portions of the essay that do not support my thesis and therefore should be eliminated or rewritten?

ABOUT *SUPPORT*

✓ Does my essay include strong details that help the reader understand my claim?

✓ Does every paragraph support my thesis in some way?

ABOUT *COHERENCE*

✓ Is my essay organized as point-by-point or one side at a time?

✓ Is the current organization the most effective choice?

✓ Do I use logical transitions to make points of comparison and/or contrast clear?

✓ Do I have a concluding paragraph that supports my overall essay and thesis?

ABOUT *SENTENCE SKILLS*

✓ Have I used a consistent point of view throughout my essay?

✓ Have I used specific rather than general words?

✓ Have I avoided wordiness and used concise wording?

✓ Are my sentences varied?

✓ Have I edited for spelling and other sentence skills errors, as listed in the checklist at the back of the book?

READING

p. 321: Seattle, Chief. "Chief Seattle's Speech." In Scraps From a Diary—Chief Seattle–A Gentleman by Instinct—His Native Eloquence by H. A. Smith. *The Seattle Sunday Star*, October 29, 1887.

Definition

This chapter will explain and illustrate how to

- develop an essay with emphasis on definition
- write an essay with emphasis on definition
- revise an essay with emphasis on definition

In addition, you will read and consider

- two student essays that emphasize definition
- one professional model essay that emphasizes definition

What does it mean to be a successful student? What qualities and attributes does a successful student possess? Looking at the photograph above and thinking about these questions, write an essay in which you define what it means to be a successful student.
Shutterstock

In talking with other people, we sometimes offer informal definitions to explain just what we mean by a particular term. Suppose, for example, we say to a friend, "Lucas is really an inconsiderate person." We might then explain what we mean by "inconsiderate" by saying, "He borrowed my accounting book 'overnight' but didn't return it for a week. And when I got it back, it was covered with coffee stains." In a written definition, we make clear in a more complete and formal way our own personal understanding of a term. Such a definition typically starts with one meaning of a term. The meaning is then illustrated with a series of details.

In this chapter, you will be asked to write an essay in which you define and illustrate a term. To prepare for this assignment, first read the student essays and the model essay that follow and work through the questions that accompany the essays.

Student Essays to Consider

Definition of a Football Fan

Not every person who likes football falls into the category of a football fan. The word "fan" is an abbreviation of "fanatic," meaning "a person marked or motivated by an extreme, unreasoning enthusiasm." In the case of football fans, the term is appropriate. They behave unreasonably, they are unreasonable about the past, and they are extremely loyal.   1

Football fans wear their official team T-shirts and warm-up jackets to the mall, the supermarket, the classroom, and even—if they can get away with it—to work. If the team offers a giveaway item, the fans rush to the stadium to claim the hat or sports bag or water bottle that is being handed out that day. Baseball fans get similarly enthusiastic when their favorite teams give away some attractive freebie. Football fans just plain behave unreasonably. Even the fact that fans spend the coldest months of the year huddling on icy metal benches in places like Chicago proves it. In addition, football fans decorate their houses with football-related items of every kind. To them, team bumper stickers belong not only on car bumpers, but also on fireplace mantels and front doors. When they go to a game, which they do as often as possible, they also decorate their bodies. True football fans not only put on their team jackets and grab their pennants but also paint their heads to look like helmets or wear glow-in-the-dark cheeseheads. At the game, these fans devote enormous energy to trying to get a "wave" going.   2

Football fans are extremely fascinated by the past. They talk about William "Refrigerator" Perry's 1985 Super Bowl touchdown as though it had happened last week. They excitedly discuss Peyton Manning and the Colts' fourth-quarter comeback over the New England Patriots in 2009. They reminisce about Patrick Mahomes's left-handed pass late in the fourth quarter that secured a Chiefs 2018 win over Denver. And if a person can't manage to get excited about such ancient history, they are considered unreasonable.   3

Last of all, football fans are extremely loyal to the team of their choice, often dangerously so. Should their beloved team lose three in a row, fans   4

continued

may begin to react negatively as a way to hide their broken hearts. They still obsessively watch each game and spend the entire day afterward reading and listening to the postgame commentary in newspapers, on TV sports segments, and on sports websites. Further, this intense loyalty makes fans dangerous. To anyone who dares to say to a loyal fan that another team has better players or coaches or to anyone wandering near the home cheering section wearing the jacket of the opposing team, physical damage is a real possibility. Bloody noses, black eyes, and broken bones are just some of the injuries inflicted on people cheering the wrong team when fans are around. In 2014, thirty-one fans were arrested and ninety-three were ejected from the game when fights broke out between Raiders and 49ers fans.

From February through August, football fans act like any other human   5
beings. They pay their taxes, take out the garbage, and complain about the high cost of living. But when September rolls around, the colors go on, and the flat screens stream endlessly, the record books come off the shelves, and the devotion returns. For the true football fan, another season of extremism has begun.

Student Zombies

Schools divide people into categories. From the early grades, students   1
are labeled "college track" or "vocational-technical" or "model citizen" or "troublemaker." Students pigeonhole their fellow students, too. We've all known the "brain," the "jock," the "clown," and the "teacher's pet." In most cases, these narrow labels are misleading and inaccurate. But there is one label for a certain type of college student that says it all: "zombie."

Zombies are the living dead. Most of us haven't known a lot of real   2
zombies personally, but we do know how they act. We have movies and television shows to guide us. The special effects in movies are much better these days. Over the years, we've learned from these sources that zombies stalk around graveyards, staring with empty, open eyes, and bumping like cheap toy robots into living people. Zombie students in college do just about the same thing. They stalk around campus, eyes glazed, staring off into space. When they do manage to wander into a classroom, they sit down mechanically and contemplate the ceiling. Zombie students rarely eat, talk, laugh, or toss Frisbees on campus lawns. Instead, they vanish when class is dismissed and return only when some mysterious zombie signal summons them back into a classroom. The signal may not occur for weeks.

Zombies are controlled by some mysterious force. According to   3
legend, real zombies are corpses that have been brought back to life to

continued

do the bidding of a magical master. Student zombies, too, seem directed by a strange power. They continue to attend school although they have no apparent desire to do so. They show no interest in college-related activities like tests, grades, papers, and projects. And yet some inner force compels them to wander through the halls of higher education.

An awful fate awaits all zombies unless something happens to break   4
the spell they're under. In the movies, zombies are often shot, stabbed, drowned, electrocuted, and run over by large vehicles, all to no avail. Finally the hero or heroine realizes that a potion is needed. Once the potion is made, with the appropriate props of chicken feet, human hair, and bats' eyeballs, the zombie-corpse can return peacefully to its coffin. The only hope for a student zombie to change is for them to undergo an awakening experience.

All college students know that it's not necessary to see *Night of the*   5
Living Dead or *The Walking Dead* in order to see zombies in action—or nonaction. They can forget the campus film series or the late-late show. All they need to do is just sit in a classroom and wait. They know what they're looking for—the students who walk in without books or papers and sit in the very last row of seats. The ones plugged constantly into their smartphone earbuds don't count as zombies—that's a whole different category of "student." *Day of the Living Dead* is showing every day at a college nearby.

ABOUT UNITY

QUESTIONS 1

1. Which supporting paragraph in "Definition of a Football Fan" has a topic sentence buried within the paragraph, rather than at the paragraph's beginning? *(Write the paragraph number and the opening words of the topic sentence.)*

_____

2. What sentence in paragraph 2 of "Definition of a Football Fan" should be omitted in the interest of paragraph unity? *(Write the opening words.)*

_____

3. Which sentence in paragraph 2 of "Student Zombies" should be omitted in the interest of paragraph unity? *(Write the opening words.)*

_____

4. What sentence in the final paragraph of "Student Zombies" introduces a new topic and so should be eliminated? *(Write the opening words.)*

_____

ABOUT SUPPORT

5. Which essay develops its definitions through a series of comparisons?

   _____

6. After which sentence in paragraph 4 of "Definition of a Football Fan" is more support needed? *(Write the opening words.)*

   _____

7. In the second paragraph of "Definition of a Football Fan," how many examples are given of fans' unreasonable and extreme behavior? *(Circle the letter of the answer.)*

   a. two

   b. four

   c. six

ABOUT COHERENCE

8. Which paragraph in "Definition of a Football Fan" begins with a transitional phrase? _____

9. Which sentence in paragraph 2 of "Student Zombies" begins with a change-of-direction transitional word? *(Write the opening words.)*

   _____

ABOUT THE INTRODUCTION AND/OR CONCLUSION

10. Which method of introduction is used in the opening paragraph of "Student Zombies"? *(Circle the letter of the answer.)*

    a. anecdote

    b. idea that is the opposite of the one to be developed

    c. quotation

    d. broad, general statement narrowing to a thesis

Developing an Essay with Emphasis on Definition

Considering Purpose and Audience

When you write an essay that emphasizes definition, your main purpose is to explain to readers your understanding of a key term or concept, while your secondary purpose is to persuade them that your definition is a legitimate one. Keep in mind that when you present a definition in your essay, you should not simply repeat a word's dictionary meaning. Instead, you should convey what a particular term means *to you* by using persuasive examples. For example, if you were to write about the term *patriotism*, you might begin by presenting your definition of the word. You might say patriotism means turning out for Fourth of July parades or displaying the flag. Or perhaps you think patriotism is about becoming politically aware and voting. Whatever definition you choose, be sure to provide specific instances so that readers can fully understand your meaning of the term. For example, in writing an essay on patriotism, you might describe three people whom you see as truly patriotic. Writing about each person will help ensure that readers see and understand the term as you do.

As with other essay forms, keep your audience in mind. If, for instance, you were proposing a new definition of "patriotism," an audience of war veterans might require different examples than would an audience of college students.

Development through Prewriting

Brian, the author of "Definition of a Football Fan," spent a few minutes jotting down a number of possible essay topics, keeping in mind the question, "What do I know a good deal about, or at least have an interest in exploring?" Here is his list of topic ideas. Notice how they reflect Brian's interest in outdoor activities, sports, and history:

<u>Definition of</u> . . .

   A person who fishes

   A soccer goalie

   A reenactor of Civil War battles

   People who vacation at national parks

   A bodybuilder

   A Green Bay Packers fan

   A history buff

   A Little League coach

After looking over his list, Brian selected "A Green Bay Packers fan" as the topic that interested him most. He thought it would lend itself well to a lighthearted essay that defined the sometimes eccentric fans of the Wisconsin football team. After giving it further thought, however, Brian decided to broaden his topic to include all football fans. "I realized I just didn't know enough specifically about Green Bay fans to support an entire essay," he said.

A person who likes to think in visual terms, Brian decided to develop ideas and details about his topic by clustering his thoughts.

FOOTBALL FANS

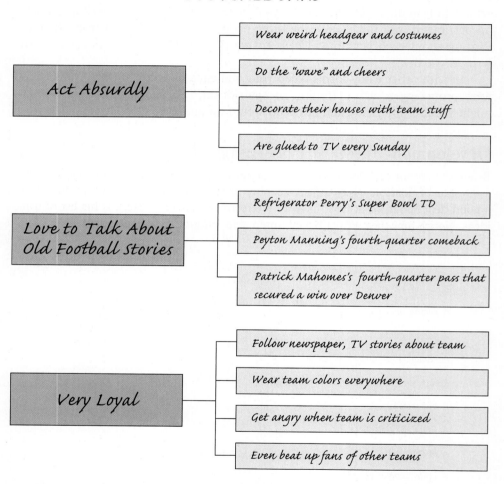

When he looked over his diagram, Brian realized that he could characterize each of his three main topics as a kind of extremism. He decided on a thesis (he would define football fans as extreme and unreasonable) that would indicate his essay's plan of development ("they behave unreasonably, they are unreasonable about the past, and they are extremely loyal").

With that thesis and plan of development in mind, Brian wrote the first draft of his essay.

First Draft

Definition of a Football Fan

Football fans are by definition eccentric. They behave unreasonably, they are unreasonable about the past, and they are extremely loyal.

If their team gives away something free, the fans rush to the stadium to get the hat or whatever. Football fans just plain behave unreasonably. Baseball fans get similarly enthusiastic when their favorite teams give away some attractive freebie. But football fans are even worse. Football fans freeze themselves in order to watch their favorite game. In addition, football fans decorate their houses with football-related items of every kind. When they go to a game, which they do as often as possible, the true football fans make themselves look ridiculous by decorating themselves in weird team-related ways. At the game, these fans do the "wave" more than they watch the game.

Football fans love to talk about the past. They talk about William "Refrigerator" Perry's 1985 Super Bowl touchdown as though it had happened last week. They discuss Peyton Manning's fourth-quarter comeback in 2009. They reminisce about Patrick Mahomes's fourth-quarter pass that secured a win over Denver. They think everyone should be as excited as they are about such old stories.

Last of all, football fans are extremely loyal to the team of their choice. Football fans wear their team T-shirts and warm-up jackets everywhere, even to work. Of course, if they have to dress up in business clothes, they can't do that. Should their beloved team lose three in a row, their fans may begin to criticize their team. But these reactions only hide their broken hearts. They still obsessively watch each game and read all the newspaper stories about it. This intense loyalty makes fans dangerous. To anyone who dares to say to a loyal fan that another team is better or to anyone wandering near the home cheering section wearing the jacket of the opposing team, physical damage is a real possibility. Incidents of violence in football stadiums have increased in recent years and are a matter of growing concern.

Football fans really act absurdly. They behave unreasonably, they are unreasonable about the past, and they're too loyal.

Development through Revising

The next day, Brian showed his first draft to a study partner from his composition class. She returned it with comments noted in the margins.

Jacob Lund/
Shutterstock

Definition of a Football Fan

Football fans are by definition eccentric. They behave unreasonably, they are unreasonable about the past, and they are extremely loyal.

If their team gives away something free, the fans rush to the stadium to get the hat or whatever. Football fans just plain behave unreasonably. Baseball fans get similarly enthusiastic when their favorite teams give away some attractive freebie. But football fans are even worse. Football fans freeze themselves in order to watch their favorite game. In addition, football fans decorate their houses with football-related items of every kind. When they go to a game, which they do as often as possible, the true football fans make themselves look ridiculous by decorating themselves in weird team-related ways. At the game, these fans do the "wave" more than they watch the game.

Football fans love to talk about the past. They talk about William "Refrigerator" Perry's 1985 Super Bowl touchdown as though it had happened last week. They discuss Peyton Manning's fourth-quarter comeback in 2009. They reminisce about Patrick Mahomes's fourth-quarter pass that secured a win over Denver. They think everyone should be as excited as they are about such old stories.

Last of all, football fans are extremely loyal to the team of their choice. Football fans wear their team T-shirts and warm-up jackets everywhere, even to work. Of course, if they have to dress up in business clothes, they can't do that. Should their beloved team lose three in a row, their fans may begin to criticize their team. But these reactions only hide their broken hearts. They still obsessively watch each game and read all the newspaper stories about it. This intense loyalty makes fans dangerous. To anyone who dares to say to a loyal fan that another team is better or to anyone wandering near the home cheering section wearing the jacket of the opposing team, physical damage is a real possibility. Incidents of violence in football stadiums have increased in recent years and are a matter of growing concern.

Football fans really act absurdly. They behave unreasonably, they are unreasonable about the past, and they're too loyal.

Reader's Comments

Huh? I guess this is about the weather—make it clearer.

Like what? Details here.

Details needed. How do they decorate themselves?

I'm not a football fan, so I don't understand these references. Can you briefly explain them?

Shouldn't this be in the second paragraph? It seems to belong to "they behave unreasonably," not "loyalty."

This doesn't support your topic statement, so take it out.

Kind of a boring way to end it. You're just repeating your thesis.

After reading his classmate's comments, Brian went to work on his next draft. As he worked, he read his essay aloud several times and noticed places where his wording sounded awkward or too informal. (Example: "If their team gives away something free, the fans rush to the stadium to get the hat or whatever.") A few drafts later, he produced the version of "Definition of a Football Fan" that appears at the beginning of this chapter.

A Model Essay to Consider

Read the following essay. Then answer the questions and read the comments that follow.

Propaganda Techniques in Today's Advertising
by Ann McClintock

Americans, adults and children alike, are being seduced. They are being brainwashed. And few of us protest. Why? Because the seducers and the brainwashers are the advertisers we willingly invite into our homes. We are victims, content—even eager—to be victimized. We read advertisers' propaganda messages on social media and news sources; we watch their alluring images on television. We absorb their messages and images into our subconscious. We all do it—even those of us who claim to see through advertisers' tricks and therefore feel immune to advertising's charm. Advertisers lean heavily on propaganda to sell products, whether the "products" are a brand of toothpaste, a candidate for office, or a particular political viewpoint. 1

Propaganda is a systematic effort to influence people's opinions, to win them over to a certain view or side. Propaganda is not necessarily concerned with what is true or false, good or bad. Propagandists simply want people to believe the messages being sent. Often, propagandists will use outright lies or more subtle deceptions to sway people's opinions. In a propaganda war, any tactic is considered fair. 2

When we hear the word "propaganda," we usually think of a foreign menace: anti-American messages broadcast by a totalitarian regime or brainwashing tactics practiced on hostages. Although propaganda may seem relevant only in the political arena, the concept can be applied fruitfully to the way products and ideas are sold in advertising. Indeed, the vast majority of us are targets in advertisers' propaganda war. Every day, we are bombarded with slogans, print and Internet pop-up ads, commercials, packaging claims, billboards, trademarks, logos, and designer brands—all forms of propaganda. One study reports that each of us, during an average day, is exposed to over *five hundred* advertising claims of various types. This saturation 3 may even increase in the future, since current trends include ads on movie screens, shopping carts, and even public television.

What kind of propaganda techniques do advertisers use? There are seven basic 4
types:

1. Name Calling. Name calling is a propaganda tactic in which negatively 5
charged names are hurled against the opposing side or competitor. By using such names, propagandists try to arouse feelings of mistrust, fear, and hate in their audiences. For example, a political advertisement may label an opposing candidate a "loser," "fence-sitter," or "warmonger." Depending on the advertiser's target market, labels such as "a friend of big business" or "a dues-paying member of the party in power" can be the epithets that damage an opponent. Ads for products may also use name calling. An American manufacturer may refer, for instance, to a "foreign car" in its commercial—not an "imported" one. The label of foreignness will have unpleasant connotations in many people's minds. A childhood rhyme claims that "names can never hurt me," but name calling is an effective way to damage the opposition, whether it is another car maker or a congressional candidate.

2. Glittering Generalities. Using glittering generalities is the opposite of name 6
calling. In this case, advertisers surround their products with attractive—and slippery—words and phrases. They use vague terms that are difficult to define and that may have different meanings to different people: *freedom, democratic, all-American, patriotic,* and *justice.* Many such words have strong affirmative overtones. This kind of language stirs positive feelings in people, feelings that may spill over to the product or idea being pitched. As with name calling, the emotional response may overwhelm logic. Target audiences accept the product without thinking very much about what the glittering generalities mean—or whether they even apply to the product. After all, how can anyone oppose "truth, justice, and the American way"?

The ads for politicians and political causes often use glittering generalities because 7
such "buzzwords" can influence votes. Election slogans include high-sounding but basically empty phrases like the following:

"He cares about people." (That's nice, but is he a better candidate than his opponent?)

"Vote for progress." (Progress by whose standards?)

"They'll make this country great again." (What does "great" mean? Does "great" mean the same thing to others as it does to me?)

"Vote for the future." (What kind of future?)

"If you love America, vote for Rosa Martineau." (If I don't vote for Martineau, does that mean I don't love America?)

Ads for consumer goods are also sprinkled with glittering generalities. Product 8
names, for instance, are supposed to evoke good feelings: *Luvs* diapers, *Stayfree*

feminine hygiene products, *Joy* liquid detergent, *Loving Care* hair color, *Almost Home* cookies, *Yankee Doodle* pastries. Product slogans lean heavily on vague but comforting phrases: . . . General Electric "brings good things to life," and Dow Chemical "lets you do great things." Chevrolet, we are told, is the "heartbeat of America," and Chrysler boasts that "Inspiration comes standard."

3. Transfer. In transfer, advertisers try to improve the image of a product by associating it with specific symbols like the American flag, a powerful animal, or an image that evokes a feeling of comfort. The advertisers hope that the prestige attached to the symbol will carry over to the product. Many companies use transfer devices to identify their products: AmeriFreight's logo is an eagle with wings reflective of the American flag; Liberty Mutual's corporate symbol is the Statue of Liberty; The Hartford's logo is a powerful buck with a full rack of antlers; Allstate's name is cradled by a pair of protective hands. 9

Corporations also use the transfer technique when they sponsor television shows. These shows function as symbols of dignity and class. Koch Industries, through multiple foundations, has supported many public television series like *Nova*; The Home Depot is a major sponsor of *Ask This Old House*; Johnson & Johnson sponsors the *PBS News-Hour*. In this way, corporations can reach an educated, influential audience and, perhaps, improve their public image by associating themselves with quality programming. 10

Political ads, of course, practically wrap themselves in the flag. Ads for a political candidate often show either the Washington Monument, a Fourth of July parade, the Stars and Stripes, a bald eagle soaring over the mountains, or a white-steepled church on the village green. The national anthem or "America the Beautiful" may play in the background. Such appeals to Americans' love of country can surround the candidate with an aura of patriotism and integrity. 11

4. Testimonial. The testimonial is one of advertisers' most-loved and most-used propaganda techniques. Similar to the transfer device, the testimonial capitalizes on the admiration people have for a celebrity to make the product shine more brightly—even though the celebrity is not an expert on the product being sold. 12

Print and television ads offer a nonstop parade of testimonials: here's Betty White eating a Snickers bar; Jennifer Garner and Samuel L. Jackson both ask "What's in your Wallet?" for Capital One; dozens of celebrities (including Rihanna) advertise clothing brands; and Sophia Vergara touts Head & Shoulders dandruff shampoo as the best. Testimonials can sell movies, too; ads for films often feature favorable comments by well-known reviewers. And, in recent years, testimonials have played an important role in pitching books; the backs of paperbacks frequently list complimentary blurbs by celebrities. 13

Political candidates, as well as their ad agencies, know the value of testimonials. Taylor Swift lent her support and music to the presidential campaign of Joe Biden, while Herschel Walker threw his support behind Donald J. Trump. Even controversial social issues are debated by celebrities. Celebrities like Leonardo DiCaprio and Shailene Woodley regularly speak out about the dangers of climate change. 14

As illogical as testimonials sometimes are (Pepsi's Michael Jackson, for in- 15 stance, was a health-food adherent who did not drink soft drinks), they are effective propaganda. We like the *person* so much that we like the *product* too.

5. Plain Folks. The plain folks approach says, in effect, "Buy me or vote for 16 me. I'm just like you." Regular folks will surely like Bob Evans's Down on the Farm Country Sausage or good old-fashioned Countrytime Lemonade. Some ads emphasize the idea that "we're all in the same boat." We see people video chatting for just the reasons we do—to put the baby on the phone to Grandma or to tell Mom we love her. And how do these folksy, warmhearted (usually saccharine[1]) scenes affect us? They're supposed to make us feel that T-Mobile—the multinational corporate giant—has the same values we do. Similarly, we are introduced to the little people at Ford, the ordinary folks who work on the assembly line, not to bigwigs in their executive offices. What's the purpose of such an approach? To encourage us to buy a car built by these honest, hardworking "everyday people" who care about quality as much as we do.

Political advertisements make almost as much use of the "plain folks" appeal 17 as they do of transfer devices. Candidates wear hard hats, farmers' caps, and assembly-line coveralls. They jog around the block and carry their own luggage through the airport. The idea is to convince voters that the candidates are average people, not the elite—not wealthy lawyers or executives but common citizens.

6. Card Stacking. When people say that "the cards were stacked against me," 18 they mean that they were never given a fair chance. Applied to propaganda, card stacking means that one side may suppress or distort evidence, tell half-truths, oversimplify the facts, or set up a "straw man"—a false target—to divert attention from the issue at hand. Card stacking is a difficult form of propaganda both to detect and to combat. When a candidate claims that an opponent has "changed his mind five times on this important issue," we tend to accept the claim without investigating whether the candidate had good reasons for changing his mind. Many people are simply swayed by the distorted claim that the candidate is "waffling" on the issue.

Advertisers often stack the cards in favor of the products they are pushing. They 19 may, for instance, use what are called "weasel words." These are small words that usually slip right past us, but that make the difference between reality and illusion. The weasel words are underlined in the following claims:

"Helps control dandruff symptoms." (The audience usually interprets this as stops dandruff.)

"Most dentists surveyed recommend sugarless gum for their patients who chew gum." (We hear the "most dentists" and "for their patients," but we don't think about how many were surveyed or whether or not the dentists first recommended that the patients not chew gum at all.)

---

[1]*saccharine: exaggeratedly sentimental*

"Sticker price $1,000 lower than <u>most comparable</u> cars." (How many is "most"? What car does the advertiser consider "comparable"?)

Advertisers also use a card stacking trick when they make an unfinished claim. For example, they will say that their product has "twice as much pain reliever." We are left with a favorable impression. We don't usually ask, "Twice as much pain reliever as what?" Or advertisers may make extremely vague claims that sound alluring but have no substance: Toyota's "Oh, what a feeling!"; Coke's "the real thing"; Cheerios' "be happy be healthy." Another way to stack the cards in favor of a certain product is to use scientific-sounding claims that are not supported by sound research. When Ford claimed that its LTD model was "400 percent quieter," many people assumed that its LTD must be quieter than all other cars. When taken to court, however, Ford admitted that the phrase referred to the difference between the noise level inside and outside the LTD. Other scientific-sounding claims use mysterious ingredients that are never explained as selling points: Retsyn, "special whitening agents," "the ingredient doctors recommend."

7. Bandwagon. In the bandwagon technique, advertisers pressure, "Everyone's doing it. Why don't you?" This kind of propaganda often succeeds because many people have a deep desire not to be different. Political ads tell us to vote for the "winning candidate." The advertisers know we tend to feel comfortable doing what others do; we want to be on the winning team. Or ads show a series of people proclaiming, "I'm voting for the senator. I don't know why anyone wouldn't." Again, the audience feels under pressure to conform.

In the marketplace, the bandwagon approach lures buyers. Ads tell us that "nobody doesn't like Sara Lee" (the message is that you must be weird if you don't). They tell us that "most people prefer Brand X two to one over other leading brands" (to be like the majority, we should buy Brand X). If we don't drink Pepsi, we're left out of "the Pepsi generation." To take part in "America's favorite health kick," the National Dairy Council asks us, "Got Milk?" Maybelline advertisements for Great Lash mascara claim it is "America's Favorite Mascara!"

Why do these propaganda techniques work? Why do so many of us buy the products, viewpoints, and candidates urged on us by propaganda messages? They work because they appeal to our emotions, not to our minds. Often, in fact, they capitalize on our prejudices and biases. For example, if we are convinced that environmentalists are radicals who want to destroy America's record of industrial growth and progress, then we will applaud the candidate who refers to them as "tree huggers." Clear thinking requires hard work: analyzing a claim, researching the facts, examining both sides of an issue, using logic to see the flaws in an argument. Many of us would rather let the propagandists do our thinking for us.

Because propaganda is so effective, it is important to detect it and understand 24 how it is used. We may conclude, after close examination, that some propaganda sends a truthful, worthwhile message. Some advertising, for instance, urges that we not drive drunk, that we become volunteers, or that we contribute to charity. Even so, we must be aware that propaganda is being used. Otherwise, we have consented to handing over to others our independence of thought and action.

QUESTIONS 2

ABOUT UNITY

1. Which sentence best expresses the main idea of McClintock's essay?

   a. Americans may be exposed daily to over five hundred advertising claims of some sort.

   b. The testimonial takes advantage of the admiration people have for celebrities, even though they have no expertise on the product being sold.

   c. People should detect and understand common propaganda techniques, which appeal to the emotions rather than to logic.

   d. Americans need to understand that advertising, a huge industry, affects their lives in numerous ways.

2. Which statement would best serve as a topic sentence for paragraph 6?

   a. Using glittering generalities is a technique that stirs positive feelings in the target audiences.

   b. Using glittering generalities is the opposite of name calling.

   c. Glittering generalities use vague terms that have different meanings to them, so they affect people differently.

   d. Glittering generalities are used by politicians and political causes.

ABOUT SUPPORT

3. In paragraph 1, McClintock's choice of words reveals her attitudes toward both propagandists and the public. What specific words reveal her attitudes, and what attitudes do they represent?

   _____

   _____

   _____

   _____

   _____

4. What key term does McClintock define in paragraph 2? Why does she define it here? Where else in the essay does she use the technique of definition?

_____

_____

_____

_____

5. McClintock provides abundant examples throughout her essay. Why does she provide so many examples? What does she accomplish with this technique?

_____

_____

_____

_____

ABOUT COHERENCE

6. List the parts of this essay that show its organization.

_____

7. The main method of organization of paragraph 3 is

   a. time order.

   b. emphatic order.

8. The author uses several transitions in paragraph 20. List four.

_____

ABOUT THE INTRODUCTION AND/OR CONCLUSION

9. What is the relationship between the essay's first paragraph and its concluding paragraph?

_____

_____

_____

10. The conclusion of "Propaganda Techniques in Today's Advertising" is made up of

   a. a summary of the techniques she discussed and a final thought.

   b. a quotation about propaganda and its effects on people.

   c. final thoughts and a recommendation about remaining vigilant.

   d. final questions that people need to ask themselves.

Writing an Essay with Emphasis on Definition

The term *hero* is used so much that it is at risk of losing its meaning. In this extended definition essay, you are to identify someone who has been a hero in your life and explain why that person is a hero. Your definition may identify sensory characteristics of your hero, compare your hero to another person who is not a hero, and/or compare your hero to the dictionary definition. You may want to review Chapter 13, "Comparison and/or Contrast," Chapter 8, "Description," and Chapter 9, "Narration," to incorporate different types of support for your profile.

PREWRITING

a.   Look up the dictionary definition of *hero* and decide if it does or doesn't support your idea of a hero.

b.   Gather information about your subject by using a prewriting method of your choice. You will want to write down as much information as possible within a ten-minute period. Don't worry about spelling, grammar, organization, or anything other than getting your thoughts down on the page. If ideas are still flowing at the end of ten minutes, keep on writing.

c.   Once you have finished getting your thoughts down, you should have a base of raw material that you can draw on in the next phase of your work. Judging from what you have produced, do you think you have enough material to support your essay? If so, keep following the steps below. If not, choose another person and spend about ten minutes generating ideas to see if they might be a better subject.

d.   As you devise your opening paragraph, *don't* begin with the overused phrase "According to Webster. . . ."

e.   Remember that the thesis of your definition is a version of "What a hero means to me." Your thesis should demonstrate why this person is a hero to you.

f.   You may find outlining to be a helpful organizational strategy for this essay.

g.   Now write the first draft of your essay.

REVISING

After you have completed the first draft of the paper, set it aside for a while if you can. Then read the paper out loud to a friend or classmate whose judgment you respect. Keep in mind the questions in the **FOUR BASES** Checklist at the end of

this chapter as you hear your own words, and ask your friend to respond to them as well. As you revise your essay through one or more additional drafts, continue to refer to that checklist until you can answer "yes" to each question.

Choose one of the terms below as the subject of an essay that emphasizes definition. Each term refers to a certain kind of person.

Personal

Shutterstock

steveallenuk/123RF

Good neighbor

Busybody

Whiner

Con artist

Optimist

Pessimist

Team player

Bully

Scapegoat

Snob

Practical joker

Procrastinator

Loner

Type A

Outlier

Character

Original

Influencer

Foodie

Visionary

Planner

Colleague

PREWRITING

a. As you devise your opening paragraph, you may want to refer to the dictionary definition of the term. If so, be sure to use only one meaning of the term. (Dictionaries often provide several different meanings for a term.) *Don't* begin your paper with the overused phrase "According to Webster. . . . "

b.   Remember that the thesis of a definition essay is a version of "What X means to me." The thesis presents what *your* experience has made *you* think the term actually means.

c.   As you plan your supporting paragraphs, think of different parts or qualities of your term. Here, for example, are the three-part divisions of the student essays considered in this chapter:

> Football fans are extreme in terms of their behavior, their fascination with the past, and their loyalty.
>
> Student zombies are the "living dead," are controlled by a "mysterious force," and are likely to suffer an "awful fate."

d.   Support each part of your division with either a series of examples or a single extended example.

e.   You may find outlining to be the most helpful prewriting strategy for your essay. As a guide, write your thesis and at least three supporting points in the spaces below.

Thesis: _____

Support: 1. _____

2. _____

3. _____

4. _____

REVISING
Once you have the first draft of your essay completed, read it aloud to a friend or classmate. The two of you should review it with the **FOUR BASES** Checklist in mind.

Jacob Lund/
Shutterstock

WRITING ASSIGNMENT 3

Academic

In this extended definition essay, you are to define a term from another course. For instance, if you are studying anthropology, you might define *culture*, or if you are studying criminal justice, you might define *environmental crime*. Not only will you need to write an extended definition, but you should also create a persuasive tone for your essay in order to convince your audience that you truly understand the term and that your definition is a correct one. You will want to check Chapter 16, "Argument," to help you create a persuasive tone.

PREWRITING

a. As you devise your opening paragraph, it would be helpful to refer to the class in which you are studying the term in order to provide an introduction for the reader and to establish a context for the term.

b. Your thesis should demonstrate why the term is important to understand in this field. It should also describe how your own experience has influenced your understanding of what the term actually means.

c. As you plan your supporting paragraphs, you may find outlining to be a helpful organizational strategy for this essay emphasizing definition.

d. Now write the first draft of your essay.

REVISING

After you have completed the first draft of the paper, set it aside for a while if you can. Then read the paper out loud to a friend or classmate whose judgment you respect. Keep in mind the questions in the FOUR BASES Checklist at the end of this chapter as you hear your own words, and ask your friend to respond to them as well. As you revise your essay through one or more additional drafts, continue to refer to that checklist until you can answer "yes" to each question.

Jacob Lund/
Shutterstock

Writing for a Specific Purpose and Audience

WRITING ASSIGNMENT 4

Work

In the past year, your school has had problems with parents demonstrating poor sportsmanship at school events. At one football game, two parents started yelling at a player because he missed a pass. At a theater production, several parents ridiculed a young girl who had forgotten her lines. At a chess tournament, a mother whose child was losing started accusing everyone else of cheating. The principal has decided to address this behavior, so he has asked you to create a handout, defining school standards and explaining what good sportsmanship is and how it applies to school events. Your definitions will need to focus on both attitudes and actions. You may want to review Chapter 8, "Description," and Chapter 10, "Exemplification," to help you develop and support your essay.

Definition Checklist: THE FOUR BASES

ABOUT *UNITY*

✔ Does my thesis statement indicate why the term is important and how I define the term?

✔ Are there portions of the essay that do not support my thesis and therefore should be eliminated or rewritten?

ABOUT *SUPPORT*

✔ Have I supported my definition with an extended example?

✔ Do my details help explain my definition of the term?

ABOUT *COHERENCE*

✔ Have I consistently used a single method of development in each supporting paragraph?

✔ Is there a clear sense of organization in my essay?

✔ Does my essay have a conclusion that emphasizes the main idea and gives an impression of resolution to the essay?

ABOUT *SENTENCE SKILLS*

✔ Have I used a consistent point of view throughout my essay?

✔ Have I used specific rather than general words?

✔ Have I avoided wordiness and used concise wording?

✔ Are my sentences varied?

✔ Have I edited for spelling and other sentence skills errors, as listed in the checklist at the back of the book?

READING

p. 341: McClintock, Ann. "Propaganda Techniques in Today's Advertising." Used by permission of Townsend Press.

Division-Classification

Visit an online library like the Library of Congress at http://www.loc. gov and browse through the various categories. If you are more interested in music, visit Pandora at http://www.pandora.com and browse the different categories of music. Or, visit a site like Overstock at http://www.overstock.com and browse the categories of items for sale. Then design your own site selling, lending, or streaming something similar. (You can be as creative as you like.) Provide at least five categories for your "product" and explain what distinguishes each one.

Library of Congress Prints and Photographs Division

This chapter will explain and illustrate how to

- develop an essay with emphasis on division-classification

- write an essay with emphasis on division-classification

- revise an essay with emphasis on division-classification

In addition, you will read and consider

- two student essays that emphasize division-classification

- one professional model essay that emphasizes division-classification

When you return home from your weekly trip to the supermarket with five bags packed with your purchases, how do you sort them out? You might separate food items from nonfood items (like toothpaste, paper towels, and detergent). Or you might divide and classify the items into groups intended for the freezer compartment, the refrigerator, and the kitchen cupboards. You might even put the items into groups like "to be used tonight," "to be used soon," and "to be used last." Sorting supermarket items in such ways is just one simple example of how we spend a great deal of our time organizing our environment in one manner or another.

In this chapter, you will be asked to write an essay in which you divide or classify a subject according to a single principle. To prepare for this assignment, first read the student essays and the model essay that follow and work through the questions that accompany the essays.

Student Essays to Consider

Academic

Over the years shopping malls have evolved from one primary type—indoor enclosed spaces—to encompass a variety of possible layouts and types, including those like the one in this photo that are set up outdoors to resemble village streets. As you read this essay, think about the types of shopping malls you have been to and the people you have observed.

randy andy/Shutterstock

Mall People

People often question what goes into "having fun." For many, "fun" involves getting out of the house, seeing other people, having something interesting to look at, and enjoying a choice of activities, all at a reasonable price. Going out to dinner or to the movies may satisfy some of those desires, but often not all. However, an attractive alternative does exist in the form of the free-admission shopping mall. Teenagers, couples on dates, and the nuclear family can all be observed having a good time at the mall.

Teenagers are drawn to the mall to pass time with pals and to see and be seen by other teens. The guys saunter by in sneakers, T-shirts, and jeans, carrying sodas and snacks from the food court. The girls stumble along in midriff-baring tank tops, with a cell phone tucked snugly in the rear pocket of their low-waisted jeans. Traveling in a gang that resembles a wolf pack, the teenagers make the shopping mall their hunting ground. Mall managers

1

2

continued

have obviously made a decision to attract all this teenage activity. The kids' raised voices and loud laughter can be heard from as far as half a mall away. They come to "pick up girls," to "meet guys," and just to "hang out."

Couples find fun of another sort at shopping malls. The young lovers   3
are easy to spot because they walk hand in hand, stopping to sneak a quick kiss after every few steps. They first pause at a jewelry store window so that they can gaze at diamond engagement rings and platinum wedding bands. Then, they wander into furniture departments in the large mall stores. Finally, they drift away, their arms wrapped around each other's waist.

Mom, Dad, little Toni, and Carlos visit the mall on Friday and Saturday   4
evenings for inexpensive recreation. Hearing the music of the antique carousel housed there, Toni begs to ride her favorite pony with its shining golden mane. Carlos shouts, "I'm starving!" and drags the family toward the food court, where he detects the seductive odor of pizza. Mom walks through a fabric store, running her hand over the soft velvets and slippery silks. Meanwhile, Dad has wandered into a cooking store and is admiring the enameled cookware he'd love to buy someday. The mall provides something special for every member of the family.

Sure, some people visit the mall in a brief, businesslike way, just   5
to pick up a specific purchase or two. But many more are shopping for inexpensive recreation. The teenagers, the dating couples, and the nuclear families all find cheap entertainment at the mall.

What to Watch

Academic

Netflix has become a mainstay in many people's lives. Even before it   1
was a streaming service, Netflix's DVD delivery service allowed people to experience the excitement and wonder of the world of movies. Netflix categorizes movies into genres like action comedy, horror, dramas, and cult films, which makes it very easy to pick a film according to one's tastes and/or moods. Netflix also allows five individual profiles for each account; these profiles allow family members to organize their own individual queues and get individualized recommendations from Netflix. The individual profiles and their corresponding queues tell a lot about the viewer.

In the group "Romance," movies like *To All the Boys I've Loved*   2
Before, Romance is a Bonus Book, and *Roped* are available. The viewer could spend hundreds of hours watching boy meets girl, boy and girl fall

continued

in love, boy and girl fight, boy and girl reunite. If, however, the viewer is looking for more holiday-specific movies, a quick search of "Romantic Christmas," reveals hours more of fun with films like *The Holiday Calendar, A Christmas Prince, The Princess Switch,* and *Operation Christmas Drop.* Finally, a quick search of "Love & Friendship" brings up another large group of movies and television shows like *Outlander, Bridgerton,* and *Orange Is the New Black.* Setting up a profile based solely on romance movies will provide hours of love and first kisses. It's clear that the Netflix viewer who wants to binge-watch only "cheesy chick flicks" can find many different movies to fill the queue.

Not all Netflix viewers want to watch romantic movies; some want 3 to spend their time watching more thoughtful and educational films. The category "Documentaries" is perfect for the more serious-minded Netflix customer; in fact, Netflix places enough importance on this category to have dedicated subcategories. In "Science & Nature Docs," the viewer can find films like *My Octopus Teacher, Night on Earth,* and *Spycraft.* By watching films in the "Biographical Documentaries" category, a person can learn about Nina Simone in *What Happened, Miss Simone?;* Natascha Kampusch in *Natascha Kampusch;* and Walter Mercado in *Mucho Mucho Amor.* The best way to learn about musicians is through documentaries because old footage is usually included. For a person who wants to travel to exotic lands, but doesn't have the money or time, the category "Travel & Adventure Documentaries" offers hours of discovery with titles like *The Summit*, a film about K2, the second highest mountain in the world; *They Call It Myanmar*, a film about Burma; and *Rock the Park*, a series of episodes about America's national parks.

For Netflix viewers who have young children in the house, the 4 category "Children & Family Movies" offers hours of family-friendly shows. Like the "Documentaries" category, this category also has subcategories to help parents quickly find shows that are age or topic appropriate. The subcategories are "Movies for Ages 2 to 4" and "Movies for Ages 11 to 12." There is also a subcategory called "Movies Based on Children's Books"; it is suited to anyone—young or old—who wants to see favorite books come to life on the screen. Films such as these that are family-friendly and based on familiar stories offer hours of safe and enjoyable viewing.

Netflix has done a great service to its customers by offering ways to 5 personalize the viewing experience. By setting up separate profiles and adding specific movie types to the queue, people can pick a profile that fits a particular mood and then quickly find movies to match. Binge-watching has never been easier.

ABOUT UNITY

1. In which supporting paragraph in "What to Watch" is the topic sentence at the end rather than, as is more appropriate for student essays, at the beginning?

2. Which sentence in paragraph 2 of "Mall People" should be omitted in the interest of paragraph unity? (*Write the opening words.*)

3. What sentence in paragraph 3 of "What to Watch" should be omitted in the interest of paragraph unity? (*Write the opening words.*)

ABOUT SUPPORT

4. After which sentence in paragraph 3 of "Mall People" are more supporting details needed? (*Write the opening words.*)

5. Which paragraph in "What to Watch" lacks sufficient specific details? _____

6. Label as *sight, touch, hearing,* or *smell* all the sensory details in the following sentences taken from "Mall People."

   a. "Hearing the music of the antique carousel housed there, Toni begs to ride her favorite pony with its shining golden mane."

   b. Carlos shouts, "I'm starving!" and drags the family toward the food court, where he detects the seductive odor of pizza."

   c. "Mom walks through a fabric store, running her hand over the soft velvets and slippery silks."

ABOUT COHERENCE

7. What are the time transition words used in paragraph 3 of "Mall People"?

   _____   _____   _____

8. Which topic sentence in "What to Watch" functions as a linking sentence between paragraphs? (*Write the opening words.*)

ABOUT THE INTRODUCTION AND/OR CONCLUSION

9. What kind of introduction is used in "What to Watch"? (*Circle the appropriate letter.*)

   a. broad, general statement narrowing to a thesis

   b. idea that is the opposite of the one to be developed

   c. quotation

   d. anecdote

10. What conclusion technique is used in "Mall People"? (*Circle the appropriate letter.*)

   a. summary

   b. prediction or recommendation

   c. quotation

Developing an Essay with Emphasis on Division-Classification

Considering Purpose and Audience

When writing an essay that emphasizes division and classification, your purpose is to present your audience with your own unique way of dividing and classifying particular topics. In order to write a successful essay, you will need to first choose a topic that interests readers and lends itself to support that can be divided and classified. Once you pick your topic and decide on the support you will use, you will then have to come up with your own specific sorting system—one that readers will be able to understand.

For example, if your essay focuses on types of clothing, there are a number of ways to sort this topic into categories. You could divide clothing by the function it serves: shirts and jackets (to cover the upper body); pants and skirts (for the lower body); and shoes and socks (for the feet). Or you could divide clothes according to the materials they are made from: animal products, plant products, and synthetic materials. A more interesting, and potentially humorous, way to divide clothes is by fashion: clothes that are stylish, clothes that are going out of style, and clothes that are so unattractive that they never were in style. Notice that in all three of these cases, the broad topic of clothing has been divided into categories according to a particular principle (function, materials, and fashion). When you divide your topic for your essay, be sure to come up with your own division principle and make it clear to your readers.

Once you've selected your topic and figured out how to divide it, you will need to provide specific details so that readers fully understand the categories you created. For the example about fashion above, you might classify plaid bell-bottom pants as part of the "going out of style" category, while blue jeans might belong in the "clothes that are stylish" group and a mustard-yellow velour jacket might fit in the "never stylish" group. Whatever divisions you establish, be sure to include enough details to make your division-classification method—your main point— clear to your readers. Equally important, keep your audience in mind. An audience of fashion-conscious young people, for instance, would probably have very different opinions about what is and isn't stylish than an audience of middle-aged bankers. Or an audience made up of the parents of middle-school students who are clamoring for "epic" clothes would have much more interest in clothing styles than the parents of students about to enter college.

Development through Prewriting

Julia, the writer of "Mall People," believed from her observations that "people at malls" would make a good topic for an essay that emphasizes division-classification. But she did not immediately know how she wanted to group those people or what she wanted to say about them. She decided to begin her prewriting by making a list of observations about mall shoppers. Here is what she came up with:

Families with kids

Lots of snacking

Crowds around special displays—automobiles, kiddie rides

Older people walking in mall for exercise

Groups of teenagers

Women getting made over at makeup counter

Dating couples

Lots of people talking and laughing rather than shopping

Interviewers stopping shoppers to fill out questionnaires

Kids hanging out, meeting each other

As Julia reviewed her list, she concluded that the three largest groups of "mall people" were families with children, groups of teens, and dating couples. She decided to organize her essay around those three groups. To further flesh out her idea, she created a scratch outline that her essay would follow. Here is the scratch outline Julia prepared:

Mall offers inexpensive fun for several groups

- *Teens*
  - *roam in packs*
  - *dress alike*
  - *meet new people*
- *Dating couples*
  - *act romantic*
  - *window-shop for future home*
  - *have lovers' quarrels*
- *Families*
  - *kids' activities*
  - *cheap food*
  - *adults shop*

Julia's list and outline prepared her to write the first draft of her essay.

First Draft

Mall People

Malls aren't only places to go shopping. They also offer free or at least cheap fun and activities for lots of people. Teenagers, dating couples, and families all like to visit the mall.

Teenagers love to roam the mall in packs, like wolves. They often dress alike, depending on the latest fashion. They're noisy and sometimes rude, and mall security officers sometimes kick them out of the building. Then they find somewhere else to go, maybe one of the warehouse-sized

continued

amusement and video-game arcades. Those places are fun, but they tend to be more expensive than just "hanging out" at the mall. Teens are usually not as interested in shopping at the mall as they are in picking up members of the opposite sex and seeing their friends.

Dating couples also enjoy wandering around the mall. They are easy to spot because they walk along holding hands and sometimes kissing. They stare at diamond rings and wedding bands and shop for furniture together. Sometimes they have spats and one of them stomps off to sulk on a bench for a while.

Little kids and their parents make up a big group of mall-goers. There is something for every member of the family there. There are usually some special displays that interest the kids, and Mom and Dad can always find things they like to window-shop for. Another plus for the family is that there is inexpensive food, like burgers and pizza, available at the mall's food court.

Development through Revising

After Julia completed her first draft, she put it aside. She knew from previous experience that she was a better critic of her own writing after she took a break from it. The following morning, when Julia read over her first draft, she noticed several places where it could be improved. Here are the observations she put in her writing journal:

- *My first paragraph does present a thesis (malls offer inexpensive entertainment), and it tells how I'm going to develop that thesis (by discussing three groups of people). But it isn't very interesting. I think I could do a better job of drawing readers in by describing what is fun about malls.*

- *Some of the details in the essay aren't necessary; they don't support my main idea. For instance, the stuff about teens being kicked out of the mall and about dating couples having fights doesn't have anything to do with the entertainment malls provide. I'll eliminate these.*

- *Some of my statements that do support the main idea need more support. For example, when I say there are special displays that interest the kids in paragraph 4, I should give an example of such a display. I should also back up the idea that many teens dress alike.*

With these observations in mind, Julia returned to her essay and revised it, producing the version that appears at the beginning of this chapter.

A Model Essay to Consider

Now read the following essay. Then answer the questions and read the comments that follow.

My Library

by A. A. Milne

When I moved into a new house a few weeks ago, my books, as was natural, moved 1
with me. Strong, perspiring men shovelled them into packing-cases, and staggered
with them to the van, cursing Caxton as they went. On arrival at this end, they
staggered with them into the room selected for my library, heaved off the lids of the
cases, and awaited orders. The immediate need was for an emptier room. Together
we hurried the books into the new white shelves which awaited them, the order in
which they stood being of no matter so long as they were off the floor. Armful after
armful was hastily stacked, the only pause being when (in the curious way in which
these things happen) my own name suddenly caught the eye of the foreman. "Did
you write this one, sir?" he asked. I admitted it. "H'm," he said noncommittally. He
glanced along the names of every armful after that, and appeared a little surprised
at the number of books which I hadn't written. An easy-going profession, evidently.

So we got the books up at last, and there they are still. I told myself that 2
when a wet afternoon came along I would arrange them properly. When the wet
afternoon came, I told myself that I would arrange them one of these fine mornings. As they are now, I have to look along
every shelf in the search for the book
which I want. To come to Keats is no guarantee that we are on the road to Shelley.
Shelley, if he did not drop out on the way,
is probably next to *How to Be a Golfer
Though Middle-aged.*

Having written as far as this, I had to 3
get up and see where Shelley really was.
It is worse than I thought. He is between
Geometrical Optics and *Studies in New
Zealand Scenery.* Ella Wheeler Wilcox,
whom I find myself to be entertaining
unawares, sits beside *Anarchy or Order,*
which was apparently "sent in the hope
that you will become a member of the
Duty and Discipline Movement"—a vain
hope, it would seem, for I have not yet

*Think of a category of people, pets, or things
in your life that mean a great deal. Create a
scratch outline, with subcategories, for a
division-classification essay on this topic.*
Milos Batinic/Shutterstock

paid my subscription. *What I Found Out*, by an English Governess, shares a corner with *The Recreations of a Country Parson*; they are followed by *Villette* and Baedeker's *Switzerland*. Something will have to be done about it. But I am wondering what is to be done. If I gave you the impression that my books were precisely arranged in their old shelves, I misled you. They were arranged in the order known as "all anyhow." Possibly they were a little less "anyhow" than they are now, in that the volumes of any particular work were at least together, but that is all that can be claimed for them. For years I put off the business of tidying them up, just as I am putting it off now. It is not laziness; it is simply that I don't know how to begin.

Let us suppose that we decide to have all the poetry together. It sounds rea- 4 sonable. But then Byron is eleven inches high (my tallest poet), and Beattie (my shortest) is just over four inches. How foolish they will look standing side by side. Perhaps you don't know Beattie, but I assure you that he was a poet. He wrote those majestic lines:

> The shepherd-swain of whom I mention made
> On Scotia's mountains fed his little flock;
> The sickle, scythe or plough he never swayed—
> An honest heart was almost all his stock.

Of course, one would hardly expect a shepherd to sway a plough in the ordi- 5 nary way, but Beattie was quite right to remind us that Edwin didn't either. Edwin was the name of the shepherd-swain. "And yet poor Edwin was no vulgar boy," we are told a little further on in a line that should live. Well, having satisfied you that Beattie was really a poet, I can now return to my argument that an eleven-inch Byron cannot stand next to a four-inch Beattie, and be followed by an eight-inch Cowper, without making the shelf look silly. Yet how can I discard Beattie— Beattie who wrote:

"And now the downy cheek and deepened voice Gave dignity to Edwin's blooming prime."

You see the difficulty. If you arrange your books according to their contents 6 you are sure to get an untidy shelf. If you arrange your books according to their size and colour you get an effective wall, but the poetically inclined visitor may lose sight of Beattie altogether. Before, then, we decide what to do about it, we must ask ourselves that very awkward question, "Why do we have books on our shelves at all?" It is a most embarrassing question to answer.

Of course, you think that the proper answer (in your own case) is an indignant 7 protest that you bought them in order to read them, and that you put them on your shelves in order that you could refer to them when necessary. A little reflec- tion will show you what a stupid answer that is. If you only want to read them, why are some of them bound in morocco and half-calf and other expensive cov- erings? Why did you buy a first edition when a hundredth edition was so much cheaper? Why have you got half a dozen copies of the *Rubaiyat*? What is the particular value of this other book that you treasure it so carefully? Why, the fact that its pages are uncut. If you cut the pages and read it, the value would go.

So, then, your library is not just for reference. You know as well as I do that it furnishes your room; that it furnishes it more effectively than does paint or mahogany or china. Of course, it is nice to have the books there, so that one can refer to them when one wishes. One may be writing an article on sea-bathing, for instance, and have come to the sentence which begins: "In the well-remembered words of Coleridge, perhaps almost too familiar to be quoted"—and then one may have to look them up. On these occasions a library is not only ornamental but useful. But do not let us be ashamed that we find it ornamental. Indeed, the more I survey it, the more I feel that my library is sufficiently ornamental as it stands. Any reassembling of the books might spoil the colour-scheme. Baedeker's *Switzerland* and *Villette* are both in red, a colour which is neatly caught up again, after an interlude in blue, by a volume of Browning and Jevons' *Elementary Logic*. We had a woman here only yesterday who said, "How pretty your books look," and I am inclined to think that that is good enough. There is a careless rapture about them which I should lose if I started to arrange them methodically. 8

But perhaps I might risk this to the extent of getting all their heads the same way up. Yes, on one of these fine days (or wet nights) I shall take my library seriously in hand. There are still one or two books which are the wrong way round. I shall put them the right way round. 9

QUESTIONS 2

ABOUT UNITY

1. Which of the following statements best represents the main idea of the selection?
   a. Milne likes his library and wants to show it off to people.
   b. Milne recognizes that his library currently lacks any type of organization.
   c. Milne thinks that all libraries should be organized alphabetically.
   d. Milne asserts that libraries are meant to furnish a room.

2. What is the topic sentence for paragraph 8? (*Write the opening words.*)

   _____

ABOUT SUPPORT

3. Milne claims that a library furnishes a room better than what?

   _____

4. Milne makes a claim that people who buy books just to read them aren't being honest with themselves. Which of the following does he NOT use as support for this claim?

a. Some books are bound in expensive coverings like morocco and half-calf.

b. First editions are more expensive than a hundredth edition.

c. Buying books and not opening them or "cutting" the pages.

d. Buying books to arrange in color-schemes in the library.

5. In paragraph 3, Milne states that his books were arranged in the order known as what?

_____

6. What three different ways does Milne suggest he could organize his library?

_____

ABOUT COHERENCE

7. Which method of organization does Milne use in his essay?

a. Time order

b. Emphatic order

8. In paragraphs 4 and 5, Milne creates continuity through repetition. What major words or names does he repeat in these paragraphs?

_____

ABOUT THE INTRODUCTION AND/OR CONCLUSION

9. Which method best describes the introduction to "My Library"?

a. quotation

b. idea that it is the opposite of the one to be developed

c. anecdote

d. broad, general statement narrowing to thesis

10. Milne ends his essay with a reference that looks back to paragraph 2. What is this reference?

_____

_____

_____

Writing an Essay with Emphasis on Division-Classification

WRITING ASSIGNMENT 1

In this essay, you are to organize the music on your iPod, smartphone, or other music medium into at least three categories and explain how these categories

reflect who you are. You might have categories like "workouts" or "studying"; you might even have more specific categories like "music to listen to after breaking up with a guy." You will want to review Chapter 8, "Description," and Chapter 9, "Narration," to help you create support and details that will appeal to your reader.

Image Source/DreamPictures/Getty Images

PREWRITING

a. For at least ten minutes, look at the songs you have on your iPod, smartphone, or tablet and group the songs into possible categories. You might create your categories by type (sad, soul, jazz) or group (BTS, Apres, The Chicks) or by when you listen to the songs (with my parents, with friends, in the car). Whichever grouping principle you choose, be sure to come up with meaningful categories.

b. Decide on a thesis statement that will introduce your topic and claim. Two possible thesis statements follow:

My iPod is filled with thousands of songs that can be categorized to explain my moods.

My tablet is filled with songs that I listen to while I am with my parents, whenever I am alone, and when I am out with friends.

c. You may need to spend some extra time generating ideas to come up with additional support for your thesis. You do not want to simply inventory the songs that are on your iPod; instead, you want to highlight one or two songs in each category, and explain why those songs are good examples for that category. You may even want to incorporate a narrative with one or two songs in your essay as added support; gathering story ideas at this point will only help you as you draft your essay.

d. Now write the first draft of your essay.

REVISING

After you have completed the first draft of the paper, set it aside for a while if you can. Then read the paper out loud to a friend or classmate whose judgment you respect. Keep in mind the questions in the FOUR BASES Checklist at the end of this chapter as you hear your own words, and ask your friend to respond to them as well. As you revise your essay, continue to refer to that checklist until you can answer "yes" to each question.

WRITING ASSIGNMENT 2

Many students find college to be more expensive than they expected, and as credit card companies continue to give cards away, more and more students are finding themselves deeper in debt than they need to be. The best way to save money, or not overspend, is to create a budget that helps you keep track of your cash flow. For this essay, you will need to classify common expenses that college students have and come up with a plan that helps students spend their money more wisely. You will want to review Chapter 10, "Exemplification," and Chapter 16, "Argument," to help you create an effective essay.

PREWRITING

a. First, you'll need to classify typical student expenses. You may want to break them down by month or semester to help organize them. You should then divide these expenses into necessary and unnecessary.

b. Once you have categorized students' typical expenses, generate some ideas that could help students save money. You should provide ideas for savings in both categories.

c. Create a thesis statement that introduces your topic and your proposal. Two possible thesis statements follow:

Students in college often go deeper into debt than they need to and should follow a simple plan to avoid this pitfall.

Students in college should organize and budget their expenses in order to avoid getting deeper in debt than necessary.

d. Now write the first draft of your essay.

REVISING

After you have completed the first draft of the paper, set it aside for a while if you can. Then read the paper out loud to a friend or classmate whose judgment you respect. Keep in mind the questions in the FOUR BASES Checklist as you hear your own words, and ask your friend to respond to them as well. As you revise your essay, continue to refer to that checklist until you and your reader can answer "yes" to each question.

Jacob Lund/
Shutterstock

Writing for a Specific Purpose and Audience

In this essay that emphasizes division-classification, you will write with a specific purpose and for a specific audience.

Imagine that your boss has asked you to prepare a section for the employee handbook. The purpose of this section is to explain to new employees the three main types of clients they can expect to deal with and how to properly handle those clients. For instance, if you work at a salon and spa, you may explain there are three kinds of clients that you must regularly handle: the over-demanding customer, the environmentally conscious client, and the customer who never knows what they want. Or maybe you work at a restaurant and the regular clients are business people, senior citizens, and families with small children. Once you have identified the types, you will need to explain in detail how to effectively work with each specific group. You will want to review Chapter 8, "Description," Chapter 10, "Exemplification," and Chapter 12, "Cause and Effect," to help you create effective support for your essay.

Division-Classification Checklist:
THE FOUR BASES

ABOUT UNITY

✔ Does my essay have a clearly stated thesis, including the topic and a dominant impression or principle of division?

✔ Does my essay describe the classifications in a clear, logical way?

✔ Are there portions of the essay that do not support my thesis and therefore should be eliminated or rewritten?

ABOUT SUPPORT

✔ Have I backed up my thesis with specific examples that support the divisions I am discussing?

✔ Is essential information missing that could help the reader understand my point?

✔ Are my support points detailed enough to create an interesting essay?

ABOUT COHERENCE

✔ Is each one of the paragraphs in the body of my essay based on one of the categories I am describing?

✔ Do I have a concluding paragraph that provides a sense of completion to the essay?

ABOUT SENTENCE SKILLS

✔ Have I used a consistent point of view throughout my essay?

✔ Have I used specific rather than general words?

✔ Have I avoided wordiness and used concise wording?

✔ Are my sentences varied?

✔ Have I edited for spelling and other sentence skills errors, as listed in the checklist at the back of the book?

READING

p. 362: Milne. A. A., "My Library," in *Not That It Matters*. New York: E. P. Dutton & Company. 1920.

Argument

This chapter will explain and illustrate how to

- develop an essay with emphasis on argument

- write an essay with emphasis on argument

- revise an essay with emphasis on argument

In addition, you will read and consider

- two student essays that emphasize argument

- one professional model essay that emphasizes argument

Should cell phones be permitted in class? Look at the photograph above and write an essay in which you argue for or against the use of cell phones in the classroom. Include at least three separate reasons that support your point of view.
Ariel Skelley/Getty Images

Do you know someone who enjoys a good argument? Such a person likes to challenge any sweeping statement we might make. For example, when we say something like "Ms. Lucci doesn't grade fairly," they come back with "Why do you say that? What are your reasons?"

Our questioner then listens carefully as we state our case, judging if we really do have solid evidence to support our point of view. We realize that saying, "Ms. Lucci just doesn't, that's all," sounds weak and unconvincing, so we try to come up with stronger evidence to back up our statement. Such a questioner may make us feel uncomfortable, but we may also feel grateful to them for helping us clarify our opinions.

The ability to put forth sound and compelling arguments is an important skill in everyday life. You can use argument to make a point in a class discussion, persuade a friend to lend you money, or talk an employer into giving you a day off. Becoming skilled in clear, logical reasoning can also help you see through faulty arguments that others may make. You'll become a better critic of advertisements, newspaper articles, political speeches, and the other persuasive appeals you see and hear every day.

In this chapter, you will be asked to write an essay in which you defend a position with a series of solid reasons. In a general way, you have done the same thing—making a point and then supporting it—with all the essays in this book. The difference here is that argument advances a *controversial* point, a point that at least some of your readers will not be inclined to accept. To prepare for this assignment, first read about five strategies you can use in advancing an argument. Then read the student essays and the model essay that follow and work through the questions that accompany the essays.

Strategies for Argument

Because argument assumes controversy, you have to work especially hard to convince readers of the validity of your position. Here are five strategies you can use to help win over readers whose viewpoint may differ from yours.

1 Use Tactful, Courteous Language

In an essay that emphasizes argument, you are attempting to persuade readers to accept your viewpoint. It is important, therefore, not to anger them by referring to them or their opinions in rude or belittling terms. Stay away from sweeping statements like "Everybody knows that . . ." or "People with any intelligence agree that. . . ." Also, keep the focus on the issue you are discussing, not on the people involved in the debate. Don't write, "*My opponents* say that orphanages cost less than foster care." Instead, write, "*Supporters of orphanages* say that orphanages cost less than foster care." Terms like *my opponents* imply that the argument is between you and anyone who disagrees with you. By contrast, a term such as *supporters of orphanages* suggests that those who don't agree with you are nevertheless open-minded people who are willing to consider differing opinions.

2 Point Out Common Ground

Another way to persuade readers to consider your opinion is to point out common ground—opinions that you share. Find points on which people on all sides of the argument can agree. Perhaps you are arguing that there should be an 11 P.M. curfew for juveniles in your town. Before going into detail about your proposal, remind readers who oppose such a curfew that you and they share certain goals: a safer city, a lower crime rate, and fewer gang-related tragedies. Readers will be more receptive to your idea once they have considered how you and they think alike.

3 Acknowledge Differing Viewpoints

It is a mistake to simply ignore points of view that conflict with yours. Acknowledging other viewpoints strengthens your position in several ways. First, it helps you spot flaws in the opposing position—as well as in your own argument. Second, and equally important, it gives the impression that you are an open-minded person, willing to look at an issue from all sides. Readers will be more likely to consider your point of view if you indicate a willingness to consider theirs.

At what point in your essay should you acknowledge opposing arguments? The earlier the better—ideally, in the introduction. By quickly establishing that you recognize the other side's position, you get your readers on board with you, ready to hear what else you have to say.

One effective technique is to *cite the opposing viewpoint in your thesis statement.* You do this by dividing your thesis into two parts. In the first part, you acknowledge the other side's point of view; in the second, you state your opinion, suggesting that yours is the stronger viewpoint. In the following example, the opposing viewpoint is underlined once; the writer's own position is underlined twice:

> Although some students believe that studying a foreign language is a waste of time, two years of foreign-language study should be required of all college graduates.

For another example of a thesis that acknowledges an opposing viewpoint, look at this thesis statement, taken from the second student essay in this chapter, "Once Over Lightly: Local TV News":

> While local TV newscasts can provide a valuable community resource, too often such programs provide mere entertainment at the expense of solid news.

Another effective technique is to use one or two sentences (separate from the thesis) in the introduction to acknowledge the alternative position. Such sentences briefly state the "other side's" argument. To see this technique at work, look at the introduction to the first student essay in this chapter, "Teenagers and Jobs," noting the sentence "Many people argue that working can be a valuable experience for the young."

A third technique is to *use a paragraph within the body of your essay to summarize opposing opinions in greater detail.* To do this successfully, you must spend some time researching those opposing arguments. A fair, evenhanded summary of the other side's ideas will help convince readers that you have looked at the issue from all angles before deciding where you stand. Imagine, for instance, that you are writing an essay arguing that the manufacture and sale of handguns should be outlawed. You would begin by doing some library research to find information on both sides of the issue, making sure to pay attention to material that argues against your viewpoint. You might also talk with local representatives of the National Rifle Association or other organizations that support gun ownership. Having done your research, you would be in a good position to write a paragraph summarizing the opposing viewpoints. In this paragraph, you might mention that many citizens believe that gun ownership is a right guaranteed by the Constitution and that gun owners fear that outlawing handguns would deprive law-abiding people of protection against gun-toting criminals. Once you had demonstrated that you understood opposing views, you would be in a stronger position to present your own point of view.

4 When Appropriate, Grant the Merits of Differing Viewpoints

Sometimes an opposing argument contains a point whose validity you cannot deny. What should you do then? The strongest strategy is to admit that the point is a good one. You will lose credibility if you argue against something that clearly makes sense. Admit the merit of one aspect of the other argument while making it clear that you still believe your argument to be stronger overall. Suppose that you were arguing against the use of computers in writing classrooms. You might say, "Granted, students who are already accustomed to computers can use them to write papers more quickly and efficiently"—admitting that the other side has a valid point. But you could quickly follow this admission with a statement making your own viewpoint clear: "But for students like me who write and think in longhand, a computer in the classroom is more a hindrance than a help; it would require too long a learning curve to be of any value to me."

5 Rebut Differing Viewpoints

Sometimes it may not be enough simply to acknowledge other points of view and present your own argument. When you are dealing with an issue that your readers feel strongly about, you may need to *rebut* the opposing arguments. To *rebut* means to point out problems with an opposing view, to show where an opponent's argument breaks down.

Imagine that you are writing an essay arguing that your college should use money intended to build a campus health and fitness center to upgrade the library instead. From reading the school paper, you know that supporters of the center say it will help attract new students to the college. You rebut that point by citing a study conducted by the admissions office that shows that most students choose a college because they can afford it and because they like its academic programs and facilities. You also emphasize that many students, already financially strapped, would have trouble paying the proposed fee for using the center.

A rebuttal can take two different forms: (1) You can first mention all the points raised by the other side and then present your counterargument to each of those points. (2) You can present the first point raised by the opposition and rebut that point, then move on to the second opposing point and rebut that, and so on.

Student Essays to Consider

Teenagers and Jobs

"The pressure for teenagers to work is great, and not just because of   1
the economic plight in the world today. Much of it is peer pressure to have
a little bit of freedom and independence, and to have their own spending
money. The concern we have is when the part-time work becomes the
primary focus." These are the words of Roxanne Bradshaw, educator and
officer of the National Education Association. Many people argue that
working can be a valuable experience for the young. However, working
more than about fifteen hours a week is harmful to adolescents because
it reduces their involvement with school, encourages a materialistic and
expensive lifestyle, and increases the chance of having problems with
drugs and alcohol.

Schoolwork and the benefits of extracurricular activities tend to   2
go by the wayside when adolescents work long hours. As more and
more teens have filled the numerous part-time jobs offered by fast-
food restaurants and malls, teachers have faced increasing difficulties.
They must both keep the attention of tired pupils and give homework
to students who simply don't have time to do it. In addition, educators
have noticed less involvement in the extracurricular activities that
many consider a healthy influence on young people. School bands
and athletic teams are losing players to work, and sports events are
poorly attended by working students. Those teens who try to do it all—
homework, extracurricular activities, and work—may find themselves
exhausted and prone to illness. A recent newspaper story, for example,
described a girl in Pennsylvania who suffered from extreme fatigue as a
result of aiming for good grades, playing on two school athletic teams,
and working thirty hours a week.

continued

Another drawback of too much work is that it may promote materialism   3
and an unrealistic lifestyle. Some parents claim that working helps teach
adolescents the value of a dollar. Undoubtedly that can be true. It's also
true that some teens work to help out with the family budget or to save
for college. However, surveys have shown that the majority of working
teens use their earnings to buy luxuries—nonessential electronic devices,
clothing, even cars. These young people, some of whom earn $500
or more a month, don't worry about spending wisely—they can just
about have it all. In many cases, experts point out, they are becoming
accustomed to a lifestyle they won't be able to afford several years down
the road, when they no longer have parents paying for car insurance,
food, lodging, and so on. At that point, they'll be hard-pressed to pay for
necessities as well as luxuries.

Finally, teenagers who work a lot are more likely than others to get   4
involved with alcohol and drugs. Teens who put in long hours may seek a
quick release from stress, just like the adults who need to drink a couple of
martinis after a hard day at work. Stress is probably greater in our society
today than it has been at any time in the past. Also, teens who have money
are more likely to get involved with drugs.

Teenagers can enjoy the benefits of work while avoiding its   5
drawbacks, simply by limiting their work hours during the school year.
As is often the case, a moderate approach will be the most healthy and
rewarding.

Once Over Lightly: Local TV News

Unfortunately, local television newscasts are not a reliable source   1
of news and don't provide in-depth coverage and analysis of issues.
While local TV newscasts can provide a valuable community resource,
too often such programs provide mere entertainment at the expense of
solid news. In their battle for high ratings, local programs emphasize news
personalities at the expense of stories. Visual appeal has a higher priority
than actual news. And stories and reports are too brief and shallow.

Local TV newscasters are as much the subject of the news as are   2
the stories they present. Nowhere is this more obvious than in weather
reports. Meteorologists spend valuable news time joking, drawing
cartoons, chatting about weather fronts as "good guys" and "bad guys,"
and dispensing weather trivia such as statistics about relative humidity
and record highs and lows for the date. Reporters, too, draw attention
to themselves. Rather than just getting the story, the reporters are
shown jumping into or getting out of helicopters to get the story. When

continued

reporters interview crime victims or the residents of poor neighborhoods, the camera angle typically includes them and their reaction as well as their subjects. When they report on a storm, they stand outside in the storm, their styled hair blowing, so we can admire how they "brave the elements." Then there are the news anchors, who are chosen as much for their looks as their skills. They, too, dilute the news by putting their personalities at center stage.

Often the selection of stories and the way they are presented are based on visual impact rather than news value. If a story is not accompanied by an interesting video, it is not likely to be shown on the local news. The result is an overemphasis on fires and car crashes and little attention to such important issues as the economy. A tractor-trailer spill on the highway slightly injures one person and inconveniences motorists for only an hour. But because it provides dramatic pictures—the big truck on its side, its load spilled, emergency personnel running around, lots of flashing lights—it is given greater emphasis in the local newscast than a rise in local taxes, which has far more lasting effect on the viewer. "If it bleeds, it leads" is the unofficial motto of many local news programs. A story that includes pictures of death and destruction, no matter how meaningless, is preferable on the local news to a solid, important story without flashy visuals. The mania for visuals is so strong that local news programs will even slap irrelevant visuals onto an otherwise strong story. A recent story on falling oil prices, for example, was accompanied by footage of a working oil well that drew attention away from the important economic information in the report.   3

On the average, about half a minute is devoted to a story. Clearly, stories that take less than half a minute are superficial. Even the longest stories, which can take up to several minutes, are not accompanied by meaningful analysis. Instead, the camera jumps from one location to another, and the newscaster simplifies and trivializes the issues. For instance, one recent "in-depth" story about the homeless consisted of a glamorous reporter talking to a homeless person and asking him what should be done about the problem. The poor man was in no condition to respond thoughtfully. The story then cut to an interview with a city bureaucrat who mechanically rambled on about the need for more government funding. Is raising taxes the answer to every social problem? There were also shots of homeless people sleeping in doorways and on top of heating vents, and there were interviews with people in the street, all of whom said that something should be done about the terrible problem of homelessness. There was, in all of this, no real exploration of the issue and no proposed solution. It was also apparent that the homeless were just the issue of the week. After the week's coverage was over, the topic was not mentioned again.   4

continued

Because of the emphasis on newscasters' personalities and on the   5
visual impact of stories and the short time span for stories, local news
shows provide little more than diversion. What viewers need instead is
news that has real significance. Rather than being amused and entertained,
we need to deal with complex issues and learn uncomfortable truths that
will help us become more responsible consumers and citizens.

ABOUT UNITY

1. Which paragraph in "Once Over Lightly" lacks a topic sentence?_____
   Write a topic sentence for the paragraph:

   _____

2. What sentence in paragraph 4 of "Once Over Lightly" should be omitted in the interest of paragraph unity? *(Write the opening words.)*

   _____

3. Which sentence in paragraph 4 of "Teenagers and Jobs" should be omitted in the interest of paragraph unity? *(Write the opening words.)*

   _____

ABOUT SUPPORT

4. Which sentence in paragraph 4 of "Teenagers and Jobs" needs to be followed by more supporting details? Which sentence in paragraph 2 of "Once Over Lightly" needs to be followed by supporting details? *(Write the opening words of each sentence.)*

   _____

   _____

5. In "Teenagers and Jobs," which supporting paragraph raises an opposing idea and then argues against that idea? _____ What transition word is used to signal the author's change of direction?_____

6. In paragraph 2 of "Once Over Lightly," the topic sentence is supported by details about three types of newscasters. What are those three types?

   _____   _____   _____

ABOUT COHERENCE

7. Which two paragraphs of "Teenagers and Jobs" begin with an addition transition, and what are those words?

   _____   _____

8. Write the change-of-direction transition and the illustration transition in paragraph 3 of "Once Over Lightly."

Change of direction: _____   *Illustration:* _____

ABOUT THE INTRODUCTION AND/OR CONCLUSION

9. Two methods of introduction are used in "Teenagers and Jobs." Circle the
letters of these two methods.
   a. broad, general statement narrowing to thesis
   b. idea that is the opposite of the one to be developed
   c. quotation
   d. anecdote

10. Both essays end with the same type of conclusion. What method do they use?
   a. summary only
   b. summary and recommendation
   c. prediction

Developing an Essay with Emphasis on Argument

Considering Purpose and Audience

When you write an essay that has an emphasis on argument, your main purpose is
to convince readers that your particular view or opinion about a controversial issue
or topic is correct. In addition, at times, you may have a second purpose for your
essay: to persuade your audience to take some sort of action.

To convince readers, it is important to provide them with a clear main point
and plenty of logical evidence to back it up. Say, for example, you want to argue
that public schools should require students to wear uniforms. In this case, you
might do research to gather as much evidence as possible to support your point.
You may check to see, for instance, if uniforms are cheaper than the alternative.
Perhaps you could find out if schools with uniforms have a lower rate of violence
than those without them. You may even look for studies to see if students' academic performance improves when school uniforms are adopted. As you search
for evidence, be sure that it clearly links to your topic and supports the main
point you are trying to get across to your audience.

While consideration of your audience is important for all essay forms, it is
absolutely critical to the success of an essay that is persuasive in tone. Depending
on the main point you choose, your audience may be firmly opposed to your view
or somewhat supportive of it. As you begin planning your essay, consider what

your audience already knows, and how it feels about the main point of your essay. Using the example above, for instance, ask yourself what opinion your audience holds about school uniforms. What are likely to be their objections to your argument? Why would people not support your main point? What, if anything, are the merits of the opposing point of view? In order to "get inside the head" of your opposition, you might even want to interview a few people you're sure will disagree with you: say, for instance, a student with a very funky personal style who you know would dislike wearing a uniform. By becoming aware of the points of view your audience might have, you will know how to proceed in researching your rebuttal to their arguments.

> For more information on how to deal with opposing views in your essay, see the section in this chapter called, "Acknowledge Differing Viewpoints." By directly addressing your opposition, you add credibility to your argument and increase the chances that others will be convinced that your main point is valid.

TIP

Development through Prewriting

Before choosing a topic for her essay, Anna, the writer of "Teenagers and Jobs," asked herself what controversial subject she was particularly well qualified to argue. She wanted to select something she cared about, something she could sink her teeth into. As a person who had been an active member of her high school community—she had worked on the newspaper, played basketball, and sung in a chorus—Anna first thought of writing about student apathy. It had always bothered her to see few students taking advantage of the opportunities available to them in school. But as she thought more about individual students she knew and their reasons for not getting more involved in school and extracurricular activities, she changed her opinion. "I realized that 'apathy' was not really the problem," she explained. "Many of them worked so much that they literally didn't have time for school life."

After narrowing her thesis to the idea of "teenagers and work," Anna made a list of what she perceived as the bad points of students' working too much:

No time for real involvement in school and school activities

Students leave right after school—can't stay for clubs, practices

Don't have time to attend games, other school functions

Students sleep in class and skip homework

continued

> *Stress, extra money contribute to drug and alcohol use*
>
> *Teachers frustrated trying to teach tired students*
>
> *Having extra money makes teens materialistic*
>
> *Some get so greedy they drop out of school to work full-time*
>
> *Students miss the fun of being young, developing talents and social abilities*
>
> *Students burn out, even get sick*
>
> *Hanging around older coworkers can contribute to drug, alcohol use*
>
> *Buying luxuries gives teens unrealistic idea of standard of living*

As she reviewed and revised her list of points, Anna identified three main points to develop in her essay. Those she identified as points 1, 2, and 3. She realized that some of the other items she had jotted down were related ideas that might be used to support her main topics. She marked those with the number of the main idea they supported, in parentheses, like this: (1). She also crossed out points that did not fit.

> *1 No time for real involvement in school and school activities*
>
> *(1) Students leave right after school—can't stay for clubs, practices*
>
> *(1) Don't have time to attend games, other school functions*
>
> *~~Students sleep in class and skip homework~~*
>
> *2 Stress, extra money contribute to drug and alcohol use*
>
> *(1) Teachers frustrated trying to teach tired students*
>
> *3 Having extra money makes teens materialistic*
>
> *(3) Some get so greedy for money they drop out of school to work full-time*
>
> *~~Students miss the fun of being young, developing talents and social abilities~~*
>
> *~~Students burn out, even get sick~~*
>
> *(2) Hanging around older coworkers can contribute to drug, alcohol use*
>
> *(3) Buying luxuries gives teens unrealistic idea of standard of living*

Referring to this list, Anna wrote the following first draft of her essay.

Teenagers and Jobs

Many people think that working is a valuable experience for young people. But when teenagers have jobs, they are too likely to neglect their schoolwork, become overly materialistic, and get into trouble with drugs and alcohol.

Schoolwork and the benefits of extracurricular activities tend to go by the wayside when adolescents work long hours. As more and more teens have taken jobs, teachers have faced increasing difficulties. They must both keep the attention of tired pupils and give homework to students who simply don't have time to do it. In addition, educators have noticed less involvement in extracurricular activities. School bands and athletic teams are losing players to work, and sports events are poorly attended by working students. Those teens who try to do it all—homework, extracurricular activities, and work—may find themselves exhausted and burned out.

Another drawback of too much work is that it may promote materialism and an unrealistic lifestyle. Most working teens use their earnings to buy luxuries. These young people don't worry about spending wisely—they can just about have it all. They are becoming accustomed to a lifestyle they won't be able to afford several years down the road, when they have to support themselves.

Finally, teenagers who work are more likely than others to get involved with alcohol and drugs. Teens who put in long hours may seek a quick release from stress, just like the adults who need to drink a couple of martinis after a hard day at work. Also, teens who have money are more likely to get involved with drugs.

In short, teens and work just don't mix.

Development through Revising

Anna's instructor had offered to look over students' first drafts and suggest improvements for revision. Here is the note she wrote at the end of Anna's work:

Anna—Good beginning. While I think your thesis is overstated, it and each of your main topics are on the right track. Here are some points to consider as you write your next draft:

- Many teenagers find working a <u>limited</u> number of hours a week to be a good experience. I think it's a mistake to state flatly that it's <u>always</u>

a negative thing for teenagers to have jobs. Think about acknowledging that there can be good points to students' working part-time.

- You do a pretty good job of supporting your first main point ("Schoolwork and the benefits of extracurricular activities tend to go by the wayside when adolescents work long hours") by noting the effect of too much work on scholastic achievement and extracurricular activities. You <u>less</u> effectively support points 2 and 3 ("Another drawback of too much work is that it may promote materialism and an unrealistic lifestyle" and "Finally, teenagers who work are more likely than others to get involved with alcohol and drugs"). <u>Show</u> how teens become too materialistic; don't just state that they do. And what evidence do you have that working teens use drugs and alcohol more than others?

- Throughout the essay, can you come up with evidence beyond your own observations to support the idea that too much working is detrimental to teens? Look in the magazine indexes in the library and on the Internet for studies or stories that might support your thesis.

I'll look forward to seeing your final draft.

After considering her instructor's comments, Anna wrote the version of "Teenagers and Jobs" that appears in the section "Student Essays to Consider" earlier in this chapter.

Arguments can be made through visual images as well. What visual argument is suggested by this photograph? Is it effective? Why or why not?
Daniel Albach/Shutterstock

A Model Essay to Consider

Read the following essay. Then answer the questions and read the comments that follow.

Essay on the Importance of Teaching Failure

by Edward Burger

What can we conclude when undergraduates bemoan, "How did anyone ever 1 come up with this stuff?" Although the students might feel confused or bedazzled, there's one thing for certain: the instructor jumped over the requisite missteps that originally led to the discovery at hand. This type of intellectual revisionism often depicts weighty concepts and conclusions as slick and sanitized, and, as a result, foreign and intangible.

In reality, every idea from every discipline is a human idea that comes from a 2 natural, thoughtful, and (ideally) unending journey in which thinkers deeply understand the current state of knowledge, take a tiny step in a new direction, almost immediately hit a dead end, learn from that misstep, and, through iteration, inevitably move forward. That recipe for success is not just the secret formula for original scholarly discovery, but also for wise, everyday thinking for the entire population. Hence, it is important to explicitly highlight how essential those dead ends and mistakes are—that is, to teach students the power of failure and how to fail effectively.

Individuals need to embrace the realization that taking risks and failing are 3 often the essential moves necessary to bring clarity, understanding, and innovation. By making a mistake, we are led to the pivotal question: "Why was that wrong?" By answering this question, we are intentionally placing ourselves in a position to develop a new insight and to eventually succeed. But how do we foster such a critical habit of mind in our students—students who are hardwired to avoid failure at all costs? Answer: Just assess it.

For the last decade or so, I've put my students' grades where my mouth is. 4 Instead of just touting the importance of failing, I now tell students that if they want to earn an A, they must fail regularly throughout the course of the semester—because 5 percent of their final grade is based on their "quality of failure." Would such a scheme provoke a change in attitude? Absolutely—with this grading practice in place, students gleefully take more risks and energetically engage in discussions.

And when a student (say, Aaron) makes a mistake in class, he exclaims, "Oh 5 well, my quality of failure grade today is really high." The class laughs and then quickly moves to the serious next step—answering: Why was that wrong? It's not enough to console an incorrect response with a nurturing, "Oh, Aaron, that's not quite right, but we still think you're the best! Now, does anyone else have another guess?" Instead, a mistake solicits either the enthusiastic yet honest response, "Congratulations, Aaron—that's wrong! Now what lesson or insight is Aaron offering us?" or the class question, "What do you think? Is Aaron correct?" Either way, the students have to actively listen and then react, while Aaron sees his comment as an important element that allows the discussion to move forward.

I often refer back again and again to someone's previous mistake to celebrate 6 just how significant it was. If we foster an environment in our classrooms in which failing is a natural and necessary component in making progress, then we allow our students to release their own genius and share their authentic ideas—even if (or especially when) those ideas aren't quite polished or perfectly formed.

After returning a graded assignment and reviewing the more challenging ques- 7 tions, I ask students to share their errors—and the class immediately comes to life: everyone wants to show off their mistakes as they now know they are offering valuable learning moments. What's more, in this receptive atmosphere, it's actually fun to reveal those promising gems of an idea that turned out to be counterfeit.

More recently, I've asked my students to intentionally fail—in the spirit of an 8 industrial stress test. I now require my students to write a first draft of an essay very quickly and poorly—long before its due date—and then have the students use that lousy draft as a starting point for the (hopefully lengthy) iterative process of revising and editing. When the work is due, they must submit not only their final version, but also append their penultimate draft all marked up with their own red ink. This strategy assures that they will produce at least one intermediate draft before the final version. Not surprisingly, the quality of their work improved dramatically.

When I consult with or lead workshops for faculty and administrators, they are 9 drawn to this principle of intentionally promoting failure, which inevitably leads to the question: How do you assess it? The first time I tried my 5 percent "quality of failure," I had no idea how to grade it. But I practiced what I preached—taking a risk and being willing to fail in the noble cause of teaching students to think more effectively. I passionately believe that assessment concerns should never squelch any creative ped-agogical experiment. Try it today, and figure out how to measure it tomorrow.

In the case of assessing "quality of failure," at the end of the semester I ask 10 my students to write a one-page reflective essay describing their productive failure in the course and how they have grown from those episodes (which might have occurred outside of class—including false starts and fruitful iterations). They conclude their essay by providing their own grade on how they have evolved through failure and mistakes (from 0—meaning "I never failed" or "I learned nothing from failing" to 10—meaning "I created and understood in profound, new ways from my failed attempts"). I read their narratives, reflect on their class par-ticipation and willingness to take risks, and then usually award them the surpris-ingly honest and restrained grades they gave themselves. To date, I've never had a student complain about their "quality of failure" grade.

To my skeptical colleagues who wonder if this grading scheme can be exploited 11
as a loophole to reward unprepared students, I remind them that we should not
create policies in the academy that police students, instead we should create
policies that add pedagogical value and create educational opportunity. And with
respect to my grading failure practice, I found no such abuse at the three institutions in which I have employed it (Williams College, the University of Colorado
at Boulder and Baylor University). On the contrary, if implemented correctly, you
will see your students more engaged, more prepared, and more thoughtful in class
discussions and in life.

Beyond the subject matter contained in the thirty-two to forty-eight courses 12
that typical undergraduates fleetingly encounter, our students' education centers
about the most important creative feat of their lives—the creation of themselves:
Creating a mind enlivened by curiosity and the intellectual audacity to take risks
and create new ideas, a mind that sees a world of unlimited possibilities. So we
as educators and scholars should constantly be asking ourselves: Have I taught
my students how to successfully fail? And if not, then: What am I waiting for?

ABOUT UNITY

QUESTIONS 2

1. What is the thesis of Burger's essay? If it is stated directly, locate the relevant
   sentence or sentences. If it is implied, state the thesis in your own words.

   _____

   _____

2. Which statement would best serve as a topic sentence for paragraphs 5 and 6?
   a. Students should celebrate all failures in learning.
   b. Helping students celebrate effective failure helps them learn.
   c. Teachers should publicize students' failures to help them learn.
   d. Failure is part of education, so students just need to accept it.

3. Which statement would best serve as a topic sentence for paragraph 10?
   a. Students are required to grade themselves on their quality of failure, and
      their grades are usually honest and correct.
   b. Students are required to grade themselves on their quality of failure, but
      their grades are often inflated.
   c. Students are assigned to write a one-page reflective essay, so they can
      fully understand the nature of failure.
   d. By examining their successes in honest reflective essays, students are
      able to demonstrate their growth.

ABOUT SUPPORT

4. Which statement best expresses the implied point in paragraph 2?
   a. Only deep thinkers are able to understand how to fail effectively.
   b. Teachers need to introduce students to the secret formula that leads to success.
   c. Students need to be taught how to fail because it is the key to true scholarly discovery.
   d. Good ideas go through numerous iterations but always last the test of time.

5. Why does the author ask students to intentionally fail?
   a. His teaching style is contrarian so he approaches learning from an atypical point of view.
   b. He deliberately promotes contradictory ideas to what he actually teaches in the classroom.
   c. He wants students to understand what failure looks like, so they can avoid the experience of failure in the future.
   d. He wants students to free themselves from the need to be perfect all the time, so they are more open to learning.

6. Which of the following best defines the author's phrase "quality of failure"?
   a. a student's ability to accept a failing grade
   b. a student's ability to learn from a failing grade
   c. a student's ability to take academic risks
   d. a student's ability to fix their mistakes

ABOUT COHERENCE

7. Burger uses time order as his primary means of organization in this essay. Find four examples of time signals. (Some are *not* in the list in Chapter 4.)

   _____

8. In paragraph 11, Burger acknowledges an opposing point of view when he addresses his "skeptical colleagues." What sentence in that paragraph contains a "change of direction" signal indicating that Burger's own argument takes a different point of view? *(Write the first few words of that sentence.)*

   _____

ABOUT THE INTRODUCTION AND/OR CONCLUSION

9. Burger's introduction consists of two very brief paragraphs. Which statement best describes the style of his introduction?

   a. It presents an anecdote that is related to the topic of why students need to learn to fail.

   b. It presents a point of view about failure that is the opposite of the one that is developed in the essay.

   c. It presents some general ideas that lead to the topic of why students need to learn to fail.

   d. It presents a quotation that connects the topic to a historical context.

10. Which of these best describes the conclusion of "Essay on the Importance of Teaching Failure"?

    a. It leaves the reader with a thought-provoking idea.

    b. It summarizes the points of the essay.

    c. It narrates an anecdote about failing educational practices.

    d. It predicts what will happen if students don't learn to fail.

Writing an Essay with Emphasis on Argument

WRITING ASSIGNMENT 1

Find an editorial in your local newspaper with which you either strongly agree or strongly disagree. Write a letter to the editor responding to that editorial. State why you agree or disagree with the position taken by the paper. Provide several paragraphs of supporting evidence for your position. When you turn in the copy of your letter to your instructor, also turn in the editorial to which you are responding. Your instructor may want you to send your letter to the newspaper, but you will want instructor feedback before doing so. The topic of the editorial will determine the additional chapters you will need to review. For instance, if the editorial focuses on an implied definition, you will need to review Chapter 14, "Definition," but if the editorial focuses on the effects of a specific city project, you will need to review Chapter 12, "Cause and/or Effect."

PREWRITING

a. As you write your opening paragraph, make sure you include the title of the editorial and the date on which it appeared. Refer to Chapter 20, "Writing a Research Essay," to properly punctuate and cite this information.

b. If you are writing to disagree with the article, you will want to pay special attention to your tone, always keeping your words as respectful as possible. If you are writing to agree with the article, you should respectfully acknowledge the opposing point of view before stating your thesis. Often, an editorial is printed on the same page as another editorial or an op-ed piece that argues the opposite point; reading both articles will help you focus your introductory material to properly set up your reader.

c. As you organize your points, keep in mind that emphatic order (in which you end with your most important reason) is often the most effective way to organize an argument. Your reader is most likely to remember your final reason.

d. Proceed to write the first draft of your essay.

REVISING

After you have completed the first draft of the paper, set it aside for a while if you can. Then read the paper out loud to a friend or classmate whose judgment you respect. Keep in mind the questions in the FOUR BASES Checklist at the end of this chapter as you hear your own words, and ask your friend to respond to them as well. As you revise your essay through additional drafts, continue to refer to that checklist until you and your reader can answer "yes" to each question.

Jacob Lund/
Shutterstock

WRITING ASSIGNMENT 2

Write an essay in which you argue *for* or *against* any one of the three comments below. Support and defend your argument by drawing on your reasoning ability and general experience.

OPTION 1

For many years, junk food was available in school cafeterias and school vending machines across the nation. For decades, school cafeteria menus did not encourage the best eating habits. A 2012 federal mandate changed the kinds of foods offered in public schools so that, for the large part, junk food was no longer available, and there was a strong emphasis on healthy eating, including fruits and vegetables. This is only right. Schools are now practicing what they preach about the importance of healthy diets and it is commendable that they have stopped serving junk food.

OPTION 2

By the time many students reach high school, they have learned the basics in most subjects. Some still have much to gain from the education that high schools offer, but others might be better off spending the next four years in other ways. For their benefit, high school attendance should be voluntary.

OPTION 3

Many of today's young people are mainly concerned with prestigious careers, making money, and owning things. It seems we no longer teach the benefits of spending time and money to help the community, the country, or the world. Our country can strengthen these human values and improve the world by requiring young people to spend a year working in some type of community service.

WRITING ASSIGNMENT 3

Personal

Throughout history, people have publicly demonstrated for and against issues they feel passionately about. In 1963, thousands marched on Washington to protest the treatment of African Americans and demand equal civil rights. In 1982, one million anti-nuclear protesters stood up against America's development of nuclear weapons and called for an end to the cold war arms race. In 2016, the Standing Rock Sioux Tribe was joined by other tribes (or Native Nations), celebrities, and politicians to take a stand against the Dakota Access Pipeline to protect sacred land and water. In 2020, Americans throughout the nation protested police brutality against Black Americans.

Having strong convictions, however, doesn't always mean that a person needs to participate in a protest or public demonstration. Some arguments are much less controversial. For instance, students may feel that parking fees at their schools are too high or student housing is inadequate. Other students may feel passionately about healthy food

Protests and calls for activism are a cornerstone of American democracy.
Allison C Bailey/Shutterstock

choices being more available to those in lower socioeconomic groups.

For this assignment, you are to think about issues you are most concerned about. Then, you should support and defend your argument by drawing on your reasoning ability, general experience, and any necessary research. You may want to review Chapter 8, "Description," Chapter 10, "Exemplification," and Chapter 12, "Cause and/or Effect." If you need to incorporate research, you will want to review Part 3, "Researching, Writing, and Documenting."

The following essay is an example written by a student who suffers from celiac disease. The writer argues that doctors need to be more proactive in diagnosing the disease, so those afflicted can manage it and heal.

Academic

Celiac Disease Needs to Be Diagnosed to Be Controlled

It is estimated that one person in one hundred suffers from celiac   1
disease, a genetic disorder that causes digestive problems. These
problems occur when gluten, a protein composite found in grains like
wheat and barley, is ingested. The symptoms of celiac disease can
range from irritability and abdominal pain to severe weight loss and
fatigue. Also called celiac sprue, non-tropical sprue, gluten-sensitive
enteropathy, and coeliac disease, the disease can cause serious
damage that ranges from malnutrition to cancer. Doctors currently don't
know exactly what causes the disease, but they do understand that
people who have the disease have an overreaction to gluten in food.
Doctors need to take this disease seriously and run tests to diagnose it,
so those suffering from the disease can take control of their lives.

Even though diagnosing celiac disease can be difficult because   2
many of the symptoms are similar to other diseases like Crohn's,
anemia, or irritable bowel syndrome, it is important that doctors learn to
properly diagnose their patients. The obvious symptoms of celiac
disease are abdominal pain and bloating. Other less obvious symptoms
can be mouth blisters, joint irritation, and painful nerve damage. More
serious symptoms include weight loss, stunted growth, and osteoporosis.

These symptoms result from what is physically occurring within the   3
small intestine. The small intestine is lined with tiny finger-like projections
called villi; the villi are covered with microvilli. The villi and microvilli increase
absorption of nutrients. Celiac disease destroys them and obstructs nutrient
absorption. Without the villi, nutrients like vitamins and protein are not
absorbed and are quickly eliminated, often resulting in painful diarrhea.
Whether the symptoms are mild or severe, patients need doctors to help
them figure out the cause, so they can get the proper treatment.

Proper diagnosis of celiac disease often requires several expensive   4
tests and procedures. A blood test to screen for transglutaminase antibody
(tTG) is the primary test used to screen for celiac. Several other tests, like a
total immunoglobulin A test or the anti-giadan antibody, may be ordered if
the tTG test is positive for celiac disease. These tests will be positive in
celiac sufferers because their bodies see gluten as an enemy substance
and produce elevated levels of antibodies to fight the substance. If blood
tests are positive, doctors will often test a sample of the small intestine to
check for damaged villi. Some doctors may have patients swallow a
camera pill to examine the entire small intestine. Even though the
procedures can be expensive, diagnosis is the only way patients can be
sure of the correct treatment, so it is vital that doctors run the needed tests.

Unfortunately, there is currently no cure for celiac disease nor   5
medicine to control it, so doctors need to educate their patients about
how to control their symptoms. Celiac disease can be effectively
managed through a rigid diet; any foods that contain gluten must be

continued

avoided. Such foods include barley, bulgur, durum, farina, graham flour, rye, semolina, spelt, triticale, and wheat. Most gluten is found in food, but people diagnosed with celiac disease should also be aware of medicines, vitamins, and lip balms that may contain gluten. Once a person has started on a gluten-free diet, the body will begin to recover. The inflammation within the intestine will subside within several weeks. Full healing and regrowth of the villi may take as long as two to three years. Trace amounts of gluten can be damaging, so it is important that once a person is diagnosed with celiac they avoid all forms of gluten.

It is believed that as many as two million people are currently   6
undiagnosed with celiac disease or gluten sensitivity. It is imperative that doctors understand this disease and do not disregard patients who complain of symptoms of the disease. Since there is currently no medication to help heal patients, it is crucial that doctors diagnose patients before serious physical damage occurs and teach their patients how to manage the disease to avoid more damage.

Writing for a Specific Purpose and Audience

WRITING ASSIGNMENT 4

In this essay with emphasis on argument, you will write with a specific purpose and for a specific audience.

The art of persuasion in the workplace is so important that many businesses bring in educational consultants to teach employees how, why, and when to be persuasive. Often these companies charge several thousands of dollars for their expertise; however, to save money, your boss has asked you to write an essay that will be given to all employees explaining the art of persuasion and why it is a necessary skill in your workplace.

In order for employees to understand what they are being asked to do, you should incorporate an extended definition of what good persuasion is, and possibly contrast it with what good persuasion is not. You may also want to incorporate scenarios that demonstrate both good and bad examples to help your audience fully understand how and when to be persuasive.

Perhaps you work at an advertising company. One of your jobs is to acquire new client accounts, and persuading them to sign with you usually involves a key presentation. As the writer of this essay, you could give an example of one of your best presentations, explaining what was done correctly and why it worked. You could also give an example of one of your worst presentations, emphasizing what was done incorrectly. You will want to review Chapter 8, "Description," Chapter 11, "Process," Chapter 13, "Comparison and/or Contrast," and Chapter 14, "Definition," to help create a strong, persuasive essay.

Argument Checklist: THE FOUR BASES

ABOUT *UNITY*

✓ Have I included a thesis statement that clearly asserts an argument?

✓ Does each paragraph in my essay have a clear topic sentence that goes back to the thesis?

✓ Are there portions of the essay that do not support my thesis and therefore should be eliminated or rewritten?

ABOUT *SUPPORT*

✓ Have I provided persuasive details to support my argument?

✓ Have I included enough specific details to persuade my reader to agree with my argument?

ABOUT *COHERENCE*

✓ Have I acknowledged the opposing point of view, to demonstrate I have considered other arguments?

✓ Have I provided a concluding paragraph to summarize my argument or to add a final persuasive touch?

ABOUT *SENTENCE SKILLS*

✓ Have I used a consistent point of view throughout my essay?

✓ Have I used specific rather than general words?

✓ Have I avoided wordiness and used concise wording?

✓ Are my sentences varied?

✓ Have I edited for spelling and other sentence skills errors, as listed in the checklist at the back of the book?

READING

p. 383: Burger, Edward, "Essay on the Importance of Teaching Failure," *Inside Higher Ed,* August 21, 2012. Used with permission.

Researching, Writing, and Documenting

Michaeljung/Shutterstock

Write an essay about an experience you have had researching for and writing a source-based essay. What struggles and successes did you have? What could have made the process better? If you haven't yet written a source-based essay, write an essay about any concerns you have about the process and any challenges you anticipate.

Information Literacy

This chapter will explain and illustrate how to

- locate online sources efficiently
- evaluate online sources
- use the library in the context of the digital world

Write a letter to yourself exploring the difficulties you have had in the past navigating the Internet and your school library while trying to do research for a paper.

Mikael Vaisanen/Getty Images

Engaging in research means dealing with a lot of information from different sources. One of the keys to good research is understanding how to navigate all the information that is available to you. Students have the option of using:

- the Internet
- college libraries
- public libraries
- television
- radio
- personal interviews
- questionnaires

Navigating all this information and choosing what type is best for the project at hand can be overwhelming. Figuring out which of the multitude of results are credible and trustworthy and will support the purpose of your paper can also be daunting.

Often, students begin their research by going online, which usually nets more results than are possible to evaluate. This can cause both frustration and wasted time as students try to figure out where to start and what to read. Especially when operating under a time crunch, students don't always select the best resources for their papers. Knowing how to properly approach online research by using the right search engines and search terms and the right databases, as well as knowing how to find credible information, will save both time and frustration.

While you will most likely do a majority of your research online, you want to keep all resource possibilities open. You should always start with your college library, as it will provide you with the best sources. Since, like most libraries, it has a variety of print, online, and media sources available, it can be challenging to navigate the resources in a college library. Even though these are "library sources," you still have to understand how to evaluate and sift through your findings to find the best information for your needs. Among the many options are:

- general reference materials
- reserved references
- books
- periodicals
- Web sources
- databases

In addition, you will need to decide whether primary sources or secondary sources are best for your research. Primary sources are original sources—documents like:

- the Constitution
- the Bill of Rights
- research reports
- novels
- autobiographies
- poems

Secondary sources include:

- analyses such as poetry interpretations
- articles evaluating the Constitution
- commentaries on a piece of research

Knowing how to identify the best and most appropriate sources for your work and how to use each source accurately will help you immeasurably in your research and significantly reduce the amount of time you'll need to spend. This chapter will introduce you to ways of managing and evaluating resources to help you efficiently research information that supports the purpose of each essay that you write.

Although this chapter focuses on finding good sources for research, you should apply these same skills to any information you read, hear, or see on any media platform. You should be aware of two types of false information.

Misinformation is information that is falsely presented as correct with or without intent to mislead.

Disinformation is false information that is deliberately disseminated to manipulate a narrative.

Knowing how to critically evaluate sources, consult multiple sources, and understand source reliability will help you in both research and daily life.

Using Online Sources Effectively

Locating Sources Efficiently

When faced with a research paper assignment, students' initial reaction is to go to Google, type in some terms and start reading the links in the order they appear. Often, the first link students will see is Wikipedia, which seems to be full of information. However, the nature of Wikipedia—a site that can be edited by anyone—makes it unreliable as a source, regardless of its position in the list of results. Understanding that rank order doesn't necessarily mean that site is the *best choice* should make students wary of beginning with a general Google search.

Another weakness of starting with Google is that this type of research can lead to an overwhelming number of results, which will take far too long to sort through. It can also take more time than necessary as students try to determine what search terms will deliver the best results. Since search engines go through a vast amount of information to find articles containing any of the words you have put into your search, knowing what search engine to use for information gathering, how best to search, and how to sift through the results is important for all researchers.

Search Engines

While most people think of Google when they look up information, it is not the only search engine option, and students should try different ones. Meta search engines can produce more results because they get information from other search engines and are not confined to only one source of indexing. There are also specialized search engines that refine results to certain types of sources. Being familiar with specialized search engines can save you time because these engines focus their searches in specific areas.

General search engines:

- Bing
- DuckDuckGo
- Dogpile

Meta search engines:

- Mamma (retrieves news, image, and videos with filter capability)
- Symbaloo (can retrieve information from social networking sites like Twitter and image-sharing platforms like Instagram)
- Turbo Scout (searches other meta search engines)

Specialized search engines:

- Google Scholar (searches scholarly articles)
- WolframAlpha (creates data comparisons)
- LivePlasma (searches books, movies, and music)

Using a specialized search engine like Google Scholar can narrow an initial search dramatically and can reduce the number of results by 97 percent. An additional benefit to using Google Scholar is that the results will all be from scholarly sources that have been evaluated by several people prior to their publication. Like professionally published print sources, scholarly sources have to be approved by editors, peer reviewers, and publishers before they are accepted. You may not be able to get access to full-text copies of all the academic sources you find through your search, so you may need to use a database to access one, several, or all of the results you want to use.

Searching with Keywords and Boolean Operators

Being familiar with strong search terms (keywords) is also important when "Googling." If you want to do a paper on *free college tuition*, using Google will get you over 65 million results. However, if you narrow your search to *debt-free college tuition debate,* the results narrow to just over 450,000.

Using Keywords Efficiently

Knowing how to best use keywords will help you save time. Keywords, like *free college* above, are the general terms that are entered into search engines. When keywords are typed into a search, documents with all those words will be included in the list of results. However, because all the words are included, no matter how insignificantly they have been used within the document, thousands, if not millions, of results will be returned. This is why you need to be as specific as possible. Narrowing a search to *debt-free college tuition debate* will net fewer results because you have expanded all the specific words that must be contained in the document.

When searching with keywords, you will want to be aware of how synonyms and different phrases can affect not only the number of results, but also the quality of results. For instance, if you started researching with the keywords *free college* you would get over one billion results because the words are all very broad. Knowing that you want to find information on either attending college for free or graduating without debt—*debt-free*—will help you find more relevant material. This same idea applies to the word *debate* in the search. If you change the word *debate* to *argument*, the number of results increases because the word *argument* has much broader meanings. Be willing to try different, more specific, words as you search.

Understanding Boolean Operators

Understanding Boolean operators can also help you narrow your searches. By adding quotation marks around words, using AND, OR, or NOT, you can quickly change your results. In the earlier Google search, changing the phrase to *debt-free and college* causes the results to jump to seven million, but by changing the phrase to "*debt-free AND college*," the results drop to just seven. Boolean operators can be used with any of the search engines.

Databases

Databases, like JSTOR and Academic Search Elite, are services that offer you the ability to search and access periodicals and journals online. Most databases have to be accessed through a subscription service, so your library will be your best source. However, if your library doesn't subscribe to a certain database that you need to use, many offer individual subscriptions for reasonable fees. In this way you can, for example, read editions of *The Harvard Review* from the past thirty years. Common library databases will be discussed in more detail later in the chapter.

Evaluating Online Sources

Keep in mind that the quality and reliability of information you find on the Internet may vary widely, and it is your responsibility to learn how to discern valuable information from propaganda. Most reputable journals, news sources, and published books have editors and other staff members to verify information, thus giving you some assurance that care has been taken with the information. Online, however, no such quality control exists. Anyone with a bit of computer know-how can create

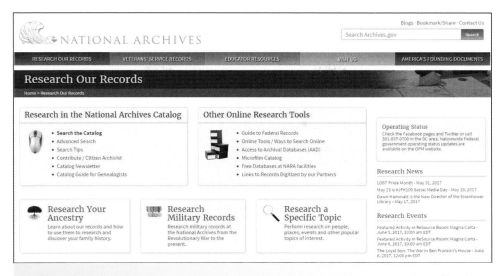

The National Archives searchable database is a good resource for reliable information.
Source: National Archives

a website, and it is very common for the information on sites to change overnight. The designer of a website may be a Nobel Prize winner, a leading authority in a specialized field, a high school student, or a conspiracy theory zealot. While the following information focuses on websites and other online sources, you should evaluate all your research (including print and media) in this manner to be sure you are using sources that are credible and support the purpose of your paper.

Determining the Reliability of an Online Source

Be careful to look closely at any source in the following ways:

1. **Internet address:** In a Web address (the Uniform Resource Locator or URL), the three letters following the "dot" are the domain. The most common domains are .com (usually a commercial organization); .edu (educational institution); .gov (government organization); and .org (non-profit or sometimes for-profit organization). A common misconception is that a website's reliability can be determined by its domain. This is not the case, as almost anyone can get a Web address ending in .com, .edu, .org, or any of the other domains. Therefore, it is important that you examine every website carefully, considering the four points that follow.

2. **Publisher or Sponsor:** Who maintains the site? Is the organization/group/individual reputable? What is the domain? Remember, these don't determine reliability, but they can help you find out who is responsible for the website.

3. **Author:** What credentials does the author have (if any)? Has the author published other material on the topic? Is the author known to have a particular stance (bias) on this topic? You may need to do some additional research through a Web search or library database search to find this information.

4. **Date:** Is the information up-to-date? Check at the top or bottom of the document for copyright, publication, or revision dates. Knowing such dates will help you decide whether the material is current enough for your purposes.

5. **Internal evidence:** Does the author seem to proceed objectively—presenting all sides of a topic fairly before arguing their own views? Does the author produce solid, adequate support for those views?

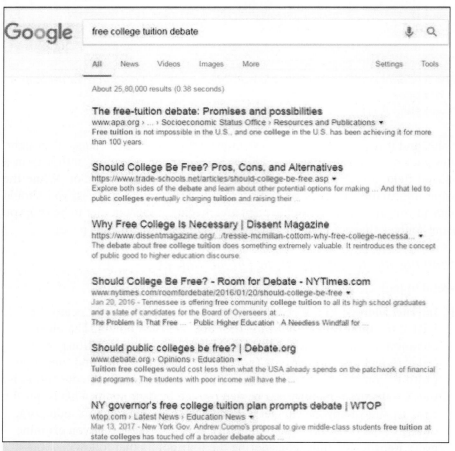

Results from a keyword search on Google using "free college tuition debate."
Source: Google

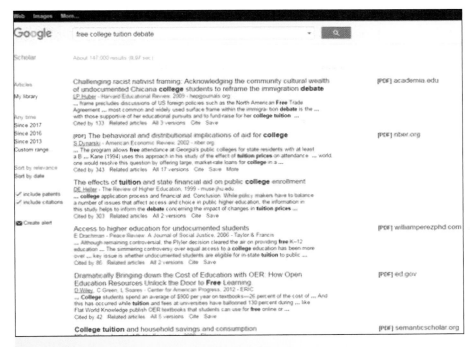

Results from a keyword search on Google Scholar using "free college tuition debate."

Source: Google

Comparing Results from Different Search Engines

The two preceding images show the different results a student could expect when using Google versus Google Scholar. Although the same search terms were used, the results on Google Scholar were not only fewer, but they were also more focused and research based.

Notice the difference in the number of results and types of results:

- In the first image, you can see that the first result is from the American Psychological Association, a well-known organization that works to advance the science of psychology. While it is a reputable source, you will still need to verify information you use from this site.

- The second result is a business-based website with information about tuition-free schools. A source like this will require you to read through the "about" section and verify the information. For instance, this website claims that Alice Lloyd College is tuition-free; you could verify this by going directly to the college's website.

- The third result is an online political and intellectual journal. This site will also require you to read the "about" section to learn who publishes the site, who the authors are, and what organization is behind the site. Politically oriented websites will always have a strong bias, so it is very important that you spend time fact-checking before you use such a source as support.

- The fourth result is from a popular news source. While it is a well-known source, you will still need to spend time validating the information and checking any claims provided for bias.

- The fifth result is an organization, and the sixth result is a commercial news site. Both of these will require you to read the "about" sections, look at biases, and verify information the authors present.

- In the second image, you can see all the results are from articles cited in other studies, based on research and published in specialized journals. These sources, while as potentially biased as organizations, do go through more steps in order to be published, so their credibility is already potentially stronger than the organizations and newspapers. You will still need to spend time analyzing the sources to determine how valuable they will be for your research, but you won't need to spend as much time determining whether or not the sources are credible.

Using Critical Thinking to Examine Online Sources

Once you have determined whether or not a source is reliable, you then need to work through the material to determine how well it will support the purpose of your essay. You will first want to analyze the author's argument, think about whether or not you have seen a similar opinion expressed elsewhere, and ask yourself if it endorses or counters the argument you are presenting (just because it counters your argument doesn't mean you cannot use it). As you look at the author's argument, you want to think about whether or not the author's support is valid and verifiable. Just because someone repeats something multiple times doesn't make it true. Another good way to verify your source is to look at the sources the author has cited. If the author is citing obviously biased sites or fake news sites, no matter how good the argument sounds, it is most likely based on poor information. When you decide that the resource will work in your research, you will want to familiarize yourself with it by reading it several times and determining how you see it fitting into your paper.

PART A

Go to www.google.com and search for *education*. Then complete the items below.

1. How many items did your search yield?_____

2. What are the first three listings?

   _____

3. Look through the first four pages of entries to find an example of each of the following domains: .edu, .gov, .org, and .com. Pick one site with each domain and write its full address.

   a. Address of one .com site: _____

   b. Address of one .gov site: _____

   c. Address of one .org site: _____

   d. Address of one .edu site: _____

PART B

Circle one of the sites you identified above and use it to complete the following evaluation.

4. Name of site's author or authoring institution: _____

5. Why did you choose this site? _____

   _____

6. Is the site's information current (within two years)? _____

7. Does the site serve obvious business purposes (with advertising or attempts to sell products)? _____

8. Does the site have an obvious connection to a governmental, commercial, business, or religious organization? If so, which one? _____

9. Does the site's information seem fair and objective? _____

   _____

10. Based on the information above, would you say the site appears reliable? _____

PART C

Try the following four search terms and compare the results on Google, Google Scholar, DuckDuckGo, Mamma, Symbaloo, WolframAlpha, and LivePlasma. On a separate sheet of paper, write down the number of returned results and the type of result that is listed in first place. Once you have compared each, choose one site and evaluate it for reliability. Explain what you have observed.

Education

"Elementary Education"

"Elementary Education" AND salary

"Elementary Education AND salary"

Using the Library in the Context of the Digital World

College libraries occupy both physical and virtual space. Getting familiar with both will benefit you well as you embark on your college journey.

The online resources can usually be accessed via your college library's home page, which typically contains information that includes location, hours, catalog of holdings, and selected databases. Some library home pages include features like:

- instant chat with a librarian
- access to other college catalogs
- research tools
- subject guides
- lists of websites that librarians have found to be useful and credible

Most students know that libraries' physical buildings provide study space, computer workstations, and copying machines. You should also be aware of a library's reading area, which contains recent copies of magazines and newspapers. Other features that you will find in the library are listed here:

- rows of books that can be perused and checked out
- DVDs and CDs that can be borrowed
- general reference materials that can be used in the library
- special materials that instructors put on reserve for specific class use

You should become familiar with your library and expect to use most, if not all, of its features at some point in your college experience. The more familiar you are with everything your library has to offer, the less time you will spend locating the information you need. Getting to know your librarians is an excellent way to start developing this familiarity and to help you navigate all the library has to offer. After a brief discussion of the role of librarians, we will examine the various resources—both print and online—a library offers.

Librarians

The number one resource available to you through your college library is the college librarian. Librarians help students and faculty with a variety of things. Often, we think of librarians acquiring, sorting, and checking out books, and while college librarians do just that, they also provide many other services. They work closely with faculty to make sure students' needs are being met, and they often set up subject guides or reserve materials that might be helpful for projects they know faculty are assigning. They are knowledgeable about the resources available to you and can quickly point you to the materials you need, often finding information for you in minutes rather than the hours or even days it might take you without assistance. Additionally, librarians often teach classes—in short sessions or sometimes over the course of a semester—about how to use the library and the library's databases, how to conduct good research, and how to strengthen the skills you need to find, manage, and evaluate resources.

Reference Materials

Primary Sources

Primary sources are original sources; they include conference presentations, dissertations, memoirs, photographs and paintings, speeches, works of literature, and government documents. Primary sources give students a direct connection to current and past events. By working directly with primary sources, students can create their own analyses of the original pieces without being influenced by others' interpretations. A good example of students' work with primary sources is an assignment requiring the writing of a literary analysis or a rhetorical analysis.

Secondary Sources

Secondary sources analyze, interpret, or comment on primary sources. Secondary sources include biographies, literature reviews, or articles written about primary sources. While secondary sources are someone else's interpretation and are often tainted by the prevailing social opinions, they can provide students with a wealth of information.

Using Both Primary and Secondary Sources Together

Often students will use secondary sources in conjunction with primary sources in order to create a full, clear picture of support. For instance, a student might be required to write an analysis of a Vincent van Gogh painting. They would first choose a painting that they find to be extremely interesting, and then analyze the piece themselves, focusing on any themes or techniques they are drawn to. To add support and weight to their analysis, they could then locate articles from art critics in the early 1900s and early 2000s. This would allow them to look at how van Gogh's paintings were critiqued in different periods and compare these critiques to their own.

General References

General references include encyclopedias, world fact books, dictionaries, atlases, manuals, and so on. Most of these can be found online, but if you do want a print source, be aware that these are often for library use only, so you will want to be prepared to spend an hour or two in the library.

Reserved References

Many libraries will have certain books, periodicals, reports, videos, and journals that cannot be taken out of the library. Instead, you will have to check out the material for a certain period, often two hours, and remain in the library while you read or view the material. It is common that professors will put such materials on reserve for students to use, but they will restrict the use to ensure all students have a chance to work with the material.

Library Catalog

The library catalog, accessible both online and on-site, is your entry point to the holdings in your library. These holdings can include print books, eBooks, downloadable audio books, CDs, and DVDs. Increasingly, more and more libraries have agreements with each other, so if a book or item isn't available at your library, you may have the option of requesting it from another library. Your college library website and librarians should have this information readily available.

Finding a Book

There are numerous ways to find books using your library's catalog. You can search by author, title, keyword(s), or subject.

Author, Title, Keywords, or Subject   If you are looking for a specific book or specific author, the easiest search would be an author or title search. For example, suppose you want to see if the library has the book *A Tribe Apart*, by Patricia Hersch. You could check for the book through:

1. An *author* search, in which you would look under *Hersch, Patricia.*

2. A *title* search, in which you would look under *Tribe Apart, A.*

However, if you are looking for books on specific topics, a *keyword* or *subject* search is your better choice. For example, if you are looking for a book about adolescent culture, you could check for a book through:

3. A *keyword* search. In this case, since the subject of the book is adolescents, you could look under words like *adolescent culture, codes,* and *values.* Keyword searches are the most common way to begin research because the system will look for that term anywhere in the record. Just as is true of the use of search engines, keyword searches are the easiest searches to employ when using online catalogs.

4. A *subject* search. Subject searches use very limited and defined vocabulary. While a good subject search can yield the best results, unless you know for sure what the subject search terms should be (in this case, "teenagers—United States"), subject searches should be done with the aid of a librarian.

Following is an example of an online catalog entry for Hersch's book, *A Tribe Apart.*

Note that in addition to giving you the publisher (Ballantine) and year of publication (1999), the entry also tells you the book's physical location and its *call number*—each of which will help you find it in the library. If you need to request the book from another library, your library will have a specific spot (front desk, reference desk, etc.) where the book will be waiting upon delivery.

Summary Points: Using Keywords and Subject Searches

- Searching by *keyword* allows for considerable flexibility of vocabulary and search parameters. Keyword searches for books in a library catalog work much the same way as keyword searches in search engines.

- Searching by *subject* requires knowledge of very controlled vocabulary and search parameters. It is best used with the aid of a librarian.

A tribe apart : a journey into the heart of American adolescence / Patricia Hersch
Hersch, Patricia.
Book/Journal | Ballantine Books | 1999 | 1st trade paperback ed.

☐ Request it

Summary
For three fascinating, disturbing years, writer Patricia Hersch journeyed inside a world that is as familiar as our own children and yet as alien as some exotic culture--the world of adolescence. As a silent, attentive partner, she followed eight teenagers in the typically American town of Reston, Virginia, listening to their stories, observing their rituals, watching them fulfill their dreams and enact their tragedies. What she found was that America's teens have fashioned a fully defined culture that adults neither see nor imagine--a culture of unprecedented freedom and baffling (...read more)

| MOBIUS - ARCHWAY | MOBIUS - BRIDGES | MOBIUS - Kansas City | | |
| MOBIUS - MERLIN | | | MOBIUS - SWAN | MOBIUS - TOWERS |

Details

Description	x, 391 pages ; 21 cm
Note	Includes index. "Featuring a Ballantine reader's companion"--Cover.
Contents	Preface to the paperback edition -- Prologue: Alone -- Stepping inside: On the brink -- Speaking out/acting out -- High school is for making memories -- Negative is positive -- Honor and other relative things -- School paper and a whole new adolescent world -- Making contact: Out of the whirlwind and on to the playing field -- Circle of friends: it's not peer pressure, it's the adolescent way of life -- Graffiti, God, and other meaningful things -- Sex: let's get it out of the way, but don't look at me naked -- Lacrosse and other challenges -- Taking care of each other and other grown-up preoccupations -- Moshing is a way to belong -- Shedding light on darkness: school is an uncomfortable place to learn -- Making sense: Rearrange your room when you can't arrange yourself -- Dilemmas of a fourteen-year-old girl: contradictions as a way of life -- Creating my own space: long cold winter and descent into darkness -- Broken promises: theirs and ours -- Doing high school the old-fashioned way -- It's my prom, my life -- Resignation: adolescence is sometimes a life-or-death issue -- Great unknown lies ahead: to the wilderness or to college -- Epilogue: Warm embrace -- Postscript -- Acknowledgments -- Index -- A reader's guide..
Subjects	Teenagers -- United States.
ISBN	034543594X (pbk.) :
OCLC #	42261321
LC CARD #	99090233
CALL #	HQ796 .H43 1999 305.235 H571t

Locations

Library	Where is it:		
MOBIUS - ARCHWAY	ECC General Collection	HQ 796 .H43 1999	AVAILABLE
MOBIUS - ARCHWAY	STLCC-W Stacks	305.235 H571t3	AVAILABLE
MOBIUS - BRIDGES	Covenant Seminary Stacks	HQ796 .H43 1999	AVAILABLE
MOBIUS - BRIDGES	Maryville Univ Main Collection	HQ796 .H43 1999	AVAILABLE
MOBIUS - Kansas City	Avila SPST Circulating	HQ796 .H43 1999	AVAILABLE
MOBIUS - Kansas City	RU Circ Top Floor	HQ796 .H43 1999	AVAILABLE
MOBIUS - MERLIN	MU Ellis	HQ796 .H43 1999	AVAILABLE
MOBIUS - SWAN	Evangel AGTS General Circulation	HQ796 .H43 1999	AVAILABLE

An example of an online catalog entry.
Source: MOBIUS

Use your library's catalog to answer the following questions.

1. What is the title of one book by Anna Quindlen? _____
   _____

2. What is the title of one book by Gabriel Garcia Marquez? _____
   _____

3. Who is the author of *A Tree Grows in Brooklyn*? (Remember to look up the title under *Tree*, not *A*.) _____

4. Who is the author of *Seven Habits of Highly Effective People*? _____
   _____

5. List two books and their authors dealing with the subject of "adoption."
   a. _____
      _____
   b. _____

6. List two books and their authors dealing with the subject of "virtual reality in education."
   a. _____ _____
      _____
   b. _____ _____
      _____

7. Look up a book titled *The Answer Is . . .: Reflections on My Life* or *White Fragility: Why It's So Hard for White People to Talk About Racism* and obtain the following information:
   a. Author _____
   b. Publisher _____
   c. Date of publication _____
   d. Call number _____
   e. One subject heading _____

8. Look up a book written by Paul Kalanithi or Elin Hilderbrand and obtain the following information:
   a. Title _____
   b. Publisher _____
   c. Date of publication _____
   d. Call number _____
   e. One subject heading _____

9. Look up a book using the keywords *community college*. On the line, write one of the titles published in 2019 or later. _____

_____

_____

10. Look up a book using the keywords *best jazz musician*. On the line, write one of the titles published in 2019 or later.

_____

_____

Book Stacks

The book stacks are the library shelves where books are arranged according to their call numbers. The call number, as distinctive as a Social Security number, always appears on the catalog entry for any book. It is also printed on the spine of every book in the library. If your library has open stacks (ones that you are permitted to enter), there is a basic procedure to finding a book. Suppose you are looking for *A Tribe Apart*, which has the call number HQ796.H43 in the Library of Congress system. (Libraries using the Dewey decimal system have call letters made up entirely of numbers rather than letters and numbers. However, you use the same basic method to locate a book.) The first place you would look is the section that holds the H's. You would then want to look for the HQ's, which will be listed alphabetically. Once you've located the section housing the HQ's, you would then look for HQ796 and finally HQ796.H43. If your library has closed stacks (ones you are not permitted to enter), you will have to write down the title, author, and call number and have a reference librarian get the book for you.

Periodicals

Periodicals—*magazines, journals*, and *newspapers*—are available in both print and electronic form. They contain recent or very specialized information about a subject, which may not be available in a book. Most libraries will have print copies of many of the magazines and journals students enjoy reading like *Rolling Stone* and *People*, and more scholarly sources like *Economic Policy, Shakespeare Quarterly,* and the *Journal of the American Medical Association*. If the source isn't available in print, check with your librarian to see if the resource is available online through one of the databases your college subscribes to. If not, the librarian may be able to secure it through an interlibrary loan or may be able to direct you to a nearby library that has that source either in print or electronic form.

Using Databases

As mentioned earlier in this chapter, most college and public libraries now provide online computer-search services known as online databases or library subscription services. Using any of these services, you will be able to type in keywords and quickly search many periodicals for articles on your subject. Some databases, such as General Science Index, are discipline-specific, but others, such as Academic Search Premier, are more general.

The search process can vary depending on the database you are using. As in searching the library catalog, your best choices are using an *author* or *title* search if you know the specific piece you are trying to locate or a *keyword* search if you are trying to gather information on a topic. Just as in a regular online search, using Boolean operators can help you narrow your results. Use a subject search only if you know exactly what vocabulary to use.

Different Formats

Often articles you find will be shown as "full text." That means that you can print out the entire article from your computer. In other cases, only an abstract (summary) of the article will be available. However, abstracts are valuable too, for they allow you to determine whether the article is relevant to your research and whether you should continue searching for the full text.

Finally, database articles appear in *html* (hypertext markup language) or *pdf* (portable document format) format or in both. Articles in .html have been reformatted for publication on the Internet. Those in .pdf are exact reproductions of a print document. Note that some databases are among many compiled by the same provider. EBSCOhost, Infotrac, and ProQuest are such providers.

Useful Databases

Following are a few online databases that have proven useful for new student researchers and are often available through college libraries. (You should become familiar with your college's offerings as not all databases are offered at all colleges.) If you are unsure which databases will be most useful for your research, reference librarians are skilled and knowledgeable in exactly this area and can help you locate the best source of information.

Academic Search Elite (EBSCO) covers a variety of disciplines and includes full-text articles and abstracts of articles from thousands of journals.

American History Online (Facts on File Reference Suite) contains hundreds of primary source documents.

ERIC (Education Resources Information Center) makes available articles from professional journals, reports, and speeches having to do with education.

JSTOR (Journal Storage) provides full-text articles found in back issues of journals in the humanities, social sciences, and natural sciences.

Lexis-Nexis Academic Universe has full-text access to over 10,000 journals, covering local and world news, legal cases, and business.

ProQuest Research Library provides articles covering a variety of topics including education, law, psychology, arts, and business.

Science Online (Facts on File Reference Suite) contains thousands of diagrams, experiments, videos, biographies, and essays.

ACTIVITY 3

1. Look up a recent article on immigration in America using one of your library's online databases and fill in the following information:

   a. Name of the index you used _____

   b. Article title _____

   c. Author (if given) _____

   d. Name of magazine _____

   e. Pages _____

   f. Date _____

2. Look up a recent article on the Supreme Court using one of your library's online databases and fill in the following information:

   a. Name of the index you used _____

   b. Article title _____

   c. Author (if given) _____

   d. Name of magazine _____

   e. Pages _____

   f. Date _____

ACTIVITY 4

Use your library or the Internet to research a subject that interests you. Select one of the following areas or (with your instructor's permission) an area of your own choice:

Animal rights movement	Immigration-related issues
Best job prospects today	LGBTQ+ resources
Censorship	Pollution of drinking water
Civil/Human rights	Prison reform
Drug treatment programs	Seat belt laws
Elections and voting	Sexual harassment
Gambling and youth	Software hacking protection
Greenhouse effect	Species nearing extinction
Health insurance reform	Stress reduction in the workplace
Holistic healing	Toxic waste disposal

Research the topic first through a keyword search in Google Scholar and one of your college library's databases. Finally, conduct a subject search in your library's catalog (enlisting the aid of a librarian, if necessary). On a separate sheet of paper, provide the following information:

1. Topic
2. Three full-text available articles on the topic published in 2012 or later. Include the following:

   Title of article

   Author (if given)

   Title of magazine/journal

   Date

   Pages (if given)
3. Three books that either cover the topic directly or at least touch on the topic in some way. Include the following:

   Author

   Title

   Place of publication

   Publisher

   Date of publication

   Whether it is available for checkout or on reserve
4. Finally, write a paragraph describing just how you went about researching your topic. In addition, include a photocopy or printout of one of the three articles.

18

Summarizing and Paraphrasing

This chapter will explain

- how to summarize an article

- how to paraphrase an article

- how to use a direct quotation

Find an article in your school or local newspaper. Choose one article and write a paragraph-length summary of that article. Then, using that same article, paraphrase one paragraph.

GM Visuals/Tetra Images, LLC/Alamy Stock Photo

Most writing will require students to use information from outside sources. In order to properly incorporate information and avoid plagiarism, you will need to first understand the material you are reading, which may require you to do a second or third reading, take careful notes, and choose how to incorporate the information. As a writer, you will need to decide whether or not to summarize or paraphrase the material or use a direct quotation. The general rule is, if the author says it brilliantly, use the author's words (quotation); if the author's ideas are great, but you can rewrite it to better fit your essay, use paraphrase or summary.

In this chapter, you will learn how to write summaries and paraphrases and be given a brief introduction to using direct quotations.
(Chapter 19, "Writing a Source-Based Essay," will further explain how to
incorporate quotations into your own writing.)

Identifying and Avoiding Plagiarism

If you fail to properly document information that you have incorporated into your
essay and is not your own, you will be stealing. The formal term is *plagiarizing*—
using someone else's work as your own. This is true whether you borrow a single
image, idea, sentence, or entire essay.

One example of plagiarism is turning in a friend's paper (or a paper you
purchased) as if it were your own. Another example is copying an article found
in a magazine, newspaper, journal, or on the Internet and turning it in as your
own. By copying someone else's work, you risk being failed or even expelled.
Equally, plagiarism deprives you of what can be a most helpful learning and
organization experience—researching and writing about a selected topic in detail.

Plagiarism presents a specific risk for each of the writing activities—
summarizing, paraphrasing, and using direct quotations—treated in this chapter.
For that reason, within each major section, you will find a brief discussion that
focuses on that activity and on what writers need to watch for specifically in order
to avoid plagiarizing.

Writing a Summary

At some point in a course, your instructor may ask you to write a summary of a book,
an article, a TV show, or the like. In a summary (also referred to as a *précis* or an
abstract), you reduce material in an original work to its main points and key supporting details. A summary may consist of a single word, a phrase, several sentences, or
one or more paragraphs. The length of any summary you prepare will depend on your
instructor's expectations and the length of the original work. Most often, you will be
asked to write a summary consisting of one paragraph. Summaries can be written as
stand-alone pieces or incorporated into essays as detailed support.

Writing a summary brings together a number of important reading, study, and
writing skills. To condense the original assigned material, you must preview, read,
evaluate, organize, and perhaps outline it. Summarizing, then, can be a real aid
to understanding; you must "get inside" the material and realize fully what is being
said before you can reduce its meaning to a few words.

Avoiding Plagiarism in Summary Writing

You need to be extra careful to avoid accidental plagiarism when writing a summary. A helpful method is to make sure you fully understand the material first, and then to avoid consulting the original piece while writing your summary. You can then inspect for plagiarism by checking your words and phrases against the original, making sure that the words used are your own and not the author's. You should also examine your sentence structure to confirm that you are not mimicking the author's sentence structure and merely inserting a new word here and there. Finally, you need to make sure you have credited the original source in your summary either by in-text citation or by crediting the author within the summary.

How to Summarize an Article

To write a summary of an article, follow the steps described below. If the assigned material is a TV show or film, adapt the suggestions accordingly.

1. Take a few minutes to preview the work. You can preview an article in a magazine by taking a quick look at the following:
    a. *Title.* A title often summarizes what an article is about. Think about the title for a minute and about how it may condense the meaning of the article.
    b. *Subtitle.* A subtitle, if given, is a short summary appearing under or next to the title. For example, in a *Newsweek* article titled "Growing Old, Feeling Young," the following caption appeared: "Not only are Americans living longer, they are staying active longer—and their worst enemy is not nature, but the myths and prejudices about growing old." In short, the subtitle, the caption, or any other words in large print under or next to the title often provide a quick insight into the meaning of an article.
    c. *First and last several paragraphs.* In the first several paragraphs, the author may introduce you to the subject and state the purpose of the article. In the last several paragraphs, the writer may present conclusions or a summary. The previews or summaries can give you a quick overview of what the entire article is about.
    d. *Other items.* Note any heads or subheads that appear in the article. They often provide clues to the article's main points and give an immediate sense of what each section is about. Look carefully at any pictures, charts, or diagrams that accompany the article. Page space in a magazine or journal is limited, and such visual aids are generally used only to illustrate important points in the article. Note any words or phrases set off in *italic type* or **boldface type;** such words have probably been emphasized because they deal with important points in the article.

2. Read the article for all you can understand the first time through. Do not slow down or turn back. Check or otherwise mark main points and key supporting details. Pay special attention to all the items noted in the preview. Also, look for definitions, examples, and enumerations (lists of items), which often indicate key ideas. You can also identify important points by turning any headings into questions and reading to find the answers to the questions.

3. Go back and reread more carefully the areas you have identified as most important. Also, focus on other key points you may have missed in your first reading.

4. Take notes on the material. Concentrate on getting down the main ideas and the key supporting points.

5. Prepare the first draft of your summary, keeping these points in mind:

   a. In the summary, identify the title and author of the work. If your summary is not part of an essay, with in-text citation and a "Works Cited" page, then you should also include the date of publication and publication name. The two examples below show the difference in format.

   b. The first sentence of your summary should also be written as a topic sentence and should contain the main idea or thesis of the original work in your own words.

   c. Do not write an overly detailed summary. Remember that the purpose of a summary is to reduce the original work to its main points and essential supporting details.

   d. Express the main points and key supporting details in your own words. Do not imitate the style of the original work.

   e. Never insert your own ideas or opinions into the summary. Be careful not to use loaded language. For instance, saying "the author tries to support her claims with studies" or "the author supports her claims with weak information" implies an opinion of how well argued the original piece is. A good summary, instead, would simply state, "the author supports her claims with studies."

   f. Periodically refer to the author (by last name) or article to emphasize that this is a summary. As well, use signal words (*argues, illustrates, asserts, observes, writes, reports*) to remind readers that the ideas being presented are directly from the article.

   g. Quote from the material only to illustrate key points. Limit your quotations. A one-paragraph summary should not contain more than one quoted sentence or phrase.

   h. Preserve the balance and proportion of the original work. If the original devoted 70 percent of its space to one idea and only 30 percent to another, your summary should reflect that emphasis.

i. Revise your first draft, paying attention to the four bases of effective writing *(unity, support, coherence,* and *sentence skills)* explained in Part 1.

j. Write the final draft of the summary.

A Model Summary of an Article

Here is a model summary of a magazine article that would stand on its own:

In the article, "Why the Campaign to Stop America's Obesity Crisis Keeps Failing," originally printed in the May 2012 *Newsweek,* Gary Taubes reports on the obesity epidemic and his beliefs that refined sugars are the cause of obesity. He begins his article by citing information from the 1930s that demonstrates children had obesity problems even during the Depression. Taubes then points out that despite government recommendations, Americans' dietary changes have not resulted in less obesity. He supports his claims about refined sugars and carbohydrates by detailing the science of fat cells, insulin, and the liver. He concludes with the assertion that the authorities like the Centers for Disease Control and Prevention and the National Institutes of Health may need to rethink what they are telling Americans (32–36).

Here is a model summary of a magazine article that is used in an essay containing a "Works Cited" page. Note that the publication information is not needed within the text, but it is available in the "Works Cited" entry. If this is the first time you are citing the article, you need to reference the article's title. However, if this is the second or subsequent time citing this article, you would refer only to the author's last name, as in "Taubes continues to remark . . . "

In his article, "Why the Campaign to Stop America's Obesity Crisis Keeps Failing," Gary Taubes reports on the obesity epidemic and his beliefs that refined sugars are the cause of obesity. He begins his article by citing information from the 1930s that demonstrates children had obesity problems even during the Depression. Taubes then points out that despite government recommendations, Americans' dietary changes have not resulted in less obesity. He supports his claims about refined sugars and carbohydrates by detailing the science of fat cells, insulin, and the liver. He concludes with the assertion that the authorities like the Centers for Disease Control and Prevention and the National Institutes of Health may need to rethink what they are telling Americans (32–36).

Works Cited

Taubes, Gary. "Why the Campaign to Stop America's Obesity Crisis Keeps Failing." *Newsweek* 14 May 2012, pp. 32–36.

Write a summary of the following article, "Power Learning," by Jerry Blythe. Your topic sentence should introduce the name of the article, the main purpose/thesis of the article, and the publication information. The rest of your summary should include only factual information that expresses the main points of the article. Your concluding sentence should express the closing idea presented in the article.

ACTIVITY 1

Power Learning

Jill had not done as well in high school as she had hoped. Since college involved even more work, it was no surprise that she didn't do better there.   **1**

The reason for her so-so performance was not a lack of effort. She attended most of her classes and read her textbooks. And she never missed handing in any assignment, even though it often meant staying up late the night before homework was due. Still, she just got by in her classes. Before long, she came to the conclusion that she simply couldn't do any better.   **2**

Then one day, one of her instructors said something to make her think otherwise. "You can probably build some sort of house by banging a few boards together," he said. "But if you want a sturdy home, you'll have to use the right techniques and tools. Building carefully takes work, but it gets better results. The same can be said of your education. There are no shortcuts, but there are some proven study skills that can really help. If you don't use them, you may end up with a pretty flimsy education."   **3**

Jill signed up for a study-skills course and found out a crucial fact— that learning how to learn is the key to success in school. Certain dependable skills have made the difference between disappointment and success for generations of students. These techniques won't free you from work, but they will make your work far more productive. They include three important areas: time control, classroom note-taking, and textbook study.   **4**

Time Control

Success in college depends on time control. *Time control* means that you deliberately organize and plan your time, instead of letting it   **5**

continued

drift by. Planning means that you should never be faced with an overdue term paper or a cram session the night before a test.

Three steps are involved in time control. *First,* you should prepare a large monthly calendar. Buy a calendar with a large white block around each date, or make one yourself. At the beginning of the college semester, circle important dates on this calendar. Circle the days on which tests are scheduled; circle the days when papers are due. This calendar can also be used to schedule study plans. At the beginning of the week, you can jot down your plans for each day. An alternative method would be to make plans for each day the night before. On Tuesday night, for example, you might write down "Read Chapter 5 in psychology" in the Wednesday block. Hang this calendar where you will see it every day—your kitchen, bedroom, even your bathroom!   6

The *second step* in time control is to have a weekly study schedule for the semester—a chart that covers all the days of the week and all the waking hours in each day. Below is part of one student's schedule: 7

Time	Mon.	Tue.	Wed.	Thurs.	Fri.	Sat.	
6:00 a.m.							
7:00	Breakfast	Breakfast	Breakfast	Breakfast	Breakfast		
8:00	Math	STUDY	Math	STUDY	Math	Breakfast	
9:00	STUDY	Biology	STUDY	Biology	STUDY	Job	
10:00	Psychology	↓	Psychology	↓	Psychology		
11:00		English		English		↓	
12:00	Lunch		Lunch		Lunch		

On your own schedule, fill in all the fixed hours in each day—hours for meals, classes, job (if any), and travel time. Next, mark time blocks that you can *realistically* use for study each day. Depending on the number of courses you are taking and the demands of these courses, you may want to block off five, ten, or even twenty or more hours of study time a week. Keep in mind that you should not block off time that you do not truly intend to use for study. Otherwise, your schedule will be a meaningless gimmick. Also, remember that you should allow time for rest and relaxation. You will be happiest, and able to accomplish the most, when you have time for both work and play.

The *third step* in time control is to make a daily or weekly to-do list. This may be the most valuable time-control method you ever use. On this list, write down the things you need to do for the following day or the following week. If you choose to write a weekly list, do it on Sunday   8

continued

night. If you choose to write a daily list, do it the night before. Here is part of one student's daily list:

```
      To Do              Tuesday
        1.       Review biology notes before class
        2.       Proofread English payer due today
        3.       See Nikola about game on Friday
        4.       Get gas for car
        5.       Read next chapter of psychology text
```

You may use a three-by-five-inch notepad or a small spiral-bound notebook for this list. Carry the list around with you during the day. Always concentrate on doing the most important items first. To make the best use of your time, mark high-priority items with an asterisk and give them precedence over low-priority items. For instance, you may find yourself wondering what to do after dinner on Thursday evening. Among the items on your list are "Clean inside of car" and "Review chapter for math quiz." It is obviously more important for you to review your notes at this point; you can clean out the car some other time. As you complete items on your to-do list, cross them out. Do not worry about unfinished items. They can be rescheduled. You will still be accomplishing a great deal and making more effective use of your time.

Classroom Note-Taking

9   One of the most important single things you can do to perform well in a college course is to take effective class notes. The following hints should help you become a better note-taker.

10   First, attend class faithfully. Your alternatives—reading the text, reading someone else's notes, or both—cannot substitute for the class experience of hearing ideas in person as someone presents them to you. Also, in class lectures and discussions, your instructor typically presents and develops the main ideas and facts of the course—the ones you will be expected to know on exams.

11   Another valuable hint is to make use of abbreviations while taking notes. Using abbreviations saves time when you are trying to get down a great deal of information. Abbreviate terms that recur frequently in a lecture and put a key to your abbreviations at the top of your notes. For example, in sociology class, *eth* could stand for *ethnocentrism;* in a psychology class, *STM* could stand for *short-term memory.* (When a lecture is over, you may want to go back and write out the terms you have abbreviated.) Also, use *e* for *example;* *def* for *definition;* *info* for

continued

information; + for and; and so on. If you use the same abbreviations all the time, you will soon develop a kind of personal shorthand that makes taking notes much easier.

A third hint for taking notes is to be on the lookout for signals of importance. Write down whatever your instructor puts on the board. If he or she takes the time to put material on the board, it is probably important, and the chances are good that it will come up later on exams. Always write down definitions and enumerations. Enumerations are lists of items. They are signaled in such ways as "The four steps in the process are . . ."; "There were three reasons for . . ."; "The two effects were . . ."; "Five characteristics of . . ."; and so on. In your notes, always number such enumerations (1, 2, 3, etc.). They will help you understand relationships among ideas and organize the material of the lecture. Watch for emphasis words—words your instructor may use to indicate that something is important. Examples of such words are "This is an important reason . . ."; "A point that will keep coming up later . . ."; "The chief cause was . . ."; "The basic idea here is . . ."; and so on. Always write down the important statements announced by these and other emphasis words. Finally, if your instructor repeats a point, you can assume that it is important. You might put an *R* for *repeated* in the margin so that later you will know that your instructor stressed it.

Next, be sure to write down the instructor's examples and mark them with an *e*. The examples help you understand abstract points. If you do not write them down, you are likely to forget them later, when they are needed to help make sense of an idea.

Also, be sure to write down the connections between ideas. Too many students merely copy terms the instructor puts on the board. They forget that, as time passes, the details that serve as connecting bridges between ideas quickly fade. You should, then, write down the relationships and connections in class. That way you'll have them to help tie together your notes later on.

Review your notes as soon as possible after class. You must make them as clear as possible while they are fresh in your mind. A day later may be too late, because forgetting sets in very quickly. Make sure that punctuation is clear, that all words are readable and correctly spelled, and that unfinished sentences are completed (or at least marked off so that you can check your notes with another student's). Add clarifying or connecting comments wherever necessary. Make sure that important ideas are clearly marked. Improve the organization if necessary so that you can see at a glance main points and relationships among them.

Finally, try in general to get down a written record of each class. You must do this because forgetting begins almost immediately. Studies have shown that within two weeks you are likely to have forgotten 80 percent or more of what you have heard. And in four weeks you are lucky if 5 percent

12

13

14

15

16

continued

remains! This is so crucial that it bears repeating: To guard against the relentlessness of forgetting, it is absolutely essential that you write down what you hear in class. Later you can concentrate on working to understand fully and to remember the ideas that have been presented in class. And then, the more complete your notes are, the more you are likely to learn.

Textbook Study

In many college courses, success means being able to read and study a textbook skillfully. For many students, unfortunately, textbooks are heavy going. After an hour or two of study, the textbook material is as formless and as hard to understand as ever. But there is a way to attack even the most difficult textbook and make sense of it. Use a sequence in which you preview a chapter, mark it, take notes on it, and then study the notes.   17

Previewing

Previewing a selection is an important first step to understanding. Taking the time to preview a section or chapter can give you a bird's-eye view of the way the material is organized. You will have a sense of where you are beginning, what you will cover, and where you will end.   18

There are several steps in previewing a selection. First, study the title. The title is the shortest possible summary of a selection and will often tell you the limits of the material you will cover. For example, the title "FDR and the Supreme Court" tells you to expect a discussion of President Roosevelt's dealings with the Court. You know that you will probably not encounter any material dealing with FDR's foreign policies or personal life. Next, quickly read over the first and last paragraphs of the selection; these may contain important introductions to, and summaries of, the main ideas. Then briefly examine the headings and subheadings in the selection. Together, the headings and subheadings are a mini-outline of what you are reading. Headings are often main ideas or important concepts in capsule form; subheadings are breakdowns of ideas within main areas. Finally, read the first sentence of some paragraphs, look for words set off in **boldface** or *italics,* and look at pictures or diagrams. After you have previewed a selection in this way, you should have a good general sense of the material to be read.   19

Marking

You should mark a textbook selection at the same time that you read it through carefully. Use a felt-tip highlighter to shade material that seems important, or use a ballpoint pen and put symbols in the margin next to the material: stars, checks, or NB (*nota bene,* Latin for "note   20

continued

well"). What to mark is not as mysterious as some students believe. You should try to find main ideas by looking for clues: definitions and examples, enumerations, and emphasis words.

1. *Definitions and examples:* Definitions are often among the most import-   21
   ant ideas in a selection. They are particularly significant in introductory courses in almost any subject area, where much of your learning involves mastering the specialized vocabulary of that subject. In a sense, you are learning the "language" of psychology or business or whatever the subject might be.

   Most definitions are abstract, and so they usually are followed by   22
   one or more examples to help clarify their meaning. Always mark off definitions and at least one example that makes a definition clear to you. In a psychology text, for example, we are told that "rationalization is an attempt to reduce anxiety by deciding that you have not really been frustrated." Several examples follow, among them: "A student, frustrated at doing poorly on an exam, convinces themself they weren't given enough time to study."

2. *Enumerations:* Enumerations are lists of items (causes, reasons, types,   23
   and so on) that are numbered 1, 2, 3, . . . or that could easily be numbered. They are often signaled by addition words. Many of the paragraphs in this book, for instance, use words like *First of all, Another, In addition,* and *Finally* to signal items in a series. Other textbooks also use this very common and effective organizational method.

3. *Emphasis words:* Emphasis words tell you that an idea is important.   24
   Common emphasis words include phrases such as *a major event, a key feature, the chief factor, important to note, above all,* and *most of all.* Here is an example: "The most significant contemporary use of marketing is its application to nonbusiness areas, such as political parties."

Note-Taking

Next, you should take notes. Go through the chapter a second time,   25
rereading the most important parts. Try to write down the main ideas in a simple outline form. For example, in taking notes on a psychology selection, you might write down the heading "Defense Mechanisms." Below the heading you would define them, number and describe each kind, and give an example of each.

Defense Mechanisms

a. *Definition: unconscious attempts to reduce anxiety*

b. *Kinds*

continued

(1) *Rationalization: An attempt to reduce anxiety by deciding that you have not*

really been frustrated

Example: An applicant who doesn't get a job says they didn't want the job in

the first place.

(2) *Projection: Projecting onto other people motives or thoughts of one's own*

Example: A person who avoids horror movies because they find them

frightening assumes that everyone avoids horror movies for the same reason.

Studying Notes

To study your notes, use repeated self-testing. For example, look   26
at the heading "Defense Mechanisms" and say to yourself, "What are
the kinds of defense mechanisms?" When you can recite them, then
say to yourself, "What is rationalization?" "What is an example of
rationalization?" Then ask yourself, "What is projection?" "What is an
example of projection?" After you learn each section, review it, and
then go on to the next section.

Do not simply read your notes; keep looking away and seeing if   27
you can recite them to yourself. This self-testing is the key to effective
learning.

Textbook Study Sequence

Remember this sequence for dealing with a textbook: preview, mark,   28
take notes, study the notes. Approaching a textbook in this methodical
way will give you very positive results. You will no longer feel bogged
down in a swamp of words, unable to figure out what you are supposed
to know. Instead, you will understand exactly what you have to do and
how to go about doing it.

Conclusion

Take a minute now to evaluate your own study habits. Do you practice   29
many of the above skills to take effective classroom notes, control your
time, and learn from your textbooks? If not, perhaps you should. The skills
are not magic, but they are too valuable to ignore. Use them carefully and
consistently, and they will make academic success possible for you. Try
them, and you won't need convincing.

ACTIVITY 2

Write a paragraph-length summary of a broadcast of the CBS television show *60 Minutes*. In your first sentence, include the date of the show. For example, "The January 3, 2021, broadcast of CBS's *60 Minutes* dealt with three subjects most people would find of interest. The first segment of the show centered on . . . ; the second segment examined . . . ; the final segment discussed. . . ." Be sure to use parallel form in describing the three segments of the show.

ACTIVITY 3

Write a paragraph-length summary of a cover story of interest to you in a recent issue of a magazine like *Sports Illustrated, Forbes,* or *Inked.*

Writing a Paraphrase

In a paraphrase, you report the information in your own words and style without condensing it. You should paraphrase when the original information is important, but you can write it more clearly in your own words. In order to successfully paraphrase something, you should read the information, set it aside, and then try to explain what you just read in your own words and writing style. Since you are not condensing it, a paraphrase usually compares in length to the original work. Unlike a summary, which can be created as a stand-alone paper, paraphrases are only used within a larger essay.

Avoiding Plagiarism in Paraphrase Writing

Students must be careful when paraphrasing in order to avoid plagiarism. As with summaries, if you don't fully understand the information you have just read, you won't be able to write a successful paraphrase. You should preview, read, and evaluate the information before trying to write about it using your own words and writing style. Once you have completed your paraphrase, you should go back and inspect your words and sentence structure against those of the original. This is particularly important because it is far easier to accidentally plagiarize when paraphrasing if, as many students do, you try to take original sentences and just replace words here and there. Simply changing one or two words from the original is not a paraphrase. This is still plagiarizing because you are plagiarizing the sentence structure and not writing it in your own words and voice. Finally, just as with summaries, you need to make sure you have credited the original source in your paraphrase either by in-text citation or by crediting the author within the paraphrase.

How to Paraphrase Information from an Article

To paraphrase information from an article, follow steps 1 and 2 for "How to Summarize an Article," then follow the steps below. If the assigned material is a TV show or film, adapt the suggestions accordingly.

1. Find and reread a paragraph or two that you have identified as important.

2. Set the article aside. Without looking at the original source and using your own words, write down what you have just read. One technique that helps many students to do this is to pretend they are telling someone about what they read.

3. Compare your version with the original source. Using quotation marks, mark any words or phrases that are directly from the original source. Using a highlighter, mark any phrases that have a sentence structure that is similar to the original source or sound too much like that source.

4. Revise any sections that are structured closely to the original source. To do this, focus first on the areas you highlighted or put in quotation marks. Don't just change a word here and there—instead, look at how you can completely rewrite and reorganize a sentence. The paraphrase should use your voice, not the voice of the original author.

5. At the bottom of your version, write down the source information, including page number, so you can properly credit the information when you use it.

Here are two model paraphrases. The first one is unacceptable. Note the sections that are too closely related to the original source. The second one properly conveys the meaning of the passage without following the original sentence structure or using the original words.

A *scratch outline* is an excellent sequel to the first four prewriting techniques. A scratch outline often follows freewriting, questioning, list-making, or diagramming; or it may gradually emerge in the midst of these strategies. In fact, trying to make a scratch outline is a good way to see if you need to do more prewriting. If you cannot come up with a solid outline, then you know you need to do more prewriting to clarify your main point or its several kinds of support.

Original passage

Paraphrase A

A *scratch outline* is a good follow-up to the first prewriting techniques. A scratch outline often follows diagramming, questioning, list-making, or freewriting; or it may emerge in the middle of these strategies. In reality, making a scratch outline is the best way to see if you need to prewrite more. If you cannot come up with a firm outline, then you know you need to do more prewriting to explain your claim and support.

Unacceptable paraphrase

**Acceptable
paraphrase**

Paraphrase B

    A *scratch outline* is a good technique to use after you have spent time prewriting with your chosen method. By creating a scratch outline, you can see the holes in your argument and support, so you can figure out where you may need to do additional prewriting. The weaker your outline, the more obvious it is you need to spend more time prewriting.

ACTIVITY 4

Here are four sets of passages from the anthology of readings at the end of this book. Each set begins with an original passage and an MLA formatted bibliographic entry demonstrating how a student would cite the use of such a passage in the Works Cited page. Each set is followed by two possible paraphrases of the passage. One is an acceptable paraphrase and the other is unacceptable in which the sentences and ideas too closely follow the original, using some of the same structure and same words as the original. Identify the acceptable paraphrase with an A and the unacceptable paraphrase with a U.

SET 1: ORIGINAL PASSAGE

During adolescence, Elkind says, kids are changing so much so fast (physically, mentally, and emotionally) that they become intensely self-centered. It is literally difficult for them to remember that other individuals have their own lives, thoughts, and feelings, and that they are not focusing their attention on the adolescents. According to Elkind, the adolescent is terrified of doing or saying something that will attract scorn or criticism. As a result, we end up with the teenager whose life is "ruined" by an outbreak of acne; an adolescent who won't leave the house on a bad hair day; or the teen who refuses to return to school after making an embarrassing slip during a speech.

Kendall, Audra. "The Certainty of Fear." *College Writing Skills with Readings.* 11th ed., authored by Zoé L. Albright and John Langan, The McGraw Hill Companies, 2022, pp. 669–672.

_____   a. Elkind says, during adolescence, kids change so fast (physically, mentally, and emotionally) that they become intensely self-centered. It is hard for them to understand that other people have their own feelings, thoughts, and lives, and that they are not focused on the adolescents. According to Elkind, adolescents are scared of doing or saying something that will attract negative attention. As a result, teenagers often think their lives are "ruined" by an outbreak of acne, won't leave the house on a bad hair day, or refuse to go back to school after making an embarrassing mistake during a speech.

_____ b. According to Elkind, teens become so self-centered during adolescence that they have a hard time looking outside of themselves and putting things into perspective. They struggle to recognize that other people are not focused on the adolescents' experiences, but are instead dealing with their own lives. Because teens are hyperfocused on themselves, this translates to small things like pimples or "bad hair" becoming overblown in importance, causing the teens to feel like their lives are ruined.

SET 2: ORIGINAL PASSAGE

Send a thank-you note. Once you've gotten past the interview, there is one more chance for you to make a fine impression. As soon as you can—certainly no more than one or two days after the interview—write a note of thanks. In it, briefly remind the interviewer of when you came in and what job you applied for. As well as thanking the interviewer for seeing you, reaffirm your interest in the job and mention again why you think you are the best candidate for it. Make the note courteous, businesslike, and brief—just a paragraph or two. If the interviewer is wavering between several equally qualified candidates, such a note could tip the scales in your favor.

Davis, Glenda. "How to Do Well on a Job Interview." *College Writing Skills with Readings.* 11th ed., authored by Zoé L. Albright and John Langan, The McGraw Hill Companies, 2022, pp. 278–281.

_____ a. After a job interview, you should consider sending a thank-you note to make one final positive impression. The note should be sent shortly after the interview, preferably the day of the interview or at the latest the next day. Sending a note gives you the opportunity to remind the interviewer of your qualifications and desire to get the job, and it could be the difference between your getting the job and someone else getting it.

_____ b. **Send a thank-you note.** There is one more chance for you to make a fine impression once you've gotten past the interview. As soon as you can, write a note of thanks. In it, remind the interviewer of when you came in and what job you applied for, reaffirm your interest in the job, and mention again why you think you are the best candidate for it. Make the note kind, businesslike, and brief—just a paragraph or two. If the interviewer is wavering between several equally qualified candidates, such a note could help.

SET 3: ORIGINAL PASSAGE

The lecture system ultimately harms professors as well. It reduces feedback to a minimum, so that the lecturer can neither judge how well students understand the material nor benefit from their questions or comments. Questions that require the speaker to clarify obscure points and comments that challenge sloppily constructed arguments are indispensable to scholarship. Without them, the liveliest mind can atrophy. Undergraduates may not be able to make telling contributions very often, but lecturing insulates a professor even from the beginner's naive question that could have triggered a fruitful line of thought.

Daniels, David. "College Lectures: Is Anybody Listening?" *College Writing Skills with Readings.* 11th ed., authored by Zoé L. Albright and John Langan, The McGraw Hill Companies, 2022, pp. 699–702.

_____ a. Lectures, by nature, inhibit scholarly exchange. The professor disseminates the material, and the student is expected to understand and digest it. Very seldom is the student able to ask questions, which hurts not only the student, but the professor as well because they are unable to gauge how well students are understanding the material. Without the exchange and discussion of ideas, or challenges to presented theories, opportunities for more in-depth knowledge and potential discovery is limited or missed.

_____ b. Lectures hurt both the professor and student. There is little feedback, so the professor doesn't know how well students understand the material and cannot profit from their questions. Students don't get to ask the professor to explain unclear ideas or challenge arguments, which are crucial to education. Without the ability to question, students can get bored. Undergraduates don't contribute new information very often, but lectures guarantee that professors don't hear naive questions.

SET 4: ORIGINAL PASSAGE

This was decades before gay characters on TV or in the movies had become commonplace. The words "gay marriage" would only have been heard in a punch line to a joke, and, in fact, most people still believed that homosexuality was a mental illness or a crime. In the town where I grew up, it was illegal to be gay—police used to stake out a little rundown cinderblock bar on the other side of the tracks where, supposedly, gay men gathered. It was not uncommon for the police to rough up and handcuff men they saw coming out of this bar. Then they were thrown in the jail for the night for little or no real reason. Most of the townspeople thought this was a good idea.

Savory, Tanya. "Stepping into the Light." *College Writing Skills with Readings.* 11th ed., authored by Zoé L. Albright and John Langan, The McGraw Hill Companies, 2022, pp. 660–665.

_____   a. This was before gay characters on TV had become commonplace. The words "gay marriage" would only have been heard in a punch line to a joke. Most people still believed that homosexuality was a crime. In the town where I grew up, it was illegal to be gay and police arrested gay men through stake-outs at a specific bar. It was not uncommon for the police to handcuff men they saw coming out of this bar. Then they were thrown in the jail for the night for little or no real reason. Most people thought this was a good idea.

_____   b. In the author's hometown, it was illegal to be gay. Gay people were treated harshly by police and were often targeted and arrested for being suspected of being gay. Because they weren't aware of a different way of thinking, most of the community thought this treatment was ok. At that time, gay people weren't widely seen in the media, and if they were, they were usually treated as a joke or punch line instead of presented as normal.

Choose two non-consecutive paragraphs from the essay, "Power Learning," you summarized in Activity 1 and write a paraphrase of each paragraph. Make sure you include the original paragraphs with your work.

ACTIVITY 5

Choose a recent article from a journal like *Popular Mechanics, Smithsonian,* or *Entrepreneur.* After reading the article, find a paragraph that could be potentially useful in a research paper. Write the original paragraph; below the original, paraphrase the paragraph. Remember to follow the steps outlined earlier in the chapter.

ACTIVITY 6

Using Direct Quotations

Unlike a summary or paraphrase, a direct quotation must be written exactly as it appears in the original work. There are three ways that direct quotations are generally presented. For shorter passages, quotation marks are used. For longer complete passages, the material is indented as a block of text and no quotation marks are used. (Each "Original Passage" in the preceding paraphrasing activity is an example of a direct quotation.) The same formatting applies to longer passages with omitted material, but for these passages, ellipses are included to indicate the omitted text.

Each of these categories is explained further and illustrated in the following sections. These examples have been taken from the "Power Learning" essay you worked with in Activity 1. The paragraph location of each quotation is explained, so you can refer to the original essay and see the quotation in its original context.

Short Quotations

If you want to include a brief sentence or two of direct text from an original source, you will use a short quotation. As you insert the quoted material into your own writing, a transition is usually needed. Examine the two examples below. Notice that in the second example, the writer builds the direct quote into a larger sentence and in so doing, places the letter "t" in brackets. This shows that the word was lowercased by the student and not by the author of the quotation.

See paragraph 5 in original text

Blythe states, "Success in college depends on time control" (419).

See paragraph 7 in original text

Blythe emphasizes there are three steps to good time control. He explains that "[t]he second step in time control is to have a weekly study schedule for the semester—a chart that covers all the days of the week and all the waking hours in each day" (420).

Long Complete Quotations

If you want to use a complete section that is longer than four lines, you should block the quotation, which means you'll need to indent it by an extra five spaces to set it off from the rest of the essay. (This will result in an indent of ½ inch from the left margin.) Block quotations do not use quotation marks. In the example below, the first paragraph was written by a student as a lead-in to the direct quotation from "Power Learning." Notice how the quotation is set off by the extra indent.

In the essay, "Power Learning," several strategies for successful studying are presented. In the section about note-taking, good attendance is stressed as the most important key to success:

See paragraph 10 in original text

> First, attend class faithfully. Your alternatives—reading the text, reading someone else's notes, or both—cannot substitute for the class experience of hearing ideas in person as someone presents them to you. Also, in class lectures and discussions, your instructor typically presents and develops the main ideas and facts of the course—the ones you will be expected to know on exams. (Blythe 421)

Quotations with Omitted Information

If you are using a longer quotation that includes information unrelated to your topic, you may omit the irrelevant words as long as you don't change the overall meaning. To show such an omission, use three spaced periods (known as *ellipsis points*) in place of the deleted words:

The author offers three clear steps to good time control, "First, you should prepare a large monthly calendar . . . circle important dates on this calendar. Circle the days on which tests are scheduled; circle the days when papers are due" (Blythe 420).

See paragraph 6 in original text

Note that in the following example there are four dots in the first line of the quotation—the first dot is the period at the end of the sentence.

The author's final step in time control focuses on lists. "The *third step* in time control is to make a daily or weekly to-do list. . . . On this list, write down the things you need to do for the following day or the following week" (Blythe 420).

See paragraph 8 in original text

Avoiding Plagiarism in Direct Quotations

Unlike summaries and paraphrases—where accidental plagiarism can occur as students try to use their own words to report others' words and ideas—there is less risk of plagiarism in the use of direct quotations. The key factor is to copy the exact words and punctuation and then enclose the text in quotation marks (or set it off as a block indent, if longer). However, if students forget to use quotation marks or block indents and/or forget to credit the author, plagiarism can occur. Thus, it is critical for students to pay careful attention to their use of another author's words throughout all their writing.

19

Writing a Source-Based Essay

This chapter will explain and illustrate

- how to plan and take notes for a source-based essay
- how to incorporate sources in an essay
- how to cite sources in an essay

This chapter also includes

- a model literary analysis
- a model rhetorical analysis

To gain a sense of how to review a text, visit the New York Review of Books *website at http://www.nybooks.com and choose a review to read. Write a short paragraph explaining why you chose that review and what you've learned from it.*

The New York Review, Inc.

Each semester, you will probably be assigned at least one paper that will require you to use outside sources to support your argument. Academic writing often calls for students to use different sources to support their arguments. For instance, a sociology class might require students to write a response to a chapter in their text, using information from that chapter as support. Students in a history class may have to write a response to an essay written during the Civil War. While these assignments don't necessarily demand research on the part of the student, they will require the student to use information from the original source as essay support. This information will need to be incorporated and cited properly.

Writing a source-based essay will require careful note-taking, proper integration of information, in-text citation, and a Works Cited page regardless of whether you are using one, two, or ten sources. The following pages will explain how to properly incorporate and document your sources.

Planning Ahead and Taking Notes

The purpose of a source-based essay is to thoroughly develop a limited topic that is neither too narrow nor too broad. You want your sources to focus on the development of that topic, not stray in multiple directions. When you are writing a source-based essay, you will need to read through and take notes on the material you plan to use to support your essay. As you learned in Chapter 17, "Information Literacy," finding the right information can often be the most difficult part of writing a source-based essay. If you have been assigned a topic and have to locate your own sources, you should read over Chapter 17 before reading the rest of this chapter. If you have been assigned a source to work with, you should be ready to create a scratch outline and begin taking notes.

Preparing a Scratch Outline

As you carefully read through the material you have gathered, think about the content and organization of your paper. Begin deciding what information you will present and how you will arrange it. Prepare a scratch outline that shows both the paper's working thesis and the areas that support the thesis. Try to include at least three areas, if not more, of support.

Working Thesis: _____

Support:

- _____

- _____

- _____

- _____

See Chapter 2 for further discussion about and additional models of scratch outlines.

Keeping Careful Notes

With this tentative outline in mind, you can begin taking notes on the information that you expect to include in your paper. For each source, you will want to create a document or use note cards. Don't use loose-leaf or notebook paper; doing so makes it harder to organize your notes as you prepare to draft your paper. Notes should be in the form of *direct quotations and summaries in your own words*. At times, you may also *paraphrase*. Since most research involves condensing, you will probably summarize much more often than you will paraphrase. Chapter 18 provides detailed information defining and differentiating these forms of writing.

When you create your notes, you want to make sure you include all relevant bibliographic information—title of source, author, page number, publication information. As you choose information that you think you are going to use, you should copy it word-for-word and enclose it within quotation marks. If you want to paraphrase or summarize the information, you should write your paraphrase or summary with the page number and a notation stating what you have created.

Always record the exact source and page from which you use information. In a source-based essay, you must document all information that is not common knowledge or not a matter of historical record. For example, the birth and death dates of Dr. Martin Luther King, Jr., are established facts and do not need documenting. On the other hand, the average number of hours worked in the United States this year compared with the average number worked in 1980 is a specialized fact and should be documented. In addition, as you read several sources on a subject, you will develop a sense of what authors regard as generally shared, or common, information and what is more specialized information that requires documentation.

Notes can be taken in two different formats—note cards and documents. Each format is discussed and illustrated below.

Taking Notes Using Note Cards

When using note cards to take notes, students should include only one quotation, summary, or paraphrase per card. Examples follow.

Direct Quotations

A *direct quotation* must be written exactly as it appears in the original work. However, you may omit words that are not relevant to your point as long as you don't change the meaning. To show such an omission, use three spaced periods (known as *ellipsis points*) in place of the deleted words. Several examples of note cards with direct quotations follow.

Alcott, Louisa M. *Little Women.* **Little, Brown, and Company, 1915**

"The dim, dusty-room, with the busts staring down from the tall book-cases, the cosey chairs, the globes, and best of all, the wilderness of books, in which she could wander where she liked, made the library a region of bliss to her. The moment Aunt March took her nap, or was busy with company, Jo hurried to this quiet place, and curling herself up in the easy-chair, devoured poetry, romance, history, travels, and pictures, like a regular book worm. But, like all happiness, it did not last long; for as sure as she had just reached the heart of the story, the sweetest verse of the song, or the most perilous adventure of her traveller, a shrill voice called, "Josy-phine! Josy-phine!" and she had to leave her paradise to wind yarn, wash the poodle or read Belsham's Essays by the hour together." (This is a direct quotation found on page 40.)

Note with Direct Quotation

Alcott, Louisa M. *Little Women.* **Little, Brown, and Company, 1915**

"The dim, dusty-room, with the busts staring down from the tall book-cases . . . and best of all, the wilderness of books, in which she could wander where she liked, made the library a region of bliss to her. The moment Aunt March took her nap, or was busy with company, Jo hurried to this quiet place, and . . . devoured poetry, romance, history, travels, and pictures, like a regular book worm. But, like all happiness, it did not last long . . . and she had to leave her paradise to wind yarn, wash the poodle or read Belsham's Essays by the hour together." (This is a direct quotation found on page 40.)

Note with Direct Quotation and Ellipsis

Zevin, Gabrielle. *The Storied Life of A. J. Fikry.* **Algonquin Books of Chapel Hill, 2014**

"Authors never look that much like their author photos, but the first thing A. J. thinks when he meets Leon Friedman is that he *really* doesn't look like his author photo. Photo Leon Friedman is thinner, clean-shaven, and his nose looks longer. Actual Leon Friedman looks somewhere between old Ernest Hemingway and a department store Santa Claus: big red nose and belly, bushy white beard, twinkly eyes." (This is a direct quotation found on page 140.)

Note with Direct Quotation

Note with Direct Quotation and Ellipsis

> **Zevin, Gabrielle. *The Storied Life of A. J. Fikry*. Algonquin Books of Chapel Hill, 2014**
>
> "Authors never look that much like their author photos, but the first thing A. J. thinks when he meets Leon Friedman is that he *really* doesn't look like his author photo. . . . [He] looks somewhere between old Ernest Hemingway and a department store Santa Claus: big red nose and belly, bushy white beard, twinkly eyes." (This is a direct quotation found on page 140.)

(Note the four dots in the above example; the first dot is the period at the end of the sentence. The word *He* in brackets shows that the word was added by the student and not by the author of the quotation.)

Summary

Remember that in a *summary*, you condense the original material and use your own words.

Note with Summary

> **Alcott, Louisa M. *Little Women*. Little, Brown, and Company, 1915**
>
> The narrator explains why the library is a place of escape for Jo even though she rarely gets to spend as much time there as she would like. (This is a summary of the first full paragraph on page 40.)

Paraphrase

Remember that, in a *paraphrase*, you report the information in your own words and style without condensing it.

Note with Paraphrase

> **Zevin, Gabrielle. *The Storied Life of A. J. Fikry*. Algonquin Books of Chapel Hill, 2014**
>
> When A. J. Fikry first meets the author Leon Friedman, A. J. is surprised at how much the author doesn't look like his photo. In real life Leon Friedman is a heavy-set, white-haired bearded man who looks like a grandpa. His photo was obviously old because in the photo, Friedman was much younger and more smartly presented than the man A. J. was standing with. (This is a paraphrase of part of the third paragraph on page 140.)

Keeping Notes in a Document

The other format for note-taking is creating a document. Unlike note cards, which have only one quotation, summary, or paraphrase per card, a document can contain all the information from one source. Students should put their citation information at the beginning of the document. Then, with each quotation, paraphrase, or summary, students should include proper citations. In this way, students can use the copy and paste feature as they write their essays, ensuring they properly cite each piece of information they get from an outside source.

An example of a document used for note-taking follows. Notice that the student included both a direct quotation and a paraphrase for the material on page 6 because they weren't sure how they would ultimately incorporate the information, and they are thus keeping their options open.

Gee, James P., and Elizabeth R. Hayes. *Language and Learning in the Digital Age.* **Routledge Taylor and Francis Group, 2011.**

"Language can be viewed as cognitive, material, or social; it is of course, all of these at one and the same time. Language is also something that is both individual and social. Language seems to belong to us as individuals—to be something we can use in distinctive ways—and yet seems also to be shaped by social conventions beyond our individual control" (Gee and Hayes 6).   ← **Direct quotation**

"Language can be viewed as cognitive, material, or social; it is of course, all of these at one and the same time. . . . Language seems to belong to us as individuals—to be something we can use in distinctive ways—and yet seems also to be shaped by social conventions beyond our individual control" (Gee and Hayes 6).   ← **Direct quotation with ellipses**

"Language seems to belong to us as individuals—to be something we can use in distinctive ways—and yet seems also to be shaped by social conventions beyond our individual control" (Gee and Hayes 6).   ← **Quotation and paraphrase**
Paraphrase: While we think that our use of language is very distinct and personal, it is actually more than that. Society impacts our language and our use of language (Gee and Hayes 6).

"Language can be viewed as cognitive, material, or social; it is of course, all of these at one and the same time. Language is also something that is both individual and social. Language seems to belong to us as individuals—to be something we can use in distinctive ways—and yet seems also to be shaped by social conventions beyond our individual control" (Gee and Hayes 6).   ← **Quotation and summary**
Summary: Language is both personal and social (Gee and Hayes 6).

Helpful Tips on Taking Notes

Keep the following in mind as you take notes.

If you are using note cards:

- Write on only one side of each card.
- Write only one kind of information, from one source, on any one card.
- Identify the source and page number on every card.
- Identify whether you have written a quotation, summary, or paraphrase on every card.

If you are keeping notes in a document:

- Create a new document for each source.
- Identify the author, title, and publication information at the top of the document. Write it in proper MLA format.
- Identify the page number at the end of each note.
- Indicate clearly whether you have written a quotation, summary, or paraphrase.

ACTIVITY 1

Read the following paragraphs from books that a student might use to gather material for a source-based essay. Then, on a separate sheet of paper, create three separate notes for each:

1. In the first note, use a direct quotation in which you indicate the omission of certain words or phrases by using ellipses.
2. In the second note, write a paraphrase of the paragraph.
3. In the third note, write a summary of the paragraph.

Be sure to provide the source information at the beginning of the notes.

PARAGRAPH A

Welker, Glen, editor. *The Constitution of the Iroquois Nations.* 1993–2016, www.indigenouspeople.net/iroqcon.htm.

"The Lords of the Confederacy of the Five Nations shall be mentors of the people for all time. The thickness of their skin shall be seven spans—which is to say that they shall be proof against anger, offensive actions and criticism. Their hearts shall be full of peace and good will and their minds filled with a yearning for the welfare of the people of the Confederacy. With endless patience they shall carry out their duty and their firmness shall be tempered with a tenderness for their people. Neither anger nor fury shall find lodgment in their minds and all their words and actions shall be marked by calm deliberation."

PARAGRAPH B

Douglass, Frederick. *My Bondage and My Freedom*. London, England: Partridge and Oakey, 1855. *Lit2Go,* http://etc.usf.edu/lit2go/45/my-bondage-and-my-freedom/1458/chapter-11-a-change-came-oer-the-spirit-of-my-dream/.

"It is easy to see, that, in entering upon the duties of a slaveholder, some little experience is needed. Nature has done almost nothing to prepare men and women to be either slaves or slaveholders. Nothing but rigid training, long persisted in, can perfect the character of the one or the other. One cannot easily forget to love freedom; and it is as hard to cease to respect that natural love in our fellow creatures. On entering upon the career of a slaveholding mistress, Mrs. Auld was singularly deficient; nature, which fits nobody for such an office, had done less for her than any lady I had known. It was no easy matter to induce her to think and to feel that the curly-headed boy, who stood by her side, and even leaned on her lap; who was loved by little Tommy, and who loved little Tommy in turn; sustained to her only the relation of a chattel. I was more than that, and she felt me to be more than that. I could talk and sing; I could laugh and weep; I could reason and remember; I could love and hate. I was human, and she, dear lady, knew and felt me to be so. How could she, then, treat me as a brute, without a mighty struggle with all the noble powers of her own soul. That struggle came, and the will and power of the husband was victorious. Her noble soul was overthrown; but, he that overthrew it did not, himself, escape the consequences. He, not less than the other parties, was injured in his domestic peace by the fall."

Rewrite each of the following quotations, omitting irrelevant words. Each quotation is followed by an MLA-formatted bibliographic entry demonstrating how a student would cite the use of the quotation in the Works Cited page.

ACTIVITY 2

1. "Another valuable hint is to make use of abbreviations while taking notes. Using abbreviations saves time when you are trying to get down a great deal of information. Abbreviate terms that recur frequently in a lecture and put a key to your abbreviations at the top of your notes."

   Blythe, Jerry. "Power Learning." *College Writing Skills with Readings*. 11th ed., authored by Zoé L. Albright and John Langan, The McGraw Hill Companies, 2022, pp. 419–425.

   _____

   _____

2. "During adolescence, Elkind says, kids are changing so much so fast (physically, mentally, and emotionally) that they become intensely self-centered. It

is literally difficult for them to remember that other individuals have their own lives, thoughts, and feelings, and that they are not focusing their attention on the adolescents."

Kendall, Audra. "The Certainty of Fear." *College Writing Skills with Readings*. 11th ed., authored by Zoé L. Albright and John Langan, The McGraw Hill Companies, 2022, pp. 669–672.

_____

_____

_____

3. "In the darkness, it was easier to hide. I made new friends that I didn't really care too much about. I lost interest in anything that was special or unique about me, not wanting to draw attention to who I was. I went entirely over-board in my devotion to Mark, even suggesting that we get married as soon as we graduated from high school. College and my future no longer mattered to me. All that mattered was escaping the light, the fear of who I really was. It didn't matter that I was confused and miserable as long as I was hidden."

Savory, Tanya. "Stepping into the Light." *College Writing Skills with Readings*. 11th ed., authored by Zoé L. Albright and John Langan, The McGraw Hill Companies, 2022, pp. 660–665.

_____

_____

_____

_____

4. "The lecture system ultimately harms professors as well. It reduces feedback to a minimum, so that the lecturer can neither judge how well students understand the material nor benefit from their questions or comments."

Daniels, David. "College Lectures: Is Anybody Listening?" *College Writing Skills with Readings*. 11th ed., authored by Zoé L. Albright and John Langan, The McGraw-Hill Companies, 2022, pp. 699–702.

_____

_____

5. "Applied to propaganda, card stacking means that one side may suppress or distort evidence, tell half-truths, oversimplify the facts, or set up a "straw man"—a false target—to divert attention from the issue at hand."

McClintock, Ann. "Propaganda Techniques in Today's Advertising." *College Writing Skills with Readings*. 11th ed., authored by Zoé L. Albright and John Langan, The McGraw Hill Companies, 2022, pp. 341–346.

Understanding How to Incorporate Sources

Knowing how to write a good summary or paraphrase or copy a quotation isn't enough. You have to know how to incorporate the information, so that it is seamless and part of your essay. There are several parts to a properly integrated quote, summary, or paraphrase.

Introduction: The source needs to be introduced to the reader, so the reader understands why the upcoming information is important and is prepared for the information. Any time a new source is used, you must introduce the important information—author and credibility of the source used. You should always refer to the author(s) by full name and title the first time; you can use the author(s)' last name(s) each time after. Never refer to an author by their first name only.

Quotation/Paraphrase/Summary: After you have introduced the source, you will need to transition into the exact words (quotation) or rewording (paraphrase/summary) of the original source. You want to avoid statements like "the following quote says" or "a summary of the source is." Instead you should employ good transitional devices to link your ideas and to make a connection as to why you are using that piece of information. See the following box for transition suggestions.

Citation: Immediately following the information you used, you need to include a citation that shows where the information originated. Citations are explained in more detail later in the chapter.

Connection: Once you have incorporated the information, you want to continue to connect it to why you are using it. Explain how the cited information supports the topic sentence of that paragraph or the thesis of your essay. By doing this, you develop the information more deeply, helping the reader to see your point.

TRANSITIONAL WORDS AND PHRASES	
According to . . .	The author . . .
In contrast . . .	. . . asserts
For instance . . .	. . . states
The point is . . .	. . . argues
Although . . .	. . . points out
To illustrate . . .	. . . writes

An Example of How to Incorporate Source Material from Document Notes

The following example demonstrates how to incorporate a direct quotation and a short summary. The student's assignment was to react to the essay "from *Self-Reliance*" located in the anthology section, Part 5, of your text. This student has chosen to keep their notes in a document instead of using note cards. At the top of the document is the bibliographic entry. The student has then included the two original quotations they have decided to use in their essay. The first quotation also includes a summary as the student wasn't sure if they were going to summarize this section or use a direct quotation. Keeping notes in this manner allows the student to keep their options open.

Emerson, Ralph Waldo. "from *Self-Reliance.*" *College Writing Skills with Readings*. 11th ed., authored by Zoé L. Albright and John Langan, The McGraw Hill Companies, 2022, pp. 648–649.

Original Quotation: "What I must do is all that concerns me, not what the people think. This rule, equally arduous in actual and in intellectual life, may serve for the whole distinction between greatness and meanness. It is the harder because you will always find those who think they know what is your duty better than you know it. It is easy in the world to live after the world's opinion; it is easy in solitude to live after our own; but the great man is he who in the midst of the crowd keeps with perfect sweetness the independence of solitude . . ." (Emerson 649)

Summary: Emerson thinks we should ignore what others think even if it is hard. It's easy to follow your ideas if you don't interact with others. It's a better person who can follow his own ideas in society even if those ideas don't follow society's ideas (649).

Original quotation: "For nonconformity the world whips you with its displeasure. And therefore a man must know how to estimate a sour face. The by-standers look askance on him in the public street or in the friend's parlor. If this aversion had its origin in contempt and resistance like his own he might well go home with a sad countenance . . ." (Emerson 649)

Following is the paragraph that resulted from this student's notes.

Student's Paragraph Using Short Quotation and Summary

A person who seeks the accomplishment embodied by the American Dream must be ready to tear barriers and stand proudly above the masses. A vast majority of the time when someone attempts to carve out a path in society, many critics and skeptics will attempt to deter that person from moving forward. According to Ralph Waldo Emerson, a noted American essayist from the 1800s, "[f]or nonconformity the world whips you with its displeasure" (649). In the early 1980s, Steve Jobs had a revolutionary idea—that idea was to make computers easier to use by using a simple visual interface with a mouse. Many dismissed the idea, and it was not initially successful. Despite the critics, Jobs was not afraid to challenge the status quo and ignore the disbelievers; he went on to become one of the leaders of the computing world. Those who dare to achieve the American Dream must be ready to wade through the sea of critics, and as Emerson asserts, ignore what others think or say of them, and no matter how hard it is, always speak their ideas (649). They must remain headstrong, dismiss the naysayers, and stray from the pack.

Notice that the student's notes are longer than what they wound up using in the final paragraph. The first quotation in that paragraph is only a small portion of the original quote (second quotation on document). Only the most important part of the quotation is used. The second citation in the paragraph is a summary. Although the student could have tried to incorporate Emerson's direct words, they were able to summarize the main points in their own words that better fit into the paragraph.

While it is best to incorporate your research within your paragraph, it is sometimes necessary to use a quotation that is longer than four lines. In this case, you will need to block your quotation. However, you should use block quotations sparingly because they don't often fit within the flow of your essay. Following is an example.

Student's Paragraph Using Block Quotation

Keeping my priorities intact while in school has been more difficult than I thought. In Emerson's essay "from *Self-Reliance*," he asserts that society makes it difficult for a person to remain true to his or her own inner beliefs:

> What I must do is all that concerns me, not what the people think. This rule, equally arduous in actual and in intellectual life, may serve for the whole distinction between greatness and meanness. It is the harder because you will always find those who think they know what is your duty better than you know it. (649)

Knowing that even in the 1800s, society made it difficult for people to be true to their own selves, has made me realize that I'm not alone. It has also made me more determined to keep my priorities straight and get the degree and career that I want, no matter what others may say.

Citing Sources

Format

The model paper in this chapter shows acceptable formats for a research paper using the style recommended by the Modern Language Association (MLA). Most English professors require this style. However, if you are writing in another class, such as psychology, sociology, or one of the physical sciences, your instructor may require a different style. So, always check with your professor first.

Documentation of Sources

You must reveal the sources (books, articles, and so on) of borrowed information in your paper. Whether you quote directly, or summarize ideas in your own words, you must acknowledge your sources. In the past, you may have used footnotes. However, the MLA now requires a simpler form of documentation.

Citations within a Paper

When citing a source, you must mention the author's name and the relevant page number. The author's name may appear either in the sentence you are writing or in parentheses following the sentence:

In *The Way We Really Are,* Stephanie Coontz writes, "Right up through the 1940s, ties of work, friendship, neighborhood, ethnicity, extended kin, and voluntary organizations were as important a source of identity for most Americans . . ." (37).

"Some . . . are looking for a way to reclaim family closeness in an increasingly fast-paced society. . . . Still others worry about unsavory influences in school—drugs, alcohol, sex, violence" (Kantrowitz and Wingert 66).

There are several points to note about citations within the paper:

- When the author's name is provided in parentheses, only the last name is given.

- There is no punctuation between the author's name and the page number.

- The parenthetical citation is placed after the borrowed material but before the period at the end of the sentence.

- If you are using more than one work by the same author, include a shortened version of the title in the citation. For example, your citation for the quotation above would be (Coontz, *Way We Really* 39). Note that a comma appears between the author's name and the title.

- The abbreviation *qtd. in* is used when citing a quotation from another source. For example, a quotation from Edward Wolff on page 2 of the paper was found in a book not by Wolff but by Sylvia Ann Hewlett and Cornel West. The citation is as follows:

  Families have been feeling this loss of time for years but have been unable to describe it. The economist Edward Wolff explains the loss of time: Over a thirty-year time span, parental time has declined 13 percent. The time parents have available for their children has been squeezed by the rapid shift of mothers into the paid labor force, by escalating divorce rates and the subsequent abandonment of children by their fathers, and by an increase in the number of hours required on the job. The average worker is now at work 163 hours a year more than in 1969, which adds up to an extra month of work annually. (qtd. in Hewlett and West 48)

Citations at the End of a Paper

End your paper with a list of works cited that includes all the sources actually used in the paper. (Don't list other sources, no matter how many you have read.) Look at the "Works Cited" page in the model research paper (in the next chapter) and note the following:

- The works-cited list begins on a new page, not on the last page of the paper's text.

- Entries are organized alphabetically according to the authors' last names. Entries are not numbered.

- Entries are double-spaced, with no extra spaces between entries.

- After the first line of an entry, a half-inch indentation separates each additional line in that entry. This arrangement is called a "hanging indent" in most formatting menus.
- *Italicize* (do not underline) titles of books, periodicals, websites, and other independently published works.
- Include a Digital Object Identifier or DOI (preferred, as it is permanently assigned to a source), a permalink, or a URL. Copy URLs in full from your browser.
- If the date of publication includes a month, then abbreviate the month in your citation, except for the months of May, June, and July.
- When you are citing a Web page that has no publication date, you can include a date of access at the end of your citation. Here is an example of how to present an access date: Accessed 24 Apr. 2022.

Model Entries for a List of Works Cited

Use the following entries as a guide when you prepare your list.

Book by One Author

Erdrich, Louise. *The Night Watchman*. Harper, 2020.

Note that the author's last name is written first.

Two or More Entries by the Same Author

—. *Future Home of the Living God: A Novel*. HarperLuxe, 2017.

If you cite two or more entries by the same author (in the example above, a second book by Louise Erdrich is cited), do not repeat the author's name. Instead, begin the line with three hyphens followed by a period. Then give the remaining information as usual. Arrange works by the same author alphabetically by title. The words *A, An,* and *The* are ignored when alphabetizing by title.

Book by Two Authors

Zoboi, Ibi, and Yusef Salaam. *Punching the Air*. Balzer + Bray, 2020.

For a source with two authors, give both authors' names but reverse only the first author's name. For a source with three or more authors, list the first author's name (reversed), followed by a comma, and then the phrase *et al.* (which means "and others").

Magazine Article
Newspaper Article

Chai, Julie. "A Growing Mission." *Martha Stewart Living*, January/February 2021, pp. 84-89.

Worland, Gayle. "Fitness Is Movement." *Wisconsin State Journal*, 4 April 2021, p. D1.

The final letter and number refer to page 1 of section D. If the article is not printed on consecutive pages, simply list the first page followed by a plus sign ("+"). In that case, the above example would read "D1+").

"Many Jobless Workers Aren't Getting Help." Editorial. *The New York Times*, 11 Feb. 2021, p. A22.

List an editorial as you would any signed or unsigned article, but indicate the nature of the piece by adding the description *Editorial* after the article's title.

Cox, Milton D. "FLC Definition and Recommendations: A Yearlong vs. a One-Semester FLC and an Honors Program Example." *Learning Communities Journal*, vol. 11, 2019, pp. 75-106.

Coleman, James. "Social Capital in the Creation of Human Capital." *Sociology of Education: A Critical Reader*, 3rd ed., edited by Alan R. Sadovnik and Ryan W. Coughlan, Routledge, 2016, pp. 97-119.

Schaefer, Richard. *Sociology Matters*. 7th ed., McGraw Hill Education, 2018.

Edition information (*revised ed., 2nd ed., 3rd ed.,* and so on) is placed right after the title.

Burford, Bill. "The Gastronomic Capital of the World." *Dirt*, Alfred A. Knopf, 2020, pp. 353-359.

Funding Your Education. United States Department of Education, Office of Federal Student Aid, 2014.

"COVID's Long Haulers." *60 Minutes*, produced by Nichole Marks and David M. Levine, reported by Anderson Cooper, season 53, episode 12, CBS, 22 Nov. 2020.

Jumanji: The Next Level. Directed by Jake Kasdan, Columbia Pictures, 2019.

Charli XCX. "Claws." *How I'm Feeling Now*, Atlantic, 2020.

Firbank, Matthew. Personal interview. 14 July 2020.

Sudmeijer, Bas. "How Carbon Capture Networks Could Help Curb Climate Change." *TED*, Oct. 2020, www.ted.com/talks/bas_sudmeijer_how_carbon_capture_networks_could_help_curb_climate_change.

Hardman, Heidi. "I've Rescued Hundreds of Special Needs Dogs." *Newsweek*, 16 Jan. 2021, www.newsweek.com/ive-rescued-hundreds-special-needs-dogs-1562001.

"The Amish Ghost Bridge of Pinecraft, Florida." *Urban Legends Online*, 3 June 2020, urbanlegendsonline.com/the-amish-ghost-bridge-of-pinecraft-florida/.

When a source has no author listed, start the citation with the title of the source. When the name of a website and the name of the publisher or sponsor for the site is the same (as with *TED* and *Urban Legends Online* above), do not include a publisher or sponsor in your citation. Include the date that the Web source was posted or was last modified or updated.

Article in a Reference Database

Hu, Zhiguo, and Hongyan Liu. "The Affective Meaning of Words Is Constrained by the Conceptual Meaning." *Journal of Psycholinguistic Research*, vol. 48, no. 6, Dec. 2019, pp. 1377–1390. EBSCO-host, search.ebscohost.com/login.aspx?direct=true&db=eric&AN=EJ1232652&site=ehost-live.

Include complete print publication information for the article, and then list the name of the database and a DOI or URL for the article. A DOI (digital object identifier) is a number assigned by publishers to some professional journal articles; if you see a DOI listed for an article, include that in your citation instead of a URL.

E-mail

Graham, Vanessa. "Teenager Problems." Received by Sonya Philips, 12 Apr. 2020.

ACTIVITY 3

On a separate sheet of paper, convert the information in each of the following into the correct form for a list of "Works Cited." Use the appropriate model above as a guide.

1. A book by Tommy Orange called *There There: A Novel* and published by Knopf in 2018.

2. An article by Tyler Hayes titled "5 Best Smart Water Bottles to Help You Drink More Water" dated January 28, 2021, found on the *Newsweek* website, at this URL: https://www.newsweek.com/5-best-smart-water-bottles-help-you-drink-more-water-1565201.

3. A book by David Newman titled *Identities and Inequalities: Exploring the Intersections of Race, Class, Gender, and Sexuality* and published in a fourth edition by McGraw Hill Education in 2022.

4. An article titled "How the Arab Spring Changed Cinema" written by Joseph Fahim and posted on January 13, 2021, on the Culture section of the BBC website at this URL: https://www.bbc.com/culture/article/20210113-how-the-arab-spring-changed-cinema.

5. The 2014 Puerto Rican documentary *Mala Mala* directed by Antonio Santini and Dan Sickles and produced by El Peligro, which you watched on Netflix.

A Model Literary Analysis

Here is a literary analysis written by a student for her class. Notice how the essay makes a claim about the literature and uses information from the novel to support the claim.

Burks 1

Kylee Burks

Professor R. Laird

English 101

5 April 2021

I Know Why the Caged Bird Sings: Depth and Emotion through Words

 In *I Know Why the Caged Bird Sings*, Maya Angelou tells the story of her earliest years. Angelou, a dancer, poet, and television producer as well as a writer, has continued her life story in three more volumes of autobiography. *I Know Why the Caged Bird Sings* is the start of Maya Angelou's story; in this book, she writes with extraordinary clarity about the pains and joys of being Black in America.

1

Introductory paragraph, including thesis.

continued

Summary:
Notice this first paragraph gives a summary of the novel.

I Know Why the Caged Bird Sings covers Maya Angelou's life from   2
age three to age sixteen. When the book opens, she is a gawky little girl
in a white woman's cut-down lavender silk dress. She has forgotten the
poem she had memorized for the Easter service, and all she can do is
rush out of the church. At this point, Angelou is living in Stamps, Arkansas,
with her grandmother and uncle. The town is rigidly segregated: "People
in Stamps used to say that the whites in our town were so prejudiced that
a Negro couldn't buy vanilla ice cream" (40). Yet Angelou has some good
things in her life: her adored older brother Bailey, her success in school,
and her pride in her grandmother's quiet strength and importance in the
Black community. There is laughter, too, as when a preacher is interrupted
in mid-sermon by an overly enthusiastic woman shouting, "Preach it, I say
preach it!" The woman, in a frenzied rush of excitement, hits the preacher
with her purse; his false teeth fly out of his mouth and land at Angelou's
feet. Shortly after this incident, Angelou and her brother are taken by her
father to live in California with their mother. Here, at age eight, she is
raped by her mother's boyfriend, who is mysteriously murdered after
receiving only a suspended sentence for his crime. She returns, silent and
withdrawn, to Stamps, where the gloom is broken when one of her
mother's friends introduces her to the magic of great books. Later, at age
thirteen, Angelou returns to California. She learns how to dance. She runs
away after a violent family fight and lives for a month in a junkyard. She
becomes the first Black female to get a job on the San Francisco
streetcars. She graduates from high school eight months pregnant. And
she survives.

Connection:
Notice the topic sentence reconnects with the thesis.

Maya Angelou's writing style is impressive and vivid. For example, she   3
describes the lazy dullness of her life in Stamps: "Weekdays revolved in a
sameness wheel. They turned into themselves so steadily and inevitably

continued

Burks 3

that each seemed to be the original of yesterday's rough draft" (93). She also knows how to bring a scene to life, as when she describes her eighth-grade graduation. For months, she has been looking forward to this event, knowing she will be honored for her academic successes. She is even happy with her appearance: her hair has become pretty, and her yellow dress is a miracle of hand-sewing. But the ceremony is spoiled when the speaker—a white man—implies that the only success available to Blacks is in athletics. Angelou remembers: "The man's dead words fell like bricks around the auditorium and too many settled in my belly. . . . The proud graduating class of 1940 had dropped their heads" (152). Later, Angelou uses a crystal-clear image to describe her father's mistress sewing: "She worked the thread through the flowered cloth as if she were sewing the torn ends of her life together" (208). With such vivid details and figures of speech, Maya Angelou re-creates her life for her readers.

Quotation:

In this quote, the student uses ellipses to signal where original material has been omitted.

The strong images of the injustices suffered by Blacks two generations ago are well done and incredibly powerful. The description of seven-year-old Maya—when some "powhitetrash" girls torment her dignified grandmother, calling her "Annie" and mimicking her mannerisms—is emotional and raw. In another incident, Mrs. Cullinan, Angelou's white employer, decides that Marguerite (Angelou's given name) is too difficult to pronounce and so renames her Mary. This loss of her name—a "hellish horror" (91)—is another humiliation suffered at white hands, and Angelou leaves Mrs. Cullinan's employ soon afterward. Later, Angelou encounters overt discrimination when a white dentist tells her grandmother, "Annie, my policy is I'd rather stick my hand in a dog's mouth than in a nigger's" (160)—and only slightly less obvious prejudice when the streetcar company refuses to

4

Connection: Topic sentence reiterates specific points found in thesis.

Page numbers reference where the quotes originate.

continued

accept her application for a conductor's job. Over and over again, Angelou is the victim of a white society.

Although these injustices are disheartening, Angelou's triumphs are   5
inspiring. Angelou is thrilled when she hears the radio broadcast of Joe Louis's victory over Primo Carnera: "A Black boy. Some Black mother's son. He was the strongest man in the world" (114). She weeps with pride when the class valedictorian leads her and her fellow eighth-graders in singing the Negro National Anthem. And there are personal victories, too. One of these comes after her father has gotten drunk in a small Mexican town. Though she has never driven before, she manages to get her father into the car and drives fifty miles through the night as he lies intoxicated in the back seat. Finally, she rejoices in the birth of her son: "He was beautiful and mine. Totally mine. No one had bought him for me" (245). Angelou shows, through these examples, that she is proud of her race—and of herself.

I Know Why the Caged Bird Sings is a remarkable book. Angelou   6
could have been just another casualty of race prejudice. Yet by using her intelligence, sensitivity, and determination, she succeeds in spite of the odds against her. And by writing with such power, she lets the readers share her defeats and joys. She also teaches a vital lesson: With strength and persistence, all people can escape their cages—and sing their songs.

Author's last name is not needed in the citations because she is mentioned in the introduction to the quotation.

Thesis reasserted in conclusion.

Student Paper: A Rhetorical Analysis

Here is a rhetorical analysis essay written by a student for her English composition course. In this assignment, the student was asked to compare two articles that discussed the same topic but had differing opinions, and decide which of the two articles was the most persuasive. Notice how the article incorporates quotations to support the student's claim. This essay is MLA formatted and shows a proper heading, headers, in-text citations, and Works Cited page.

Cruz 1

Malori Cruz

Professor Sullivan

English Composition 1

4 December 2021

Kill or No-Kill

A recent growth in the popularity of no-kill animal shelters has sparked a debate over the effectiveness of no-kill policies. In this debate, both sides share a common interest—the well-being of animals. In the article, "Growth of no-kill policies can jam animal shelters," author Mike Hendricks presents arguments that support no-kill policies. On the other side of the debate, author Brian Palmer takes a stance against no-kill policies in his article, "Are No-Kill Shelters Good for Cats and Dogs?" While both articles are well-written and compelling, Mike Hendricks's article proves to be more persuasive.

Hendricks attempts to convince readers in favor of no-kill policies in his article, "Growth of no-kill policies can jam animal shelters." To begin, Hendricks describes a local animal shelter with its "cages upon cages of cats" to appeal to the readers' emotions. He explains that no-kill policies cause overcrowding, resulting in dismal living conditions for shelter animals. By immediately

Article titles are placed in quotation marks.

Thesis statement

Topic sentence goes back to the thesis statement and asserts information about the first article.

Cruz 2

addressing one of the negative outcomes of no-kill shelters, he engages readers on both sides of the issue. He follows these descriptions with information about the deadly fate of many thousands of animals that are euthanized to prevent overcrowding. In doing so, Hendricks anticipates the audience will find the killing of animals to be the unfavorable option, thus downplaying his opposition before even supporting his own argument.

To continue compelling the reader to agree that no-kill policies are beneficial, despite possible overcrowding, Hendricks explains how shelters have reevaluated how they do things. "By putting greater emphasis on finding homes for stray and unwanted animals," shelters are changing their focus from simply housing animals, euthanizing when necessary, to becoming actively involved in communities as a community partner. Hendricks provides numerous successful cases by reputable organizations, including one local shelter who was "euthanizing 25,000 animals a year [in 2002] . . . and now it's about 2,000 [in 2016]." Without specifically saying that no-kill shelters should be the choice, Hendricks uses multiple sources to show how thousands of animals are being adopted rather than being killed, leading the reader to agree that this is a much better option than euthanizing.

Brian Palmer's article, "Are No-Kill Shelters Good for Cats and Dogs," starts off using an emotional appeal just like Hendricks's article, but it has a very different message—no-kill shelters do more harm than good. Palmer originally grabs the readers' attention with a grisly tale of Victorian-era euthanasia—drowning dozens of dogs in an iron cage—and then goes on to discuss the history of euthanasia. As he explains, however, the means of euthanasia

Paragraph gives a brief summary of the article.

Topic sentence continues the argument made by the previous paragraph.

Student has used ellipses to signal missing information. The brackets show where the student has added information for clarification.

Topic sentence introduces the second article and connects to both the thesis and the previous paragraphs by signaling this article contradicts the other article.

Cruz 3

improved over time; gas chambers provided a more efficient option. His historic narrative, cruel as it may appear, is actually a potentially strong emotional appeal. The reader, unaware, is being eased into supporting the author's claim. This, however, requires the reader to view euthanasia as a humane option from the beginning in order to be open to the idea that practices have become more humane over time. If the reader is against euthanasia of any kind, however, Palmer runs the risk of actually turning the reader away from his claim, rather than supporting it.

To appeal to those who are against euthanasia, Palmer admits that most Americans think no-kill shelters are more humane. Palmer does illustrate that no-kill shelters are a good idea, but his examples focus on shelters that need to be regulated more than they are because of terrible overcrowding issues. While he acknowledges that no-kill shelters are working hard to avoid these problems by increasing volunteer staff, marketing heavily and hosting mass reduced and free adoptions, he counters these measures by questioning whether these conditions are better than humane methods of euthanasia. To provide credible proof of issues with failed no-kill policies, he cites Daphna Nachminovitch, senior vice president of cruelty investigations at PETA, who states, "Adoption can be bad—far worse than euthanasia" because many people who adopt have unethical reasons for adopting and vetting cannot be done properly in these situations.

To conclude his article, Palmer targets the readers' emotions, once again, by describing the negative practices of no-kill shelters, providing examples of shelters turning away animals deemed

Topic sentence connects to the previous paragraph by the use of the author's last name.

Because these are online sources, page numbers are not needed in the citations.

Cruz 4

un-adoptable, and including instances of overcrowding leading to fights between the animals that cause aggression and injury, often leading to slow, painful deaths. While Palmer's article has a strong emotional appeal, his reliance upon PETA as his main source of credibility weakens his overall argument.

Topic sentence goes back to the introduction.

Both articles present compelling, well-developed arguments for their claim. However, it was Hendricks's understanding of his audience that allowed him to make a more effective argument. His continual appeal to the reader's emotions allowed him to distract from and downplay his opposition successfully. By taking advantage of the reader's presumed predisposition, Hendricks manages to increase the effectiveness of each example used; in comparison to Palmer, Hendricks tailors each case to appeal to the audience immediately. Palmer, on the other hand, relies on the reader's ability to synthesize information and make rational decisions, regardless of emotional inclinations. Unfortunately for Palmer, animals are an emotionally driven subject for most individuals, putting him at a disadvantage from the start. Additionally, Palmer's lack of variety in sources, only citing PETA, as well as the absence of statistical information, caused his credibility to be inadequate and weakened his article, giving Hendricks an advantage. As a result, Hendricks produced a more effective article in persuading readers in favor of no-kill policies for animal shelters.

Thesis statement is reasserted.

Works Cited

Hendricks, Mike. "Growth of No-Kill Polices Can Jam Animal Shelters."
   The Kansas City Star, 30 Aug. 2014, www.kansascity.com/news/local/
   article1332523.html.

Palmer, Brian. "Are No-Kill Shelters Good for Cats and Dogs?" *Slate*,
   19 May 2014, www.slate.com/articles/health_and_science/
   science/2014/05/no_kill_animal_shelters_and_peta_what_is_the_
   most_humane_way_to_treat_stray.html.

The Works Cited page should always begin on a new page.

Writing a Research Essay

This chapter will explain and illustrate

- the major steps in writing a research paper:

  Step 1: Get started by creating a schedule.

  Step 2: Select a topic that you can readily research.

  Step 3: Limit your topic and make the purpose of your paper clear.

  Step 4: Brainstorm and gather information on your limited topic.

  Step 5: Keep track of your sources and take notes.

  Step 6: Write the paper.

  Step 7: Create a Works Cited page.

This chapter also provides

- a model research essay

Reimar Gaertner/Pixtal/age fotostock

Irina Zharkova31/Shutterstock

If you were to write a research essay on climate change, what would you focus on? Climate change is too broad a topic to cover in one research paper. You would need to select a more limited topic to write about, for example the effects of different types of farming on climate change. Looking at the above photographs, can you think of some other limited topics about climate change you might cover in a research paper?

Writing a research essay will require many of the same skills as writing a source-based essay; however, it will also require good organization and time management. Many students who are assigned research papers find themselves running out of time because they spend too many hours trying to gather research, reading the research, or changing the focus of their papers at the last minute. This chapter will explain how to create a realistic schedule, organize your notes, and break down the writing of the essay into smaller, more manageable steps.

Getting Started and Creating a Schedule

Writing a research essay will require you to be very organized in order to complete all the steps necessary in a timely fashion. Getting started is often the hardest part. The inclination is that your paper isn't due for several weeks, so there is no rush to begin. This type of attitude can get you in trouble. Instead, you should figure out your schedule and get started as soon as you have been assigned the paper.

Creating an effective and realistic schedule is an important first step. It is best to work backward from the date your paper is due. You should always build in more time than you think it will take and have a contingency plan that will allow you to handle unexpected interruptions and changes.

At the end of this chapter is a model research essay that was written by a student, Jacob Lashley, for his English 101 class. His professor gave students three weeks to produce a rough draft with a due date of April 27, 2021, and a final draft due date of May 4, 2021. Since Jacob knew time would be tight, he mapped out his schedule. First he filled in the due dates for the rough and final drafts. He then worked backward to create a timeline to keep on track. He knew he would need as much time as possible to complete this task, so he built in quite a few weekend days. A working version of his schedule is shown on the next page.

Selecting a Topic That You Can Readily Research

Many professors will assign a topic, but if you need to select your own topic, you will want to add time in your research schedule to find one that interests you enough to work with for an extended period of time. Remember, if your professor has given you a list of topics to avoid, don't waste your time trying to figure out a way to write about one of those topics.

To quickly find a topic that interests you and has enough material to work with, you should first consult your library resources. For example, if you initially choose the broad topic "climate change," try to find at least three academic

Final Draft Due	_May 4, 2021_
Edit	
Revise	
Rough Draft Due	_April 27, 2021_
Works Cited Created & Checked	
Rough Draft	
Outline	_April 18, 2021_
Bibliography Created & Checked	
Research Read and Annotated	_April 14, 2021_
Research Collected	
Creating a Working Thesis	_April 10, 2021_
Limiting the Topic	
Choose Topic	
Preliminary Research	_April 8, 2021_

resources on climate change. These sources could be current science books or journal articles on climate change. For instance, when Jacob Lashley, author of the model research essay "Environmental Health," visited his college library, he connected to EBSCOhost and typed "climate change" in the search box. In seconds, EBSCOhost came back with hundreds of hits—titles, publication information, and the complete text of articles about climate change.

If you decide you need more information and are planning to use the Internet, you don't necessarily want to start with Google. So many results will come back that you will not be able to work your way through them all in the time you have allotted for research. As was discussed in Chapter 17, search engines like Google Scholar will enable you to search specific types of online sources. This will prove a great time-saver for you as you gather your research.

Limiting Your Topic and Making the Purpose of Your Paper Clear

Like any paper that is source-based, a research essay should thoroughly develop a limited topic. Your paper's length will determine how broad or narrow your topic will need to be. While a ten-page essay will allow you to address a broader topic than one that is four pages, you will still need to fully develop your argument and go beyond surface-level information. Therefore, as you read through books and articles, look for ways to limit your general topic. While you are doing this, you should also be thinking about your purpose—a working thesis—that will help you focus your essay. One good way to do this is to question yourself as you are reading your material. Consider what questions you find yourself asking as you read about the topic. Could one of these questions be turned into a working thesis?

For instance, as Jacob read materials on the general topic "climate change," he chose to limit his topic to ways in which the general population could make a positive impact on climate change. As he read, he found himself asking, "What are some of the causes of climate change?" and "What can people in developed countries do to offset climate change?" He then decided to limit his topic even further by focusing on the problem of food waste as a factor of climate change.

A few other examples of limiting a research topic include:

- narrowing the general topic "drug abuse" to "successful drug treatment programs for adolescents"

- or, refocusing a topic on conservation practices so that it is limited to controlling the overpopulation of deer in suburban areas.

Do not expect to limit your topic and make your purpose clear all at once. You may have to do quite a bit of reading as you work out a narrowed focus for your paper. Note that many research essays have one of two general purposes: (1) to defend a point—for example, to provide evidence that elected officials should serve no more than a single term; or (2) to present information—for example, to discuss the effects of diet on heart disease.

Brainstorming What You Know

Once you have narrowed your topic, you should brainstorm what you already know about the topic. This will help you focus your research and save you time. For instance, as Jacob thought about his own lifestyle and how his habits contributed to climate change, he realized there were several changes he could make. He spent time writing down things he knew he should be doing but wasn't, and things he was doing but could be doing better. He also thought about how having an impact on climate change meant large-scale modifications in societal behavior, and how hard it might be to get people to make those changes. As he worked through his list, he realized that food waste was a large problem in developed economies and was something that the general population and industries could work together on to create positive change.

Gathering Information on Your Limited Topic

After limiting your topic and brainstorming what you already know, begin gathering relevant information. Remember that your time is limited, so you want to find the best sources in the shortest amount of time. If you are having problems, a good resource is a reference librarian at your college who has the knowledge and skill set to point you in the right direction.

A helpful way to proceed is to access your college library's databases and catalog to find necessary resources. If you do find a book that you think will be relevant, you will want to request it as soon as possible so you have time to work with it. You will also want to start locating credible articles from the databases or the Internet. Don't be tempted to save every article you find. Instead, as you locate articles, look at the subject headings in the catalog entry, skim the material, and save it or print it for further consideration only if you feel it will support your topic (or offer a good counterargument). Jacob had allotted only ten days to spend on research, so he used his first day to find potential articles. As he skimmed through each article, he checked to see if it was general climate change information or related to food waste. If the article looked like it had potential, he quickly saved it to read for further consideration.

Reading research material is not the same as reading a novel or magazine. Instead, you should read through the material once for an overview. As you read through the first time, you will want to pay attention to any unfamiliar vocabulary, headings, and emphasized words. During the second read, you should note areas that seem to work with your limited topic and create research questions to help you focus your essay. Depending on your understanding, you may need a third read. It is important that you allow yourself enough time to really focus on your research, but you don't want to spend so much time on it that you run short on the time needed to outline, draft, and write your essay.

For instance, Jacob knew that he had limited his research time to ten days, so as he worked through his research, he continuously asked himself whether or not a particular source focused on his working thesis—ways that people can eliminate food waste to have an impact on climate change. Knowing that he needed to address all sides of the issue, he didn't automatically eliminate a source if it didn't claim that food waste was a facet of climate change. He also knew that because he had a relatively brief amount of time to complete his research, any source that was unrelated to his limited topic should be set aside quickly so that he could move on to a new piece of research.

Keeping Track of Your Sources and Taking Notes

As you are researching, you need to keep careful and thorough track of your sources. As you learned in Chapter 19, "Writing a Source-Based Essay," doing this is important because you have to know where your information originates so that you can cite it properly. To keep track of your sources, you should create a working bibliography, a list of everything you have read and consulted. This should be formatted just as a "Works Cited" page is formatted. If you printed any of your sources, you should staple documents to keep them organized, so the individual pages don't get lost or mixed up. All print sources should be kept in a single folder that is dedicated to that writing assignment. To keep electronic sources organized, save each source as a separate document, and store all sources in one folder that is dedicated to that writing assignment.

You will make use of your sources by creating a scratch outline and taking good notes in preparation for the writing of your essay. Chapter 19 provides detailed coverage of how to create a scratch outline and of the kinds of notes you should take.

Writing the Paper

Many professors will require a research essay plan or a formal outline. Both are extremely helpful as you write your essay, so even if your instructor doesn't require an essay plan or a formal outline, you should consider creating one or both to help you focus your paper. Both will build from your informal scratch outline, giving you a more thorough detailed road map.

A detailed plan helps you figure out where your research will best fit into your essay before you even begin writing. Because a research essay plan includes the thesis statement and topic sentences, students can easily organize their research based upon the claims of each topic sentence.

Some students also find formal outlines to be helpful as a follow-up to a research essay plan because formal outlines include complete sentences and organize the information in a hierarchy. Formal outlines allow students to fully envision what their essay will look like. If you choose to create a formal outline, you can prepare either a topic outline (thesis plus supporting words and phrases) or a sentence outline (complete sentences). Formal outlines use roman numerals for first-level headings, capital letters for second-level headings, and Arabic numbers for third-level headings. (See Chapter 2 for further discussion of formal outlines.)

After Jacob completed his scratch outline, he decided to use a research essay plan to help him organize his research. As he read through his notes, he determined where the information would best fit, and then he placed the quotes, paraphrases, and summaries under the topic sentences. He included his citations just to make sure he didn't accidentally forget to cite something when he began writing his essay. Working with such a plan offered him the chance to organize and reorganize his information and to start writing with a very clear purpose in mind.

Jacob's research essay plan also enabled him to work on his essay as the ideas developed. It wasn't necessary for him to get his introduction completed before he could move on to the next paragraph, so he was able to avoid wasting time and experiencing "writer's block." If he found himself stuck, he could move on to another point in the essay, then later go back to the area that was giving him difficulty.

Once Jacob was finished with his rough draft, he created his Works Cited page. To create a Works Cited page, go back to your working bibliography and check through your essay. As you note a source that you used in your essay, check off that source on your bibliography. Once you have read through the essay and checked each source used, you can then refer to your notes to transfer the used sources into a Works Cited page. This page will always be located at the end of your essay on a separate page.

Throughout the process of writing your draft, your goal is to maintain unity and coherence and provide enough support to develop your thesis. Before turning in your rough draft for peer or professor review, you should use the checklist at the back of this text to make sure that your essay follows all four bases of effective writing.

A Model Research Essay

Writing a research essay takes time and organization, and students should employ a good writing process and follow the steps laid out in this chapter. This section presents Jacob's work: his initial scratch outline, his research essay plan, and his full written paper, including the Works Cited page.

Scratch Outline

Working thesis idea: Food waste and climate change

- food composting
- small-scale composting versus large-scale composting
- excess food from grocery stores and restaurants
- federal initiatives and incentives

Building on his scratch outline, Jacob created a research essay plan and organized his research to help him prepare to write his rough draft. In this plan, notice that Jacob has put quotation marks around direct quotations to make sure he reports his information correctly when he writes his paper. He has written some research as a summary or a paraphrase. As he organized his research, he did not create complete sentences because he was focused on simply organizing his ideas. He can make sure his sentences are complete as he writes his draft. By taking careful notes when he researched and carefully planning his essay development, Jacob ensured that he properly presented and cited his information to avoid possible plagiarism.

Research Essay Plan

Introduction

THESIS: As the public cautiously warms to the idea of less-than-photo-worthy bell peppers, the next steps toward food waste reduction present themselves: both small- and large-scale composting efforts and Life Cycle Assessment labeling.

Potential source information to incorporate:

BioCycle Magazine, a 1977 study estimated American food waste around 20% of all food produced for human consumption. By 1997, number had risen to 27%. Risen again to 40% by 2012. In 2011, 96% of all food waste was either sent to landfills or incinerated (Walls 42-43).

"unsold food... has been one of 'waste' — a seemingly necessary cost of doing business that needed to be discarded as quickly and inexpensively as possible to avoid disruption to future operations" (Walls 43).

Body Paragraph 1

TOPIC SENTENCE: Small-scale, residential composting has a relatively simple learning curve and can reduce a household's total contribution to landfills, thereby curbing its greenhouse gas emissions and creating usable topsoil in the process.

Potential source information to incorporate:

Compost ingredients broken down: brown materials, green materials, and water. Brown materials are high carbon items like branches, dead leaves, sawdust, and even uncoated cardboard. Green materials, such as lawn trimmings, coffee grounds, and fruit and vegetable waste, add the nitrogen necessary for cellular respiration (Environmental Protection Agency).

High-nitrogen and high-carbon materials are not suitable to be composted on their own. However, when mixed with material with a more compost friendly C/N ratio of 30:1, like coffee grounds, the results were much better (H'ng 17).

Body Paragraph 2

TOPIC SENTENCE: Providing easier access to composting in large cities and even capable of processing high fat items and bones, commercial composting sites have demonstrated the viability of processing food waste at existing medium- and large-scale composting sites.

Potential source information to incorporate:

yard trimmings and green waste only, could be easily converted to food waste composting sites with little added cost to their operation (Goldstein 20).

University of California Davis study published in 2019 showed that mixing food waste into green waste windrows did not significantly alter the greenhouse gas emissions of the composting process (S. Williams 43).

Body Paragraph 3

TOPIC SENTENCE: From grocers to restaurants, the excess left on shelves and plates leads to an alarming volume of food waste annually, and local governments are beginning to take action.

Potential source information to incorporate:

> New York City Sanitation Department (DSNY) implemented a zero-waste plan that will reduce landfill use by 90% (Simpson 23).

> "I live on the 6th floor of a 150-unit apartment building, so I can't simply build a compost bin in my backyard. In fact, most of New York City's 8.6 million residents do not have backyards. However, food waste recycling and composting is a viable option in NYC, and it's only growing. Indeed, DSNY Commissioner Kathryn Garcia said she wants DSNY to lead the nation in food waste recycling" (Simpson 23).

> Newtown Creek Wastewater Treatment Plant uses food waste to collect methane, enough to offset the heating of 2,500 homes (Simpson 25).

Body Paragraph 4

TOPIC SENTENCE: On a federal level, there has been much discussion around implementation of carbon labeling based on the life cycle assessment of a product.

Potential source information to incorporate:

> As recently as 2008, naysayers have criticized carbon labeling as an inconsistent and unfair metric ("Carbon Labeling" 6).

> Effort has been put into managing and accounting for uncertainty in carbon labeling modeling, which will increase the system's reliability and foster public trust (E. Williams 940-941).

Conclusion

TOPIC SENTENCE: Food waste is a preventable issue that requires immediate and effective public action and education.

Summarize information from essay:

> consumers have several options to significantly reduce their organic waste, implementing zero waste policies, expanding food waste collection, crafting policies that create incentive to properly dispose of organic waste, and championing public education efforts.

Here is a full model paper, as written by Jacob Lashley.

Academic

Model First Page of MLA-style Paper

1/2 inch

Lashley 1

1 inch

Jacob Lashley

Dr. M. Smith

English 101

4 May 2021

Center the title. Do not use boldface, quotation marks, or underlining.

Environmental Health

Human-induced climate change is an enormous issue whose causes are large and interconnected. Many of its solutions require the cooperation of entire nations and thorough regulation of industry. With the roots of climate change embedded so deeply, many have become understandably overwhelmed by the scale of climate change. As lawmakers begin to address climate change at the federal level, there is a growing need for public action on social issues like food waste. In the United States, food waste is historically on the rise. According to *BioCycle Magazine,* a 1977 study

Double-space lines of text. Leave a one-inch margin all the way around the page. Your name and the page number should be typed in the upper right corner one-half inch from the top of the page.

Lashley 2

estimated that American food waste was around 20% of all food produced for human consumption. By 1997, that number had risen to 27%, and then risen again to 40% by 2012. In 2011, 96% of all food waste was either sent to landfills or incinerated (Walls 42-43). Food waste is a growing crisis, but consumers, especially those in developed economies, have many options at their disposal. There are many cultural undertones that increase food waste, from a consumer preference for specific produce aesthetics to confusing sell-by/best-by dates that do not have a clear industry standard. As a result, for many years the narrative of "unsold food . . . has been one of 'waste' — a seemingly necessary cost of doing business that needed to be discarded as quickly and inexpensively as possible to avoid disruption to future operations" (Walls 43). Thankfully, as the public has become aware of their individual environmental footprint, we have seen these trends shifting in a positive direction. As the public cautiously warms to the idea of less-than-photo-worthy bell peppers, the next steps toward food waste reduction present themselves: both small- and large-scale composting efforts and Life Cycle Assessment labelling.

Small-scale, residential composting has a relatively simple learning curve and can reduce a household's total contribution to landfills, thereby curbing its greenhouse gas emissions and creating usable topsoil

This typical citation shows the source by giving the author's last name or (if no author is provided) the title of the article (and if relevant, a page number). "Works Cited" then provides full information about the source.

Ellipsis points show where the student has omitted material from the original source. The quoted material is not capitalized because the student has blended it into a sentence with an introductory phrase.

Thesis followed by plan of development.

Lashley 3

When citing a work in general, not part of a work, it is best to include the author's name in the text instead of using a parenthetical citation. No citation is needed, as the citation refers to the overall findings of the source.

in the process. Composting in a backyard is as simple as finding a dry, shady spot near a water source and placing your bin, or as little as a tarp-covered pile. Composting indoors is possible as well and done in bins either purchased from a hardware store or made at home. The Environmental Protection Agency's web page on the process explains the process in brief. All composting ingredients can be broken down into three easy-to-remember categories: brown materials, green materials, and water. Brown materials are high-carbon items like branches, dead leaves, sawdust, and even uncoated cardboard. Green materials, such as lawn trimmings, coffee grounds, and fruit and vegetable waste, add the nitrogen necessary for cellular respiration. A 2018 study showed that high-nitrogen and high-carbon materials are not suitable to be composted on their own. However, when mixed with material with a more compost-friendly C/N ratio of 30:1, like coffee grounds, the results were much better (H'ng 17). The parameters of the study were a one-to-one mixture, but most home composters start with two parts brown material per one part green material. It is advisable to avoid composting meat, dairy, and other high-fat items at home because they decompose much more slowly. Therefore, they may cause your compost to develop a terrible odor and even attract vermin. A well-managed home compost

Lashley 4

bin will neither draw pests nor putrefy and will reduce the carbon footprint of the family kitchen.

Providing easier access to composting in large cities and even capable of processing high-fat items and bones, commercial composting sites have demonstrated the viability of processing food waste at existing medium- and large-scale composting sites. As it decomposes in a landfill, food waste generates methane, a greenhouse gas, but when composted the anaerobic processes that produce that methane do not occur. As cities begin to adopt policies that divert food waste away from landfills, many seasonal composting sites, previously used for yard trimmings and green waste only, could be easily converted to food waste composting sites with little added cost to their operation (Goldstein 20). A University of California Davis study published in 2019 showed that mixing food waste into green waste windrows did not significantly alter the greenhouse gas emissions of the composting process (S. Williams 43). As local authorities implement plans and infrastructure to address climate change, food waste diversion to these sites will prove an integral part of that effort.

From grocers to restaurants, the excess left on shelves and plates leads to an alarming volume of food waste annually, and local governments are beginning to take action. Many large cities, like New York City, have

Lashley 5

adopted measures to drastically reduce the amount of food waste that will see a landfill. The New York City Sanitation Department (DSNY) has implemented a zero-waste plan that will reduce landfill use by 90% (Simpson 23). This is happening despite the logistical challenges of city living. James Simpson, Assistant Counsel for New York State's Department of Environmental Conservation, writes:

> I live on the 6th floor of a 150-unit apartment building, so I can't simply build a compost bin in my backyard. In fact, most of New York City's 8.6 million residents do not have backyards. However, food waste recycling and composting is a viable option in NYC, and it's only growing. Indeed, DSNY Commissioner Kathryn Garcia said she wants DSNY to lead the nation in food waste recycling. (23)

By offering both drop off and curbside options for compost collection and distributing brown bins for residents to dispose of food waste on the street, New York City has begun to combat food waste directly. The city has also implemented public education campaigns to ensure what is collected complies with composting standards. One of the more interesting implementations of this program occurs at the Newtown Creek Wastewater Treatment Plant, which uses food waste to collect methane, enough to offset the heating of 2,500 homes (25). As local and state governments begin to implement better environmental policy, we can expect pressure on the federal government to begin to do the same.

Source is identified by name and area of expertise.

Direct quotations of four typed lines or more are indented five spaces (or one-half inch) from the left margin. Quote marks are not used.

Only the page number is needed, as the author has already been named earlier in the paragraph.

Lashley 6

On a federal level, there has been much discussion around implementation of carbon labelling based on the life cycle assessment of a product. As more farms begin the conversion to green agricultural practices and climate continues to be a central issue, the average consumer will need to be better informed about the processes that bring them their food. For that reason, we have seen a growing push to label products according to their carbon footprint. Carbon labelling supporters hold that if we were to label a product's environmental impact, then consumers could make better-educated decisions about their own carbon footprint at the point of sale. Though as recently as 2008, naysayers have criticized carbon labelling as an inconsistent and unfair metric ("Carbon Labeling" 6). However, as the conversation grows, much effort has been put into managing and accounting for uncertainty in modelling, which will increase the system's reliability and foster public trust (E. Williams 940–941). To apply a more pragmatic metric, it may also be necessary to widen the scope beyond carbon to include other environmental concerns like total water use and soil conservation factors, because carbon is not the monolithic troublemaker in agriculture that it is in other industries. As the methodology is refined, one could certainly expect to see carbon life cycle assessment labelling on our food products in the future. A discerning

Cited material extends from one page to another, so both page numbers are given.

Lashley 7

consumer may then determine a product's environmental impact, from the harvest of its raw materials to whichever disposal method the consumer may elect, with a quick glance at its packaging.

The conclusion provides a summary and restates the thesis.

Food waste is a preventable issue that requires immediate and effective public action and education. From home composting to large-scale efforts, consumers have several options to significantly reduce their organic waste. In the past, a lack of public awareness and little infrastructural support from local governments have led our cities to overlook the opportunity presented by this challenge. Today, this trend is slowly changing course as the public's desire for a green future expands. Cities can begin to address this by implementing zero waste policies, expanding food waste collection, crafting policies that create incentive to properly dispose of organic waste, and championing public education efforts. Individuals can get involved by reducing their food waste through mindful shopping, civic engagement, raising public awareness, and composting. These actions not only have a direct impact on the health of our planet, but they also signal to our leaders that the time for meaningful change is now and that the public is ready.

Works Cited

"Carbon Labelling on Farm Products Is a 'Nonsense.'" *Food Manufacture*, vol. 83, no. 10, Oct. 2008, p. 6. *EBSCOhost*, search.ebscohost.com/login.aspx?direct=true&db=8gh&AN=35184629&site=ehost-live.

"Composting at Home." Environmental Protection Agency, 12 April 2021, https://www.epa.gov/recycle/composting-home#basics.

Goldstein, Nora, and Coryanne Mansell. "Is Your Yard Trimmings Composting Site Food Waste Ready?" *BioCycle*, vol. 60, no. 8, Nov. 2019, pp. 17–21. *EBSCOhost*, search.ebscohost.com/login.aspx?direct=true&db=8gh&AN=140030170&site=ehost-live.

H'ng, P. S., et al. "Evolution of Organic Matter Within Sixty Days of Composting of Lignocellulosic Food Industry Waste in Malaysia." *Compost Science & Utilization*, vol. 26, no. 1, Jan. 2018, pp. 16–26. EBSCOhost, doi:10.1080/1065657X.2017.1342105.

Simpson, James L. "Food Waste in the City: Composting, Fighting Climate Change, and Creating Energy in the 'City That Never Sleeps.'" *New York State Conservationist*, vol. 74, no. 4, Feb. 2020, pp. 22–25. *EBSCOhost*, search.ebscohost.com/login.aspx?direct=true&db=sch&AN=142031498&site=ehost-live.

Walls, Matthew, et al. "The Time Is Ripe for Food Recovery." *BioCycle*, vol. 55, no. 8, Sept. 2014, pp. 42–47. *EBSCOhost*, search.ebscohost.com/login.aspx?direct=true&db=8gh&AN=98416961&site=ehost-live.

Williams, Eric D., et al. "Hybrid Framework for Managing Uncertainty in Life Cycle Inventories." *Journal of Industrial Ecology*, vol. 13, no. 6, Dec. 2009, pp. 928–944. *EBSCOhost*, doi:10.1111/j.1530-9290.2009.00170.x.

Williams, Sequoia R., et al. "Impact of Composting Food Waste with Green Waste on Greenhouse Gas Emissions from Compost Windrows." *Compost Science & Utilization*, vol. 27, no. 1, Jan. 2019, pp. 35–45. *EBSCOhost*, doi:10.1080/1065657X.2018.1550023.

Works cited should be double-spaced and should always appear on a separate, titled page.

Titles of books, magazines, and the like should be italicized.

Include the date you accessed a Web source if no publication or posting date is available for that source.

Several of these sources are online. Include the DOI or a complete URL for all online sources.

After reading the research essay, consider and evaluate the programs your town or city has in place to reduce food waste and encourage composting.
pixinoo/Shutterstock

Handbook of Sentence Skills

tzahiV/Getty Images

What sentence-skills error can you find in the sign pictured above? How does this error affect the message the sign is supposed to convey? How can you correct the error?

Grammar

What sentence-skills error can you find in the sign pictured above? How can you correct it? How does this error affect the message the sign is intended to convey?
Yuri_Arcurs/Getty Images

Subjects and Verbs

This chapter will explain two of the basic building blocks of English sentences: subjects and verbs.

Key Terms

auxiliary verbs: verbs that work with the main verb to make up the complete verb in a sentence; also called helping verbs. Example: *The woman is working.* (Auxiliary verb: *is*)

linking verbs: verbs that help describe a subject by connecting it to another word. Example: *The man is handsome.* (Linking verb: *is*)

preposition: one of a group of words that precede a noun or pronoun and indicate direction, position, placement, duration, or another kind of connection to the other words in the sentence. Examples: *about, above, through, under, with*.

subject: who or what a sentence speaks about; usually a noun or pronoun that acts, is acted upon, or is described. Example: *The boy cries.* (Subject: *boy*)

verb: what the sentence says about the subject; a word that shows what a subject does or that helps describe the subject by linking it to an adjective. Example: *The boy cries.* (Verb: *cries*)

Every sentence has a subject and a verb. Who or what the sentence speaks about is called the *subject;* what the sentence says about the subject is the *verb*. In the following sentences, the subject is underlined once; the verb is underlined twice.

The <u>boy</u> <u>cried</u>.
That <u>fish</u> <u>stinks</u>.
Many <u>people</u> <u>applied</u> for the job.
The <u>show</u> <u>is</u> a documentary.

A Simple Way to Find a Subject

If you ask *who* or *what* the sentence is about, your answer will be the subject.

Who is the first sentence about? The <u>boy</u>
What is the second sentence about? That <u>fish</u>
Who is the third sentence about? Many <u>people</u>
What is the fourth sentence about? The <u>show</u>

A Simple Way to Find a Verb

If you ask what the sentence *says about* the subject, your answer will be the verb.

What does the first sentence *say about* the boy? He <u>cried</u>.
What does the second sentence *say about* the fish? It <u>stinks</u>.
What does the third sentence *say about* the people? They <u>applied</u>.
What does the fourth sentence *say about* the show? It <u>is</u> a documentary.

A second way to find the verb is to put *I, you, we, he, she, it,* or *they* in front of the word you think is a verb. If the result makes sense, you have a verb. For example, you could put *he* in front of *cried* in the first sentence, with the result, *he cried,* making sense. Thus, you know that *cried* is a verb.

Also remember that most verbs show action. In the sentences above, there are three action verbs: *cried, smells,* and *applied.* Other verbs, known as *linking verbs,* do not show action; they give information about the subject. In "The show is a documentary," the linking verb *is* joins the subject (*show*) with a word that identifies or describes it (*documentary*). Other common linking verbs include *am, are, was, were, feel, appear,* and *become.*

ACTIVITY 1

In each of the following sentences, draw one line under the subject and two lines under the verb.

1. The ripening tomatoes glistened on the sunny windowsill.

2. Acupuncture reduces the pain of my headaches.

3. Elena finished her genetics research project.

4. My brother built his bookshelves from cinder blocks and wood planks.

5. A jackrabbit bounds up to fifteen feet in one leap.

6. The singer's diamond earrings sparkled in the spotlight.

7. Walt Disney created the cartoon character Mickey Mouse.

8. The Federal Bureau of Investigation (FBI) pursues violators of federal laws.

9. Ferdinand and Isabella of Spain sponsored Columbus's voyages.

10. On April 9, 1865, General Robert E. Lee surrendered to General Ulysses S. Grant.

In each of the following sentences, draw one line under the subject and two lines under the verb.

ACTIVITY 2

1. Slovenia is a very small country in Europe with a population of 1.9 million.

2. Slovenia borders Italy, Austria, Croatia, and Hungary.

3. Ljubljana is the largest city, with a population of 400,000 people.

4. Mountains cover most of the Slovenian region.

5. The Alpine regions offer several fantastic family-friendly ski resorts.

6. A devastating ice storm destroyed 15 percent of the forests in 2013–2014 by covering the ground with over three feet of ice.

7. The country has an extensive cave system numbering over 8000 caves!

8. Farmers grow olives and grapes in the lower elevations near the Adriatic Sea.

9. The famous Lipizzaner stallions originate from Slovenia, not Austria.

10. Slovenia became an independent country in 1991.

More about Subjects and Verbs

1. A sentence may have more than one verb, more than one subject, or several subjects and verbs.
   The engine coughed and sputtered.
   Broken glass and empty cans littered the parking lot.
   Marta, Nilsa, and Robert met after class and headed downtown.

2. The subject of the sentence never appears within a prepositional phrase. A *prepositional phrase* is simply a group of words that begins with a preposition. Following is a list of common prepositions.

Prepositions

about	behind	except	on	under
above	below	for	onto	up
across	beneath	from	out	upon
after	beside	in	outside	with
among	between	inside	over	within
around	beyond	into	past	without
as	by	like	through	
at	down	of	to	
before	during	off	toward	

Crossing out prepositional phrases will help you find the sentence's subject or subjects.

A ~~stream~~ of cold air comes ~~through the space below the door~~.

~~Specks~~ of dust dance gently ~~in a ray of sunlight~~.

The amber lights ~~on its sides~~ outlined the tractor-trailer ~~in the hazy dusk~~.

~~Members~~ of the club are entitled to use the exercise room.

The golden rays ~~of the May sun~~ reflect ~~on the crystal-clear waters of the icy lake~~.

3. Many verbs consist of *helping, or auxiliary,* verbs, as seen here in several forms of the verb *work*. (See Chapter 26 for a list of other helping verbs.)

Forms of *work*

work	worked	should work
works	were working	will be working
does work	have worked	can work
is working	had been working	could be working

4. Words like *not, just, never, only,* and *always* are not part of the verb, although they may appear within the verb.

Ruby <u>has</u> never <u>liked</u> cold weather.

Our boss <u>will</u> not <u>be singing</u> with the choir this year.

The intersection <u>has</u> not always <u>been</u> this dangerous.

5. A verb preceded by *to* is never the verb of a sentence.

At night, my son <u>likes</u> to read under the covers.

Evelyn <u>decided</u> to move to a new city.

6. An *-ing* word by itself is never the verb of a sentence. (It may be part of the verb, but it must have a helping verb in front of it.) The following is *not* a sentence, because the verb is not complete:

They going on a trip this weekend.

This *is* a sentence:

They <u>are going</u> on a trip this weekend.

Draw a single line under subjects and a double line under verbs. Cross out prepositional phrases as necessary to find the subjects.

ACTIVITY 3

1. A large segment of the population supports the new legislation.

2. Two of the films we chose to write about were first released in the 1970s.

3. After more than 2,000 years, some Roman aqueducts are still supplying water to large European cities.

4. Every dog in the house barked as the mailman came to the door.

5. The fantastic advertisement about the new perfume inspired me to try the scent.

6. The novels of John Steinbeck portray the lives of the poor and powerless.

7. The smoke detector's tiny green light suddenly started to flicker.

8. A colleague of mine works at home and submits her reports by e-mail.

9. The large jar of marbles fell off the bookshelf and crashed on the floor.

10. A memorial of beautifully sculpted granite stands as tribute to Abraham Lincoln, our sixteenth president.

ACTIVITY 4

In each of the following sentences, draw one line under subjects and a double line under verbs. Cross out prepositional phrases as necessary to find the subjects.

1. One of the most popular ways of traveling is on a cruise ship.

2. The cheapest and most popular cruise line in the Caribbean is Carnival.

3. With a variety of activities, Carnival cruise passengers can enjoy themselves regardless of age.

4. For the budget traveler, cruise lines like Celebrity and Disney are a good choice.

5. With itineraries from three to seventeen days, budget cruise lines offer a good experience for kids and families.

6. Cruise companies like Viking and Uniworld offer luxurious cruises on the rivers of Europe.

7. With smaller ships, luxury river cruises deliver a more intimate experience for travelers.

8. Adventurous travelers with time and money can experience exciting destination cruises with phenomenal itineraries.

9. Unusual destinations like Antarctica, the Arctic, or Mauritius are accessible to people on Windstar or Metropolitan Touring ships.

10. From massive ships like *Harmony of the Seas* to smaller ships like the *River Princess*, travelers can find the perfect cruise for their vacation.

REVIEW TEST 1

Draw a single line under subjects and a double line under verbs. Cross out prepositional phrases as necessary to find the subjects. Many sentences contain multiple subjects and verbs.

1. Maria Sklodowka was born in 1867 in Warsaw in the country now known as Poland.

2. Her father was a mathematics and physics professor, and her mother managed a boarding school for girls.

3. Maria's mother died in 1878 of complications from tuberculosis.

4. Maria attended a clandestine university where she learned about Dostoevsky and Karl Marx.

5. Maria briefly moved to Paris to be a governess and to help her sister; her sister repaid Maria several years later when she insisted that Maria move back to Paris.

6. While in Paris, Maria met Pierre Curie and, after a courtship, married him in 1895, becoming Marie Curie.

7. Marie and Pierre worked together on the study of radiation.

8. In 1903, Marie and Pierre were awarded the Nobel Prize for physics, making Marie the first woman ever to win a Nobel Prize.

9. Pierre was killed in a wagon accident, and Marie took a job as a teacher at the Sorbonne.

10. When Marie was awarded a second Nobel Prize in 1911 for chemistry, she became the only woman to win two Nobel Prizes in different disciplines.

REVIEW TEST 2

In each of the following sentences, draw one line under subjects and a double line under verbs. Cross out prepositional phrases as necessary to find the subjects. Many sentences contain multiple subjects and verbs.

One of children's favorite authors, Roald Dahl authored stories such as *Charlie and the Chocolate Factory, James and the Giant Peach, The BFG, Matilda*, and *Fantastic Mr. Fox*. Dahl was born in Wales and served in the Royal Air Force before becoming a renowned author. Many of his short stories are tales of children overcoming cruelty. In *Matilda*, Matilda uses telekinesis on the dictatorial Miss Trunchbull to trick her into revealing the theft of Miss Honey's inheritance. In *James and the Giant Peach*, young James is treated horribly by his cruel aunts, Spiker and Sponge. They are killed when the peach rolls over them. Sophie, a young orphaned girl in *The BFG*, escapes a cruel, abusive orphanage when she goes to live with the Big Friendly Giant. Dahl's stories are also famous for their dark comedy and unanticipated endings. In *Charlie and the Chocolate Factory*, Charlie wins the factory. The other children all meet with disasters due to their spoiled and ill-tempered attitudes. At the end of *The Magic Finger*, the young narrator turns the Cooper family into tiny humans with bird wings as punishment for their bird hunting activities. Even though Dahl's books were written in the mid-twentieth century, the stories are timeless and will continue to entertain readers for generations to come.

REVIEW TEST 3

Write five complete sentences that contain prepositional phrases that come between the subject and the verb. Remember that prepositional phrases begin with words such as *with, to, in, into, about,* and *for.* Then, draw a single line under the subject and a double line under the verb. Finally, draw a line through each prepositional phrase.

Fragments

This chapter will explain how to avoid the most common types of fragments. A fragment is a word group that lacks a subject or a verb and/or one that does not express a complete thought.

Fragment:

Whenever I go to school.

"Whenever," a dependent word, cannot introduce a complete thought, so it cannot stand alone.

Correct Sentence:

Whenever I go to school, I take the bus.

The dependent word group is attached to a complete thought, so this is a full sentence.

Every sentence must have a subject and a verb and must express a complete thought. A word group that lacks a subject or a verb and/or fails to express a complete thought is a *fragment*. Here are the most common types of fragments:

1. Dependent-word fragments
2. *-ing* and *to* fragments
3. Added-detail fragments
4. Missing-subject fragments

Dependent-Word Fragments

Some word groups that begin with *dependent words* are fragments. When you start a sentence with a dependent word, be careful not to create a fragment.

Dependent Words

after	if, even if	when, whenever
although	in order that	where, wherever
as	since	whether
because	that, so that	which, whichever
before	unless	while
even though	until	who, whom, whose
how	what, whatever	

Below, the word group beginning with *after* is a fragment:

After I cashed my paycheck. I treated myself to dinner.

A *dependent statement*—one starting with a dependent word like *after*—cannot stand alone. It depends on another statement to complete the thought. *After I cashed my paycheck* is a dependent statement. It leaves us hanging. We expect to find out, in the same sentence, *what happened after* the writer cashed the check. When a writer does not follow through and complete a thought, a fragment results.

To correct the fragment, simply follow through and complete the thought:

After I cashed my paycheck, I treated myself to dinner.

Remember, then, that *dependent statements by themselves are fragments*. They must be attached to a statement that makes sense standing alone.

Here are two other examples of dependent-word fragments:

I won't leave the house. Until I hear from you.

The cat threw up the little rubber band. That it had swallowed recently.

Until I hear from you is a fragment; it does not make sense standing by itself. We want to know in the same statement what *until* refers to. The writer must complete the thought. Likewise, *That it had swallowed recently* is not in itself a complete thought. We want to know in the same statement what *that* refers to.

Additional information about dependent words and phrases can be found in Chapter 5. In that chapter, dependent words are also referred to as subordinating words.

How to Correct a Dependent-Word Fragment

Often, you correct a dependent-word fragment by attaching it to the sentence that comes after it or to the one that comes before it.

After I cashed my paycheck, I treated myself to dinner.

(The fragment has been attached to the sentence that comes after it.)

The cat threw up the little rubber band that it had swallowed recently.

(The fragment has been attached to the sentence that comes before it.)

You can also connect a dependent-word fragment by removing the dependent word and rewriting the sentence:

I cashed my paycheck and then treated myself to dinner.

I will wait to hear from you.

It had swallowed it recently.

---

a. Use a comma if a dependent-word group comes at the beginning of a sentence, but not generally if it comes at the *end* of a sentence.

Comma: After I cashed my paycheck, I treated myself to dinner.

No comma: I won't leave the house until I hear from you.

b. Sometimes *who, that, which,* or *where* appear not at the very start but near the start of a word group. A fragment can result:

I drove slowly past the old brick house. The place where I grew up.

The place where I grew up is not a complete thought. We want to know in the same statement *where was the place?* To correct the fragment, attach it to the sentence that came before:

I drove slowly past the old brick house, the place where I grew up.

TIPS

Turn each of the following dependent-word groups into a sentence by adding a complete thought. Use a comma after the dependent-word group if a dependent word starts the sentence. Note the examples.

ACTIVITY 1

EXAMPLES

Before I became a vegetarian.

Before I became a vegetarian, I would eat fish four times a week.

My neighbor who competitively barbeques.

My neighbor who competitively barbeques has won several prizes.

1. Unless I start practicing more.

_____

_____

2. Although I had studied for several hours.

_____

_____

3. Because I had just gotten paid.

_____

_____

4. Until the new mall opened.

_____

_____

5. The car that I bought.

_____

_____

ACTIVITY 2

Underline the dependent-word fragment in each item. Then rewrite the items, correcting each fragment by attaching it to the sentence that comes before or the sentence that comes after it—whichever sounds more natural. Use a comma after the dependent-word group if it starts the sentence.

1. My cat flattens herself and tries to get out of the room. Whenever I turn on the vacuum. Apparently, she thinks something is coming to eat her.

_____

_____

2. Philadelphia was originally a Quaker colony. That was founded by William Penn in 1681. By 1777, it had become the capital of the new United States.

_____

_____

3. Sakinah is the manager of the new neighborhood garden. That was started to encourage people to grow their own food. She has been making sure everyone is using only organic products.

_____

_____

4. Since Connor first began watching NOVA. He has been fascinated with space travel. He has decided to become an astronaut.

_____

_____

5. Roman law was first recorded in 450 B.C. in what was known as the "twelve tablets." It lasted for many centuries. Until the fall of the eastern Roman Empire nearly 2,000 years later.

_____

_____

-*ing* and *to* Fragments

When an -*ing* word appears at or near the start of a word group, a fragment may result. Such fragments often lack a subject and part of the verb. In the items below, underline the word groups that contain -*ing* words. Each is a fragment.

1. Enola walked all over the neighborhood yesterday. Trying to find her dog Bo. Several people claimed they had seen him only hours before.
2. We sat back to watch the movie. Not expecting anything special. To our surprise, we clapped, cheered, and cried for the next two hours.
3. I telephoned the balloon store. It being the day before our wedding anniversary. I knew my wife would be surprised to receive a dozen heart-shaped balloons.

People sometimes write -*ing* fragments because they think that the subject of one sentence will work for the next word group as well. Thus, in item 1 the writer thinks that the subject *Enola* in the opening sentence will also serve as the subject for *Trying to find her dog Bo*. But the subject must be in the same sentence.

How to Correct -*ing* Fragments

1. Attach the fragment to the sentence that comes before it or to the sentence that comes after it, whichever makes sense. Item 1 could read, "Enola walked all over the neighborhood yesterday trying to find her dog Bo."
2. Add a subject and change the -*ing* verb part to the correct form of the verb. Item 2 could read, "We didn't expect anything special."
3. Change *being* to the correct form of the verb *be (am, are, is, was, were)*. Item 3 could read, "It was the day before our wedding anniversary."

How to Correct *to* Fragments

When *to* appears at or near the start of a word group, a fragment sometimes results:

At the Chinese restaurant, Jacy used chopsticks. To impress his date. He spent one hour eating a small bowl of rice.

The second word group is a fragment and can be corrected by adding it to the preceding sentence:

At the Chinese restaurant, Jacy used chopsticks to impress his date.

ACTIVITY 3

Underline the *-ing* fragment in each of the following items. Then correct the item by using the method described in parentheses.

EXAMPLE

<u>Including the Arctic Ocean and parts of Canada, the United States, and other countries.</u> The Arctic Circle is the area that surrounds the Earth's North Pole. (Add the fragment to the sentence that comes after it.)

Including the Arctic Ocean and parts of Canada, the United States, and other countries,

the Arctic Circle is the area that surrounds the Earth's North Pole.

1. Ramses II ruled over Egypt from 1279 to 1212 B.C. Making his country stronger than ever before. He was both ambitious and intelligent.
   (Add the fragment to the preceding sentence.)

   _____

2. A noisy fire truck suddenly raced down the street. Coming to a stop at my house. My home security system had sent a false alarm.
   (Correct the fragment by adding the subject *it* and changing *coming* to the proper form of the verb, *came*.)

   _____

3. I couldn't find any books on Egyptian history in the library. They had all been checked out. The reason for this being that a research paper had just been assigned to students in an ancient history class.
   (Correct the fragment by changing *being* to the proper form of the verb, *was*.)

   _____

   _____

ACTIVITY 4

Underline the *-ing* or *to* fragment in each item. Then rewrite each item, correcting the fragment by using one of the three methods described above.

1. Knowing she had not finished the book. Madelyn was very nervous about going to class. She was sure the teacher was going to give a quiz.

   _____

   _____

2. I hired some teenage neighbors. To mow my lawn and weed the garden. They have been doing a great job.

    _____

    _____

3. Searching for the right filament for his incandescent light bulb. Thomas Edison (1847–1931) found that a strip of carbonized bamboo could glow for 1,200 hours.

    _____

    _____

4. Estevo and Bryson have been friends since first grade. Graduating from high school this May.

    _____

    _____

5. Sofia Vergara cofounded EBY with Renata Black. Their company donates 10 percent of the profits to the Seven Bar Foundation. Providing small business loans to women around the world.

    _____

    _____

Added-Detail Fragments

Added-detail fragments lack a subject and a verb. They often begin with one of the following words:

also	especially	except	for example
like	including	such as	

Underline the one added-detail fragment in each of the following items:

1. Before a race, I eat starchy foods. Such as bread and spaghetti. The carbohydrates provide quick energy.
2. Ana is taking a night course in auto mechanics. Also, one in plumbing. She wants to save money on household repairs.
3. My son keeps several pets in his room. Including hamsters and mice.

People often write added-detail fragments for much the same reason they write *-ing* fragments. They think the subject and verb in one sentence will serve for the next word group. But the subject and verb must be in *each* word group.

How to Correct Added-Detail Fragments

1. Attach the fragment to the complete thought that precedes it. Item 1 could read "Before a race, I eat starchy foods such as bread and spaghetti."

2. Add a subject and a verb to the fragment to make it a complete sentence. Item 2 could read "Ana is taking a night course in auto mechanics. Also, she is taking one in plumbing."

3. Insert the fragment within the preceding sentence. Item 3 could read "My son keeps several pets, including hamsters and mice, in his room."

ACTIVITY 5

Underline the fragment in each of the following items. Then make it a sentence by rewriting it, using the method described in parentheses.

EXAMPLE

My mother loves reading books written in the eighteenth and nineteenth centuries. Especially books by Jane Austen. She says they are more interesting than modern novels. (Add the fragment to the preceding sentence.)

My mother loves reading books written in the eighteenth and nineteenth centuries,

especially books by Jane Austen.

1. Carly likes working at the coffee shop. She enjoys the perks. For example, getting a free pound of coffee each week.
   (Correct the fragment by adding the subject and verb *she gets*.)

   _____

   _____

2. Henry Ford (1863–1947) is credited with the invention of the assembly line, not the automobile. Several nineteenth-century inventors had designed self-propelled vehicles. Like the one that ran on high-pressure steam.
   (Attach the fragment to the preceding sentence.)

   _____

   _____

3. I love to eat "b" vegetables because they are full of vitamins. Such as broccoli, Brussels sprouts, and beans. They also taste great.
   (Correct the fragment by inserting it in the preceding sentence.)

   _____

   _____

Underline the added-detail fragment in each item. Then rewrite to correct the fragment. Use one of the three methods described on the previous page.

1. The music festival had an amazing lineup. For example, The Ballroom Thieves, Blind Pilot, and Walk Off the Earth. I was very excited when I was able to purchase tickets.

   _____

   _____

   _____

2. Some European countries remained neutral during World War II. Such as Switzerland and Portugal. Most South American countries refused to take sides as well.

   _____

   _____

3. The house was overrun with cats. At least twenty of them. It was incredibly smelly and filled with fur balls.

   _____

   _____

4. Xavier loves to collect rare pieces of pottery. Like jasperware. His most prized piece is a Yixing teapot that is several hundred years old.

   _____

   _____

5. I know why I had to learn certain subjects in high school. Such as American history. Becoming a responsible citizen requires knowledge of our country's past and of its system of government.

   _____

   _____

Missing-Subject Fragments

Missing-subject fragments are dependent word groups that lack a subject. In each item below, underline the word group in which the subject is missing:

1. Alicia loves getting presents. But hates writing thank-you notes.

2. Mickey has orange soda and potato chips for breakfast. Then eats more junk food, like root beer and cookies, for lunch.

How to Correct Missing-Subject Fragments

1. Attach the fragment to the preceding sentence. Item 1 could read "Alicia loves getting presents but hates writing thank-you notes."

2. Add a subject (which can often be a pronoun standing for the subject in the preceding sentence). Item 2 could read "Then he eats more junk food, like root beer and cookies, for lunch."

ACTIVITY 7   Underline the missing-subject fragment in each item. Then rewrite that part of the item needed to correct the fragment. Use one of the two methods of correction described above.

1. Padrina loves to study math and science. But refuses to study history. She says she doesn't want to focus on the past.

   _____

   _____

2. My favorite pizza place is Sammy's Pizza and Pub. They make an amazing gluten-free spinach pizza with fresh nut-free pesto. And brew the best iced tea in the Midwest.

   _____

   _____

3. Kendall is allergic to dairy. She goes into anaphylactic shock. And loses her ability to breathe.

   _____

   _____

4. When we arrived in Chicago, we took a train from the airport to the center of the city. Then walked a few blocks to our hotel. The trip was easy.

   _____

   _____

5. Next fall, I plan to take a course in calculus. And to join the mathematics club. By the time the year is over, I will have decided whether to become a mathematics teacher.

   _____

   _____

A Review: How to Check for Sentence Fragments

1. Read your paper aloud from the *last* sentence to the *first*. You will be better able to see and hear whether each word group you read is a complete thought.

2. If you think a word group may be a fragment, ask yourself, Does this contain a subject and a verb and express a complete thought?

3. More specifically, be on the lookout for the most common fragments:
   - Dependent-word fragments (starting with words like *after, because, since, when,* and *before*)
   - *-ing* and *to* fragments (*-ing* and *to* at or near the start of a word group)
   - Added-detail fragments (starting with words like *for example, such as, also,* and *especially*)
   - Missing-subject fragments (a verb is present but not the subject)

REVIEW TEST 1

Each word group in the following student paragraph is numbered. In the space provided, write C if a word group is a complete sentence; write F if it is a fragment. You will find eight fragments in the paragraph.

Personal

_____ 1. [1]For children in areas that get snow. [2]There are stages of snow

_____ 2. days. [3]The first day is always fun, exciting, and filled with

_____ 3. possibilities. [4]It usually consists of sledding. [5]Making snowmen,

_____ 4. drinking hot chocolate, and watching movies. [6]The kids know

_____ 5. they have been given a gift of a day away from school. [7]If the

_____ 6. first day is followed by more, days two through four continue

_____ 7. with the initial excitement of day one. [8]But often lead into cabin

_____ 8. fever, boredom, and frustration. [9]This is especially true if

_____ 9. days two through four are very cold. [10]Although movies are

_____ 10. still an option. [11]Parents begin to feel guilty that their kids are not

_____ 11. learning anything; this begins a tug-of-war. [12]And studying

_____ 12. suggested. [13]If school is reopened, family sanity can be saved.

_____ 13. [14]However, if more snow days occur. [15]Reality sets in and

_____ 14. despondency grows in the parents. [16]Parents' sanity is

_____ 15. jeopardized as they try to maintain normalcy. [17]And

_____ 16. start bargaining with the school district by offering to

_____ 17. do whatever is necessary to reopen the schools. [18]The final stage

_____ 18. for parents is despair. [19]As the kids grow more and more

_____ 19. restless. [20]Countless families have been known to abandon hope

_____ 20. that the snow will ever melt and life will become normal.

Now (on separate paper) correct the fragments you have found. Attach the fragments to sentences that come before or after them or make whatever other change is needed to turn each fragment into a sentence.

REVIEW TEST 2

Underline the two fragments in each item below. Then make whatever changes are needed to turn the fragments into sentences.

EXAMPLE

Sharon was going to charge her new laptop._x *b* ~~But then decided to pay cash instead.~~
She remembered her New Year's resolution._x *t* ~~To cut down on her use of credit cards.~~

1. We both began to tire. As we passed the halfway mark in the race. But whenever I'd hear Reggie's footsteps behind me. I would pump my legs faster.

2. The American Southwest is home to several Native American nations. Such as the Navajo, the Apache, and the Pueblo. The East is the land of the Huron and Iroquois. Along with the Delaware and the Mohegan.

3. Punching all the buttons on his radio in sequence. Thiago kept looking for a good song. He was in the mood to cruise down the highway. And sing at the top of his voice.

4. My children joke that we celebrate "Hanumas." With our Jewish neighbors. We share Hanukkah and Christmas activities. Including making potato pancakes at their house and decorating our tree.

5. Pop artists gained fame in the 1950s. Reacting to the more established art forms like expressionism, which preceded them. They portrayed common images from everyday life. Such as Coke bottles and soup cans.

6. Our landlord often invites her tenants to dinner. And allows them to use her washer and dryer. By doing such things. She has become known as the kindest person in our neighborhood.

7. The alley behind our house was flat. Except for a wide groove in the center. We used to sail paper boats down the groove. Whenever it rained hard enough to create a "river" there.

8. Don passed the computer school's aptitude test Which qualifies him for nine months of training. Don kidded that anyone could be accepted. If he or she had $4,000.

REVIEW TEST 3

Read the paragraph below. In the space between the lines, correct each fragment.

It is very common for college students and young adults to find themselves in debt. As a result of poor spending habits. In order to learn how to effectively manage money. Students should be required to take personal finance classes. From elementary school all through high school. Starting in elementary school. Students could learn how to budget allowances. How to save for items like toys and college, and how to run small businesses like lemonade stands or lawn mowing services. Games could be used in the classroom to offer students hands-on learning opportunities. As students get older. Classes could be more sophisticated. Students could learn about different concepts. Like compound interest, opportunity costs, and trade-offs. They could also be taught about the history of economics. How the government influences the economy, and how and why countries trade. High school students' courses would take economics even further. Explaining general investing, paying for college, and planning for retirement. Students could be required to intern at various businesses. To learn economics from the business side. Teaching economics on all educational levels could help many students avoid poor spending choices. And enjoy better financial situations throughout their lives.

Run-Ons

Run-ons are two complete thoughts that are run together with no adequate sign given to mark the break between them. In this text, the term
"run-on" refers to both comma splices and fused sentences.

Key Terms

clause: a group of words having a subject and a verb.

comma splice: a comma incorrectly used to connect ("splice" together)
two complete thoughts. Example:

> Comma splice: *I go to school, my siblings stay home.*
>
> Correct sentences: *I go to school. My siblings stay home.*

dependent clause: a group of words having a subject and a verb that
does not express a complete thought and is not able to stand alone;
also called a subordinate clause.

fused sentence: a run-on with no punctuation to mark the break
between thoughts. Example:

> Fused sentence: *I go to school my siblings stay home.*
>
> Correct sentences: *I go to school. My siblings stay home.*

independent clause: a group of words having a subject and a verb that
expresses a complete thought and is able to stand alone.

What Are Run-Ons?

A *run-on* consists of two complete thoughts run together without adequate punctuation to signal the break between them.[*] There are two
types of run-ons: fused sentences and comma splices.

---

[*]Some instructors regard all run-ons as fused sentences. But for many other instructors, and for our
purposes in this book, the term *run-on* applies equally to fused sentences and comma splices. The
bottom line is that you do not want either fused sentences or comma splices in your writing.

Some instructors refer to each complete thought in a run-on as an independent clause. A
clause is simply a group of words having a subject and a verb. A clause may be independent
(expressing a complete thought and able to stand alone) or dependent (not expressing a complete
thought and not able to stand alone). Using this terminology, we'd say that a run-on is two
independent clauses run together with no adequate sign given to mark the break between them.
Chapter 5, "The Fourth Step in Essay Writing," demonstrates how to take simple sentences and
make them compound or complex sentences without creating run-ons.

Fused sentences have no punctuation to mark the break between the two thoughts.

> The bus stopped suddenly I found myself thrown onto the floor.

> We heard a noise in the garage two birds had flown in through the open window.

Comma splices are the most common kind of run-on. Students sense that some kind of connection is needed between two thoughts, so they often put a comma at the dividing point.

> The bus stopped suddenly, I found myself thrown onto the floor.

> We heard a noise in the garage, two birds had flown in through the open window.

But the comma alone is *not sufficient*. A stronger, clearer mark is needed between the two complete thoughts

> People often write run-ons when the second complete thought begins with one of the following words:
>
> | I | we | there | now |
> |---|---|---|---|
> | you | they | this | then |
> | he, she, it | that | next | |
>
> Be on the alert for run-ons whenever you use one of these words.

Three Ways to Correct Run-Ons

Here are three common methods of correcting a run-on:

1. Use a period and a capital letter to separate sentences:

    The bus stopped suddenly. I found myself thrown onto the floor.

    We heard a noise in the garage. Two birds had flown in through the open window.

2. Use a comma and a joining word *(and, but, for, or, nor, so, yet)*:

    The bus stopped suddenly, and I found myself thrown onto the floor.

    We heard a noise in the garage, for two birds had flown in through the open window.

3. Use a semicolon to connect the two complete thoughts:

    The bus stopped suddenly; I found myself thrown onto the floor.

    We heard a noise in the garage; two birds had flown in through the open window.

A fourth way to correct a run-on is to use *subordination*, which is discussed later in this chapter.

Method 1: Period and a Capital Letter

Use a period and a capital letter between two complete thoughts if the thoughts are not closely related or if another method would make the sentence too long.

In the following run-ons, locate the point at which one complete thought ends and another begins. Each is a fused sentence: two sentences joined with no punctuation. Reading a sentence aloud helps you hear where the break is. At this point, your voice may drop and pause. Correct each run-on by putting a period at the end of the first thought and a capital letter at the start of the next.

EXAMPLE

    Mia's cell phone doesn't work anymore. She dropped it in the toilet.

1. I got stuck in rush hour traffic today it took me an extra hour to get home.

2. Bats have gotten a bad image they actually help reduce the mosquito population.

3. Since I got my smartphone, I spend too much time texting my friends i hardly ever send e-mails anymore.

4. The flower is the most important part of a plant it contains the seeds that enable the plant to reproduce.

5. Angel has a unique sense of style his house is filled with brightly colored walls in oranges, yellows, and purples.

6. Galileo discovered that two solid objects of different weights fall at the same velocities he also made the first practical telescope for observing the heavens.

7. On our trip to Africa, we traveled to Mozambique and Zimbabwe then we went north to Zambia.

8. The man at the door was offering tree and lawn services he claimed to be the cheapest company in town.

9. Simeon is fluent in Chinese, French, Arabic, and Spanish he is often hired to help translate paperwork for businesses.

10. Jessica loved to solve mysteries she entered college to become a forensic scientist.

Method 2: Comma and a Joining Word

Another way of correcting a run-on is to use a comma and a joining word to connect the two complete thoughts. Joining words (also called *conjunctions*) include *and, but, for, or, nor, so,* and *yet.* Here are what the five most common joining words mean:

and   in addition

Teresa works full time for an accounting firm, and she takes evening classes.

(*And* means *in addition:* Teresa works full time for an accounting firm; *in addition,* she takes evening classes.)

but   however, on the other hand

I turned to the want ads, but I knew my dream job wouldn't be listed.

(*But* means *however:* I turned to the want ads; *however,* I knew my dream job wouldn't be listed.)

for   because

Lizards become sluggish at night, for they need the sun's warmth to maintain an active body temperature.

(*For* means *because:* Lizards become sluggish at night *because* they need the sun's warmth to maintain an active body temperature.)

so   as a result, therefore

The canoe touched bottom, so Dave pushed it toward deeper water.

(*So* means *as a result:* The canoe touched bottom; *as a result,* Dave pushed it toward deeper water.)

yet   but, however, on the other hand

The defenders of the Alamo were vastly outnumbered, yet they refused to surrender.

(*Yet* means *however:* The defenders of the Alamo were vastly outnumbered; *however,* they refused to surrender.)

ACTIVITY 2

Insert the joining word *(and, but, for, so)* that logically connects the two thoughts in each sentence.

1. Jordan spends a lot of time doing his homework in his room, _____ he usually listens to his iPod at the same time.

2. King Macbeth of Scotland (1040–1057) defeated King Duncan in battle, _____ he later became the title character in one of Shakespeare's tragedies.

3. The school started a new organic garden, _____ the students don't like doing the weeding.

4. I needed to deposit the cash I made from my garage sale, _____ the ATM machine wasn't working.

5. Maria Montessori is known as a pioneer of modern education, _____ she created a system that included "learning games" designed especially for children.

6. The tomato is very popular today, _____ it was once thought to be poisonous.

7. We were awakened by a huge bang in the middle of the night, _____ it turned out to be our cats knocking over our large ficus plant.

8. My paycheck is not enough to pay all my bills, _____ I have started riding my bike to and from work.

9. My favorite restaurant serves steak and lobster, _____ I don't get to go very often because my husband is a vegetarian.

10. I avoided spending money eating out over the last three months, _____ I rewarded myself by purchasing a vinyl album.

Add a complete and closely related thought to go with each of the following statements. Use a comma and the indicated joining word when you write the second thought.

ACTIVITY 3

EXAMPLE

for I decided to leave school an hour early, _____

for I had a pounding headache.

1. The corner store is convenient _____ **but**

_____

2. Leo attended night class _____ **for**

_____

3. Aisha studied for an hour before dinner _____ **and**

_____

4. Marcia was unable to take Prof. Samuelson's history class _____ **so**

_____

5. I had enough money to buy dinner _____ **but**

_____

ACTIVITY 4

Correct each run-on with either (1) a period and a capital letter or (2) a comma and a logical joining word. Do not use the same method of correction for every sentence.

Some of the run-ons are fused sentences (there is no punctuation between the two complete thoughts), and some are comma splices (there is only a comma between the two complete thoughts). One sentence is correct.

EXAMPLE

There was a strange odor in the house,⁵⁰ Burt called the gas company immediately.

1. Oxygen is an odorless gas discovered independently by Joseph Priestly and Karl Scheele, it is the third most abundant element in the universe.

2. Cockroaches adapt to any environment they have even been found living inside nuclear reactors.

3. My dog was panting from the heat I decided to wet him down with the garden hose.

4. Our science class is working on a weather project with students from Russia, we communicate by computer almost every day.

5. My grandfather is eighty-five years old, he goes to work every day.

6. The bristles of the paintbrushes were very stiff, soaking them in turpentine made them soft again.

7. Chen borrows CDs from the library to listen to on the way to work, some are music, and some are recordings of best-selling books.

8. Thomas Paine, who supported the American Revolution, was accused of treason in England, he escaped to France in 1793.

9. Today, there are only eight major planets in our solar system, for astronomers have downgraded Pluto to a dwarf planet.

10. I volunteered to run the Meals on Wheels service in our city, we deliver hot meals to sick or housebound people.

Method 3: Semicolon

A third way to correct a run-on is to use a semicolon to mark the break between thoughts. When used to correct run-ons, a semicolon can be used alone or with a transitional word.

Semicolon Alone   Unlike the comma alone, a semicolon can be used to connect the two complete thoughts:

> Lonnie heard a noise and looked out the window; the only thing he saw was his reflection.

> Lizards become sluggish at night; they need the sun's warmth to maintain an active body temperature.

> We knew a power failure had occurred; all the clocks were forty-seven minutes slow.

Using semicolons can add to sentence variety. For some people, however, the semicolon is a confusing punctuation mark. Keep in mind that if you are not comfortable using it, you can and should use one of the the first two methods of correcting run-ons.

Insert a semicolon where the break occurs between the two complete thoughts in each of the following sentences.

ACTIVITY 5

EXAMPLE

The plumber gave me an estimate of $260; I decided to repair the faucet myself.

1. The children stared at the artichokes on their plates they didn't know how to eat the strange vegetable.

2. Ecuador is in South America it is bordered by Colombia and Peru.

3. The Great Wall of China is immense it is more than 13,000 miles long.

4. Elana woke up at 3 A.M. to the smell of sizzling bacon her husband was having another insomnia attack.

5. Maya curled up under the covers she tried to get warm by grasping her icy feet with her chilly hands.

6. Honshu is the largest island in Japan it is also the most densely populated.

7. Ice had formed on the inside edge of our window Joey scratched a *J* in it with his finger.

8. Charles peered into the microscope he saw only his own eyelashes.

9. A man in a bear suit walked slowly down the street the children stopped their play to stare at him.

10. Ceylon was declared independent in 1948 later it became known as Sri Lanka.

Semicolon with a Transitional Word   A semicolon can be used with a transitional word and a comma to join two complete thoughts.

> I tried to cash my paycheck; however, I had forgotten to bring my identification.

> Athletic shoes must fit perfectly; otherwise, wearers may injure their feet.

> People use seventeen muscles when they smile; on the other hand, they use forty-three muscles when they frown.

Here is a list of transitional words, also known as *adverbial conjunctions*.

Transitional Word	Meaning
however	but
nevertheless	however
on the other hand	however
instead	as a substitute
meanwhile	in the intervening time
otherwise	under other conditions
indeed	in fact
in addition	also, and
also	in addition
moreover	in addition
furthermore	in addition
as a result	thus, therefore
thus	as a result
consequently	as a result
therefore	as a result

ACTIVITY 6

For each sentence, choose a logical transitional word from the box above, and write it in the space provided. Use a semicolon *before* the connector and a comma *after* it.

EXAMPLE

I dread going to parties; _____*however*_____, my husband loves meeting new people.

1. Lily always attends every class session _____ she hopes to get the best grade possible.

2. Kryptonite is a fictitious substance that is supposed to be harmful to Super-man _____ krypton is a real element, which was discovered in 1989.

3. Yoga is my favorite form of exercise _____ I enjoy running and hiking.

4. We were asleep in our tent _____ two bears crept into our camp-site and began searching for food.

5. The sheriff was very popular _____ she won reelection quite easily.

A Note on Subordination

A fourth method of joining related thoughts is to use subordination. *Subordination* is a way of showing that one thought in a sentence is not as important as another thought. (Subordination is explained in full in Chapter 5.) Below are three earlier sentences, recast so that one idea is subordinated to (made less important than) the other idea. In each case, the subordinate (or less important) thought is under-lined. Note that each subordinate clause begins with a dependent word.

<u>Because my dog was panting from the heat</u>, I decided to wet him down with the garden hose.

<u>Since her husband was having another insomnia attack</u>, Elana woke up at 3 A.M. to the smell of sizzling bacon.

Maria Montessori is known as a pioneer of modern education <u>because she created a system that included "learning games" designed especially for children</u>.

A Review: How to Check for Run-Ons

1. To see if a sentence is a run-on, read it aloud and listen for a break marking two complete thoughts. Your voice will probably drop and pause at the break.

2. To check an entire paper, read it aloud from the *last* sentence to the *first*. Doing so will help you hear and see each complete thought.

3. Be on the lookout for words that can lead to run-on sentences:

I	he, she, it	they	this	then	now
you	we	there	that	next	

continued

> 4. Correct run-ons by using one of the following methods:
>
> Period and a capital letter
>
> Comma and a joining word *(and, but, for, or, nor, so, yet)*
>
> Semicolon, alone or with a transitional word
>
> Subordination

REVIEW TEST 1

Correct each run-on by using (1) a period and a capital letter; (2) a comma and a joining word; or (3) a semicolon. Do not use one method exclusively.

Some of the run-ons are fused sentences (there is no punctuation between the two complete thoughts), and some are comma splices (there is only a comma between the two complete thoughts). Two sentences are correct.

1. Slovakia, a country in Eastern Europe, was once ruled by the Austro-Hungarian Empire, it is now an independent country.

2. Slovakia has had a long history of being ruled by other countries in the fifth century, the kingdom of Greater Moravia was settled and founded by Slavic tribes.

3. In the tenth century, Magyar tribes invaded they formed Greater Hungary.

4. In 1526, Hungary was defeated by the Ottoman Turks, the Hapsburgs began their rule of Upper Hungary.

5. Pozony became the Hungarian capital the city is now known as Bratislava.

6. Austria-Hungary was formed in 1867, Franz Josef, the Hapsburg emperor, negotiated with Hungarian nobles to form the new country.

7. The Austro-Hungarian Empire was dissolved in 1918 at the end of World War I, Slovakia then became part of Czechoslovakia.

8. At the end of World War II, Czechoslovakia was ruled by Czech Communists in 1948 the Soviet Union tightened its control over the country.

9. In 1989, when the Soviet Union fell, Czechoslovakians demonstrated in the Velvet Revolution, which brought some democracy to the country.

10. In 1992, Czechoslovakia was known as the Czech and Slovak Federal Republics Prime Minister Meciar began talks to disband the confederation.

11. In 1993, the Slovak Republic and the Czech Republic became two separate countries, this was nicknamed the Velvet Divorce.

12. In 2000, Slovakia began the process to join the European Union and was granted membership in 2004.

REVIEW TEST 2

Correct each run-on by using (1) a period and a capital letter; (2) a comma and a joining word; or (3) a semicolon. Do not use one method exclusively.

1. The nervous system works by transmitting signals from all parts of the body to the brain then it sends return signals to various organs and muscles.

2. With a groan, Margo pried off her running shoes, then she plunged her swollen feet into a bucket of baking soda and hot water.

3. At 2 a.m. the last customer left the diner, a server began stacking chairs on the tables for the night.

4. Hypnosis has nothing to do with the occult it is merely a state of deep relaxation.

5. Many young adults today live at home with their parents this allows them to save money.

6. Many politicians wanted America to remain neutral during World War II the attack on Pearl Harbor in 1941 made that impossible.

7. Early in life, Thomas Edison suffered with deafness, he taught his wife-to-be Morse code while he was courting her.

8. Originally, horses were too small to carry riders very far larger horses had to be bred for use in warfare.

9. The words *month, silver, purple,* and *orange* have something in common, no other English words rhyme with them.

10. I had heard that the Taj Mahal was one of the wonders of the world I planned a special excursion to visit this magnificent tomb.

REVIEW TEST 3

Locate and correct the five run-ons in the passage that follows.

Personal

   My worst experience of the week was going home for lunch, rather than eating at work. My children didn't know I was coming, they had used most of the bread. All I had to make a sandwich with were two thin, crumpled pieces of crust. I sat there eating my tattered sandwich and trying to relax, then my daughter's phone rang. My daughter, who was in the bathroom, called down to me that I should not answer her phone. As soon as I responded to her, someone knocked on the door, it was two salespeople who wanted to talk with me about their special pest control service. I politely got rid of them and went back to finish lunch. I thought I would relax over my coffee, I had to break up a fight between my two young sons about which television channel to watch. As a last bit of frustration, my daughter came downstairs she asked me to drive her over to a friend's house before I went back to work.

Regular and Irregular Verbs

This chapter will review the principal characteristics of regular and irregular verbs.

Key Terms

irregular verb: a verb that has an irregular form in the past tense and past participle. For example, *choose* becomes *chose* or *chosen*.

past participle: one of the principal parts of every verb; formed by adding *-d* or *-ed* to the present; used with the helping verbs *have*, *has*, or *had*, or with a form of *be* (with passive verbs).

present participle: one of the principal parts of every verb; formed by adding *-ing* to the present.

principal parts of verbs: the four parts of every verb: present, past, past participle, and present participle.

verb tense: the times shown by verbs: present, past, and future.

Regular Verbs

A Brief Review of Regular Verbs

Every verb has four principal parts: *present, past, past participle*, and *present participle*. These parts can be used to build all the verb *tenses*— the times shown by verbs.

Most verbs in English are regular. The past and the past participle of regular verbs are formed by adding *-d* or *-ed* to the present. The *past participle* is the form of the verb used with the helping verbs *have, has*, or *had* (or some form of *be* with passive verbs). The *present participle* is formed by adding *-ing* to the present.

For a more in-depth look at verb tense and helping verbs, refer to Chapters 25 and 26.

Here are the principal parts of some regular verbs:

Present	Past	Past Participle	Present Participle
shout	shouted	shouted	shouting
prepare	prepared	prepared	preparing
surprise	surprised	surprised	surprising
tease	teased	teased	teasing
frighten	frightened	frightened	frightening

Present Tense Endings

The verb ending -s or -es is needed with a regular verb in the present tense when the subject is *he, she, it,* or any one person or thing.

He reads every night.

She watches television every night.

It appears they have little in common.

ACTIVITY 1   Some verbs in the sentences that follow need -s or -es endings. Cross out each incorrect verb form and write the correct form in the space provided.

_____ 1. My radio wake me up every morning with soft music.

_____ 2. Sonya always rave about the beaches in Costa Rica.

_____ 3. My wife watch our baby in the morning, and I take over afternoons.

_____ 4. Alexander live on Puget Sound in Tacoma, Washington.

_____ 5. My brain work much better at night than it does in early morning.

Past Tense Endings

The verb ending -d or -ed is needed with a regular verb in the past tense.

This morning I completed my research paper.

The recovering hospital patient walked slowly down the corridor.

Some students hissed when the new assignment was given out.

Some verbs in the sentences that follow need -*d* or -*ed* endings. Cross out each incorrect verb form and write the correct form in the space provided.

_____ 1. In 1609, an Italian astronomer named Galileo use the telescope to view the moons of Jupiter.

_____ 2. At one time, the F. W. Woolworth Company own more than one thousand five-and-dime stores across the United States.

_____ 3. We realize a package was missing when we got back from shopping.

_____ 4. Bill was incorrect when he said that Henry Ford invent the automobile.

_____ 5. The driver edge the car into the intersection just as the light turned green.

Irregular Verbs

Irregular verbs have irregular forms in past tense and past participle. For example, the past tense of the irregular verb *choose* is *chose;* its past participle is *chosen.*

Almost everyone has some degree of trouble with irregular verbs. When you are unsure about the form of a verb, you can check the following list of irregular verbs. (The present participle is not shown on this list because it is formed simply by adding -*ing* to the base form of the verb.) Or you can check a dictionary, which gives the principal parts of irregular verbs.

A List of Irregular Verbs

Present	Past	Past Participle
arise	arose	arisen
awake	awoke *or* awaked	awoken *or* awaked
be (am, are, is)	was (were)	been
become	became	become
begin	began	begun
bend	bent	bent
bite	bit	bitten
blow	blew	blown
break	broke	broken

continued

Present	Past	Past Participle
bring	brought	brought
build	built	built
burst	burst	burst
buy	bought	bought
catch	caught	caught
choose	chose	chosen
come	came	come
cost	cost	cost
cut	cut	cut
do (does)	did	done
draw	drew	drawn
drink	drank	drunk
drive	drove	driven
eat	ate	eaten
fall	fell	fallen
feed	fed	fed
feel	felt	felt
fight	fought	fought
find	found	found
fly	flew	flown
freeze	froze	frozen
get	got	got *or* gotten
give	gave	given
go (goes)	went	gone
grow	grew	grown
have (has)	had	had
hear	heard	heard
hide	hid	hidden
hold	held	held
hurt	hurt	hurt
keep	kept	kept

continued

Present	Past	Past Participle
know	knew	known
lay	laid	laid
lead	led	led
leave	left	left
lend	lent	lent
let	let	let
lie	lay	lain
light	lit	lit
lose	lost	lost
make	made	made
meet	met	met
pay	paid	paid
ride	rode	ridden
ring	rang	rung
run	ran	run
say	said	said
see	saw	seen
sell	sold	sold
send	sent	sent
shake	shook	shaken
shrink	shrank	shrunk
shut	shut	shut
sing	sang	sung
sit	sat	sat
sleep	slept	slept
speak	spoke	spoken
spend	spent	spent
stand	stood	stood
steal	stole	stolen
stick	stuck	stuck
sting	stung	stung
swear	swore	sworn
swim	swam	swum
take	took	taken

continued

Present	Past	Past Participle
teach	taught	taught
tear	tore	torn
tell	told	told
think	thought	thought
throw	threw	thrown
wake	woke *or* waked	woke *or* waked
wear	wore	worn
win	won	won
write	wrote	written

ACTIVITY 3

Cross out the incorrect verb form in each of the following sentences. Then write the correct form of the verb in the space provided.

EXAMPLE

flown   After it had ~~flew~~ into the picture window, the dazed bird huddled on the ground.

_____   1. Before they bought their first house, my parents had chose to live with my grandparents in order to save money.

_____   2. Before we could find seats, the theater darkened and the opening credits begun to roll.

_____   3. To be polite, I drunk the slightly sour wine that my grandfather poured from his carefully hoarded supply.

_____   4. In 1803, the United States payed France fifteen million dollars for the Louisiana Territory.

_____   5. After crossing over land, the power of the hurricane shrinked significantly.

_____   6. After a day on the noisy construction site, Sam's ears rung for hours with a steady hum.

_____   7. Because Sophia had been stinged by wasps, she was taken to the hospital.

_____   8. If I had went to work ten minutes earlier, I would have avoided being caught in the gigantic traffic snarl.

_____   9. After the bicycle hit a patch of soft sand, the rider was throwed into the thorny bushes along the roadside.

_____   10. Anne Sullivan teached Helen Keller to speak and read.

_____   11. I was concerned that the refrigerator had broke, but it was just unplugged.

_____   12. The cat had did nothing but lie around all day.

_____   13. On Thanksgiving Day, more than three hundred geese flown over our house.

_____   14. By the time my wife had arrived home, I had ate all the chocolate in the house.

_____   15. By the end of the board meeting, she had spoked so much that her throat was sore.

Three Problematic Common Irregular Verbs

The verbs *be*, *have*, and *do* are often problematic because they are irregular even in the present tense. The following charts have the proper conjugations of *be*, *have*, and *do*.

Be

Present Tense		Present Tense Examples	
I am	we are		
you are	you are		
he/she/it is	they are	the dog is	the dogs are

Past Tense		Past Tense Examples	
I was	we were		
you were	you were		
he/she/it was	they were	the dog was	the dogs were

Have

Present Tense		Present Tense Examples	
I have	we have		
you have	you have		
he/she/it has	they have	the professor has	the professors have
Past Tense		**Past Tense Examples**	
I had	we had		
you had	you had		
he/she/it had	they had	the professor had	the professors had

Do

Present Tense		Present Tense Examples	
I do	we do		
you do	you do		
he/she/it does	they do	the chef does	the chefs do
Past Tense		**Past Tense Examples**	
I did	we did		
you did	you did		
he/she/it did	they did	the chef did	the chefs did

TIP   Many people have trouble with one negative form of *do*. They will say, for example, "He don't agree," instead of, "He doesn't agree," or they will say, "The door don't work," instead of, "The door doesn't work." Be careful to avoid the common mistake of using *don't* instead of *doesn't*.

ACTIVITY 4   Fill in the blank with the correct form of *be*, *have*, or *do*.

My boss _____ a very fair and kind supervisor. Last week, I _____ late because I _____ a flat tire. My boss _____ extremely upset at my tardiness because she _____ to reschedule an important meeting. Once I told her what happened, she _____ more understanding. She _____ like it, however,

when people take advantage of her kindness. My colleague _____ absent for two weeks because of a funeral, but he _____ not tell our boss where he _____.
He _____ out of a job now.

Cross out the incorrect verb form or tense in each sentence. Then write the correct form or tense in the space provided.

EXAMPLE

_____is_____   The National World War I museum ~~be~~ located in Kansas City, Missouri.

_____   1. In 1918, at the end of World War I, concerned citizens in Kansas City begin the Liberty Memorial Association.

_____   2. R. A. Long, the founding president, said the memorial would be "a living expression for all time of the gratitude of a grateful people to those who offered and who gives their lives in defense of liberty and our country."

_____   3. Once the members of the association beginned fundraising, it took only ten days to raise $2.5 million.

_____   4. H. Van Buren Magonigle winned the competition to design the memorial.

_____   5. When the site for the memorial were dedicated, Admiral David Beatty of Great Britain, General Armando Diaz of Italy, Marshal Ferdinand Foch of France, Lieutenant General Baron Jacques of Belgium, and General John J. Pershing of the United States, the supreme Allied commanders, spoke to the crowd of people.

_____   6. In 1994, the memorial was closed because its structure had deteriorated and safety had became a concern.

_____   7. In the late 1990s, concerned citizens in Kansas City once again rally to restore the memorial.

_____   8. After an additional sales tax was initiated, enough money is raised to restore the memorial and to expand the museum.

_____   9. The museum is now an 80,000-square-foot facility that housed over 75,000 items.

_____ 10. The National Museum received its official status as the United States' official World War I museum in 2004 after Congress had gave it the designation.

_____ 11. Visitors to the museum enter by crossing a bridge over a field of nine thousand poppies; each poppy stands for one thousand combatant deaths, representing the nine million who die during the war.

_____ 12. A favorite item of many visitors be the 1917 Harley Davidson motorcycle.

_____ 13. Children especially enjoyed the interactive displays that explain the war on a level they can understand.

_____ 14. Many of the exhibits, like the walk through the crater, allow visitors to experience what the soldiers and civilians experience during and after the devastating war.

_____ 15. A visit to Kansas City and the National World War I Museum be an educational experience.

REVIEW TEST 2

Write short sentences that use the form requested for the following verbs.

EXAMPLE

Past of *think* _I thought I would purchase a car this week._____

1. Past participle of *bring* _____

2. Past of *choose* _____

3. Present of *speak* _____

4. Past of *teach* _____

5. Present of *hide* _____

6. Past participle of *shrink* _____

7. Past of *light* _____

8. Past of *lend* _____

9. Past participle of *hurt* _____

10. Present of *spend* _____

Subject–Verb Agreement

Subject–verb agreement is the correspondence in number between the subject and the verb of a sentence; plural subjects take plural verbs, and singular subjects take singular verbs. This chapter will review the necessity for subject–verb agreement.

Incorrect:

The crinkly lines around Nia's mouth gives her a friendly look.

The subject "crinkly lines" is a plural, so the verb should be "give," not "gives."

Correct:

The crinkly lines around Nia's mouth give her a friendly look.

The verb "give" agrees with the plural "crinkly lines."

Key Terms

compound subject: two subjects separated by a joining word such as *and*.

indefinite pronoun: a word that refers to people and things that are not named or are not specific. Many indefinite pronouns (such as *one, nobody, nothing,* and *each*) take a singular verb; others, such as *both* or *few*, take plural verbs.

A verb must agree with its subject in number. A *singular subject* (one person or thing) takes a singular verb. A *plural subject* (more than one person or thing) takes a plural verb. Mistakes in subject–verb agreement are sometimes made in the following situations:

1. When words come between the subject and the verb
2. When a verb comes before the subject
3. With compound subjects
4. With indefinite pronouns

Each of these situations is explained in this chapter.

Words between Subject and Verb

Words that come between the subject and the verb do not change subject–verb agreement. In the sentence

The sharp <u>fangs</u> in the dog's mouth <u><u>look</u></u> scary.

the subject (*fangs*) is plural, and so the verb (*look*) is plural. The words that come between the subject and the verb are a prepositional phrase: *in the dog's mouth*. They do not affect subject–verb agreement. (A list of prepositions can be found in Chapter 21.)

To help find the subject of certain sentences, you should cross out prepositional phrases.

The lumpy <u>salt</u> ~~in the shakers~~ <u><u>needs</u></u> to be changed.

An old <u>chair</u> ~~with broken legs~~ <u><u>has sat</u></u> in our basement for years.

ACTIVITY 1

Underline the subject and lightly cross out any words that come between the subject and the verb. Then double-underline the verb in parentheses that you believe is correct.

1. Some members of Abraham Lincoln's cabinet (was, were) his political rivals.

2. The woman in the yoga pants with the Star Wars design (teaches, teach) at Zen Zone Yoga Studio.

3. The Prado, one of the world's greatest art museums, (is, are) located in Madrid, Spain.

4. The wind in the long, cold tunnels (sounds, sound) like an old-fashioned pipe organ.

5. Aline's bike, with fat tires, a titanium frame, and a big bell, (is, are) a Why Big Iron.

6. The lilies alongside the neighbor's garage (blooms, bloom) all summer.

7. The slow-cooked pulled pork in the crock-pot on the countertop (smells, smell) absolutely divine.

8. The Grand Canyon, with its deep valleys and colorful rock formations, (is, are) a popular place to visit.

9. In my opinion, an ocean-side resort that has rooms with balconies overlooking the ocean (make, makes) the perfect place to vacation.

10. John Glenn, who was the first American to orbit the Earth in 1962 and who flew in the *Discovery* in 1998, (holds, hold) the record for being the oldest person to fly in space.

Verb before Subject

A verb agrees with its subject even when the verb comes *before* the subject. Words that may precede the subject include *there, here,* and, in questions, *who, which, what,* and *where.*

Here are some examples of sentences in which the verb appears before the subject:

> There <u>are</u> wild <u>dogs</u> in our neighborhood.
>
> In the distance <u>was</u> a <u>billow</u> of black smoke.
>
> Here <u>is</u> the <u>newspaper</u>.
>
> Where <u>are</u> the children's <u>coats</u>?

If you are unsure about the subject, ask *who* or *what* of the verb. With the first example above, you might ask, "*What* are in our neighborhood?" The answer, *wild dogs,* is the subject.

Write the correct form of each verb in the space provided.

ACTIVITY 2

1. Where _____ the locker filled with books?   **(is, are)**

2. Near the top of the hill _____ two gigantic pines covered with snow.   **(was, were)**

3. _____ Hunter shop at Trader Joe's or Target?   **(do, does)**

4. There _____ four cats eating out of our garbage can last night.   **(was, were)**

5. In our school, there _____ six sets of twins.   **(is, are)**

Compound Subjects

A *compound subject* is two subjects separated by a joining word, such as *and.* Subjects joined by *and* generally take a plural verb.

> A patchwork <u>quilt</u> and a sleeping <u>bag</u> <u>cover</u> my bed in the winter.
>
> <u>Clark</u> and <u>Lois</u> <u>are</u> a contented couple.

When subjects are joined by *either . . . or, neither . . . nor, not only . . . but also,* the verb agrees with the subject closer to the verb.

> Neither the <u>negotiator</u> nor the union <u>leaders</u> <u>want</u> the strike to continue.

The nearer subject, *leaders,* is plural, and so the verb is plural.

> Neither the union <u>leaders</u> nor the <u>negotiator</u> <u>wants</u> the strike to continue.

In this version, the nearer subject, *negotiator,* is singular, so the verb is singular.

Write the correct form of the verb in the space provided.

(know, knows)

1. Neither the students nor the teacher _____ what caused the classroom bird to start singing.

(look, looks)

2. A watchtower and several cabins _____ over the valley.

(need, needs)

3. Either the cupcakes or the pie _____ to be eaten.

(cover, covers)

4. Spidery cracks and a layer of dust _____ the ivory keys on the old piano.

(taste, tastes)

5. Chicken and fish _____ completely different, but I like them both.

(belong, belongs)

(was, were)

6. Not only France and Great Britain but also Italy _____ to NATO.

7. In eighteenth-century France, makeup and high heels _____ worn by men.

(catch, catches)

8. Tanya and her dad _____ fish every time they go fishing.

(has, have)

9. Neither the director nor the writers of this film _____ ever received an Academy Award.

(freeze, freezes)

10. Water and alcohol _____ at different temperatures.

Indefinite Pronouns

The following words are known as *indefinite pronouns*. Indefinite pronouns usually take singular verbs.

(-*one* words)	(-*body* words)	(-*thing* words)	
one	nobody	nothing	each
anyone	anybody	anything	either
everyone	everybody	something	neither
someone	somebody	everything	

TIP *Both* always takes a plural verb.

Write the correct form of the verb in the space provided.

1. Neither of the essays _____ plagiarized.

2. Somebody in my office always _____ how terrible the coffee is.

3. Both countries _____ great coffee.

4. Everyone _____ the college kite-flying contest in the spring

5. One of the students in my history class _____ Polish.

(was, were)

(mention, mentions)

(produce, produces)

(enter, enters)

(speak, speaks)

REVIEW TEST 1

In the space provided, write the correct form of the verb shown in the margin.

1. Yellowstone National Park, located in Wyoming, Idaho, and Montana, _____home to Old Faithful, the world's most famous geyser. (are, is)

2. Each of their children _____ given a name picked at random from a page in the dictionary. (was, were)

3. Near the top of the company's organizational chart _____ the vice president for sales and the director of personnel. (were, was)

4. Envelopes, file folders, and an old telephone book _____ jammed into Lupe's kitchen drawers. (is, are)

5. Neither of the main dishes at tonight's dinner _____ any meat. (contains, contain)

6. A drop in the price of gasoline and other fuels _____ the chances that bus fares will go up soon. (decrease, decreases)

7. Many people in my neighborhood _____ to be recycling paper, cans, glass, and plastic. (appear, appears)

8. A good grounding in mathematics _____ it easier to learn physics. (make, makes)

9. In exchange for reduced rent, Karla and James _____ the dentist's office beneath their second-floor apartment. (cleans, clean)

10. One of the hospital's delivery rooms _____ furnished with bright carpets and curtains to resemble a room at home. (is, are)

REVIEW TEST 2

Double-underline the correct verb in parentheses. In addition, underline the subject that goes with the verb.

1. According to Hasbro, the game of MONOPOLY (was created, were created) in 1935, and over 200 million copies have been sold since it first entered the market.

2. When Mr. Charles B. Darrow first presented the game to the Parker Brothers game company, they rejected it because "fifty-two errors" (was found, were found).

3. The inventor then produced the game on his own and (was able, were able) to sell five thousand handmade sets to a department store in Philadelphia.

4. Mr. Darrow contacted Parker Brothers a second time and, by that point, the game (was, were) so popular that the company decided to produce it.

5. Since 1935, the Parker Brothers company (have manufactured, has manufactured) more than 5,120,000,000 little green plastic houses.

6. During World War II, Allied forces (was able, were able) to hide escape maps, files, compasses, and real money inside MONOPOLY game boards that were smuggled into POW camps.

7. Over the years, players (have landed, has landed) on three squares—GO, B&O Railroad, and Illinois Avenue—most often.

8. The total amount of money in a standard MONOPOLY game (is, are) $15,140.

9. Since the 1970s, international MONOPOLY tournaments (occurs, occur) every four years.

10. The documentary *Under the Boardwalk: The MONOPOLY Story* (focuses, focus) on the international tournaments and the stories behind the players.

11. Multiple versions of MONOPOLY (have been, has been) created since it first started.

12. Some of the special editions of MONOPOLY (is, are) *Disney, SpongeBob SquarePants, Star Wars: Clone Wars,* and *James Bond.*

13. MONOPOLY (continues, continue) to have such a strong following that multiple Facebook pages have been dedicated to the game.

14. Currently, MONOPOLY (is, are) published in twenty-seven languages and is licensed in more than eighty-one countries.

15. Multiple online and computer versions of MONOPOLY (is, are) also available.

More about Verbs

This chapter will provide additional information about verbs, specifically:

- verb tense
- helping verbs
- verbals

Key Terms

gerund: a verbal; the *-ing* form of the verb used as a noun. Example: I love *dancing*.

infinitive: a verbal; *to* plus the base form of the verb. Example: I love *to dance*.

participle: a verbal; the *-ing* or *-ed* form of the verb used as an adjective. Example: I love *dancing* bears.

verbals: words formed from verbs that often express action; these include gerunds, infinitives, and participles.

Verb Tense

As mentioned in Chapter 24, the time that a verb shows is usually called *tense*. The most common tenses are the simple present, past, and future. In addition, nine other tenses enable us to express more specific ideas about time than the simple tenses do.

Tenses	Examples
Present	I *work*. Tony *works*.
Past	Ellen *worked* on her car.
Future	You *will work* on a new project next week.

continued

Tenses	Examples
Present perfect	He *has worked* on his research paper for a month. They *have worked* out a compromise. *Note:* The present perfect tense is used for an action that began in the past and continues in the present.
Past perfect	The nurse *had worked* two straight shifts. *Note:* The past perfect tense is used for a past action that came *before* another past action.
Future perfect	Next Monday, I *will have worked* here exactly two years.
Present progressive	I *am working* on my speech for the debate. You *are working* too hard. The toaster *is* not *working* properly.
Past progressive	He *was working* in the basement. The contestants *were working* on their robot design.
Future progressive	My son *will be working* in our store this summer.
Present perfect progressive	Adriel *has been working* late this week.
Past perfect progressive	Until recently, I *had been working* nights.
Future perfect progressive	My mother *will have been working* as a nurse for forty-five years by the time she retires.

On a separate sheet of paper, write twelve sentences using the twelve verb tenses. **ACTIVITY 1**

Helping Verbs

These common verbs can either stand alone or "help" other verbs.

be (am, are, is, was, were, being, been)
have (has, having, had)
do (does, did)

Here are examples of the helping verbs:

USED ALONE	USED AS HELPING VERBS
I *was* angry.	I *was growing* angry.
Izabel *has* the key.	Izabel *has forgotten* the key.
He *did* well in the test.	He *did fail* the previous test.

Nine helping verbs (traditionally known as *modals,* or *modal auxiliaries*) are always used in combination with other verbs. Here are the nine verbs and a sentence example of each:

can	I *can see* the rainbow.
could	I *could* not *find* a seat.
may	The game *may be postponed*.
might	Hannah *might resent* your advice.
shall	I *shall see* you tomorrow.
should	He *should get* his car serviced.
will	Luke *will want* to see you.
would	They *would* not *understand*.
must	You *must* visit us again.

Note from the examples that these verbs have only one form. They do not, for instance, add an *-s* when used with *he, she, it,* or any one person or thing.

ACTIVITY 2   On a separate sheet of paper, write nine sentences using the nine helping verbs.

Verbals

Verbals are words formed from verbs. Verbals, like verbs, often express action. They can add variety to your sentences and vigor to your writing style. The three kinds of verbals are *infinitives, participles,* and *gerunds.* Additional information about infinitives can be found in Chapter 22. Additional information about participles and gerunds can be found in Chapters 22, 24, and 31.

Infinitive

An infinitive is *to* plus the base form of the verb.

> I love *to dance.*
>
> Lina hopes *to write* for a newspaper.
>
> I asked the children *to clean* the kitchen.

Participle

A participle is a verb form used as an adjective (a descriptive word). The present participle ends in *-ing.* The past participle ends in *-ed* or has an irregular ending.

> *Peering* into the cracked mirror, the *laughing* clown waved to the reflection.
>
> The *astounded* man stared at his *winning* lottery ticket.
>
> *Swinging* a sharp ax, the worker split the *rotted* beam.

Gerund

A gerund is the *-ing* form of a verb used as a noun.

> *Swimming* is the perfect exercise.
>
> *Eating* junk food is my diet downfall.
>
> Through *doodling,* people express their inner feelings.

ACTIVITY 3

PART A

On a separate sheet of paper, write three sentences using infinitives, three sentences using participles, and three sentences using gerunds.

PART B

Identify the infinitives, participles, and gerunds in the following sentences. Write *I* for infinitive, *P* for participle, and *G* for gerund on the line.

_____ 1. To teach mathematics is her fervent ambition.

_____ 2. Holding the instrument in the correct manner, the violin teacher demonstrated the importance of position.

_____ 3. Sleeping is one of my favorite activities, but unfortunately I can't indulge in it often.

_____ 4. Receiving an award for their work with homeless people was the last thing Dakota and Finley expected.

_____ 5. Entering the hotdog contest, Charli set a high personal goal, but her stomach had other ideas.

Pronoun Agreement and Reference

This chapter will provide information on pronoun agreement and reference.

Incorrect:

Johan was annoyed when they failed his car for a faulty turn signal.

In this case, "they" should be replaced by a specific noun, such as "the inspectors," so the reader knows who the word "they" refers to.

Correct:

Johan was annoyed when the inspectors failed his car for a faulty turn signal.

Now it is made clear that it was the inspectors who failed the car.

Key Terms

indefinite pronouns: words that refer to people and things that are not named or are not specific. Many indefinite pronouns take a singular verb; some take plural verbs; and others can take either a singular or a plural verb.

nouns: words that name persons, places, or things.

pronouns: words that take the place of nouns. Pronouns are shortcuts that keep you from unnecessarily repeating words in writing.

pronoun agreement: correspondence in number between the pronoun and the noun it replaces. Example: *Students enrolled in the art class must prove that they can paint.*

pronoun reference: the relationship between the pronoun and the noun in the sentence to which it refers. A sentence may be confusing if a pronoun appears to refer to more than one noun or does not appear to refer to any specific noun. Example: See above "Incorrect" and "Correct" example sentences.

Nouns name persons, places, or things. *Pronouns* are words that take the place of nouns. In fact, the word *pronoun* means "for a noun." Pronouns are shortcuts that keep you from unnecessarily repeating words in writing. Here are some examples of pronouns:

> Eddie left *his* camera on the bus.
>
> (*His* is a pronoun that takes the place of *Eddie's*.)
>
> Sandra drank the coffee even though *it* was cold.
>
> (*It* replaces *coffee*.)
>
> As I turned the newspaper's damp pages, *they* disintegrated in my hands.
>
> (*They* is a pronoun that takes the place of *pages*.)

This chapter presents rules that will help you avoid two common mistakes people make with pronouns. The rules are the following:

1. A pronoun must agree in number with the word or words it replaces.

2. A pronoun must refer clearly to the word it replaces.

Pronoun Agreement

A pronoun must agree in number with the word or words it replaces. If the word a pronoun refers to is singular, the pronoun must be singular; if that word is plural, the pronoun must be plural. (Note that the word a pronoun refers to is known as the *antecedent*.)

> Marie showed me her antique watch collection.
>
> Students enrolled in the art class must provide their own supplies.

In the first example, the pronoun *her* refers to the singular word *Marie;* in the second example, the pronoun *their* refers to the plural word *Students*.

It's important to note that language usage is evolving; the pronouns *they/ them/their*, once considered only plural, can be now be used as either singular or plural pronouns. Many people choose not to use *he/she* pronouns and instead choose to use *they/them* as non-gendered pronouns. In the following example, *their* refers to one person, Lindz Amer, who uses *they/them* pronouns.

> Lindz Amer hosts a phenomenal website and YouTube channel to tell their story and educate others.

Write the appropriate pronoun (*their, they, them, it*) in the blank space in each of the following sentences.

EXAMPLE

    I opened the wet umbrella and put   <u>it</u>   in the bathtub to dry.

1. Kate and Omar left for the movies earlier than usual because _____ knew the theater would be packed.

2. The area around San Jose, California, produces fine wines, but _____ is also the home of many high-tech companies.

3. Jiang and Takashi spent the entire holiday playing _____ new video games.

4. Many people immigrate to America to make a better life for _____ families.

5. The salesperson said the store usually carried Birkenstocks, but _____ hadn't received any shipments in a while, so the stock was depleted.

6. The young girl liked to read graphic novels because _____ were filled with exciting adventures and intricate artwork.

7. The clothes were still damp, but I decided to fold _____ anyway.

8. Tom said he enjoyed the play *Les Misérables* even though _____ was a sad story filled with death.

9. Jabari's grandparents renewed _____ marriage vows at a huge fiftieth wedding anniversary celebration.

10. Samantha and Tom were walking quickly to algebra class, but I managed to catch up with _____.

Indefinite Pronouns

Indefinite pronouns follow slightly different rules from other pronouns. They don't always replace a specific noun nor do they always require an antecedent. Some are considered singular, some are considered plural, and some can be either, depending on the context of the sentence.

> Traditionally, writers used the masculine pronoun (*he, him, his*) to refer to people, regardless of gender. To become more inclusive, writers then began using *he or she, him or her,* and *his or hers* to avert an implied gender bias. This construction was often awkward and wordy. As mentioned in the preceding section, language has evolved to become more inclusive and nonbiased, and the use of *they, them, their* has now become the preferred, clearer pronoun to use when referring to people if gender is unknown or irrelevant to the context or it is an individual's expressed choice.

Common Indefinite Pronouns That Are Treated as Singular

anybody	everybody	no one
anyone	everyone	somebody
anything	everything	someone
each	neither	something
either	nobody	

If a pronoun in a sentence refers to one of these singular words, that pronoun should be singular. In the examples that follow, each circled pronoun is singular because it refers to a singular indefinite pronoun. If there is a clear gender indication, as in these examples, it is acceptable to use *he/him/his* or *she/her/hers* as the singular pronoun.

Somebody left (her) gym bag in the women's locker room.

One of the boys on the soccer team said (he) would be an hour late.

In the next example, there is no information about what type of club it is; thus, the use of *their* is appropriate as a neutral singular pronoun. (However, if everyone in the club was a woman, the pronoun would be *her*.)

Everyone in the club must pay (their) dues next week.

Here are other examples:

Everybody has (their) own opinion about the election.

No one in the class remembered to bring (their) books.

Anybody who doesn't have (their) ticket won't get onto the plane.

Another option, which does not employ an indefinite pronoun, is to rewrite the sentence in plural form:

Club members must pay (their) dues next week.

People have (their) own opinions about the election.

No students in the class remembered to bring (their) books.

Travelers who don't have (their) tickets won't get onto the plane.

Common Indefinite Pronouns That Are Treated as Plural

both	fewer	others
few	many	several

If a pronoun in a sentence refers to one of these plural words, that pronoun should be plural.

Both players left (their) gym bags in the women's locker room.

Several of the boys on the soccer team said (they) would be an hour late.

Many in the club must pay (their) dues next week.

Each circled pronoun is plural because it refers to a plural indefinite pronoun.

Common Indefinite Pronouns That Can Be Singular or Plural

all	most	some
any	none	

If a pronoun in a sentence refers to one of these indefinite pronouns, the context of the sentence determines whether a singular or plural pronoun should be used.

Most of the players left (their) gym bags in the women's locker room.

Most of the locker room is in (its) cleanest condition ever.

Underline the correct pronoun.

ACTIVITY 2

1. Each of the three sisters was willing to donate (her, their) inheritance to charity.

2. Everybody should bring (his, their) own camera to class next week.

3. Some of the sidewalk had footprints in (its, their) newly poured sections.

4. All of the Seattle Sounders soccer players celebrated (his, their) championship win.

5. Anyone who witnesses a crime should contact (her, their) local police immediately.

6. Neither of the men had organized (his, their) office by the end of the day.

7. Somebody left (his or her, their) books in the classroom today.

8. Each of the women in the choir had to have (her, their) choir outfit dry cleaned after each wearing.

9. All new skiers should expect (his or her, their) muscles to ache the next day.

10. Some of the cupcakes were missing (its, their) icing flowers.

Pronoun Reference

A sentence may be confusing and unclear if a pronoun appears to refer to more than one word or does not refer to any specific word. Look at this sentence:

> Johan was annoyed when they failed his car for a faulty turn signal.

Who failed his car? There is no specific word that *they* refers to. Be clear:

> Johan was annoyed when the inspectors failed his car for a faulty turn signal.

Here are sentences with other faulty pronoun references. Read the explanations of why they are faulty and look carefully at how they are corrected.

FAULTY	CLEAR
Peter told Alan that his dog was goofy and lovable.	Peter told Alan, "My dog is goofy and lovable."
(Whose dog is goofy and lovable: Peter's or Alan's? Be clear.)	
Kia is really a shy person, but she keeps it hidden.	Kia is really a shy person, but she keeps her shyness hidden.
(There is no specific word that *it* refers to. It would not make sense to say, "Kia keeps shy hidden.")	
The representative supports the new bill, which upsets her constituents.	The representative's support of the new bill upsets her constituents.
(Does *which* mean that the representative's support upsets her constituents or that the new bill upsets her constituents?)	*Or:* The new bill upsets the representative's constituents.

ACTIVITY 3 Working with a fellow classmate, rewrite each of the following sentences to make clear the vague pronoun reference. Add, change, or omit words as necessary.

EXAMPLE

Grace's mother wondered if she was fast enough to be a competitive runner.

Grace's mother wondered if Susan was fast enough to be a competitive runner.

1. Jim is a talkative person; sometimes he just can't control it.

_____

Jacob Lund/
Shutterstock

2. At that fast-food restaurant, they give you free glasses with your soft drinks.

_____

3. Jada told Anna that she had just been promoted to assistant manager.

_____

4. Dipping her spoon into the pot of simmering spaghetti sauce, Olivia felt it slip out of her hand.

_____

5. Evan visited the tutoring center because they can help him with his economics course.

_____

6. Sam and Liam went to see the symphony last week because he is a budding violinist.

_____

7. After sorting her old albums from her new ones, Emma sold them at a garage sale.

_____

8. Caleb unhooked the DVD player from the TV and fixed it.

_____

9. The teachers told the students that they were going to see a special performance.

_____

10. In our college library, they check out books and help students with research problems.

_____

REVIEW TEST 1

Underline the correct word or words in parentheses.

1. Last year, my Art 210 class went to Planet Comicon to listen to artists discuss (his or her, their) artwork.

2. Although our teacher had discouraged it, several students dressed up as (his or her, their) favorite comic characters.

3. Some of the artists like Ben Templesmith are not as famous as Stan Lee, but (he, they) still had huge followings.

4. Students in the class got very excited when Dan Parent demonstrated how (he, they) created Archie, Jughead, Betty, and Veronica.

5. Adam Smith and Matthew Fox were signing copies of (his, their) graphic novel, *Long Walk to Valhalla*, which is set in rural Arkansas.

6. Many of the attendees were dressed in Steampunk fashions; (they, the clothes) were available to purchase from several vendors.

7. Michelle Thorstrom, owner of Damsel in this Dress, gave a presentation about (her, their) sumptuous Victorian bustle skirts, which she said have been tested "against zombies, krakens, dinosaurs, and angler fish with prodigious success!"

8. Several girls in my class purchased complete outfits including dresses, corsets, boots, hats, and goggles; (they, the dresses) were very elaborately embellished with velvet, lace, and silk.

9. One of the highlights of the day for my friend Jabril was getting into an elevator with Chris Claremont and having a chance to talk to him briefly because (he, Chris Claremont) is such an icon in the comic world.

10. By the end of the day, each of the students had (his, their) hands full of bags of clothes, autographs, and artwork.

REVIEW TEST 2

Underline the correct word or words in parentheses. Then, in the space provided, write whether the issue is one of pronoun agreement or of pronoun reference.

EXAMPLE

p. agreement   My brother's major was English literature; (he, they) had to read a lot of novels.

_____ 1. Many students in English literature courses have to read the works of the Brontë sisters, who spent (her, their) lives writing poems, stories, and novels.

_____ 2. Charlotte Brontë was born in 1816 and is most famous for (her, their) novel *Jane Eyre*.

_____ 3. Jane is an orphan who is treated poorly by her cruel aunt, oppressive teachers, and initially Mr. Rochester, but she eventually gets away from (them, her aunt and teachers) and finds love with Mr. Rochester.

_____ 4. Emily Brontë was born in 1818 and is best known for (her, their) novel, *Wuthering Heights.*

_____ 5. In *Wuthering Heights,* Heathcliff and Hindley lead cruel, revenge-filled lives, and (he, Heathcliff) eventually slips into insanity.

_____ 6. Anne Brontë was born in 1820 and is famous for (her, their) poetry and the novel *The Tenant of Wildfell Hall.*

_____ 7. Anne's novel is not as famous as her sisters' novels, but (it, she) was more progressive and controversial.

_____ 8. The main character, Helen, abandons (her, their) abusive, alcoholic husband and lives as a widow.

_____ 9. By leaving her husband, Helen breaks both the social conventions and English law of the 1800s because even if (they, women) were beaten and abused, they were not allowed to leave or divorce their husbands.

_____ 10. More than 150 years later, the Brontë sisters' books are still read by thousands of literature majors and bibliophiles everywhere because of (their, the works') timeless themes.

28 Pronoun Types

This chapter will describe some common types of pronouns:

- subject pronouns
- object pronouns
- possessive pronouns
- demonstrative pronouns

Key Terms

subject pronouns: pronouns that function as the subjects of verbs. Example: *They are all in the high school orchestra.*

object pronouns: pronouns that function as the objects of verbs or prepositions. Example: *Nathan helped me.*

possessive pronouns: pronouns that show ownership or possession. Example: *The keys are mine.*

demonstrative pronouns: pronouns that point to or single out a person or thing. The four demonstrative pronouns are *this, that, these,* and *those.*

Subject and Object Pronouns

Most pronouns change their form depending on what place they occupy in a sentence. In the box that follows is a list of subject and object pronouns.

Subject Pronouns	Object Pronouns
I	me
you	you (no change)
he	him
she	her
it	it (no change)
we	us
they	them

Subject Pronouns

Subject pronouns are subjects of verbs.

> *He* served as a soldier during the war in Iraq. (*He* is the subject of the verb *served*.)
>
> *They* are moving into our old apartment. (*They* is the subject of the verb *are moving*.)
>
> *We* students should have a say in the decision. (*We* is the subject of the verb *should have*.)

Following are several rules for using subject pronouns—and several kinds of mistakes people sometimes make with subject pronouns.

Rule 1

Use a subject pronoun when you have a compound subject (more than one subject).

INCORRECT	CORRECT
My brother and *me* are Billie Eilish fanatics.	My brother and *I* are Billie Eilish fanatics.
Him and *me* know the lyrics to all of Billie's songs.	*He* and *I* know the lyrics to all of Billie's songs.

Rule 1

If you are not sure what pronoun to use, try each pronoun by itself in the sentence. The correct pronoun will be the one that sounds right. For example, "Him knows the lyrics to all of Billie's songs" does not sound right; "He knows the lyrics to all of Billie's songs" does.

TIP

Rule 2

Use a subject pronoun after forms of the verb *be*. Forms of *be* include *am, are, is, was, were, has been, have been,* and others.

> It was *I* who left the light on.
>
> It may be *they* in that car.
>
> It is *he*.

The sentences above may sound strange and stilted to you because they are seldom used in conversation. When we speak with one another, forms such as "It was me," "It may be them," and "It is him" are widely accepted. In formal writing, however, the grammatically correct forms are still preferred.

TIP

> *Rule 2*
>
> You can avoid having to use a subject pronoun after *be* by simply rewording a sentence. Here is how the preceding examples could be reworded:
>
> I was the one who left the light on.
>
> They may be in that car.
>
> He is here.

Rule 3

Use subject pronouns after *than* or *as*. The subject pronoun is used because a verb is understood after the pronoun.

You play better than I (play). (The verb *play* is understood after *I*.)

Jenna is as bored as I (am). (The verb *am* is understood after *I*.)

We don't need the money as much as they (do). (The verb *do* is understood after *they*.)

TIP

> *Rule 3*
>
> Avoid mistakes by mentally adding the "missing" verb at the end of the sentence.

Object Pronouns

Object pronouns (me, him, her, us, them) are the objects of verbs or prepositions. (*Prepositions* are connecting words like *for, at, about, to, before, by, with,* and *of.* See Chapter 23 for a list of prepositions.) Notice that in each of the sentences below, the object pronoun directly follows the verb or preposition.

Ali helped me. (*Me* is the object of the verb *helped.*)

We took *them* to the college. (*Them* is the object of the verb *took.*)

Leave the children with *us*. (*Us* is the object of the preposition *with.*)

I got in line behind *him*. (*Him* is the object of the preposition *behind.*)

People are sometimes uncertain about what pronoun to use when two objects follow a verb or a preposition and will sometimes incorrectly use a subject pronoun instead of an object pronoun.

INCORRECT	CORRECT
I gave a gift to Ray and *she*.	I gave a gift to Ray and *her*.
She came to the movie with Lindsey and *I*.	She came to the movie with Lindsey and *me*.

> If you are not sure what pronoun to use, try each pronoun by itself in the sentence. The correct pronoun will be the one that sounds right. For example, "I gave a gift to she" does not sound right; "I gave a gift to her" does.

TIP

Underline the correct subject or object pronoun in each of the following sentences. Then show whether your answer is a subject or object pronoun by circling the S or O in the margin.

ACTIVITY 1

S   O   1. The chickens that Laura gave my sister and (I, me) were extremely noisy.

S   O   2. Morgan and (she, her) visited the Valle De La Luna during their trip to Chile.

S   O   3. The senator praised her opponent by saying that no one had ever run a cleaner campaign than (he, him).

S   O   4. Your piano performance proved that you practiced more than (they, them).

S   O   5. My sister drove my friends and (I, me) to Whataburger.

S   O   6. Aalia asked (he, him) to the dance last week.

S   O   7. (We, Us) students spent over three weeks painting the sets for the school play.

S   O   8. Jonah and (him, he) did the editing on the class film.

S   O   9. The teachers told Lucia and (I, me) not to run in the hallways.

S   O   10. Reading about the ancient Greeks became an obsession for Eliza and (him, he).

S   O   11. (She, Her) and Ashar love to bake cookies.

S   O   12. The professor informed Quinn and (I, me) that our project was well done.

S   O   13. Caleb doesn't like it when Tenley and (he, him) get into arguments.

S   O   14. (She, Her) and Tristan have been friends since kindergarten.

S   O   15. The tow-truck driver rescued (we, us) from the side of the highway.

Possessive Pronouns

Here is a list of possessive pronouns:

my, mine	our, ours
your, yours	your, yours
his	their, theirs
her, hers	
its	

Possessive pronouns show ownership or possession.

> Adam revved up *his* motorcycle and blasted off.
>
> The keys are *mine*.

TIP ▶ A possessive pronoun *never* uses an apostrophe. (See also Chapter 34.)

INCORRECT

That coat is *hers'*.

The inflatable projection screen is *theirs'*.

CORRECT

That coat is *hers*.

The inflatable projection screen is *theirs*.

ACTIVITY 2

Cross out the incorrect pronoun form in each of the following sentences. Write the correct form in the space at the left.

EXAMPLE

hers   Those dogs are ~~hers'~~.

_____ 1. I discovered that my car had somehow lost its' rear license plate.

_____ 2. Are those seats theirs'?

_____ 3. The mayor said that the task of cutting the budget was not hers' alone.

_____   4. The prize-winning entry in the science fair was our's.

_____   5. These books are yours' if you want them.

Demonstrative Pronouns

Demonstrative pronouns point to or single out a person or thing. There are four demonstrative pronouns:

this	these
that	those

Generally speaking, *this* and *these* refer to things close at hand; *that* and *those* refer to things farther away. The four demonstrative pronouns are also commonly used as demonstrative adjectives.

Is anyone using *this* spoon?

I am going to throw away *these* magazines.

I just bought *that* black pickup truck at the curb.

Pick up *those* toys in the corner.

> Do not use *them, this here, that there, these here,* or *those there* to point to or single out. Use only *this, that, these,* or *those.*

 TIP

Cross out the incorrect form of the demonstrative pronoun, and write the correct form in the space provided.

ACTIVITY 3

EXAMPLE

Those   ~~Them~~ tires look worn.

_____   1. This here map is out of date.

_____   2. Leave them keys out on the coffee table.

_____   3. Them two movies are about life in early New England.

_____   4. Jack entered that there dog in an obedience contest.

_____   5. Where are them concert tickets I left here?

Read the paragraph and underline the correct word in the parentheses.

Ben & Jerry's ice cream is a multi-million-dollar business that has quite an interesting history. Ben Cohen and Jerry Greenfield opened (their, their's) first shop in 1978 in Burlington, Vermont. (That, That there) shop was housed in an old gas station that (they, them) renovated using scraps of aluminum to fix the roof and second-hand items to furnish the store. By 1981, Ben & Jerry's had grown very popular, and the first franchise opened (its', its) doors in Shelburne, Vermont. In 1983, Ben & Jerry's ice cream was used "to build the world's largest ice cream sundae." (That, These) same year, pints of the ice cream began to be sold in Boston. In 1984, Ben & Jerry's went head-to-head against Haagen-Dazs in a campaign known as "What's the Doughboy Afraid Of?" The following year, Ben & Jerry's began building (its', its) first ice cream manufacturing plant. In 1987, "Cherry Garcia" was introduced. Jerry Garcia was the guitarist for the Grateful Dead; the ice cream was named after (he, him). Also in 1987, the waste from the manufacturing plant began to be used as pig feed and the pigs went wild for almost every flavor. However, (they, them) didn't like "Mint with Oreo® Cookie" because pigs don't like mint. In 1988, Ben & Jerry's gave 7.5 percent of (it's, its) pre-tax income to non-profit organizations, winning (this, this here) company an award for giving. The company also started a non-profit group that is now known as the Business for Social Responsibility. Ben and Jerry were socially conscious when (they, them) chose to renovate the old building. (They, them) continued to be socially conscious as (their, their') company grew larger. In 2005, to protest drilling for oil in the Arctic National Wildlife Refuge, Ben & Jerry's created a nine-hundred-pound Baked Alaska dessert from "Fossil Fuel" ice cream. (That there, That) dessert was served on the lawn of the U.S. Capitol. For over thirty years, Ben & Jerry's has been giving back to (its', its) communities and customers. One of the most popular celebrations is Free Cone Day, an annual event since 1979, because everyone gets a free scoop of ice cream.

Adjectives and Adverbs

This chapter will describe the principal characteristics of adjectives and adverbs.

Key Terms

adjectives: words that describe nouns or pronouns.
Example: Sofia is a *wise* economist.

adverbs: words that describe verbs, adjectives, or other adverbs.
Example: I walked *quickly* to the store.

Adjectives

What Are Adjectives?

Adjectives describe nouns (names of persons, places, or things) or pronouns.

> Sofia is a *wise* economist. (The adjective *wise* describes the noun *economist*.)
> She is also *funny*. (The adjective *funny* describes the pronoun *she*.)
> I'll carry the *heavy* bag of groceries. (The adjective *heavy* describes the noun *bag*.)
> It is *torn*. (The adjective *torn* describes the pronoun *it*.)

Adjectives usually come before the word they describe (as in *wise* economist and *heavy* bag). But they also come after forms of the verb *be* (*is, are, was, were,* and so on). They also follow verbs such as *look, appear, seem, become, sound, taste,* and *smell*.

> That road is *slippery*. (The adjective *slippery* describes the road.)
> The dogs are *noisy*. (The adjective *noisy* describes the dogs.)
> Those customers were *impatient*. (The adjective *impatient* describes the customers.)
> Your room looks *neat*. (The adjective *neat* describes the room.)

Using Adjectives to Compare

Adjectives are often used to compare things or people. Use the comparative form of the adjective if two people or things are being compared. Use the superlative form of the adjective if three or more people or things are being compared.

For all one-syllable adjectives and some two-syllable adjectives, add *-er* when comparing two things and *-est* when comparing three or more things.

> Phil's beard is *longer* than mine, but Noah's is the *longest*.

> Kana may be the *quieter* of the two sisters; but that's not saying much, since they're the *loudest* girls in school.

For some two-syllable adjectives and all longer adjectives, use *more* when comparing two things and *most* when comparing three or more things.

> Liza Minnelli is *more famous* than her sister; but their mother, Judy Garland, is still the *most famous* member of the family.

> The red letters on the sign are *more noticeable* than the black ones, but the Day-Glo letters are the *most noticeable*.

You can usually tell when to use *more* and *most* by the sound of a word. For example, you can probably tell by its sound that "carefuller" would be too awkward to say and that *more careful* is thus correct. But there are many words for which both *-er* or *-est* and *more* or *most* are equally correct. For instance, either "a more fair rule" or "a fairer rule" is correct.

To form negative comparisons, use *less* and *least*.

> During my first dance class, I felt *less graceful* than an injured elephant.

> When the teacher came to our house to complain to my parents, I offered her the *least* comfortable chair in the room.

Points to Remember about Comparing

Point 1

Use only one form of comparison at a time. That is, do not use both an *-er* ending and *more* or both an *-est* ending and *most*:

INCORRECT	CORRECT
My brother's suitcase is always *more heavier* than my father's.	My brother's suitcase is always *heavier* than my father's.
Get Out is still the *most frighteningest* movie I've ever seen.	*Get Out* is still the *most frightening* movie I've ever seen.

Point 2

Learn the irregular forms of the words shown below.

	COMPARATIVE (For Comparing Two Things)	SUPERLATIVE (For Comparing Three or More Things)
bad	worse	worst
good, well	better	best
little (in amount)	less	least
much, many	more	most

Do not use both *more* and an irregular comparative or *most* and an irregular superlative.

INCORRECT

It is *more better* to give than to receive.
Last night I got the *most worst* snack attack I ever had.

CORRECT

It is *better* to give than to receive.
Last night I got the *worst* snack attack I have ever had.

Add to each sentence the correct form of the word in the margin.

ACTIVITY 1

EXAMPLES

The solutions that Mary offered were ___*better*___ than mine.   good

The Rockies are the world's _*most beautiful*_ mountains.   beautiful

1. Javon makes the _____ blueberry crumble I have ever tasted.   good

2. Akiko and her sister, Chiaki, are twins; Akiko is the _____ one.   old

3. Maria and Colin are the _____ spellers in the class.   bad

4. Jacob painted the _____ scene in the class.   unusual

5. The three-legged cat was _____ than the dog.   ferocious

6. Stephen King writes the _____ horror books of any author.   scary

7. It is _____ this winter than it was last year.   warm

8. Manny's Mexican restaurant has the _____ nachos in the city.   good

9. Poppy is _____ than I am when it comes to planning pranks.   skillful

10. *Game of Thrones* is _____ than *Fuller House*.   interesting

Adverbs

What Are Adverbs?

Adverbs describe verbs, adjectives, or other adverbs. They usually end in *-ly*.

> The father *gently* hugged the sick child. (The adverb *gently* describes the verb *hugged*.)
>
> Newborns are *totally* innocent. (The adverb *totally* describes the adjective *innocent*.)
>
> The lecturer spoke so *terribly* fast that I had trouble taking notes. (The adverb *terribly* describes the adverb *fast*.)

A Common Mistake with Adverbs and Adjectives

People often mistakenly use an adjective instead of an adverb after a verb.

INCORRECT	CORRECT
Galen needs a haircut *bad*.	Galen needs a haircut *badly*.
She gets along *easy* with others.	She gets along *easily* with others.
You might have lost the race if you hadn't run so *quick* at the beginning.	You might have lost the race if you hadn't run so *quickly* at the beginning.

ACTIVITY 2   Underline the adjective or adverb needed.

 HINT   Remember that adjectives describe nouns, and adverbs describe verbs and other adverbs.

1. As Mac danced, his head bounced (rapid, rapidly).

2. We back up all of our files in case there is a (sudden, suddenly) power surge that could damage our computers.

3. I hiccuped (continuous, continuously) for fifteen minutes.

4. The detective opened the door (careful, carefully).

5. The Salvation Army is (heavy, heavily) dependent upon donations from the public.

6. We begged him to call the police (quick, quickly).

7. He is (complete, completely) exhausted from studying all semester.

8. The lake was (peaceful, peacefully) in the early hours of the morning.

9. The losing team (sad, sadly) walked back to their locker room.

10. *Legally Blonde* was a (humorous, humorously) musical.

Well and *Good*

Two words that are often confused are *well* and *good*. *Good* is an adjective; it describes nouns. *Well* is usually an adverb; it describes verbs. But *well* (rather than *good*) is used as an adjective when referring to how healthy one is feeling.

Team up with a fellow classmate and write *well* or *good* in each of the sentences that follow.

ACTIVITY 3

Jacob Lund/
Shutterstock

1. Miami fared _____ during the last hurricane because the people took adequate precautions.

2. The governor commended the literacy volunteers for the _____ work they had accomplished.

3. In high school, Tiara always did _____ in history.

4. After Jameson won the lottery, he discovered who his _____ friends really were.

5. Grant and Alyssa organized the fundraiser so _____ that everything went perfectly.

6. DeAndré did a phenomenal job on his report last week and received a raise because of his _____ work.

7. The musicians played so _____ at the concert they were asked to perform for an additional night.

8. Because she had a high fever, Aaliyah didn't feel _____ enough to go to school.

9. Emilie was a _____ student and always did her homework on time.

10. Miles was surprised at how _____ he did during his first yoga class.

REVIEW TEST 1

Underline the correct word in parentheses.

1. We could not have asked for a (more good, better) teacher in math.

2. The Beatles seemed to burst onto the scene very (quick, quickly), but they had been singing for years before they became so popular.

3. John Roebling's prediction that he could build a bridge across New York's East River turned out (good, well); today that structure is known as the Brooklyn Bridge.

4. The cleaner was very (abrasive, abrasively) and scratched my countertops.

5. As soon as I set down the food, the puppy (hungry, hungrily) wolfed it down.

6. The (stranger, strangest) of the two pictures featured an owl with three eyes.

7. The young boy was the (lazier, laziest) one in the whole family and refused to move off the couch.

8. William took his classes very (serious, seriously) and studied several hours a day.

9. Tara told the (more clever, most clever) jokes I've ever heard.

10. As the little boy (gentle, gently) snuggled the tiny kitten, the kitten purred.

REVIEW TEST 2

There are ten adjective and adverb errors in the following paragraph. In the spaces between the lines, correct the mistakes.

The Disney Corporation has been producing films since 1937.

One of the most earliest films was *Snow White and the Seven Dwarfs.*

Fantasia followed soon after and is still considered to be a real iconic,

groundbreaking film. Two other films, *Saludos Amigos* and *The Three*

Caballeros, targeted Latin American audiences; they are not known

as good. In 1950, *Cinderella* was released and is believed to be Walt

Disney's most favoritest film. *Alice in Wonderland* was released short after *Cinderella* and introduced the beloved novel, *Alice's Adventures in Wonderland*, to a new audience. In 1960, another deep loved novel of younger audiences, *Swiss Family Robinson*, was brought to the screen; however, it was not animated. In 1995, Pixar Studios released *Toy Story* as part of a three-picture deal with Disney. Pixar's computer animation and innovatively technicians forever changed the way that animated films are made. In recent decades, films such as *Inside Out* and *Soul* have mesmerized audiences by their high detailed animations that are extreme dynamic. As technology advances, audiences can look forward to even more creative designed 2-D and 3-D films produced by these studios and others like them.

30

Misplaced Modifiers

This chapter will describe misplaced modifiers, which are words that, because of awkward placement, do not describe what the author intended them to describe.

Incorrect:

Miguel couldn't get on his bike with a broken leg.

The sentence makes it sound as if the bike has the broken leg, not Miguel.

Correct:

With a broken leg, Miguel couldn't get on his bike.

The phrase "with a broken leg" has been moved so that it is closer to "Miguel"; now it is clearer whose leg is broken.

Identifying and Correcting Misplaced Modifiers

Misplaced modifiers are words that, because of awkward placement, do not describe what the writer intended them to describe. A misplaced modifier can make a sentence confusing or unintentionally funny. To avoid this, place words as close as possible to what they describe.

MISPLACED WORDS	CORRECTLY PLACED WORDS
Miguel couldn't get on his bike *with a broken leg.* (The bike had a broken leg?)	With a broken leg, Miguel couldn't get on his bike. (The words describing Miguel are now placed next to *Miguel.*)
The toaster was sold to us by a charming salesperson *with a money-back guarantee.* (The salesperson had a money-back guarantee?)	The toaster with a money-back guarantee was sold to us by a charming salesperson. (The words describing the toaster are now placed next to it.)

MISPLACED WORDS	CORRECTLY PLACED WORDS
He *nearly* brushed his teeth for twenty minutes every night. (He came close to brushing his teeth but in fact did not brush them at all?)	He brushed his teeth for nearly twenty minutes every night. (The meaning—that he brushed his teeth for a long time—is now clear.)

Underline the misplaced word or words in each sentence. Then rewrite the sentence, placing related words together and thereby making the meaning clear.

ACTIVITY 1

EXAMPLES

Frozen shrimp lay in the steel pans <u>that were thawing rapidly</u>.

Frozen shrimp that were thawing rapidly lay in the steel pans.

The speaker discussed the problem of crowded prisons <u>at the college</u>.

At the college, the speaker discussed the problem of crowded prisons.

1. The hotel patrons ate the free snacks on the lobby couch.

2. The crowd watched the tennis players with swiveling heads.

3. Vonnie put four hamburger patties on the counter, which she was cooking for dinner.

4. Steve carefully hung the new suit that he would wear to his first job interview in the bedroom closet.

5. The novel was about a pioneer family that Annie had borrowed from her cousin.

6. The latest Denzel Washington movie has almost opened in 2,200 theaters across the country.

7. To be cooked properly, the chef advised us to place the casserole in a pre-heated oven.

_____

8. The tenants left town in a dilapidated old car owing two months' rent.

_____

9. The plan was to construct a church on an acre of land made of brick and stone.

_____

10. I discovered an unusual plant in the greenhouse that oozed a milky juice.

_____

REVIEW TEST 1

Write MM for *misplaced modifier* or C for *correct* in the space provided for each sentence.

_____   1. I nearly napped for twenty minutes during the biology lecture.

_____   2. I napped for nearly twenty minutes during the biology lecture.

_____   3. The spacecraft traveled nearly 142 million miles to reach Mars.

_____   4. The spacecraft nearly traveled 142 million miles to reach Mars.

_____   5. My grandfather prepared breakfast for his family wearing his bathrobe.

_____   6. Wearing his bathrobe, my grandfather prepared breakfast for his family.

_____   7. We couldn't read the advertisement on the billboard written in tiny letters.

_____   8. We couldn't read the advertisement written in tiny letters on the billboard.

_____   9. I ordered a children's lamp from the catalog shaped like a cartoon character.

_____   10. I ordered from the catalog a children's lamp shaped like a cartoon character.

Make the changes needed to correct the misplaced modifier in each sentence.

1. Henry Wadsworth Longfellow was born a poet and professor in 1907 in Portland, Maine.

   _____

   _____

2. One of Longfellow's most famous poems during the Revolutionary War is "Paul Revere's Ride," depicting an historically important night.

   _____

   _____

3. Longfellow wrote that rainbows are flowers that have died and gone to heaven in a poem.

   _____

   _____

4. Longfellow's wife, Frannie, died when her dress caught fire from terrible burns.

   _____

   _____

5. Eighteen years later, in the sonnet, "The Cross of Snow," Longfellow never fully recovered and commemorated his wife's death.

   _____

   _____

Dangling Modifiers

This chapter will describe dangling modifiers—descriptive words that open a sentence but do not describe what the author intended them to describe.

Incorrect:

While reading the newspaper, my dog sat with me on the steps.

The sentence misleadingly states that the dog was reading the newspaper.

Correct:

While I was reading the newspaper, my dog sat with me on the steps.

The sentence makes it clear that the subject "I" was reading the newspaper.

Identifying and Correcting Dangling Modifiers

A modifier that opens a sentence must be followed immediately by the word it is meant to describe. Otherwise, the modifier is said to be dangling, and the sentence takes on an unintended meaning. For example, in the sentence

While reading the newspaper, my dog sat with me on the front steps.

the unintended meaning is that the *dog* was reading the newspaper. The writer should have said,

While reading the newspaper, *I* sat with my dog on the front steps.

The dangling modifier could also be corrected by placing the subject within the opening word group:

While *I* was reading the newspaper, my dog sat with me on the front steps.

DANGLING

Shaving in front of the steamy mirror, the razor nicked Eli's chin. (*Who* was shaving? The subject *Eli* must be added.)

While turning over the bacon, hot grease splashed my arm. (Who was turning over the bacon? *I* was, not the *hot grease*. The subject *I* must be added.)

To impress the interviewer, punctuality is essential. (Who is to impress the interviewer? The interviewee is, not *punctuality*.)

CORRECT

Shaving in front of the steamy mirror, *Eli* nicked his chin with the razor.
Or When *Eli* was shaving in front of the steamy mirror, he nicked his chin with a razor.

While *I* was turning over the bacon, hot grease splashed my arm.
Or While turning over the bacon, *I* was splashed with hot grease.

To impress the interviewer, the *interviewee* must be punctual.
Or For the *interviewee* to impress the interviewer, punctuality is essential.

The examples above show two ways to correct a dangling modifier.

1. Place the subject *within* the opening word group:

   When *Eli* was shaving in front of the steamy mirror, he nicked his chin.

> In some cases, a subordinating word such as *when* must be added, and the verb may have to be changed.

2. Place the subject right *after* the opening word group:

   Shaving in front of the steamy mirror, *Eli* nicked his chin.

Look at the opening words in each sentence and ask *who* or *what*. The subject that answers the question should be nearby in the sentence. If it is not, provide the logical subject by using either method of correction described above.

ACTIVITY 1

EXAMPLE

   While pitching his tent, a snake bit Josiah on the ankle.

   While Josiah was pitching his tent, a snake bit him on the ankle.

OR

   While pitching his tent, Josiah was bitten on the ankle by a snake.

1. Applying an ice pack to the burn on my leg, the pain soon subsided.

   _____

2. Marching across the field, a distant river could be seen by the soldiers.

   _____

   _____

3. Practicing relaxation techniques daily, stress can be relieved.

   _____

   _____

4. Avoiding foods high in fat and calories, Vicente's health drastically improved.

   _____

   _____

5. Lit by several floodlights, the audience was able to see the stage clearly.

   _____

   _____

6. Running through the rain, the puddles soaked my pants.

   _____

   _____

7. Crammed tightly in the elevator, the doors wouldn't close.

   _____

   _____

8. Hoping to make her employees more comfortable, a dozen new chairs were purchased by the new boss.

   _____

   _____

9. Fixing the potholes, the roadway was smooth.

   _____

   _____

10. Screaming loudly, the roller coaster scared the young children.

   _____

   _____

Write DM for *dangling modifier* or C for *correct* in the space provided for each sentence.

_____ 1. Having considered several models, the Ford Mustang was finally agreed upon.

_____ 2. Having considered several models, we finally agreed upon the Ford Mustang.

_____ 3. After eating shellfish for the first time, Renata had a frightening allergic reaction.

_____ 4. After eating shellfish for the first time, Renata's allergic reaction was frightening.

_____ 5. At sixteen, my parents bought me a car.

_____ 6. When I was sixteen, my parents bought me a car.

_____ 7. Waddling slowly along the path, the overweight cat made the girls laugh.

_____ 8. Waddling slowly along the path, the young girls laughed at the overweight cat.

_____ 9. Large and impressive, I was amazed by the size of the tree.

_____ 10. Large and impressive, the tree amazed me by its size.

Make the changes needed to correct the dangling modifier in each sentence.

1. Hoping to achieve higher test scores, SAT and other standardized tests are sometimes taken by one top-performing student for other students.

   _____

   _____

2. Embarrassed by the widespread cheating, tighter rules have been introduced by the testing companies.

   _____

   _____

3. Required to upload verified photo ID pictures when they register and take the exam, the testing companies have set stricter identification standards for students.

   _____

   _____

4. Stored in databases, high school and college admissions personnel can access the photos.

   _____

   _____

5. Cheating on the SAT and ACT, the new rules have made it harder.

   _____

   _____

REVIEW TEST 3

Complete the following so that a logical subject follows the opening words.

EXAMPLE

   Looking through the door's peephole, *I couldn't see who rang the doorbell.*

1. Noticing the light turn yellow, _____

   _____

2. Being fragile, _____

   _____

3. While washing the car, _____

   _____

4. Graduating at the top of her class, _____

   _____

5. Driving past the cemetery, _____

   _____

Mechanics and Punctuation

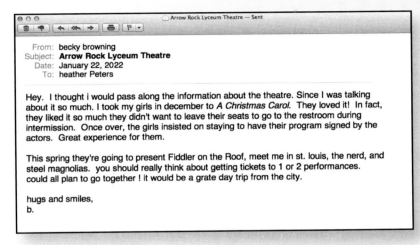

From: becky browning
Subject: **Arrow Rock Lyceum Theatre**
Date: January 22, 2022
To: heather Peters

Hey. I thought i would pass along the information about the theatre. Since I was talking about it so much. I took my girls in december to *A Christmas Carol*. They loved it! In fact, they liked it so much they didn't want to leave their seats to go to the restroom during intermission. Once over, the girls insisted on staying to have their program signed by the actors. Great experience for them.

This spring they're going to present Fiddler on the Roof, meet me in st. louis, the nerd, and steel magnolias. you should really think about getting tickets to 1 or 2 performances. could all plan to go together ! it would be a grate day trip from the city.

hugs and smiles,
b.

People often forget to apply sentence skills to their writing when composing e-mails. Identify the sentence-skills mistakes in the e-mail pictured here. How could you correct them? Do you think such mistakes should be excusable in e-mails?

32

Capital Letters

This chapter will describe

- the main uses of capital letters
- secondary uses of capital letters
- unnecessary use of capital letters

Incorrect:

The Bank is located on the corner.

"The" is capitalized correctly because it appears at the beginning of the sentence, but "bank" is not the building's official, specific name.

Correct:

The bank is located on the corner.

"The" is capitalized to start the sentence, but "bank" is left lowercase.

Main Uses of Capital Letters

Capital letters are used with

1. First word in a sentence or direct quotation
2. Names of persons and the word *I*
3. Names of particular places
4. Names of days of the week, months, and holidays
5. Names of commercial products
6. Titles of books, magazines, newspapers, articles, stories, poems, films, television shows, songs, papers that you write, and the like
7. Names of companies, associations, unions, clubs, religious and political groups, and other organizations

Each use is illustrated in this chapter.

First Word in a Sentence or Direct Quotation

The corner grocery was robbed last night.

The alien said, "Take me to your leader."

"If you need help," said Tamako, "call me. We'll work together."

In the third example above, *If* and *We'll* are capitalized because they start new sentences. But *call* is not capitalized, because it is part of the first sentence.

Names and Titles

Names of Persons and the Word I

Last night, I started watching *Ted Lasso*, a hilarious series starring Jason Sudeikis.

Names of Particular Places and Institutions

Although Ju-Long dropped out of Port Charles High School, he eventually earned his degree and got a job with Atlas Realty Company.

But Use small letters if the specific name is not given.

Although Ju-Long dropped out of high school, he eventually earned his degree and got a job with a real estate company.

Names of Days of the Week, Months, and Holidays

On the last Friday afternoon in May, the day before Memorial Day weekend, my boss is having a barbecue for all the employees.

But Use small letters for the seasons—summer, fall, winter, spring.

Most people feel more energetic in the spring and fall.

Names of Commercial Products

Luke installed a new Blaupunkt stereo and a Garmin GPS system into his old Ford Ranger pickup.

But Use small letters for the *type* of product (stereo, cell phone, pickup, and so on).

Titles of Books, Magazines, Newspapers, Articles, Stories, Poems, Films, Television Shows, Songs, Papers That You Write, and the Like

We read the book *Hiroshima*, by John Hersey, for our history class.

In the doctor's waiting room, I watched *Fixer Upper*, read an article in *Popular Mechanics*, and leafed through the *Miami Herald*.

Names of Companies, Associations, Unions, Clubs, Religious and Political Groups, and Other Organizations

Joe Naples is a Roman Catholic, but his wife is a Methodist.

The Hilldale Square Dancers' Club has won many competitions.

Kevin, a member of Bricklayers Local 431 and the Knights of Columbus, works for Ace Construction.

ACTIVITY 1

Underline the words that need capitals in the following sentences. Then write the capitalized form of each word in the space provided. The number of spaces tells you how many corrections to make in each case.

EXAMPLE

Sammy's <u>pizza</u> and <u>pub</u>, which is located at 19 <u>federal</u> <u>street</u>, has phenomenal pizzas. _Pizza_   _Pub_   _Federal_   _Street_

1. We visited several theme parks in orlando, florida, including disney world.

   _____   _____   _____   _____

2. Zion was a big eater. For lunch he had a mcdonald's quarter-pounder, a big mac, and a large coke.

   _____   _____   _____   _____   _____

3. Sydney's favorite download from *born and raised* is "shadow days."

   _____   _____   _____   _____

4. Austin and brianna had a baby this july; his name is connor matteo campbell.

   _____   _____   _____   _____   _____

5. Kaia is a huge fan of the black eyed peas and has several T-shirts, concert stubs, and a pair of fergie's shoes that she wore on tour in 2009.

   _____   _____   _____   _____   _____

6. My children, rory, maggie, and noah, love to read *highlights* magazine.

   _____   _____   _____   _____

7. Martha's vineyard—especially the town of west chop—is a great place to vacation.

   _____   _____   _____

8. Since my mother is the leader of our local daisy troop, she holds the meetings at cedar creek elementary, which is where she works.

   _____   _____   _____   _____

9. To find out was what causing his wrist pain, Isaiah went to visit dr. landown.

   _____   _____

10. The first day of classes was on the tuesday following labor day that year, and I had to report to moore hall to register.

   _____   _____   _____   _____   _____

Other Uses of Capital Letters

Capital letters are used with

1. Names that show family relationships
2. Titles of persons when used with their names
3. Specific school courses
4. Languages
5. Geographic locations
6. Historical periods and events
7. Ethnicities, nations, and nationalities
8. Opening and closing of a letter

Each use is illustrated on the following pages.

Names and Titles

Names That Show Family Relationships

All his life, Father has been addicted to gadgets.

I browsed through Grandmother's collection of old photographs.

Aunt Florence and Uncle John bought a mobile home.

But Do not capitalize words like *mother, father, grandmother, grandfather, uncle, aunt,* and so on when they are preceded by a possessive word (such as *my, your, his, her, our, their*).

All his life, my father has been addicted to gadgets.

I browsed through my grandmother's collection of old photographs.

My aunt and uncle bought a mobile home.

Titles of Persons When Used with Their Names

I contributed to Senator McGrath's campaign fund.

Is Dr. Gomez on vacation?

Professor Adams announced that there would be no tests in the course.

But Use lowercase letters when titles appear by themselves, without specific names.

I contributed to my senator's campaign fund.

Is the doctor on vacation?

The professor announced that there would be no tests in the course.

Specific School Courses

The college offers evening sections of Introductory Psychology I, Abnormal Psychology, Psychology and Statistics, and Educational Psychology.

But Use lowercase letters for general subject areas.

The college offers evening sections of many psychology courses.

Miscellaneous Categories

Languages

My grandfather's Polish dishes like pampuchy are really popular with my friends.

Geographic Locations

He grew up in the Midwest but moved to the South to look for a better job.

But Use lowercase letters in directions.

Head west for five blocks and then turn south on State Street.

Historical Periods and Events

During the Middle Ages, the Black Death killed over one-quarter of Europe's population.

Ethnicities, Nations, and Nationalities

> The questionnaire asked whether the head of our household was Caucasian, African American, Asian, Latino, or Native American.
>
> Tanya has lived on army bases in Germany, Italy, and Spain.
>
> Maya's beautiful features reflect her Chinese and Mexican parentage.

Opening and Closing of a Letter

> Dear Sir: Sincerely yours,
>
> Dear Ms. Henderson: Truly yours,

Capitalize only the first word in a closing.

Underline the words that need capitals in the following sentences. Then write the capitalized form of each word in the spaces provided. The number of spaces tells you how many corrections to make in each case.

ACTIVITY 2

1. The boston tea party was an act of defiance against the british government's policy of taxation in the american colonies.

   _____ _____ _____ _____ _____

2. On their jobsite in spain, the french, swiss, and chinese coworkers used English to communicate.

   _____ _____ _____ _____

3. When uncle harvey got the bill from his doctor, he called the American Medical Association to complain.

   _____ _____

4. Dr. Freeling of the business department is offering a new course called introduction to web design.

   _____ _____ _____

5. A new restaurant featuring vietnamese cuisine has just opened on the south side of the city.

   _____

Unnecessary Use of Capitals

ACTIVITY 3

Jacob Lund/
Shutterstock

Many errors occur when capitalization is used when it is not needed. Working with a fellow classmate, underline the incorrectly capitalized words in the following sentences, and write the correct forms in the spaces provided. The number of spaces tells you how many corrections to make in each sentence.

1. Minnesota is bordered by the Canadian Provinces of Manitoba and Ontario to the North, by Wisconsin to the East, and by North and South Dakota to the West.

   _____   _____   _____   _____

2. North America is the World's third largest Continent. It includes Canada, the United States, Mexico, the Countries of Central America, and the island Nations of the Caribbean.

   _____   _____   _____   _____

3. Einstein's theory of relativity, which he developed when he was only twenty-six, led to the invention of the Electron Microscope, Television, and the Atomic bomb.

   _____   _____   _____   _____

4. Homer's Poem, *The Iliad,* is an Epic Poem and tells about the dispute between King Agamemnon and the Warrior Achilles.

   _____   _____   _____   _____

5. The *Harry Potter* Saga comprises eight films depicting the Rise and Fall of Lord Voldemort.

   _____   _____   _____

REVIEW TEST 1

Add capitals where needed and remove unnecessary capitals in the following sentences.

Academic

EXAMPLE:

The åmerican řevolution began in 1775 when the Ċolonists decided that they were tired of the taxes ềngland was imposing.

1. The colonies set up a new government in 1776, and with the aid of the french were able to defeat the british government.

2. Not long after the defeat of the british and the establishment of the united states of america, the french also had a Revolution.

3. The majority of the french population consisted of merchants and peasants known as the third estate; They were tired of paying taxes to the upper class, also known as the second estate.

4. In july 1789, a parisian mob stormed the bastille, a political prison.

5. Unfortunately, the abolishment of the Monarchy didn't lead to peace right away, and the time known as the reign of terror began in 1792.

6. a slightly more peaceful france was restored when napoleon Bonaparte rose to power in 1799.

7. However, he quickly declared himself emperor napoleon I, and in 1812 led a french invasion of russia.

8. Russia and the european alliance defeated napoleon twice, first in 1814 and again in 1815.

9. Despite Napoleon's defeat, his ideals helped create a spirit of Nationalism throughout europe.

10. After Napoleon was defeated, the congress of vienna met to restore legitimate Monarchs to their thrones; the regulations set up by this congress kept europe largely at peace until the end of the Nineteenth Century.

REVIEW TEST 2

On separate paper, write
1. Seven sentences demonstrating the seven main uses of capital letters.
2. Eight sentences demonstrating the eight other uses of capital letters.

Numbers and Abbreviations

This chapter will describe the proper use of numbers and abbreviations.

Incorrect:

It took us 5 weeks to find an apt. we both liked.

"5" can be written as one word ("five") so it should be spelled out. "Apartment" can be abbreviated on an envelope, but should be written out in a sentence.

Correct:

It took us five weeks to find an apartment we both liked.

Spelling out "five" and "apartment" is correct in this format.

Incorrect:

We'll have the report for you in 72 hours.

"72" can be written out as "seventy-two," which is fewer than three words.

Correct:

We'll have the report for you in seventy-two hours.

Because the number can be expressed in fewer than three words, it is spelled out.

Key Term

abbreviations: shortened forms of words, often used for convenience in writing. Certain abbreviations (such as *Mr., A.M.,* and *e.g.*) are acceptable in formal writing; in general, however, the complete form of words is preferred.

Numbers

Here are three helpful rules for using numbers.

Rule 1

Spell out numbers that take no more than two words. Otherwise, use the numbers themselves.

> In Jody's kitchen is her collection of seventy-two cookbooks.
>
> Jody has a file of 350 recipes.
>
> It will take about two weeks to fix the computer database.
>
> Since a number of people use the database, the company will lose over 150 workdays.
>
> Only twelve students have signed up for the field trip.
>
> Nearly 250 students came to the lecture.

Rule 2

Be consistent when you use a series of numbers. If some numbers in a sentence or paragraph require more than two words, then use numbers for the others, too.

> After the storm, maintenance workers unclogged 46 drains, removed 123 broken tree limbs, and rescued 3 kittens who were stuck in a drainpipe.

Rule 3

Use numbers to show dates, times, addresses, percentages, and chapters of a book.

> The burglary was committed on October 30, 2021, but was not discovered until January 2, 2022.
>
> Before I went to bed, I set my alarm for 6:45 A.M. (But spell out numbers before *o'clock*. For example: I didn't get out of bed until seven o'clock.)
>
> The library is located at 45 West 52nd Street.
>
> When you take the skin off a piece of chicken, you remove about 40 percent of the fat.
>
> The name of the murderer is revealed in Chapter 8 on page 290.

ACTIVITY 1

Cross out the mistakes in numbers and write the corrections in the spaces provided.

1. The Puerto Rican Pride Parade will begin at three-thirty in front of the news-paper office at one sixteen South Forty-Second Street.

   _____   _____   _____

2. The governor is scheduled to arrive at four P.M., but she isn't going to arrive until four forty-five P.M.

   _____   _____

3. We expect to have fifty percent of the work completed by March tenth.

   _____   _____

Abbreviations

Using abbreviations can save you time when you take notes. In formal writing, however, you should avoid most abbreviations. Listed below are some of the few abbreviations that are considered acceptable in compositions. Note that a period is used after most abbreviations.

1. Mr., Mrs., Ms., Jr., Sr., Dr. when used with names:

   Ms. Johnson   Dr. Garcia   Howard Kelley Jr.

2. Time references:

   A.M.   P.M.   B.C., A.D.

3. Initials in a person's name:

   J. Edgar Hoover   John F. Kennedy   Michael J. Fox

4. Organizations, technical words, and company names known primarily by their initials:

   IBM   UNICEF   ABC   IRS   NBA   AIDS

ACTIVITY 2

Cross out the words that should not be abbreviated, and correct them in the spaces provided.

1. Between mid-Nov. and the beginning of Jan., I typically gain about five lbs.

   _____   _____   _____

2. I have an appointment this A.M., but I can meet you for lunch in the caf. at noon.

   _____   _____

3. I stopped at the p.o. for a few min. and bought five dol. worth of stamps.

   _____   _____   _____   _____

Rewrite the following e-mail to correct problems with numbers and abbreviations.

From: Thomas S.

Sent: Saturday, September 15, 2018

To: Prof. Michael Hatzenberg

Subject: Psychology 2 Schedule, Weeks 2–four

Hi Prof. Hatzenberg:

I wanted to make sure I had our assignments clear for the next 3 weeks in our Psych. class. By Sept. twenty, I am supposed to understand how Psych drs. study behavior with exp. methods and read Chapters One & 2 in the textbook. In the 3rd week of class, I will need to read Chapters 5 and 6 and complete the 7 exercises on pg. fifty-six. In the fourth week of class, I will need to visit Saint Louis Children's Hosp. from 9:30 A.M. until one-thirty P.M. each day. During the visit, I am to observe the ped. psych dept. Is this right?

Thx,

Tom

Apostrophe

This chapter will describe the two main uses of the apostrophe. The sentences below will introduce you to one of these uses—to show ownership or possession. The other main use, to form contractions, is defined below.

Incorrect:

Because of the dogs constant barking, I could not sleep all night.

An apostrophe is needed before the *s* in dogs to show possession of the constant barking.

Correct:

Because of the dog's constant barking, I could not sleep all night.

With the apostrophe included it is clear that the dog is the possessor of the constant barking.

Key Terms

apostrophe: a punctuation mark generally used in order to (1) show the omission of one or more letters in a contraction, and to (2) show ownership or possession.

contraction: the combination of two words through omission of one or more letters and use of an apostrophe. Example: *hasn't* (for *has not*)

The two main uses of the apostrophe are

1. To show the omission of one or more letters in a contraction
2. To show ownership or possession

Apostrophe in Contractions

A contraction is formed when two words are combined. An apostrophe shows where letters are omitted.

have + not = haven't (the *o* in *not* has been omitted)

I + will = I'll (the *wi* in *will* has been omitted)

Following are some other common contractions:

I + am = I'm	it + is = it's
I + have = I've	it + has = it's
I + had = I'd	is + not = isn't
who + is = who's	could + not = couldn't
do + not = don't	I + would = I'd
did + not = didn't	they + are = they're
	we + are = we're

Will + not has an unusual contraction: won't.

Write the contractions for the words in parentheses.

ACTIVITY 1

1. (Are not) _____ the reserve books in the library kept at the circulation desk?

2. If (they are) _____ going to Israel, they (do not) _____ want to miss visiting Jerusalem.

3. (I am) _____ the kind of student (who is) _____ extremely nervous before tests.

4. (Who is) _____ the clerk who discovered that (it is) _____ cheaper to buy supplies online? (We are) _____ always interested in recognizing employees with good ideas.

5. I (cannot) _____ remember if (there is) _____ gas in the car or not.

> Even though contractions are common in everyday speech and in written dialogue, it is often best to avoid them in formal writing.

TIP

Apostrophe to Show Ownership or Possession

To show possession, we can use such words as *belongs to,* or *possessed by.*

the umbrella that belongs to Mark
the toys possessed by children
the aquatic center owned by the school district
the gentleness of my father

But the apostrophe and *s* (if the word doesn't end in *s*) is often the easiest way to do this.

Mark's umbrella

the children's toys

the school district's aquatic center

my father's gentleness

Points to Remember

1. The *'s* goes with the owner or possessor (in the examples given, *Mark, children, the school, my father*). What follows is the person or thing possessed (in the examples given, *the umbrella, the toys, the aquatic center, gentleness*).

2. There should not be a break between the word and *'s*.

Mark's
↗
Yes

not

Mark 's
↗
No

3. An apostrophe and *s* are used to show possession with a singular word even if the word already ends in *s:* for example, Elias's book (the book belonging to Elias).

ACTIVITY 2   Working in groups of two or three, rewrite the *italicized* part of each of the sentences below, using *'s* to show possession. Remember that the *'s* goes with the owner or possessor.

EXAMPLE

The wing of the bluejay was broken.

The bluejay's wing was broken.

1. *The capital of Scotland* is Edinburgh.

_____

2. *One of the major attractions of New York City* is the Empire State Building.

_____

3. *The three official languages of Switzerland* are German, French, and Italian.

_____

4. *The piano belonging to the Previn family* was once used in a symphony orchestra.

_____

5. *The computer belonging to John* was a top-of-the-line Apple.

_____

6. A cat ran out in front of *the car belonging to Abigail.*

_____

7. *In the window of the bakery* was the largest cupcake I had ever seen.

_____

8. *The apartment belonging to Caden* was located in an old converted warehouse.

_____

9. *The tennis shoes owned by Gabrielle* were original Chuck Taylor All-Stars.

_____

10. Keenan offered to paint *the house of Whitney Parker.*

_____

Add *'s* to each of the following words to make it the possessor or owner of something. Then write sentences using the words. The first one is done for you.

ACTIVITY 3

1. The train conductor *The train conductor's* _____

   The train conductor's announcement reassured the passengers that they would arrive on time.

_____

2. The government _____

_____

3. Annalise _____

_____

4. The grocery store _____

_____

5. The golden retriever _____

_____

6. The ski resort _____

_____

Apostrophe versus Possessive Pronouns

Do not use an apostrophe with possessive pronouns. They already show owner-ship. Possessive pronouns include *his, hers, its, yours, ours,* and *theirs.*

INCORRECT	CORRECT
The sun warped his' albums.	The sun warped his albums.
The restored Model T is theirs'.	The restored Model T is theirs.
The decision is yours'.	The decision is yours.
The lion charged its' prey.	The lion charged its prey.

Apostrophe versus Simple Plurals

To make a word plural, add only *s,* not an apostrophe. For example, the plural of the word *movie* is *movies,* not *movies'.*

Look at this sentence:

Tim coveted his roommate's collection of video games and compact discs.

The words *games* and *discs* are simple plurals, meaning more than one game, more than one disc. The plural is shown by adding *s* only. On the other hand, the *'s* after *roommate* shows possession—that the roommate owns the games and discs.

ACTIVITY 4

Jacob Lund/
Shutterstock

Insert an apostrophe where needed to show possession in the following sentences. Write *plural* above words where the *s* ending simply means more than one. Then, compare your answers with that of a classmate.

EXAMPLE

                         plural   *plural*
Gabriella's tinted contact lenses protect her eyes from glare.

1. Hannah grasped her wifes arm as she stood on ice skates for the first time.

2. Vonettes decision to study computer science is based on predictions of good opportunities for women in that field.

3. Pablo Picassos paintings are displayed in museums all over the world.

4. At the doctors request, Lyndon pulled up his shirt and revealed the zipperlike scars from his operation.

5. Of all the peoples names in all the worlds countries, the most common is Muhammad.

6. Sevilles many attractions include the beautiful Alcazar district built by the Moors, who ruled this Spanish city for five centuries.

7. The childrens shouts of delight grew louder as the clown added eggs, lightbulbs, and a bowling ball to the items he was juggling.

8. Tinas camping handbook suggests that we bring water purification tablets and nylon ropes.

9. *Black Beauty,* a childrens novel, has entertained young readers for more than a hundred years.

10. The rattlesnakes head has a sensitive pit below the eyes, capable of detecting the body heat of warm-blooded prey.

Apostrophe with Plurals Ending in *s*

Plurals that end in *s* show possession simply by adding the apostrophe, rather than an apostrophe and *s*.

the Thompsons' porch
the players' victory
her parents' motor home
the Rolling Stones' last album
the soldiers' hats

Add an apostrophe where needed.

1. Several campers tents collapsed during the storm.

2. Both of the Johnsons daughters have become attorneys.

3. Many cities subway and bus systems provide inexpensive and efficient transportation.

4. The twins habit of wearing similar clothes was started by their mother when they were children.

5. At the crowded intersection, several young men rushed out to wash the cars windshields.

REVIEW TEST 1

In the following paragraph, underline the words that either need apostrophes or have misused apostrophes. Then, in the spaces between the lines, correct the mistakes.

Academic

Learning the fifty state's capital's can often be a difficult task, but by using mnemonic devices and practicing, students can find success. Virginias capital is Richmond; a student can picture a rich man and his wife Virginia dancing at a ball to remember this capital. The capital of Maine is Augusta. This wouldnt be hard to forget if a student pictured a huge lion basking in the sun, while a gust of wind tousles the lions mane. Kentuckys capital is Frankfurt, easily remembered by picturing two boys' named Ken and Tuck sharing a hotdog. Connecticuts capital is Hartford, so a student could picture a heart connected to a Ford truck. Arkansas' capital, Little Rock, can be remembered by picturing a huge ark that is hit by a bunch of little rocks'. A fun way to remember Washington States capital, Olympia, is to picture George Washington receiving a gold medal at the Olympics. Mnemonic devices are creative ways to remember information and can help ensure students success in school.

Quotation Marks

Quotation marks are punctuation marks that indicate exact words or the titles of short works. This chapter will describe the two main uses of quotation marks. The sentences below will introduce you to one of these uses—to set off the exact words of a speaker or writer. The other main use is listed below.

Incorrect:

I'm interviewing for a new job tomorrow said Jason.

Because it is a direct quote, what Jason said should be in quotation marks.

Correct:

"I'm interviewing for a new job tomorrow," said Jason.

Jason's words are directly attributed by the quotation marks.

The two main uses of quotation marks are

1. To set off the exact words of a speaker or writer
2. To set off the titles of short works

Quotation marks are also used in research papers to signify material that has been directly quoted from a source. See Chapter 18.

Quotation Marks to Set Off the Words of a Speaker or Writer

Use quotation marks to show the exact words of a speaker or writer.

U.S. Congresswoman Barbara Jordan once said, "I never intended to become a run-of-the-mill person."
(Quotation marks set off the exact words that Barbara Jordan said.)
"I don't consciously try to be a role model," said Wilma Rudolph, "so I don't know if I am or not. That's for other people to decide."

(Two pairs of quotation marks are used to enclose Wilma Rudolph's exact words.)

The biology professor said, "Ants are a lot like human beings. They farm their own food and raise smaller insects as livestock. And like humans, ants send armies to war."

(Note that the end quotation marks do not come until the end of the biology professor's speech. Place quotation marks before the first quoted word and after the last quoted word. As long as no interruption occurs in the speech, do not use quotation marks for each new sentence.)

> **TIP** ▶ In the three examples above, notice that a comma sets the quoted part off from the rest of the sentence. Also, observe that commas and periods at the end of a quotation always go *inside* quotation marks.

Complete the following statements, which explain how capital letters, commas, and periods are used in quotations. Refer to the three examples above as guides.

1. Every quotation begins with a _____ letter.

2. When a quotation is split (as in the sentence from Wilma Rudolph), the second part does not begin with a capital letter unless it is a _____ sentence.

3. _____ are used to separate the quoted part of a sentence from the rest of the sentence.

4. Commas and periods that come at the end of a quotation go _____ the quotation marks.

The answers are *capital, new, Commas,* and *inside.*

ACTIVITY 1 Place quotation marks around the exact words of a speaker or writer in the sentences that follow.

1. Several people have been credited with saying, The more I see of people, the more I like dogs.

2. Let nature be your teacher, advised the poet William Wordsworth.

3. According to the Bible, The laborer is worthy of his hire.

4. The ballot, said Abraham Lincoln, is stronger than the bullet.

5. When chefs go to great lengths, the woman at the culinary school said, the dishes they create expand a diner's imagination.

6. My friend said that when she dies, she wants her headstone to read, She lived life to the fullest!

7. I apologize that my homework is tattered and stained, said the child, but I dropped it in a mud puddle.

8. Marilyn Monroe said, I restore myself when I'm alone.

9. The article warned residents, Severe weather is expected to arrive within the next two days.

10. Although he was most known for being funny, when Robin Williams said, No matter what people tell you, words and ideas can change the world, he was giving serious advice.

ACTIVITY 2

Jacob Lund/
Shutterstock

1. Write a sentence in which you quote a favorite expression of someone you know. In the same sentence, identify the person's relationship to you.

   EXAMPLE *My grandfather loves to say, "It can't be as bad as all that."*

   _____

   _____

   _____

2. Write a quotation that contains the words *Pablo asked Teresa*. Write a second quotation that includes the words *Teresa replied*.

   _____

   _____

   _____

   _____

   _____

3. Quote an interesting sentence or two from a book or magazine. In the same sentence, identify the title and author of the work.

   EXAMPLE *In The Dilbert Desk Calendar, by Scott Adams, the cartoon character Dilbert says,*

   "I can please only one person per day. Today isn't your day, and tomorrow isn't looking

   good either."

   _____

   _____

continued

_____

_____

_____

_____

4. Write a sentence in which the speaker of a quotation is identified in the middle of the quotation.

EXAMPLE *"Ralph ate a pound of pasta, six meatballs, and a slice of chocolate cake,"*

said his wife, Alice, "but he was still hungry!"

_____

_____

_____

_____

Indirect Quotations

An indirect quotation is a rewording of someone else's comments rather than a word-for-word direct quotation. The word *that* often signals an indirect quotation.

DIRECT QUOTATION	INDIRECT QUOTATION
The nurse said, "Some babies cannot tolerate cow's milk." (The nurse's exact spoken words are given, so quotation marks are used.)	The nurse said that some babies cannot tolerate cow's milk. (We learn the nurse's words indirectly, so no quotation marks are used.)
Vicky's note to Dan read, "I'll be home by 7:30." (The exact words that Vicky wrote in the note are given, so quotation marks are used.)	Vicky left a note for Dan saying that she would be home by 7:30. (We learn Vicky's words indirectly, so no quotation marks are used.)

ACTIVITY 3

Rewrite the following sentences, changing words as necessary to convert the sentences into direct quotations. The first one has been done for you as an example.

1. Dominic asked Julia whether she wanted to see his spider collection.

   Dominic asked Julia, "Do you want to see my spider collection?"

_____

2. According to Monica, her grandmother has been the role model for several women in her family.

_____

_____

3. Angelo said that he wanted a box of the extra-crispy chicken.

_____

_____

4. My history professor told us that tomatoes were first grown in Peru.

_____

_____

5. The instructor announced that Thursday's test had been canceled.

_____

_____

Quotation Marks to Set Off Titles of Short Works

Titles of short works are usually set off by quotation marks, while titles of long works are italicized. Use quotation marks to set off titles of such short works as articles in books, newspapers, or magazines; chapters in a book; short stories; poems; and songs. But you should italicize titles of books, newspapers, magazines, plays, movies, CDs, and television shows. Following are some examples.

QUOTATION MARKS	ITALICS
the essay "On Self-Respect"	in the book *Slouching Towards Bethlehem*
the article "The Problem of Acid Rain"	in the newspaper *The New York Times*
the article "Living with Inflation"	in the magazine *Time*
the chapter "Chinese Religion"	in the book *Paths of Faith*
the story "Hands"	in the book *Winesburg, Ohio*
the poem "When I Have Fears"	in the book *Complete Poems of John Keats*
the song "Ziggy Stardust"	in the album *Changes*
	the television show *60 Minutes*
	the movie *High Noon*

> When you are typing a paper, you should always italicize longer works; however, if you are handwriting a paper, you should underline longer works. For example, *Catching Fire* by Suzanne Collins would be handwritten <u>Catching Fire</u> by Suzanne Collins.

Jacob Lund/
Shutterstock

ACTIVITY 4

Use quotation marks as needed. Underline titles that should be italicized. Review your answers with a partner.

1. The movie Rogue One, starring Felicity Jones, explains how the Rebel Alliance learned how to blow up the Empire's Death Star.

2. We read the chapter Pulling Up Roots in Gail Sheehy's book Passages.

3. The book Small Great Things by Jodi Picoult addresses the issue of racism in modern America.

4. Pinned on Jeffrey's wall is the cover of a recent issue of Rolling Stone. The cover has a photo of the British rock group The Rolling Stones.

5. Madhuri Vijay's short story Lorry Raja is a poignant story about Indian children who work in the mines in Asia.

6. The sociology test will cover the first two chapters: Culture and Diversity and Social Stratification.

7. Over spring break, Sadie read the science fiction thriller Dark Matter by Blake Crouch.

8. An article in Golf magazine called Kiwi's Big Adventure entices the reader to plan a trip to New Zealand to golf at the Tara Iti Golf Club.

9. The January issue of Real Simple magazine included an article entitled This Is the Year To Get Better at Saying No.

10. Ta-Nehisi Coates writes for The Atlantic and has published many articles, including But This Latter Person, I Am Not Trying To Convince and When the World Runs Out of Room for Monsters.

Other Uses of Quotation Marks

Quotation marks are also used as follows:

1. To set off special words or phrases from the rest of a sentence:

> In grade school, we were taught a little jingle about the spelling rule "*i* before *e*."

What is the difference between "it's" and "its"?

(In this and other books, *italics* are often used instead of quotation marks to set off words.)

2. To mark off a quotation within a quotation:

The physics professor said, "For class on Friday, do the problems at the end of the chapter titled 'Work and Energy.'"

Cameron remarked, "Did you know that Humphrey Bogart never actually said, 'Play it again, Sam,' in the movie *Casablanca*?"

A quotation within a quotation is indicated by *single* quotation marks, as shown above.

 TIP

REVIEW TEST 1

Directions: Insert quotation marks where needed in the sentences that follow. One sentence is correct; mark that sentence with a C.

1. In *Monty Python and the Holy Grail*, John Cleese famously says, I fart in your general direction. Your mother was a hamster and your father smelt of elderberries.

2. In *Black Panther*, Shuri explains, Just because something works doesn't mean it can't be improved.

3. Tom Hanks plays a coach in *A League of Their Own*, but it certainly isn't his finest moment when he yells at one of his players, "Are you crying? There's no crying! There's no crying in baseball!"

4. In *Hidden Figures*, Katherine rebuts Colonel Johnson's doubts about women's capabilities by saying, And it's not because we wear skirts. It's because we wear glasses.

5. In *Guardians of the Galaxy*, Drax the Destroyer expresses his emotional side when he says, I just wanted to tell you how grateful I am that you've accepted me despite my blunders.

6. Find a truly original idea. It is the only way I will ever distinguish myself. It is the only way I will ever matter, John Nash moans in *A Beautiful Mind*.

7. In *Crazy Rich Asians*, when Rachel is in Singapore's famous Changi Airport, she exclaims, I can't believe this airport has a butterfly garden and a movie theater. JFK is just salmonella and despair.

8. Emily Blunt's character in *The Devil Wears Prada* explains,   I'm just one stomach flu away from my goal weight.

9. *Fast & Furious Presents: Hobbs & Shaw* includes many quotable lines, such as,   The key to immortality is first living a life worth remembering   and   In life, things happen. You may not want them to, but they do.

10. Robin Williams inspires his students in *Dead Poets Society* when he says,   If you listen real close, you can hear them whisper their legacy to you. Go on, lean in. Listen, you hear it? *Carpe*—hear it—*Carpe, Carpe diem*. Seize the day, boys. Make your lives extraordinary.

REVIEW TEST 2

In a newspaper's comic section find an amusing comic strip. Choose one where two or more characters speak to each other. Write a description that enables people who have not read the comic strip to appreciate its humor. Describe the setting and action in each panel, and enclose the speakers' words in quotation marks.

Comma

This chapter will describe the six main uses of the comma. The sentences below will introduce you to one of these uses—to set a direct quotation off from the rest of the sentence. The other five main uses of the comma are included below.

Incorrect:

The journalist pleaded "Just one more question."

A comma is needed to set the direct quotation off from the rest of the sentence.

Correct:

The journalist pleaded, "Just one more question."

With the comma included, the direct quotation is properly set off from the rest of the sentence.

Six Main Uses of the Comma

Commas are used mainly as follows:

1. To separate items in a series
2. To set off introductory material
3. On both sides of words that interrupt the flow of thought in a sentence
4. Between two complete thoughts connected by *and, but, for, or, nor, so, yet*
5. To set off a direct quotation from the rest of a sentence
6. For certain everyday material

You may find it helpful to remember that the comma often marks a slight pause or break in a sentence. Read aloud the sentence examples given for each rule, and listen for the minor pauses or breaks that are signaled by commas.

Comma between Items in a Series

Use commas to separate items in a series.

> The street vendor sold watches, necklaces, and earrings.
> The pitcher adjusted his cap, pawed the ground, and peered over his shoulder.
> The exercise instructor told us to inhale, exhale, and relax.
> Owen peered into the hot, still-smoking engine.

A. The final comma in a series is optional, but it is often used. If you use a final comma in one series in an essay, use one in all the other series in the same essay.

B. A comma is used between two descriptive words in a series only if *and* inserted between the words sounds natural. You could say:

> Owen peered into the hot *and* still-smoking engine.

But notice in the following sentence that the descriptive words do not sound natural when *and* is inserted between them. In such cases, no comma is used.

> Micah wore a pale green tuxedo. (A pale *and* green tuxedo does not sound right, so no comma is used.)

ACTIVITY 1

Place commas between items in a series.

1. The American alligator lives in southern swamps streams lakes and other bodies of water.

2. Rudy stretched out on the swaying hammock popped open a frosty can of soda and balanced it carefully on his stomach.

3. The children splashed through the warm deep swirling rainwater that flooded the street.

4. The police officer's warm brown eyes relaxed manner and pleasant smile made her easy to talk to.

5. The soft warm woolen blankets comforted us as we heard the cold north wind blow through the pines.

Comma after Introductory Material

Use a comma to set off introductory material.

> Just in time, Leah applied the brakes and avoided a car accident.
> Muttering under his breath, Hassan reviewed the terms he had memorized.
> In a wolf pack, the dominant male holds his tail higher than the other pack members.

Although he had been first in the checkout line, Deion let an elderly woman go ahead of him.

After the fire, we slogged through the ashes of the burned-out house.

If the introductory material is brief, the comma is sometimes omitted. In the activities here, you should include the comma.

Place commas after introductory material. Once you have completed the activity, review your answers with a partner.

ACTIVITY 2

1. Although it cannot kill certain bacteria penicillin is still a useful antibiotic.

2. His heart pounding wildly Jesse opened the letter that would tell him whether he had been accepted to college.

3. Passing through fourteen states the Appalachian trail is over two thousand miles long.

4. When the band hadn't taken the stage forty-five minutes after the concert was supposed to begin the audience started shouting and stamping their feet.

5. Along the side of the brook we noticed a newborn speckled fawn.

Jacob Lund/ Shutterstock

Comma around Words That Interrupt the Flow of Thought

Use a comma on both sides of words or phrases that interrupt the flow of thought in a sentence.

The vinyl car seat, sticky from the heat, clung to my skin.

Jake's gaming system, which his wife got him as a birthday gift, occupies all his spare time.

The hallway, dingy and dark, was illuminated by a bare bulb.

Usually, by reading a sentence aloud, you can hear the words that interrupt the flow of thought. In cases where you are not sure if certain words are interrupters, remove them from the sentence. If it still makes sense without the words, you know that the words are interrupters and that the information they give is nonessential. *Such nonessential or extra information is set off with commas.* In the sentence

Sue Dodd, who goes to drumming class with me, was in a serious car accident.

the words *who goes to drumming class with me* are extra information not needed to identify the subject of the sentence, *Sue Dodd*. Commas go around such nonessential information. On the other hand, in the sentence

> The woman who goes to drumming class with me was in a serious accident.

the words *who goes to drumming class with me* supply essential information— information needed for us to identify the woman being spoken of. If the words were removed from the sentence, we would no longer know exactly who was in the accident: "The woman was in a serious accident." Here is another example:

> *Watership Down*, a novel by Richard Adams, is the most thrilling adventure story I've ever read.

Here the words *a novel by Richard Adams* could be left out, and we would still know the basic meaning of the sentence. Commas are placed around such nonessential material. But in the sentence

> Richard Adams's novel *Watership Down* is the most thrilling adventure story I've ever read.

the title of the novel is essential. Without it the sentence would read, "Richard Adams's novel is the most thrilling adventure story I've ever read." We would not know which of Richard Adams's novels was so thrilling. Commas are not used around the title, because it provides essential information.

Most of the time you will be able to hear which words interrupt the flow of thought in a sentence and will not have to think about whether the words are essential or nonessential.

ACTIVITY 3   Use commas to set off interrupting words.

1. Two large pines located near my cabin were swaying in the cold winter wind.

2. Hawaii which became the fiftieth state in 1959 is made up of eight major islands.

3. Nathan Bage an avid football fan watches college football on Saturdays and professional football on Sundays.

4. The weather windy and wild created twenty-foot swells on the lake.

5. A talented actress who has starred in many plays lives across the street.

Comma between Complete Thoughts

Use a comma between two complete thoughts connected by *and, but, for, or, nor, so, yet*.

> Sam closed all the windows, but the predicted thunderstorm never arrived.
>
> I like wearing comfortable clothing, so I buy oversize shirts and sweaters.

Riley attended The Culinary Institute of America, for she has a goal to become the best chef possible.

A. The comma is optional when the complete thoughts are short.

> The Ferris wheel started and Wilson closed his eyes.
>
> Many people left but the band played on.
>
> I made a wrong turn so I doubled back.

B. Be careful not to use a comma to separate two verbs that belong to one subject. The comma is used only in sentences made up of two complete thoughts (two subjects and two verbs). In the sentence

> The doctor stared over his bifocals and lectured me about smoking.

there is only one subject (*doctor*) and a double verb (*stared* and *lectured*). No comma is needed. Likewise, the sentence

> Dean switched the lamp on and off and then tapped it with his fingers.

has only one subject (*Dean*) and a double verb (*switched* and *tapped*); therefore, no comma is needed.

ACTIVITY 4

Place a comma before a joining word that connects two complete thoughts (two subjects and two verbs). Remember, do *not* place a comma within a sentence that has only one subject and a double verb. Some items are correct as given. For these items, write "Correct" at the end of the sentence.

1. The television sitcom sounded silly but I poked my head out of the kitchen to listen anyway.

2. Before he published his first novel, *Go Tell It on the Mountain*, James Baldwin moved to Paris, France.

3. The fluffy frizzle chicken ran noisily around the coop for it was afraid of the raccoon sitting outside the chicken wire.

4. Orangutans are ideally suited for living in trees and they rarely climb down to the ground.

5. Plastic surgery was developed to repair damaged tissue and it has helped many war victims heal from injuries.

6. Allison was tired of summer reruns so she visited the town library to pick up some interesting books.

7. You can spend hours driving all over town to look for a particular type of camera or you can visit a few stores' websites to find it quickly.

8. Many people strolled among the exhibits at the comic book collectors' convention and stopped to look at a rare first edition of *Superman*.

9. Our neighborhood crime patrol escorts elderly people to the local bank and installs free dead-bolt locks on their apartment doors.

10. Brendan tapped the small geraniums out of their pots and carefully planted them on his grandfather's grave.

Comma with Direct Quotations

Use a comma to set off a direct quotation from the rest of a sentence.

> The carnival barker cried, "Step right up and win a prize!"
> "Be a good person to all around you," the fortune cookie read.
> "I'm sorry," said the restaurant hostess. "You'll have to wait."
> "For my first writing assignment," said Scott, "I have to turn in a five-hundred-word description of a stone."

TIP Commas and periods at the end of a quotation go inside quotation marks. See also Chapter 35.

ACTIVITY 5 Use commas to set off direct quotations from the rest of the sentence.

1. The child heard her mother whisper "Ladybird, ladybird, fly away home."

2. "My heart is bursting" said Stella. "How can I ever repay you for all you've done?"

3. The teacher announced "Tomorrow will be our last day of state testing."

4. "I know you did it" the detective accused the murderer "and I can prove it!"

5. "Please remember to watch the gap" the conductor warned.

Comma with Everyday Material

Use a comma when a person is spoken to.

Persons Spoken To
> If you're the last to leave, Nicholas, please switch off the lights.
> Dylan, I think we're on the wrong road.

Use a comma after the salutation of a friendly letter and after the salutation and closing of a friendly and a formal letter.

Openings and Closings of Letters
> Dear Liam,   Sincerely yours,
> Dear Roberto,   Yours truly,

> **TIP**
>
> In formal letters, a colon is used after the opening: Dear Sir: *or* Dear Madam: *or* Dear Allan: *or* Dear Ms. Mohr:

Use commas in numbers of four digits or more, except for years and street numbers.

Numbers

    In 2008, the insurance agent sold me a $50,000 term life insurance policy.

Use commas in dates and in addresses as illustrated.

Dates

    July 4, 1980, is my brother's birthday.

Addresses

    The Brown Elementary School is located at 20 Milk Street, Wareham, Massachusetts 02571.

> **TIP**
>
> No comma is used before a ZIP code.

Place commas where needed.

ACTIVITY 6

1. On July 15 2009, Philip Vassallo opened a legal office at 2600 Woodbridge Avenue Fort Myers Florida.

2. The city of Kinshasa Tanisha is the capital of the Democratic Republic of Congo.

3. The mileage chart shows Ava that we'll have to drive 1 329 miles to get to Ashburn Georgia.

4. My friend's new address is 5533 Edith Boulevard NE Santa Fe New Mexico 87107.

5. Rod Stewart's 1994 concert in Rio de Janeiro Brazil had an estimated attendance of 3 500 000 people, making it one of the most attended concerts in history.

REVIEW TEST 1

Insert commas where needed. In the space provided below each sentence, summarize briefly the rule that explains the comma or commas used.

1. "Kleenex tissues" said the history professor "were first used as gas mask filters in World War I."

    _____

2. The large juicy Bartlett pear that I bit into was sweet cold and refreshing.

    _____

3. While waiting to enter the movie theater we studied the faces of the people just leaving to see if they had liked the show.

    _____

4. I had left my wallet on the store counter but the clerk called me at home to say that it was safe.

_____

5. The demonstrators protesting nuclear arms carried signs reading "Humans have never invented a weapon that they haven't used."

_____

6. Large cactus plants which now sell for very high prices are being stolen from national parks and protected desert areas.

_____

7. At the age of twenty-one Tiger Woods won the 1997 Masters Tournament with the highest margin of victory in the golfing tournament's history.

_____

8. Tucson a large city in Arizona is quite near the border with Mexico.

_____

9. The North African nation of Algeria is bordered by seven other countries: Tunisia Libya Niger Mali Mauritania Western Sahara and Morocco.

_____

10. Cats and dogs like most animals love the taste of salt and will lick humans' hands to get it.

_____

REVIEW TEST 2

In the following passage, there are ten missing commas. Add the commas where needed. The types of mistakes to look for are shown in the box below.

> 3 commas missing between items in a series
> 2 commas missing after introductory material
> 2 commas missing between complete thoughts
> 2 commas missing around interrupting words
> 1 comma missing with a direct quotation

Instructor Performance Review: Ms. J. Thompson

It is evident that Ms. Thompson is well liked by her students engenders an atmosphere of fun in her classroom, and has continued to improve as an instructor. During Ms. Thompson's evaluation she presented a lesson on creating parallelism in writing. Students then partnered up, read their essays, and tried to incorporate parallel statements in their own pieces of writing. Most students except two remained focused during the activity and Ms. Thompson quickly addressed both students "Either pay attention and complete the activity, or remove yourself from the class." She then continued to walk about the classroom and used her presence to remind the class to stay focused. When students finished this activity they moved to a discussion about the English Portfolio Assessment. Students presented their portfolios and Ms. Thompson offered insight and advice. Students' portfolios were very innovative and included items such as a "Bucket List," creative covers that reflected something about the contents of the portfolio and a bio-poem. Although Ms. Thompson's students exhibited success in their approaches, Ms. Thompson should refocus her course goals to include more academic and longer pieces that follow the outcomes laid out in the faculty handbook. These pieces should demonstrate expressive, expository and persuasive writing techniques that use the principles of organization, unity, coherence, and theme development. It is suggested that Ms. Thompson work with a tenured professor chosen by the English department to reconfigure her syllabus to meet the course outcomes as laid out by the college.

REVIEW TEST 3

Insert commas where needed. Mark the one sentence that is correct with a C.

1. Before leaving for the gym Nikki added extra socks and a tube of shampoo to the gear in her duffel bag.

2. My father said "Golf isn't for me. I can't afford to buy lots of expensive sticks so that I can lose lots of expensive white balls."

3. Reviewed by a committee of college faculty Jason's application for the scholarship was approved unanimously.

4. Oscar took a time-exposure photo of the busy highway so the cars' taillights appeared in the developed print as winding red ribbons.

5. A line of dancing numerals on *Sesame Street* kicked across the screen like a chorus line.

6. During the summer graduation ceremony students fanned themselves with commencement programs and parents hid in the shade of trees.

7. Leaving seven astronauts dead the space shuttle *Columbia* broke apart as it returned to Earth on February 1 2003.

8. "When I was little " said Angel "my brother told me it was illegal to eat fried chicken with utensils in a town in Georgia. I still don't know if that's true or not."

9. The Cloisters a museum of medieval art which is part of the New York Metropolitan Museum of Art includes buildings brought to the United States from Europe.

10. On June 24 1948 the Soviet Union closed the German city of Berlin to traffic from the West. However this ill-fated venture lasted only until May 11 1949 when the Soviets were forced to reopen the city.

REVIEW TEST 4

On separate paper, write six sentences, one illustrating each of the six main comma rules.

Word Use

What errors can you find on this sign? How can you correct them?

Kim Karpeles/Alamy Stock Photo

Commonly Confused Words

This chapter will list homonyms and other commonly confused words. These words are especially troublesome for students who rely on spell-checking applications to catch all their errors. Spell-check programs can be misleading and unreliable because a word that shows up as spelled correctly may actually not be the right word. This chapter's information and activities are designed to help you learn to distinguish the differences.

Key Term

homonym: words such as *brake* and *break* that have the same sounds but different meanings.

Homonyms

Some words are commonly confused because they have the same sounds but different meanings and spellings; such words are known as *homonyms*. Following are a number of homonyms. Complete the activity for each set of words. Check off and study the words that give you trouble.

all ready   completely prepared

already   previously; before

It was *already* four o'clock by the time I thought about lunch.

My report was *all ready,* but the class was canceled.

Fill in the blanks: Tyrone was _____ to sign up for the course when he discovered that it had _____ closed.

brake   stop

break   come apart

The mechanic advised me to add *brake* fluid to my car.

During a commercial *break,* Angel got a snack and made a cup of tea.

Fill in the blanks: I didn't want to _____ my promise, but since the _____ on my bike wasn't working, I couldn't take my son biking.

course	part of a meal; a school subject; direction
coarse	rough

> At the movies, I tried to decide on a *course* of action that would put an end to the *coarse* language of the man behind me.

Fill in the blanks: Over the _____ of time, jagged, _____ rocks will be polished to smoothness by the pounding waves.

hear	perceive with the ear
here	in this place

> I can *hear* the performers so well from *here* that I don't want to change my seat.

Fill in the blanks: "_____ is the best place to _____ the birds," said Reagan as she pointed out a shaded spot near the river.

hole	an empty spot
whole	entire

> A *hole* in the crumbling brick mortar made a convenient home for a small bird and its *whole* family.

Fill in the blanks: It took a _____ weekend for the two workers to dig a _____ for the new waterfall and pond.

its	belonging to it
it's	shortened form (contraction) of "it is" or "it has"

> The tall giraffe lowered *its* head (the head belonging to the giraffe) to the level of the car window and peered in at us.
>
> *It's* (it is) too late to sign up for the theater trip to New York.

Fill in the blanks: I decided not to take the course because _____ too easy; _____ content offers no challenge whatsoever.

knew	understood; past form of *know*
new	not old

> No one *knew* our *new* phone number, but the obscene calls continued.

Fill in the blanks: Bryan and Courtney _____ that having a _____ car was a luxury they couldn't afford.

know   to understand

no   a negative

By the time students complete that course, they *know* two computer languages and have *no* trouble writing their own programs.

Fill in the blanks: The students _____ that anytime the teacher says _____, they need to listen.

passed   went by; succeeded in; handed to

past   a time before the present; by, as in "I drove past the house"

As Yvonne *passed* exit six on the interstate, she knew she had gone *past* the correct turnoff.

Fill in the blanks: Lewis asked for a meeting with his boss to learn why he had been _____ over for promotion twice in the _____ year.

peace   calm

piece   a part

The best *piece* of advice she ever received was to maintain her own inner *peace.*

Fill in the blanks: I will have _____ of mind once I know this expensive _____ of jewelry is in the safe-deposit box.

plain   simple

plane   aircraft

The *plain* box contained a very old model *plane* kit.

Fill in the blanks: After studying and practicing for months, Pierce finally executed a solo landing of his _____ on the highway near his _____ brown house.

principal   main; a person in charge of a school

principle   a law or standard

If the *principal* ingredient in this stew is onion, I'll abandon my *principle* of trying everything at least once.

Fill in the blanks: The _____ of the school announced that the _____ behind exams was to test students' learning.

| right | correct; opposite of "left" |
| write | to put words on paper |

Without the *right* amount of advance planning, it is difficult to *write* a good research paper.

Fill in the blanks: Farha tried to take detailed notes during the presentation, but she could not _____ fast enough to get all the _____ information down before the presentation ended.

their	belonging to them
there	at that place; a neutral word used with verbs like *is, are, was, were, have,* and *had*
they're	contraction of "they are"

The tenants *there* are complaining because *they're* being cheated by *their* landlord.

Fill in the blanks: _____ hoping to move _____ campsite over _____ near the tall oak tree.

| threw | past form of *throw* |
| through | from one side to the other; finished |

As the inexperienced pizza-maker *threw* the pie into the air, he punched a hole *through* its thin crust.

Fill in the blanks: As the parade moved slowly _____ the cheering crowd, the people on the floats _____ candy and flowers into the crowd.

to	verb part, as in *to smile;* toward, as in "I'm going *to* heaven."
too	overly, as in "The pizza was *too* hot"; also, as in "The coffee was hot, *too.*"
two	the number 2

I ran *to* the car *to* roll up the windows. (The first *to* means "toward"; the second *to* is a verb part that goes with *roll.*)

That amusement park is *too* far away; I hear that it's expensive, *too.* (The first *too* means "overly"; the second *too* means "also.")

The *two* players (2 players) jumped up to tap the basketball away.

Fill in the blanks: I wanted _____ take the _____ young girls to see the roses at the botanical garden, but the girls were _____ interested in the Japanese garden _____ comply.

wear   to have on

where   in what place

Where I will *wear* a purple feather boa is not the point; I just want to buy it.

Fill in the blanks: My husband and son like to go to parties _____ they can _____ colorful ties and suits.

weather   atmospheric conditions

whether   if it happens that; in case; if

Although meteorologists are *weather* specialists, even they can't predict *whether* a hurricane will change course.

Fill in the blanks: I didn't know _____ to wear long pants or shorts because the _____ kept changing so suddenly.

whose   belonging to whom

who's   contraction of "who is" and "who has"

"*Who's* the patient *whose* filling fell out?" the dentist's assistant asked.

Fill in the blanks: _____ the salesperson _____ customers are always complaining about his high-pressure tactics?

your   belonging to you

you're   contraction of "you are"

You're making a fool of yourself; *your* Elvis imitation isn't funny.

Fill in the blanks: If _____ having trouble filling out _____ tax return, why don't you call the IRS's toll-free hotline?

Other Words Frequently Confused

Not all frequently confused words are homonyms. Here is a list of other words that people often confuse. Complete the activities for each set of words. Check off and study the words that give you trouble.

a, an   Both *a* and *an* are used before other words to mean, approximately, "one."

Generally you should use *an* before words starting with a vowel (*a, e, i, o, u*) or a vowel sound:

    an orange   an umbrella   an indication   an ape   an effort

    an hour   an X-ray

Generally you should use *a* before words starting with a consonant (all other letters) or a consonant sound:

a genius   a movie   a speech   a study   a typewriter

a unique   a useless

Fill in the blanks: Mrs. Surface's classroom had _____ old, comfy couch and _____ plush easy chair for the students to enjoy while reading.

| accept | (ăk sĕpt′) | to receive; agree to |
| except | (ĭk sĕpt′) | excluding; but |

It was easy to *accept* the book's plot, *except* for one unlikely coincidence at the very end.

Fill in the blanks: Shaurya would _____ the position, _____ that it would add twenty minutes to his daily commute.

| advice | (ăd vīs′) | noun meaning "an opinion" |
| advise | (ăd vīz′) | verb meaning "to counsel, to give advice" |

I have learned not to take my sister's *advice* on straightening out my life.

A counselor can *advise* you about the courses you'll need next year.

Fill in the blanks: The professor often liked to _____ his students, but they didn't always welcome his _____.

| affect | (uh fĕkt′) | verb meaning "to influence" |
| effect | (ĭ fĕkt′) | verb meaning "to cause something"; noun meaning "result" |

The bad weather will definitely *affect* the outcome of the election.

If we can *effect* a change in Sebastian's attitude, he may do better in his courses.

One *effect* of the strike will be dwindling supplies in the supermarkets.

Fill in the blanks: People who bikepack long distances without proper training often have the side _____ of saddle sores, which can _____ their moods.

| among | implies three or more |
| between | implies only two |

After the team of surgeons consulted *among* themselves, they decided that the bullet was lodged *between* two of the patient's ribs.

Fill in the blanks: _____ halves, one enthusiastic fan stood up _____ the crowd of equally fanatic spectators and took off his coat and shirt.

beside	along the side of
besides	in addition to

Besides doing daily inventories, I have to stand *beside* the cashier whenever the store gets crowded.

Fill in the blanks: _____ my glass of water and book, I always place my glasses on the table _____ my bed.

fewer	used with things that can be counted
less	refers to amount, value, or degree

I've taken *fewer* classes this semester, so I hope to have *less* trouble finding time to study.

Fill in the blanks: Since I am working _____ hours, I am making _____ money than I used to.

former	refers to the first of two items named
latter	refers to the second of two items named

Delia yelled at her sons, Greg and John, when she got home; the *former* (Greg) had left the refrigerator open and the *latter* (John) had left wet towels all over the bathroom.

Fill in the blanks: Oliver collects coupons and parking tickets; the _____ saves him money and the _____ is going to cost him a great deal of money someday.

learn	to gain knowledge
teach	to give knowledge

I can't *learn* a new skill unless someone with lots of patience *teaches* me.

Fill in the blanks: My philosophy professor likes to _____ about the great philosophers of the past, and I have enjoyed this opportunity to _____ about the brilliant minds behind my favorite theories.

loose	(lo͞os)	not fastened; not tight-fitting
lose	(lo͞oz)	to misplace; fail to win

In this strong wind, the house may *lose* some of its *loose* roof shingles.

Fill in the blanks: The _____ screw caused us to _____ a wheel on our garden wagon, thus making our vegetables spill all over the yard.

quiet	(kwī′ĭt)	peaceful
quite	(kwīt)	entirely; really; rather

Avery seems *quiet* and demure, but she is *quite* able to voice her opinions when she wants to.

Fill in the blanks: I am _____ certain that _____, relaxing mornings are the perfect way to start a day.

than   (thăn)   used in comparisons
then   (thĕn)   at that time

I made more money *then,* but I've never been happier *than* I am now.

Fill in the blanks: I wanted to attend New York University more _____ the University of Chicago, but _____ I was offered a scholarship to the University of Chicago, so that is where I went to school.

These sentences check your understanding of *its, it's; there, their, they're; to, too, two;* and *your, you're.* Underline the two incorrect spellings in each sentence. Then spell the words correctly in the spaces provided.

ACTIVITY 1

_____
_____   1. "Its not a very good idea," yelled Alexandra's boss, "to tell you're customer that the striped couch she plans to buy is overpriced."

_____
_____   2. You're long skirt got stuck in the car door, and now its sweeping the highway.

_____
_____   3. When your young, their is a tendency to confuse a crush with true love.

_____
_____   4. After too hours of typing, Lin was to tired to type any longer.

_____
_____   5. In its' long history, the island of Sicily has been a colony of Greece, a Norman kingdom, and an Arab emirate; today its part of the Republic of Italy.

_____
_____   6. The vampires bought a knife sharpener in order too sharpen there teeth.

_____
_____   7. Your never alone if your loved ones are in you're heart.

_____   8. When the children get to quiet, we know their getting

_____   into trouble.

_____   9. There friendship developed into love as the years passed, and

_____   now, in midlife, their newlyweds.

_____   10. It is to far to swim too Nantucket Island—the Massachusetts

_____   mainland is thirty miles away.

REVIEW TEST 1

Read the following paragraph to find the twelve incorrectly used words. Draw a line through those words. In the space between the lines, write the correct word.

Woodrow Wilson served as the twenty-eighth president of the United States from 1913–1921. President Wilson earned his doctorate at Johns Hopkins University and then began a academic career. In 1902, he became the president of Princeton University. In 1910, he ran for governor of New Jersey and, in 1912, was nominated as the Democratic candidate in the presidential race. The race of 1912 was very important because three candidates with very different ideologies ran against each other. Wilson's policy stood for the principals of individualism and states' writes with a platform called the Knew Freedom. The incumbent, President Taft, was the conservative Republican candidate who represented big business. Theodore Roosevelt was the Bull Moose Party (Progressive) candidate, representing the reform-minded majority of America. Even though Wilson received only 42 percent of the popular vote, he won the electoral vote too become president. While in office, he managed to get the Federal Reserve Act past and established the Federal Trade Commission. He was able two win a second election in 1916 with the slogan, "He kept us out of war." However, in 1917, he had to ask Congress for a declaration of war. America than entered World War I. In 1918, the Treaty of Versailles was signed by the League of Nations; the affect of this treaty was an end to the war and a

tentative worldwide piece. Congress wouldn't except Wilson's support of

the treaty and would not agree to sign the treaty. This greatly devastated

President Wilson. As he campaigned to gain public support for the United

States to enter into agreement with the League of Nations, he suffered a

massive stroke. President Wilson was cared for by his second wife and

died a quite death in 1924.

On separate paper, write short sentences using the ten words shown below.

1. accept
2. its
3. you're
4. too
5. then
6. course
7. their
8. passed
9. fewer
10. all ready

CHAPTER 38

Effective Word Choice

This chapter will give you practice in avoiding slang, clichés, and pretentious words.

Key Terms

cliché: an expression that has been worn out through constant use. Example: *short but sweet*

pretentious language: artificial or stilted expressions that more often obscure meaning than communicate it clearly. Example: *It was a splendid opportunity to obtain some slumber* could be more simply expressed as *It was a good chance to get some sleep.*

slang: nonstandard language particular to a time and often to a specific locale; acceptable in everyday speech, slang should be avoided in formal contexts and, with few exceptions, in writing. Example: *I'm going to have to sweat it out for the next couple of days until the test results are posted* would be more appropriately expressed as *I'm going to have to wait anxiously for the next couple of days until the test results are posted.*

Choose your words carefully when you write. Always take the time to think about your word choices rather than simply use the first word that comes to mind. You want to develop the habit of selecting words that are precise and appropriate for your purpose. One way you can show sensitivity to language is by avoiding slang, clichés, and pretentious words.

Slang

We often use slang expressions when we talk because they are so vivid and colorful. However, slang is usually out of place in formal writing. Here are some examples of slang:

Someone *ripped off* Ken's new Adidas running shoes from his locker.

After the game, we *stuffed our faces* at the diner.

I finally told my parents to *get off my case*.

The movie really *grossed me out*.

Slang expressions have a number of drawbacks. They go out of date quickly, they become tiresome if used excessively in writing, and they may communicate clearly to some readers but not to others. Also, the use of slang can be an evasion of the specific details that are often needed to make one's meaning clear in writing. For example, in "The movie really grossed me out," the writer has not provided the specific details about the movie necessary for us to clearly understand the statement. Was it acting, special effects, or violent scenes that the writer found so disgusting? In general, then, you should avoid slang in your writing. If you are in doubt about whether an expression is slang, it may help to check a recently published hardbound or electronic dictionary.

Rewrite the following sentences, replacing the italicized slang words with more formal ones.

EXAMPLE

Theo was so wiped out after his workout at the gym that he couldn't *get it together* enough to heat up a microwave meal.

Theo was so exhausted *after his workout at the gym that he couldn't* find the energy to heat up a microwave meal.

1. I was *psyched* to go to the concert; the lead singer just *slayed* it!

_____

_____

2. When Joshua tried to *chat up* Caitlin at the dance, she totally *roasted* him.

_____

_____

3. Last week I was in the most *boujie* neighborhood with *totes adorbs* boutiques.

_____

_____

4. Kylie is so *extra*! We were planning to *keep things chill*, but she showed up in a full velvet ensemble and insisted we *hit the clubs*.

_____

_____

5. My parents took me on a surprise trip that I thought was going to be *dank*, but it turned out to be a total *graycation*.

_____

_____

_____

Clichés

A *cliché* is an expression that has been worn out through constant use. Here are some typical clichés:

short but sweet	at a loss for words
drop in the bucket	taking a big chance
had a hard time of it	took a turn for the worse
word to the wise	singing the blues
it dawned on me	in the nick of time
sigh of relief	too close for comfort
too little, too late	saw the light
last but not least	easier said than done
work like a dog	on top of the world
all work and no play	time and time again
it goes without saying	make ends meet

Clichés are common in speech but make your writing seem tired and stale. Also, they are often an evasion of the specific details that you must work to provide in your writing. You should, then, avoid clichés and try to express your meaning in fresh, original ways.

ACTIVITY 2

Jacob Lund/
Shutterstock

Underline the cliché in each of the following sentences. Then substitute specific, fresh words for the trite expression. Partner with a classmate and go over your answers together.

EXAMPLE

My boyfriend has stuck with me <u>through thick and thin</u>.

through good times and bad.
_____

1. As the only girl in an otherwise all-boy family, I got away with murder.

   _____

2. I was on top of the world when the doctor told me I was as healthy as a horse.

   _____

3. My suggestion is just a shot in the dark, but it's better than nothing.

   _____

4. Eve got more than she bargained for when she offered to help Larry with his math homework.

   _____

5. A stone's throw from the Colosseum in Rome are some restaurants, where the food is as good as it gets.

   _____

6. On a hot, sticky midsummer day, iced tea or any frosty drink really hits the spot.

   _____

7. Nadia thanks her lucky stars that she was born with brains, beauty, and humility.

   _____

8. Anything that involves mathematical ability has always been right up my alley.

   _____

9. The Montessori system of education is old hat now, but when it came on the scene, it raised a few eyebrows.

   _____

10. Even when we are up to our eyeballs in work, our boss wonders if we have enough to do.

    _____

ACTIVITY 3

Write a short paragraph describing the kind of day you've had. Try to put as many clichés as possible into it. For example, "I got up at the crack of dawn, ready to take on the world. I grabbed a bite to eat. . . ." By making yourself aware of clichés in this way, you should lessen the chance that they will appear in your writing.

Pretentious Words

Some people feel that they can improve their writing by using fancy, elevated words rather than simple, natural words. They use artificial, stilted language that more often obscures their meaning than communicates it clearly. This frequently occurs when students attempt to use a dictionary or thesaurus, but just pick words at random to replace the simpler words. Using college-level vocabulary is a way to improve your writing, but you must be careful in choosing words. Not only can certain choices sound artificial, but another problem may arise when words are chosen without enough thought. Because many words can act as nouns, verbs, adjectives, and adverbs, using the wrong part of speech often leads to obscured meaning.

Here are some unnatural-sounding sentences:

It was a marvelous gamble to procure some slumber.
We relished the delectable noon-hour repast.
The officer apprehended the imbibed operator of the vehicle.
The female had an affectionate spot in her heart for domesticated canines.

The same thoughts can be expressed more clearly and effectively by using plain, natural language, as below:

It was an excellent chance to get some sleep.
We enjoyed the delicious lunch.
The officer arrested the drunk driver.
The woman had a warm spot in her heart for dogs.

Here are some other inflated words and simpler words that could replace them:

Inflated Words	Simpler Words
amplitude	fullness or abundance
terminate	finalize or finish
delineate	describe or explain
facilitate	assist or help
moribund	dying or wasting away
manifested	established or shown
to endeavor	to attempt or to try
habituated	accustomed or familiar

Cross out the inflated words in each sentence. Then substitute clear, simple language for the inflated words.

ACTIVITY 4

EXAMPLE

The ~~conflagration~~ was ~~initiated~~ by an arsonist.

. . . fire was started by an arsonist. _____

1. Rico and his brother do not interrelate in a harmonious manner.

   _____

2. The meaning of the movie's conclusion eluded my comprehension.

   _____

3. The departmental conference will commence promptly at two o'clock.

   _____

4. Utilization of the left lane is proscribed except for buses.

   _____

5. When my writing implement malfunctioned, I asked the professor for another.

   _____

REVIEW TEST 1

Certain words are italicized in the following paragraph. These words are either clichés, slang, or inflated. In the space between the lines, replace the italicized words with more effective diction. In a few cases, the italicized words are not needed at all. Simply cross those words out.

Immigration in the United States has some costs and risks, but it can be _strategically advantageous_ for the country _time and time again_. Many people fear or resent _persons who have emigrated from foreign lands_, afraid that they may be involved in dangerous, illegal activities or simply planning to _purloin_ jobs from American citizens. Thinking about immigrants in these _nullifying_ terms ignores all the _indisputably wonderful augmentations_ that immigrants have made to our country. In fact, it is often said that this country wouldn't exist if it weren't for immigrants. Over the past decades, millions of average citizens, as well as some of our most

Academic

influential residents, have immigrated to the United States. Henry Kissinger, fifty-sixth Secretary of State and 1973 Nobel Peace Prize winner, was born in Germany and immigrated in 1938 when he was fifteen. Ang Lee, writer and director, was born in Taiwan and moved to the United States, *and got his act together* to study at the University of Illinois at Urbana-Champaign and to complete his Master's degree in Film Production at New York University. Without immigration, people like Albert Einstein, Madeleine Albright, and I.M. Pei wouldn't have had *the golden opportunities that come once in a lifetime* to affect American society as they did. Without immigration, American palates would not know *the delectations of the palatableness* of salsa, foie gras, paprika-based dishes, or pizza. Without immigration, about 25 percent of American *physicians of medicine* would not be in the United States. Without immigration, the United States of America would not have the history it does. *Last but not least,* when the discussion of immigration comes up, people *should be cognizant that it isn't an either-or issue.*

Tests

Bradley Sauter/Alamy Stock Photo

What is it about these signs that makes them funny? How could each one be fixed so that its message is clearer?

Mark Bourdillon/Alamy Stock Photo

CHAPTER
39

Editing Tests

This chapter will give you practice in editing to correct sentence-skills mistakes.

Key Terms

editing: correcting sentence-skills mistakes.

proofreading: carefully examining written text to correct typographical mistakes and other related errors.

proofreading symbols: shorthand notations intended to call attention to typographical mistakes and other related errors.

The ten editing tests in this chapter provide practice in correcting sentence-skills mistakes. Remember that if you don't edit carefully, you run the risk of sabotaging much of the work you have put into a paper. If readers see too many surface flaws, they may assume that you don't place much value on what you have to say, and they may not give your ideas a fair hearing. Checking your work to eliminate sentence-skills errors is a basic part of clear, effective writing.

In five of the tests, the spots where errors occur have been underlined; your job is to identify and correct each error. In the other five tests, you must locate as well as identify and correct the errors.

EDITING HINTS

1. Have at hand two essential tools: a good dictionary and a sentence-skills handbook (you can use Part 4 of this book).

2. Use a sheet of paper to cover your essay so that you will expose only one sentence at a time. Look for errors in grammar, spelling, and typing. It may help to read each sentence out loud. If a sentence does not read clearly and smoothly, chances are something is wrong.

3. Pay special attention to the kinds of errors you tend to make. For example, if you tend to write run-ons or fragments, be especially on the lookout for those errors.

4. Refer to the boxed proofreading symbols in the "Proofreading" section of Chapter 5 for help in marking corrections.

EDITING TEST 1

In the spaces at the bottom, write the numbers of the eight word groups that contain fragments or run-ons. Then, in the spaces between the lines and in the margin, edit by making necessary corrections.

Academic

[1]Filming a television show is much more difficult than many viewers know. [2]On screen, viewers may see one or two hosts, but behind the scenes, dozens of people are working hard to create the show. [3]The person with the money behind the show is the executive producer. [4]Whose role is to oversee the work of the producer. [5]The producer, on the other hand, coordinates and supervises all aspects of the production. [6]Production assistants perform various tasks. [7]Like office work, cleaning up, organizing people, and doing whatever the producer needs. [8]The best boy is the primary electrician on the crew, this person coordinates all the lighting technicians, manages the logistics, organizes the equipment, and keeps track of the paperwork. [9]The lighting supervisor works with the script and the lighting department to set up the studio's lighting for overall design. [10]As the title implies, the camera operator operates the camera. [11]But not alone, as the operator is often aided by several camera assistants. [12]The director is the person responsible for getting the script to the screen. [13]And getting the actors to perfect their roles. [14]The film editor actually assembles all the footage this person then organizes it into the final product. [15]Researchers do a variety of jobs like checking facts, developing ideas, and checking for possible legal issues. [16]Script supervisors sit on set and observe every shot closely they take detailed notes on the script to help ensure that the final production has verbal and visual continuity. [17]These are but a few of the many jobs that intertwine to produce the comedies, news shows, and dramas that people enjoy. [18]Watching on their televisions.

1. _____   3. _____   5. _____   7. _____

2. _____   4. _____   6. _____   8. _____

EDITING TEST 2

Identify the ten sentence-skills mistakes at the underlined spots in the student paper that follows. From the box below, choose the letter that describes each mistake and write that letter in the space provided. (The same kind of mistake may appear more than once.) Then, in the spaces between the lines, edit and correct each mistake.

a. fragment	d. dangling modifier
b. run-on	e. missing comma
c. inconsistent verb tense	f. misuse of capital letter

Academic

George Washington was a land <u>surveyor during</u> the French and Indian
                                    1
Wars, he led the Virginia militia. Twenty years later, when the American

Revolution <u>broke out. Washington</u> commanded the Continental armies. In
            2

1776, <u>after blockading Boston</u>, the city was taken from the British. Later,
        3
however, Washington yielded New York City to the <u>enemy, he</u> retreated to
                                                    4
Pennsylvania. In December, he boosted the sagging morale of

<u>his men crossing</u> the Delaware River on Christmas night he <u>attacks</u> Trenton,
    5   **6**
where Hessians (British allies) were <u>stationed. Then went</u> on to defeat a
                                        7
British army at Princeton. In 1777–1778, the <u>Army</u> spent a miserable winter
                                                8
at <u>Valley Forge Pennsylvania</u>. Later, however, it defeated the British at
    9
Monmouth, New Jersey. This battle marked a turning point. In 1781, by

winning the battle of <u>Yorktown Washington</u> brought the war to an end.
                        10

1. _____   3. _____   5. _____   7. _____   9. _____
2. _____   4. _____   6. _____   8. _____   10. _____

EDITING TEST 3

Identify the eight sentence-skills mistakes at the underlined spots in the student paper that follows. From the box below, choose the letter that describes each mistake and write that letter in the space provided. (The same kind of mistake may appear more than once.) Then, in the spaces between the lines, edit and correct each mistake.

a. fragment	e. dangling modifier
b. run-on	f. missing comma
c. homonym error	g. wordiness
d. misplaced modifier	h. cliché

Anyone who doubts the possibility of <u>falling in love at first sight</u> without
1
meeting in person should reconsider <u>they're</u> beliefs. John G. Neihardt and
2
his wife, Mona Martinson, fell in love through the magic of letters. Mona, a

sculptor who studied with Auguste Rodin, first heard of <u>Neihardt. When</u> she
3
read his book of poetry, *A Bundle of Myrhh*. <u>Shortly after reading the

book, Neihardt received</u> her first letter, and a correspondence between the
4
two ensued. They finally met six months after the first letter exchange. <u>Their

love had grown, they married the next day.</u> For the next fifty <u>years</u> the couple
5 6
remained faithful to each other. They had four daughters, Enid, Sigurd, Hilda,

and Alice. When Neihardt died, his ashes were mixed and scattered over the

Missouri River <u>with</u> Mona's. <u>Therefore, one could make the observation that</u>
7 8
long before e-mail, Match.com, and eHarmony, people were falling in love by

writing letters and getting to know each other without actually meeting.

1. _____   3. _____   5. _____   7. _____

2. _____   4. _____   6. _____   8. _____

EDITING TEST 4

Identify the ten sentence-skills mistakes at the underlined spots in the student paper that follows. From the box below, choose the letter that describes each mistake and write that letter in the space provided. (The same kind of mistake may appear more than once.) Then, in the spaces between the lines, edit and correct each mistake.

a. run-on	d. wordiness
b. mistake in subject–verb agreement	e. cliché
c. faulty parallelism	f. fragment

It is this writer's opinion that taking care of the environment is not a
                    1
political issue, but an ethical issue. The environment is not simply pretty

mountains, fields of wild grass, and glacial ice; it is the air we breathe,

the drinking water, and the food we eat. Our air is more polluted than it
        2
were one hundred years ago. We have added cars, factories, and refineries
3
to the world. It goes without saying that as we have built up cities, we have
          4
cut down trees. Thereby upsetting the earth's natural balance. The water we
              5
drink is not only at risk of being overly polluted as more and more people
                                6
need water, it is also becoming a rare resource. Too many people waste

water as they unnecessarily leave faucets running and water lawns too

frequently. Another threat to healthy drinking water is the run-off from all

the fertilizers and pesticides that people are using on lawns, gardens, and

farms. The polluted air, polluted water, and overcrowded world is all also
                                                    7

continued

affecting the food we eat. Not only is it going to be increasingly difficult to

produce the amount of food needed to feed the <u>world</u>, the quality of food
                                              8

is also becoming poorer. If humans <u>doesn't</u> start taking better care of the
                                     9

environment soon, it will <u>be too little too late.</u>
                                10

1. _____   3. _____   5. _____   7. _____   9. _____
2. _____   4. _____   6. _____   8. _____   10. _____

EDITING TEST 5

Identify the ten sentence-skills mistakes at the underlined spots in the paper that follows. From the box below, choose the letter that describes each mistake and write that letter in the space provided. (The same kind of mistake may appear more than once.) Then, in the spaces between the lines, edit and correct each mistake.

a. fragment	e. mistake in pronoun point of view
b. run–on	f. homonym error
c. mistake in subject–verb agreement	g. missing comma
d. mistake in verb tense	

College should be a time to expand horizons by meeting new people,

getting exposure to new <u>ideas and</u> becoming a better critical thinker.
1

Meeting new people <u>are</u> one of the best parts about college. Many
2

colleges have students from around the country, as well as from different

countries. <u>Four</u> example, college students in Texas may meet and perhaps
3

room with students from New York City, Seattle, London, and Tokyo.

Getting to know new people is not only exciting because of possible new

<u>friendships. But</u> it also helps expose <u>you</u> to new ideas. People who grow
4   5

up in different cultures often look at things differently. A student from

London will have a very different perspective on European politics than a

student who lives in Seattle. Meeting new <u>people</u> however, is not the only
6

way college students get exposed to new ideas. Every class that a college

student <u>took</u> exposes that individual to new ideas. Whether <u>its</u> American
7   8

continued

Indian Literature or College Algebra 101, the professor instructing the class

will introduce concepts and methods that will be new to students. These

new ideas, along with new friendships and relationships, will help students

become critical thinkers. With each new experience, students will need <u>too</u>

9

make decisions and form reactions. Many students think they should know

everything when they enter <u>college they</u> should be prepared for all the

10

new people, ideas, and experiences that await them.

1. _____   3. _____   5. _____   7. _____   9. _____
2. _____   4. _____   6. _____   8. _____   10. _____

EDITING TEST 6

Identify the ten sentence-skills mistakes at the underlined spots in the student paper that follows. From the box below, choose the letter that describes each mistake and write that letter in the space provided. (The same kind of mistake may appear more than once.) Then, in the spaces between the lines, edit and correct each mistake.

a. fragment	e. missing capital letter
b. run-on	f. dangling modifier
c. mistake in subject–verb agreement	g. homonym mistake
	h. missing apostrophe
d. missing comma	i. cliché

At one <u>time doctors</u> believed that diseases generated spontaneously—
1

on their own. Louis Pasteur (1822–95), a <u>french</u> scientist, disproved that.
2

Demonstrating that germs cause many <u>diseases. Pasteur</u> worked <u>like a dog</u>
3   **4**

to convince doctors to sterilize their instruments and wash their hands

before delivering a baby. Pasteur <u>new</u> this would reduce the chances of
5

<u>infection as a result,</u> it would save the lives of many women who otherwise
6

would have died giving birth. Another of <u>Pasteurs</u> discoveries was a vaccine
7

for rabies. Retarding the progress of the disease, <u>a boy bitten by a rabid</u>
8

<u>dog was saved.</u> Finally, Pasteur is responsible for a <u>process that stop</u> the
9

growth of bacteria in wine and <u>milk,</u> it now bears his name: pasteurization.
10

1. _____   3. _____   5. _____   7. _____   9. _____

2. _____   4. _____   6. _____   8. _____   10. _____

Locate the ten sentence-skills mistakes in the following passage. The mistakes are listed in the box below. As you locate each mistake, write the number of the word group in the space provided. Then, in the space between the lines, edit and correct each mistake.

---

2 fragments _____ _____

2 run-ons _____ _____

1 mistake in verb tense _____

1 missing capital letter _____

1 nonparallel structure _____

1 missing comma after introductory material _____

2 missing apostrophes _____ _____

Academic

[1]Sicily is an island situated just west of the southern tip of mainland Italy. [2]The Strait of Messina separates the island from the mainland at its narrowest point, it is two miles wide. [3]Over the years, Sicily has been ruled by Phoenicians, Greeks, Romans, Spanish, British, and people from France. [4]It is currently part of Italy. [5]Because of its colorful history. [6]Sicily has a lot to offer tourists. [7]Tourists interested in Greek architecture can visit the beautiful Greek theater of Syracuse, the Temple of Apollo, and the Altar of Hieron II they were all built between the 6th and 5th centuries BC! [8]For those interested in Roman mosaics the Villa Romana del Casale at Piazza Armerina contains the largest collection of ancient mosaics in the world. [9]Architecture lovers will enjoy a side trip to the hill town, Monreale, where they can visit the towns splendid Romanesque cathedral. [10]not every tourist attraction in Sicily has to do with history. [11]Visitors can wander among the salt pans along the west coast. [12]And experience some of the most spectacular sunsets and ocean views. [13]The most adventurous of tourists, however, should visit Mount Etna, one of the worlds most active volcanoes. [14]Sicily may be a small island, but it offered a world full of adventures.

EDITING TEST 8

Locate the ten sentence-skills mistakes in the following passage. The mistakes are listed in the box below. As you locate each mistake, write the number of the word group in the space provided. Then, in the space between the lines, edit and correct each mistake.

2 fragments _____ _____	1 verb tense mistake _____
1 mistake in subject–verb agreement _____	2 apostrophe mistakes _____ _____
1 missing capital letter _____	3 comma mistakes _____ _____ _____

Academic

¹This weeks history and geography lesson was incredibly fascinating. ²Because it focused on countries that have experienced major changes in the past century. ³The first countries our teacher told us about were countries' that were part of the former Soviet Union. ⁴After the collapse of the Soviet Union, multiple countries like Latvia, Lithuania Georgia, and Uzbekistan eventually gained their independence. ⁵Our teacher also educates us about many countries on the african continent that changed their names to reflect the culture they knew, before they were colonized by other countries. ⁶For instance, in 1975 Dahomey became the People's Republic of Benin, and in 2018 Swaziland changed its name back to its original name eSwatini. ⁷Finally, our teacher explained that several countries on the continent of Asia decided on name changes. ⁸When their governments changed. ⁹For instance, the country of Cambodia were known as the Kingdom of Cambodia, Democratic Kampuchea, and State of Cambodia. ¹⁰Learning about these countries' histories through their name changes was one of the best classroom lessons I have experienced.

EDITING TEST 9

Locate the ten sentence-skills mistakes in the following passage. The mistakes are listed in the box below. As you find each mistake, write the number of the word group in the space provided. Then, in the space between the lines, correct each mistake.

---

2 fragments _____ _____

1 run-on _____

1 mistake in verb tense _____

1 dangling modifier _____

2 missing capital
letters _____ _____

1 mistake in pronoun point of
view _____

1 mistake in pronoun
agreement _____

1 mistake in subject–verb
agreement _____

---

¹The earliest type of paper appeared about five thousand years ago in Egypt it took its name from the papyrus plant. ²The fibers of which were used in its manufacture. ³The kind of paper that you use today probably originated in china in the second century. ⁴However, some historians argue that paper have been invented in that country hundreds of years earlier. ⁵Made of hemp fiber and tree bark, the Arabs brought this new paper to Europe in the fifteenth century via spain. ⁶A country they controlled at the time. ⁷When printing was invented, the manufacture of paper increased greatly. ⁸Today, most paper consist of wood fiber, but they may also contain cotton and other textiles.

EDITING TEST 10

Locate the ten sentence-skills mistakes in the following passage. The mistakes are listed in the box below. As you locate each mistake, write the number of the word group in the space provided. Then, in the space between the lines, edit and correct each mistake.

1 fragment _____	2 missing apostrophes
1 run-on _____	_____ _____
1 mistake in subject-verb agreement _____	1 nonparallel structure _____
2 missing commas after introductory material	1 dangling modifier _____
_____ _____	1 mistake in pronoun point of view _____

Work

¹Being a server is an often underrated job. ²A server needs the tact of a diplomat, they must be as organized as a business executive, and the ability of an acrobat. ³Serving as the link between customers and kitchen, the most demanding diners must be satisfied, and the often temperamental kitchen help must be kept tamed. ⁴Both groups tend to blame servers whenever anything goes wrong. ⁵Somehow, servers are held responsible by the customers for any delay (even if it's the kitchens fault), for an overcooked steak, or for an unavailable dessert. ⁶While the kitchen automatically blames servers for the diners who change their orders or return those burned steaks. ⁷In addition servers must simultaneously keep straight who ordered what at each table, who is yelling for the check, and whether the new arrivals want cocktails or not.

continued

[8]They must be sure empty tables are cleared, everyone has refills of coffee, and no one is scowling because a request for more rolls are going unheard. [9]Finally servers must travel a hazardous route between the busy kitchen and the crowded dining room, they have to dodge a diners leg in the aisle or a swinging kitchen door. [10]Additionally, you must do this while balancing a tray heaped with steaming platters. [11]The hardest task of servers, though, is trying to maintain a decent imitation of a smile most of the time.

Correction Symbols

Here is a list of symbols the instructor may use when marking papers.

Agr	Correct the mistake in agreement of subject and verb or pronoun and the word the pronoun refers to
Apos	Correct the apostrophe mistake
Bal	Balance the parts of the sentence so they have the same (parallel) form
Cap	Correct the mistake in capital letters
Coh	Revise to improve coherence
Comma	Add a comma
CS	Correct the comma splice
DM	Correct the dangling modifier
Det	Support or develop the topic more fully by adding details
Frag	Attach the fragment to a sentence or make it a sentence
Ital	*Italics*
lc	Use a lowercase (small) letter rather than a capital
MM	Correct the misplaced modifier
¶	Indent for a new paragraph
No¶	Do not indent for a new paragraph
Pro	Correct the pronoun mistake
Quot	Correct the mistake in quotation marks
R-O	Correct the run-on
Sp	Correct the spelling error
Trans	Supply or improve a transition
Verb	Correct the verb or verb form
Wordy	Omit needless words
WW	Replace the word marked with a more accurate one
?	Write the illegible word clearly
/	Eliminate the word, letter, or punctuation mark so slashed
∧	Add the omitted word or words
; /: /- /—	Add semicolon, colon, hyphen, or dash
✔	You have something fine or good here: an expression, a detail, an idea

Readings for Writers

PART 5

Scott Mullin

Juleyka Lantigua-Williams addresses the audience at a Voices of Poetry Thanks for the Giving event.

Education has power. In Juleyka Lantigua-Williams's essay, she argues that students who have criminal histories need to be welcomed at institutions of higher learning in order to better themselves. Can you think of examples of people you know who have been held back because they lacked the educational credentials required?

The eighteen reading selections in Part 5 will help you find topics for writing. (Note that there are also nine professional essays in Part 2.) These selections deal in various ways with interesting, often thought-provoking concerns or experiences of contemporary life. Subjects of the essays include the power of family and self; life goals; practical advice on surviving the first year of college; ways in which the Internet may be affecting our thinking; ways people change society; a comparison of academic writing and public writing; and the challenges of everyday life. The varied subjects should inspire lively class discussions as well as serious individual thought. The selections should also provide a continuing source of high-interest material for a wide range of writing assignments.

The selections serve another purpose as well. They will help develop reading skills, with direct benefits to you as a writer. One benefit is that, through close reading, you will learn how to recognize the thesis in a selection and to identify and evaluate the supporting material that develops the thesis. In your own writing, you will aim to achieve the same essential structure: an overall thesis followed by detailed, valid support for that thesis. A second benefit is that close reading will also help you explore a selection and its possibilities thoroughly. The more you understand about what is said in a piece, the more ideas and feelings you may have about writing on an assigned topic or a related topic of your own. A third benefit of close reading is that you will become more aware of authors' stylistic devices—for example, their introductions and conclusions, their ways of presenting and developing a point, their use of transitions, and their choice of language to achieve a particular tone. Recognizing these devices in other people's writing will help you enlarge your own range of ideas and writing techniques.

The Format of Each Selection

Each selection begins with a short overview that gives helpful background information as well as a brief idea of the topic of the reading. The selection is followed by three sets of questions:

- First, ten "Reading Comprehension" questions help you measure your understanding of the material. These questions involve several important reading skills: understanding vocabulary in context, recognizing a subject or topic, determining a thesis or main idea, identifying key supporting points, and making inferences. Answering the questions will enable you and your instructor to quickly check your basic understanding of a selection. More significantly, as you move from one selection to the next, you will sharpen your reading skills as well as strengthen your thinking skills—two key factors in making you a better writer.

- Following the comprehension questions are four questions on "Structure and Technique" that focus on aspects of a writer's craft, and four questions on "Critical Reading and Discussion" that involve you in reading carefully and thinking actively about a writer's ideas.

Finally, several writing assignments accompany each selection. The assignments range from personal narratives to expository and persuasive essays about issues in the world at large. Many assignments provide detailed guidelines on how to proceed, including suggestions for prewriting and appropriate methods of development. When writing your essay responses to the readings, you will have opportunities to apply all the methods of development presented in Part 2 of this book.

How to Read Well: Four General Steps

Skillful reading is an important part of becoming a skillful writer. Following is a series of four steps that will make you a better reader—of the selections here and in your reading at large.

1. Concentrate as You Read

To improve your concentration, follow these tips:

- First, read in a place where you can be quiet and alone. Don't choose a spot where there are a lot of distractions like TV, music, friends, or family.

- Next, sit upright when you read. If your body is in a completely relaxed position, sprawled across a bed or nestled in an easy chair, your mind is also going to be completely relaxed. The light muscular tension that comes from sitting in a straight chair promotes concentration and keeps your mind ready to work.

- Third, consider using your index finger (or a pen) as a pacer while you read. Lightly underline each line of print with your index finger as you read down a page. Hold your hand slightly above the page and move your finger at a speed that is a little too fast for comfort. This pacing with your index finger, like sitting upright in a chair, creates a slight physical tension that will keep your body and mind focused and alert.

2. Skim Material Before You Read It

In skimming, you spend about two minutes rapidly surveying a selection, looking for important points and skipping secondary material. Follow this sequence when skimming:

- Begin by reading the overview that precedes the selection.

- Then study the title of the selection for a few moments. A good title is the shortest possible summary of a selection; it often tells you in a single word or a few words what a selection is about. For example, the title "The Professor Is a Dropout" suggests that you're going to read about an intriguing, important aspect of someone's work and life.

- Next, form a question (or questions) based on the title. For instance, for the selection titled "The Professor Is a Dropout," you might ask, "What exactly did the professor drop out of? Did the professor drop out of teaching? Did the professor drop out of school? If so, how would that person become a professor?" Using a title to form questions is often a key to locating a writer's thesis, your next concern in skimming.

- Read the first and last couple of paragraphs in the selection. Very often a writer's thesis, if it is directly stated, will appear in one of these places and will relate to the title. For instance, in "The Certainty of Fear" the author says in her final paragraph that "[e]very stage of life brings them; while we may say goodbye to childish fears, there are always others in the wings, waiting to take their place."

- Finally, look quickly at the rest of the selection for other clues to important points. Are there any subheads you can relate in some way to the title? Are there any words the author has decided to emphasize by setting them off in *italic* or **boldface** type? Are there any major lists of items signaled by words such as *first, second, also, another,* and so on?

3. Read the Selection Straight Through with a Pen in Hand

Read the selection without slowing down or turning back; just aim to understand as much as you can the first time through. Write a check or star beside answers to basic questions you formed from the title and beside other ideas that seem important. Number lists of important points: 1, 2, 3, and so on. Circle words you don't understand. Write question marks in the margins next to passages that are unclear and that you will want to reread.

4. Work with the Material

Go back and reread passages that were not clear the first time through. Look up words that block your understanding of ideas and write their meanings in the margin. Also, reread carefully the areas you identified as most important; doing so will enlarge your understanding of the material. Now that you have a sense of the whole, prepare a short written outline of the selection by answering these questions:

- What is the thesis?
- What key points support the thesis?
- What seem to be other important ideas in the selection?

By working with the material in this way, you will significantly increase your understanding of a selection. Effective reading, just like effective writing, does not happen all at once. Rather, it must be worked on. Often you begin with a general impression of what something means, and then, by working at it, you move to a deeper level of understanding.

How to Answer the Comprehension Questions: Specific Hints

The ten reading comprehension questions that follow each selection involve several important reading skills:

- understanding vocabulary in context
- summarizing the selection in a title
- determining the main idea
- recognizing key supporting details
- making inferences

The following hints will help you apply each of these reading skills:

- *Vocabulary in context.* To decide on the meaning of an unfamiliar word, consider its context. Ask yourself, "Are there any clues in the sentence that suggest what this word means?"

- *Subject or title.* Remember that the title should accurately describe the entire selection. It should be neither too broad nor too narrow for the material in the selection. It should answer the question "What is this about?" as specifically as possible. Note that you may at times find it easier to answer the title question after the main-idea question.

- *Main idea.* Choose the statement that you think best expresses the main idea—also known as the *central point*, or *thesis*—of the entire selection. Remember that the title will often help you focus on the main idea. Then ask yourself, "Does most of the material in the selection support this statement?" If you can answer yes, you have found the thesis.

- *Key details.* If you were asked to give a two-minute summary of a selection, the key, or major, details are the ones you would include in that summary. To determine the key details, ask yourself, "What are the major supporting points for the thesis?"

- *Inferences.* Answer these questions by drawing on the evidence presented in the selection and your own common sense. Ask yourself, "What reasonable judgments can I make on the basis of the information in the selection?"

The readings in Part 5 are categorized according to three main themes: Building Self-Awareness; Education and Learning; and Challenging Societal Values. Additionally, these readings represent how authors use a variety of rhetorical modes within their essays to support their points. A complete list of these readings, grouped by rhetorical mode, is provided at the front of this book. It is titled "Readings Listed by Rhetorical Mode" and directly follows the Table of Contents. Note that that list includes the Part 2 essays as well.

Building Self-Awareness

■ READINGS

from Self-Reliance

Ralph Waldo Emerson

Ralph Waldo Emerson was born on May 25, 1803, in Boston, Massachusetts. He is known as an essayist, poet, and the "philosophical voice of the nineteenth century in America." He graduated from Harvard Divinity School and was ordained as a minister, but resigned after the death of his first wife. After his marriage to his second wife, Emerson settled into a life of reading, writing, and lecturing. He died of pneumonia in 1882. This excerpt from *Self-Reliance* demonstrates Emerson's philosophy of individualism.

1 There is a time in every man's education when he arrives at the conviction that envy is ignorance; that imitation is suicide; that he must take himself for better for worse as his portion; that though the wide universe is full of good, no kernel of nourishing corn can come to him but through his toil bestowed on that plot of ground which is given to him to till . . .

2 Trust thyself: every heart vibrates to that iron string. Accept the place the divine providence has found for you, the society of your contemporaries, the connection of events. Great men have always done so, and confided themselves childlike to the genius of their age, betraying their perception that the absolutely trustworthy was seated at their heart, working through their hands, predominating in all their being . . .

3 Whoso would be a man, must be a nonconformist. He who would gather immortal palms must not be hindered by the name of goodness, but must explore if it be goodness. Nothing is at last sacred but the integrity of your own mind. Absolve you to yourself, and you shall have the suffrage of the world. I remember an answer which when quite young I was prompted to make to a valued adviser, who was wont to importune me with the dear old doctrines of the church. On my saying, "What have I to do with the sacredness of traditions, if I live wholly from within?" my friend suggested,—"But these impulses may be from below, not from above." I replied, "They do not seem to me to be such; but if I am the Devil's child, I will live then from the Devil." No law can be sacred to me but that of my nature.

Good and bad are but names very readily transferable to that or this; the only right is what is after my constitution, the only wrong what is against it . . .

What I must do is all that concerns me, not what the people think. This rule, 4 equally arduous in actual and in intellectual life, may serve for the whole distinction between greatness and meanness. It is the harder because you will always find those who think they know what is your duty better than you know it. It is easy in the world to live after the world's opinion; it is easy in solitude to live after our own; but the great man is he who in the midst of the crowd keeps with perfect sweetness the independence of solitude . . .

For nonconformity the world whips you with its displeasure. And therefore a 5 man must know how to estimate a sour face. The by-standers look askance on him in the public street or in the friend's parlor. If this aversion had its origin in contempt and resistance like his own he might well go home with a sad countenance; but the sour faces of the multitude, like their sweet faces, have no deep cause, but are put on and off as the wind blows and a newspaper direct . . .

The other terror that scares us from self-trust is our consistency; a reverence 6 for our past act or word, because the eyes of others have no other data for computing our orbit than our past acts, and we are loath to disappoint them . . .

A foolish consistency is the hobgoblin of little minds, adored by little states- 7 men and philosophers and divines. With consistency a great soul has simply nothing to do. He may as well concern himself with his shadow on the wall. Speak what you think now in hard words, and tomorrow speak what tomorrow thinks in hard words again, though it contradict every thing you said today.—"Ah, so you shall be sure to be misunderstood."—Is it so bad, then, to be misunderstood? Pythagoras was misunderstood, and Socrates, and Jesus, and Luther, and Copernicus, and Galileo, and Newton, and every pure and wise spirit that ever took flesh. To be great is to be misunderstood.

READING COMPREHENSION

1. The word *bestowed* in "through his toil bestowed on that plot of ground" (paragraph 1) means

   a. used or applied to.

   b. given as a gift.

   c. provided with housing.

   d. taken.

2. The word *predominating* in "working through their hands, predominating in all their being" (paragraph 2) means

   a. to have advantages in numbers.

   b. to have insignificance.

c. to exert controlling influence.

d. to dominate.

3. The word *absolve* in "Absolve you to yourself" (paragraph 3) means

    a. blame.

    b. free from guilt.

    c. release from sin.

    d. to incriminate.

4. Which of the following would be a good alternative title for this selection?

    a. Inconsistency Is Key

    b. Be Understood

    c. Good vs. Bad

    d. Don't Conform

5. Which sentence best expresses the main idea of the selection?

    a. People should trust in themselves and say what they truly believe, regardless of what others think.

    b. People should conform to the standards set by the church and great philosophers.

    c. People should do everything they can to avoid being misunderstood.

    d. People should always act to do good and never do wrong.

6. According to Emerson, what is the main source of greatness in a person?

    a. religion

    b. beauty

    c. a person's individuality

    d. conforming among people

7. Emerson refers to the "integrity of your own mind" (paragraph 3) and defines it within the paragraph. Which of the following is part of his definition?

    a. following the teachings of the church

    b. following the teachings of the Devil

    c. following one's conscience

    d. following the teaching of great philosophers

8. *True or False?* _____ Emerson values traditional wisdom over original thoughts.

9. Emerson calls "foolish consistency" the "hobgoblin of little minds." What does he mean by this?

   a. People need to remain consistent in their beliefs forever.

   b. People should never remain consistent in their beliefs.

   c. People who stay consistent in their beliefs, despite new knowledge, could make mistakes.

   d. People should change their beliefs every time they learn new ideas.

10. According to Emerson's essay, which virtue does society demand the most?

   a. self-reliance

   b. conformity

   c. consistency

   d. truth

STRUCTURE AND TECHNIQUE

1. Emerson begins his second paragraph with "Trust thyself: every heart vibrates to that iron string." What does he mean by this? Why do you think he placed it this early in the essay?

2. Emerson uses several metaphors in his essay. Find one that you identify with and explain your connection.

3. Emerson ends his essay by listing important historical figures who were misunderstood. What is his purpose in ending on such an important note?

4. A title can offer interesting insights into an essay, especially if the title acquires unexpected meanings. Before reading this essay, what did you think the title *Self-Reliance* might refer to? What additional meaning have you gleaned after reading the essay?

CRITICAL READING AND DISCUSSION

1. What does Emerson mean by "envy is ignorance; . . . imitation is suicide"?

2. Emerson states that "the only right is what is after my constitution; the only wrong what is against it." Do you think he means that people can be totally selfish and do whatever they want? Explain your answer.

3. In paragraph 4, Emerson says "it is easy in the world to live after the world's opinion; it is easy in solitude to live after our own." What does he mean by this? What is his purpose in making this statement?

4. What does Emerson say is a consequence of being a nonconformist, and why does he feel this consequence shouldn't put you off?

WRITING ASSIGNMENTS

Assignment 1

Respond to Emerson's essay and his central idea that all people have the potential to be great, if they trust themselves. Do you agree or disagree with what he says? Explain your reaction to his ideas.

Assignment 2

Emerson mentions several accomplished men in his essay. Choose one of the men mentioned, research about his life, and then explain how he fits the statement at the end of the essay: "To be great is to be misunderstood." Alternately, choose a person who has lived since Emerson's time who fits the statement and is known for their accomplishments.

Assignment 3

The promise of the American Dream prevails, but many people think it is a right, not an earned privilege. Most people who have achieved the American Dream have worked hard and haven't simply waited for someone to hand them the prize. People like Steve Jobs and Larry Page started out working long hours in a garage or dorm room, taking risks when necessary (often with unexpected consequences), and pushed themselves to achieve. Write an essay in which you use the principles laid out in *Self-Reliance* as a guide for achieving the dream. You may want to incorporate examples of people who have demonstrated these principles as extra support.

Kimberly White/Stringer/Getty Images

I Became Her Target

Roger Wilkins

Any newcomer in school often has an awkward time breaking the ice with classmates. For Roger Wilkins, being the only Black student in his new school made the situation considerably worse. He could easily have become the focus of the other students' prejudice and fear. Instead, help came in the form of a teacher who quickly made it clear how she saw him—as a class member with something to contribute.

DOMINIC BRACCO II/UPI/Alamy Stock Photo

My favorite teacher's name was "Deadeye" Bean. Her real name was Dorothy. She 1 taught American history to eighth-graders in the junior high section of Creston, the high school that served the north end of Grand Rapids, Michigan. It was the fall of 1944. Franklin D. Roosevelt was president; American troops were battling their way across France; Joe DiMaggio was still in the service; the Montgomery bus boycott was more than a decade away, and I was a twelve-year-old black newcomer in a school that was otherwise all white.

My mother, who had been a widow in New York, had married my stepfather, a 2 Grand Rapids physician, the year before, and he had bought the best house he could afford for his new family. The problem for our new neighbors was that their neighborhood had previously been pristine[1] (in their terms) and that they were ignorant about black people. The prevailing wisdom in the neighborhood was that we were spoiling it and that we ought to go back where we belonged (or alternatively, ought not intrude where we were not wanted). There was a lot of angry talk among the adults, but nothing much came of it.

But some of the kids, those first few weeks, were quite nasty. They threw 3 stones at me, chased me home when I was on foot and spat on my bike seat when I was in class. For a time, I was a pretty lonely, friendless and sometimes

---

[1]*pristine:* pure.

frightened kid. I was just transplanted from Harlem, and here in Grand Rapids, the dominant culture was speaking to me insistently. I can see now that those youngsters were bullying and culturally disadvantaged. I knew then that they were bigoted, but the culture spoke to me more powerfully than my mind and I felt ashamed for being different—a nonstandard person.

I now know that Dorothy Bean understood most of that and deplored it. So 4 things began to change when I walked into her classroom. She was a pleasant-looking single woman, who looked old and wrinkled to me at the time, but who was probably about forty. Whereas my other teachers approached the problem of easing in their new black pupil by ignoring him for the first few weeks, Miss Bean went right at me. On the morning after having read our first assignment, she asked me the first question. I later came to know that in Grand Rapids, she was viewed as a very liberal person who believed, among other things, that Negroes were equal.

I gulped and answered her question and the follow-up. They weren't brilliant 5 answers, but they did establish the facts that I had read the assignment and that I could speak English. Later in the hour, when one of my classmates had bungled an answer, Miss Bean came back to me with a question that required me to clean up the girl's mess and established me as a smart person.

Thus, the teacher began to give me human dimensions, though not perfect ones 6 for an eighth-grader. It was somewhat better to be an incipient[2] teacher's pet than merely a dark presence in the back of the room onto whose silent form my class-mates could fit all the stereotypes they carried in their heads.

A few days later, Miss Bean became the first teacher ever to require me to think. 7 She asked my opinion about something Jefferson had done. In those days, all my opinions were derivative.[3] I was for Roosevelt because my parents were, and I was for the Yankees because my older buddy from Harlem was a Yankee fan. Besides, we didn't have opinions about historical figures like Jefferson. Like our high school building or old Mayor Welch, he just was.

After I had stared at her for a few seconds, she said: "Well, should he have 8 bought Louisiana or not?"

"I guess so," I replied tentatively.   9

"Why?" she asked   10

Why! What kind of question was that, I groused silently. But I ventured an 11 answer. Day after day, she kept doing that to me, and my answers became stronger and more confident. She was the first teacher to give me the sense that thinking was part of education and that I could form opinions that had some value.

Her final service to me came on a day when my mind was wandering and I 12 was idly digging my pencil into the writing surface on the arm of my chair. Miss Bean impulsively threw a hunk of gum eraser at me. By amazing chance, it hit

---

[2]*incipient:* about to become.
[3]*derivative:* not original.

my hand and sent the pencil flying. She gasped, and I crept mortified after my pencil as the class roared. That was the icebreaker. Afterward, kids came up to me to laugh about "Old Deadeye Bean." The incident became a legend, and I, a part of that story, became a person to talk to. So that's how I became just another kid in school and Dorothy Bean became "Old Deadeye."

READING COMPREHENSION

1. The word *deplored* in "But some of the kids, those first few weeks, were quite nasty. . . . Dorothy Bean understood most of that and deplored it" (paragraphs 3–4) means
    a. supported.
    b. imitated.
    c. often taught.
    d. disapproved of.

2. The word *groused* in "Why! What kind of question was that, I groused silently" (paragraph 11) means
    a. complained.
    b. agreed.
    c. answered.
    d. yelled.

3. Which of the following would be a good alternative title for this selection?
    a. Education in the Forties
    b. A True Teacher's Pet
    c. Eighth Grade
    d. Teacher's Help

4. Which of the following sentences best expresses the main idea of the selection?
    a. After moving from Harlem to Grand Rapids, Michigan, the author had numerous adjustments to make.
    b. Eighth grade can be a challenging time for a new student.
    c. Using unusual methods, Miss Bean helped her eighth-grade students learn to think for themselves.
    d. A teacher helped the first Black student in school to be accepted and to learn to think for himself.

5. After moving to Grand Rapids, Wilkins felt ashamed of
   a. having a stepfather.
   b. being smart.
   c. having lived in Harlem.
   d. being different.

6. By involving Wilkins in class discussion, Miss Bean helped the other students see him as more than a
   a. stereotype.
   b. liberal.
   c. legend.
   d. bigot.

7. Wilkins writes that before entering Miss Bean's class, he held
   a. no opinions.
   b. no original opinions.
   c. opinions based on careful thought.
   d. opinions on various historical figures.

8. The author implies that some of the bigotry in Grand Rapids was the result of
   a. anger about the war.
   b. ignorance about Black people.
   c. his youth.
   d. ignorance about physicians.

9. In stating "the teacher began to give me human dimensions, though not perfect ones for an eighth-grader" (paragraph 6), the imperfection that Wilkins refers to is his
   a. different race.
   b. inadequate answers.
   c. becoming a teacher's pet.
   d. coming from another state.

10. We can conclude that Dorothy Bean threw an eraser at the author because she
    a. knew the event would become an icebreaker for him.
    b. wanted to knock the pencil from his hand.
    c. wanted to ask his opinion about something.
    d. wanted him to pay attention in class.

STRUCTURE AND TECHNIQUE

1. Which pattern of development—comparison, narration, or description—does Wilkins use in most of his essay? Explain.

2. Which kind of transition signal—addition, time, or space—does Wilkins use to move his essay smoothly from one event to the next? Find at least four different words that are examples of this signal.

3. In the first paragraph, Wilkins chooses to provide some historical background for his story. Why do you think he chose the specific details mentioned there? What might have been lost if these details had been excluded from the essay?

4. A title can offer interesting insights into an essay, especially if the title acquires unexpected meanings. Before reading this essay, what did you think the title "I Became Her Target" might refer to? What additional meanings do you think Wilkins intended?

CRITICAL READING AND DISCUSSION

1. What does Wilkins mean by the term *nonstandard person* (paragraph 3)? Do you think he later felt more like a "standard" person? Why or why not?

2. Wilkins mentions several ways Miss Bean treated him differently from the way he was treated by the other teachers at Creston. How did her approach differ from theirs? What does this approach reveal about Miss Bean—as a teacher and as a person?

3. Wilkins says that initially he was Miss Bean's "incipient teacher's pet" (paragraph 6). But how did Miss Bean's behavior toward him go beyond mere favoritism? In what way did her treatment of Wilkins affect how his peers regarded him?

4. In paragraph 7, Wilkins says, "Miss Bean became the first teacher ever to require me to think." Before Miss Bean's class, what do you suspect Wilkins—and his classmates—were being taught to do in school? Describe a teacher who gave you "the sense that thinking was part of education." In your opinion, what can teachers do to get students to think?

WRITING ASSIGNMENTS

Assignment 1

Dorothy Bean, Wilkins's favorite teacher, obviously had an important influence on him in more ways than one. She helped him become accepted by the other students, she strengthened his self-image, and she helped him learn to think for himself. Write an essay on one of your favorite teachers and the ways that person influenced you.

Like Wilkins, dramatize specific incidents to show how this teacher affected you. Provide whatever background is necessary to put the teacher's influence into perspective. Your thesis will be a general statement that summarizes the teacher's impact on your life, such as this one: "Mrs. Croson, my sixth-grade teacher, helped me in ways that strengthened all of the rest of my education." Then go on in your introduction to list three specific ways the teacher influenced you. An example of such a plan of development is "She gave me confidence and taught me the joys of reading and writing."

Alternatively, write an essay on three of your favorite teachers. Your thesis might be about the characteristics the three teachers shared or how they influenced you.

Assignment 2

Wilkins suggests that the students in his new school misjudged him because at first they saw him only as a stereotype, a stranger with no particular personal characteristics. Perhaps we are all subject to prejudging people, if not because of their race, then for another reason. Did a person who made a good impression on you ever turn out to be boring and mean? Did a boss you thought was overly strict ever turn out to be supportive and teach you a lot? Write an essay about someone who was really quite different from what you initially thought they would be. You may wish to consider the following characteristics, which often lead people to prejudge each other:

age

gender

race

sexual preference

size

clothing

job

Begin your essay by explaining in vivid detail your first impression and what caused it. Then go on to narrate some experiences you had with the person and how these experiences changed your mind about them.

Alternatively, write about an individual or individuals who have prejudged you. Explain what those people thought of you and why, and describe how they treated you. If they came to change their minds, explain why and how your relationship changed.

Assignment 3

Mike Watson Images Limited/Glow Images

Write an essay in which you contrast your best teacher and your worst teacher. Make a list of the qualities that made one teacher excellent and the other ineffective or worse. Focus on three pairs of contrasting qualities, using either a *one-side-at-a-time* or a *point-by-point method* of development (see Chapter 13, "Comparison and/ or Contrast"). Following are some elements of teaching to consider as you plan your essay:

grasp of the subject

ability to communicate

ability to motivate

interest in students

classroom presentation

sense of humor

In addition, consider what you or other students learned or did not learn, such as the following:

subject matter

ways to learn

ways to think

self-confidence

methods of cooperation

Stepping into the Light

Tanya Savory

PREVIEW

What would you do if you were convinced that people would reject, even despise you if they knew who you really were? Would you dare to be yourself and risk their condemnation? Or would you do your best to conform to their expectations? In this selection, Tanya Savory tells how she came to terms with her identity as a gay woman. In doing so, she draws a parallel between fair treatment for gays and the civil rights struggles of her youth.

One night in April when I was barely seven years old, my mother told me to put   1
on my Sunday dress—Dad was taking the family to a church across town. None of this made sense to me. After all, it was a Thursday, it was nearly bedtime, and our church was right next door. Dad was the minister, so all we did was walk across a parking lot to get to church. Why were we going across town?

After what seemed like an endless drive, we were winding slowly through a   2
neighborhood I'd never seen before. Suddenly we were in front of a big wooden building with no windows. Streams of people were pouring in, all of them quiet and many of them hugging or holding hands. When our family walked into the church, many people turned to stare at us for a moment—nearly everyone in the church was Black, and we were white. But then a friend of my father's, a young Black minister, rushed over to greet us and led us to a pew.

Throughout that evening, the tall Black woman sitting next to me turned to smile   3
at me again and again even though there were tears in her eyes. I was amazed by her hat full of flowers and even some bird feathers, so I smiled back. No one wore hats like that in our church. I gazed at her hat until I became drowsy and drifted in and out of sleep, occasionally waking up to hear voices joined in song. Many songs were sung that night that I knew, but at the end of the service everyone joined hands and sang a slow, moving song that I'd never heard before: *We shall overcome, we shall overcome, we shall overcome some day. . . .* The tall woman next to me put one arm around me and lifted the other into the air, tears streaming down her face.

It was April 4th, 1968, and Martin Luther King Jr. had been shot and killed just   4
five hours earlier.

When I was a senior in high school, I sat on the front porch with my dad 5 one warm South Carolina afternoon and asked him about that night.

"Weren't you afraid?" I asked   6

"Afraid? Of what?" my dad asked, giving me a kind of funny look.   7

"Well, you know," I said awkwardly, "afraid of the kind of white people who 8 hate Blacks. What if they had found out that we were at that service that night? Weren't you afraid of what they might think or do?"

My dad stared at me for a long moment before he answered. "Your mother and I 9 have never been *afraid* of what bigots think of us. And we certainly weren't going to be bullied into hiding the way we felt just because some racists thought we were wrong."

"Yeah, but when everyone found out, you lost a lot of friends. Even Aunt Jo 10 still doesn't speak to you," I pointed out.

"Not a lot of friends—a few. But that's a small price to pay to be true to 11 yourself. I'm sorry to lose some friends, but I'd be sorrier to be living my life according to how other people think I should live it."

"Really? I asked. "You really think that?"   12

"Yes. I really *know* that," my dad answered.   13

That night I lay awake for hours thinking about what my dad had said. I knew 14 he was right, but I was 100 percent afraid to be true to myself. I was in a small town in the South in 1978, and I was afraid, very afraid, that I was someone that even open-minded people would despise. Someone who, if I were true to myself, would be laughed at, abandoned by my friends, and worse. Someone whose own mother and father might turn against her. I was afraid I was gay.

This was decades before gay characters on TV or in the movies had become com- 15 monplace. The words "gay marriage" would only have been heard in a punch line to a joke, and, in fact, most people still believed that homosexuality was a mental illness or a crime. In the town where I grew up, it was illegal to be gay—police used to stake out a little rundown cinderblock bar on the other side of the tracks where, supposedly, gay men gathered. It was not uncommon for the police to rough up and handcuff men they saw coming out of this bar. Then they were thrown in the jail for the night for little or no real reason. Most of the townspeople thought this was a good idea.

Every day in the halls at school, I would wonder and worry if my classmates 16 could tell by looking at me. I pretty much looked and acted like any other seventeen-year-old girl. I passed notes in geometry, wore too much mascara, and worried about what I would wear to the prom in April. And like most of my friends, I had a boyfriend that I loved. But something had begun to creep into my conscious-ness about a year earlier—something like the slightest pinprick of light that had grown just a bit brighter every day until I was sure that everyone could see it like a spotlight on me: I didn't love my boyfriend, Mark, the same way I loved my best friend, Karla. I loved her more—I was in love with her. Midway through my senior year in high school, I became so afraid and confused about how I felt that I simply made the choice to stop being friends with Karla. The way I saw it, if I turned off the spotlight, no one would be able to see the real me.

In the darkness, it was easier to hide. I made new friends that I didn't really 17 care too much about. I lost interest in anything that was special or unique about me, not wanting to draw attention to who I was. I went entirely overboard in my devotion to Mark, even suggesting that we get married as soon as we graduated from high school. College and my future no longer mattered to me. All that mattered was escaping the light, the fear of who I really was. It didn't matter that I was confused and miserable as long as I was hidden.

Strange as it may sound today, I was actually relieved when, one Sunday 18 morning, I came across a short and angry article in a Christian magazine that insisted that homosexuality was a sin and that it was a choice. Apparently, all one had to do was change his or her mind about who they loved, *choose* to hate that kind of love, and everything would be okay. Supposedly it was as simple as deciding not to rob a bank or choosing not to eat too much pie. Choose heterosexuality and you get heaven. Otherwise, you get hell. I had made the right choice! In a burst of satisfaction, I decided to tell my father everything I had been through and how I had made the right decision. After all, he was a minister. Surely he'd be proud of me.

Thankfully, he was not.   19

"Is your decision based on who you really are or who you want people to 20 think you are?" was my dad's first question.

I was stunned. This was not how I had expected my father to respond at all. 21 No one I knew had ever said anything about it being okay to be gay. In fact, no one ever talked about it at all except to make fun of it. I paused for a long time before answering. Finally, I quietly said, "I'm not sure."

I don't remember what else was said, but my father hugged me. And that was 22 a great turning point, a great source of light in my life.

Decades later, I look back on that year as a strange, murky time full of con- 23 fusion about myself and about the world around me. Luckily, I had parents who, though they worried about how the world around me would treat me, did not try to change me. They never once suggested that there was anything "wrong" with me. But most of the gay people I know who grew up in that same era were not so lucky: One friend tells a story of his seventy-five-year-old grandmother chasing him down the street with a shotgun when she found out he was gay. "She thought I'd be better off dead," he explained. "Luckily, her aim was bad." Another friend describes how her parents changed the locks on the doors, leaving a note that simply read, "Don't come back." Perhaps worst of all was a friend whose own family boycotted his funeral when he died of AIDS.

It's hard to imagine where that kind of hate comes from. What is it about love 24 between two people of the same sex that creates such anger and hostility? Some people, like my friend's seventy-five-year-old grandmother, have an uninformed idea of what gay people are like. They believe all the ridiculous stereotypes that they've read about or seen on TV or in the movies. The stereotypes are frightening to them—and fear is always one step away from hate. To them, gay people are a big group of creepy and weird outcasts full of prissy men who wear dresses and angry women who look like lumberjacks. In reality, of course, gay people are no different from anyone else. We work in the same jobs, eat the same foods, have the same worries, and experience the same joys and sorrows as any other human beings.

Other people, like the parents who locked their daughter out of their house, 25 feel that it is immoral—that it is just plain wrong for two people of the same sex to fall in love. They feel that it is best to just lock it out and hope it goes away. This, in fact, was the same way many people felt about Black and white people falling in love years ago. It just seemed wrong and it made people feel uneasy. They didn't want to have to see it or think about it. So until 1948, it was against the law in the United States for interracial couples to marry. But laws designed to keep people from loving one another and labeling something "immoral" just because it makes some people uncomfortable are always bad ideas.

Still other people, like the family that refused to attend their own son's 26 funeral, claim that God doesn't approve of homosexuality. Like the author of the article I had read so many years ago, they feel it's a sin. There is rarely any argument one can present that can change the minds of people who point to the Bible as their reason for disliking, even hating, gay people. But using religion to justify the way we can mistreat other people, however, is nothing new. In the past, the Bible has been used to justify slavery, segregation, and even denying women the right to vote. As the daughter of a minister, all of this seems strange to me. Like my father, I would like to think that religion is better suited to promoting love—not hate.

Luckily, things are changing. It is definitely not the same dark and mysterious 27 world for a young gay person that it was when I was seventeen. Being gay is actually discussed, and it is no longer considered cool or socially acceptable to make fun of gay people or tell jokes about them. And the majority of Americans say that they think homosexuals should be accepted the same as anyone else. It is no longer unusual to hear about gay actors, singers, athletes, ministers, teachers, firefighters, senators, or even a gay wizard in *Harry Potter*! Even so, there is a long road ahead. In many states it is still legal to fire an employee simply because he or she is gay. And nearly every day there are acts of violence directed at gay people who refuse to hide who they are.

But somewhere in the future, there will certainly come a day when no one 28 has to worry about "coming out" any longer because no one will really care one way or the other about sexual orientation. It will become a non-issue. As it is, gay people rarely spend their time focusing on the fact that they are gay, regardless of how big a deal the media likes to make of a celebrity or politician who has suddenly come out. As talk show host Ellen Degeneres once explained, "I never think about being gay, you know? I'm just living my life . . . I don't wake up every morning and say, 'I'm gay!'" Like any minority, gay people are not looking for special recognition—just fair treatment and the same rights everyone has that make it possible just to live one's life.

Not long ago, I read a story that made me very angry. In a small town in the Midwest, an elderly woman named Sarah had just lost her partner of forty-two years, Laura, to leukemia. As Laura lay dying in the hospital, Sarah pleaded with the hospital staff to allow her to see Laura, but the staff refused—only family was allowed in the rooms of critical patients. That was the law. Laura died alone, and Sarah never got to tell her goodbye. 29

Within a couple days of Laura's death, Laura's only surviving relative, a nephew who hadn't seen his great-aunt in twenty years, came to claim possession of the home Sarah and Laura had shared for decades. The home was in Laura's name, so now the law said it belonged to the nephew. Additionally, the nephew was happy to be legally entitled to all of the home's possessions and all of the money in his aunt's savings. Sarah was left with nothing—no laws protected her because no laws recognized her relationship with Laura. Legally, Sarah and Laura were no more than strangers to one another. Sarah would spend her remaining years in a rundown facility for penniless elderly people. 30

And, legally, Sarah could even have been denied the right to attend her partner's funeral if the nephew hadn't wanted her there. However, the nephew had no interest in attending the service once he secured the deed to the house. 31

On a cold April morning, Sarah and a handful of friends gathered at Laura's gravesite. But just as the service began, shouts were heard. Ten members of an anti-gay hate group had gathered across the road from the rural cemetery. Somehow, they had gotten wind of the fact that a gay person was about to be buried. Standing in a line and holding signs with slogans such as "Fags Burn in Hell" and "God Hates Homos," the group shouted cruel and angry comments throughout the funeral service. *Legally*, they had the right to do this. 32

As I read this story and looked at the pictures of the faces of those holding the signs and yelling, I felt hate. I felt like jumping in my car and driving nonstop to that little town and giving them a dose of their own darkness. I wanted to pay them back for all the despair their kind of hatred brought to gay teens who were, like I had once been, lost and confused. I wanted to spew venom right back at this group. 33

But then, near the end of the story, a comment by the elderly woman, Sarah, stopped me in my tracks. Reporters, who had crassly rushed to the scene, asked Sarah how she felt about the group picketing across the street. "Well," she had said, "I'm sorry they feel that way. But it won't do no good to hate them back." 34

And suddenly, Sarah's words were like a light—a light that seemed to shine all the way back to nearly forty years ago. To a night in April amidst a group of mourners who chose to sing and hold hands in response to hate and violence. A group that was certainly angry and weary of being treated unfairly. And surely, 35 somewhere during that evening, the young Black minister who had led us to a seat must have reminded the congregation of the wisdom of Dr. King's teachings that love would ultimately overcome hate and that light would always overcome darkness.

READING COMPREHENSION

1. The word *crassly* in "Reporters, who had crassly rushed to the scene, asked Sarah how she felt about the group picketing across the street" (paragraph 34) means
   a. crudely.
   b. sensitively.
   c. violently.
   d. cleverly.

2. Which of the following would be a good alternative title for this selection?
   a. The Bigots Among Us
   b. An Unusual Church Service
   c. How I Learned to Love Myself—and My Neighbor
   d. Special Rights for Gays

3. Which sentence best expresses the main idea of the selection?
   a. The author had a difficult time growing up in a small town in the South.
   b. Attitudes toward same-sex relationships have changed over the past several years.
   c. Over time, the author learned to accept her gayness and love her enemies.
   d. Gays have often been the target of cruel and unfair treatment.

4. When Savory read an article in a Christian magazine about being gay, she decided
   a. that the author didn't know what he was talking about.
   b. she had made the right decision in 'choosing' to be straight.
   c. she must keep her sexual orientation a secret from everyone.
   d. to reveal her sexual orientation to her father.

5. According to the article, the majority of Americans
   a. despise gays.
   b. think of gays as a big group of creepy and weird outcasts.
   c. believe in gay marriage.
   d. think gays should be accepted the same as anyone.

6. The hospital staff told Sarah she could not see her partner Laura because

    a. Laura had a highly contagious disease.

    b. Sarah was not a family member.

    c. Sarah was gay.

    d. Laura didn't want any visitors.

7. We can infer that the author would agree that

    a. gay couples should have the same rights as straight couples.

    b. while some people are born gay, others choose to be gay.

    c. it's useless to try to change people's minds about same-sex orientation.

    d. gay couples should be given special rights.

8. Based on paragraphs 18–22, we can infer that the author's dad

    a. believed that people could choose to be gay or straight.

    b. did not think same-sex orientation was sinful.

    c. had little to do with his daughter after she came out as a gay woman.

    d. knew a lot of gay people.

9. In telling the story of Sarah and Laura, the author implies that

    a. Sarah should have inherited Laura's home, possessions, and money.

    b. Laura's nephew didn't care about her, just her money.

    c. Sarah is a forgiving person.

    d. all of the above.

10. We can infer that the picketers at the funeral

    a. will some day change their minds about same-sex orientation.

    b. were basically decent people.

    c. used religion to support their hateful views.

    d. may have been gay themselves.

STRUCTURE AND TECHNIQUE

1. What method of introduction—brief story, stating importance of topic, or broad-to-narrow—does Savory use? Why do you think she chose this way to begin her essay?

2. Which pattern of development—comparison, narration, or description—does Savory use in most of her essay? Explain.

3. A symbol is something that represents something else. In the title and through-out the selection, Savory uses light in a symbolic sense. What does light represent to her? What does the absence of light represent?

4. Savory concludes her essay by going back to where it began—her childhood. In your opinion, is this an effective way to conclude her essay? Why or why not?

CRITICAL READING AND DISCUSSION

1. How does Savory's attitude toward same-sex orientation change in the course of the selection? What incident marks the turning point in her attitude toward her own sexuality?

2. According to the Christian magazine that Savory read as a youth, people can choose to be straight in the same way that they can decide not to rob a bank or eat too much pie. In your view, do members of the LGBTQ community choose their sexual orientation? Explain.

3. What did Savory feel was so unjust about the story of Sarah and Laura? If you agree with her attitude toward the couple, what steps could be taken to make sure that unfortunate situations like these no longer occur?

4. In paragraph 28, Savory states that there will come a day when no one will really care one way or the other about sexual orientation. Do you agree or disagree with her belief? Explain.

WRITING ASSIGNMENTS

Assignment 1

Clearly, Savory's minister father was an important figure in her life. Not only did he show her that it was important to stand up for one's beliefs and to treat others with respect, but he made it easier for her to accept her own sexual orientation. Write an essay about a person in your life who has had a positive influence on you. Provide whatever background is necessary to put the person's influence into perspective. Your thesis will be a general statement that summarizes the person's impact on your life, such as this one: "_____ helped me in ways that affected my life." Then go on in your introduction to list three specific ways that person influenced you. An example of such a plan of development is, "He (she/they) helped me to believe in myself, showed me that it was important to listen to others, and taught me the value of hard work."

Assignment 2

Savory was outraged by the picketers who appeared at Laura's funeral. Although most of us have probably not experienced this level of hatred, we've all seen or heard about situations that have awakened our sense of injustice. Write an essay about three situations you've experienced or learned about that awakened your sense of injustice. In your essay, devote each supporting paragraph to one such anecdote, describing the incident in detail and your response to it. Like Savory, the incident you describe could be something you read about or saw on TV. If you wish, you may suggest ways in which similar incidents might be avoided. Your thesis for the essay might be similar to the following:

> In my life, three incidents in particular have awakened my sense of injustice.

Assignment 3

Although, as Savory points out, LGBTQ people are now more accepted by society than they once were, the question of same-sex marriage is still a controversial topic. Write an essay that takes as its thesis one of the following statements:

> The Supreme Court made the right decision in 2015 to legalize same-sex marriage.

> The word *marriage* should apply only to a union between a man and a woman.

Support your thesis with several points, each developed in its own paragraph. Before you begin, you may wish to research arguments for and against same-sex marriage on the Internet. To access the Internet, use a search engine such as Google (www. google.com) and refer to Chapter 17, "Information Literacy."

The Certainty of Fear

Audra Kendall

PREVIEW

What are you afraid of? Were your fears different five years ago? Will they change as you grow older? In this selection, Audra Kendall shows us that every stage of life brings its own fears—and that all fears revolve around the threat of loss. Do your fears fit the pattern?

I had all the usual childhood fears. I couldn't go to sleep unless the light in my 1 bedroom closet was on. I dreaded that someday when my mother was distracted, Crazy Betty (our local small-town oddball) would grab me in the grocery store. On the hottest summer nights, my feet had to be wrapped tightly in my bedsheets; if one of them hung bare over the side of the bed, who knew what might grab it in its cold, slimy claw?

But all other frights paled before the Great Fear, the *Titanic* of my childhood 2 terrors. That fear—and I admit, I feel a tightening in my stomach typing the words even today—was that something would happen to Monk-Monk.

Looking at Monk-Monk today, you wouldn't see what I see. You'd see a torn, 3 discolored sock monkey, very much past his prime, stuffing leaking from his stumpy tail, holes on his sock-body inexpertly stitched up with thread that doesn't match. I see my dearest childhood friend, my companion of a thousand nights. When I was only two and very ill, an aunt made him for me and delivered him to the hospital. I bonded with him fiercely and rarely let him out of my sight. When no one else was around, Monk-Monk played endless games with me, soaked up my tears, and listened to my secrets.

And then Uncle Ken came to visit. I didn't know Uncle Ken well, and I didn't 4 like him very much. I had the feeling he didn't really like me, either. He clearly thought it was pretty silly that a big first-grader was dragging a sock monkey around, and he teased me by saying he thought he'd take Monk-Monk home to Ohio with him. I clutched Monk-Monk more tightly.

I was at school a few days later when Uncle Ken left. When I came home, I 5 couldn't find Monk-Monk anywhere. I can hardly describe the depths of my panic. I don't think I cried; my terror was beyond that. I could barely breathe. My thoughts raced like a wild animal in a tiny cage. Where was Monk-Monk? What had Uncle Ken done to him? Was he safe somewhere, or had Uncle Ken (and this thought made my heart nearly stop) thrown him out the car window? Was Monk-Monk lying in a weedy strip along the interstate, lonely and cold, never to be loved again?

When we found Monk-Monk wedged behind the sofa (could Uncle Ken really 6 have been mean enough to do that? I never found out), I was limp with relief. For days afterwards I was shaken, crying at the least provocation.

As far as I can remember, that near-loss of Monk-Monk was my first encoun- 7 ter with real, deep-down fear. I felt the threatened loss of something precious to me. And that, I think, is the essence of fear—the threat of loss.

Small children fear the loss of a favorite toy. The fears of adolescents are 8 different. Above almost anything, adolescents fear losing their cool—looking "stupid." They will risk almost anything in order to maintain the illusion that they are cool, composed and in control.

Let me give you an example. A friend of mine had the opportunity to work 9 in Florence, Italy, for a few months. While he was gone, he arranged for his two teenage sons to visit him for a week. The excited boys arrived at the airport and checked in. After sitting down to wait for their flight, one nudged the other. "Look at the tickets," he told his brother. "They don't say 'Florence.'" Indeed, the tickets did not list Florence as the destination. They said "Firenze."

Now, it so happens that Firenze is the Italian name for Florence, so everything 10 was fine. But the boys didn't know that. They thought that through some error, they were being put on the wrong plane for the wrong destination.

So what did they do?   11

Nothing.   12

At the appointed time, they unhappily boarded the plane for Firenze, sat down, 13 and worried silently for six hours that they were going to end up in, oh, maybe South America. Possibly Asia. They had no idea. But the thought of admitting to a ticket agent that they didn't know what "Firenze" meant was more terrifying than the prospect of being dumped, alone, in a strange city on an unknown continent.

The fear of being conspicuous does not usually land teenagers on jet airplanes 14 bound for unknown destinations. But for many adolescents, it rules their daily lives. Such fear is rooted in the enormous self-consciousness that afflicts many adolescents. Psychologist David Elkind has come up with what he calls the "Imaginary Audience Theory" to help explain this period of life.

During adolescence, Elkind says, kids are changing so much so fast (physi- 15 cally, mentally, and emotionally) that they become intensely self-centered. It is literally difficult for them to remember that other individuals have their own lives, thoughts, and feelings, and that they are not focusing their attention on the adolescents. According to Elkind, the adolescent feels as though he or she is on an enormous stage before a watchful audience that is noticing every aspect of his or her behavior. As a result, the adolescent is terrified of doing or saying something that will attract scorn or criticism. As a result, we end up with the teenager whose life is "ruined" by an outbreak of acne; an adolescent who won't leave the house on a bad hair day, or the teen who refuses to return to school after making an embarrassing slip during a speech.

In general, typical adolescent fears don't do great harm. Kids mature and eventually realize a moment's embarrassment isn't that big a deal, and that, in fact, most people aren't paying much attention to them at all. But the fear of being conspicuous can have serious, even tragic results. Adolescents can be so fearful of being criticized that they sometimes go along with the crowd when it is in their best interests not to. Teens get into cars with obviously intoxicated drivers; they go along with the crowd on a shoplifting expedition; they engage in risky sexual behavior, etc., in large part because they are afraid to speak up and risk the scorn of the "audience." 16

In midlife, we generally become more confident and less obsessed with what others are thinking of us. But underneath that veneer of confidence, a new kind of fear grips many middle-aged people. That fear has been expressed in timeless fashion by the Italian poet Dante in his famous poem *The Inferno:* "In the middle of the road, I found myself in a dark wood, with no clear path through." 17

The key word here is "middle." As people enter middle age, they face the unsettling fact that their lives are halfway over. They are no longer youngsters, looking ahead at decades filled with unlimited potential. In looking back at what they have accomplished, many people feel unsatisfied. They may not have achieved the career success they had hoped for. They fear they do not have time to reach goals that they had once dreamed of. They become critical of their own aging bodies. As their parents die and their children grow up and leave home, they feel adrift, no longer certain of their roles in life. Frightening thoughts press in: "My life is heading downhill. I'm running out of time." 18

The result of all this inner turmoil is what is often termed a midlife crisis. Movies and sitcoms often present such a crisis in tragicomic style: the middle-aged guy dumps his wife, dyes his hair, buys a sports car, and begins romancing a woman young enough to be his daughter. The middle-aged woman gets liposuction and a facelift and has an affair with a young personal trainer. 19

There is plenty of evidence that such behavior does occur. Many long-term marriages break up as a result of one or both partners' midlife crisis. The panicky feelings that can result from thinking "Is this all there is?" can make even a formerly happy marriage seem suffocating. 20

However, most midlife crises do not have such dramatic results. More typically, the midlife crisis is a time of inner exploration, of reconsidering one's priorities. It may involve a period of depression, but, fortunately, most people emerge from a midlife crisis feeling relatively satisfied. They come to terms with the idea that youth and its promise are behind them, and learn to appreciate the perhaps quieter joys of mature life. 21

Those joys and a sense of certainty about life's priorities often carry over into the elderly years. Senior citizens' self-knowledge often allows them to state their opinions and explore new interests in a way they did not feel free to in their younger years. 22

But along with the relief from self-consciousness comes another set of fears 23
for the elderly. Those fears center around the increasing frailty of the body and
the accompanying loss of independence.

Some years ago, a television ad featured an elderly woman saying, "Help! I've 24
fallen and I can't get up." The ad became the punch line of many jokes, but the
message was serious. Many elderly people report falling as their greatest fear. They
are not simply concerned with the injury they might suffer. They worry that a fall
might lead to being institutionalized, a step that many elderly people fear deeply.
After a lifetime of independence and, often, of taking care of others, they dread
the idea of being helpless, even a burden to their families.

As a result, many elderly people—especially after having suffered a fall or 25
another injury—become increasingly reluctant to go out into the world to try new
things and keep up with friends. Afraid of being hurt, they become hermit-like,
staying within the confines of their homes. Ironically, this isolation and lack of
exercise can actually hasten the dreaded loss of independence. Mental and physical
activity are both key elements in keeping elderly people in good health.

Benjamin Franklin once wrote, "In this world nothing is certain but death 26
and taxes." Franklin might have added, "and fears." Every stage of life brings
them; while we may say goodbye to childish fears, there are always others in the
wings, waiting to take their place. By being aware of them, we can keep their dark
shadows from adversely affecting our lives.

READING COMPREHENSION

1. The word *turmoil* in "The result of all this inner turmoil is what is often
   termed a midlife crisis" (paragraph 19) means

   a. confusion.

   b. calmness.

   c. sickness.

   d. anger.

2. The word *frailty* in "Those fears center around the increasing frailty of the
   body and the accompanying loss of independence" (paragraph 23) means

   a. physical weakness.

   b. restlessness.

   c. tiredness.

   d. slowness.

3. Which of the following would be a good alternative title for this selection?

   a. Don't Let Fear Rule Your Life

   b. The *Titanic* of My Childhood Fears

 c. Death, Taxes, and Fears

 d. Every Stage of Life Brings Fear

4. Which of the following sentences best expresses the main idea of the selection?

 a. It is impossible to be totally fearless.

 b. Many people allow their fears to negatively affect their behavior.

 c. People fear different things at different stages in their lives.

 d. Some people handle fear better than others.

5. According to the selection, the thing that adolescents fear most of all is

 a. looking "stupid."

 b. flying to overseas destinations.

 c. appearing to be self-conscious.

 d. engaging in risky behavior.

6. The author states that elderly people

 a. are better off leading a quiet existence.

 b. need both mental and physical activity to stay healthy.

 c. sometimes feel relief when they are institutionalized.

 d. have less to fear than adolescents and middle-aged people.

7. Many elderly people report their greatest fear to be

 a. fear of outliving their spouse.

 b. fear of falling.

 c. fear of getting cancer.

 d. fear of becoming deaf and blind.

8. The author infers that Uncle Ken was

 a. an insensitive, mean-spirited man.

 b. kind-hearted, but silly.

 c. wise to conclude that a first-grader should not be dragging around a sock monkey.

 d. probably a child molester.

9. On the basis of paragraphs 20–21, we can infer that the author

 a. strongly disapproves of middle-aged people who have affairs with younger partners.

 b. respects middle-aged people who do new things, like taking up with younger partners, buying sports cars, and having plastic surgery.

 c. is not yet middle-aged.

 d. believes it is important for middle-aged people to learn to appreciate the quieter joys of mature life.

10. Paragraph 26 suggests that

    a. recognizing our fears helps us to keep them from becoming crippling.

    b. Ben Franklin was himself fearless.

    c. all fears are childish.

    d. it is possible, with effort, to become completely fearless.

STRUCTURE AND TECHNIQUE

1. The author uses the first-person approach to introduce her topic. Why do you think she uses this approach? Do you think this approach is effective?

2. In paragraph 5, Kendall writes a series of four questions. Why does she employ this technique? Do you think it is effective?

3. Which kind of transition signal—addition, change of direction, or illustration—does Kendall use to move from a discussion of adolescent fears to a discussion of fears that occur in middle age? From midlife fears to fears of the elderly? Which transitional word does she use in each case?

4. In paragraph 2, Kendall begins a personal anecdote about her own greatest childhood fear. Starting in paragraph 9, she relates another anecdote about the teenage sons of a friend of hers. What do these anecdotes contribute to the essay? How do they relate to the larger point she is trying to make?

CRITICAL READING AND DISCUSSION

1. Kendall calls her greatest childhood fear "the *Titanic* of my childhood terrors." What does the use of this metaphor add to her essay? What was your own greatest childhood fear? Did it actually happen?

2. According to Kendall, different stages of life are characterized by different fears. Which fears accompany which stages? Based upon your observations, is Kendall's thesis accurate? Why or why not?

3. The author writes, "And that, I think, is the essence of fear—the threat of loss." Do you agree with her? What are some examples you can think of in which fears are caused by the threat of loss? If you disagree with her statement, what other fears can you think of that would lie outside this description?

4. What do you think of psychologist David Elkind's "Imaginary Audience Theory" of adolescence? Did you feel the kind of self-consciousness he describes when you were an adolescent? Do you observe that kind of behavior in other teens?

WRITING ASSIGNMENTS

Assignment 1

Clearly, the loss of Monk-Monk was a frightening incident in Kendall's childhood. Write an essay about a frightening incident that occurred during your childhood. Begin by providing some background information about yourself. How old were you when this incident occurred? Where did it take place? Was another person involved besides you? Was this incident something you had feared might happen, or did it happen unexpectedly? Then organize your supporting paragraphs into two or three time phases. First, you may want to review Chapter 9 on the narrative essay. You might conclude your essay by summing up what this incident says about childhood fears in general.

Alternatively, write an essay in which you describe in detail three of your childhood fears. The thesis of your essay might be similar to this:

Like Audra Kendall in "The Certainty of Fear," I had my own childhood fears.

Assignment 2

Kendall writes about fears that characterize different life stages. Think of some people you know of different ages. Then write an essay about three of them who exhibit fears characteristic of their age group. The thesis of your essay might be similar to this:

It is clear to me that my little brother Ben, my thirteen-year-old cousin Ted, and my grandmother Rose have fears that are specific to their age group.

A supporting paragraph about a little brother, for instance, might begin, "Since I'm often around him, I've come to realize that my little brother Ben has some typical childhood fears."

Assignment 3

Often the things we fear never happen, such as the fear the teens in the selection had of landing someplace other than in Florence, Italy. Write an essay in which you contrast your fears about what could have happened on three different occasions with what actually happened. Below are a few possible situations you might describe:

starting school	learning a new skill
going on a first date	beginning a new job
making a class presentation or giving a speech	giving birth
going on a job interview	playing a sport
performing on stage	taking an exam

100 Years of
The Secret Garden

Gretchen Holbrook Gerzina

PREVIEW

Gretchen Holbrook Gerzina holds a Ph.D. from Stanford University and has taught at Vassar College and Barnard College, Columbia University. In this essay, Dr. Gerzina discusses the life of Frances Hodgson Burnett and what influenced her to write *The Secret Garden*.

Gretchen Holbrook Gerzina/Commonwealth Honors College

"With regard to *The Secret Garden*," Frances Hodgson Burnett wrote to her English 1 publisher in October 1910, "do you realize that it is not a novel, but a childs [sic] story though it is gravely beginning life as an important illustrated serial in a magazine for adults. . . . It is an innocent thriller of a story to which grown ups listen spell bound to my keen delight." The "thriller of a story" made its first appearance that fall in *The American Magazine*, but appeared as an actual book a year later.

Now, as the novel is celebrated during its centennial year, it's fascinating to go 2 back and see the modest beginning of a book that is repeatedly cited as one of the most influential and beloved children's books of all time. Yet Burnett would be astonished today to learn that she is known primarily as a writer for children, when the majority of her fifty-three novels and thirteen produced plays were for adults.

When Burnett sat down to write the story of an orphaned girl sent from India 3 to the Yorkshire moors, where she helps herself and others find redemption and health by reviving a forgotten garden, she composed it not in the north of England but in her new home on Long Island. Born in 1849 and raised in Manchester, England, into a middle class family, she moved as a teenager to Tennessee when her widowed mother decided they should emigrate at the end of the Civil War. Although they were poor, Burnett was delighted at giving up the grit and smoke of a factory city for the stunning landscapes of eastern Tennessee. In America she soon began to publish her romantic stories in some of the most popular magazines, eventually becoming hugely famous when she published her sixth novel, *Little Lord Fauntleroy*, in 1886. From the first her work had never been turned down by any publisher, but with *Fauntleroy* she became, and remained, the highest paid woman writer of her time, churning out books and stories with great regularity. Despite the enormous success of *Fauntleroy*, and later of *A Little Princess*, most of her novels and plays were not for a juvenile audience.

By this time a married mother of two living in Washington, DC, she capitalized on her English background in most of her work. Over the years, England remained an active and important part of her life. She crossed the Atlantic no fewer than thirty-three times over her lifetime, often living abroad for a year or two at a time. At the same time, she maintained homes in Washington, and later in New York, and doted upon her very American sons, even when her marriage to their father broke down and through some surprisingly long absences from them. **4**

Two life-changing events contributed to the genesis of *The Secret Garden*, which was written late in her life. The first was the death of her sixteen-year-old son Lionel, who became increasingly ill in Washington while she was living away. Her husband, Dr. Swan Burnett, wrote her urgent letters about their son's failing health, but it was not until the diagnosis turned out to be tuberculosis that she rushed home to take Lionel on a desperate circuit of European spas. When he died in her arms in Paris at the end of 1890, she was completely devastated. For years she threw herself into starting and supporting a clubhouse for boys in London, and in spoiling her remaining son, Vivian. **5**

The second loss was that of her beloved home Maytham Hall in Kent, in southern England, which she had leased for ten years. In 1908 the leaseholder decided to sell the grand house, and Burnett was forced to leave the home where she had spent the happiest months of each year, after shedding her abusive second husband. There she cultivated extensive gardens, held parties, and tamed a robin as she wrote outdoors at a table in a sheltered garden. Both the robin and the gardens made their way into *The Secret Garden*. **6**

With the loss of Maytham Hall, Burnett returned to America where she built adjoining houses for herself and her sister Edith, and for Vivian and his family in Plandome, on Long Island. She returned for several long sojourns to England, and spent her winters with Edith in Bermuda. In both Bermuda and Plandome she threw herself into gardening, with the help of gardeners, designing extensive gardens that produced award-winning blooms. Roses were her favorite, and her trademark, just as they were for Lilias Craven in *The Secret Garden*. **7**

Every year Burnett published a book in time for the Christmas market, and in 1910 she found herself intrigued by the thought of a sallow and unlikeable little girl, her disabled cousin, and a strong nature-loving boy and his benevolent mother. Always taken with her own writing—she often declared that they "came" to her rather than being invented, and she could sometimes be found reading her own books on a stairway, with evident pleasure—she wrote to her publisher that "I love it myself. There is a long deserted **8** garden in it whose locked door is hidden by ivy and whose key has been buried for ten years. It contains also a sort of Faun who charms wild creatures and tame ones and there is a moorland cottage woman who is a sort of Madonna with twelve children—a warm bosomed, sane, wise, simple Mother thing."

Burnett loved the combination of the gothic and the natural worlds, and the 9 ability of children to understand and appreciate them in everyday life. In this new story, she was able, whether she recognized it or not, to recover from her two enormous losses. Unlike her son Lionel, Colin Craven is restored to health at the end of the novel. And unlike Maytham Hall, the gardens at Misselthwaite Manor continually bloomed. When Burnett died in 1924, her friends helped erect a memorial to her in Central Park, consisting of a fountain surrounded by gardens and reading benches. Their prescient choice of *The Secret Garden* for the fountain sculpture surprised the public, for it was, at the time, one of her lesser known and appreciated books, but they knew these were things that were close to the author's heart.

Although it sold well enough at first, *The Secret Garden* lapsed into a kind of 10 near oblivion for many decades. Critics ignored or disparaged it, even at a time when children's literature began receiving more and more critical and scholarly attention. It was the children, along with librarians, who saved it, passing on the book to readers and friends, and creating a special place in their hearts for the story. By the 1960s, its fortunes began to revive, and when the book went out of copyright in 1986, dozens of illustrators and publishers rushed to reproduce it.

As we celebrate 100 years of *The Secret Garden*, the book has never been more 11 popular or influential. Whole shelves in bookstores carry its many editions, and it has been translated into nearly every known language. Children around the world continue to love the story of the children, who with the help of nature and positive thinking, bring the world back to life. As Burnett said to a friend, "I know quite well that it is one of my best finds." Children and adults one hundred years later, still agree.

READING COMPREHENSION

1. The phrase *churning out* in "churning out books and stories with great regularity" (paragraph 3) means

   a. producing in large numbers.

   b. making excessively active.

   c. stirring violently.

   d. producing mechanically.

2. The word *emigrate* in "they should emigrate at the end of the Civil War" (paragraph 3) means

   a. temporarily move to a new home.

   b. move away from one's current homeland.

    c. move to a different neighborhood.

    d. move to a country with a different culture.

3. The word *oblivion* in "*The Secret Garden* lapsed into a kind of near oblivion for many decades" (paragraph 10) means

    a. the fact or condition of forgetting.

    b. removed from existence.

    c. a state of damage or disrepair.

    d. a state of being forgotten or unknown.

4. Which of the following would be a good alternative title for this selection?

    a. The Life of a Children's Author

    b. A Contemporary Woman

    c. Honoring an Important Book

    d. The Secret Behind the Garden

5. Which sentence best expresses the main idea of the selection?

    a. Burnett had a tough life but a prosperous writing career.

    b. Children and adults around the world love *The Secret Garden* because it is such a wonderful story.

    c. Burnett was a novel and play writer and hated being known only for her children's book, *The Secret Garden*.

    d. Burnett's life-changing events helped her create one of the most beloved children's books of all time.

6. According to the author, *The Secret Garden* is now

    a. unfamiliar to children growing up in the twenty-first century.

    b. one of the most influential and beloved children's books of all time.

    c. banned from most reading lists and libraries.

    d. ignored by critics.

7. According to the author, which of the following statements is true?

    a. Burnett's sister was in an abusive relationship.

    b. Burnett remarried after her first husband died.

    c. Burnett struggled with money her entire life.

    d. Burnett was the highest paid woman writer of her time.

8. What was the second loss that "contributed to the genesis of *The Secret Garden*"?

    a. Burnett's divorce from Dr. Swan Burnett

    b. the death of her son Lionel

   c.   her long trips away from her sons

   d.   the loss of her home Maytham Hall

9. Burnett traveled from America to England

   a.   once.

   b.   ten times.

   c.   over thirty times.

   d.   twenty times.

10. After Burnett's death, where did her friends erect a monument?

   a.   Central Park

   b.   Maytham Hall

   c.   Plandome, Long Island

   d.   Washington, DC

STRUCTURE AND TECHNIQUE

1. What method of introduction does the author use in the essay? Why do you think she uses this method?

2. In the beginning of the essay, Gerzina uses a quote from Burnett, but punctuates the quote in the following manner, ". . . but a childs [sic] story though it is gravely . . ." What is the purpose of [sic]?

3. What is the main organizational method used in the essay?

4. The author uses several transitional words in the essay. What are they?

CRITICAL READING AND DISCUSSION

1. In paragraph 4, the author claims that Burnett doted on her sons. Reread paragraphs 4 and 5; do you feel Burnett was a doting mother? Why or why not?

2. In paragraph 9, the author states, "Burnett loved the combination of the gothic and the natural worlds, and the ability of children to understand and appreciate them in everyday life." Do you agree or disagree with the author's opinion? Explain your answer.

3. The author claims that "children, along with librarians" saved *The Secret Garden* by "passing on the book to readers and friends, and creating a special place in their hearts for the story." Can you think of other books that have had similar fates?

4. In 1986, *The Secret Garden* went out of copyright. What does this mean? Why would illustrators and publishers be interested in something going out of copyright?

WRITING ASSIGNMENTS

Assignment 1

The book *The Secret Garden* is about a neglected garden that is brought back to life with love and attention. The garden is a metaphor for people; when people are neglected or forgotten, they wither away. Using this idea of metaphor, write an essay in which you discuss a time you felt neglected, but someone stepped in and helped you blossom. You might focus on a teacher who helped you personally or academically; a family member who helped you find your talents; or a coach who helped you achieve goals others didn't think you would reach.

Assignment 2

Write an essay in which you discuss the merits of one of your favorite children's (or young adult's) books and why it should be celebrated as *The Secret Garden* has been. Your essay should focus on the strengths of the book, why it is significant enough to its genre, and why others should read it.

Assignment 3

Urban gardening has become a widespread phenomenon over the past decade. Gardens have been popping up everywhere—windowsills and decks, rooftops, abandoned city lots, and even in the back of truck beds. Many cities have begun urban gardens to help bring fresh fruits and vegetables to people who have normally been unable to acquire or afford these foods.

In this essay, you are to research the affordability and availability of fresh fruits and vegetables in your town or city. Does your city have farmers' markets? Are grocery stores widely available? Do you have any food deserts (areas where it is difficult to purchase fresh food)? Once you have learned about what your city or town has to offer, create a plan that will increase the availability of affordable fresh food to the citizens of your community. This plan may include locating abandoned or untended lots and getting a community volunteer program together to begin prepping the soil; partnering with local nurseries; and/or working with local colleges and universities. Once you have created a plan, you will want to write your essay as if you are presenting it to your city council. This means that you will need to develop a formal argument that will include an explanation of the process (how it will be created and how people will access the food) and answer potential questions about costs, workers, and logistics.

Education and Learning

Colleges Must Confront Structural Racism

Here are steps they should take now

Kevin V. Collymore

PREVIEW

Kevin V. Collymore received his M.A. in higher education and student affairs from New York University. In this essay, in which he analyzes what colleges should be doing to stop structural racism, he writes from his current perspective as the Assistant Director of Advisement and Student Services at New York University.

Kevin Collymore

The protest movement spurred by the killing of George Floyd aims to dismantle not 1 only instances of overt racism and violence but also institutional racism in every sector of American life. Higher education will not be immune from this reckoning. Whether colleges end up operating in person, online, or in a hybrid format this fall, they will have to confront structural racism head-on.

For students, who have made clear their dissatisfaction with the status quo, 2 empty gestures from administrators will not be enough. They will demand meaningful change. They will demand leadership that is proactive, not reactive. Here are some concrete steps colleges can take to combat structural racism in higher education:

Require implicit-bias training for anyone involved in admissions. Admissions 3 workers are the gatekeepers of institutions. They must understand the importance of their role, as well as the biases they bring to it. All application readers should undergo training to recognize their unconscious biases before every admissions cycle. In her decision upholding affirmative action at Harvard University, Judge Allison D. Burroughs advised implicit-bias training for its admissions team. This valuable and necessary intervention should be adopted at all colleges, even when a federal judge doesn't recommend it.

Guarantee financial aid beyond the first year.   Stop front-loading financial-aid 4 packages to lure first-generation and underrepresented students to your institution. This includes the practice of offering merit-aid scholarships with preconditions for continued funding beyond the first year. A bachelor's degree is a key way for this population to improve not only their lives but also the lives of their immediate families. If students are increasingly burdened by the stress of making payments, it can affect their academic performance, including their ability to stay enrolled. Those who do manage to graduate are likely to become disaffected alumni.

Require de-escalation training for public-safety officers.   The physical safety and 5 well-being of students are core responsibilities of all colleges. Public-safety officers should be required to undergo racial-bias and de-escalation training annually. Further, public-safety administrators should make an effort to participate in stu-dent town halls and student-government meetings to build trust. Students shouldn't hear from the campus police only during a crisis. At Barnard College, for exam-ple, a community-safety group is "charged with discussing broad issues related to campus safety, including concerns about racial and other forms of bias and their consequences."

Adopt a transparent student-protest policy.   At public colleges, students are 6 guaranteed their constitutional right to free assembly. At private institutions, there should be a well-defined process to allow students to organize on campus. Make all processes for student protest transparent and accessible. At Middlebury College and the University of Southern California, for example, student-demonstration policies are embodied in student handbooks, and a single student or a recognized student club can request event space on campus for a demonstration. This differs from many private institutions, where demonstrations require a sponsoring department or group, a policy that can discourage and suppress enthusiasm.

Conduct a campuswide review of building and school names.   Colleges have 7 existed in America since colonial times. The names on all buildings should be examined for potential links to the country's dark history of slavery, Jim Crow, and white supremacy. Princeton University's recent announcement that it will remove Woodrow Wilson's name from its public-policy school is a reminder that reviews should not be limited to Confederate names. Colleges are better off using an independent third party to investigate and provide recommendations. It's not easy to tell a benefactor that his or her money is not welcome at your institution, especially if the benefactor is a trustee or someone else with close ties to the college. Using a third party makes the decision easier.

Punish racial profiling on campus.   Just as we've seen in the larger society, students 8 of color have been forced to engage with campus safety officers or the local police because employees or other students reported them as suspicious. Race-based calls to public safety should be an infraction punishable under the rules governing student and employment conduct.

Create a strategic plan to hire a diverse faculty and staff.   Recruiting to hire a more   9
diverse work force should not be limited to the equal-employment-opportunity statement in a job ad or an additional statement on the value of diversity. Institutions must think creatively about and invest money in hiring and retaining full-time professors and administrators of color. Administrators should ask themselves the following: Have we developed a faculty pipeline to recruit, hire, retain, and tenure full-time faculty of color? Does campus leadership resemble the student body? How diverse is our faculty-tenure committee? Should the chief diversity officer be a standing member of the tenure committee? How often are professional-development opportunities given to administrators of color compared with their white counterparts?

Diversify health and wellness personnel.   After a disturbing national or local event,   10
leaders often urge students by email to take advantage of the college's health and wellness services. But how diverse is that staff at your institution? If your college is like most, the answer is "not very." For too long, we have asked minority students to enter a health and wellness space staffed by professionals who do not resemble them. Hire diverse psychologists, physicians, nurses, social workers, and nutritionists on your campus.

Expand the scope of your chief diversity officer.   If your campus does not have a chief   11
diversity officer, now is a good time to hire one. If your campus already has one, take a closer look at the role. Is it a one-person job? Is there an office dedicated to the work of inclusion? Will the officer's work also encompass faculty development? It should.

Engage in proactive dialogue.   Speak often about race, privilege, diversity, equity,   12
and inclusion. The model and philosophy of proactive advising should not be limited to academic advising. It can be applied across campus. And regardless of the frequency of extracurricular dialogues on campus, students will be looking to further conversations of diversity and inclusion in the curriculum and in course readings. Faculty members should be pressed to show that they are incorporating these ideas into their courses.

Those recommendations are not exhaustive, but they are a start. The time has   13
come for higher education to identify and dismantle all echoes of institutional racism in its midst. Statements disavowing the murders of black men and women are not enough. Sooner or later, the spotlight will be on your college. Will people like what they see?

READING COMPREHENSION

1. The word *disaffected* in "Those who do manage to graduate are likely to become disaffected alumni" (paragraph 4) means
   a. uncompliant.
   b. indifferent.
   c. antagonistic.
   d. mutinous.

2. The word *embodied* in "student-demonstration policies are embodied in student handbooks" (paragraph 6) means
   a. represented in concrete form.
   b. formatted as a set of body paragraphs.
   c. incorporated within.
   d. collected and organized.

3. Which of the following would be a good alternative title for the selection?
   a. Colleges Aren't Doing Enough to Protect Students
   b. College Hiring Practices Aren't Working
   c. Colleges Need to Hire More Diverse Faculty
   d. Colleges Need to Do More for Equity

4. Which sentence best expresses the main idea of the selection?
   a. Colleges need to require implicit-bias training for all admissions counselors.
   b. Colleges have the ability to confront structural racism through concerted actions.
   c. Colleges need to publicly disavow the murders of Black men and women.
   d. Colleges should eliminate racist names from campus buildings and programs.

5. What does the author mean when he states that students will "demand leadership that is proactive, not reactive" (paragraph 2)?
   a. College students expect colleges to put steps into place before things happen rather than put steps into place in a reaction to something happening.
   b. College students expect colleges to put steps into place as a reaction to something happening instead of wasting time planning for things that might happen.

c. College students expect the student government leaders to push for changes in college practices instead of relying on college administrators to make decisions.

d. College students expect student government leaders and college administrators to work together toward positive change.

6. According to the essay, which of the following is NOT a question administrators should ask when creating a plan to hire a more diverse faculty and staff?

a. Have we developed a faculty pipeline to recruit, hire, retain, and tenure full-time faculty of color?

b. Does campus leadership resemble the student body?

c. Should the chief diversity officer be a member of the hiring committee?

d. How often are professional-development opportunities given to administrators of color compared with their white counterparts?

7. True or False? _____ According to the essay, most medical professionals on college campuses reflect the diversity of the student population.

8. When the author says, "Faculty members should be pressed to show that they are incorporating these ideas into their courses" (paragraph 12), he is suggesting that

a. students should hold faculty accountable.

b. administrators should be observing college lectures to check that faculty are properly teaching.

c. faculty should have their lesson plans approved before they teach.

d. faculty should have end-of-semester presentations to show what they taught.

9. We can infer from this essay that the practice of front-loading financial aid means that students

a. are offered good merit-aid scholarships that will be easily renewable every year the students are in college.

b. are offered financial aid that often increases students' stress because of required monthly payments.

c. are offered good financial aid for their first year, but then end up struggling to raise enough money for the next three years.

d. are offered good financial aid for their first year, but it is usually in high-interest loans.

10. After reading the essay, we can infer that *structural racism* is

a. a set of beliefs built into the structure of institutions.

b. the tradition of naming college structures and buildings for racist people.

c. a system of offering financial aid only in the first year.

d. a process of not hiring diverse faculty and staff.

STRUCTURE AND TECHNIQUE

1. In the introduction, Collymore begins with a reference to the killing of George Floyd. What is his purpose in using this reference?

2. The author uses boldfaced statements positioned before each paragraph's topic sentence. What is the purpose of this, and is it effective?

3. In paragraph 6, Collymore references Middlebury College and University of Southern California. What is his purpose in naming these two specific schools?

4. The author ends his essay by addressing the reader. Why do you think he does this, and how do you think his intended audience will react to this ending?

CRITICAL READING AND DISCUSSION

1. In paragraph 3, the author suggests that implicit-bias training should be required. Think about some implicit biases you might have. Why do you think you have these biases, and how do you think they formed?

2. According to the author, how do "student town halls and student-government meetings build trust" (paragraph 5)?

3. In paragraph 8, Collymore states that "race-based calls to public safety officials" should come with punishments in accordance with the college or university rules. Explain what a race-based call is. Do you agree with the author that people should be punished? Have you witnessed or experienced a race-based action? What did you do? What do you think people should do?

4. Collymore points out that public colleges and private colleges are held to different rules regarding student protest policies and argues that all colleges should make the rules public and easy to access. Do you think students should have a right to protest? Should they be required to have a sponsor or fill out a permit? What are the rules at your college, and do you agree or disagree with the rules?

WRITING ASSIGNMENTS

Assignment 1

Write an essay in which you agree or disagree with Collymore's claims. Use specific examples from the essay and your personal experience to support your thesis.

Assignment 2

In paragraph 11, Collymore suggests colleges should "expand the scope" of their chief diversity officer. For this essay, ascertain whether your campus has a chief diversity officer. If so, write a profile on that person. If not, write a letter to your campus president explaining why a chief diversity officer is imperative. You may want to review Chapter 16, "Argument," to help you create a well-developed assignment.

Assignment 3

Collymore argues that de-escalation training for public-safety officers should be mandatory. For this assignment you will research what de-escalation training is, and then write an essay explaining to your college president why the safety officers at your college should be required to have such training. Because this essay may require research, you should review Part 3 to ensure you use credible sources and integrate and cite your sources properly.

How to Make It in College, Now That You're Here

Brian O'Keeney

PREVIEW

The author of this selection presents a compact guide to being a successful student. He will show you how to pass tests, how to avoid becoming a student zombie, how to find time to fit in everything you want to do, and how to deal with personal problems while keeping up with your studies. These and other helpful tips have been culled from the author's own experience and his candid interviews with fellow students.

Today is your first day on campus. You were a high school senior three months ago. 1 Or maybe you've been at home with your children for the last ten years. Or maybe you work full time and you're coming to school to start the process that leads to a better job. Whatever your background is, you're probably not too concerned today with staying in college. After all, you just got over the hurdle (and the paperwork) of applying to this place and organizing your life so that you could attend. And today, you're confused and tired. Everything is a hassle, from finding the classrooms to standing in line at the bookstore. But read my advice anyway. And if you don't read it today, clip and save this article. You might want to look at it a little further down the road.

By the way, if this isn't your very first day, don't skip this article. Maybe you 2 haven't been doing as well in your studies as you'd hoped. Or perhaps you've had problems juggling your work schedule, your class schedule, and your social life. If so, read on. You're about to get the inside story on making it in college. On the basis of my own experience as a final-year student, and after dozens of interviews with successful students, I've worked out a no-fail system for coping with college. These are the inside tips every student needs to do well in school. I've put myself in your place, and I'm going to answer the questions that will cross (or have already crossed) your mind during your stay here.

What's the Secret of Getting Good Grades?

It all comes down to getting those grades, doesn't it? After all, you came here for 3 some reason, and you're going to need passing grades to get the credits or degree you want. Many of us never did much studying in high school; most of the learning we did took place in the classroom. College, however, is a lot different. You're really on your own when it comes to passing courses. In fact, sometimes you'll feel as if nobody cares if you make it or not. Therefore, you've got to figure out a study system that gets results. Sooner or later, you'll be alone with those books. After that, you'll be sitting in a classroom with an exam sheet on your desk. Whether you stare at that exam with a queasy stomach or whip through it fairly confidently depends on your study techniques. Most of the successful students I talked to agreed that the following eight study tips deliver solid results.

1. Set Up a Study Place.   Those students you see "studying" in the cafeteria or 4 game room aren't learning much. You just can't learn when you're distracted by people and noise. Even the library can be a bad place to study if you constantly find yourself watching the clouds outside or the students walking through the stacks. It takes guts to sit, alone, in a quiet place in order to study. But you have to do it. Find a room at home or a spot in the library that's relatively quiet—and boring. When you sit there, you won't have much to do except study.

2. Get into a Study Frame of Mind.   When you sit down, do it with the attitude 5 that you're going to get this studying done. You're not going to doodle in your note-book or make a list for the supermarket. Decide that you are going to study and learn *now,* so that you can move on to more interesting things as soon as possible.

3. Give Yourself Rewards.   If you sweat out a block of study time, and do a good 6 job on it, treat yourself. You deserve it. You can "psych" yourself up for studying by promising to reward yourself afterward. A present for yourself can be anything from a favorite TV show to a relaxing bath to a dish of double chocolate ice cream.

4. Skim the Textbook First.   Lots of students sit down with an assignment like 7 "Read chapter five, pages 125–150" and do just that. They turn to page 125 and start to read. After a while, they find that they have no idea what they just read. For the last ten minutes, they've been thinking about their five-year-old or what they're going to eat for dinner. Eventually, they plod through all the pages but don't remember much afterward.

In order to prevent this problem, skim the textbook chapter first. This means: 8 look at the title, the subtitles, the headings, the pictures, the first and last paragraphs. Try to find out what the person who wrote the book had in mind when he or she organized the chapter. What was important enough to set off as a title or in bold type? After skimming, you should be able to explain to yourself what the main points of the chapter are. Unless you're the kind of person who would step into an empty elevator shaft without looking first, you'll soon discover the value of skimming.

5. Take Notes on What You're Studying.   This sounds like a hassle, but it works. 9
Go back over the material after you've read it, and jot down key words and phrases
in the margins. When you review the chapter for a test, you'll have handy little things
like "definition of rationalization" or "example of assimilation" in the margins. If
the material is especially tough, organize a separate sheet of notes. Write down definitions, examples, lists, and main ideas. The idea is to have a single sheet that boils
the entire chapter down to a digestible lump.

6. Review After You've Read and Taken Notes.   Some people swear that talking to 10
yourself works. Tell yourself about the most important points in the chapter. Once
you've said them out loud, they seem to stick better in your mind. If you can't talk to
yourself about the material after reading it, that's a sure sign you don't really know
it.

7. Give Up.   This may sound contradictory, but give up when you've had enough. 11
You should try to make it through at least an hour, though. Ten minutes here and
there are useless. When your head starts to pound and your eyes develop spidery red
lines, quit. You won't do much learning when you're exhausted.

8. Take a College Skills Course If You Need It.   Don't hesitate or feel embarrassed 12
about enrolling in a study skills course. Many students say they wouldn't have made
it without one.

How Can I Keep Up with All My Responsibilities without Going Crazy?

You've got a class schedule. You're supposed to study. You've got a family. You've got a 13
husband, wife, boyfriend, girlfriend, child. You've got a job. How are you possibly going
to cover all the bases in your life and maintain your sanity? This is one of the toughest
problems students face. Even if they start the semester with the best of intentions,
they eventually find themselves tearing their hair out trying to do everything they're
supposed to do. Believe it or not, though, it is possible to meet all your responsibilities.
And you don't have to turn into a hermit or give up your loved ones to do it.

The secret here is to organize your time. But don't just sit around half the 14
semester planning to get everything together soon. Before you know it, you'll be
confronted with midterms, papers, family, and work all at once. Don't let yourself
reach that breaking point. Instead, try these three tactics.

1. Monthly Calendar.   Get one of those calendars with big blocks around the 15
dates. Give yourself an overview of the whole term by marking down the due dates
for papers and projects. Circle test and exam days. This way those days don't sneak
up on you unexpectedly.

2. Study Schedule.   Sit down during the first few days of this semester and make 16
up a sheet listing the days and hours of the week. Fill in your work and class hours
first. Then try to block out some study hours. It's better to study a little every day

than to create a huge once-or-twice-a-week marathon session. Schedule study hours for your hardest classes for the times when you feel most energetic. For example, I battled my tax law textbook in the mornings; when I looked at it after 7:00 P.M., I might as well have been reading Chinese. The usual proportion, by the way, is one hour of study time for every class hour.

In case you're one of those people who get carried away, remember to leave 17 blocks of free time, too. You won't be any good to yourself or anyone else if you don't relax and pack in the studying once in a while.

3. "To Do" List. This is the secret that, more than any other, got me through 18 college. Once a week (or every day if you want to), write a list of what you have to do. Write down everything from "write English paper" to "buy cold cuts for lunch." The best thing about a "to do" list is that it seems to tame all those stray "I have to" thoughts that nag at your mind. Just making the list seems to make the tasks "doable." After you finish something on the list, cross it off. Don't be compulsive about finishing everything; you're not Superman or Wonder Woman. Get the important things done first. The secondary things you don't finish can simply be moved to your next "to do" list.

What Can I Do If Personal Problems Get in the Way of My Studies?

One student, Roger, told me this story: 19

> Everything was going OK for me until the middle of the spring semester. I went through a terrible time when I broke up with my girlfriend and started seeing her best friend. I was trying to deal with my ex-girlfriend's hurt and anger, my new girlfriend's guilt, and my own worries and anxieties at the same time. In addition to this, my mother was sick and on a medication that made her really irritable. I hated to go home because the atmosphere was so uncomfortable. Soon, I started missing classes because I couldn't deal with the academic pressures as well as my own personal problems. It seemed easier to hang around my girlfriend's apartment than to face all my problems at home and at school.

Another student, Marian, told me: 20

> I'd been married for eight years and the relationship wasn't going too well. I saw the handwriting on the wall, and I decided to prepare for the future. I enrolled in college, because I knew I'd need a decent job to support myself. Well, my husband had a fit because I was going to school. We were arguing a lot anyway, and he made it almost impossible for me to study at home. I think he was angry and almost jealous because I was drawing away from him. It got so bad that I thought about quitting college for a while. I wasn't getting any support at home, and it was just too hard to go on.

Personal troubles like these are overwhelming when you're going through 21
them. School seems like the least important thing in your life. The two students
above are perfect examples of this. But if you think about it, quitting or failing
school would be the worst thing for these two students. Roger's problems, at least
with his girlfriends, would simmer down eventually, and then he'd regret having
left school. Marian had to finish college if she wanted to be able to live independently. Sometimes, you've just got to hang tough.

But what do you do while you're trying to live through a lousy time? First of 22
all, do something difficult. Ask yourself, honestly, if you're exaggerating small problems as an excuse to avoid classes and studying. It takes strength to admit this, but
there's no sense in kidding yourself. If your problems are serious, and real, try to
make some human contacts at school. Lots of students hide inside a miserable shell
made of their own troubles and feel isolated and lonely. Believe me, there are plenty
of students with problems. Not everyone is getting A's and having a fabulous social
and home life at the same time. As you go through the term, you'll pick up some
vibrations about the students in your classes. Perhaps someone strikes you as a
compatible person. Why not speak to that person after class? Share a cup of coffee
in the cafeteria or walk to the parking lot together. You're not looking for a best
friend or the love of your life. You just want to build a little network of support for
yourself. Sharing your difficulties, questions, and complaints with a friendly person
on campus can make a world of difference in how you feel.

Finally, if your problems are overwhelming, get some professional help. Why do 23
you think colleges spend countless dollars on counseling departments and campus
psychiatric services? More than ever, students all over the country are taking advantage of the help offered by support groups and therapy sessions. There's no shame
attached to asking for help, either; in fact, almost 40 percent of college students
(according to one survey) will use counseling services during their time in school.
Just walk into a student center or counseling office and ask for an appointment. You
wouldn't think twice about asking a dentist to help you get rid of your toothache.
Counselors are paid—and want—to help you with your problems.

Why Do Some People Make It and Some Drop Out?

Anyone who spends at least one semester in college notices that some students 24
give up on their classes. The person who sits behind you in accounting, for example, begins to miss a lot of class meetings and eventually vanishes. Or another
student comes to class without the assignment, doodles in a notebook during
the lecture, and leaves during the break. What's the difference between students
like this and the ones who succeed in school? My survey may be nonscientific,
but everyone I asked said the same thing: attitude. A positive attitude is the key
to everything else—good study habits, smart time scheduling, and coping with
personal difficulties.

What does "a positive attitude" mean? Well, for one thing, it means avoiding 25 the zombie syndrome. It means not only showing up for your classes, but also doing something while you're there. Really listen. Take notes. Ask a question if you want to. Don't just walk into a class, put your mind in neutral, and drift away to never-never land.

Having a positive attitude goes deeper than this, though. It means being mature 26 about college as an institution. Too many students approach college classes like six-year-olds who expect first grade to be as much fun as *Sesame Street*. First grade, as we all know, isn't as much fun as *Sesame Street*. And college classes can sometimes be downright dull. If you let a boring class discourage you so much that you want to leave school, you'll lose in the long run. Look at your priorities. You want a degree, or a certificate, or a career. If you have to, you can make it through a less-than-interesting class in order to achieve what you want. Get whatever you can out of every class. But if you simply can't stand a certain class, be determined to fulfill its requirements and be done with it once and for all.

After the initial high of starting school, you have to settle in for the long haul. 27 If you follow the advice here, you'll be prepared to face the academic crunch. You'll also live through the semester without giving up your family, your job, or *Monday Night Football*. Finally, going to college can be an exciting time. You do learn. And when you learn things, the world becomes a more interesting place.

READING COMPREHENSION

1. The word *queasy* in "with a queasy stomach" (paragraph 3) means
   a. strong.
   b. healthy.
   c. full.
   d. nervous.

2. The word *tactics* in "try these three tactics" (paragraph 14) means
   a. proofs.
   b. problems.
   c. methods.
   d. questions.

3. Which of the following would be a good alternative title for this selection?
   a. Your First Day on Campus
   b. Coping with College
   c. How to Budget Your Time
   d. The Benefits of College Skills Courses

4. Which sentence expresses the main idea of the selection?

   a. In high school, most of us did little homework.

   b. You should give yourself rewards for studying well.

   c. Sometimes personal problems interfere with studying.

   d. You can succeed in college by following certain guidelines.

5. According to the author, "making it" in college means

   a. studying whenever you have any free time.

   b. getting a degree by barely passing your courses.

   c. quitting school until you solve your personal problems.

   d. getting good grades without making your life miserable.

6. If your personal problems seem overwhelming, you should

   a. drop out for a while.

   b. exaggerate them to teachers.

   c. avoid talking about them.

   d. get help from a professional.

7. Which of the following is *not* described by the author as a means of time control?

   a. monthly calendar

   b. to-do list

   c. study schedule

   d. flexible job hours

8. We can infer that the writer of this essay

   a. cares about college students and their success.

   b. dropped out of college.

   c. is very disorganized.

   d. is an A student.

9. From the selection we can conclude that

   a. college textbooks are very expensive.

   b. it is a good practice to write notes in your textbook.

   c. taking notes on your reading takes too much time.

   d. a student should never mark up an expensive book.

10. The author implies that

   a. fewer people than before are attending college.

   b. most college students experience no problems during their first year.

c. all college students experience overwhelming problems.

d. coping with college is difficult.

STRUCTURE AND TECHNIQUE

1. O'Keeney uses a highly structured format in his essay. What are some of the features of this format? Why do you think O'Keeney structured his essay in this way?

2. Does the author clearly state his thesis? If so, where is it stated, and how?

3. What method of introduction does the author use in the section on personal problems (starting with paragraph 19)? What is the value of using this method?

4. In his essay, O'Keeney addresses his audience in the second person—using the word *you*. How does such a technique advance his main point?

CRITICAL READING AND DISCUSSION

1. What, according to O'Keeney, is the secret of getting good grades? Have you used any of O'Keeney's study methods? If so, how useful do you think they have been for you? Are there any that you haven't used but might try? Explain your answer.

2. What does O'Keeney recommend students do to manage their time and responsibilities more effectively? Which of these suggestions are you most likely to use? Which are you least likely to use? Why?

3. What is the secret the author says got him through college? What do you think is the most helpful or important suggestion the author makes in the selection? Give reasons for your choice.

4. Do you agree with the author that Roger and Marian should stay in school? Are there any situations in which it would be better for students to quit school or leave, at least temporarily? Explain, giving examples to support your answer.

WRITING ASSIGNMENTS

Assignment 1

Write an essay similar to the one you've just read that explains how to succeed in some other field—for example, a job, a sport, marriage, child rearing. First, brainstorm three or four problem areas a newcomer to this experience might encounter. Then, under each area you have listed, jot down some helpful hints and techniques for overcoming these problems. For example, a paper on "How to Succeed as a Restaurant Server" might describe the following problem areas:

developing a good memory

learning to do tasks quickly

coping with troublesome customers

Each supporting paragraph in this paper would discuss specific techniques for dealing with these problems. Be sure that the advice you give is detailed and specific enough to really help a person in such a situation. You may find it helpful to look over the essays in Chapter 11.

Assignment 2

Write a letter to Roger or Marian, giving advice on how to deal with the personal problem mentioned in the article. You might recommend the following:

Make other contacts at school. (How? Where?)

See a counselor. (Where? What should this person be told?)

Realize that the problem is not so serious. (Why not?)

In your introductory paragraph, explain why you are writing the letter. Include a thesis statement that says what plan of action you are recommending. Then, in the rest of the paper, explain the plan of action in detail.

Assignment 3

Write an essay contrasting college *as you thought it would be* with college *as it is*. You can organize the essay by focusing on three specific things that are different from what you expected. Or you can cover three areas of difference. For instance, you may decide to contrast your expectations about (1) a college dorm room, (2) your roommate, and (3) dining-hall food with reality. Or you could contrast your expectations about (1) fellow students, (2) college professors, and (3) college courses with reality.

Refer to the section in Chapter 13 on methods of developing comparison or contrast essays to review point-by-point and one-side-at-a-time development. Be sure to make an outline of your essay before you begin to write.

College Lectures:
Is Anybody Listening?

David Daniels

PREVIEW

College students are doodling in their notebooks or gazing off into space as their instructor lectures for fifty minutes. What is wrong with this picture? Many would say that what is wrong is the students. However, the educator and author David Daniels would say that the lecture itself is the problem. As you read this article, see if you agree with Daniels's analysis of lectures and their place in a college education.

Courtesy of David Daniels

A former teacher of mine, Robert A. Fowkes of New York University, likes to tell the story of a class he took in Old Welsh while studying in Germany during the 1930s. On the first day the professor strode up to the podium, shuffled his notes, coughed, and began, "*Guten Tag, Meinen Damen und Herren*" ("Good day, ladies and gentlemen"). Fowkes glanced around uneasily. He was the only student in the course. 1

Toward the middle of the semester, Fowkes fell ill and missed a class. When he returned, the professor nodded vaguely and, to Fowkes's astonishment, began to deliver not the next lecture in the sequence but the one after. Had he, in fact, lectured to an empty hall in the absence of his solitary student? Fowkes thought it perfectly possible. 2

Today, American colleges and universities (originally modeled on German ones) are under strong attack from many quarters. Teachers, it is charged, are not doing a good job of teaching, and students are not doing a good job of learning. American businesses and industries suffer from unenterprising, uncreative executives educated not to think for themselves but to mouth outdated truisms[1] the rest of the world has long discarded. College graduates lack both basic skills and general 3

---

[1]*truisms:* self-evident truths.

culture. Studies are conducted and reports are issued on the status of higher education, but any changes that result either are largely cosmetic or make a bad situation
worse.

One aspect of American education too seldom challenged is the lecture sys- 4
tem. Professors continue to lecture and students to take notes much as they did in
the thirteenth century, when books were so scarce and expensive that few students
could own them. The time is long overdue for us to abandon the lecture system and
turn to methods that really work.

To understand the inadequacy of the present system, it is enough to follow a 5
single imaginary first-year student—let's call her Mary—through a term of lectures
on, say, introductory psychology (although any other subject would do as well). She
arrives on the first day and looks around the huge lecture hall, taken a little aback to
see how large the class is. Once the hundred or more students enrolled in the course
discover that the professor never takes attendance (how can he?—calling the roll
would take far too much time), the class shrinks to a less imposing size.

Some days Mary sits in the front row, from where she can watch the profes- 6
sor read from a stack of yellowed notes that seem nearly as old as he is. She is
bored by the lectures, and so are most of the other students, to judge by the way
they are nodding off or doodling in their notebooks. Gradually she realizes the
professor is as bored as his audience. At the end of each lecture he asks, "Are
there any questions?" in a tone of voice that makes it plain he would much rather
there weren't. He needn't worry—the students are as relieved as he is that the
class is over.

Mary knows very well she should read an assignment before every lecture. However, 7
as the professor gives no quizzes and asks no questions, she soon realizes she needn't
prepare. At the end of the term she catches up by skimming her notes and memorizing
a list of facts and dates. After the final exam, she promptly forgets much of what she
has memorized. Some of her fellow students, disappointed at the impersonality of it all,
drop out of college altogether. Others, like Mary, stick it out, grow resigned to the system
and await better days when, as juniors and seniors, they will attend smaller classes and
at last get the kind of personal attention real learning requires.

I admit this picture is overdrawn—most universities supplement lecture courses 8
with discussion groups, usually led by graduate students; and some classes, such as
first-year English, are always relatively small. Nevertheless, far too many courses
rely principally or entirely on lectures, an arrangement much loved by faculty and
administrators but scarcely designed to benefit the students.

One problem with lectures is that listening intelligently is hard work. Reading 9
the same material in a textbook is a more efficient way to learn because students
can proceed as slowly as they need to until the subject matter becomes clear to
them. Even simply paying attention is very difficult; people can listen at a rate of
four hundred to six hundred words a minute, while the most impassioned[2] professor

---

[2]*impassioned*: enthusiastic.

talks at scarcely a third of that speed. This time lag between speech and comprehension leads to daydreaming. Many students believe years of watching television have sabotaged their attention span, but their real problem is that listening attentively is much harder than they think.

Worse still, attending lectures is passive learning, at least for inexperienced 10 listeners. Active learning, in which students write essays or perform experiments and then have their work evaluated by an instructor, is far more beneficial for those who have not yet fully learned how to learn. While it's true that techniques of active listening, such as trying to anticipate the speaker's next point or taking notes selectively, can enhance the value of a lecture, few students possess such skills at the beginning of their college careers. More commonly, students try to write everything down and even bring tape recorders to class in a clumsy effort to capture every word.

Students need to question their professors and to have their ideas taken seri- 11 ously. Only then will they develop the analytical skills required to think intelligently and creatively. Most students learn best by engaging in frequent and even heated debate, not by scribbling down a professor's often unsatisfactory summary of complicated issues. They need small discussion classes that demand the common labors of teacher and students rather than classes in which one person, however learned, propounds his or her own ideas.

The lecture system ultimately harms professors as well. It reduces feedback to a 12 minimum, so that the lecturer can neither judge how well students understand the material nor benefit from their questions or comments. Questions that require the speaker to clarify obscure points and comments that challenge sloppily constructed arguments are indispensable to scholarship. Without them, the liveliest mind can atrophy. Undergraduates may not be able to make telling contributions very often, but lecturing insulates a professor even from the beginner's naive question that could have triggered a fruitful line of thought.

If lectures make so little sense, why have they been allowed to continue? 13 Administrators love them, of course. They can cram far more students into a lecture hall than into a discussion class, and for many administrators that is almost the end of the story. But the truth is that faculty members, and even students, conspire with them to keep the lecture system alive and well. Lectures are easier on everyone than debates. Professors can pretend to teach by lecturing just as students can pretend to learn by attending lectures, with no one the wiser, including the participants. Moreover, if lectures afford some students an opportunity to sit back and let the professor run the show, they offer some professors an irresistible forum for showing off. In a classroom where everyone contributes, students are less able to hide and professors less tempted to engage in intellectual exhibitionism.

Smaller classes in which students are required to involve themselves in discussion 14 put an end to students' passivity. Students become actively involved when forced to question their own ideas as well as their instructor's. Their listening skills improve dramatically in the excitement of intellectual give-and-take with their instructors and fellow students. Such interchanges help professors do their job better because they allow them to discover who knows what—before final exams, not after. When exams are given in this type of course, they can require analysis and synthesis from the students, not empty memorization. Classes like this require energy, imagination, and commitment from professors, all of which can be exhausting. But they compel students to share responsibility for their own intellectual growth.

Lectures will never entirely disappear from the university scene both be- 15 cause they seem to be economically necessary and because they spring from a long tradition in a setting that values tradition for its own sake. But the lectures too frequently come at the wrong end of the students' educational careers—during the first two years, when they most need close, even individual, instruction. If lecture classes were restricted to junior and senior undergraduates and to graduate students, who are less in need of scholarly nurturing and more able to prepare work on their own, they would be far less destructive of students' interests and enthusiasms than the present system. After all, students must learn to listen before they can listen to learn.

READING COMPREHENSION

1. The word *enhance* in "techniques of active listening . . . can enhance the value of a lecture" (paragraph 10) means
   a. ruin.
   b. ignore.
   c. increase.
   d. claim.

2. The word *atrophy* in "Without [questions and comments], the liveliest mind can atrophy" (paragraph 12) means
   a. waste away.
   b. be unchanged.
   c. compete.
   d. strengthen.

3. Which of the following would be a good alternative title for this selection?
   a. How to Benefit from Lecture Classes
   b. The Necessity of Classroom Lecturing
   c. Problems with Lecture Classes
   d. College Lectures: An Inspirational Tradition

4. Which sentence best expresses the main idea of the selection?

   a. American colleges and universities are being attacked from many sides.

   b. Colleges and universities should offer interactive, not lecture, classes to first-year and second-year students.

   c. College graduates lack basic skills and general culture.

   d. American colleges and universities are modeled on German ones.

5. According to the author, the lecture system

   a. encourages efficient learning.

   b. encourages students to ask questions.

   c. helps professors teach better.

   d. discourages students' attendance and preparation.

6. An example of passive learning is

   a. attending lectures.

   b. writing essays.

   c. doing experiments.

   d. debating a point.

7. To develop their thinking skills, students do not need to

   a. bring recording devices to class.

   b. question professors.

   c. debate.

   d. attend small discussion classes.

8. The author implies that large lecture classes

   a. require students to have well-developed listening skills.

   b. encourage participation.

   c. are more harmful for juniors and seniors than for first-year students.

   d. are a modern invention.

9. *True or False?* _____ Daniels suggests that small classes demand greater effort from both faculty and students.

10. The author implies that administrators love lectures because

    a. students learn better in lectures.

    b. professors teach better through lecturing.

    c. schools make more money on lecture classes.

    d. professors can show off in lectures.

STRUCTURE AND TECHNIQUE

1. Daniels begins his essay with an anecdote about a former teacher of his. How does this introduction relate to his thesis?

2. Does Daniels directly state his thesis? If so, where is it stated?

3. In describing Mary's classroom experience (paragraphs 5–7), Daniels provides numerous details. What are some of these details? How do they relate to the essay's main idea?

4. Daniels's essay is an argument against the lecture system of education. What argumentation techniques does he employ? (See Chapter 16 for information on argumentation.)

CRITICAL READING AND DISCUSSION

1. Daniels states that "listening intelligently is hard work" (paragraph 9) and "[a]ctive learning . . . is far more beneficial for those who have not yet fully learned how to learn" (paragraph 10). Why might Daniels feel that listening is so hard? And why does he feel that active learning is so good?

2. In paragraph 8, Daniels acknowledges that he has exaggerated Mary's negative classroom experience, saying, "I admit this picture is overdrawn." Does this admission strengthen or weaken his argument? Explain.

3. According to Daniels, the lecture system harms professors by reducing feedback from students to a minimum. What is useful about feedback from students?

4. How do your experiences in both lecture classes and smaller classes compare with Daniels's descriptions? As a student, which type of class do you prefer? Why? If you were an instructor, which type of class would you prefer to teach? Why?

WRITING ASSIGNMENTS

Assignment 1

Write an essay in which you contrast a lecture class with a smaller, more interactive class. First make a list of the differences between the two classes. Following are some possible areas of difference you might consider:

opportunities for asking questions

opportunities for discussions

quality of feedback from the instructor

Choose three of the differences you found, and then decide which class you learned more in. You will then have the basis for a thesis statement and three supporting topic sentences. An example of a thesis statement for this essay is

> Because of the different approaches to students' questions, class discussion, and feedback from the instructor in grading papers, I learned a lot more in my first-year English class than in my business lecture class.

That thesis statement could be shortened to

> I learned a lot more in my first-year English class than in my business lecture class.

The three supporting points for this thesis statement are about

> different approaches to students' questions,
>
> class discussion, and
>
> personal feedback on assignments.

Change each of the points listed above into a sentence, and you have your three topic sentences. A topic sentence based on the last point above might be "While my English instructor gave me a lot of useful feedback on my assignments, my business instructor put only a grade on papers." Use specific details from your experience to develop your supporting paragraphs.

Assignment 2

In this selection, Daniels has given some disadvantages of lectures. Write an essay on the advantages of lectures. To support your points, use examples from your personal experience and the experiences of others. Begin by jotting down a list of advantages. Then choose the advantages you have the most to say about and develop those in your essay.

Assignment 3

Which teachers or instructors have you had who were not in a rut, who conducted classes that made you glad to learn? Write a description of your idea of a very good teacher or instructor. Your description may be of someone who actually taught you, or it may be of a fictional person who combines all the traits you have enjoyed (or missed) in your teachers and instructors through the years. Be sure to include plenty of specific examples of classroom activities and their effects on students. Here are a few aspects of teaching that you may wish to use in your description:

mastery of subject matter

ability to excite students about subject

types of activities used

Brainology

Carol S. Dweck

PREVIEW

Carol S. Dweck earned her Ph.D. in Social and Developmental Psychology from Yale University and is the Lewis and Virginia Eaton Professor of Psychology at Stanford University. This article explains her recent research on growth mindset.

Carol Dweck

This is an exciting time for our brains. More and more research is showing that our brains change constantly with learning and experience and that this takes place throughout our lives. 1

Does this have implications for students' motivation and learning? It certainly does. In my research in collaboration with my graduate students, we have shown that what students believe about their brains—whether they see their intelligence as something that's fixed or something that can grow and change—has profound effects on their motivation, learning, and school achievement (Dweck, 2006). These different beliefs, or mindsets, create different psychological worlds: one in which students are afraid of challenges and devastated by setbacks, and one in which students relish challenges and are resilient in the face of setbacks. 2

How do these mindsets work? How are the mindsets communicated to students? And, most important, can they be changed? As we answer these questions, you will understand why so many students do not achieve to their potential, why so many bright students stop working when school becomes challenging, and why stereotypes have such profound effects on students' achievement. You will also learn how praise can have a negative effect on students' mindsets, harming their motivation to learn. 3

Mindsets and Achievement

Many students believe that intelligence is fixed, that each person has a certain 4 amount and that's that. We call this a *fixed mindset,* and, as you will see, students with this mindset worry about how much of this fixed intelligence they possess. A fixed mindset makes challenges threatening for students (because they believe that their fixed ability may not be up to the task) and it makes mistakes and failures demoralizing (because they believe that such setbacks reflect badly on their level of fixed intelligence).

Other students believe that intelligence is something that can be cultivated 5 through effort and education. They don't necessarily believe that everyone has the same abilities or that anyone can be as smart as Einstein, but they do believe that everyone can improve their abilities. And they understand that even Einstein wasn't Einstein until he put in years of focused hard work. In short, students with this *growth mindset* believe that intelligence is a potential that can be realized through learning. As a result, confronting challenges, profiting from mistakes, and persevering in the face of setbacks become ways of getting smarter.

To understand the different worlds these mindsets create, we followed several 6 hundred students across a difficult school transition—the transition to seventh grade. This is when the academic work often gets much harder, the grading gets stricter, and the school environment gets less personalized with students moving from class to class. As the students entered seventh grade, we measured their mindsets (along with a number of other things) and then we monitored their grades over the next two years.

The first thing we found was that students with different mindsets cared about 7 different things in school. Those with a growth mindset were much more interested in learning than in just looking smart in school. This was not the case for students with a fixed mindset. In fact, in many of our studies with students from preschool age to college age, we find that students with a fixed mindset care so much about how smart they will appear that they often reject learning opportunities—even ones that are critical to their success (Cimpian, *et al.*, 2007; Hong, *et al.*, 1999; Nussbaum and Dweck, 2008; Mangels, *et al.*, 2006).

Next, we found that students with the two mindsets had radically different 8 beliefs about effort. Those with a growth mindset had a very straightforward (and correct) idea of effort—the idea that the harder you work, the more your ability will grow and that even geniuses have had to work hard for their accomplishments. In contrast, the students with the fixed mindset believed that if you worked hard it meant that you didn't have ability, and that things would just come naturally to you if you did. This means that every time something is hard for them and requires effort, it's both a threat and a bind. If they work hard at it that means that they aren't good at it, but if they don't work hard they won't do well. Clearly, since just about every worthwhile pursuit involves effort over a long period of time, this is a potentially crippling belief, not only in school but also in life.

Students with different mindsets also had very different reactions to setbacks. 9
Those with growth mindsets reported that, after a setback in school, they would
simply study more or study differently the next time. But those with fixed mindsets
were more likely to say that they would feel dumb, study *less* the next time, and seriously consider cheating. If you feel dumb—permanently dumb—in an academic
area, there is no good way to bounce back and be successful in the future. In a
growth mindset, however, you can make a plan of positive action that can remedy a
deficiency (Hong, *et al.*, 1999; Nussbaum and Dweck, 2008; Heyman, *et al.*, 1992).

Finally, when we looked at the math grades they went on to earn, we found 10
that the students with a growth mindset had pulled ahead. Although both groups
had started seventh grade with equivalent achievement test scores, a growth mindset quickly propelled students ahead of their fixed-mindset peers, and this gap
only increased over the two years of the study.

In short, the belief that intelligence is fixed dampened students' motivation 11
to learn, made them afraid of effort, and made them want to quit after a setback.
This is why so many bright students stop working when school becomes hard.
Many bright students find grade school easy and coast to success early on. But
later on, when they are challenged, they struggle. They don't want to make mistakes and feel dumb—and, most of all, they don't want to work hard and feel
dumb. So they simply retire.

It is the belief that intelligence can be developed that opens students to a love 12
of learning, a belief in the power of effort and constructive, determined reactions
to setbacks.

How Do Students Learn These Mindsets?

In the 1990s, parents and schools decided that the most important thing for kids to 13
have was self-esteem. If children felt good about themselves, people believed, they
would be set for life. In some quarters, self-esteem in math seemed to become more
important than knowing math, and self-esteem in English seemed to become more
important than reading and writing. But the biggest mistake was the belief that you
could simply hand children self-esteem by telling them how smart and talented they
are. Even though this is such an intuitively appealing idea, and even though it was
exceedingly well-intentioned, I believe it has had disastrous effects.

In the 1990s, we took a poll among parents and found that almost 85 percent 14
endorsed the notion that it was *necessary* to praise their children's abilities to give
them confidence and help them achieve. Their children are now in the workforce
and we are told that young workers cannot last through the day without being
propped up by praise, rewards, and recognition. Coaches are asking me where all
the coachable athletes have gone. Parents ask me why their children won't work
hard in school.

Could all of this come from well-meant praise? Well, we were suspicious of the 15 praise movement at the time. We had already seen in our research that it was the most vulnerable children who were already obsessed with their intelligence and chronically worried about how smart they were. What if praising intelligence made all children concerned about their intelligence? This kind of praise might tell them that having high intelligence and talent is the most important thing and is what makes you valuable. It might tell them that intelligence is just something you have and not something you develop. It might deny the role of effort and dedication in achievement. In short, it might promote a fixed mindset with all of its vulnerabilities.

The wonderful thing about research is that you can put questions like this to 16 the test—and we did (Kamins and Dweck, 1999; Mueller and Dweck, 1998). We gave two groups of children problems from an IQ test, and we praised them. We praised the children in one group for their intelligence, telling them, "Wow, that's a really good score. You must be smart at this." We praised the children in another group for their effort: "Wow, that's a really good score. You must have worked really hard." That's all we did, but the results were dramatic. We did studies like this with children of different ages and ethnicities from around the country, and the results were the same.

Here is what happened with fifth graders. The children praised for their intel- 17 ligence did not want to learn. When we offered them a challenging task that they could learn from, the majority opted for an easier one, one on which they could avoid making mistakes. The children praised for their effort wanted the task they could learn from.

The children praised for their intelligence lost their confidence as soon as the 18 problems got more difficult. Now, as a group, they thought they *weren't* smart. They also lost their enjoyment, and, as a result, their performance plummeted. On the other hand, those praised for effort maintained their confidence, their motivation, and their performance. Actually, their performance improved over time such that, by the end, they were performing substantially better than the intelligence-praised children on this IQ test.

Finally, the children who were praised for their intelligence lied about their 19 scores more often than the children who were praised for their effort. We asked children to write something (anonymously) about their experience to a child in another school and we left a little space for them to report their scores. Almost 40 percent of the intelligence-praised children elevated their scores, whereas only 12 or 13 percent of children in the other group did so. To me this suggests that, after students are praised for their intelligence, it's too humiliating for them to admit mistakes.

The results were so striking that we repeated the study five times just to be 20 sure, and each time roughly the same things happened. Intelligence praise, compared to effort (or "process") praise, put children into a fixed mindset. Instead of giving them confidence, it made them fragile, so much so that a brush with difficulty erased their confidence, their enjoyment, and their good performance, and made them ashamed of their work. This can hardly be the self-esteem that parents and educators have been aiming for.

Often, when children stop working in school, parents deal with this by reas- 21 suring their children how smart they are. We can now see that this simply fans the flames. It confirms the fixed mindset and makes kids all the more certain that they don't want to try something difficult—something that could lose them their parents' high regard.

How *should* we praise our students? How *should* we reassure them? By focus- 22 ing them on the process they engaged in—their effort, their strategies, their concentration, their perseverance, or their improvement.

"You really stuck to that until you got it. That's wonderful!"   23

"It was a hard project, but you did it one step at a time and it turned out 24 great!"

"I like how you chose the tough problems to solve. You're really going to 25 stretch yourself and learn new things."

"I know that school used to be a snap for you. What a waste that was. Now 26 you really have an opportunity to develop your abilities."

Brainology

Can a growth mindset be taught directly to kids? If it can be taught, will it enhance 27 their motivation and grades? We set out to answer this question by creating a growth mindset workshop (Blackwell, *et al.*, 2007). We took seventh graders and divided them into two groups. Both groups got an eight-session workshop full of great study skills, but the "growth mindset group" also got lessons in the growth mindset—what it was and how to apply it to their schoolwork. Those lessons began with an article called "You Can Grow Your Intelligence: New Research Shows the Brain Can Be Developed Like a Muscle." Students were mesmerized by this article and its message. They loved the idea that the growth of their brains was in their hands.

This article and the lessons that followed changed the terms of engagement 28 for students. Many students had seen school as a place where they performed and were judged, but now they understood that they had an active role to play in the development of their minds. They got to work, and by the end of the semester the growth-mindset group showed a significant increase in their math grades. The control group—the group that had gotten eight sessions of study skills—showed no improvement and continued to decline. Even though they had learned many useful study skills, they did not have the motivation to put them into practice.

The teachers, who didn't even know there *were* two different groups, singled 29 out students in the growth-mindset group as showing clear changes in their motivation. They reported that these students were now far more engaged with their schoolwork and were putting considerably more effort into their classroom learning, homework, and studying.

Joshua Aronson, Catherine Good, and their colleagues had similar findings 30 (Aronson, Fried, and Good, 2002; Good, Aronson, and Inzlicht, 2003). Their studies and ours also found that negatively stereotyped students (such as girls in math, or African-American and Hispanic students in math and verbal areas) showed substantial benefits from being in a growth-mindset workshop. Stereotypes are typically fixed-mindset labels. They imply that the trait or ability in question is fixed and that some groups have it and others don't. Much of the harm that stereotypes do comes from the fixed-mindset message they send. The growth mindset, while not denying that performance differences might exist, portrays abilities as acquirable and sends a particularly encouraging message to students who have been negatively stereotyped—one that they respond to with renewed motivation and engagement.

Inspired by these positive findings, we started to think about how we could 31 make a growth mindset workshop more widely available. To do this, we have begun to develop a computer-based program called "Brainology." In six computer modules, students learn about the brain and how to make it work better. They follow two hip teens through their school day, learn how to confront and solve schoolwork problems, and create study plans. They visit a state-of-the-art virtual brain lab, do brain experiments, and find out such things as how the brain changes with learning—how it grows new connections every time students learn something new. They also learn how to use this idea in their schoolwork by putting their study skills to work to make themselves smarter.

We pilot-tested Brainology in twenty New York City schools. Virtually all of 32 the students loved it and reported (anonymously) the ways in which they changed their ideas about learning and changed their learning and study habits. Here are some things they said in response to the question, "Did you change your mind about anything?"

I did change my mind about how the brain works . . . I will try harder because 33 *I know that the more you try, the more your brain works.*

Yes . . . I imagine neurons making connections in my brain and I feel like I am 34 *learning something.*

My favorite thing from Brainology is the neurons part where when u learn some- 35 *thing, there are connections and they keep growing. I always picture them when I'm in school.*

Teachers also reported changes in their students, saying that they had become 36 more active and eager learners: "They offer to practice, study, take notes, or pay attention to ensure that connections will be made."

What Do We Value?

In our society, we seem to worship talent—and we often portray it as a gift. Now we 37 can see that this is not motivating to our students. Those who think they have this gift expect to sit there with it and be successful. When they aren't successful, they get defensive and demoralized, and often opt out. Those who don't think they have the gift also become defensive and demoralized, and often opt out as well.

We need to correct the harmful idea that people simply have gifts that trans- 38 port them to success, and to teach our students that no matter how smart or talented someone is—be it Einstein, Mozart, or Michael Jordan—*no one* succeeds in a big way without enormous amounts of dedication and effort. It is through effort that people build their abilities and realize their potential. More and more research is showing there is one thing that sets the great successes apart from their equally talented peers—how hard they've worked (Ericsson, *et al.*, 2006).

Next time you're tempted to praise your students' intelligence or talent, 39 restrain yourself. Instead, teach them how much fun a challenging task is, how interesting and informative errors are, and how great it is to struggle with something and make progress. Most of all, teach them that by taking on challenges, making mistakes, and putting forth effort, they are making themselves smarter.

References

Aronson, J., Fried, C., & Good, C. (2002). Reducing the effects of stereotype threat on African American college students by shaping theories of intelligence. *Journal of Experimental Social Psychology, 38,* 113–125. https://psycnet.apa.org/doi/10.1006/jesp.2001.1491

Binet, A. (1909/1973). *Les idées modernes sur les enfants* [Modern ideas on children]. Paris: Flamarion.

Blackwell, L., Trzesniewski, K., & Dweck, C.S. (2007). Implicit theories of intelligence predict achievement across an adolescent transition: A longitudinal study and an intervention. *Child Development, 78,* 246–263. https://doi.org/10.1111/j.1467-8624.2007.00995.x

Cimpian, A., Arce, H., Markman, E.M., & Dweck, C.S. (2007). Subtle linguistic cues impact children's motivation. *Psychological Science, 18,* 314–316. http://dx.doi.org/10.1111/j.1467-9280.2007.01896.x

Dweck, C.S. (2006). *Mindset.* Random House.

Ericsson, K.A., Charness, N., Feltovich, P.J., & Hoffman, R.R. (Eds.) (2006). *The Cambridge handbook of expertise and expert performance.* Cambridge University Press.

Good, C., Aronson, J., & Inzlicht, M. (2003). Improving adolescents' standardized test performance: An intervention to reduce the effects of stereotype threat. *Journal of Applied Developmental Psychology, 24,* 645–662. https://psycnet.apa.org/doi/10.1016/j.appdev.2003.09.002

Hong, Y.Y., Chiu, C., Dweck, C.S., Lin, D., & Wan, W. (1999) Implicit theories, attributions, and coping: A meaning system approach. *Journal of Personality and Social Psychology, 77,* 588–599. https://psycnet.apa.org/doi/10.1037/0022-3514.77.3.588

Kamins, M., & Dweck, C.S. (1999). Person vs. process praise and criticism: Implications for contingent self-worth and coping. *Developmental Psychology, 35,* 835–847. https://psycnet.apa.org/doi/10.1037/0012-1649.35.3.835

Mangels, J.A., Butterfield, B., Lamb, J., Good, C.D., & Dweck, C.S. (2006). Why do beliefs about intelligence influence learning success? A social-cognitive-neuroscience model. *Social, Cognitive, and Affective Neuroscience, 1,* 75–86. https://dx.doi.org/10.1093%2Fscan%2Fnsl013

Mueller, C.M., & Dweck, C.S. (1998). Intelligence praise can undermine motivation and performance. *Journal of Personality and Social Psychology, 75,* 33–52. https://psycnet.apa.org/doi/10.1037/0022-3514.75.1.33

Nussbaum, A.D., & Dweck, C.S. (2008). Defensiveness vs. remediation: Self-theories and modes of self-esteem maintenance. *Personality and Social Psychology Bulletin, 34*(5), 599–612. https://doi.org/10.1177%2F0146167207312960

READING COMPREHENSION

1. The word *demoralizing* in "it makes mistakes and failures demoralizing" (paragraph 4) means
   a. discouraging.
   b. without morals.
   c. destructive.
   d. weakening.

2. The word *engagement* in "changed the terms of engagement for students" (paragraph 28) means
   a. a hostile encounter between military forces.
   b. the state of being interested and committed.
   c. the state of being in gear.
   d. a promise to be present at a specific time and place.

3. The word *virtually* in "Virtually all of the students loved it" (paragraph 32) means
   a. being powerful or forceful.
   b. simulated or extended by computer software.
   c. for all practical purposes.
   d. almost entirely or nearly all.

4. Which of the following would be a good alternative title for this selection?
   a. Experimenting with Students
   b. Researching the Brain
   c. Why Brains Are Like Muscles
   d. How Students Learn to Study

5. Which sentence best expresses the main idea of the selection?
   a. Students can increase their intelligence through learning and practice.
   b. Intelligence is determined at birth and doesn't change.
   c. Students' success depends on their grades in middle school.
   d. People's brains are muscles that need to be exercised.

6. According to the essay, in the 1990s, parents and schools focused on helping students
   a. get more work done in class to lessen the amount of homework.
   b. get in touch with tutoring services that could provide help.
   c. achieve high grades.
   d. achieve high self-esteem.

7. In the study of fifth graders, those who had been praised for their intelligence
    a. achieved higher grades.
    b. frequently exaggerated their test scores.
    c. approached challenges with confidence.
    d. typically improved their performance in class.

8. The author monitored "several hundred students across a difficult school transition." What transition was this?
    a. the transition from preschool to elementary school
    b. the transition from elementary school to middle school
    c. the transition from middle school to high school
    d. the transition from high school to college

9. *True or False?* _____ According to the author, in our society, we seem to worship talent more than effort.

10. The author implies that
    a. psychological studies like the one she conducted involve risks for students.
    b. an individual's attitude toward intelligence can affect their achievement.
    c. a student's future achievement is largely determined by the fifth grade.
    d. intelligence and talent are established, or fixed, at an early age.

STRUCTURE AND TECHNIQUE

1. Several of the sections throughout the essay explain the methods Dr. Dweck and her graduate students used. Why would she explain her methods to the reader? Does this section affect your opinion of the research and findings?

2. Dweck employs the use of headings in her essay. What is the purpose of these headings? When should a student use headings in an essay?

3. Throughout the essay, Dweck presents several questions. Why do you think she does this, especially when asking questions within an essay is often discouraged in college English courses?

4. Paragraphs 33–35 are statements from some of the students in the study. What is the author's purpose in including these quotations?

CRITICAL READING AND DISCUSSION

1. In paragraph 8, Dweck discusses the idea of effort. Think back to something you had to work very hard to achieve. How did you feel after achieving it?

How does this feeling compare to how you felt when you were given something without any effort on your part?

2. How do you feel about the ethics of the growth mindset study (explained in paragraphs 27–36)? How would you feel if you found out you were in the group who hadn't received the growth mindset information?

3. After reading this essay, has your opinion about intelligence changed? Explain your answer.

4. How could you, your classmates, and teacher create a growth mindset atmosphere in your class?

WRITING ASSIGNMENTS

Assignment 1

React to the essay. Do you think you have had a growth mindset or a fixed mindset in the past? How do you think you could achieve a growth mindset? You may need to review Chapter 9, "Narration," and Chapter 10, "Exemplification," to help you create a strong, thesis-driven essay.

Assignment 2

The author states that seventh grade is the time "when the academic work often gets much harder, the grading gets stricter, and the school environment gets less personalized . . . bright students find grade school easy and coast to success early on. But later on, when they are challenged, they struggle." Think back to your seventh grade experience. Did you find it more challenging than elementary school? Did you struggle or did you find success? Why do you think you had the experience you did? What could you have done differently? Write a response that addresses these questions in a well-organized, thesis-driven essay. You may want to review Chapter 9, "Narration," and Chapter 10, "Exemplification."

Assignment 3

In paragraph 27, Dweck references the article "You Can Grow Your Intelligence: New Research Shows the Brain Can Be Developed Like a Muscle." She asserts that "students were mesmerized by this article and its message." Locate this article, read it, and discuss what you think of the article, whether or not you agree with Dweck's claim, and how your opinion of the article affects your opinion of her essay. You may need to review Part 3, especially Chapters 18, 19, and 20, to help you properly incorporate any quotations or paraphrases you use and to help you create a Works Cited page.

Is Google Making Us Stupid?*

Nicholas Carr

PREVIEW

Nicholas Carr is a well-known author who writes about society, culture, and technology. This passage was originally published in *The Atlantic* and then revised to become the first chapter in his book *The Shallows: What the Internet Is Doing to Our Brains*.

Geraint Lewis/Shutterstock

"Dave, stop. Stop, will you? Stop, Dave. Will you stop, Dave?" So the supercomputer 1
HAL pleads with the implacable astronaut Dave Bowman in a famous and weirdly
poignant scene toward the end of Stanley Kubrick's *2001: A Space Odyssey*. Bowman, having nearly been sent to a deep-space death by the malfunctioning machine,
is calmly, coldly disconnecting the memory circuits that control its artificial "brain."
"Dave, my mind is going," HAL says, forlornly. "I can feel it. I can feel it."

I can feel it, too. Over the past few years I've had an uncomfortable sense 2
that someone, or something, has been tinkering with my brain, remapping the
neural circuitry, reprogramming the memory. My mind isn't going—so far as I
can tell—but it's changing. I'm not thinking the way I used to think. I can feel it
most strongly when I'm reading. Immersing myself in a book or a lengthy article
used to be easy. My mind would get caught up in the narrative or the turns of
the argument, and I'd spend hours strolling through long stretches of prose. That's
rarely the case anymore. Now my concentration often starts to drift after two or
three pages. I get fidgety, lose the thread, begin looking for something else to do.
I feel as if I'm always dragging my wayward brain back to the text. The deep
reading that used to come naturally has become a struggle.

---

*This essay is abridged from the original.

I think I know what's going on. For more than a decade now, I've been spend-   3
ing a lot of time online, searching and surfing and sometimes adding to the great
databases of the Internet. The Web has been a godsend to me as a writer. Research that once required days in the stacks or periodical rooms of libraries can
now be done in minutes. A few Google searches, some quick clicks on hyperlinks,
and I've got the telltale fact or pithy quote I was after. Even when I'm not working,
I'm as likely as not to be foraging in the Web's info-thickets, reading and writing
e-mails, scanning headlines and blog posts, watching videos and listening to pod-
casts, or just tripping from link to link to link. (Unlike footnotes, to which they're
sometimes likened, hyperlinks don't merely point to related works; they propel
you toward them.)

For me, as for others, the Net is becoming a universal medium, the conduit for   4
most of the information that flows through my eyes and ears and into my mind. The
advantages of having immediate access to such an incredibly rich store of information
are many, and they've been widely described and duly applauded. "The perfect recall
of silicon memory," *Wired*'s Clive Thompson has written, "can be an enormous boon
to thinking." But that boon comes at a price. As the media theorist Marshall McLu-
han pointed out in the 1960s, media are not just passive channels of information.
They supply the stuff of thought, but they also shape the process of thought. And
what the Net seems to be doing is chipping away my capacity for concentration and
contemplation. My mind now expects to take in information the way the Net distrib-
utes it: in a swiftly moving stream of particles. Once I was a scuba diver in the sea
of words. Now I zip along the surface like a guy on a Jet Ski.

I'm not the only one. When I mention my troubles with reading to friends   5
and acquaintances—literary types, most of them—many say they're having similar
experiences. The more they use the Web, the more they have to fight to stay
focused on long pieces of writing. Some of the bloggers I follow have also begun
mentioning the phenomenon. Scott Karp, who writes a blog about online media,
recently confessed that he has stopped reading books altogether. "I was a lit major
in college, and used to be [a] voracious book reader," he wrote. "What happened?"
He speculates on the answer: "What if I do all my reading on the web not so
much because the way I read has changed, i.e. I'm just seeking convenience, but
because the way I THINK has changed?"

Bruce Friedman, who blogs regularly about the use of computers in medicine, also   6
has described how the Internet has altered his mental habits. "I now have almost totally
lost the ability to read and absorb a longish article on the web or in print," he wrote
earlier this year. A pathologist who has long been on the faculty of the University of
Michigan Medical School, Friedman elaborated on his comment in a telephone conversation with me. His thinking, he said, has taken on a "staccato" quality, reflecting
the way he quickly scans short passages of text from many sources online. "I can't read
War and Peace anymore," he admitted. "I've lost the ability to do that. Even a blog
post of more than three or four paragraphs is too much to absorb. I skim it."

Anecdotes alone don't prove much. And we still await the long-term neurological 7 and psychological experiments that will provide a definitive picture of how Internet use affects cognition. But a recently published study of online research habits, conducted by scholars from University College London, suggests that we may well be in the midst of a sea change in the way we read and think. As part of the five-year research program, the scholars examined computer logs documenting the behavior of visitors to two popular research sites, one operated by the British Library and one by a U.K. educational consortium, that provide access to journal articles, e-books, and other sources of written information. They found that people using the sites exhibited "a form of skimming activity," hopping from one source to another and rarely returning to any source they'd already visited. They typically read no more than one or two pages of an article or book before they would "bounce" out to another site. Sometimes they'd save a long article, but there's no evidence that they ever went back and actually read it. The authors of the study report:

> It is clear that users are not reading online in the traditional sense; indeed there 8 are signs that new forms of "reading" are emerging as users "power browse" horizontally through titles, contents pages and abstracts going for quick wins. It almost seems that they go online to avoid reading in the traditional sense.

Thanks to the ubiquity of text on the Internet, not to mention the popularity 9 of text-messaging on cell phones, we may well be reading more today than we did in the 1970s or 1980s, when television was our medium of choice. But it's a different kind of reading, and behind it lies a different kind of thinking—perhaps even a new sense of the self. "We are not only *what* we read," says Maryanne Wolf, a developmental psychologist at Tufts University and the author of *Proust and the Squid: The Story and Science of the Reading Brain*. "We are *how* we read." Wolf worries that the style of reading promoted by the Net, a style that puts "efficiency" and "immediacy" above all else, may be weakening our capacity for the kind of deep reading that emerged when an earlier technology, the printing press, made long and complex works of prose commonplace. When we read online, she says, we tend to become "mere decoders of information." Our ability to interpret text, to make the rich mental connections that form when we read deeply and without distraction, remains largely disengaged.

Reading, explains Wolf, is not an instinctive skill for human beings. It's not 10 etched into our genes the way speech is. We have to teach our minds how to translate the symbolic characters we see into the language we understand. And the media or other technologies we use in learning and practicing the craft of reading play an important part in shaping the neural circuits inside our brains. Experiments demonstrate that readers of ideograms, such as the Chinese, develop a mental circuitry for reading that is very different from the circuitry found in those of us whose written language employs an alphabet. The variations extend across many regions of the brain, including those that govern such essential cognitive functions as memory and the interpretation of visual and auditory stimuli. We can expect as well that the circuits woven by our use of the Net will be different from those woven by our reading of books and other printed works. . . .

. . . In Google's world, the world we enter when we go online, there's little 11 place for the fuzziness of contemplation. Ambiguity is not an opening for insight but a bug to be fixed. The human brain is just an outdated computer that needs a faster processor and a bigger hard drive.

The idea that our minds should operate as high-speed data-processing machines 12 is not only built into the workings of the Internet, it is the network's reigning business model as well. The faster we surf across the Web—the more links we click and pages we view—the more opportunities Google and other companies gain to collect information about us and to feed us advertisements. Most of the proprietors of the commercial Internet have a financial stake in collecting the crumbs of data we leave behind as we flit from link to link—the more crumbs, the better. The last thing these companies want is to encourage leisurely reading or slow, concentrated thought. It's in their economic interest to drive us to distraction.

Maybe I'm just a worrywart. Just as there's a tendency to glorify technological 13 progress, there's a countertendency to expect the worst of every new tool or machine. In Plato's *Phaedrus*, Socrates bemoaned the development of writing. He feared that, as people came to rely on the written word as a substitute for the knowledge they used to carry inside their heads, they would, in the words of one of the dialogue's characters, "cease to exercise their memory and become forgetful." And because they would be able to "receive a quantity of information without proper instruction," they would "be thought very knowledgeable when they are for the most part quite ignorant." They would be "filled with the conceit of wisdom instead of real wisdom." Socrates wasn't wrong—the new technology did often have the effects he feared—but he was shortsighted. He couldn't foresee the many ways that writing and reading would serve to spread information, spur fresh ideas, and expand human knowledge (if not wisdom).

The arrival of Gutenberg's printing press, in the 15th century, set off another 14 round of teeth gnashing. The Italian humanist Hieronimo Squarciafico worried that the easy availability of books would lead to intellectual laziness, making men "less studious" and weakening their minds. Others argued that cheaply printed books and broadsheets would undermine religious authority, demean the work of scholars and scribes, and spread sedition and debauchery. As New York University professor Clay Shirky notes, "Most of the arguments made against the printing press were correct, even prescient." But, again, the doomsayers were unable to imagine the myriad blessings that the printed word would deliver.

So, yes, you should be skeptical of my skepticism. Perhaps those who dismiss 15 critics of the Internet as Luddites or nostalgists will be proved correct, and from our hyperactive, data-stoked minds will spring a golden age of intellectual discovery and universal wisdom. Then again, the Net isn't the alphabet, and although it may replace the printing press, it produces something altogether different. The kind of deep reading that a sequence of printed pages promotes is valuable not just for the knowledge we acquire from the author's words but for the intellectual vibrations those words set off within our own minds. In the quiet spaces opened up by the sustained, undistracted reading of a book, or by any other act of contemplation, for that matter, we make our own associations, draw our own inferences and analogies, foster our own ideas. Deep reading, as Maryanne Wolf argues, is indistinguishable from deep thinking.

If we lose those quiet spaces, or fill them up with "content," we will sacrifice 16 something important not only in our selves but in our culture. In a recent essay, the playwright Richard Foreman eloquently described what's at stake:

> I come from a tradition of Western culture, in which the ideal (my ideal) was 17 the complex, dense and "cathedral-like" structure of the highly educated and articulate personality—a man or woman who carried inside themselves a personally constructed and unique version of the entire heritage of the West. [But now] I see within us all (myself included) the replacement of complex inner density with a new kind of self—evolving under the pressure of information overload and the technology of the "instantly available."

As we are drained of our "inner repertory of dense cultural inheritance," Foreman 18 concluded, we risk turning into "'pancake people'—spread wide and thin as we connect with that vast network of information accessed by the mere touch of a button."

I'm haunted by that scene in *2001*. What makes it so poignant, and so weird, is 19 the computer's emotional response to the disassembly of its mind: its despair as one circuit after another goes dark, its childlike pleading with the astronaut—"I can feel it. I can feel it. I'm afraid"—and its final reversion to what can only be called a state of innocence. HAL's outpouring of feeling contrasts with the emotionlessness that characterizes the human figures in the film, who go about their business with an almost robotic efficiency. Their thoughts and actions feel scripted, as if they're following the steps of an algorithm. In the world of *2001*, people have become so machinelike that the most human character turns out to be a machine. That's the essence of Kubrick's dark prophecy: as we come to rely on computers to mediate our understanding of the world, it is our own intelligence that flattens into artificial intelligence.

READING COMPREHENSION

1. The word *pithy* in "I've got the telltale fact or pithy quote I was after" (paragraph 3) means

   a. perfect.

   b. meaningful.

   c. redundant.

   d. lengthy.

2. The word *ubiquity* in "thanks to the ubiquity of text on the Internet" (paragraph 9) means

   a. simplicity.

   b. complexity.

   c. restricted access.

   d. presence everywhere.

3. The word *myriad* in "the doomsayers were unable to imagine the myriad blessings" (paragraph 14) means

   a. undefined.

   b. abundant.

   c. versatile.

   d. wonderful.

4. Which of the following would be a good alternative title for this selection?

   a. Why We No Longer Read

   b. Rewiring the Brain

   c. The Truth as Socrates Saw It

   d. Dangerous Internet

5. Which sentence best expresses the main idea of the selection?

   a. Our reliance on technology is affecting our ability to think.

   b. The Internet is providing a multitude of ways to better research.

   c. Technology is making research much quicker and easier.

   d. Reading is not an instinctive skill in the way that speaking is.

6. According to the author, what does it mean to "power browse"?

   a. browse the Internet for hours and hours with no break

   b. browse the Internet quickly searching for the exact information

   c. browse sites horizontally and quickly through titles and abstracts

   d. browse sites quickly, jumping from one web page to another

7. Why did Socrates express distress over the development of writing?

   a. He was illiterate and was worried that he would no longer be able to keep up with society and its ideas.

   b. He was worried that easy availability of books would lead to intellectual laziness and weakened minds.

c. He was fearful that as people wrote things down, they would lose their ability to commit things to memory.

d. He was worried that as people wrote down an increasing number of ideas, human knowledge would expand too quickly.

8. *True or False?* _____ According to the author, the Internet is going to create the next golden age of intellectual discovery and universal wisdom.

9. According to the essay, being turned into a "pancake" person means becoming

a. someone who is able to navigate and contextualize all the information available to them.

b. someone who has so many things to get done that they are unable to get any work done.

c. someone who is able to create a wide web of concentration that allows them to complete great amounts of work.

d. someone who is stretched thin as they attempt to connect to all the available information.

10. We can infer that the author believes which of the following statements?

a. He is grateful for the way the Internet has changed the way he researches.

b. He is worried he has forgotten how to properly research.

c. He embraces the Internet, but he is wary of what it is doing to us.

d. He is fearful of the Internet and uses it only because he has to.

STRUCTURE AND TECHNIQUE

1. Carr uses a metaphor to compare how he used to read to how he now reads. Find the metaphor and explain it.

2. In paragraph 5, Carr says that when he mentions "my troubles with reading to friends and acquaintances—literary types, most of them—many say they're having similar experiences." Why does he emphasize that he is talking to literary types?

3. Throughout the essay, Carr quotes several people like Bruce Friedman, Maryanne Wolf, and Clay Shirky. Why does he include these quotations?

4. Explain how the author uses paragraphs 1 and 19 to frame his essay. How do these two paragraphs work together to enhance the essay?

CRITICAL READING AND DISCUSSION

1. Think of all the reading you do, as described in paragraph 9. How much do you think you actually read each day? Does what you've discovered change your belief about yourself as a reader?

2. Carr references Scott Karp, who asserts that the way people think has changed. Do you agree or disagree with this assessment? If the way people think has changed, do you believe this should affect the way teachers teach? Support your answer.

3. Carr writes, in paragraph 9, "When we read online, she [Wolf] says, we tend to become 'mere decoders of information.' Our ability to interpret text, to make the rich mental connections that form when we read deeply and without distraction, remains largely disengaged." Why do you think he believes this could be a problem? Do you agree with him? Explain your answer.

4. What point is Carr making in paragraph 12? Do you agree? Can you think of additional examples? Explain your answer.

WRITING ASSIGNMENTS

Assignment 1

React to the essay. Do you agree or disagree with the author's perception that the Internet is changing how we think? Do you think this is something to worry about or is it similar to the printing press—that is, something people feared at the time but that has proven to be incredibly valuable? You may need to review Chapter 10, "Exemplification," and Chapter 16, "Argument," to help you create a strong, thesis-driven essay.

Assignment 2

Carr reminds us that Google and other companies collect information about their users to focus advertisements to specific tastes. For instance, if you decide to visit Athleta.com to browse yoga gear, days later when you are reading an article about current events, you may see advertisements pop up for the yoga outfit you were browsing.

For this essay, you are going to discuss your reaction to the idea that Google is collecting your browsing information. First, you will need to go to an online news site you frequent and scroll through the ads to see how they reflect your browsing history. (Be sure you don't "go incognito" or use "private browsing," and make sure you disable any ad blocker feature.)

Your introduction should include a quotation from Carr's essay. Paragraph 12 may be especially helpful. The rest of your introduction should connect your chosen quote to your thesis, which should assert whether you find the idea of focused advertisements to be worrisome or helpful.

Your first paragraph should describe the types of advertisements you noticed and how these advertisements reflect your browsing history. You will also want to react to the types of advertisements. For instance, if you had been researching yoga gear and an ad for a company you had never even heard of popped up, would this be more or less worrisome than ads from actual sites you had visited?

The rest of your paper should then discuss why or why not this type of data gathering is acceptable; whether or not you feel it violates privacy; and whether or not regulations should be put into place. You will want to review Chapter 8, "Description," and Chapter 16, "Argument," to help you write a strong essay.

Assignment 3

For this essay, you are going to profile someone who regularly works on computers. Your profile should focus on what this person thinks about computers, data gathering, and the effects computer use has on people, so you will want to ask guiding questions such as the following. Make sure you ask for explanations and any clarifications you need to write a lengthy profile.

- How often do you use a computer? What types of things do you do on a computer?
- What are the sites you most often visit?
- Whenever you search for information using Google, the company collects, stores, and analyzes your data. This data is used for targeted ads, among other things. How do you feel about this type of data gathering?
- Do you feel data gathering is a violation of privacy? Why or why not?
- Have you noticed the targeted ads on any of the sites you are visiting?
- Do you think computers have affected our health or our brains? Please explain your answer.
- Do you think computers are becoming dangerous, like HAL in *2001: A Space Odyssey*?

Once you have asked all your questions, you will need to create a thesis that introduces the person you are profiling and the main claim you will support in your essay. The following sample thesis statements should help you develop your own thesis:

fizkes/Shutterstock

- Although my mom, Jane Smith, regularly works on computers, she fears that we are relying on them too much.
- My dad, Allan Jones, believes that Google's data gathering has made his life online much better.

You may want to consult Chapter 9, "Narration," and Chapter 10, "Exemplification," to help guide your profile.

The Quiet Struggle of College Students with Kids

Gillian B. White

PREVIEW

Gillian B. White received her B.A. Economics and Political Science degree from Columbia University and her M.S. Journalism degree from Northwestern. She is a freelance writer and a Senior Associate Editor for *The Atlantic*. In this article, she highlights some of the challenges college students who are parents face.

Gillian B. White

More than one-quarter of American undergraduates have dependent children, but affordable, on-campus childcare is still hard to find.

In 2001, Michelle Marie enrolled at Oregon State University. After two years 1 of community college, and then another two years at home taking care of her baby, Marie was ready to complete her bachelor's degree. But that meant she'd need to find someone to watch her daughter, who was nearly two years old, and both resources and information were scarce. "At the time nobody was asking me if I was a student parent. Nobody was saying, 'Hey, we're aware that you're a member of a population that is perhaps not served by the services and resources that are available,'" Marie says. "I felt like I had to set aside my parent status in order to be a student."

Marie was lucky; a nearby aunt was able to provide childcare until her daugh- 2 ter was old enough for kindergarten. Without her aunt's help, Marie says she's not sure how, or if, she could have juggled both school and a young child.

Now, nearly 15 years later, she's working on her Ph.D. and participating in 3 student-parent advocacy on campus, in hopes of creating a better experience for others who will follow in her footsteps. But Marie says things haven't improved all that much. "Childcare is actually even less available on campus, and more expensive than it was then," she says. "Student-parents are still an invisible population."

According to a 2014 study from the Institute for Women's Policy Research, 4.8 million college students were parents of dependent children in 2011, the most recent year for which data is available—that's about 26 percent of all college undergraduates. The vast majority of these students, 71 percent, are women. But while the number of enrolled students who have children has grown (increasing by 50 percent between 1995 and 2011, according to IWPR), the availability of childcare on campuses hasn't. In fact, the number of overall childcare facilities available at public colleges (where more than 60 percent of students with children enroll) has decreased over the past decade or so. In 2002, 54 percent of public, four-year colleges had on-campus childcare; by 2013 that number had dropped to 51 percent. For public, two-year colleges, those figures declined from 52 percent to 46 percent during the same period.

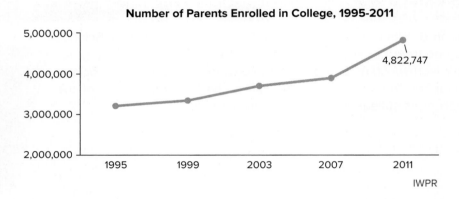

Number of Parents Enrolled in College, 1995-2011

4,822,747

1995   1999   2003   2007   2011

IWPR

The reasons behind the declining availability in childcare are varied, potentially a mix of both budget constraints and academic culture, says Barbara Gault, the executive director at IWPR. "It's taking a long time for institutions of higher education to undergo a culture shift that reflects the changing demographics, and to begin to view themselves as organizations that are family-friendly—not just for faculty, but for students," she says. It might also be true that these types of facilities aren't yet considered a financial priority. "Institutions are looking desperately for places to cut. Because there's so little awareness of the prevalence of students with children I think it often ends up looking like something that's an extra rather than something that's essential," Gault says.

Graduate student Kimberly Lewis is a soon-to-be parent who is currently wrestling with the lack of both funds and childcare programs as she anticipates the arrival of a child in February. While she's excited, she's also a bit nervous. Lewis works as a graduate assistant at Western Illinois University in Macomb. In exchange she receives a stipend that helps cover her expenses while she furthers her education. She also receives assistance from SNAP and WIC in order to make ends meet each month. But when it comes to finding help for childcare, so that she can head back to work and school after the baby, Lewis can't seem to find a solution.

She says that she looked into childcare on campus, but that the facility 7 wouldn't hold a spot open for her until March, when her child will be old enough to finally start daycare. And then a nearby Early Head Start program bumped her to the wait-list after originally confirming her registration. "They told me, 'Hey, you're pretty poor, you qualify for Early Head Start,'" she said. But then two weeks later they called to say that she had been moved to the wait-list and her child's spot was no longer confirmed. She says that the daycare facility cited the fact that enrollment was need-based, not first-come, first-served, but that they told a friend of hers the opposite. Plus, Lewis says, she does in fact need the help. If she can't arrange childcare, she'll lose her graduate-assistant job and along with it her $800 monthly stipend and tuition assistance.

If she can't find a solution by the time she has to go back to work, after the 8 school's 2015 spring break, she's considered going into debt in order to fund both her studies and the cost of childcare.

It's a solution that other student-parents have had to rely on while in school. 9 Andrea Fitch turned to loans while she pursued her bachelor's almost five years ago. She managed to earn scholarships or grant money for nearly all of her education expenses while she studied at Colorado State University. She says she looked into the daycare on-site, but "it was still charging $40 a day, per kid—and there was a wait-list because a lot of the children at that facility were from faculty and staff." Fitch says that she also looked into subsidies for childcare, but at the time, Colorado's Child Care Assistance Program was frozen, leaving little financial help available. In the end, she took out nearly $30,000 in loans in order to pay for in-home childcare while she earned her degree. "I felt like it was my only option for creating a next step," she said.

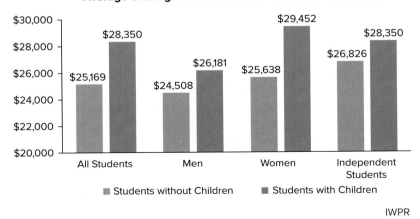

Average Undergraduate Debt One Year After Graduation

All Students: Students without Children $25,169; Students with Children $28,350
Men: Students without Children $24,508; Students with Children $26,181
Women: Students without Children $25,638; Students with Children $29,452
Independent Students: Students without Children $26,826; Students with Children $28,350

■ Students without Children   ■ Students with Children

IWPR

Students who have kids tend to have higher student-loan debt than their 10 childless peers, according to IWPR. That's particularly problematic given the fact that these parents are also more likely to have low-incomes than their fellow students. That makes subsidies, like the federal funds that support childcare at colleges, particularly important. But some of those services have also been reduced. In 2013 around $14.9 million was allocated to the Child Care Access Means Parents in School program, which provides funding for on-campus child-care services. That's a far cry from the funding that was allocated in 2001, when $25 million was made available for such programs. And in many states, programs that offer funding for student-parents are facing frozen funds, require a certain number of work hours per week, or inflict limits on total school hours, making subsidies more difficult to qualify for and imposing more stringent schedules on those who do receive funds, according to IWPR's research.

So why is on-campus childcare so important? Well, it's partially because it 11 could help more parents graduate, allowing them to secure better jobs and provide a more stable home for themselves and their children. According to IWPR, par-ents with dependent children drop out of college at a higher rate than any other demographic, with only 33 percent of students with children obtaining a degree or certificate within six years. Placing these facilities on-campus not only simpli-fies daily routines for parents, allowing them to spend less time (and money) commuting from home, to daycare to school, and back again, but also gives them peace-of-mind while at school, since they could easily reach their children in case of emergency. According to Gault, both advocacy groups and politicians who have touted educational attainment as a key component to moving families out of poverty, should be particularly concerned with the presence of childcare facilities on college campuses.

But the availability of on-campus childcare and the funds to help students pay 12 for these services vary widely by state. In Delaware, Rhode Island, and Nevada, all community colleges offer an on-campus childcare facility, according to the American Association of University Women. In New York, 32 out of the state's 36 community colleges provide the service; and in California, 84 percent of the state's 118 commu-nity colleges offer childcare. On the other hand, less than 20 percent of community colleges in Louisiana and South Carolina offer such services, and only 10 percent of Tennessee's 39 community colleges have on-campus childcare.

According to Catherine Hill, vice president for research at the AAUW, these 13 variations suggest that the presence of both childcare programs and the sup-portive funding that would help needy student-parents pay for them is as much an issue of state politics and policies as it is higher-education culture. "There is a little bit of a regional difference, and I think that that suggests that some of the state policies are no doubt making a difference," Hill says. "States that are providing childcare should be a model for those that are not doing it at the same level or same scale."

READING COMPREHENSION

1. The word *prevalence* in "Because there's so little awareness of the prevalence of students with children" (paragraph 5) means
    a. frequency.
    b. dominance.
    c. popularity.
    d. power.

2. The word *anticipates* in "as she anticipates the arrival of a child" (paragraph 6) means
    a. to think about calmly and happily.
    b. to meet before a due date.
    c. to foresee and deal with in advance.
    d. to look ahead to an event or experience.

3. The word *touted* in "both advocacy groups and politicians who have touted educational attainment" (paragraph 11) means
    a. to spy on or watch.
    b. to give a tip or solicit bets.
    c. to praise or publicize loudly.
    d. to take one side in an argument.

4. Which of the following would be a good alternative title for this selection?
    a. Students' Uphill Climb
    b. Colleges' Hidden Shame
    c. Wasteful Federal Spending
    d. Why Students Fail College

5. Which sentence best expresses the main idea of the selection?
    a. College students who are parents have much higher debt when they finish college than traditional college students.
    b. College students who are parents shouldn't be enrolling in college because there are no services to help them.
    c. College students who are parents face additional struggles in order to achieve their college degrees.
    d. College students who are parents rely on childcare facilities and families in order to complete their degrees.

6. What does the author mean by "student-parents are still an invisible population"?

   a. Student-parents are nonexistent.

   b. Student-parents are ignored.

   c. Student-parents are incompetent.

   d. Student-parents are a burden.

7. According to the essay, how many students were parents of dependent children in 2014?

   a. 26 percent of all college undergraduates

   b. 46 percent of all college undergraduates

   c. 51 percent of all college undergraduates

   d. 60 percent of all college undergraduates

8. According to the essay, how much did federal funding that supports childcare at colleges drop between 2001 and 2013?

   a. $39.9 million

   b. $25 million

   c. $14.9 million

   d. $10.1 million

9. According to the Institute for Women's Policy Research (IWPR), how many students with dependent children complete their undergraduate degrees within six years?

   a. 20 percent

   b. 33 percent

   c. 67 percent

   d. 84 percent

10. All of the following states, except one, provide on-campus childcare at 100 percent of the community colleges. Which of these states does NOT provide on-campus childcare at 100 percent of its community colleges?

    a. Rhode Island

    b. New York

    c. Nevada

    d. Delaware

STRUCTURE AND TECHNIQUE

1. What type of introduction does White use? How does it enhance the essay?

2. What point of view does the author employ? Why do you think she uses this approach? Do you think this approach is effective?

3. What rhetorical modes does White use to create a well-written essay?

4. White doesn't create a traditional concluding paragraph that looks back at the thesis. Why do you think she does this, and do you think her conclusion is adequate?

CRITICAL READING AND DISCUSSION

1. Reread the first three paragraphs. Hints have been provided to explain how long it took Michelle Marie to complete her bachelor's degree. Using the hints, try to determine an approximate length, and then discuss how this differs from "traditional" college students. What kind of impact do you think this different experience has on the lives of students who are parents?

2. The author provides several reasons for the decline in childcare facilities on college campuses. Explain the reasons she gives and discuss what you think of these factors. Do you agree with her assertion that on-campus childcare facilities are essential?

3. In paragraph 10, the author states, "programs that offer funding for student-parents are facing frozen funds, require a certain number of work hours per week, or inflict limits on total school hours, making subsidies more difficult to qualify for and imposing more stringent schedules on those who do receive funds." What is she implying about the effect this has on students' studies and their chances of completing a degree?

4. The author describes Andrea Fitch's experience at Colorado State University. What circumstances did she face, and what do you think of the choices she wound up making?

WRITING ASSIGNMENTS

Assignment 1

Think about what you have to juggle in your own life in order to attend college and do well. If you are a student-parent, how does your college experience compare to those described in the article? If you aren't a student-parent, how do the experiences compare to your own college experience?

Assignment 2

For this assignment, you will need to do a little research into your college. If your college has an on-site childcare center, answer question a. If your college does not have an on-site childcare center, answer question b. You may need to look at Chapter 16, "Argument," and Chapter 19, "Writing a Source-Based Essay," to help you integrate quotes, paraphrases, and summaries from the article into your essay.

a. First, you will need to visit the center to find out what types of services it offers, what the costs are for students, and any other information that could help you describe the center to someone who hasn't been there. Second, you will need to decide why this childcare center provides an important service to your campus. Your target audience should be either students with children who don't know about the center or administrators who are considering shutting down the center. Your essay should focus on supporting the argument that (a) students who are unaware are missing out on a great opportunity, or that (b) administrators need to understand why this center is so valuable.

b. You will need to argue why your college should have an on-site childcare center. Your target audience will be the administrators at your school, and you should focus on explaining why this added budget expense is a vital and needed service.

Assignment 3

Critique the essay. Are the arguments in White's essay clear? Do you feel that White successfully supports her arguments? If not, in what areas should she have gone deeper? What types of support would have helped her argument? Have any ideas been overemphasized or underemphasized? Are there any statements that you think are unclear? Has the author made any assumptions about her readers that could have an impact on how well the essay is received? Does the author have an evident bias that affects how her information is presented?

Once you have read through the essay and answered as many questions as possible, you will need to create a thesis that presents your overall impression of the essay. You will then need to organize your ideas around your thesis, so you can create a strong argument. You may need to look at Chapter 16, "Argument," and Chapter 19, "Writing a Source-Based Essay," to help you integrate quotes, paraphrases, and summaries from the article into your essay.

Shalom Ormsby Images Inc/Getty Images

What Academics Misunderstand about 'Public Writing'

Popular writing should be as rigorous as scholarship—but much easier to read

Irina Dumitrescu

PREVIEW

Irina Dumitrescu received her Ph.D. in English from Yale University. She has taught at Columbia University and Southern Methodist University and is currently a professor of English medieval studies at the University of Bonn.

Irina Dumitrescu

Public writing can be a touchy subject. From one perspective, we are living in a golden age of public intellectualism. Today's scholars have numerous ways to reach a broad audience—from online magazines hungry for fresh takes on the topics of the day to print magazines looking for authoritative essays. Writing coaches and programs such as the OpEd Project offer training in how to pitch to general-interest publications, while grant agencies in Europe and North America increasingly require recipients to communicate with the public. To some scholars, public writing has even started to seem like yet another skill they are expected to master to stay competitive.

At the same time, academics often approach newspapers, magazines, and websites with assumptions drawn from the outlets we're used to writing for: scholarly journals and, since the early 2000s, the blogs that flourish as a faster, more casual medium of scholarly exchange. Trying to write for the public can mean a series of unpleasant surprises about what happens to our work at every stage of editing and publication.

Even as readers, however, scholars tend to misunderstand how public writing— 3
or as the public would call it, "writing"—works, what it's for, and what makes it
good. The result is both unnecessary frustration for academics making that first
foray into newspapers and online outlets, and misplaced indignation among certain
scholars who think their colleagues' public essays should read just like scholarship.

In more than a decade of writing essays and reviews for the public, both in 4
my academic wheelhouse and outside of it, I have gathered a number of lessons
that I offer here to spare other freelance writers some pain and annoyance. My
comments are specifically about the process of writing—sometimes with a contract, and preferably for pay—for editors at established print and online publications aimed at a general audience.

Control. As a scholar, you are used to having an enormous amount of say 5
over your writing and how it is presented. It may not always feel that way, particularly when you are responding to Reader B and revising that article for the fifth
time. Yet the final work represents your vision.

The moment you write for general-interest outlets, however, you are subject 6
to their editorial vision. What that means in practical terms: Headlines, illustrations, and publication dates are decided for you. Sometimes the headline will
misrepresent the article it accompanies, or exaggerate your message to attract
clicks. Readers angered by the headline tend to direct their rage at you, the writer.
In some cases, you will see the draft headline during the editing process, but it
can still change after that point.

All of the above holds for art, too, which can range from subtly inaccurate 7
to deeply offensive. The worst headlines usually appear online, but the good news
is that you can sometimes persuade the editors at online outlets to change a
particularly egregious headline.

Much the same goes for the publication date. Unless a piece is pegged to a 8
quickly developing news event, it's likely to go into a publication queue and appear
anywhere from weeks to months later. That can be challenging for writers impatient
to see their work appear. Even when an outlet gives you a publication date, it can
be delayed without notice, either due to more pressing pieces or because the editors
saved it for use with other articles on the same theme. In one case, I had a book
review appear online as announced, but in print a month later.

Meanwhile, readers used to the fast publishing potential of Medium or per- 9
sonal blogs might wrongly assume that a newly published essay reflects your
current thinking, when, in fact, it may only reflect how you viewed the matter six
months ago. Just as work in scholarly journals suffers from a time lag, so does
much popular writing.

Even once your essay has been published, you may be surprised to find it 10
syndicated to other outlets or translated into foreign languages—all without your
knowledge or permission. In some cases you will receive a permission request and
a fee for the reprint, but in others you will not even be informed.

Before you allow your work to be published by a particular venue, ask your 11 editor to spell out the copyright arrangement (since it's not always clear in the outlet's "terms and conditions"). If the terms don't include nonexclusive reprint rights, you can sometimes negotiate for that. Check the publication to make sure it fits your ethics, but know that the moment you agree to sell the rights, you have limited say over how your work will be presented.

Editing. Editors for general-interest publications usually like to play an active 12 role in shaping articles, to an extent that can be bracing for scholars used to solitary writing. With a few exceptions, such as op-eds and literary essays, you will usually land assignments with a pitch outlining the story you plan to tell and how you will go about it. Most editors prefer a pitch to a draft, as it allows them input at an early stage of the work.

Once a draft is done, the fun really begins. Some editors make only general 13 comments or tiny changes, while others revise the text intensively. We academics tend to be precious about our prose. It can be hard to receive a draft in which the editor has mercilessly slashed our darling paragraphs, rewritten our brilliant sentences, and inserted her own writing.

Viewing writing as a collaborative endeavor has been one of the most difficult 14 lessons I have had to learn as a crossover writer. Once I learned not to be so prickly about what happened to my prose, however, I began to see the bright side. If you have a hands-on editor, you can ask for advice early in the process, and worry less about providing a perfect draft—the editor will work with you to improve it.

I knew I had reached a new point in my freelancing education when I received 15 page proofs from a new publication and marveled that the editors had not changed a word. Later, when I compared the proofs to my original draft, I realized that every single sentence had been rewritten.

Style. Much has been written about bad academic prose, and I do not need 16 to repeat it here. Even good academic prose, however, is ill suited to a general audience.

The habits we learn in writing scholarship serve us poorly in popular writing. 17 Graduate school teaches us to craft our prose defensively—to ward off possible attacks from colleagues. We shy away from strong claims, watering down every sentence with "perhaps" or "one could say." In the worst cases, we make our prose completely impenetrable, figuring that if our critics can't understand what we're saying, they won't be able to tear it down. But the qualities that make scholarly writing unassailable turn off general readers.

One of our key defenses is citation, which is what makes it so unsettling to 18 write something without footnotes—particularly if the essay is related to our research. A public-facing piece will not cite all of its sources. It may not cite any.

I have seen that prompt consternation among colleagues, who grumble that 19 the foundational work of Professor X wasn't mentioned in that (enviable) *New*

Yorker feature written by Professor Z. But the public does not want to read about Professor X's contributions. Readers of your general-interest essay don't expect in-text citations of everything you read that went into writing it.

Purpose. Public writing has a different ethos from scholarly prose. We write 20 scholarship to establish our credentials in a field, to lay stake to original claims, and to build a name for ourselves in the profession. For general-interest writing, however, you should follow Horace's advice for poetry: Aim to instruct or delight—ideally, do both. Tell your readers a story, and give them the basic information they need to take it in. Avoid jargon for the most part, but teach your readers a key term when it will help them understand your topic better.

One genre that can be confusing in this respect is book reviews. They are an 21 easy entry point into public writing, as they draw on skills that scholars already have. But the point of writing a book review for the public is not to show how clever you are or what typos you have caught in the text. Rather, it is to help readers decide if they want to buy the book, and to offer them insights and information to enjoy even if they choose not to.

To be fair, the most useful book reviews in academic journals do that, too, in 22 their own register, but general publications usually are more interested in the experience of the reader than in the egos of the reviewer or the author whose work is being reviewed. This also means that if your book is the one being reviewed in a mainstream publication, you may be dismayed to find the "review" is an independent essay using your book as a hook. Try to appreciate the publicity.

Quality. Academics sometimes make the mistake of thinking that their stan- 23 dards do not need to be particularly high when writing for the public. Even though you will not be writing with the precision of scholarly prose or citing every source, you should still strive to be as accurate and careful as you would be in your scholarly publications, especially if you are drawing on your specialization.

A few mainstream publications still have fact-checking departments, but, in 24 general, assume you bear full responsibility for ensuring the truth of what you write. You owe the public an even higher standard of rigor than you do your colleagues, since the public is more likely to trust your credentials and has less access to your sources. If you get proofs before publication, check them carefully to make sure that no inaccuracies have slipped in.

The uncomfortable reality is that—while crossover work counts for little in 25 the way of raises or promotions in academe—it can still hurt your reputation if you do a sloppy job.

Given all of those warnings, why write for the public at all?   26

There are strategic reasons, such as raising your visibility or showing the 27 relevance of your research. It is also satisfying to reach readers who are curious about your field, but do not have the training necessary to appreciate your scholarship. As a public scholar, you have the freedom to write about topics beyond your area of specialization, which in turn can enrich your research and teaching. Finally, many of the qualities that make for good public essays—clarity, conviction, style—can improve your scholarly writing too.

READING COMPREHENSION

1. The word *subject* in "you are subject to their editorial vision" (paragraph 6) means
    a. obedient.
    b. course.
    c. exposed.
    d. susceptible.

2. The word *egregious* in "persuade the editors at online outlets to change a particularly egregious headline" (paragraph 7) means
    a. tolerable and minor.
    b. outrageous and terrible.
    c. shocking and distinguished.
    d. extraordinary and noteworthy.

3. The word *pegged* in "unless a piece is pegged to a quickly developing news event" (paragraph 8) means
    a. estimated to be of a certain value.
    b. expected to be something based on a stereotype.
    c. identified, labeled, classified, or assigned.
    d. attached to a certain variable as a measure of value.

4. Which of the following would be a good alternative title for the selection?
    a. Two Different Types of Writing
    b. Different Genres, Different Rules
    c. How Editors Make Revisions
    d. Quality, Quantity, and Time

5. Which sentence best expresses the main idea of the selection?
    a. There is a place for academic writers in public writing, but the writers need to recognize different rules and constraints.
    b. Academic writing is more important than public writing, and academic writers should not lower themselves to writing general-interest pieces.

    c. Academic writers should have control over what they write and shouldn't be influenced by the editors.

    d. Editors are more involved with the writing process when they work with freelance writers than scholarly writers.

6. Why might writing for a general-interest publication be difficult for an academic writer?

    a. Academic writers are not used to submitting a finished piece of work to an editor.

    b. Academic writers like to pitch several ideas before they begin a writing project.

    c. Academic writers aren't used to working closely with editors during the writing process.

    d. Academic writers don't like to publish their writing online and prefer print.

7. What is one of the most difficult lessons the author has had to learn as a crossover writer?

    a. knowing what works and what makes writing good

    b. dealing with readers angered by a headline

    c. asking the editor for the copyright arrangement

    d. viewing writing as a collaborative endeavor

8. According to the author, general-interest writing should

    a. instruct and entertain the reader.

    b. instruct and persuade the reader.

    c. entertain and challenge the reader.

    d. challenge and persuade the reader.

9. True or False? _____ According to the author, newly published essays may appear to reflect a writer's current thinking but may actually reflect a writer's earlier ideas.

10. The author's comment about her "freelancing education" (paragraph 15) is a reference to

    a. an education that is free, like public school.

    b. an education that is available online in a free format, like Khan Academy.

    c. an education that someone has gained through experience.

    d. an education that someone has been granted through a scholarship.

STRUCTURE AND TECHNIQUE

1. What type of introduction does the author use?

2. The author breaks her article into five separate sections. What are these sections and how does she signal them? Why do you think the author has organized her essay this way?

3. Sarcasm is defined as a form of criticism that expresses ridicule or contempt and often uses irony. In paragraph 13, the author employs the use of sarcasm. Find the example and discuss why you think the author chose sarcasm. Explain why you think its use is effective or not.

4. In paragraphs 6 and 7, the author compares art and writing when she explains how general-interest articles move through the publication process. What is the author's purpose in making this comparison? How does creating a comparison like this help the reader?

CRITICAL READING AND DISCUSSION

1. Why does the author suggest that writers should "check the publication to make sure it fits your ethics" (paragraph 11)?

2. In paragraph 13, the author states, "Some editors make only general comments or tiny changes, while others revise the text intensively." How do you think each approach affects writers' confidence and the final products? Which approach do you think is more appropriate? Why do you feel this way? How does this apply to academic writing/peer review?

3. In paragraph 18, the author makes the statement, "A public-facing piece will not cite all of its sources. It may not cite any." Do you think this could be problematic? Do you think requiring citations might help with misinformation? Why or why not?

4. According to the author, what is the point of a book review? Do you read book reviews? If so, what do you hope to get out of reading a book review?

WRITING ASSIGNMENTS

Assignment 1

Online blogs are very prevalent. Readers can find blogs on a multitude of subjects like travel, pets, and fashion; blogs can also function, as the author states, as "a faster, more casual medium of scholarly exchange." Not all blogs, however, are created equal. For this assignment, find two blogs on the same topic, and write a comparison and/or contrast essay. You may need to quote and paraphrase some of the information from the blogs, so you will want to pay special attention to Chapter 18, "Summarizing and Paraphrasing," Chapter 19, "Writing a Source-Based Essay," and Chapter 20, "Writing a Research Essay," to ensure you properly present and cite your information.

Assignment 2

In this essay, the author discusses the difference between public writing and academic writing, and gives tips to writers who want to cross over. In order to do this, writers must first reflect on their own way of writing to determine what they may need to do differently. If they are used to working alone, how will they embrace working with a more hands-on editor? If they are used to publishing extremely complex academic papers, how will they embrace a more casual tone? For this assignment, reflect on your own writing process. In a well-developed essay, discuss your process. Explain what you do well and how it benefits your final writing pieces and what you need to improve upon. You may want to review Chapter 11, "Process," to help you explain your own process, and you may want to review Chapter 12, "Cause and/or Effect," to help you articulate how your current process positively and negatively affects your polished pieces of writing.

Assignment 3

The author discusses the purpose of book reviews in paragraphs 21 and 22. For this assignment, you are to write a review of a favorite book. The purpose of your review is to get your reader excited about reading the book, so you will need to include good details without giving away the plot. You may want to review Chapter 8, "Description," to help you pick vibrant details to excite your reader.

Challenging Societal Values

■ READINGS

The Professor Is a Dropout

Beth Johnson

After being mistakenly labeled "retarded"* and humiliated into dropping out of first grade, Lupe Quintanilla knew she wanted nothing more to do with formal education. Life as a wife and mother would satisfy her— and it did, until she saw her own children being pushed aside as "slow learners." Driven to help them succeed, Lupe took steps that dramatically changed her life.

Courtesy of Beth Johnson

Guadalupe Quintanilla is an assistant professor at the University of Houston. She 1
is president of her own communications company. She trains law enforcement officers all over the country. She was nominated to serve as the U.S. Attorney General. She's been a representative to the United Nations.

That's a pretty impressive string of accomplishments. It's all the more impressive 2
when you consider this: "Lupe" Quintanilla is a first-grade dropout. Her school records state that she is retarded, that her IQ is so low she can't learn much of anything.

How did Lupe Quintanilla, "retarded" nonlearner, become Dr. Quintanilla, 3
respected educator? Her remarkable journey began in the town of Nogales, Mexico, just below the Arizona border. That's where Lupe first lived with her grandparents. (Her parents had divorced.) Then an uncle who had just finished medical school made her grandparents a generous offer. If they wanted to live with him, he would support the family as he began his medical practice.

Lupe, her grandparents, and her uncle all moved hundreds of miles to a town 4
in southern Mexico that didn't even have paved roads, let alone any schools. There, Lupe grew up helping her grandfather run his little pharmacy and her grandmother keep house. She remembers the time happily. "My grandparents were wonderful,"

---

*When the professor was young, the word "retarded" was often used to label anyone who was seen as having cognitive and mental limitations. That word is no longer accepted as appropriate; however, in this piece, it is used to emphasize the negativity of the word.

she said. "Oh, my grandfather was stern, authoritarian, as Mexican culture demanded, but they were also very kind to me." When the chores were done, her grandfather taught Lupe to read and write Spanish and do basic arithmetic.

When Lupe was twelve, her grandfather became blind. The family left Mexico 5 and went to Brownsville, Texas, with the hope that doctors there could restore his sight. Once they arrived in Brownsville, Lupe was enrolled in school. Although she understood no English, she was given an IQ test in that language. Not surprisingly, she didn't do very well.

Lupe even remembers her score. "I scored a sixty-four, which classified me as 6 seriously retarded, not even teachable," she said. "I was put into first grade with a class of six-year-olds. My duties were to take the little kids to the bathroom and to cut out pictures." The classroom activities were a total mystery to Lupe—they were all conducted in English. And she was humiliated by the other children, who teased her for being "so much older and so much dumber" than they were.

After four months in first grade, an incident occurred that Lupe still does not 7 fully understand. As she stood in the doorway of the classroom waiting to escort a little girl to the bathroom, a man approached her. He asked her, in Spanish, how to find the principal's office. Lupe was delighted. "Finally someone in this school had spoken to me with words I could understand, in the language of my soul, the language of my grandmother," she said. Eagerly, she answered his question in Spanish. Instantly her teacher swooped down on her, grabbing her arm and scolding her. She pulled Lupe along to the principal's office. There, the teacher and the principal both shouted at her, obviously very angry. Lupe was frightened and embarrassed, but also bewildered. She didn't understand a word they were saying.

"Why were they so angry? I don't know," said Lupe. "Was it because I spoke 8 Spanish at school? Or that I spoke to the man at all? I really don't know. All I know is how humiliated I was."

When she got home that day, she cried miserably, begging her grandfather 9 not to make her return to school. Finally he agreed.

From that time on, Lupe stayed at home, serving as her blind grandfather's 10 "eyes." She was a fluent reader in Spanish, and the older man loved to have her read newspapers, poetry, and novels aloud to him for hours.

Lupe's own love of reading flourished during these years. Her vocabulary was 11 enriched and her imagination fired by the novels she read—novels which she learned later were classics of Spanish literature. She read *Don Quixote*, the famous story of the noble, impractical knight who fought against windmills. She read thrilling accounts of the Mexican revolution. She read *La Prensa*, the local Spanish-language paper, and *Selecciones*, the Spanish-language version of *Reader's Digest*.

When she was just sixteen, Lupe married a young Mexican-American dental 12 technician. Within five years, she had given birth to her three children, Victor, Mario, and Martha. Lupe's grandparents lived with the young family. Lupe was quite happy with her life. "I cooked, sewed, cleaned, and cared for everybody," she said. "I listened to my grandmother when she told me what made a good wife. In the morning I would actually put on my husband's shoes and tie the laces—anything to make his life easier. Living with my grandparents for so long, I was one generation behind in my ideas of what a woman could do and be."

Lupe's contentment ended when her children started school. When they brought home their report cards, she struggled to understand them. She could read enough English to know that what they said was not good. Her children had been put into a group called "Yellow Birds." It was a group for slow learners. 13

At night in bed, Lupe cried and blamed herself. It was obvious—not only was she retarded, but her children had taken after her. Now they, too, would never be able to learn like other children. 14

But in time, a thought began to break through Lupe's despair: Her children didn't seem like slow learners to her. At home, they learned everything she taught them, quickly and easily. She read to them constantly, from the books that she herself had loved as a child. *Aesop's Fables* and stories from *1,001 Arabian Nights* were family favorites. The children filled the house with the sounds of the songs, prayers, games, and rhymes they had learned from their parents and grandparents. They were smart children, eager to learn. They learned quickly—in Spanish. 15

A radical idea began to form in Lupe's mind. Maybe the school was wrong about her children. And if the school system could be wrong about her children— maybe it had been wrong about her, too. 16

Lupe visited her children's school, a daring action for her. "Many Hispanic parents would not dream of going to the classroom," she said. "In Hispanic culture, the teacher is regarded as a third parent, as an ultimate authority. To question her would seem most disrespectful, as though you were saying that she didn't know her job." That was one reason Lupe's grandparents had not interfered when Lupe was classified as retarded. "Anglo teachers often misunderstand Hispanic parents, believing that they aren't concerned about their children's education because they don't come visit the schools," Lupe said. "It's not a lack of concern at all. It's a mark of respect for the teacher's authority." 17

At her children's school, Lupe spoke to three different teachers. Two of them told her the same thing: "Your children are just slow. Sorry, but they can't learn." A third offered a glimmer of hope. He said, "They don't know how to function in English. It's possible that if you spoke English at home they would be able to do better." 18

Lupe pounced on that idea. "Where can I learn English?" she asked. The teacher shrugged. At that time there were no local English-language programs for adults. Finally he suggested that Lupe visit the local high school. Maybe she would be permitted to sit in the back of a classroom and pick up some English that way. 19

Lupe made an appointment with a counselor at the high school. But when the two women met, the counselor shook her head. "Your test scores show that you are retarded," she told Lupe. "You'd just be taking space in the classroom away from someone who could learn." 20

Lupe's next stop was the hospital where she had served for years as a volunteer. 21
Could she sit in on some of the nursing classes held there? No, she was told, not
without a diploma. Still undeterred, she went on to Texas Southmost College in
Brownsville. Could she sit in on a class? No; no high-school diploma. Finally she
went to the telephone company, where she knew operators were being trained.
Could she listen in on the classes? No, only high-school graduates were
permitted.

That day, leaving the telephone company, Lupe felt she had hit bottom. She had 22
been terrified in the first place to try to find an English class. Meeting with rejection
after rejection nearly destroyed what little self-confidence she had. She walked home
in the rain, crying. "I felt like a big barrier had fallen across my path," she said. "I
couldn't go over it; I couldn't go under it; I couldn't go around it."

But the next day Lupe woke with fresh determination. "I was motivated by 23
love of my kids," she said. "I was not going to quit." She got up; made breakfast
for her kids, husband, and grandparents; saw her children and husband off for
the day; and started out again. "I remember walking to the bus stop, past a dog
that always scared me to death, and heading back to the college. The lady I spoke
to said, 'I told you, we can't do anything for you without a high-school degree.'
But as I left the building, I went up to the first Spanish-speaking student I saw.
His name was Gabito. I said, 'Who really makes the decisions around here?' He
said, 'The registrar.'" Since she hadn't had any luck in the office building, Lupe
decided to take a more direct approach. She asked Gabito to point out the
registrar's car in the parking lot. For the next two hours she waited beside it until
its owner showed up.

Impressed by Lupe's persistence, the registrar listened to her story. But instead 24
of giving her permission to sit in on a class and learn more English, he insisted that
she sign up for a full college load. Before she knew it, she was enrolled in four classes:
basic math, basic English, psychology, and typing. The registrar's parting words to
her were, "Don't come back if you don't make it through."

With that "encouragement," Lupe began a semester that was part nightmare, 25
part dream come true. Every day she got her husband and children off to school,
took the bus to campus, came home to make lunch for her husband and grandparents, went back to campus, and was home in time to greet Victor, Mario, and
Martha when they got home from school. In the evenings she cooked, cleaned, did
laundry, and got the children to bed. Then she would study, often until three in
the morning.

"Sometimes in class I would feel sick with the stress of it," she said. "I'd go 26
to the bathroom and talk to myself in the mirror. Sometimes I'd say, 'What are
you doing here? Why don't you go home and watch *I Love Lucy?*'"

But she didn't go home. Instead, she studied furiously, using her 27
Spanish-English dictionary, constantly making lists of new words she wanted to
understand. "I still do that today," she said. "When I come across a word I don't

know, I write it down, look it up, and write sentences using it until I own that word."

Although so much of the language and subject matter was new to Lupe, one 28 part of the college experience was not. That was the key skill of reading, a skill Lupe possessed. As she struggled with English, she found the reading speed, comprehension, and vocabulary that she had developed in Spanish carrying over into her new language. "Reading," she said, "reading was the vehicle. Although I didn't know it at the time, when I was a girl learning to love to read, I was laying the foundation for academic success."

She gives credit, too, to her Hispanic fellow students. "At first, they didn't 29 know what to make of me. They were eighteen years old, and at that time it was very unfashionable for an older person to be in college. But once they decided I wasn't a 'plant' from the administration, they were my greatest help." The younger students spent hours helping Lupe, explaining unfamiliar words and terms, coaching her, and answering her questions.

That first semester passed in a fog of exhaustion. Many mornings Lupe doubted 30 she could get out of bed, much less care for her family and tackle her classes. But when she thought of her children and what was at stake for them, she forced herself on. She remembers well what those days were like. "Just a day at a time. That was all I could think about. I could make myself get up one more day, study one more day, cook and clean one more day. And those days eventually turned into a semester."

To her own amazement perhaps as much as anyone's, Lupe discovered that 31 she was far from retarded. Although she sweated blood over many assignments, she completed them. She turned them in on time. And, remarkably, she made the dean's list her very first semester.

After that, there was no stopping Lupe Quintanilla. She soon realized that 32 the associate's degree offered by Texas Southmost College would not satisfy her. Continuing her Monday, Wednesday, and Friday schedule at Southmost, she enrolled for Tuesday and Thursday courses at Pan American University, a school 140 miles from Brownsville. Within three years, she had earned both her junior college degree and a bachelor's degree in biology. She then won a fellowship that took her to graduate school at the University of Houston, where she earned a master's degree in Spanish literature. When she graduated, the university offered her a job as director of the Mexican-American studies program. While in that position, she earned a doctoral degree in education.

How did she do it all? Lupe herself isn't sure. "I hardly know. When I think 33 back to those years, it seems like a life that someone else lived." It was a rich and exciting but also very challenging period for Lupe and her family. On the one hand, Lupe was motivated by the desire to set an example for her children, to prove to them that they could succeed in the English-speaking academic world. On the other hand, she worried about neglecting her family. She tried hard to attend important activities, such as parents' meetings at school and her children's sporting events.

But things didn't always work out. Lupe still remembers attending a baseball game that her older son, Victor, was playing in. When Victor came to bat, he hit a home run. But as the crowd cheered and Victor glanced proudly over at his mother in the stands, he saw she was studying a textbook. "I hadn't seen the home run," Lupe admitted. "That sort of thing was hard for everyone to take."

Although Lupe worried that her children would resent her busy schedule, she 34 also saw her success reflected in them as they blossomed in school. She forced herself to speak English at home, and their language skills improved quickly. She read to them in English instead of Spanish—gulping down her pride as their pronunciation became better than hers and they began correcting her. (Once the children were in high school and fluent in English, Lupe switched back to Spanish at home, so that the children would be fully comfortable in both languages.) "I saw the change in them almost immediately," she said. "After I helped them with their homework, they would see me pulling out my own books and going to work. In the morning, I would show them the papers I had written. As I gained confidence, so did they." By the next year, the children had been promoted out of the Yellow Birds.

Even though Victor, Mario, and Martha all did well academically, Lupe realized 35 she could not assume that they would face no more obstacles in school. When Mario was in high school, for instance, he wanted to sign up for a debate class. Instead, he was assigned to woodworking. She visited the school to ask why. Mario's teacher told her, "He's good with his hands. He'll be a great carpenter, and that's a good thing for a Mexican to be." Controlling her temper, Lupe responded, "I'm glad you think he's good with his hands. He'll be a great physician someday, and he is going to be in the debate class."

Today, Lupe Quintanilla teaches at the University of Houston, where she has 36 developed several dozen courses concerning Hispanic literature and culture. Her cross-cultural training for law enforcement officers, which helps bring police and firefighters and local Hispanic communities closer together, is renowned throughout the country. Former President Ronald Reagan named her to a national board that keeps the White House informed of new programs in law enforcement. She has received numerous awards for teaching excellence, and there is even a scholarship named in her honor. Her name appears in the Hispanic Hall of Fame, and she has been co-chair of the White House Commission on Hispanic Education.

The love of reading that her grandfather instilled in Lupe is still alive. She 37 thinks of him every year when she introduces to her students one of his favorite poets, Amado Nervo. She requires them to memorize these lines from one of Nervo's poems: "When I got to the end of my long journey in life, I realized that I was the architect of my own destiny." Of these lines, Lupe says, "That is something that I deeply believe, and I want my students to learn it before the end of their long journey. We create our own destiny."

Her love of reading and learning has helped Lupe create a distinguished des- 38 tiny. But none of the honors she has received means more to her than the success of her own children, the reason she made that frightening journey to seek classes in English years ago. Today Mario is a physician. Victor and Martha are lawyers, both having earned doctor of law degrees. And so today, Lupe likes to say, "When someone calls the house and asks for 'Dr. Quintanilla,' I have to ask, 'Which one?' There are four of us—one retarded and three slow learners."

READING COMPREHENSION

1. The word *flourished* in "Lupe's own love of reading flourished during these years. Her vocabulary was enriched and her imagination fired by the novels she read" (paragraph 11) means
   a. grew.
   b. stood still.
   c. was lost.
   d. remained.

2. The word *instilled* in "The love of reading that Lupe's grandfather instilled in Lupe is still alive" (paragraph 37) means
   a. frightened.
   b. established.
   c. forced.
   d. forgot.

3. Which of the following would be a good alternative title for this selection?
   a. Difficulties Facing Spanish-Speaking Students
   b. Unfair Labeling
   c. Balancing School and Family
   d. A Courageous Mother's Triumph

4. Which sentence best expresses the main idea of the selection?
   a. Lupe, a first-grade dropout, eventually earned a doctoral degree and created a professional career.
   b. Lupe Quintanilla's experience proves that the educational system has been set up to accommodate non-English-speaking children.
   c. Through hard work and persistence combined with a love of reading and learning, Lupe has created a distinguished career and helped her children become professionals.
   d. In school, Spanish-speaking students may experience obstacles as they aim for professional careers.

5. Lupe realized that her children were not "slow," as they'd been labeled, when
   a. they got good grades at school.
   b. she saw how quickly they learned at home.
   c. they were put in the group called "Yellow Birds."
   d. they read newspapers, poetry, and novels to her.

6. Lupe's training for law enforcement officers
   a. teaches them to speak Spanish.
   b. teaches Hispanic literature and culture.
   c. offers a scholarship named in her honor.
   d. brings police, firefighters, and local Hispanic communities together.

7. According to Lupe, Hispanic parents rarely visit their children's schools because they
   a. do not consider schoolwork important.
   b. think doing so would be disrespectful to the teacher.
   c. are ashamed of their English language skills.
   d. are usually working during school visitation hours.

8. "Once they arrived in Brownsville, Lupe was enrolled in school. Although she understood no English, she was given an IQ test in that language. Not surprisingly, she didn't do very well" (paragraph 5). From these sentences, we might conclude that
   a. an IQ test in a language that the person tested doesn't know is useless.
   b. although Lupe was not very intelligent at first, she became more intelligent once she learned English.
   c. Lupe really did know English.
   d. there are no IQ tests in Spanish.

9. We might conclude from the reading that
   a. a school system's judgment about an individual is always accurate.
   b. it is often better for a child to stay home rather than attend school.
   c. by paying attention and speaking up, parents may remove obstacles to their children's education.
   d. working parents should accept the fact that they cannot attend important events in their children's lives.

10. The last line of the reading suggests that
    a. slow learners can become successful professionals.
    b. people should not blindly accept other people's opinions of them.

   c. Lupe's children are smarter than she is.

   d. all of the above

STRUCTURE AND TECHNIQUE

1. Johnson begins the essay by listing Lupe Quintanilla's accomplishments, then revealing that Quintanilla was once classified as "retarded." What introductory technique is Johnson employing? Why is it effective here?

2. Paragraphs 3–11 are devoted to the first fifteen years of Lupe's life. But the next decade or so is covered in only two paragraphs (12–13). Why might Johnson have presented Lupe's earlier life in so much more detail? Do you agree with her decision?

3. In paragraph 2, Johnson writes that "[Lupe's] school records state that she is retarded. . . ." But in the next sentence, she writes, "How did Lupe Quintanilla, 'retarded' nonlearner, become Dr. Quintanilla, respected educator?" Why does Johnson put the word "retarded" in quotation marks in the second sentence, but not in the first? What is she implying? Can you find another place where Johnson makes similar use of quotation marks?

4. At one point, Johnson switches from the topic of Lupe's success in college to the topic of the challenges that continued to face her children in school. In what paragraph does she make that switch? What transitional words does she use to alert the reader to her new direction?

CRITICAL READING AND DISCUSSION

1. In the course of the essay, what characteristics and attitudes does Lupe suggest are typical of Hispanic culture? Does she seem sympathetic, critical, or neutral about those qualities or attitudes? How has she dealt with cultural expectations in her own life?

2. How has Lupe handled the question of what language to use with her children? If you grew up in a two-language household, how did your family deal with the issue? How would you approach the issue with children of your own?

3. Do you think Lupe's grandfather was right in allowing her to quit school? What factors do you imagine might have gone into his decision?

4. Lupe credits her fellow Hispanic students with giving her valuable support in college. Is there anyone in your life—a teacher, family member, or friend—who has helped you through challenging times in your education? Explain what obstacles you faced and how this person helped you overcome them.

WRITING ASSIGNMENTS

Assignment 1

Write an essay that takes as its thesis one of the following statements:

> Schools need to be prepared to help non-English-speaking students catch up with other students at their grade level.

> The responsibility for catching non-English-speaking students up to their grade level rests solely with the students and their families.

Support your thesis with several points, each developed in its own paragraph.

Assignment 2

Lupe Quintanilla is an outstanding example of someone who has taken charge of her life. She has been, to echo the poet whose work she teaches, the architect of her own destiny. Choose a person you know who, in your opinion, has done a fine job of taking charge of their own destiny. Write an essay about this person. You might describe three areas of life in which the person has taken control. Alternatively, you might narrate three incidents from the person's life that illustrate their admirable self-determination.

Assignment 3

Lupe had to struggle in order to balance her school responsibilities with her duties as a wife and mother. Write an essay in which you identify aspects of your life that you need to juggle along with your responsibilities as a student. They may include a job, a spouse or significant other, children, housekeeping duties, pets, extracurricular activities, a difficult living situation, or anything else that poses a challenge to your academics. Provide vivid, real-life illustrations of how each of those responsibilities sometimes conflicts with your studies.

Purposefully Mispronouncing Kamala Harris's Name Is Racist, Plain and Simple

Duaa Israr

PREVIEW

Duaa Israr graduated in 2021 from DePaul University in Illinois, where she double-majored in journalism and political science. In this piece that she wrote for her college newspaper, Israr explores the importance of a person's name and the significance of its proper pronunciation.

Duaa Israr

There are two stages in a name for people of color. First, it begins when you change 1 your name to fit the mouths of others. It's easier to let people pronounce your name the way they want to instead of the immigrant dialect it's supposed to be said in. It's easier, simpler and it allows you to shed a bit of your identity to fit in. You may not look like everyone, but simplifying your name will make you stand out less.

The second stage comes years later. When you've grown a little and you 2 understand the power of names, the importance of the culture and heritage you were given. Your name is your identity. It encompasses who you are, so why would you change that to make it easier for someone else? It belongs to you.

So when Republican Sen. David Perdue mocked Senator and Vice Presidential 3 nominee Kamala Harris's name by saying "Ka-MAL-a, Ka-MAL-a or Kamala, Kamala, Ka-mala, -mala, -mala, I don't know, whatever," at a rally in Georgia, not only was it disrespectful to a highly qualified colleague, but it also brought up a conversation about how people of color have faced years of microaggressive behavior for simply having names.

His team later stated that Perdue "simply mispronounced" Harris's name and 4 it "didn't mean anything." Harris and Perdue have served in the Senate for three years together and they serve on the budget committee. It wasn't a simple mistake when you've known a person for multiple years, it was willfully ignorant.

"The first time someone mispronounces a name, there's a pass. Maybe they're 5 unfamiliar with the name or they sincerely can't pronounce it, that's one thing. But when someone mispronounces it consistently because they don't want to bother, it's highly problematic, demeaning, personal and intolerable," said DePaul Professor of Political Science Christina Rivers.

Plainly put, Perdue was racist.   6

The mispronunciation of a name is not a minuscule topic that can be brushed 7 off as an honest mistake. Not for people who have been brushed off their entire lives. For people of color, our names prevent us from getting interviews, let alone offers, jobs and promotions. The concept that our names are not "white-sounding" is just another obstacle that places us behind our white counterparts.

This isn't the first incident of Harris's name being mocked. When Harris was 8 announced as Joe Biden's running mate, Fox News Host Tucker Carlson proceeded to mispronounce Harris's name multiple times until Democratic political consultant Richard Goodstein corrected Carlson, calling the action "the bare minimum."

Carlson responded with "so what?"   9

"To me, this indicates his disrespect for the Senator who might be the VP of 10 the country. Not only that, but I do think that it's an indicator that to him, everything including people's identity must be modified to fit his heritage, the way he speaks. It's not like her name has a letter or a combination of letters that are difficult to articulate," said DePaul Islamic Studies professor Ahmed Hashim.

But the mispronunciation behind Harris's name goes beyond just a form of 11 racism. It also has to do with her being a female in politics.

Over the past year, we've seen an increase in blatant disrespect and violence 12 towards women in politics and how they have been treated by their male coworkers. From President Trump stating that Sen. Ilhan Omar was an al-Qaeda sympathizer to Rep. Ted Yoho calling Sen. Alexandria Ocasio-Cortez a "f***ing bitch," to even the plot to kidnap Gov. Gretchen Whitmer, women in politics have been criticized for simply existing.

The focus on Harris's name is partly because she's a woman of color in a 13 position of power, and her name makes her an easy target to point out to people that she's different. She doesn't fit the mold of what a politician looks like. She's not white, and she's not a man.

"Her name is something, repeating it like this. It's used like a smoke screen, 14 dismissing someone because they are an immigrant. She's an immigrant, she's Black, but people can't go there. They can't attack her publicly for that. There's a concept called the neutrality of a name. It's the intentional concentration on her name that's coded for the objection to who she is as a woman of color," Rivers said.

My name is Duaa. In Islam, it's the basis for all acts of worship. The action 15 of cupping your hands, closing your eyes and asking God for what you need. It's calling on a superior being, Allah, for help. Simply put, a dua is a prayer.

My name gives away I'm a woman of color, writing about politics. My name 16
makes me an easy target for those who would like to use it to deny me a job, attack
me for my religion and remind others that I'm different. But, there's also a chance
that my name comes across to people—to women—who look like me. A form of
representation in a world filled with men named David and Tucker and Ted.

In the meantime, if Kamala is too hard for Perdue and Carlson to pronounce, 17
they can start referring to her as Vice President Harris.

READING COMPREHENSION

1. The word *blatant* in "we've seen an increase in blatant disrespect and violence" (paragraph 12) best means

   a. obvious.

   b. unblushing.

   c. prominent.

   d. glitzy.

2. The word *representation* in "a form of representation in a world filled with
   men" (paragraph 16) means

   a. an artistic rendering or image.

   b. people who stand in for those who are absent.

   c. the members who symbolize a group or population.

   d. the members who comprise a legislative body.

3. Which of the following would be a good alternative title for the selection?

   a. The Power of a Name

   b. The Struggles of Racist Politicians

   c. Republicans Versus Democrats

   d. A Clear Demonstration of Racism

4. Which sentence best expresses the main idea of the selection?

   a. The author believes that women in politics are treated poorly by male
      politicians.

   b. The author asserts that racism is exhibited in more common everyday
      actions than people often realize.

   c. The author believes people should learn how to properly pronounce peo-
      ple's names.

   d. The author believes men like Tucker Carlson and David Perdue are racist.

5. How many stages does the author claim people of color have in a name?

    a. 1

    b. 2

    c. 3

    d. 4

6. Why does the author dismiss Perdue's claim that he "simply mispronounced" Harris's name?

    a. Perdue had a habit of mispronouncing the names of women in the Senate.

    b. Richard Goodstein had corrected Perdue several times.

    c. Perdue and Harris had worked together for three years.

    d. Harris's name has a combination of letters that are difficult to articulate.

7. According to the author, who was guilty of purposely mispronouncing Kamala Harris's name?

    a. Christina Rivers

    b. Tucker Carlson

    c. Joe Biden

    d. Ahmed Hashim

8. According to the author, what is the "mold" that most politicians fit?

    a. White and male

    b. Young and male

    c. White and wealthy

    d. Old and wealthy

9. According to the essay, what is "the neutrality of a name"?

    a. It is a way for someone to offer a nickname to use for colleagues who have a hard time with the pronunciation of the legal name.

    b. It is a way to embrace a name that is less indicative of a person's ethnicity.

    c. It is a way to demonstrate racist and dismissive behavior without being blatantly racist or dismissive.

    d. It is a way to dismiss people because their names are not English-sounding enough.

10. We can infer from the essay that the author
    a. is proud of her name and heritage.
    b. is a regular viewer of Fox News Channel.
    c. doesn't think women should be in politics.
    d. regularly lets people mispronounce her name.

STRUCTURE AND TECHNIQUE

1. Although students are told to use a consistent point of view in their writing, Israr uses first-, second-, and third-person point of view in her essay. Find examples of each point of view, explain why she has used these different points of view as she has, and discuss whether or not you think Israr's essay works well as it is.

2. Paragraph development in academic writing usually requires a topic sentence and good supporting details. However, in paragraphs 6, 9, and 17, the author uses only one simple sentence. Why does the author do this? Is it effective? Why or why not?

3. In paragraph 12, the author uses several very specific examples. What is the purpose of these examples? Do you think their use is effective? Explain your answer.

4. The author includes several fragments in her essay. Find two and explain why you think the author chooses to break grammar rules this way.

CRITICAL READING AND DISCUSSION

1. Reread paragraph 4. Have you ever had an experience in which someone mispronounced your name even after you'd corrected them? If so, how did you handle it? If not, suggest some potential ways that the situation might be handled well.

2. In paragraph 7, the author explains that people of color are often prevented from getting job offers and promotions because their names are not "white-sounding." Have you or someone you know experienced this? How do you think companies can avoid being guilty of this?

3. In paragraph 10, the author quotes Ahmed Hashim. Why would the author use this person's words as support for her argument?

4. Kamala Harris is the first female, first Black, and first Asian-American vice president of the United States. After reading this essay, explain how you think Israr feels about these "firsts" and discuss how you personally feel about these "firsts."

WRITING ASSIGNMENTS

Assignment 1

In paragraph 2, the author asserts, "Your name is your identity." Discuss this statement, using your own name and experiences as support. As the author did in paragraph 15, you may want to include the origin of your name and the meaning behind the name, and you may want to discuss whether or not you feel you "fit" your name. If you go by a name other than your legal name, you might want to explain how that chosen name better encompasses your identity.

Assignment 2

In paragraph 3, the author states that "people of color have faced years of microaggressive behavior." For this assignment, you have two options.

1. The first option is to write a personal exemplification essay about microaggressions you have experienced yourself. You will want to review Chapter 10, "Exemplification," to help you create a strong thesis and organized support.

2. The second option is to research common microaggressions experienced by college students in the classroom. You may want to interview some of your classmates about their experiences. You should then write a letter to your college president explaining the students' experiences and what training and policies should be put into place at your college to educate your college community. You may want to review Chapter 16, "Argument," to help you develop a strong essay.

Assignment 3

Our history is filled with people who have been "firsts" like Vice President Kamala Harris. For this essay, you are to research someone who was a first in their field and write a profile of that person. For instance, you might write about the first female engineer at NASA or the first Black politician in your state, or you might find information about the first person to swim across the English Channel or the first person to win the Tour de France. Because this essay will require you to research and integrate that research into a well-developed essay, you will want to review Chapter 17, "Information Literacy," to make sure you choose good sources. As well, you should review Chapter 18, "Summarizing and Paraphrasing," and Chapter 19, "Writing a Source-Based Essay," to make sure you properly present and cite the sources in your essay.

Memes and the Art of Nonsense

Serena G. Pellegrino

PREVIEW

Serena G. Pellegrino is a philosophy major at Harvard University. This article, in which she discusses the phenomenon of memes, was published in the university newspaper, *The Harvard Crimson*.

Serena G. Pellegrino

I believe in the importance of nonsense. More specifically, that a little bit of non- 1
sense in life is very valuable. Nonsense, in this case, being internet memes.

Usually, I'm quick to criticize the internet. I have dedicated a significant 2
amount of time to blaming it for many of our generation's social conflicts. And
honestly, contemplating social media and the web at large frequently leads me
down a path of existential desperation. But memes are, for me, an exception. They
are deceivingly relevant and their function is more profound than their shallow
perceptions afford them. Of course, not all memes are funny, many are pointless,
and offensive ones are unacceptable. But the concept of a meme is significant. It
is an authentic, unfiltered expression rarely seen elsewhere online. It is a sign of
humanity, something we often try to erase from our virtual selves.

Evolutionary biologist Richard Dawkins coined the term "meme" in his 1976 3
book "The Selfish Gene," where he defines it as "a unit of cultural transmission."
From the Greek word "mimema," meaning "imitated," memes are contingent on
imitating relevant cultural patterns. Dawkins considers memes to be cultural
genes—they have heredity, undergo replication, and require fitness to survive. His
analogy, while so unfortunately untimely, explains meme fitness in terms of virus:
ideas worth passing on are contagious.

The fittest, most contagious memes allow us to feel and relate to others. Their 4
images—the face of Sulley from "Monsters, Inc." superimposed onto Mike Wazows-
ki's, Kermit the Frog drinking tea, or Baby Yoda—are so detached from reality,

that we feel free to laugh at their captions because there is distance between us and them. Without feeling exposed, we empathize.

But memes are so refreshing because they remind us to take ourselves less seri- 5 ously. When an online audience is constantly watching and judging, they render our every action a performance—an evaluation of self. So choosing what information to disclose and how we should look on our profiles is in itself an act. Who we so carefully portray is a character. However, memes are a break in character—a sigh of relief when we're off stage. Through memes' ridiculousness, we acknowledge the show can't go on forever. We're flawed and our flaws can be funny. We take off our masks to laugh at the fact that we can be a mess. Sometimes, relating to a comic of a dog sitting in flames drinking coffee insisting "this is fine" can be therapeutic.

This critique through parody is no novelty. In the early 1700s, Italian playwright 6 Carlo Goldoni innovated the theatre* scene and revitalized "commedia dell'arte," a then-declining dramatic art form, to realize a vision proving quite meme-like. Just as memes unveil a more authentic emotional and human experience, Goldoni elimi- nated the use of masks and replaced stock characters with more realistic personali- ties. And like our trove of recycled meme images, Goldoni created a fixed set of these personalities. Their scripted jokes were scattered into improvised acting, func- tioning much like captions we apply according to context.

In addition to emotional release, Goldoni's dramatic arts offered cultural com- 7 mentary and political criticism. His productions were popular for their transgressive humour*, actors often speaking in Italian dialects to criticize the different regions of Italy. And we see much the same online, memes calling out the odd idiosyncrasies of different states or disagreeing with our government. Especially in the COVID era, we are in constant disagreement with laws, politicians, and each other. As Goldoni's productions did so many years ago, memes give us grounds to transgress. In the guise of ridiculousness, we can push the boundaries and express contentious opinions without direct, explicit confrontation. After all, where else would we be able to overlay a "Karen" wig onto Donald Trump's hair?

Yet the real beauty of Goldoni's art and the world of memes is their ability 8 to pantomime and portray the world as it is. As viewers, we enjoy watching sce- narios in which we can see ourselves—joyful, tragic, awkward, or hopeless as they may be. Experiencing objectively helps us process. It takes the edge off the lives we live so seriously.

But while history repeats itself to a large extent, it evolves, too. Memes are 9 far more abstract than people playing parts on stage. That we can feel seen by seeming gibberish may go to show just how critical of ourselves we have become; we don't like it when things get too real. Our solution, then, is both escape and catharsis. Teary-eyed cats, SpongeBob imitating a chicken, or Bernie Sanders "once again asking" for something cushions the blow of discomfort or dissent.

---

*The author has chosen to use the British spelling "theatre" for the word "theater," as well as the British spelling "humour" for the word "humor." Authors will sometimes use British spellings to highlight certain words.

The internet has become a place full of dividing constructs like artificial hier- 10
archies, popularity contests, or assessments of perceived success. But we're not
walking LinkedIn profiles or Facebook bios and we all know it. We're more
memeish than we are post-like, so embrace the memeishness. To accept ourselves,
organically human and imperfect as we are, we have to laugh a little. Of course,
there are sides of us that are less than brag-worthy, but there is no need to deny
them. No one is spared by the truth of memes; they're an unexpectedly equalizing
online presence. Regardless of status and online artifice, we naturally react and
relate to one another in the same way. We all feel the joy of laughter when we
come across that meme that resonates. The power of a meme shouldn't be under-
estimated just because it seems like nonsense—nonsense isn't worthless. It allows
us to laugh together. And there's no nonsense more meaningful than that.

READING COMPREHENSION

1. The word *existential* in "down a path of existential desperation" (paragraph
   2) means having
   a. an observed understanding.
   b. a sense of reality and a feeling of being peaceful.
   c. a sense of pragmatism and subjectivity.
   d. a sense of anxiety and a feeling of being overwhelmed.

2. The word *pantomime* in "their ability to pantomime and portray the world"
   (paragraph 8) means
   a. caricature.
   b. reflect.
   c. deceive.
   d. gesture.

3. The word *catharsis* in "Our solution, then, is both escape and catharsis" (paragraph 9) means
   a. release.
   b. disinfection.
   c. sanctification.
   d. atonement.

4. Which of the following would be a good alternative title for the selection?
   a. The History of Memes
   b. Critiquing Yoda, SpongeBob, and Politics
   c. Reality through a New Kind of Lens
   d. Laughter Is the Best Medicine

5. Which sentence best expresses the main idea of the selection?

    a.   Even though memes seem to be frivolous and a waste of time, they serve a positive purpose.

    b.   Even though most memes are inappropriate and offensive, they are an important part of the online society.

    c.   Memes remind us to take ourselves less seriously, so they should be shared widely.

    d.   Effective memes offer emotional release, cultural commentary, and political criticism.

6. Which of the following is NOT something the author asserts about memes?

    a.   Memes allow people to publicly disagree with their governments.

    b.   Memes allow people to connect and relate to each other.

    c.   Memes are silly, pointless, and inappropriate.

    d.   Memes can be extremely significant and authentic.

7. When was the term "meme" first used?

    a.   1700s

    b.   1976

    c.   2000

    d.   2018

8. According to the author, what is the concept of a meme?

    a.   It is an authentic, unfiltered expression of humanity.

    b.   It is a simple, funny, ridiculous thing to read on the Web.

    c.   It is a nonsensical, fleeting, social connection people make.

    d.   It is a cultural commentary that changes people's minds.

9. According to the author, what do we often try to erase from our virtual selves?

    a.   our imperfections

    b.   our humanity

    c.   our social conflicts

    d.   our emotions

10. What can we infer is the author's main point in paragraph 5?

    a.   It is important to carefully choose what we post online and share publicly.

    b.   It is important to recognize that we are characters in our own lives.

    c.   It is important to embrace our flaws as long as we don't post them online.

    d.   It is important to embrace our flaws and laugh about ourselves.

STRUCTURE AND TECHNIQUE

1. The author creates a very short introduction that contains two fragments. Find the fragments and try to fix them. Then discuss why you think she has broken academic writing rules to create this introduction.

2. In paragraph 2 the author uses a lot of adjectives to create very poignant statements. Find an example and discuss what you like about the word choices.

3. In paragraph 3 the author examines the origin of the word *meme*. Why do you think she does this? How does it add to the essay?.

4. With her statement in paragraph 7 about overlaying a "'Karen' wig onto Donald Trump's hair," the author is making several assumptions about the reader. What assumptions does she make? How can this be problematic?

CRITICAL READING AND DISCUSSION

1. Do you agree with the author that "a little bit of nonsense in life is very valuable"? Explain your answer.

2. The author asserts that memes allow us to empathize without feeling exposed (paragraph 4). What do you think she means by this? Do you agree with this sentiment?

3. What does the author mean when she states that "we're more memeish than we are post-like"? Do you agree with this statement? Explain your answer.

4. According to the author, what is the "truth of memes"? Find her statement and then explain what she means.

WRITING ASSIGNMENTS

Assignment 1

Do you agree or disagree with Pellegrino's claims about memes? Why or why not? If you do agree with her claims, explain why. You can use personal examples and examples from her essay to support your essay. Or, if you don't agree with her claims, you can use examples from her essay that you feel are weak and counter those examples with your personal examples.

Assignment 2

Find a meme online and write an essay explaining why it is "deceivingly relevant" as stated in paragraph 2. Because you will need to describe the meme, you should review Chapter 8, "Description." You will also need to create an argument to support your explanation, so you should review Chapter 16, "Argument."

Assignment 3

In paragraph 5, the author asserts that online audiences are "constantly watching and judging." Additionally, in paragraph 10, the author asserts that we are "not walking LinkedIn profiles or Facebook bios." For this assignment, you are to review and analyze one of your social media profiles and answer the following questions:

- How realistic is your profile?
- How much truth have you incorporated?
- Do you filter it to make your online presence better than reality?
- What impact do your online audiences' reactions have on your sense of self?

An Example of a Meme

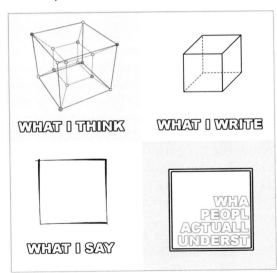

Courtesy of Reichart Von Wolfsheild.

Moving Beyond Pain

bell hooks

bell hooks, born Gloria Jean Watkins, received her B.A. from Stanford University, her M.A. from the University of Wisconsin, and her Ph.D. from University of California, Santa Cruz. She is known for her strong feminist pieces. In this piece, she analyzes Beyoncé's *Lemonade*.

Anthony Barboza/Archive Photos/Getty Images

Fresh lemonade is my drink of choice. In my small Kentucky town, beautiful black, 1 brown, and white girls set up their lemonade stands and practice the art of money making—it's business. As a grown black woman who believes in the manifesto "Girl, get your money straight" my first response to Beyoncé's visual album, *Lemonade*, was WOW—this is the business of capitalist money-making at its best.

Viewers who like to suggest *Lemonade* was created solely or primarily for black 2 female audiences are missing the point. Commodities, irrespective of their subject matter, are made, produced, and marketed to entice any and all consumers. Beyoncé's audience is the world and that world of business and money-making has no color.

What makes this production—this commodity—daring is its subject matter. 3 Obviously *Lemonade* positively exploits images of black female bodies—placing them at the center, making them the norm. In this visual narrative, there are diverse representations (black female bodies come in all sizes, shapes, and textures with all manner of big hair). Portraits of ordinary everyday black women are spotlighted, poised as though they are royalty. The unnamed, unidentified mothers of murdered young black males are each given pride of place. Real-life images of ordinary, overweight not dressed up bodies are placed within a visual backdrop that includes stylized, choreographed, fashion plate fantasy representations. Despite all the glamorous showcasing of Deep South antebellum fashion, when the show begins Beyoncé as star appears in sporty casual clothing, the controversial hoodie. Concurrently, the scantily-clothed dancing image of athlete Serena

Williams also evokes sportswear. (Speaking of commodification, in the real-life frame Beyoncé's new line of sportswear, Ivy Park, is in the process of being marketed right now.)

Lemonade offers viewers a visual extravaganza—a display of black female 4 bodies that transgresses all boundaries. It's all about the body, and the body as commodity. This is certainly not radical or revolutionary. From slavery to the present day, black female bodies, clothed and unclothed, have been bought and sold. What makes this commodification different in *Lemonade* is intent; its purpose is to seduce, celebrate, and delight—to challenge the ongoing present day devaluation and dehumanization of the black female body. Throughout *Lemonade* the black female body is utterly-aestheticized—its beauty a powerful in your face confrontation. This is no new offering. Images like these were first seen in Julie Dash's groundbreaking film *Daughters of the Dust* shot by the brilliant cinematographer Arthur Jafa. Many of the black and white still images of women and nature are reminiscent of the transformative and innovative contemporary photography of Carrie Mae Weems. She has continually offered decolonized radical revisioning of the black female body.

It is the broad scope of *Lemonade's* visual landscape that makes it so distinc- 5 tive—the construction of a powerfully symbolic black female sisterhood that resists invisibility, that refuses to be silent. This in and of itself is no small feat—it shifts the gaze of white mainstream culture. It challenges us all to look anew, to radically revision how we see the black female body. However, this radical repositioning of black female images does not truly overshadow or change conventional sexist constructions of black female identity.

Even though Beyoncé and her creative collaborators daringly offer multi- 6 dimensional images of black female life, much of the album stays within a conventional stereotypical framework, where the black woman is always a victim. Although based on the real-life experience of Beyoncé, *Lemonade* is a fantasy fictional narrative with Beyoncé starring as the lead character. This work begins with a story of pain and betrayal highlighting the trauma it produces. The story is as old as the ballad of "Frankie and Johnny" ("he was my man alright, but he done me wrong"). Like the fictional Frankie, Beyoncé's character responds to her man's betrayal with rage. She wreaks violence. And even though the father in the song "Daddy's Lessons" gives her a rifle warning her about men, she does not shoot her man. She dons a magnificently designed golden yellow gown, boldly struts through the street with baseball bat in hand, randomly smashing cars. In this scene, the goddess-like character of Beyoncé is sexualized along with her acts of emotional violence, like Wagner's "Ride of the Valkyries" she destroys with no shame. Among the many mixed messages embedded in *Lemonade* is this celebration of rage. Smug and smiling in her golden garb, Beyoncé is the embodiment of a fantastical female power, which is just that—pure fantasy. Images of female violence undercut a central message embedded in *Lemonade* that violence in all its forms, especially the violence of lies and betrayal, hurts.

Contrary to misguided notions of gender equality, women do not and will not 7 seize power and create self-love and self-esteem through violent acts. Female violence is no more liberatory than male violence. And when violence is made to look sexy and eroticized, as in the *Lemonade* sexy-dress street scene, it does not serve to undercut the prevailing cultural sentiment that it is acceptable to use violence to reinforce domination, especially in relations between men and women. Violence does not create positive change.

Even though Beyoncé and her creative collaborators make use of the powerful 8 voice and words of Malcolm X to emphasize the lack of respect for black womanhood, simply showcasing beautiful black bodies does not create a just culture of optimal well being where black females can become fully self-actualized and be truly respected.

Honoring the self, loving our bodies, is an appropriate stage in the construc- 9 tion of healthy self-esteem. This aspect of *Lemonade* is affirming. Certainly, to witness Miss Hattie, the 90-year-old grandmother of Jay Z, give her personal testimony that she has survived by taking the lemons life handed her and making lemonade is awesome. All the references to honoring our ancestors and elders in *Lemonade* inspire. However, concluding this narrative of hurt and betrayal with caring images of family and home do not serve as adequate ways to reconcile and heal trauma.

Concurrently, in the world of art-making, a black female creator as powerfully 10 placed as Beyoncé can both create images and present viewers with her own interpretation of what those images mean. However, her interpretation cannot stand as truth. For example, Beyoncé uses her non-fictional voice and persona to claim feminism, even to claim, as she does in a recent issue of *Elle* magazine, "to give clarity to the true meaning" of the term, but her construction of feminism cannot be trusted. Her vision of feminism does not call for an end to patriarchal domination. It's all about insisting on equal rights for men and women. In the world of fantasy feminism, there are no class, sex, and race hierarchies that breakdown simplified categories of women and men, no call to challenge and change systems of domination, no emphasis on intersectionality. In such a simplified worldview, women gaining the freedom to be like men can be seen as powerful. But it is a false construction of power as so many men, especially black men, do not possess actual power. And indeed, it is clear that black male cruelty and violence towards black women is a direct outcome of patriarchal exploitation and oppression.

In her fictive world, Beyoncé can name black female pain, poignantly articu- 11 lated by the passionate poetry of Somali-British poet Warsan Shire, and move through stages evoked by printed words: Intuition, Denial, Forgiveness, Hope, Reconciliation. In this fictive world, black female emotional pain can be exposed and revealed. It can be given voice: this is a vital and essential stage of freedom struggle, but it does not bring exploitation and domination to an end. No matter how hard women in relationships with patriarchal men work for change, forgive, and reconcile, men must do the work of inner and outer transformation if emotional violence against black females is to end. We see no hint of this in *Lemonade*. If change is not mutual then black female emotional hurt can be voiced, but the reality of men inflicting emotional pain will still continue (can we really trust the caring images of Jay Z which conclude this narrative).

It is only as black women and all women resist patriarchal romanticization 12 of domination in relationships can a healthy self-love emerge that allows every black female, and all females, to refuse to be a victim. Ultimately *Lemonade* glamorizes a world of gendered cultural paradox and contradiction. It does not resolve. As Beyoncé proudly proclaims in the powerful anthem "Freedom": "I had my ups and downs, but I always find the inner-strength to pull myself up." To truly be free, we must choose beyond simply surviving adversity, we must dare to create lives of sustained optimal well-being and joy. In that world, the making and drinking of lemonade will be a fresh and zestful delight, a real-life mixture of the bitter and the sweet, and not a measure of our capacity to endure pain, but rather a celebration of our moving beyond pain.

READING COMPREHENSION

1. The word *exploits* in "*Lemonade* positively exploits images of black female bodies" (paragraph 3) means
   a. to make use of meanly.
   b. to act nobly or heroically.
   c. to put to productive use.
   d. to take advantage of.

2. The word *transgresses* in "a display of black female bodies that transgresses all boundaries" (paragraph 4) means
   a. violates.
   b. breaks.
   c. offends.
   d. infringes.

3. The word *construction* in "it is a false construction of power" (paragraph 10) means
   a. the result of interpreting or explaining.
   b. the process or manner of building something.
   c. the connection of words in a sentence.
   d. a sculpture of separate pieces put together.

4. Which of the following would be a good alternative title for this selection?

   a. Beyoncé's New Album

   b. An Artistic Statement

   c. Daughters of the Dust

   d. Violence and Betrayal

5. Which sentence best expresses the main idea of the selection?

   a. Beyoncé's album is extremely important and as many people as possible should buy and copy and listen to it.

   b. Beyoncé's album is a visual and musical masterpiece, but it doesn't contain a strong enough message.

   c. Beyoncé's album contains the important message that Black women are strong and should be heard.

   d. Beyoncé's album contains the important message that Black women should accept their fate and learn to work with it.

6. According to the essay, female _____ is no more liberatory than male _____.

   a. power

   b. vandalism

   c. violence

   d. domination

7. Who are given "pride of place?"

   a. ordinary, everyday Black women

   b. Black girls with lemonade stands

   c. elders and ancestors

   d. mothers of murdered Black males

8. What, according to the author, is the intent of *Lemonade*?

   a. to celebrate Beyoncé's triumph over the struggles she had with Jay Z

   b. to encourage young Black women to stand up against violence

   c. to challenge ongoing devaluation of the Black female body

   d. to politicize the ongoing treatment of Black women in society

9. *True or False?* _____ Beyoncé uses her interview in *Elle* magazine to gain more power for women and weaken men.

10. The author implies that

    a. Beyoncé based her album on the ballad of "Frankie and Johnny."

    b. *Lemonade* is one of Beyoncé's most important statements to date.

    c. Jay Z inflicted emotional pain on Beyoncé and cannot be trusted.

    d. Beyoncé created this album solely to "get her money straight."

STRUCTURE AND TECHNIQUE

1. What type of introduction does hooks use? What is her purpose?

2. hooks uses imagery as support in paragraphs 3 and 6. Find two examples and be prepared to discuss how they support (or don't support) the purpose of the essay.

3. The use of clichés should be avoided in academic writing, yet in paragraph 9, hooks uses a cliché. Find the cliché and discuss why her use is appropriate.

4. The author references Julie Dash and Carrie Mae Weems. What is the purpose of including these women in the essay?

CRITICAL READING AND DISCUSSION

1. In paragraph 5, hooks writes "[h]owever, this radical repositioning of black female images does not truly overshadow or change conventional sexist constructions of black female identity." What do you think she means by this statement?

2. hooks asserts that Beyoncé's album does not "create a culture of optimal well-being where black females can become fully self-actualized and be truly respected." What do you think it will take for Black females, all females, and other minority groups to be truly respected?

3. "Violence in all its forms, especially the violence of lies and betrayal, hurts." React to this statement. Explain your answers.

4. In paragraph 10, hooks states that Beyoncé's "vision of feminism does not call for an end to patriarchal domination." Based on what she writes, what do you think hooks's vision of feminism is?

WRITING ASSIGNMENTS

Assignment 1

Most people need music in their lives because it speaks to them in a multitude of ways. We each have our favorite artists and favorite songs. For this assignment, you are to choose one of the following assignments.

- Write about your favorite album. You will need to explain who the artist is, what the album is, and why it is your favorite.

- Write about your three favorite songs. You will need to describe the artist behind each song and explain why that song is one of your favorites.

Assignment 2

In this analysis of Beyoncé's *Lemonade*, the author explores themes she sees woven throughout the album. Most artists' albums are like essays—multiple songs that work together to support the thesis of the album. For this assignment, you are to pick one of your favorite albums and analyze its themes and messages. You may want to review the rhetorical analysis sample essay in Chapter 19, "Writing a Source-Based Essay," to understand how to keep an analytic tone. You will also need to review Chapter 8, "Description," to help you create such strong descriptions in your paper that even someone unfamiliar with the album will be able to understand your point.

Assignment 3

As the author discusses specific parts of Beyoncé's album, she focuses on a specific scene in which the character in the video smashes cars and "destroys with no shame." Do you think this is a radical idea in the twenty-first century? Does shame affect people negatively? What does it mean for marginalized people to destroy with no shame, and has shame played a part in their struggles?

For this assignment you will want to focus on only one question and answer that question using support either from history or current events. This will require you to read Chapter 17, "Information Literacy," Chapter 18, "Summarizing and Paraphrasing," and Chapter 19, "Writing a Source-Based Essay," so you can properly integrate the information you find in your research.

When a Classmate Is a Former Inmate

Juleyka Lantigua-Williams

Juleyka Lantigua-Williams is a writer, editor, and journalist who has had articles appear in the *Chicago Tribune*, *L.A. Times*, *JET*, and *The Atlantic*. She received her B.A. from Skidmore College and her M.S. in Journalism from Boston University.

Jason Honyotski/Juleyka Lantigua-Williams

These days, American colleges are eager to boast about their number of women enrollees, their percentage of ethnic minorities, even their ratio of low-income students. They're very proud of their inclusiveness and outreach. But many colleges are mum when it comes to the students on their campuses with criminal records. 1

To be fair, it's a very delicate issue, one that requires reassuring students and parents that safety has not been compromised while also ensuring that some students with records are not singled out or treated differently. Finding that balance has proved elusive for some colleges, but others have successfully untangled the complexities created by this increasingly common phenomenon. At hundreds of colleges, students have to disclose any criminal history during the admissions process and may be prescreened by a special committee. A quick online search yields multiple websites—like the one at the University of Colorado, Boulder—with guidelines for admissions for students with criminal records. At some schools, a formerly incarcerated student's movements on campus and his or her access to facilities may be restricted. At a number of colleges and universities, students who have committed certain crimes may be jointly monitored by campus authorities and state officials. The measures are set up based on state requirements, school policy, and the institution's comfort level. 2

"It's just incredibly stigmatizing," said Emily NaPier, the director of justice strat- 3
egies at the Center for Community Alternatives, which conducts research in this
area. She said that some students with records complain that some schools "don't
allow them to live on campus housing," "some have a probation period," and others
"have some level of tracking and surveillance regarding their grades." NaPier added
that the center is also aware of schools that require students with criminal records "to
sign a declaration that they will only come to campus for classes and will not participate in any extracurricular activity on campus, that they will not linger on campus,
that they will not be on campus for any other reason other than classes."

That used to be the case at Indiana University-Purdue University Indianapolis. 4
For students who had answered "yes" to an application question asking if they had
a criminal history, their admissions letter informed them that they could enroll in
school, but they couldn't live on campus. However, the school recently removed
the measure after it expanded the use of the background question to applications
that are given to high-schoolers, which could have meant that "freshmen would
not be able to live on campus housing," said Pamela Brown, IUPUI's associate
director of undergraduate admissions for operations. She said the school regularly
modifies its policies as conflicts come up. "It just didn't make sense to exclude
them from campus housing," she said. Now, the incoming fall 2016 class will be
the first to be allowed to live on campus no matter their backgrounds.

But, in some instances, there are situations that are entirely out of a school's 5
control. Students with criminal records who want to apply for certain professional
programs often hit dead-ends. "People are not rejected solely based on having a
criminal record but can end up being excluded from certain academic programs
that do not allow those with criminal histories to work in the field," said Jason
Ebbeling, executive director of the Student Success Center at Connecticut State
Colleges & Universities. Due to licensure requirements or clinical-rotation guidelines, future teachers, nurses, and others who might work in sensitive areas are
not allowed to have past criminal histories.

"Why is someone in a classroom with a record more dangerous than someone 6
sitting next to me in a movie theater or a restaurant?" asked Barmak Nassirian
during my conversation with him. Nassirian has worked in higher education for
25 years and is the director of policy analysis at the American Association of State
Colleges and Universities. "People do have a responsibility for maintaining safe
campuses, I don't dismiss that." But he fervently opposes asking students to divulge
the information, considering it as part of admissions, and subsequently monitoring
students once on campus. "We essentially condemn people to a life of underem-
ployment and poverty if we deny them the one medicine that actually cures criminal behavior: education."

"We have a number of students that do have a criminal background," Ebbeling 7
said. "We work at the community-college level with people that have been sex
offenders and people who have other convictions." CSCU asks questions about

criminal backgrounds and felony convictions at its universities but not at its community colleges. Some cases don't necessarily even require a background question. "We have a very formalized process for sex offenders: The state has a registry for sex offenders; deans of students at the community-college level meet with students to discuss behavioral expectations; in fact, we place a hold on their account until the meeting happens," Ebbeling said. "We start from a place where they are given the opportunities any other students are given until there are any behavioral disruptions," he said. But he also explained that for the sexual-assault registry, there are state requirements that Connecticut schools must comply with and of course they must collaborate with state agencies on any pending investigations.

College administrators, according to several of the experts I spoke to, try to 8 put in place as many mechanisms and safety precautions as possible to reinforce how safe their campuses are, especially for the peace of mind of prospective families. And yet, there are no statistically valid relationships between asking about criminal histories, the ratio of such students on campus, and the incidences of campus crime. One glaring example of this is sexual assault, one of the most common campus crimes.

Walter DeKeseredy, a professor of sociology and the director of the Research 9 Center on Violence at West Virginia University, has spent over 30 years conducting research on violence against women, but he is best known for his work on sexual assault on college campuses. He sees no merit in efforts to identify and monitor students with prior criminal records on campus. "Two of the high-risk groups on campus are fraternity brothers and men who are in combative sports—football, hockey, and lacrosse," DeKeseredy said. "We have the data. They are among the highest-risk men on campus for committing sexual assault. You have a subculture that promotes and rewards a hyper masculine masculinity."

Another researcher believes there are other important factors at play. "The issue 10 of race and class are primary, and they get focused on young black men, but it's really young white men who created the problem," said Natalie Sokoloff, professor emerita of sociology at John Jay College of Criminal Justice. So even though in the United States black men are more likely to have a record and thus more likely to be under scrutiny by collegiate safety policies, it is actually white men who commit the majority of serious crimes, like sexual assault, on campus. "What we try to highlight is that these kinds of practices really are a de facto form of race-based discrimination . . . They undermine the goal of higher education, restrict access, and result in less diverse applicant pools. It's so counterproductive."

One measure that has emerged from the growing awareness of crimes on campus 11 is the practice of signaling in students' transcripts when disciplinary action has been taken against them. In most instances, schools do this of their own volition, but in several states, it is the law. One university has even started tracking states and colleges that annotate transcripts. "An issue that pops up is perpetrators of sexual violence who leave campus just ahead of the sheriff, who quietly transfer before any evidence is gathered against them," Nassirian said, referring to troublemaking students who voluntarily leave school before any disciplinary or legal measures have been taken against them—only to later transfer into a new college with a fresh start. "There is a real risk, and real pressure, to annotate the transcript with any instances of disciplinary actions to warn the future institution about the student."

A student could in theory simply not admit to a criminal background and circumvent all of the hassle and stigma—but hiding it can have severe consequences. In Connecticut's state-university system, it "could be grounds for dismissal if the student does not self-identify in [the] admissions process, and there's an issue later on," according to Ebbeling. The same is true at the University of Washington. "It could be grounds for disciplinary action or dismissal if it were discovered later on," said Paul Seegert, U.W.'s director of admissions. "But it's the same for lying or withholding information on any part of the application." 12

Educators want to welcome and serve qualified students. But they are also charged with maintaining safe and conducive atmospheres for learning. And so, for the student with a criminal background who wants an education, it can seem like there is no easy way around having a record—stigmatization now or dismissal later. 13

READING COMPREHENSION

1. The word *elusive* in "finding that balance has proved elusive for some colleges" (paragraph 2) means
   a. insubstantial.
   b. baffling.
   c. evasive.
   d. mysterious.

2. The word *delicate* in "it's a very delicate issue" (paragraph 2) means
   a. dainty.
   b. exquisite.
   c. superior.
   d. sensitive.

3. The word *stigmatizing* in "It's just incredibly stigmatizing" (paragraph 3) means
   a. having a scar or physical deformity.
   b. having a mark of shame or discredit.
   c. having a destructive personality characteristic.
   d. having wounds resembling those of the crucified Christ.

4. Which of the following would be a good alternative title for this selection?
   a. Colleges and Criminals
   b. Keeping Campuses Safe
   c. Colleges Offer Opportunity
   d. No Criminals on Campus

5. Which sentence best expresses the main idea of the selection?
   a. Colleges are trying to figure out how to handle students who have criminal records.
   b. Students who have criminal records should not be allowed on college campuses.
   c. Students with criminal records should be required to register with the campus police and to live in separate housing.
   d. Colleges have tried many means of handling students with criminal records but are now realizing it does not work out.

6. According to the essay, what is the one medicine that actually cures criminal behavior?
   a. incarceration
   b. meditation
   c. admonition
   d. education

7. According to the essay, which of the following represent one of the highest-risk groups for committing sexual assault?
   a. students who are past sexual offenders
   b. students who have criminal records
   c. male students who play football and lacrosse
   d. male students who play any sport

8. As explained in the essay, which school now allows freshman students with a criminal record to live on campus?
   a. West Virginia University
   b. John Jay College of Criminal Justice
   c. University of Washington
   d. Indiana University-Purdue University Indianapolis

9. *True or False?* _____ According to the author, a student could simply not admit to having a criminal background, thus eliminating any of the problems.

10. The author implies that

   a. students who have criminal records pose a great danger to other students.

   b. students who have criminal records should be given better chances at an education.

   c. students who have criminal records should be allowed to enroll in college, but only in certain fields.

   d. students who have criminal records should not be allowed to enroll in college.

STRUCTURE AND TECHNIQUE

1. What method of introduction—brief story, stating importance of topic, or broad-to-narrow—does Lantigua-Williams use? Why do you think she chose this way to begin her article?

2. Lantigua-Williams employs the use of dialogue throughout her article. Why do you think she does this, and do you find it effective?

3. What patterns of development are the most dominant in the essay?

4. What type of tone does the author use throughout the essay? Why do you think she adopts this tone? Do you find it effective? Would a different tone be more effective?

CRITICAL READING AND DISCUSSION

1. In paragraph 3, a researcher explains that some schools require students to "sign a declaration that they will only come to campus for classes and will not participate in any extracurricular activity on campus." What might be the results of these requirements? Explain your reasoning.

2. In paragraph 6, the following question is posed: "Why is someone in a classroom with a record more dangerous than someone sitting next to me in a movie theater or a restaurant?" What would your answer to this question be?

3. In paragraph 10, the author states, "even though in the United States black men are more likely to have a record and thus more likely to be under scrutiny by collegiate safety policies, it is actually white men who commit the majority of serious crimes, like sexual assault, on campus." What is your reaction to this information?

4. When should a person's past decisions stop affecting their future? Should there be a statute of limitations regarding how long someone should be required to report past criminal records? Should this vary depending on the offense?

WRITING ASSIGNMENTS

Assignment 1

React to the essay. Do you agree or disagree that students with records should be allowed on campus? Why or why not? If you do think students with records should be allowed on campus, do you believe restrictions should be placed on these students? Explain your reasoning.

Assignment 2

This essay discusses college students who have criminal records. Prisons often offer education for inmates to help them acquire knowledge and skills that will prepare them for life after they are released. Do you think prisons should offer education to prisoners? If so, what types of education should be available to prisoners? If you don't think education should be offered, explain your reasons. You will want to review Chapter 16, "Argument," to help you create a persuasive tone to your essay.

Assignment 3

The author brings up the topic of sexual assault on campuses, a crime that has been prevalent for decades. For this article, you have two choices.

- Choice 1: Write a letter to your college administration (deans, president, chancellor) expressing why student safety should be more strongly emphasized, especially in regard to sexual assault, and what would help make your campus safer. You might suggest classes or seminars that college students could attend that could help them avoid unsafe situations or intervene when they see someone in an unsafe situation.

- Choice 2: Write a letter to the students on your campus persuading them to engage in safer behavior and to become knowledgeable about how to help others avoid unsafe behavior.

A Memoir Reflects on What Happens to the 'Fairest' of Them All

Hope Wabuke

Hope Wabuke is a Ugandan American poet, writer, and assistant professor at the University of Nebraska Lincoln. She received her B.S. from Northwestern University and her M.F.A. from New York University. What follows is her review of the book *Fairest: A Memoir* by Meredith Talusan.

Hope Wabuke

As a young child, Marc Talusan was enthralled with the music of Lea Salonga 1 upon first listen, connecting with Salonga's lyric "I am the girl with golden hair."

Writes Talusan: "But by the time she sang, "What a joy! What a life! What a 2 chance!" a few moments later, I had already returned to my own body, the body of a boy in the Philippines who just happened to have her hair. My future may hold riches, but I would not live it as a beautiful woman."

What Talusan did receive, throughout a childhood in the Philippines, was 3 positive affirmation based upon the white skin-tone and blonde hair that came with Talusan's albinism. Talusan's grandmother would always say: "'Those other kids aren't white like you,'" writes Talusan. "And when she said white, puti, I could tell she also meant beautiful, intelligent, better, more special."

Everywhere the young Talusan went, from grocery shopping to a bus ride to 4 visit family, Talusan was met with positive affirmation because of this whiteness. This deification of whiteness in a culture in which whiteness is alien speaks to the immense power of the narrative of white supremacy that anchored Western colonization.

Yet, the same white body that makes Talusan so desirable at home—the same 5 body, when migrated to the United States, the land of whiteness—is faced with the lack of desirability based on race; indeed, a meditation on this forms much of the opening section of the memoir, itself anchored in a reunion event for Harvard's queer alumni. Here, Talusan interrogates "how our looks determined our place in the gay pecking order and how our lack of attractiveness had so much to do with our race and femininity," before noting that Talusan and the other person of color at the reunion, Kit Clark, a queer black man, "both occupied liminal spaces in our white-dominated Harvard gay society" due to race.

In *Fairest's* carefully nuanced and detailed analysis, Talusan articulates the 6 ways in which people of color create solidarity when there are only one or two non-white individuals in these elite, predominantly white spaces of privilege. At times, this solidarity is in simply seeing each other—in un-erasing the erasure whiteness creates. Writes Talusan movingly of the importance of Kit Clark's queer POC presence in that elite, white LGBTQ space:

> "He recognized me as an albino Asian when everyone else thought I was white; he could tell my workout regimen was cover for a femininity I obscured because it was not attractive."

And yet Talusan, despite constant positive affirmation because of "fair" skin 7 and hair, while still known as Marc Talusan, always felt something was missing. Although Talusan had had a lifelong understanding of queerness, it would not be until years later and a chance meeting with a student's trans friend that Talusan would realize life could be lived as Meredith Talusan instead: "Me, a child from a Philippine province, descendant of peasant farmers, son of derelict immigrants."

But before this moment is the journey: We see Talusan's move from childhood 8 sanctuary with grandmother Nanay Coro in the Filipino countryside to freshman year at Harvard learning queer theory in the classroom and the easy cruelty and cool disposability of dating and sex in American culture outside of the classroom; we see Talusan study abroad in London; we see Talusan having found a fulfilling relationship with a mature and loving partner, faced with this horrific impasse: As Talusan transitions to living as a woman, Talusan's partner "didn't see the person he fell in love with when he looked at me."

This nuance, this careful attention to looking and attempting to understand 9 this journey not just from her own perspective, but also from those affected by it, gives a welcome maturity, depth and resonance to Talusan's memoir. One of the most touching scenes in the book is in the beginning of Talusan's transition to womanhood. Talusan's partner, Ralph, just wants her to look "normal," as he calls it and asks Talusan to dress like a man, without make-up, for a friend's important event at Carnegie Hall. Talusan promises—but when she goes to the bathroom to scrub her face free of make-up, she cannot, eventually collapsing crying on the floor. To erase her make-up, to erase her femininity—to make herself look like a man when she is a woman—is destroying her in that moment. And Ralph, hearing her pain, comes into the bathroom and hugs her. He tells Talusan that he will never ask her to take off her make-up again.

The make-up, a stand-in for true selfhood and identity, functions in conver- 10
sation with the usage of the mirror, a central grounding conceit for Talusan's
flights into astute analysis of race, gender and sexuality not just here, but elsewhere in the book. While an argument can be made that the vehicle of a mirror
as a tool for self-reflection is a bit on-point, a bit overused, it does hold a
productive presence both narratively and structurally in this gorgeous and lyrical
debut.

It is worth noting how Talusan begins to unpack the uneasy conversation 11
between herself and the figure of the white, golden-blonde female as the ideal
woman still proliferated by post-colonial white supremacy. Writes Talusan toward
the end of *Fairest*:

> "Barrett's words kept playing in my head, 'I don't see you as trans,' coupled
> with 'I can't tell you're Asian.' The way he looked at me was exactly what I'd
> honed over many years, this trick of perception, and it puzzled me that I was
> dissatisfied over having accomplished it, a state of being so many trans women
> sacrifice so much to achieve."

Here, Talusan points to the problematic trans and racial double erasure 12
endemic to the cis white gaze. Later, Talusan again pushes back against this erasure of her trans identity: "I couldn't bring myself to wish I had never been a
man, because my life as a man was part of the complexity of my being, this
unusual person I had become, someone whose insights I cherished."

In the time in which Talusan was coming into adulthood after immigrating 13
to the United States, there was less space for duality and gender fluidity. Now,
however, that Talusan is more centered in her own culture rather than global white
supremacy, she is more aware of gender fluidity in her own cultural history:
"among my own indigenous ancestors, select male-bodied people who lived their
lives as women were held in high esteem and found themselves husbands, in
domestic life treated identically as other women."

Now, too, that we are living in a time with more acceptance of nonbinary 14
gender expression, Talusan questions if she even needs the language of identifying
as a "woman" anymore. Indeed, at the university reunion in 2018 that structurally
grounds the narrative, Talusan wonders: "why becoming a woman had seemed so
urgent then, when it felt so mundane now, as I realized that being a woman was
less important to me than having experienced being a woman, that I'd grown
much less precious about how people gendered me, even though I still felt alienated from the toxic parts of manhood."

The language we have now, the spaces and community support to exist firmly 15
within a gender fluid and/or nonbinary gender identity are developments made
mostly within the last 50 years. They have been made, in large part, because of
the work of inspiring trans activists like Talusan. Because of them, people are no
longer faced with erasure or binary opposition as the only realities.

Just as there are multiple feminisms, there are multiple genders and multiple 16 sexualities along a spectrum. And Talusan, like everyone else, is no longer forced into a binary at either end of this spectrum to exist in this world, but can now exist at various points on this spectrum, engaging with masculinity and femininity in a happy balance that most aligns with her authentic self.

READING COMPREHENSION

1. The word *liminal* in "both occupied liminal spaces in our white-dominated Harvard gay society" (paragraph 5) means

   a. unfamiliar.

   b. invisible.

   c. noticeable.

   d. conspicuous.

2. The word *unpack* in "begins to unpack the uneasy conversation" (paragraph 11) means

   a. to remove the contents of.

   b. to undo from a container or packaging.

   c. to analyze by examining in detail.

   d. to unburden or decompress.

3. The word *precious* in "I'd grown much less precious about how people gendered me" (paragraph 14) means

   a. affected.

   b. refined.

   c. valuable.

   d. beloved.

4. Which of the following would be a good alternative title for the selection?

   a. A Memoir Reflects on the Girl with the Golden Hair

   b. A Memoir Reflects on the Story of a Filipino Girl

   c. A Memoir Reflects on an Activist's Inspiring Journey

   d. A Memoir Reflects on the Journey from the Philippines to Harvard

5. Which sentence best expresses the main idea of the selection?

   a. The memoir by Talusan is an important read with a strong message for the twenty-first century.

   b. The memoir by Talusan will be tough to read for those who are in the LGBTQ community.

    c. Books by people with albinism offer significant perspectives.

    d. Books by people in the LGBTQ community convey important messages.

6. Where did the author of *Fairest: A Memoir* spend her childhood?

    a. Uganda

    b. the United States

    c. the Philippines

    d. London

7. According to the essay, who recognized Talusan as both albino and Asian?

    a. Coro

    b. Barrett

    c. Clark

    d. Salonga

8. According to the author, Talusan grew up in a society that had a "deification of whiteness in a culture in which whiteness is alien." What does the author mean by this?

    a. Religion in Talusan's country was not common and only white people were religious.

    b. White-skinned people were adored in Talusan's country and often had positions of power.

    c. Even though most of the people in Talusan's country were not white, they felt that white-skinned people were more valuable.

    d. Most of the people in Talusan's country were white, and they felt that white-skinned people were more valuable.

9. What has Talusan learned about her own culture as she has aged?

    a. Her indigenous ancestors all lived as women.

    b. Her indigenous ancestors embraced gender fluidity.

    c. Her indigenous ancestors were dominated by white settlers.

    d. Her indigenous ancestors were immigrants from another country.

10. We can infer from reading this article that the author believes

    a. the rights of members of the LGBTQ community are equal to the rights of people who are not in the LGBTQ community.

    b. gender and sexuality should not be discussed in a public forum or an educational setting.

c. it is important that LGBTQ community members' stories be told, heard, and understood.

d. it is insignificant whether LGBTQ community members' stories are told, heard, and understood.

STRUCTURE AND TECHNIQUE

1. The author includes a number of direct quotations from Talusan's memoir to illustrate her argument. Do you think these quotations add to the essay? Explain your answer.

2. Reread paragraph 3 and pay special attention to the final sentence. Why do you think Talusan uses a Filipino word as she does?

3. Reread paragraph 7. Unlike some of the paragraphs in this essay that focus on one small incident or time period, this paragraph does something different. What is it? Why do you think the author writes this paragraph this way? Do you think it is effective? Explain your answer.

4. Throughout the essay, the author refers to Meredith Talusan by her last name. In only a few spots does Wabuke include Talusan's first name before she transitioned and first name after she transitioned. Why does Wabuke refer to Talusan most often by her last name? What is the purpose of including the first names?

CRITICAL READING AND DISCUSSION

1. Wabuke points out that Talusan received "positive affirmation" for her albinism in one country but not the other. Explain what Wabuke is illustrating.

2. Explain why Talusan didn't feel part of the LGBTQ community at her university.

3. In paragraph 9, the author highlights an incident in which Talusan struggles to take off her makeup. What does this incident demonstrate? Why do you think Wabuke considered this incident one that needed to be shared in her review?

4. In paragraph 11, the author states that "the figure of the white, golden-blonde female" is still seen as the ideal in white-dominated society. Do you agree with this statement? Explain your answer.

Adam Hester/Tetra Images, LLC/Alamy Stock Photo

WRITING ASSIGNMENTS

Assignment 1

In paragraph 9, Wabuke highlights an incident in which Talusan's partner, Ralph, asks her to look "normal." Here, Ralph is asking Talusan to be something other than she is. Have you ever had to erase or negate something about yourself to please others? Have you had to hide things from family or friends? Perhaps you had a partner who didn't like the way you dressed, acted, talked? For this assignment, describe a situation in which you found yourself pleasing someone else but hurting your own self in the process. You should provide enough background and details so that the reader understands the conflict you experienced and how that situation changed you. You will want to review Chapter 10, "Exemplification," to help you create an essay that helps your reader understand your experience.

Assignment 2

The author opens the essay by sharing Talusan's connection to the music of Lea Salonga, stating that "Talusan was enthralled with the music of Lea Salonga upon first listen, connecting with Salonga's lyric 'I am the girl with golden hair.'" Music, regardless of type, is extremely important to most people and most societies. For this assignment, you are to write about a song or an artist with whom you connect. With the assumption that some of your readers won't know the artist, you will need to explain to the reader who the artist is. You will then need to provide a detailed explanation as to why you connect with that artist or a specific song by the artist. You may want to review Chapter 8, "Description," to help you use vibrant details. You may also want to review Chapter 19, "Writing a Source-Based Essay," to help you integrate any song quotations you choose to include in your essay.

Assignment 3

This essay is Hope Wabuke's review of Meredith Talusan's book. To clearly support her claims, Wabuke integrates Talusan's words within the review. For this assignment, you are to write a review of a favorite book. The purpose of your review is to get your reader excited about reading the book, so you will need to include good details without giving away the plot. You may want to review Chapter 8, "Description," to help you select vibrant details to excite your reader. You will also want to review Chapter 18, "Summarizing and Paraphrasing," and Chapter 19, "Writing a Source-Based Essay," to help you properly incorporate quotations from your chosen book.

READINGS

p. 648: Source: Emerson, Ralph Waldo, *Self-Reliance* (1841).

p. 653: Wilkins, Roger, "I Became Her Target," *Newsday*, September 6, 1987. Reprinted by permission of the author.

p. 660: Savory, Tanya, "Stepping into the Light." Used by permission of Townsend Press.

p. 669: Kendall, Audra, "The Certainty of Fear." Used by permission of Townsend Press.

p. 676: Gerzina, Gretchen Holbrook, "100 Years of *The Secret Garden*," *The Public Domain Review*, March 8, 2011. Reprinted by permission of the author.

p. 683: Collymore, Kevin V. "Colleges Must Confront Structural Racism." July 1, 2020. The Chronicle of Higher Education. https://www.chronicle.com/article/Colleges-Must-Confront/249102?cid=wcontentlist_hp_5. Used with permission.

p. 690: O'Keeney, Brian, "How to Make it in College, Now That You're Here." Used by permission of Townsend Press.

p. 699: Daniels, David, "College Lectures: Is Anybody Listening?" Used by permission of Townsend Press.

p. 706: Dweck, Carol S., "Brainology: Transforming Students' Motivation to Learn," *Independent School Magazine*, Winter 2008. Used with permission of Carol S. Dweck.

p. 716: Carr, Nicholas, "Is Google Making Us Stupid?" *The Atlantic*, July/August 2008. Copyright © 2008 The Atlantic Media Co, as first published in The Atlantic Magazine. All rights reserved. Distributed by Tribune Content Agency, LLC.

p. 725: White, Gillian B., "The Quiet Struggle of College Students with Kids," *The Atlantic*, December 11, 2014. Copyright © 2014 The Atlantic Media Co, as first published in The Atlantic Magazine. All rights reserved. Distributed by Tribune Content Agency, LLC.

p. 733: Dumitrescu, Irina. "What Academics Misunderstand About 'Public Writing.'" July 2, 2020. Chronicle of Higher Education. https://www.chronicle.com/article/what-academics-misunderstand-about-public-writing. Used with permission.

p. 742: Johnson, Beth, "The Professor Is a Dropout." Used by permission of Townsend Press

p. 752: Israr, Duaa. "Opinion: Purposefully Mispronouncing Kamala Harris' Name Is Racist, Plain and Simple." The DePaulia. Nov. 1, 2020. https://depauliaonline.com/51129/special-issues/the-election-issue/opinion-women-in-politics-deserve-the-respect-of-their-name/. Used with permission.

p. 758: Pellegrino, Serena G. "Memes and the Art of Nonsense." Harvard Crimson. Nov. 20, 2020. https://www.thecrimson.com/column/whats-left-unsaid/article/2020/11/20/pellegrino-memes-arts-of-nonsense/. ©2021 The Harvard Crimson, Inc. All rights reserved. Reprinted with permission.

p. 764: bell hooks, "Moving Beyond Pain," Blog, May 9, 2016. Used with permission of the bell hooks Institute.

p. 771: Lantigua-Williams, Juleyka, "When a Classmate Is a Former Inmate," *The Atlantic*, May 5, 2016. Copyright © 2016 The Atlantic Media Co, as first published in The Atlantic Magazine. All rights reserved. Distributed by Tribune Content Agency, LLC.

p. 778: Wabuke, Hope. "A Memoir Reflects on What Happens to the 'Fairest' of Them All." May 27, 2020. NPR. https://www.npr.org/2020/05/27/862238651/a-memoir-reflects-on-what-happens-to-the-fairest-of-them-all. Used with permission.

INDEX